PERRY COMO

PERRY COMO

A Biography and
Complete Career Record

Malcolm Macfarlane *and*
Ken Crossland

Foreword by Michael Feinstein

McFarland & Company, Inc., Publishers
Jefferson, North Carolina, and London

LIBRARY OF CONGRESS CATALOGUING-IN-PUBLICATION DATA

Macfarlane, Malcolm, 1942–
Perry Como : a biography and complete career record / Malcolm
Macfarlane and Ken Crossland ; foreword by Michael Feinstein.
p.   cm.
Includes bibliographical references and index.

ISBN 978-0-7864-3701-6
illustrated case binding : 50# alkaline paper ∞

1. Como, Perry, 1912–2001.   2. Singers—United States—Biography.
I. Crossland, Ken.   II. Title.
ML420.C657M33   2009   782.42164092—dc22 [B]   2009009927

British Library cataloguing data are available

Cover photograph: Perry Como, 1966 (Photofest)

Manufactured in the United States of America

McFarland & Company, Inc., Publishers
Box 611, Jefferson, North Carolina 28640
www.mcfarlandpub.com

To Ray Charles, Nick Perito, Mitchell Ayres
and all the other special people who helped make
Perry's music so memorable over so many years.

Acknowledgments

MANY PEOPLE AND MANY ORGANIZATIONS have helped us prepare this biography of Perry Como.

We were particularly fortunate to have the help of Ray Charles, who was Perry's choral director for over 35 years. Ray, seemingly ageless, could not have done more to aid us in bringing the project to fruition. He patiently answered the host of questions with which we bombarded him over a 12-month period, and he welcomed us to his home in Beverly Hills for a long interview. The clarity of his recall has helped us immensely, and through his contacts he was able to introduce us to others we might not have been able to reach.

Perry's son, David, was also a major help to us. He entertained us at his home in the Napa Valley and consented to a long interview, as well as responding to a range of ad hoc queries by email and phone. Perry's brother, Gene, who still lives in the area of Canonsburg, Pennsylvania, where he and Perry were born, accompanied us to see the former Como family homes, along with Mayor Anthony L. Colaizzo. Local historians Jim Herron and Gina Nestor gave us detailed background about the history of Canonsburg. Jim introduced us to Luigi Falcocchio, who helped us to understand the genealogy of Perry's Italian ancestors. Ken White of the Archives & Records Center in the Diocese of Pittsburgh kindly arranged for the details of Perry and Roselle's baptisms to be released to us to supplement this aspect of our research.

Perry Como has always had a loyal base of fans, and many of them provided invaluable assistance. George Townsend's comprehensive web site, www.kokomo.ca, was a constant source of information, and George also helped us at every stage of our undertaking. We are especially grateful to him for his permission to use his discographical research in one of our appendices. Matthew Long of the Perry Como Appreciation Society in Birmingham, U.K., was tireless in his support and willingly supplied a colossal number of items to help with our book. Another U.K. Como collector, Michael Dunnington from Pedmore, generously allowed us to borrow his substantial Como archive for several weeks. Larry and Judy Trompeter of Denver, Colorado, enthusiastically undertook the task of researching Perry's TV appearances using the archives at the University of Colorado. Colleen Zwack also has been only too willing to help in any way she could, and the interview she taped with Mickey Glass for the University of Colorado has added very useful background. To all of them we give grateful thanks.

Cassandra M. Volpe, Archivist at the American Music Research Center in the University of Colorado at Boulder where most of the documentation relating to Perry's career is stored, guided Larry and Judy Trompeter and relayed their findings back to us. Cassandra also made available to us some fascinating interviews with Nick Perito and Mickey Glass which are held in the university archives. In addition, research was undertaken at a number of other libraries and museums in the U.S. and the U.K., either in person or by email. Taking the U.S. first, we should like to thank the staff of the National Archives and Records Administration in Washington, D.C.; Rachel Moninger of Greater Canonsburg Public Library, Canonsburg; Laura Morgan, Chicago Public Library; the Los Angeles Public Library; the staff at the Carnegie Library of Pittsburgh; Allison Botelho, Reference Librarian at New Haven Public Library (Connecticut); Mira P. Waller, MLS Assistant Director Reference, Outreach, & Education Librarian, Duke University Medical Center Archives; and the Museum of Broadcast Communications, Chicago. In the U.K., thanks go to Louise North of the BBC Written Archives Centre, Caversham, the staff at the British Library in London; the Newspaper Library, Colindale Avenue, London and Manchester Public Library.

Those from the show business world who have given us tremendous assistance are (in alphabetical order): Bob Banner, Ken Barnes, Ron Cannatella, John Corrado, Michael Feinstein (who kindly contributed the Foreword), Bob Finkel, Will Friedwald, Bill Harbach, the late Dwight Hemion, Anita Kerr, Bill Klages, Buz Kohan, Rich Little, Yvonne Littlewood, Vera Lynn, Jeff Margolis, Tony Martin, Cassie Miller, Stephen Pouliot, Jack Swersie, Terry Terajima, Felisa Vanoff, Rob Waldman, Andy Williams, Dick Williams and Bob Wynn. It was a pleasure and an honor to engage with these members of the entertainment profession. All were extremely helpful and very happy to give us their time to talk about Perry.

Interviews with Bob Banner, Bob Finkel, Dwight Hemion and Bill Klages which were made available on YouTube by the Academy of Television Arts & Sciences Foundation's Archive of American Television were very useful in supplementing our direct contact with these individuals. Jenni Matz of the Academy kindly provided source details of the interviews and permission to reproduce extracts.

Our thanks are also given to the following, all of whom made significant contributions to the preparation of this book: Mike Costello, Richard Grudens, Gary Hamann, Elizabeth Leonard, Martin McQuade, Gilbert Nelson, Jon Oye, Keith Parkinson, Graham Pascoe, Lee Pecue, Judy Schmid, Allison Scott, Mike Schnurr, Greg Van Beek and Wig Wiggins.

Last, but certainly not least, we must make special mention of our spouses, Pat and Linda, whose tolerance, love and support we too easily take for granted! Thank you, girls.

Malcolm Macfarlane and Ken Crossland • Spring 2009

Contents

Foreword by Michael Feinstein

SOMETIMES IT TAKES DOGGED DEDICATION AND assiduous research to help restore a once iconic name to its rightful position in history. The name of Perry Como is famous, but only with a certain generation, and it has not been treated kindly by time and taste. How very unfair and inappropriate considering Como's success, influence, achievements, and most of all, his talent. Anyone who reads this book, even without hearing his music, will immediately grasp the scope of his effect on the Golden Age of popular music in the U.S., the U.K. and beyond. It's amazing that most people don't know what a big star Como was or that he survived the decades of change in music without altering his essential style.

Perry was the real thing, and his famously understated delivery made a multitude of fans believe that singing was easy. For him it was, yet his ease of delivery should not be confused with how seriously he regarded his art or how high a level of musicianship he maintained. The nonchalant vocal style that became the butt of jokes was indeed his birthright, but it was what he did with it that elevated him to the pantheon of great singers.

Perry's story is fascinating and gives the reader a great sense of what the entertainment world was like in the last century. It is about innovators and originators of music who were unknowingly creating history and elevating their art along the way. It's about exploration and new beginnings as the electronic age came into full bloom. It's about an era that happened only a few years ago yet is vastly distant from the world we know today. And it's all seen through the eyes of one fascinating man.

Perry sailed through the years with pop record hits that ranged from the flowery ballads of the Gilded Age, through rock 'n' roll and into the mellow rock sounds of the seventies. He also displayed talent that transcended song, for he was noted as a television natural and became one of the most familiar faces on the small screen for many years. His long forgotten films reveal a handsome movie star face that looked swell in Technicolor, almost transcending the improbable celluloid stories. Those who saw him perform live in his later years hold the memory dear. He gave generously to his public and they gratefully returned the affection.

His is a wonderful story told on a broad canvas, and will go a long way toward reminding the fickle public that Perry Como was here and made a difference in many, many lives. And every time one of his records is played, he continues to do so.

Michael Feinstein is a four-time Grammy-nominated singer and pianist. An interpreter, scholar and archivist of the Great American Songbook, he is an advisor to the National Recording Preservation Board of the Library of Congress.

Introduction

WHEN PERRY COMO DIED PEACEFULLY, sleeping in an armchair ("how else?" asked one obituary[1]), the tributes reflected the man; warm, sensitive, understated. His death was not headline news because the days when he filled the headlines were long gone. Anyone over the age of 50 remembered him as the ever-present face of music on 1950s television. Anyone 30 to 50 years old remembered him as a somnambulant singer who turned up once a year to sing Christmas songs. Yes, he had been a big star. Everybody was agreed on that. As for the rest.... He wore cardigans, didn't he? And what did he sing? Ah, yes, "Catch a Falling Star" and.... Oh well, there was lots more too, but even the obituarists didn't seem too sure. "One supposes that there are biographies out there about Como," William F. Buckley wrote, "because there are biographies out there about everybody."[2]

Everybody except Perry Como. When the idea for this book was first conceived, the first question people asked was how many other books there were about him. None. None? No one would believe it. This was a singer who first walked up to a microphone in 1933 and kept on doing so for 61 years; a singer who, by the time gramophone records became obsolete in the mid–1980s, had sold over 100 million records. He had 17 gold discs and 14 chart toppers; in the 1950s, he sold more records than anyone bar Elvis. When music historian Joel Whitburn published his list of the top ten chart performers from 1950 to 1999, the only representative of the pre–rock era was Perry Como.[3] Not Sinatra or Crosby, not Tony Bennett or Nat King Cole, not even Dean Martin or Barbra Streisand, but the former barber from Canonsburg, Pa. It was inconceivable—wasn't it?—that nobody had bothered to tell the story of a man who stood as a colossus in the history of American television, hosting over 1,000 weekly shows during an unbroken 15-year dominance of the medium. But it was true. The career that once loomed large now stood undocumented and increasingly forgotten.

When finally the message struck home, the next question was "Why?" Was there perhaps a dark side to the avuncular Mr. Como that had been expertly concealed for 60 years or more? Or was it simply that Perry Como's life was so bland and blameless that there was no story to tell? Perry himself would probably have subscribed to the latter view, although he would probably twitch a cheek muscle at the idea that he was "blameless." He was an ordinary guy who happened to be able to sing. That he could sing better than almost anyone else on the planet seemed to pass him by. His long time friend and choral director, Ray Charles, said he was "the most underrated singer of the century," which is exactly how his boss would have liked it.[4] Perry, said the people who knew him, never wanted a biography to be written about him. Such a stance was in part an extension of his ordinariness. For years and years, he turned down requests to appear on television talk shows partly because he believed that he had nothing to say, or at least nothing that would be of interest to anyone watching. But the main reason that he preferred to stay in the shadows was because he valued the privacy of himself and his family almost as much as anything else in his life. "He consents to spotlights beamed on him only as necessary to perform for his audiences," wrote William Buckley. "Otherwise, he was happiest serving merely as a presence in the room."[5]

In writing the first biography of Perry Como, we have sought to respect the privacy that he treasured so dearly. He was married to the same woman for 65 years until her death, three years before his own. They raised three children, had homes in New York, Florida and North Carolina, were practicing Roman Catholics and quietly supported a host of worthy causes. They appear to have lived full and rewarding lives as a devoted couple. Our probing of the private life of Perry Como has extended no further.

Outside the boundaries that he set and guarded, however, Perry Como chose to make himself public property. He loved to sing, he loved to work with writers, arrangers, singers, producers, directors, musicians, and above all, he loved the rapport that he created with his audiences and his fans. But as Michael Feinstein points out in his introduction to this book, the name of Perry Como is fast fading. Without a documented record of his life and career, eventually no one will know who Perry Como was, what he contributed to music and entertainment in the 20th century and why he was ever famous. Left untended, his achievements in public life will soon wash away with the sands of time.

Those achievements are enormous. "Bing Crosby created microphone singing, Louis Armstrong made it swing and Frank Sinatra made it the stuff of consenting adults," Richard Cook wrote in 2000. "All three of them, though, might have to defer to another as the most enduring singer in pop. Perry Como has outlived all his peers and every fashion in popular singing."[6]

When Perry Como put down his barber's shears and started singing, everybody was copying Bing Crosby, the man who started it all. By the time World War II arrived, Frank Sinatra had emerged as the first real challenger to Crosby in over a decade. It was in the slipstream to the two greatest and most enduring crooners that Como found his niche. Musically, it took the form of a series of dramatic ballads that began with "Till the End of Time," the biggest hit record in the U.S. in 1945, followed swiftly by "Prisoner of Love," "Temptation," "Because" and more.

For a time, Como seemed content to ease along as the third man of popular singing, until his radio sponsors, Chesterfield Cigarettes, decided to experiment with the new medium of television. Where others were wary and uncertain about the small box in the corner of the living room, Perry Como made it his home. Through the 1950s, he was the incarnation of Eisenhower's America. Cool and casual, his appeal crossed generations, time zones and seasons. His weekly TV show became an institution, "Saturday Night with Mr. C," the TV show that everyone watched and everyone remembered. He was the voice of Christmas, the herald of Easter, and the Kewpie Doll singer at the high-school hop. Television created a succession of hit records for him with novelty songs such as "Hot Diggity" and "Round and Round." In recent years, critics have thumbed their noses at Como's espousal of such novelty material, but they miss the point that Como's TV routines built around such songs were the forerunner of the modern music video.

With perfect timing, he exited his weekly show in 1963, just before the arrival of the Beatles turned the musical world on its head. For the rest of the Sixties, Perry Como virtually disappeared, leaving his golf cart and his fishing boat only for the occasional TV special or record date. Then a song called "It's Impossible" and a Las Vegas debut at the age of 58 relaunched his career, which endured for another quarter century. Even at the age of 80, Como could sing with a vocal range and purity of tone that few could match.

The statistics tell their own story:

• Between 1936 and 1987, he recorded over 700 songs, and in the 25 years from 1945 to 1970, his record sales exceeded 100 million—only Bing Crosby, Elvis Presley and the Beatles sold more in that period.

• Between 1945 and 1976, he scored 131 charted records in the U.S., fourteen of which reached the top spot.[7] He also enjoyed chart successes in many other parts of the world, particularly the U.K. and Australia.

• Seventeen of his records were accredited Gold status, from "Till the

The avuncular Mr. Como in a 1962 television image (courtesy Colleen Zwack).

End of Time" in 1945 to "Catch a Falling Star" in 1958. The last-named song had the distinction of being the first record officially certified Gold by the Recording Industry Association of America (RIAA).

• He received a Grammy in 1958 for Best Vocal Performance, Male, for "Catch a Falling Star" (the first such award to a male singer) and was posthumously awarded the Grammy Lifetime Achievement Award in 2002.

• He recorded 33 albums, all of which sold consistently well over the years with four of them being accorded gold status by the RIAA.

• As a pioneer of television, he made his debut on Christmas Eve 1948 and went on to host an incredible 1,049 shows as well as making more than 80 guest appearances on other programs. His Christmas specials became a holiday fixture and were invariably highly rated by the audience measurement organizations.

• He made headlines in 1959 when he signed a television contract worth $25 million over a two-year period. The deal, described as the biggest in the history of show business, gave the exclusive services of Perry to the Kraft Foods Company, for a total of 66 color TV shows on Kraft's Wednesday 9 to 10 P.M. hour.

• He won the Emmy awarded by the Academy of Television Arts and Sciences for Best Male Singer in 1955 and 1956. Also in 1956 he won the Emmy for Best M.C. or Program Host (Male or Female). He followed this in 1957 by winning the Emmy for Best Male Personality (Continuing Performance). The Academy inducted Perry into its Hall of Fame in 1990.

• After a long absence, he returned to the live concert stage in 1966 and gave more than 570 performances in the period up to 1994.

• A practicing Catholic, he was made a Knight Commander of the Holy Sepulchre in 1952, one of the top honors of the Church. In addition he received the Club of Champions Medal for 1965, the highest award conferred by the Catholic Youth Organization.

• A supporter of many charities, he was particularly associated with the Duke University Children's Hospital in Durham, North Carolina, where he helped raise millions of dollars over a 20-year period. The university gave him an honorary doctorate in 1977 when he was made a Doctor of Humane Letters. He also held an honorary degree from Niagara University.

• Perry was presented with the Kennedy Center Honor in 1987 by President Reagan. He had performed at the White House in 1982 and in 1983 he entertained the visiting British queen, Elizabeth II, at a prestigious event in Hollywood.

• A single-handicap golfer, he sponsored the Perry Como Amateur Invitational golf tournament each Thanksgiving weekend from 1962 to 1969 at Port St. Lucie Country Club in Florida. Over the years, he played in numerous fund-raising tournaments for various charities.

Perry Como continues to hit the charts. His recording of "Jingle Bells" topped the Ringtones chart published by *Billboard* in December 2006 and 2007. His 21st century success provides a postscript to the career of a great singer, but no more than that. No history of popular music can be considered complete without an examination of the career of Perry Como. In a show business world where chivalry often took second place to blind ambition, Perry Como was the nice guy who came out on top. It is time that his story was told.

⬭ Chapter 1 ⬭

The Barber Business

THE TOWN OF CANONSBURG SITS IN Washington County in the state of Pennsylvania, some 18 miles south of Pittsburgh. Its origins date back to 1789 when Colonel John Canon laid out the first settlement there and gave the town its name. Incorporation for the town came as early as 1802 and it grew steadily throughout the 19th century, the area's rich natural reserves fueling industrial growth built on coal and steel. By the dawn of the 20th century, the town's population supported a population of around 5,000, many of the townsfolk being newly arrived Greek and Italian immigrants who settled in the East End of the town. Between 1910 and 1920, the town doubled in size, with immigration again a major factor.

It was in Canonsburg on May 18, 1912, that Perry Como was born at 227 (later renumbered 527) Franklin Avenue.[1] Perry was the first American-born child of Pietro and Lucia Como. Perry's father, Pietro, had been born in Palena in the province of Chieti in the Abruzzi e Molise region of Italy in 1877. His wife, Lucia Travaglini, was born six years later in the same town. They married in October 1901, and their first child, Basilica, was born the following year. The Comos settled to married life in the town of Palena, which stands on a gentle hill in the Aventino valley. Its history dates back to the 11th century,[2] but by the time Pietro and Lucia exchanged their vows, living conditions in the Abruzzi region were hard. The wool trade that had sustained the town for most of the 19th century was dying. The industrial revolution had finally reached southern Italy and handcrafted woolens had no place in the new industrial landscape that worshipped the twin gods of coal and iron. It was the same all over the south of the country. A series of natural disasters made life harder still. Many families looked to America for salvation. By the time the 19th century turned, 10 percent of the *palenesi* had joined the tidal wave of emigrants to the United States. Between 1900 and 1910, over two million Italians left their homeland to settle there.

Pietro's younger brother, Falco, was the first Como to make the crossing, arriving in New York in 1902. In May 1904, Pietro followed him aboard the *SS Roma*. Pietro's intended destination was the town of McKeesport, Pennsylvania, where Falco had settled, but he seems never to have got beyond Ellis Island. Why Pietro Como's voyage proved abortive is a mystery; perhaps there were medical or other issues preventing his entry into the U.S. Perhaps he was simply overcome by homesickness. What is clear is that within weeks of setting sail from Naples, Pietro Como was back home, working as a farmer in Palena.[3]

Six years passed before a severe drought[4] in Palena caused Pietro to try again. Traveling aboard the *San Giovanni*, Pietro entered the U.S. through Ellis Island on May 23, 1910. U.S. government immigration records detail that he was 5 feet 3 inches tall, with brown hair and brown eyes and carrying with him the sum of $24.[5] This time, Pietro's destination was Canonsburg where his brother-in-law Giuseppe Travaglini had settled a few years before.

From the moment he arrived, Pietro's sole ambition was to earn enough money for his wife Lucia and their children to join him. By the end of the year, he had realized his goal, and Lucia made the arduous seven-day voyage from Naples aboard the *Duca degli Abruzzi*. She arrived in New York on December 21, 1910, with her three Italian-born children, Basilica, Giuseppina (Josephine) and Domenico. The Comos were reunited in Canonsburg and celebrated their first American Christmas as a family.

Pietro would soon learn enough English to get by in his new homeland but Lucia never mastered the language, although she did find a way of communicating. Her youngest son, Gene, recalled his mother talking over the garden fence to the Greek lady who

lived next door. Neither could speak English or each other's language but somehow they knew what the other meant.[6] Pietro adopted the Anglicized name of "Peter," while his wife became "Lucy." Their first American-born child was baptized at the Church of the Immaculate Conception, Washington, Pennsylvania, on March 10, 1913.[7] The name they chose was Pierino Petrum, but this was soon given an English treatment, and the newborn baby became Perry Ronald Como. The middle name was apparently an anglicization of Rinaldo, the name of his maternal grandfather. Despite his English name, Perry Como spoke only Italian until he started school at the age of six.

Conventional Perry Como wisdom holds that he was one of thirteen children and more particularly, the seventh son of a seventh son. In many cultures such a child is blessed with special powers and good fortune. Perry Como did indeed have special gifts—and a modicum of good fortune—but neither arose from being the seventh son of a seventh son. The idea that Perry Como grew up in a family of thirteen is another myth that has endured

Perry's birthplace at 227 (now 527) Franklin Avenue as seen in 2007 (photograph by authors).

down the years, fostered in part by Como's willingness to discuss it in television interviews later in his life as a statement of fact. Even Como's youngest brother, Gene, believed that his parents had produced thirteen children.[8]

The reality is that Perry Como was one of ten who were born to Pietro and Lucia between 1902 and 1923, seven of whom survived to adulthood.[9] Three infants, including a pair of twins, died before the Comos left their native Italy. The three infant deaths plus Basilica, Giuseppina and Domenico meant that Perry was the seventh child of Pietro Como, which may be the basis for the notion that he was a "seventh son of a seventh son." Over time, such stories often develop a life of their own, and in later years, virtually every interview that Como gave opened with that suggestion.[10] Perry usually shrugged off the idea that he had any special gifts because of it, although he never denied its veracity, despite knowing full well that he had only one elder brother.

The Como children grew up in East Canonsburg where the Cecil Improvement Company had made land available for the development of an industrial site that became the Standard Tinplate Corporation factory in 1903. Their rapidly increasing workforce needed houses and the Improvement Company was happy to oblige, laying out the adjoining site and selling the land in lots for $400 each. Before long, there was a large estate occupied by workers and their families from all over Europe. As it developed, East Canonsburg became a rough area with many crime problems. Events there rarely featured in the local newspaper, which preferred to concentrate its stories on the more prosperous south end of town. The Ku Klux Klan was active in the East End and there was a backlash by the indigenous Presbyterians against the many Catholic immigrants. Rival religious leaders discouraged their congregations from mixing outside their religions.

Perry went to the First Ward School, which had no less than eighteen different nationalities in attendance, with Italian and Polish pupils predominant. In 1926, he entered Canonsburg High School but would leave within two years without graduating.[11] At that time, children could withdraw from school with their parent's permission at age 14. With Pietro's blessing, Perry left school to pursue the career that his father had already mapped out for him: the barber business.

The Como family fitted the stereotype of the Italian-immigrant family—hard working, musical and entrepreneurial. Pietro Como encouraged his children to learn to play a musical instrument. His own love was for opera and the music of Enrico Caruso and later, Beniamino Gigli.[12] Perry recalled his father as a relaxed man. "He was laid back, although we didn't call it that, then," said Perry,[13] who attributed much of his own easygoing nature to his father's influence. Despite Pietro's diminutive size and calm exterior, he could be forceful when he needed to be. "You always knew he was the boss," said Perry.[14] Pietro also had a keen eye for money and knew how to supplement his factory wages.

Taking his father's lead, Perry borrowed a hundred dollars or so to buy his first musical instrument, a double-bell euphonium. This was the late 1920s and Perry by then was working in his own barbershop. A friend invited him to play in a marching band at a local Italian festival. It meant taking the weekend off from cutting hair, but Perry proudly returned with twenty bucks to show for his playing. Perry expected praise from his father. What he received was anything but. "So you made twenty bucks playing a horn," said Papa Como. "What about the $100 you lost in the barbershop?" With that, Pietro Como took the euphonium from his son and disappeared into his work shed. When he returned, the horn was minus its two bells, which, Perry said, his dad used for wine funnels. "So I wound up with no euphonium and a $100 debt," said Perry.[15]

After Perry's birth, the Como family grew further with the births of another daughter, Venzie, in 1918, and two more sons, Albert in 1920 and Gene in 1923. They remained a devoutly Catholic family. Gene Como recalled their regular attendance at St. Patrick Catholic Church in Canonsburg. In later years, after Pietro lost his sight in one eye in an accident at work, he abandoned his Catholic faith. At his death in 1945, his funeral service took place at the Greenside United Presbyterian Church, although Lucia and her children remained with the Roman church for the rest of their lives.

Pietro Como's easy-going nature disguised a strong entrepreneurial spirit. His regular income came from his job as a mill hand at the Standard Tinplate Corporation. It gave him around $35 per week, marginally above the average for skilled male labor in U.S. manufacturing industry at that time. Yet by the time Perry had the chance to set up his own barbershop in the mid–1920s, Pietro had amassed sufficient capital to bankroll him in the venture. Pietro's income source was property. Not long after Perry's birth, the family moved across the street to 530 Franklin Avenue but Pietro retained the ownership of their old home at 527 and took in boarders. Standing outside 530 some 80 years later, Gene Como recalled that his father owned several properties adjoining their home.[16] They had, he said, provided the money that kept the family afloat through his father's time as an invalid.

Despite Pietro Como's ability to find money, his upbringing meant that he thought

about a trade for his sons ahead of any ideas of high school learning. He resolved that his first-born American son should enter the barber business. Of all the Italian workers arriving in America in the first decade of the 20th century, almost half claimed to be *barbieri*. It was a trade that offered a good living and a secure income. Every man needed a haircut and a shave. Nick Tosches, in his biography of Dean Martin, likened the role of the barber to that of the local priest. "Men came to him whether they wanted to or not, because it made them feel clean, because it was something that one did. A haircut was a sacrament, a ritual, a communion not with God but with other men."[17]

The former Como family home at 220 (now 530) Franklin Avenue, 2007 (photograph by authors).

Perry started work in Stefano (Steve) Fragapane's three-chair barbershop at 214 Third Street at the age of 10. Fragapane's shop was not far from the Como residence and young Perry would work in the morning before heading off to school. After school, he

Christmas season in the early 1920s. Steve Fragapane (left) is cutting Antonio Terlingo's hair while a diminutive Perry Como (right) attends to another customer (courtesy Jim Herron, Canonsburg historian).

returned and worked through to 7:30 in the evening. He earned 50 cents per week, shining shoes and sweeping the floor, although it wasn't long before Perry started to try his hand with the shears and a razor. "I trained on my dad," Como later said. "He had one of those wonderful Italian handlebar moustaches." Little by little, Como trimmed—first one side and then the other until eventually the moustache was not much more than "a smudge under my dad's nose." "He'd have killed me if I did it all at once," said Perry.[18]

Perry progressed rapidly to become an after-school apprentice to Fragapane and soon had his own chair in the shop. He was always proud of his skills as a barber. He had big hands but shaved very lightly, he later recalled, with an open razor. "I cut myself with a safety razor," he joked.[19] By the age of 14, Perry felt confident enough to open his own shop. Pietro Como provided the necessary funding, although Perry maintained for the rest of his life that he never knew how his father had raised the cash. The impression given by Perry was that his shop had been a new venture, a bold step in the direction of entrepreneurial freedom. Local Canonsburg historians, however, offer a different spin, one that illustrates the seventh son-style good fortune that seemed to accompany Perry.

In 1926, Perry had left Fragapane and was working at a shop at 520 Blaine in Canonsburg's Greek quarter. One morning Perry turned up for work to find that his new boss had passed away suddenly. The barbershop was located in a building that also housed a Greek coffee shop, and its owner, Mike Pihakis, offered Perry the chance to take on the two-chair barber business. Pihakis's coffee shop served as the center for the Hellenic community in Canonsburg and in the absence of a Greek Orthodox Church also served as a venue for weddings and baptisms. Before a Greek wedding, custom was for the groom to visit the barber while the wedding party sang during the haircut. The tips were good—gold pieces, 5- and 10-dollar coins. "He could make three months' wages in one day," Pihakis's son Manuel recalled in 2004.[20]

The money might have been good in his own shop, but the dawn to dusk regime soon began to take its toll. Perry was not a strong youth and his father grew unhappy about the way the strain was beginning to show. "So he sold the shop!" said Perry in 1988.[21] Perry returned to having his own chair in someone else's barbershop, but at the same time started out on a new apprenticeship in the music business. Perry had learned to read music as part of his abortive foray with the euphonium. He also learned to play the organ and the guitar, but it was his vocal cords that began to catch people's ears. Perry's soft crooning as he clipped away with the shears helped to keep the tips flowing and soon he was supplementing his income by singing at local chapters of the Sons of Italy and other fraternal organizations.

Perry's next step was to form a vaudevillian double act with a local comedian named Lou Marchione.[22] Their billing was "Perry & Lou—The Comedy Boys." Forty years later, Perry recalled his partner as "a short man—that's something for me to say, isn't it [Como was around 5' 8" in height]—much shorter than me with a cherub-looking face."[23] Perry played guitar and sustained the duo through their opening song:

> How do you do, everybody, how do you do
> We are the comedy boys, Perry and Lou
> From Maine up to Alaska
> This is all we wanna ask you
> How do you do, everybody, how do you do?[24]

From then on, Marchione's corny comedy took over, and Como cringed visibly when he recounted some of the jokes in a TV interview years later. Despite their "Maine to Alaska" billing, the duo was strictly a local act. Their impact on show business history is now invisible, but the experience gave Perry his first taste of performing to a live audience—and made him want to do more.[25]

By the time Perry teamed up with Lou Marchione, a more important partnership in his life was taking shape. Sometime around 1927, Perry and a group of friends took a trip to a weiner roast on the banks of Chartiers Creek that runs through Canonsburg. There he met a pretty young blonde girl whose parents lived in the nearby town of Meadowlands. Her name was Roselle and for the rest of his life, Perry referred to her as "my girl."

According to baptism records, Roselle Bellino was born on May 11, 1912, although there is some uncertainty about both her date of birth and the spelling of her maiden name; June 11, 1914, is a more commonly quoted date, and her family name is often shown as "Belline."[26] Her parents were Domenico and Joannia Bellino. Like the Comos, the Bellinos were Italian immigrants. They were born in Locana, close to Turin in Italy's

Piedmont region. Locana was just across the border from France and when the Bellinos chose to leave Italy, it was there that they headed first. Joannia bore two sons during their time in France before they decided to join the emigrant trail west.

By the time the stock market crashed in 1929, Perry and Roselle were dating steadily. Canonsburg survived the worst ravages of the Great Depression, thanks mainly to the resilience of the largest plant in town, Standard Tinplate, and the adjacent Continental Can Co. Tin cans were one of the few products for which demand held up. Demand for haircuts and shaves fared well too, and Perry was able to make a steady living. But in 1932, he made a decision that would change his life. He left his work in Canonsburg to move 100 or so miles north to Meadville in Crawford County, in western Pennsylvania.[27] Perry's new chair was in his uncle's barbershop run at the Hotel Conneaut on Conneaut Lake Park. The hotel, built in 1905, had a reputation as a leisure and music resort and offered Perry a distinct step up in terms of his musical interests.

Conneaut Lake is Pennsylvania's largest natural lake, located 40 miles south of Erie and 80 miles from both Cleveland and Pittsburgh. The early years of the century saw it establish a reputation as a summer resort getaway. As such, it was a regular stopping point for the dance bands that worked their way up and down the Ohio Valley. The arrival of just such a band gave Perry the break he needed. The hotel booked the mighty Duke Ellington and his orchestra to do a one-nighter in the Dreamland Ballroom on August 5, 1932. To open the show, they hired the Freddie Carlone band from nearby Cleveland. Carlone and his 13-piece band were on the lookout for new singer. Within a year, the young barber who watched from the floor that night would hang up his shears and pick up the microphone as the Freddie Carlone band's resident vocalist. A sixty-year show business career was about to take shape.

Perry Como's "audition" with the Freddie Carlone band came early in 1933. Some sources have suggested that the audition was pre-arranged, with Como having been introduced to Carlone by mutual friends. Como's own account, however, suggested that it was more of a chance encounter. He said that he, Roselle and a gang of friends spent a weekend having fun in nearby Cleveland. There they found the Carlone band playing at the Crystal Slipper Ballroom, Cleveland's newest and biggest dance hall. The group of friends was having a good time dancing when Freddie Carlone issued an open invitation to any would-be vocalist to come on stage and take a turn with the band. Perry's friends pushed him forward. "Go on, get up there," they told him. Recounting the occasion in a radio interview in 1994, Perry recalled the terror he felt. "I can't get up there," he told his friends "I don't know the band, their music...."[28] Carlone, a fellow Italian-American, saw Perry's dilemma. He was, said Perry, "a very nice guy" and encouraged Perry to come up and take a turn. "I don't even remember what I sang," said Perry years later, but Carlone liked what he heard. Soon he was offering Perry a regular spot with the band at a salary of $28 per week. "Twenty-eight dollars," said Perry. "I was shocked. I was earning twice that in the barbershop."[29]

The offer of a job singing with a band came out of the blue for Perry. He loved singing and was already enough of a ham to like the spotlight and the reaction of an audience, but he had never thought of it as any more than a sideline to the barber business. That was his trade, what he was good at. He knew that touring with the band would be fun, but still his mind focused on the downside. What if he failed? What if he got fired within a week? What if Carlone found a better singer—and surely, there were lots of singers who were better than him? And how could he justify to his family taking a job that might end tomorrow when he already had a regular job that paid twice as much? The answer to him seemed to be "No."

Perry headed back to Canonsburg and discussed it with his father. In his mind, he was expecting his father to tell him that his doubts were well founded and that he should forget any ideas of trying to earn a living as a singer. That, after all, was the reaction that he remembered from the euphonium episode. Once again, Perry found himself surprised by his father's response. Later, Perry reflected that perhaps his father had started to enjoy the fact that his son had become a local celebrity, singing in the local festivals and the Fourth of July Parade. "He walked right alongside me in the crowd," said Perry. "You know, 'That's-a-my-boy.'"[30]

Pietro told his son that he understood his doubts and his uncertainty but said that he had been given an opportunity and he owed it to himself to see if he could make good. If he didn't give it a try, then he would never know whether he might have made it as a singer. To go through life not knowing and ever wondering would, he said, only lead to unhappiness and frustration.[31]

Perry's girlfriend, Roselle, took the same view as her future father-in-law. "She saw a little more in me than I did," Perry said in later years.[32] The clincher for Perry came when Roselle agreed to join him and travel with the band, although that meant another big step. As children of devout Catholic families, neither Perry nor Roselle could contemplate such a lifestyle without being married. On July 31, 1933, they stood before a Justice of the Peace in Meadville, Pennsylvania, and became Mr. and Mrs. Perry Como.

The Carlone band that Como joined was a modest, 13-piece outfit that had been formed by three brothers in 1927. Other members of the band included saxophonist Nick Lovano, violinist Maurice Cancasi, trumpeter Lennie "Buzz" Lenassi, pianist Fred Kaiser, and two more saxophonists, Arthur Circillo and Johnny Singer (aka John Mensinger). The Carlone outfit was essentially a "territory band," playing mainly at ballrooms up and down the Ohio Valley. Carlone managed to secure the occasional radio broadcast on local stations but was never able to gain a commercial recording contract. The band was a creature of its time. The twenties were a decade when America started "going out dancing."[33] It was a time of enormous cultural and technological change. Before World War I, social dancing had been reserved for the upper echelon of society. Dances were formal balls, dancers were chaperoned and the experience had a stately, regal air to it. By the mid-twenties, ballrooms and dance halls were spreading across the country. Hotels and clubs competed for the best dance bands, which in turn competed for the best musicians, whether ragtime, sweet, or hot—the epithets applied to the bands of the day.

When Carlone formed his band in 1927, he had no need of a resident vocalist. It was tunes, not songs, that dancers demanded, and in the days before a microphone became commonplace, a singer struggled to make himself heard above the band. Yet as the decade wore on, the Tin Pan Alley tunes started to take on the complexion of the modern popular song, complete with lyrics and requiring someone in the band to give them articulation. Every band needed someone to sing. It might be a saxophone player, or maybe the trombonist. Indeed any regular musician who thought he could sing might take a turn at the mike. Nobody employed a vocalist *per se* until a young man from Spokane, Washington, came on the scene.

His name was Harry Lillis Crosby, but the world came to know him as Bing. Even he had to go along with the convention of the day and in his early days with the Paul Whiteman Orchestra, the best-known band in America at the time, Crosby had to pretend to be a musician. Whiteman offered a variety of instruments, mainly in the brass and percussion sections, but each time, Crosby caused havoc. "I'd oompah along," said Crosby "and sometimes I'd oompah in tune and sometimes I'd be out of tune. Finally Whiteman had had enough and he gave me a violin with rubber strings."[34]

Technology added to the pace of change. Movies found their voice in 1927, while acoustic recording, a mechanical process, gave way to electrical around the same time. Radios brought voices into the living room and the advent of the microphone permitted a new style of singing. Bing Crosby was the first singer to realize that if the microphone could hear him, then so could everybody else. He developed a style of singing where the notes escaped gently from the back of his throat rather than exploding from his lungs. The crooner was born.

Como's entry into the Carlone band gave it a new dimension and style that people noticed. One reviewer commenting on Como's arrival said that the band had made "more progress within the last year than in the other six combined"[35] and was in no doubts as to why that should be. "The change," he said, "may be attributed in no small measure to the popularity of Perry Como, the featured vocalist with the orchestra." Perry's debut in the Carlone band came early in 1933, possibly as early as March 4. That date was significant because it represented the Carlone band's most high-profile booking ever as one of several bands playing at the Inaugural Ball for President Franklin Roosevelt in Washington, D.C. On March 7, the Canonsburg *Daily Notes* carried a story in its "Personals" column to the effect that "Perry Como, a local boy, is being featured by Fred Carlone's Band of Cleveland, Oh. This band is at present touring the country and played at the Inaugural Ball Saturday night." While the Canonsburg press stopped short of saying that Perry had actually appeared that night, another local paper, the Monessen *Daily Independent*, went a step further and talked of Perry having been "such a sensation at the Presidential Inaugural Ball."[36]

The young Bing Crosby in an early publicity shot (courtesy The International Club Crosby).

Como himself never made any mention of appearing at such a function and it is unlikely that even his none-too-great memory would have forgotten such a debut. What is clear is that Como was with the band some months ahead of his marriage to Roselle in July 1933. Saxophonist John Mensinger recalled that he and Perry joined the band around the same time. Every Sunday when their last performance was done, "I'd jump into my little 1930 Ford roadster and drive Perry to Canonsburg to visit his family and his girlfriend. We'd sleep in the basement at Perry's family home," Singer said.[37] Gene Como recalled the excitement that he felt as a young boy when the members of the Carlone band suddenly descended upon the Como household.[38]

Como's first identifiable billing with the Carlone band came in his hometown. On April 7, 1933, the band played at a "Big Dance" at Canonsburg's Mapleview Park. Not surprisingly, the Canonsburg press made great play of the local boy made good.[39] The band's main stream of bookings, however, was still in its native Cleveland. The Crystal Slipper Ballroom at 9810 Euclid Avenue was a regular venue,[40] but as Como's impact and popularity extended, so too did the band's. Soon Carlone was fielding bookings from venues as far afield as the Rice Hotel in Houston, Danceland in New York and the Edgewater Beach Hotel in Chicago.[41] For Perry and Roselle, traveling around on the band bus just added to the fun. "It was like an extended honeymoon," said Perry in 1977.[42]

Como's apprenticeship as a band singer, however, was far from smooth sailing and he had issues of both temperament and technique to overcome. First, he needed to get comfortable standing on the stage in front of the band. "How do you go from being a barber to singing with a band?" he reflected during a BBC interview in 1994.[43] Perry also needed to get familiar with singing into a microphone, something that was new to him. It took a while for him to adjust. Perry's natural singing voice was melodic but soft. He possessed a wide vocal range, which became apparent as soon as he embarked upon a solo career. But when Perry wasn't hitting the high notes, his liking for singing softly—something he retained throughout his career—meant that there was a problem of making himself heard. Prior to joining Carlone, Perry had used a megaphone in his occasional appearances on stage. This was the acoustic solution to the amplification problem that singers adopted before the invention of the microphone. Its best-known exponent was Rudy Vallee.

Vallee was the first singer to whom the term "crooner" was applied. It was used both as a term of endearment—generally by ladies, attracted by Vallee's handsome good looks—and ridicule.[44] Vallee first used a megaphone one evening in 1925, choosing a cut-down cheerleader's megaphone to project his voice. "For the first time, soft, sexy singing was wafted beyond the front row. The era of crooners had been born," wrote George T. Simon.[45] "My use of the megaphone came through absolute necessity," said Vallee. "My voice is very loud when I speak or shout yet when I use it musically, it's not penetrating or strong."[46]

Perry had the same problem. Joining Carlone meant that he was required, literally, to step up to the microphone (ironically, first introduced by Vallee himself in 1930[47]). Reluctant to discard his megaphone, Perry first tried singing through his megaphone into the microphone. The results were bizarre—the hollow, nasal sound that the megaphone created was amplified such that the voice itself disappeared into a massive echo chamber. Perry's stardust-painted megaphone had to go.[48]

Once it did, Perry's progress was spectacular. Six months after joining the band, he was its star attraction and by the summer of 1934, Perry was being talked of in the same breath as his idol, Bing Crosby. When the Carlone band came to Canonsburg in July of that year, the *Daily Notes* headlined, "Canonsburg Youth Rated as Modern Edition Bing Crosby." Featuring a full column photograph of a darkly handsome Como, complete with Ronald Colman moustache, the paper trumpeted the young Canonsburg boy who "threatens to snatch the crown from Bing Crosby's head."[49]

The labeling of Perry as a Bing Crosby disciple and clone would stay with him for the rest of his career. It was a comparison that Perry took more as a compliment than a burden. "If it wasn't for him, I'd still be cutting hair," Perry told his audience at the Boston Symphony Hall in 1988.[50] It was a standard line in Como's act by that time, usually followed by the punch line, "And at the prices they're getting these days, that wouldn't be a bad idea." In his more serious moments, though, Como acknowledged

The Carlone band, dressed for the occasion. Perry is in the center of the main row, just under Freddie Carlone, who stands at the back (courtesy Colleen Zwack).

the impact of Crosby but also the need to find a style of his own. "We all took something from Bing; me, Frank, the rest of the guys," Como told Michael Parkinson in a TV interview in 1977. "But there comes a time when you have to make a left turn somewhere; there was no future as a second somebody. You have to become the first."[51]

Not everyone saw Crosby as Perry's role model. "He patterned his singing style after Russ Columbo," saxophonist John Mensinger recalled.[52] Like Como, Columbo was the child of first generation Italian immigrants and his Neapolitan features were much closer to Como's than those of the half–Irish Crosby. Como and Columbo met in Cleveland in 1933 while Columbo was playing the Golden Pheasant. Como's later recollection that the crooner had been a "good friend"[53] might have been an overstatement, but Perry was certainly struck by the success that came the way of the handsome young singer from New Jersey. That success came to a tragic end in September 1934 when Columbo met his death in a bizarre shooting accident. Como however never forgot the influence that Columbo had on him. "When I was about 20, if you didn't sing like Bing or Russ Columbo, you didn't work," he said in 1973.[54]

By the time of Columbo's death, the Carlone band was touring extensively through the Midwest, picking up several radio spots along the way. It wasn't long before Freddie Carlone's young singer started attracting offers from the bigger bands. Vincent Lopez was one bandleader who courted Perry. Lopez's sweet-band style rivaled that of Guy

Lombardo and later, Lawrence Welk. Carlone's response was to offer Perry more money, and Perry agreed to stay. The Monessen *Daily Independent* carried the story of the deal "which assures the dancing public that Perry Coma [sic] will positively appear with Freddie Carlone."[55]

Despite the confusion over his name—"Como" often became "Coma," and one billing referred to the new singing sensation "Harry" Como[56]—there was no doubting that Perry Como was destined for bigger things. Freddie Carlone knew it, and when the time came, he would not stand in the way of the young singer from Canonsburg. It was just a question of who and when. The answer came one night in December 1935, in a gambling casino in Warren, Ohio.

Chapter 2

Beat the Band—
The Ted Weems Years

ONE OF THE BANDS THAT FOLLOWED a touring itinerary similar to Freddie Carlone's was the Ted Weems band. The Weems outfit was the same size and shape as Carlone but occupied a position at least two notches higher in the show business hierarchy. The band went back to 1923, formed by Weems—born Wilfred Theodore Wemyes in Pitcairn, Pennsylvania, on September 26, 1901—with his brother, Art, while they were students at the University of Pennsylvania. Success came quickly. Within a year, they had a recording contract and their first hit, "Somebody Stole My Gal," came a year later.[1] There followed a string of minor hits—often titles with an element of novelty or frivolity about them—although it wasn't until the band moved to Chicago in 1928 that people started to sit up and take notice.

It was radio however that made the Ted Weems band's name. By the time Weems made it to Chicago, radio had become a national phenomenon. NBC began broadcasting in 1926 and CBS a year later. By 1930, there were over 600 radio stations and over 12 million radio sets in the country. That number doubled over the next five years, while 2½ million car radio sets sold during the same period.[2] Weems' first significant radio contract was *The Canada Dry Ginger Ale Program* in 1932, with an up-and-coming comedian called Jack Benny as its emcee. Weems provided some humorous musical interludes although by now, the band was well on the way to developing a broader personality. Hot jazz and swing numbers sat alongside novelty and comedy material. Art Jarrett joined as a vocalist in 1927, followed in 1931 by Elmo Tanner, whose whistling gave the band a unique identity. By the time Perry Como joined, the band had become more of a show band than a serious jazz or swing unit. Big Band historian George T. Simon said the Weems band was a "good but never great musical outfit that turned in a whale of job entertaining in a modest, intimate sort of a way."[3] Como choral director Ray Charles was more direct. "It was a Mickey Mouse band, musically," he said, "with a small number of musicians and four entertainers."[4] Como described the band in a similar way. The singers, he said, were the heart and soul of the band. "I can't recall that it ever played a straight instrumental," he told George Simon.[5]

Como's chance to join Weems came through another piece of typical Perry Como good fortune. The Carlone band was booked to play a gambling casino in Warren, Ohio, sometime late in 1935. When Perry came to the microphone, Ted Weems was sitting at one of the roulette tables. Weems almost certainly knew of the young singer's growing

reputation but with no recordings and only a limited amount
of broadcasts, it was probably
Weems' first chance to hear Como
sing. He liked what he heard. By
now, Carlone had realized that
Como was destined for a bigger
stage and was encouraging offers
to come his way. One competing
offer was from the Paul Whiteman Orchestra in New York.
Singer Frankie Laine, in his autobiography, recalled that Weems
had lined him up as a possible
alternative to Perry, should
Como decide to take the Whiteman offer. When Perry decided in
the end to throw in his lot with
Weems, the wheel of fortune took
another turn and Laine ended up
as Como's replacement in the
Carlone Band.[6]

Como's salary with Weems
was $50 and he joined the band's
other featured performers including Red Ingle, Parker Gibbs and
Country Washburne. Ingle played

One of Perry's publicity photographs from his days with
Weems (courtesy Colleen Zwack).

sax, sang and had a talent as a human sound-effects machine. Como said, "He was one
of the most talented men I ever met."[7] Parker Gibbs shared the singing duties while future
Spike Jones City Slicker Country Washburne brought a hillbilly style to the band via his
tuba playing, occasional vocals and songwriting. Female vocalists Mary Lee and, later,
Marvel Maxwell[8] completed the vocal lineup. The star of the band, however, was Elmo
Tanner. "The whistler was the whole band," Como said in 1975, with a tongue-in-cheek
complaint that Tanner got all the good songs. "Any dumb song—the kind of stuff that
some guy had written on the back of a menu—was the stuff that Weems said, 'Arrange
that for Como,'" Perry said.[9] When Como hosted a Ted Weems reunion on his TV show
in 1961, the band played out a sketch where Perry was relegated to last place at the
microphone and then found his solo was drowned out by the backup singing of Ingle,
Tanner *et al.* Elmo Tanner was responsible for the Weems band's biggest hit record,
"Heartaches," which reached #1 in 1947, 14 years after the band had cut the record.
(Como's vocal refrain on "I Wonder Who's Kissing Her Now," recorded in 1939, was
another delayed hit for Weems, charting in 1947.)

Como's debut with the Weems band came early in 1936 at the Palmer House Hotel
in Chicago, but did not live up to Weems' expectations. The band broadcast from there
each evening over station WGN, but the new singer's slurred diction brought an immediate complaint from the station. Weems later said that it was so bad that WGN was
on the point of issuing an ultimatum—either the singer goes or the band. Weems was
reluctant to give up his new singer and had some transcriptions made of the broadcasts.
He asked Perry to stay behind one night to hear them. "I can't understand a word I'm

singing," said Como. The answer, Weems told his young singer, was simple—cut out the vocal tricks and give your voice the freedom it deserves. The advice did the trick. "His enunciation and performance improved overnight," wrote Weems in 1962. "He was on his way."[10]

Weems' recording contract was with Decca Records and on May 15, 1936, Perry Como made his recording debut. Two of the five sides cut that day are the earliest surviving examples of the Como voice and represent the first time that the name "Perry Como" appeared on a record label. Como's songs were "You Can't Pull the Wool over My Eyes" and "Lazy Weather." The first title was a quickstep tempo, with little scope for any vocalist to make much of an impact, but "Lazy Weather," an Oscar Levant–Irving Kahal composition, was more typical of the ballad style that would later become part of Como's stock-in-trade.

The influence of both Bing Crosby and Russ Columbo was very evident in Como's debut recordings, although they revealed the problem that any singer faced when trying to imitate Bing. Crosby's greatest talent was that his style of singing was effortless and free of any obvious technique—"the art that conceals the art," said music critic Henry Pleasants.[11] This art form—or lack of—presented a problem for anyone who sought to copy it. What was there to copy? It was like looking for the man who wasn't there. The consequence was that any Crosby copyist ended up presenting a caricature of Bing, and like any caricature, the results were full of exaggeration. Where Crosby's phrasing was smooth and effortless, his copyists sounded jagged and forced. While Crosby's bass notes reflected the natural timbre of his voice, his imitators sounded as if they were the scooping out the deep notes to match him. And where Crosby's range allowed him an effortless progression to a high note at the end of a phrase, his imitators' attempts to match his ability to soar often sounded weak and uncertain.[12] Taken in isolation, any good Crosby imitator could, for a fleeting moment, sound more like the real thing than Crosby did. Bing himself said that he once entered a Bing Crosby Sound-Alike Competition and finished third![13] It is only when the listener returns to the genuine article—a Crosby record or aircheck from that time—that the differences between real gold and fools' gold become apparent.

Como's "Lazy Weather" is an archetypal Crosby copy. His vocal is full of mannerisms and tricks, many of which Crosby had already discarded. His voice mimics the huskiness that Crosby had displayed in 1931, when over-use had almost destroyed his voice, and his pitch is lower than its natural level. Como often said that in the early days of his career, "if you didn't sing like Bing, you didn't work," and "Lazy Weather" is testament to that statement.[14] In the mid-thirties, only the Canadian crooner Dick Todd was delivering more obvious Crosby caricatures than the young Perry Como. None of which is to say that Crosby was the only influence, because there are echoes too of Russ Columbo in "Lazy Weather." Columbo's voice had a higher pitch than Crosby's (and indeed, Como's) but in some of Columbo's covers of Crosby's hits—notably Bing's theme song "Where the Blue of the Night"—his efforts to match Crosby's bass notes produce an unnatural and slightly slurred vocal effect. Como's attempts to deepen his register caused the same thing, resulting in the slurred diction that worried Weems' radio hosts.

Como's likeness to Crosby brought other complications. American Decca as a label had been founded on the basis of Jack Kapp's success in luring Bing away from Brunswick Records.[15] Kapp became president of Decca Records and his brother Dave also worked there. When Dave Kapp heard Perry sing, all he heard was a Crosby copyist. "Why are you letting him sing? Hell, we got one Crosby," he said to Weems. Kapp had made his comment out of earshot of Perry but it got back to him via one of the sound engineers.

"It was like someone stabbing me," Como said later.[16] A decade and a half later, Como arrived at the RCA studios in New York for a recording session and found Dave Kapp in the studio. "What the hell is he doing here?" Como asked. On being told that Kapp had recently joined RCA, Como took the studio mike and said, "Hi Dave, get the hell out of here!" and went on to tell him, and everyone else in the studio, just why.[17]

In June 1936, the Weems band took over as the featured band on the popular radio show *Fibber McGee and Molly*. The show, which premiered on April 16, 1935, went on to become one of the best-remembered radio comedies and stayed on the air until September 1959. It featured a real-life husband-and-wife pairing of Jim and Marian Jordan of Peoria, Illinois. The Jordans had toured throughout the vaudeville circuit before moving into radio. Their 15-minute show *Smackout* premiered on NBC in April 1933 and ran for two years until writer Donald Quinn developed the Jordans' characters into those of Fibber, a braggart and ne'er do well, and his honey-natured wife, Molly. Each week, the show featured the couple in a new situation. The Weems band provided incidental music as the plot moved along, together with a featured song in the middle of the show. It gave Como the occasional solo and his first coast-to-coast radio exposure.

The band continued its work on the show until January 1938. Live weekly broadcasts from Chicago meant that other work—touring spots, one-night stands and recording dates—had to fit around the weekly commitment to be in Chicago. Throughout 1937, *Fibber McGee & Molly* locked the Weems band firmly into the Midwest. For Perry, it meant that his lifestyle with Weems was much the same as it had been with the Carlone band. Roselle still toured with him and together, they enjoyed the here-today, gone-tomorrow style of life on the road. Como later recalled that they saw themselves as two kids—both were still in their early twenties—having fun rather than pursuing a career.

The Weems band was back in the Decca studios in August 1936, and Como featured on two songs, "Until Today" and "Fooled by the Moon." Once again, his vocals were full of the same Crosby mannerisms from the May session, although on "Fooled by the Moon," there were traces too of an Al Jolson influence. Como also featured along with just about every other member of the band in a third song recorded that day. "Knock Knock, Who's There?" was an archetypal Weems piece, based on the music hall joke that provided the song's title. Como's turn at providing the one-line answer to the knock-knock question was unbilled and unmemorable. The song nevertheless was a modest hit. On the next Weems session in September 1936 Como featured more prominently, handling the vocal refrain on four songs, "Picture Me Without You," "Rainbow on the River," "Darling Not Without You" and a Cliff Friend composition, "(Trouble Ends) Out Where the Blue Begins." The first three titles show a more composed and relaxed Como with fewer Crosby touches, although his rendition on "Out Where the Blue Begins" holds enough Crosby trademarks to fill all four records. The lyric's emphasis of the "B" consonant offered lots of "bu-boo-blue" phraseology that was Crosby's trademark and which Como was unable to resist.

Fibber McGee & Molly dominated the band's schedule for 1937 and Perry rode along as one of the gang until November of that year when he reached another milestone in his career: on Sunday, November 28, 1937, he made a solo radio broadcast for the Chicago station WMAQ. Como's show went out from noon to 12:15 P.M. and featured Perry with piano accompaniment. Appropriately enough, given his former life, a hair oil company was the sponsor.[18] The show later switched to a 10:45 A.M. Sunday slot and ran on a weekly basis for two months, the December 19 broadcast having the title "Perry Como Goes 'Bing!'"

In January 1938, the Weems band made its last appearance on *Fibber McGee &*

Perry Como never lost his adulation of Bing Crosby. Here they are seen together rehearsing for Crosby's guest spot on *Perry Como's Kraft Music Hall* in 1960.

Molly and set out on a national theatre tour. In the first two months of 1938, they played a series of dates in the East, with a heavy recording session in New York in February 1938. The band cut eleven sides over two days, five of them featuring Como's vocals. The strongest was "In My Little Red Book," a song that was a hit that year for Guy Lombardo. In March, the band was back in Chicago, where it opened at the Trianon Ballroom on March 5, 1938, and resumed radio work, both for the Mutual Broadcasting System and the NBC Red Network. Perry also resumed his solo career this time via an independent station, WCFL. The break from touring, however, was short-lived and by August 1938, Como found himself with the band in California. Engagements on Santa Catalina Island ran alongside a series of West Coast radio broadcasts, in which Elmo Tanner attracted most of the interest and publicity. While in Hollywood, Weems filmed a cameo appearance at Universal Studios for the movie *Swing Sister, Swing* and also found time to fit in a recording session in Los Angeles, cutting five sides. Two of the titles featured Como vocals. "Simple and Sweet" was easily his most assured performance on disc to that date, with the first hints of the more relaxed style that would become a trademark a decade later.

The year 1939 brought more of the same for Weems and the band. En route back from the West Coast, the band made stops in Salt Lake City, Denver and Kansas City before reaching Chicago. A young Italian musician called Nick Perito grew up in Denver and recalled spending his Sunday afternoons listening to the bands of Kay Kyser,

Bob Crosby, Les Brown and others as they passed through his hometown. "The orchestra of Ted Weems featured a handsome young Italian singer who immediately captured the hearts of all the ladies, especially those in my family," Perito later wrote.[19] Twenty-five years later, Perito would become Como's musical director and Man Friday, a constant figure at his side. The band stayed in the Midwest through the early part of 1939, heading east to New York in March for two days of recording. Como was the featured vocalist on two titles, an eminently forgettable "Song of the Cuban Money Divers (Ad-De-Day)" and a more suitable ballad, "Class Will Tell," in which the Crosby upper mordent, the distinctive "wobble" on a high note at the end of a phrase, was still strongly evident.[20] Soon, the band was back on the road and in June 1939, they returned to California, playing a season at the Casino Ballroom on Santa Catalina Island, with broadcasts each Monday evening, before heading east for a series of engagements through the fall of 1939.

Perry and Roselle celebrated their sixth wedding anniversary in July 1939 with the news that Roselle was pregnant. Their son was born on January 15, 1940, in the Passavant Memorial Hospital, Chicago. They named the baby Ronald, taking Perry's middle name, although the child was soon known as Ronnie. Perry was working with the band in Chicago at the time of the birth and risked his job by leaving the stage in mid-performance to be with Roselle at the hospital. Becoming parents did little to change the Comos' way of life. Once Roselle and the baby were strong enough to travel, she resumed traveling with Perry and the band, although the days on the band bus were over. "We had an old Packard," Como later recalled, "and we made the back seat into a form of crib."[21]

A new radio show, however, meant that Perry and Roselle could spend much of their first year as parents in Chicago. The show was *Beat the Band*, which made its debut on NBC on January 28, 1940. Sponsored by General Mills, makers of a new "ready to eat" corn cereal called *Kix*, and hosted by Garry Moore (later, the host of his own *Garry Moore Show*), the show was a musical quiz with listener participation. Quiz shows were, for a time, the hottest thing on radio and for this one, listeners sent in a musical question for the band, earning $10 if their question was used and a further $10 if their question "beat the band." The range of questions varied; almost all were corny to the extreme, and some bordered on the obtuse and the inane. When one questioner asked, "What would a dentist say to a tooth that he is pulling out?" the anticipated answer was "Aren't You Coming Out," which a band member was expected to come up with and then play. The humor went downhill from there:

> QUESTION: What would a near-sighted ballplayer say as he was rounding third base?
> ANSWER: "Show Me the Way to Go Home."
> QUESTION: What favorite song of a famous Scotch-entertainer are you reminded of by the picture of an Italian gentleman taking a walk early in the evening?
> ANSWER: "Aroamin' in the Gloamin'."

Any musician who missed an answer tossed 50 cents into the bass drum. The musician with the biggest tally of right answers walked off at the end of the show with the cash in the drum. *Variety* was lukewarm in its review of the first show, preferring the Weems band's "sample or two of good snappy dance music" to the quiz that it called "sluggish and uncertain."[22] In the first show, five of the 13 questions flummoxed the band members. *Variety* lamented the demise of a quiz-free evening. "Until [now]," it said, "the listener knew that at least on Sunday nights he could escape these adolescent mental or memory tests. The last refuge is gone and to top it all, the invader represents the curious spectacle of musicians being paid to play games instead of their instruments."

Recordings of many of the *Beat the Band* shows have survived, and the musical spots provide an indication of the type of material that was part of Weems' touring repertoire. Whereas most of the titles that Weems recorded commercially are long forgotten, many of the tunes they featured both live and in broadcasts went on to become standards. Como found himself tackling material such as "Indian Summer," "A Nightingale Sang in Berkeley Square" (which he would eventually record 37 years later) and "Our Love Affair," and the exposure to better quality material undoubtedly contributed to his development as a top-level vocalist.

Beat the Band occupied the Sunday evening slot for 13 months, the last show going out on February 23, 1941.[23] Its demise was hastened by a dispute over royalties between the National Broadcasters' Association and the American Society of Composers, Authors and Publishers (ASCAP). With ASCAP withdrawing permission for radio networks to play its material, the Weems band's on-air repertoire was limited to tunes by writers registered with Broadcasting Music Inc. Because such a constraint struck at the very heart of the show's concept, *Beat the Band* vanished from the airwaves. Free once more from a weekly commitment, Weems took the band back on the road, playing venues as far afield as the Shubert Theater in Cincinnati, the El Patio Ballroom in Denver and the Roosevelt Hotel in New Orleans. The trip south gave Perry his first exposure to the game of golf, using a set of clubs that he borrowed from the band manager, Bill Black. The love affair with golf lasted almost to the end of Como's life.

Between October 1939 and December 1941, the Weems band had only one further recording session, in New York in January 1941. Weems featured Perry on three vocals, "May I Never Love Again," "Rose of the Rockies" and "It All Comes Back to Me Now." Five years into his Weems experience, Como had finally begun to cast off his more obvious Crosby mannerisms. On "May I Never Love Again," Perry sang a full solo rather than merely a refrain chorus, and it was a more confident Como who stepped up to the microphone. His phrasing is more assured and deliberate and there are the first hints of the great reserve of power that the Como voice had in its peak years. The song is the first from all of the Weems recordings to display a distinct Perry Como sound.

Perry had by now been singing professionally for eight years. His development as a vocalist was slow—certainly much slower than that of Frank Sinatra, who arguably made greater strides during his two and a half years with the Tommy Dorsey Orchestra than Como did in his eight with Weems and Carlone. Indeed the Sinatra of the early forties was probably an influence on Como. Certainly, their paths crossed and in later years, Como suggested that they had been close friends for a time. There are definite hints in Como's vocals from 1941 and 1942 of the slower phrasing that was such a feature of Sinatra at that time—the first indication of a different influence on Como since the Crosby-Columbo parallels were drawn in 1934.

Touring the country with a small child was turning out to be less fun than the Comos had first thought. Perry later said that the worries about what it might do to Ronnie first hit him during the band's engagement in New Orleans early in 1941. "We were playing the Roosevelt Grill," Perry told Colin Escott in 1993, "and I noticed a little boy about eight ... sitting there among the strangers, lonely and restless. I said to Roselle, 'Is this what's going to happen to Ronnie?'"[24] As the baby grew, the Comos had to face the reality that they could not spend their whole life on the road. Roselle headed home to Canonsburg while Perry continued to tour with the band.[25] His earnings were now $250 per week but he found the price of separation from a family to be much higher. Thoughts about quitting, however, were put into sharper context by events elsewhere. With war in Europe and the Far East, debate at home was about if and how the United States might be drawn into the conflict. Those debates ended early one Sunday morning in 1941 with the Japanese attack on Pearl Harbor. When it came, Perry was in Los Angeles for a recording session that was scheduled for December 9, two days after the attack.

That session was Perry's last with the Weems band. He featured prominently on each of the four titles the band cut that day. Two were conventional ballads that provided a good platform for the maturing Como style; the third was a new up-tempo song called "Deep in the Heart of Texas." Written by Don Swander and June Hershey, the song went on to become the unofficial state song of Texas. The Weems band was the first to record it, and they scored a minor hit, although the main chart honors went to Alvino Rey and His Orchestra and Bing Crosby, who teamed up with the Woody Herman Woodchoppers to offer a jazz treatment.

The fourth title on the session was a song called "Ollie Ollie Outs in Free" and holds the dubious distinction of being Como's first recorded novelty song. The title was a variation on the phrase "olly olly oxen free" used in children's games.[26] Although the song itself was unmemorable—and indeed is one of only a handful of Como's recordings with Weems not to have enjoyed a reissue in LP or CD form—it provides the earliest example of Como dealing with novelty and nonsense material. Posthumously, critics were quick to accuse Como for selling his musical soul to novelty songs, but such criticism failed to recognize two things. One was that the novelty material was an indelible part of Como's mastery of music on television throughout the fifties. The second was that all of Como's peers, including Crosby, Sinatra *et al.* chanced their arm with similar material at times in their careers. The difference with Como was that he could carry it off better than anyone else. Where other vocalists might be heard to cringe audibly at the rhyming scheme of these songs, Como gave them a non-judgmental delivery, which was light, pleasant and fun. The songs were not "Night and Day," and no one pretended that they were.

With America on a war footing, the days of the touring bands were ending. Styles and tastes were changing too and gradually, the spotlight shifted until it shone as much on the vocalists in the bands as on the bands themselves. Bob Eberly with the Jimmy Dorsey band, Dick Haymes with Harry James and Sinatra with Tommy Dorsey were all emergent soloists, competing for the right to take on Crosby, who was still the undisputed champ. Frank Sinatra recalled that the competition was a factor in his leaving Dorsey and starting out on his own. "I thought if I don't make a move out of this band and try to do it on my own soon, one of those guys will do it, and I'll have to fight all three of them to get a position."[27] The remark says much about Sinatra's drive, energy and competitive nature. Como was a different animal. Languid and easy-going, Como rarely displayed any sense of ambition. When quizzed on television in 1979 whether he felt competitive with Sinatra, he said he did not. "It was all about getting the best songs. There was no sense of personal competition, just some joking and friendly name calling," he said.

Sinatra made his break from Tommy Dorsey in September 1942 and by the end of the year, Perry Como was a free agent too. On December 1, 1942, Ted Weems announced that the band's current engagement in Memphis would be its last for the duration of the war. Most of the band was to join the Merchant Marine at San Mateo Point on December 20. The band's final radio appearance came on December 13 on the *Fitch Bandwagon* show, when each member of the band said his or her public farewell. As a married man with a child, Como was somewhere down the pecking order for the draft, with a 3A ranking.[28] Rather than enlist, he decided to wait until he was drafted, which he never was. In the meantime, he had a family to support and a living to earn. His mood, as he watched Weems and his friends in the band head off for California, was melancholic. He spent Christmas Eve alone in Chicago—the worst Christmas he ever had, he said.[29] It had been nine years since he had joined the Carlone band. His sense now was that it was time to start living a real life, the one that his father had mapped out for him. His plans were to go back to Canonsburg, open up a barbershop, find a house and provide a home for Roselle and Ronnie.

A telephone call from a booking agent changed his mind.

Chapter 3

Till the End of Time

THE VOICE ON THE OTHER END of the telephone belonged to Tommy Rockwell. He was one of the doyens of the agency business, having started out as a recording executive in the twenties. He worked alongside Bing Crosby, Louis Armstrong and the Mills Brothers, but it was not until he formed the Rockwell-O'Keefe Agency with Francis (Cork) O'Keefe in the early 1930s that he began to develop his personal reputation. By the early forties, Rockwell-O'Keefe had become the General Artists Corporation (GAC), with clients who included most of the swing bands that mattered. Rockwell's list had on it names such as Glenn Miller, Artie Shaw, Jimmy Dorsey and Bob Crosby, and only the Music Corporation of America (MCA) was bigger. Even they struggled to match GAC's swing band pedigree.[1] One other client of Rockwell's was Ted Weems. It meant that Rockwell knew full well of the potential of Weems' Italian singer.

Rockwell was not the first agent to call Como and tell him that his ideas about going back to the barber business were crazy. Nevertheless, Como's lack of ambition and ordinariness seemed set to win the day. He already had a property in mind for his new shop and was well into negotiations with a realtor for the lease. Fortunately, two other Como characteristics—indecisiveness and a tendency to procrastinate—meant that the deal was slow in coming together.

Rockwell's pitch to Perry was different. Where the other agents offered more of the itinerant lifestyle that Como had tired of, Rockwell offered a radio deal in New York. He also told Perry that he could land him a recording contract. Most importantly, his pitch was that Perry could do it all from New York. No more life on the road. Como was tempted, but, as ever, uncertain. He genuinely did not think of himself as a star or even as somebody who was known in the music business. It seems inconceivable now that Como could have just flicked the "off" switch on his career, something that BBC interviewer Chris Stuart quizzed him about in a program to mark his eightieth birthday. "Surely that was just a press story," said Stuart. "No," said Perry, "I'd had my fun and I thought it was time to go home. Nothing had really happened, career-wise. I was a Chicago singer. Take me out of Chicago, and they would say, 'Perry who?'"[2]

Why then did Tommy Rockwell succeed where others had failed? Part of the answer was to do with Rockwell himself. Como felt that he could trust him. "I liked Tommy right away," Perry said. "He became my agent, but he was more like my father. He steered me. All my major career moves, he made. He had everybody. I'd have been a fool not to go with him."[3] There was also someone much closer to Como who had an influence. "My lady said, 'Stick with it,'" Como said in 1979.[4]

Como arrived in New York just as the swooner-crooner era was getting up a head of steam, renting an apartment at 45 E. 85th St. where he lived with Roselle and Ronnie.[5] It was an exciting time to be in New York, especially if you were a young, Italian singer. Frank Sinatra had made his first solo appearance at the Paramount in New York on December 30, 1942, heralding the arrival of the girl fans who became known as the bobby-soxers. Como's handsome Italian looks put him in pole position for the same kind of adulation. Como took a more down to earth view, however, of what he thought Rockwell should give him. "I wanted to get on radio and make records," he said later.[6] Rockwell duly delivered, and Perry made his New York solo radio debut in a 15-minute program for CBS on March 12, 1943. His contract was worth $100 per week.

Other one-off airings followed until April 12, 1943, when Perry started a regular series of sustaining (i.e. non-sponsored) broadcasts for CBS called *Columbia Presents Perry Como*. These 15-minutes shows aired in New York immediately behind the news at 4:30 P.M., with a simultaneous broadcast on the West Coast at 1:30 P.M. Perry had the Raymond Scott Orchestra backing him, together with guitarist Tony Mottola. With Warren Sweeney as the announcer, it was a thoroughbred cast. Scott was well known as a composer and musical inventor and had led his own Raymond Scott Quintette, a six-piece (despite its name) jazz-swing fusion, prior to joining CBS in 1942. Mottola went on to become one of the pre-eminent guitarists in the business, working extensively with Frank Sinatra as well as being Como's featured guitarist in his television years.

The daily shows were an exercise in soft melodies and gentle singing. Each show opened with Perry singing the theme "For a Little While," before moving into three songs, interrupted by an orchestral piece. Perry's songs were mainly ballads, some old, some new, but always easy on the ear. Warren Sweeney topped and tailed the show but in between, Como did his own linking of the songs, calling his audience "friends," the term he would use on stage and television for the rest of his career. *Variety* liked the show without going overboard, saying Como had a "polished delivery and phrasing" but criticizing his choice of songs. Como's first show had included two Crosby numbers, "It's Always You" and "I Surrender Dear." Como, said *Variety*, was finding the challenge of not sounding like his mentor hard enough without choosing Bing's material as well. Perry's third song, "Dream of Tomorrow," was, said *Variety*, "messed up at the outset by faltering accompaniment and a poor arrangement."[7]

Como's broadcasts continued each weekday throughout the summer of 1943. He took heed of what the reviewers said, staying clear of the Crosby catalogue and devoting his time to newer ballads. His singing was pleasant, but unexceptional. Most of the Crosby mannerisms had gone by now but he had yet to put a style of his own in its place. *Variety* thought his work "a bit too studied, resulting in a lack of warmth and excitement in his voice."[8] Perry exhibited the same characteristics when Tommy Rockwell brought him his first nightclub booking at the Copacabana on June 10, 1943, where Como turned a two-week booking into a three-month stay. Harriet Van Horne, radio critic of the New York *World-Telegram*, found him "darkly handsome, pleasantly wholesome, and mercifully unaffected. His voice is clear, full-throated baritone, and when he sings he appears to be suffering no pain at all. Not even that private exquisite pain that is peculiar to nightclub crooners."[9] A wordy Abel Green, future editor-in-chief of *Variety*, saw enough to persuade him that Como was destined for bigger things. "He has poise, showmanship and unction.... He croons with intelligence. He pitches and modulates with effect.... Como won't send the Copa customers into any comas, but neither does he sing them into a stupor. He manifests wise handling: better yet, he is interpreting his skillful auspices with a highly merchandisable songalog. Between the Copa acclaim, plus the CBS buildup, Como is on the ascension."[10]

In his usual style, Como played down the significance of his debut. He looked back on it in an interview with journalist Pete Martin in 1960. "Pretty cruel" was how he described it. "They didn't know who I was, just an ex-band singer." Como said. He was, he said, especially "frightened" during the dinner shows "where there'd be two guys, a little drunk, who only wanted to talk to each other about selling washing machines or automobiles—and all I did was to annoy them." When Martin asked how Como had responded, Perry said that the first line of defense was to turn up the volume on the mike, but that hadn't worked. "What then?" asked Martin. "I'd just sing a couple of songs and politely go away," said Perry. It was, he said, only the fact that "a couple of my records started to mean something" that kept him there so long.[11] (When confronted with a similar challenge of being heard in Las Vegas 25 years later, Como adopted a different tactic, singing without a microphone and forcing the noise to stop.)

The young crooner in an early 1940s publicity photograph (courtesy Colleen Zwack).

Perry Como's debut as a solo recording artist came 10 days after he opened at the Copa. Two long established labels dominated the recording business. One was Columbia Records, the oldest surviving brand in the business, dating back to the days of cylinder recordings in the 1880s. The other big player was RCA-Victor, usually referred to as Victor. In 1943, Columbia held Frank Sinatra's contract and Decca Records had Crosby. Victor needed a crooner to go head to head with the two giants and when Tommy Rockwell took his Como demonstration record to them, they bit straight away.[12] Perry signed his RCA contract on June 17 and three days later entered their Studio 2 in New York to cut three sides. It was the beginning of a business relationship that would endure for 44 years, the longest time ever spent by a major artist with the same company. Perry Como would go on to cut over 650 records for RCA, with 131 making the charts and 17 receiving Gold discs. Only Elvis Presley sold more records for RCA and together, Presley and Como stood head and shoulders above any other artist on the label.

Como could not have picked a worse time to start his recording career. On August 1, 1942, the American Federation of Musicians (AFM) had launched a strike, seeking royalty payments every time that a record was played on a jukebox or on radio. The newer boys in the industry, Decca and Capitol, settled within a year, but the old stagers, Victor and Columbia, held out until 1944. The ban kept any union member out of a recording studio and denied any jazz or swing band the ability to make records during that period. Singers such as Crosby, Sinatra and Como who were not members of the musicians' union were untouched by the ban, but while they were free to record, no musician could enter a studio to back them. All they could do was to hire a vocal group to provide an *a capella* backing. It was fine for the occasional outing but nothing more, and the recorded output of the big singers almost dried up while the ban was in place.[13]

In 1993, Como looked back on his first session as "murder." Rehearsals started at 11:30 A.M.; he cut his first take at 1:30 and was still there ten hours later. The problem, he said, was that he was flanked at the microphone by two backing singers "with perfect pitch."[14] Managing the vagaries of pitch and volume caused take after take to fall by the wayside. These were the days when a record was still cut into wax—mixing and editing were terms that did not yet exist in the recording business. When someone made a mistake, whether it was on the first note or the last, there was no option but to go back and start again. Eventually, RCA wound up with three finished masters from the session, although one, "Secretly," was never issued. The other two sides, "Goodbye Sue" and "There'll Soon Be a Rainbow," were issued together and reached #18 in the Billboard listings, with sales of 200,000 copies,[15] although neither attracted great reviews. Even when RCA reissued "Goodbye Sue" on the back of Como's 1946 hit stream, *Billboard* said that it "drips with sentimentality as Como gushes out the wordage out of tempo."[16]

In July 1943, Como made his Broadway debut in a five-week engagement at the Strand Theatre as part of a cine-variety show. This combination of film and live show was a popular feature on Broadway at the time. Como's show ran alongside the film *The Constant Nymph* starring Charles Boyer and Joan Fontaine. From there, Como went straight on to another four-week stint at the Copacabana. There was no question that by the middle of the year, New York was beginning to take notice of the young barber. The *New York Times* ran an editorial feature about him in August 1943.[17]

Between August 1943 and December 1944, Perry Como continued to climb the show business ladder. He cut more records for Victor, but had to wait until December 1944 before he was able to make a disc with instrumentalists, rather than singers, behind him. Until then, his strongest performance on disc had come in February 1944 when he recorded "Long Ago (And Far Away)" and a new Cole Porter song, "I Love You," from the show *Mexican Hayride*. Como's vocals were strong and his disc scored in the Hit Parade, although he found himself competing on both counts with Bing Crosby, whose Decca recordings were no longer affected by the musicians' ban and who enjoyed a #1 hit with the same Porter piece. On radio, Como opened 1944 with a new show, still called *Columbia Presents Perry Como* but now airing weekly rather than daily. Paul Baron's orchestra replaced Raymond Scott on the show, which aired at 7:15 P.M. on Sundays. It was a prime time slot and ostensibly a step forward for Perry although the bad news was that he was scheduled against Jack Benny's popular NBC show. *Variety* brought him a reminder that he was still some way short of the major league. Having replaced Frank Sinatra in the same spot, the journal said that his "name value is much lighter than Sinatra's and will make his task much more difficult."[18]

Columbia Presents Perry Como ran through mid–June 1944, ending its season one week after Allied troops completed the Normandy landings. Freed from his weekly commitment, Como played a three week cine-variety presentation at the New York Paramount, before taking to the road in a sustained way for the first time since he had moved to New York 18 months before. A week in Chicago was followed by short spells in Columbus, Boston and Washington, D.C. Reviewing his New York appearance, *Variety* noted real progress in his style. "Como's former weakness of sounding too much like Crosby has been corrected and amply demonstrated here when he gives the oldie [Crosby's "Temptation"] individual and effective treatment," its review said.[19]

Como returned to New York in December 1944. By now, he and Roselle had moved out to Queens but despite his growing fame and wealth, Perry still took the subway into the city each day. Two weeks before Christmas on Monday, December 11, 1944, Como headed into town to begin the most significant phase of his career so far. After completing a recording session at the RCA studios, he headed straight for the NBC radio studios on 5th Avenue. There, he made his debut as the host of the *Chesterfield Supper Club*, a 15-minute show that would go out each weekday evening from 7:00 to 7:15 P.M. It was the beginning of a road that would take Perry Como from radio to television and make him one of the biggest stars in the world.

Chesterfield was one of the major radio sponsors of the forties. The brand was the most famous of the Liggett and Myers Tobacco Company (L&M) line. L&M had started making cigarettes in 1878 but it was "Chesterfields"—named for Chesterfield County in Virginia and launched in 1911—which made the company famous.[20] "Chesterfields," the propaganda said, were "faultless in manufacture, incomparable in purity and aroma and made of the finest selections of tobacco."[21] "Chesterfields satisfy" was the tag-line, dominating Chesterfields' marketing to such an extent that Perry's first group of backing singers on his new show took "The Satisfiers" (sometimes referred to as "The Satisfyers") as their name. Como's association with a tobacco company may look strange in the 21st century, but in 1945, smoking, as a social habit, was at its peak. It was an indelible part of life. All the major cigarette makers spent heavily on radio sponsorships, the name of the sponsor being at least as prominent as the stars of the shows. When radio gave way to television, the sponsorship deals moved seamlessly across. Smoking was associated with pleasure and relaxation. Some of the marketing said that it was positively good for you too. Few people took seriously the rumors that cigarettes could be harmful to health.

Like most men of his generation, Perry himself was a regular smoker. His son David recalled the complimentary cases of Chesterfield and L&M cigarettes that arrived at their home each week, which his father would put on display in a large bowl on a coffee table. Once the dangers of smoking were known, Roselle would illustrate them to her children by smoking a cigarette through a tissue and then showing the residue that remained.[22] Eventually, after pressure from Roselle, Perry gave up smoking in the early 1970s, around the time that cigarette advertising finally disappeared from television screens.

The 15-minute duration of Como's new show was an indication that NBC still saw him as untested. As far as the network was concerned, he had not yet demonstrated sufficient appeal to warrant the half-hour show that was a mark of the top-drawer personalities. Despite its limited time-slot, however, the show had a large cast list. Perry acted as co-host with singer Mary Ashworth. Ted Steele's Orchestra provided the musical support with Martin Block as the announcer. Block was a personality in his own right and was directly responsible for the invention of the term "disc jockey," which journalist Walter Winchell coined to described Block's role on the show *Make Believe Ballroom*. It was a radio program that Block hosted, and although it purported to be a live broadcast of dance music, Block was in fact playing records in a studio. The show ran for almost 20 years, making Block the first disc jockey to become a star in his own right.[23]

Despite Block's fame, Como was determined that he, rather than the announcer, would be the star of the show. He told BBC interviewer David Jacobs in 1994 that he crossed swords with Block because of his unhappiness about not being able to talk to and introduce the guests. It was the norm on most shows for the announcer to link the various parts of the show together. All that the singer was expected to do was turn up and sing. Como realized that if he wanted to promote his own personality, he needed to do more than that. Doubtless, he had an eye once more to his role model, Bing Crosby. Many people attributed the development of Crosby's highly engaging public persona to the scripts that writer Carroll Carroll wrote for him on his *Kraft Music Hall* show. Como was quick to tell NBC—and Block—that he wanted a bigger role. It led, he said, to a "big fall out" with Block, until the announcer saw that Como's growing popularity made the move irresistible.[24]

As with his previous shows, Perry did two broadcasts each night—one at 7:00 P.M. for the Eastern Seaboard and a repeat at 11:00 P.M. for the West Coast. The shows went out from the NBC radio studios at Radio City and each one featured a guest star as well as the regular cast. Despite Block's fame, Como was the focal point of the show although he didn't get off to the best of starts. *Variety* said that his opening night delivery was "hampered by a nervousness that disturbed his phrasing several times." Nevertheless, they liked his two songs—"Goodbye Sue" and "I Dream of You"—and forecasted a big future for him. "As steady fare on the dial, he's likely to prove that he's big stuff. His voice and delivery have taken on a new warmth and personality."[25] With Como tucking away top spot in a national poll to name the Most Romantic Singer of 1944, his first full year as a solo performer ended on a high note.

As well as starting his new *Chesterfield* show, December 1944 was also the month when Perry Como was able to begin making records for RCA with instrumentalists rather than just a choral group to back him. Victor had finally settled its dispute with the American Federation of Musicians and on December 8, Perry recorded three titles with an orchestra conducted by Lew Martin. The more natural musical setting allowed Como to sing with more warmth and relaxation in his voice than on his recordings so far, but although two of the songs—"I Dream of You" and "I'm Confessin'"—scored as hits, they were merely hors d'oeuvres to the main course that Como was about to serve. By the end of 1945, he would be the best selling singer in America. In six sessions during that year, Como cut 13 titles, four of which became Gold records.[26]

The sequence began on March 27, 1945, when he recorded three titles. "Temptation," a dramatic piece by Nacio Herb Brown and Arthur Freed, had been a hit for Bing Crosby in 1933 and was a favorite of Como's. The song had been a regular part of his radio and stage repertoire since he had launched his solo career. Once it became a million-seller, it was forever associated with him and he was still singing it 50 years later in his final concert appearance in Japan. Como's rendition of "Temptation" owed much to producer Lew Martin, who persuaded Como to sing the song at the very limit of his vocal range, as Crosby had in 1933. Como's earlier radio versions of the song had been less ambitious and didn't exploit the drama in Freed's lyric. Martin's arrangement for Como had him stretching for, but reaching, the climax that the song demands. When Crosby included the song in a medley of hits at one of his final concerts, he did the same but didn't attempt the final note. "I'll leave that one to Perry Como," he jokingly told the audience.[27]

Surprisingly, RCA did not expect "Temptation" to be the big seller from the March session. They saw another of the titles, "I'll Always Be with You," as the strongest offering. Written by the team that had composed "I Dream of You," the song offered more of the same. Both songs were gentle ballads that Perry crooned with minimum effort but neither was an outstanding recording. "Temptation," which appeared as the B-side of "I'll Always Be with You," was altogether different. Coincidentally, Bing Crosby also re-recorded his 1933 hit in March 1945, but neither Crosby's nor Como's version made any serious impact in the charts. A year and three Gold discs later, RCA thought the song was just the thing to keep up a succession of dramatic songs from Como and when they re-released it, with Como's debut single "Goodbye Sue" on the flip side, it went Gold.[28]

Como worked in similar vein at his next session in May 1945. Once again, RCA came up with a song that would test Como's vocal range. "If I Loved You" was the big love song from the new Rodgers and Hammerstein show *Carousel*. Russ Case conducted the session, the first of 23 collaborations with Como during 1945–46. Case had spent much of his career as a freelance arranger during the pre-war big band days, but took over briefly as director of pop music for RCA after the war. "If I Loved You" was also a target for other performers and when Como, Crosby and Sinatra all brought records out at the same time, it was the first occasion on which the three most popular crooners in the land went head to head. It was also the first time that Perry Como outsold his two rivals, his disc peaking at #3 in the charts while Sinatra and Crosby could only reach #7 and #8 respectively.[29] Como, it seemed, had finally hit on a distinctive style. What differentiated him from other crooners was the power and range of his voice. Dick Haymes, Buddy Clark and Andy Russell led a host of crooners who could murmur sweet nothings, but what set Perry Como apart was that he could project and sustain music that was almost light opera in nature, as well as hold his own in the ballad department. "Temptation" and "If I Loved You" were the first indicators of this new style, but it was Como's next record that put clear daylight between him and his competitors.

"Till the End of Time" had its roots in a classical piece of music, Frederic Chopin's "Polonaise in A flat major, Op. 53." A film biography of Chopin—*A Song to Remember*—was released early in 1945 and with classical pianist Jose Iturbi playing the "Polonaise" in the film, it brought Chopin's music to a wider audience. In the rush to jump on an accelerating bandwagon, popular pianist Carmen Cavallaro was first off the mark and his playing of the "Polonaise" entered the *Billboard* charts in June 1945 on its way to the #3 position.[30] Its success prompted Ted Mossman and Buddy Kaye to turn the piece into a popular song. Perry Como recorded it on July 3, 1945, under the direction of A&R man Herb Hendler. Dick Haymes led a batch of other singers who also recorded it but the only version that mattered came from Perry Como. His rendition opens with a piano introduction from Dave Bowman, which is faithful to Chopin's original piece. Como's vocal is then a model of diction and breath control and he sings the song in an open, full-throated way, moving smoothly from the tenderness of the song's opening to the drama of its conclusion. Case's orchestration, with violins and five saxophones in evidence, complements the vocal perfectly.

RCA felt that they had a winner on their hands from the moment that the song was released and pushed it heavily in the trade journals. Not everybody shared their view. *Billboard's* review of the disc said that Como's singing on "Till the End of Time" was "not as easy to take" as on the disc's flip side, a light and inconsequential song called "(Did You Ever Get) That Feeling in the Moonlight." Como's singing on the Chopin piece was, they said, "not nearly as relaxed as for the rhythm ballad. The song holds little melodic charm as a pop song, despite the familiarity of its theme."[31] Despite *Billboard's* lack of enthusiasm, the disc took Perry Como to #1 in the Billboard chart for the first time. It stayed in the top spot for an amazing 10-week stint from September 15 to November 10, 1945, and also topped both the Disc Jockey and the Juke Box charts for nine weeks. It was the best selling record of 1945,[32] Como's first Gold record and the biggest hit that he would ever have. The song would be a regular part of Como's repertoire to the end of his career and there would be few, if any, better examples of his vocal art. Its success changed his life and career.

By the time that Perry Como had turned himself into a million-selling singer, he had also embarked upon a new career in Hollywood. News that he had signed a movie deal with 20th Century-Fox had broken in the summer of 1943. Although Como's movie deal came earlier than he expected, it was the norm for a successful singer to look to Hollywood as the next step on the career path. Pre-television, the only way that audiences saw singers they had heard on records or radio was on the big screen. Every singer since Al Jolson had wound up in the movies. Movie musicals, as a genre, had developed somewhat since the all-singing, all-dancing extravaganzas of the early thirties, but plots were still usually wafer thin. An ability to look good, kiss well and sing a few songs was, it seemed, all that was needed.

Como's contract with Fox called for him to make two pictures per year for seven years. It gave options to both sides but over its full term, Como could make over $1 million for 108 weeks' work. His take for the first picture would be $25,000, increasing over the term of the contract to $125,000 per movie.

Hollywood, it seemed, would make Perry Como both rich and famous. When he headed west, it was with stars in his eyes—but his days as a movie star turned out to be the unhappiest of his show business career.

Chapter 4

Hollywood and Bust

NOBODY REMEMBERS THE CHARACTERS OF Laddie Green, Nicky Ricci, Allen Clark and Eddie Lorrison Anders. The one thing they have in common is that they were all brought to life on the movie screen—just—by Perry Como. His film career lasted from March 1944 to May 1948. Four years, four films, four flops. "I'd rather not talk about it," was Como's standard answer when the inevitable question about "what happened in Hollywood" came his way.[1] But talk about it he did. There was nothing that he could recall about the experience of picture making that he liked. "I didn't know anything about acting and still don't," he said in 1983.[2] His films were, he said, "all terrible."[3]

In truth, Perry Como's tenure in Hollywood was not the unmitigated disaster that he liked to claim. His unhappiness had more to do with the alienation he sensed from the movie colony than his inadequacies as an actor. Film-making and acting were trades to be learned just like any other and the early screen appearances of most of Como's crooning contemporaries were hardly thespian highlights. Looking at his films now, Como on the big screen was stiff and uneasy—a long way from the loose guy that people would soon see on their television screens. That in itself didn't make him a bad actor. The difference with Perry was that he was never comfortable in Hollywood—either with the place or with its way of working.

The first problem was location. Como was an Easterner and lived most of his adult life on the Eastern Seaboard. He had worked in California during his Weems days, but he had no roots or associations there. When he arrived in Hollywood from New York, he felt like he was arriving in a foreign country. Producers and directors didn't know him and as a result, they had no feel for who he was and what he could do. By the same token, Como didn't know them, and he wasn't much interested in getting to know them. "Hooray for Hollywood" might have been the anthem for the movie colony, but not for Perry. "Perry wasn't in show business," his choral director, Ray Charles, said. "He didn't have friends in show business. He wasn't a social person."[4] The glitz and glamour of the Hollywood lifestyle was alien to a man who liked to turn up, do his job and go home to his family. Como also found the moviemaking process tedious. Shooting was generally stretched out over a three-month stint. "A half page of script took a week," he said in 1975.[5] Added to that, he disliked the impersonal nature of the soundstage that was so different from the live audience he had been used to. "There was no immediate reaction," he said, "just the director saying 'Cut.' I got sick and tired of it."[6]

Como's frustration and boredom wasn't helped by the roles that he played. While

36

his billing rose from sixth to third to second over his first three films, his characters—Messrs. Green, Ricci and Clark—were never central to the action or the plot. Even in the role of Allen Clark, the singer who winds up running for governor in *If I'm Lucky,* he is constantly overshadowed by Carmen Miranda and Phil Silvers, both of whom took lower billing (although neither was known for a shy and retiring nature!). Virtually all of Como's songs were staged pieces—a rehearsal for a show, a demo for a music publisher—rather than devices that advanced the story line. That made the songs incidental and largely forgettable. None of them proved any more durable than the names of the characters who sang them.

Perry Como's life in Hollywood started on March 20, 1944, when he reported to the 20th Century-Fox studios in Los Angeles to begin work on *Something for the Boys.* The omens from the beginning were not good. Como left New York's La Guardia Airport earlier that month, only to find himself bumped off the plane at Newark in favor of a general with a wartime priority. From there, he took a plane to Chicago and then another to Denver. His coast-to-coast trip took five days.[7] Nevertheless, by the time he finally made it to Hollywood, his dreams, said one magazine, were well ahead of him. Yet instead of landing a role that would catapult him to the Oscars, Como found himself cast as Laddie Smith "with two songs and no encores."[8] Lewis Seiler was the director with Carmen Miranda, Vivian Blaine, Michael O'Shea and Phil Silvers taking main billing in the screen presentation of the Cole Porter show of the same name. Porter's stage version opened on Broadway on January 7, 1943, and closed a year later, almost to the day, after playing 422 performances. The Broadway version starred Ethel Merman in the role of Blossom Hart, played by Vivian Blaine on the big screen.

Perry in a publicity shot for *Something for the Boys* (courtesy Colleen Zwack).

The plot, from a book by Herbert and Dorothy Fields, revolved around three cousins in the Hart family who inherit a Southern plantation, Magnolia Manor. Cousin Blossom Hart is a revue singer, cousin Chiquita (Carmen Miranda) is a machinist who can mysteriously receive radio broadcasts through her teeth (!), and the third cousin, Harry Hart, is a con man played by Phil Silvers in a prototype Sgt. Bilko role. Magnolia Manor is near an army base and a local sergeant decides to convert it for use as a hotel for army wives, only to have his superiors mistake it for a brothel. Eventually, he persuades them that his intentions are strictly on the level and in the time-honored Hollywood tradition, he comes up with the idea of putting on a show to raise money.

Como's Sergeant Laddie Green is a handsome soldier who is always on the fringe of the action without seeming to be in it. He sings to his girl, and he has a couple of lines of dialogue that don't go much beyond "yes," "no" and "okay." He sings his two songs—"In the Middle of Nowhere" and "I Wish We Didn't Have to Say Goodnight"—effortlessly, the latter with a warmer baritone than was apparent on any of his commercial recordings so far. And that was it. Three months' work, a $25,000 check and lots of sitting around.

The show and the film had the right amount of music, romance, risqué humor and patriotism to be a modest success with a wartime audience. Fox didn't skimp on taking the show to the big screen, with a Technicolor presentation that was still a rarity in 1944. On the film's release on November 1, 1944, *Variety* thought that it was "sufficiently diverting and tuneful to warrant more than moderate success at the box-office." Como, they said, "makes a good appearance before the cameras" and his two songs were "quite listenable and well sold."[9] Bosley Crowther in the *New York Times* added that both "Mr. O'Shea and Mr. Como look, act and sing agreeably. Indeed, Mr. Como's soft crooning of 'I Wish We Didn't Have to Say Goodnight' is a very good reason for remarking that there is something here for the girls too."[10]

Como returned to New York in June 1944 but was back in Hollywood the following July for his second picture role in *Doll Face*. Perry's return to the West Coast came on the back of personal tragedy following the sudden death, from a heart attack, of his father, Pietro Como, on July 8, 1945. Perry flew immediately from New York on hearing the news and stayed in Canonsburg until his father was laid to rest in Oak Spring Cemetery. From there, he headed to Los Angeles.

Doll Face, filmed this time in black and white, gave Perry a strong sense of déjà vu. Lewis Seiler was the director once more and his fellow cast members included both Vivian Blaine and Carmen Miranda. Dennis O'Keefe joined the cast and Perry was promoted to take third billing behind Blaine and O'Keefe. A play called *The Naked Genius*, written by the stripper Gypsy Rose Lee under her birth name of Louise Hovick, provided the basis for the film. The story involves a burlesque queen (Doll Face Carroll, played in the film by Vivian Blaine) who is turned down for a role in a major Broadway show because of her background and "lack of class." Her boyfriend and manager, Mike Hannegan (played by O'Keefe), comes up with the idea of promoting an autobiography of Doll Face as a vehicle for gaining both publicity and "class." The plot then twines around the love triangle that develops between Doll Face, Hannegan and the ghostwriter he hires to write the book.

Como's role is much the same as the one he played in *Something for the Boys*. This time he is Nicky Ricci, a singer with the burlesque group run by Hannegan, who somehow manages to slipstream along as Doll Face makes it to the Broadway stage. Como's role is certainly more prominent than in his debut movie, but his billing owed more to his burgeoning record sales than to anything else. Once more, he is always present without ever influencing the plot. His only truly dramatic scene comes when he is required to bawl out one of the girl singers. Como is clearly uncomfortable, blinking rapidly in a scene that cried out for a long, hard stare. Genial Perry didn't do sternness—at least, not in public.

Como has four songs in *Doll Face*, all from the pens of Jimmy McHugh and Harold Adamson. "Here Comes Heaven Again" is a pleasant ballad that Como sings twice, once to demonstrate the song at a party, and again in duet with Blaine. Interestingly, Como is far more effective in the second rendition, playing a support role to Blaine, than in any of the scenes where he is called up to play a leading role. In later years, critics would comment that Como's natural character—understated, reticent and self-effacing—was part of the reason for his success on the small screen medium of television. Just as much

Perry sings "Here Comes Heaven Again" in *Doll Face*, watched by (left to right) Carmen Miranda, Dennis O'Keefe and Martha Stewart (courtesy Colleen Zwack).

as those characteristics were right for television, they were wrong for the movies. The duet with Blaine, however, shows just how effective they could be in the right setting.

The big song from *Doll Face* was "(A Hubba-Hubba-Hubba) Dig You Later." Como's recording of the song gave him one of his first million-sellers and Perry and Vivian Blaine feature the song in the film. The song was Como's first big novelty hit, the lyric being built around the "hubba-hubba-hubba" phrase that was a popular contemporary expression of pleasure or delight. Como and Blaine perform the song in a coffee bar, complete with supporting dancers. The routine requires Perry to do more than simply move his vocal cords. While many dancers—Fred Astaire, Gene Kelly, Danny Kaye—made more than passable singers, the same cannot be said for singers who tried their hand at dancing. Bing Crosby suffered the embarrassment of always being named, tongue-in-cheek, by Astaire as his favorite dancing partner, and Frank Sinatra would joke that he "taught Gene Kelly all he knows" when anyone mentioned his dancing. It was the same with Perry Como. On television, whenever a number called for some form of dance routine, Como would invariably twitch a muscle or two and then stand in the middle while the cast danced around him. His "Hubba-Hubba-Hubba" routine in the film is much the same.

Doll Face hit the cinema screens in March 1946, coinciding with a decision by *Billboard* to feature Como on the cover of its March 16 edition. *Billboard's* feature on

Como had everything to do with his impact on radio and records and nothing to do with his appearance in the film. The critics, *New York Times'* Bosley Crowther in particular, panned it. The film, said Crowther, "is just another backstage theatrical tale.... Its only distinction is its persistence in grammatical mistakes. The only remarkability about its pattern is a monotonous fidelity to form."[11]

Perry returned to New York in October 1945 after completing *Doll Face*, and six months passed before he was required to head back to Hollywood for what would be his third and final movie for 20th Century-Fox. This time, Roselle and son Ronnie traveled with him, and although Como was already frustrated by picture-making, the Comos nevertheless enjoyed spending the early spring of 1946 in the California sun. Despite the post-war housing shortages, they managed to rent an apartment on Sunset Boulevard and in the gaps between shooting, they enjoyed the sun and the beach. They took trips out to Catalina, where Como had spent time in his Weems days, and Perry also enjoyed the freedom to play golf whenever he wanted, away from the frost and the snow that blighted much of the year in the East. By now, Como had met and befriended his idol, Bing Crosby, who helped in getting Ronnie into the same school as his four sons. ("The funniest sight in town,' said one magazine, "was the small Como worshipfully trailing the larger Crosbys wherever they wandered.")[12]

Shooting of *That's for Me*, subsequently retitled *If I'm Lucky*, began on April 8, 1946. Once more there was considerable overlap of personnel. Vivian Blaine, Carmen Miranda and Phil Silvers were again in the cast with Lewis Seiler in the director's chair.

Harry James (left), Vivian Blaine and Perry in a publicity shot for *If I'm Lucky*.

The film also featured bandleader Harry James, enabling Blaine, a former band singer, to finally achieve an ambition of singing with the James band. Blaine took top billing in the film, with Como promoted to #2.

The film was a re-make of the 1935 hit *Thanks a Million*, in which crooner and later Hollywood tough-guy Dick Powell had played the role given to Como and set a benchmark that his successor struggled to match. The far-fetched plot for *If I'm Lucky* has an out-of-work swing band picking up work supporting a political candidate for state governorship. The candidate turns out to be a stooge for a corrupt political machine, and when he finally falls down drunk, the party bosses decide that Como's character, a handsome band singer called Allen Clark, is just the man to step into the void. Clark is just as much a reluctant politician as Como was, by now, a reluctant actor. The outcome is as predictable as it is unlikely. Clark succeeds not only in exposing the corruptness of the machine that is by now blackmailing him but also in winning the election in a three-week campaign.

If I'm Lucky offered Perry Como the most significant of his three roles for 20th Century-Fox, and his performance unquestionably shows some development from the woodenness of his previous outings. He seems more comfortable with his dialogue, delivers a strong soliloquy towards the end of the movie, and—again in black and white— cuts a handsome figure on the screen, with a likeness to the young Dean Martin. Nevertheless, Como still found the three-month shoot a difficult time. He suffered for much of it with eye problems, missing three days of shooting because of treatment for an infected cyst on his left eye.[13] There were also reports that he had developed an allergy to the heat of the studio lights, requiring antibiotic treatment.[14] Even after he returned to New York in July 1946, his eye problems continued.

One more factor in Como's unhappiness in Hollywood may have been his discomfort with the technique of lip-syncing. It was standard practice on all movie sets for songs to be recorded ahead of a scene and then for the singer to mouth the words of the song to the playback. This meant that the quality of the audio soundtrack was preserved, free from any extemporaneous noises that arose on the set. It also meant that the singer could move and dance without having to worry about finding the breath for the notes. Some singers—Bing Crosby in particular—developed a liking for the technique and became very comfortable with it. Others, like Frank Sinatra and Perry Como, disliked it and preferred to sing live wherever possible.[15] Como has three songs in *If I'm Lucky*, the title song plus a confusing pair of songs entitled "One More Vote" and "One More Kiss." All the songs for the film, including the inevitable Latin pieces for Carmen Miranda, were written by the team of Josef Myrow and Edgar de Lange and were generally weak affairs. Como's recording of "If I'm Lucky" was a minor hit, reaching #19 in the Hit Parade and spending one week in the charts.

When *If I'm Lucky* was released on September 2, 1946, it coincided with record shops all over the United States designating the week as "Perry Como Week." Como's discs were breaking records in all directions and the contrast between his success on wax and his limitations on celluloid was becoming more and more apparent. The reviews—both of the film and Como's performance in it—weren't bad, although Bosley Crowther called it "rather grim."[16] Nelson Bell, writing in *The Washington Post*, said that the film was aimed "strictly at thoughtless and ephemeral diversion"[17] while others dismissed the plot as no more than a vehicle for transporting the audience from one musical scene to another. Edwin Schallert in the *Los Angeles Times* said that the film's implausibility wouldn't bother most viewers. "I don't suppose anyone who wants to hear Como and Vivian Blaine warble, either dreamily or hep-cat fashion, will care," he wrote.[18]

The badge issued by record dealers during Perry Como Week, September 1946.

By the time *If I'm Lucky* hit the movie theaters, Perry Como was already a rich man. His deal with Fox contributed, but it was Como's record sales, radio and personal appearance earnings that catapulted him into the millionaire ranks.[19] He certainly didn't need the movies and was doing nothing to suggest that his heart was in them. After one film appeared, he told reporters, "If this picture doesn't ruin Hollywood, then nothing ever will."[20] He also took every chance to ridicule the Hollywood lifestyle, telling a reporter that that he had "only attended one party in Hollywood" (itself an indicator of his discomfort) and that all he had found there were butlers. "A guy wants to wash his hands and a butler leads him to a bathroom," he said, contrasting the occasion with the beer and poker parties he was used to in New York. It was no surprise, then, that in April 1947, Perry Como terminated his 20th Century-Fox contract. "I'm not romantic; I hate this monkey suit [the tuxedo]; I'm no glamour boy with the dames," he told the press.[21] But a glamour boy with dames was what Fox wanted; the goodbyes didn't break anybody's heart. The only real surprise was that Como put another movie contract in its place.

Despite the limited success of Como's Fox films, his new contract was a step up, not down. There was nothing bigger in the movie business than the mighty Metro-Goldwyn-Mayer empire, and they announced early in 1948 that they had signed Perry to a seven-year contract requiring one film a year. His first film would be *Words and Music*, the upcoming biopic of Broadway lyricist Lorenz Hart. MGM made much of the signing of another Italian-American crooner to their list (Frank Sinatra was already signed to them), and their publicity crew worked hard to create a sense of rivalry between Como and Sinatra. Perry returned to Hollywood on April 17, 1948, to begin work. Lyricist and producer Arthur Freed greeted him at a special party at the *Mocambo*. As with his earlier sojourns in Hollywood, Perry continued with his radio work throughout the filming, his shows going out from NBC studios in Hollywood rather than New York. By 1948, however, Perry was in a position to finance the cost of taking the full orchestra and cast of the radio show out to Hollywood for the duration of the picture's shooting schedule.[22]

That schedule ran from April 17 to July 14, the usual three-month spell, and if ever a film was designed to frustrate a reluctant star, *Words and Music* was it. The storyline was a bitty affair, with a turgid and repetitive plot constantly interrupted by stand-alone musical numbers. A succession of MGM stars turned up to play themselves playing other parts from previous Broadway shows. Mickey Rooney as Hart and Tom Drake as Richard Rodgers headed the core cast for the film. Ann Sothern played the role of Hart's failed (and imaginary) love interest. Como and Cyd Charisse filled in as Eddie Lorrison Anders and Margo Grant, fictitious friends of the songwriting team.

The movie offered a heavily sanitized version of Hart's troubled life, with Rooney's portrayal owing far more to his usual bright and bouncy film persona than to Hart's complex and depressive personality. Stars playing themselves included June Allyson, Judy Garland, Gene Kelly and Lena Horne. The overall effect was labored and at times confusing, never more so than towards the end of the film when Gene Kelly, playing himself, introduces "Perry Como" to sing at the memorial concert for Hart. Until then, Como had spent the entire film in the fictional role of Anders. The saving grace was that by then, most audiences would have lost all interest in the plot.

Despite the change of studio, there was little change in Como's impact on the movie. He filmed six songs, three of which did not survive the rough cut. Rather than a progression from *If I'm Lucky*, Como's role had regressed to the marginality of his work in *Something for the Boys*. Perry's surviving songs—"Mountain Greenery," "Blue Room" and "With a Song in My Heart" came across well in the MGM Technicolor print, although two of the deleted songs probably offered truer representations of the real Perry Como. "Lover" was the song chosen to run over the movie's opening credits. A mega–Hollywood presentation was lined up with Lennie Hayton conducting an orchestra of forty-plus pieces and a mixed chorus providing some oohing and aahing. Como's vocal, filmed with him face on to the orchestra, should have provided the climax to the opening. Instead, the scene was edited to fade out just at the point where the camera focuses on Perry. The other song was the ballad "You're Nearer." Como sings the song

Perry in a scene from his film *Words and Music,* with (left to right) Cyd Charisse, Betty Garrett and Mickey Rooney.

as a demo to a music publisher in what is arguably his most effective input to the entire film. Leaning against a piano, Perry delivered three takes, all lip-synced to an effortless vocal. In the end, the song disappeared from the film entirely, but Como's outtakes appeared on the DVD version of the film, released in 2007.[23] The footage shows Como struggling with the lip-syncing but, more significantly, offering a facial expression that turns to misery as soon as the director calls "Cut!"

Words and Music opened at Radio City Music Hall in New York on December 9, 1948. The reviews were poor. "Nice music, shame about the plot" seemed to be the consensus view. Indeed, the *Los Angeles Times'* headline said almost precisely that ("Fine Music, Inept Plot Mark Film").[24] Bosley Crowther in the *New York Times* talked about the "the heavy treacle of a sluggish, maudlin plot" although he singled out Perry's duet with Cyd Charisse on "Blue Room" as one of the musical highlights.[25]

By then, Perry Como probably didn't care about the reviews. Before *Words and Music* went on general release, he had severed his links with Hollywood once and for all. Hollywood gossip has it that Como brought about the end of his short spell at MGM even before the filming of *Words and Music* was concluded. It was at a party for studio chief L.B. Mayer, who adopted July 4 as his "official" birthday (he was born in Russia in 1882 and never knew his true birthday). As was customary, the MGM stars turned out in 1948 to celebrate the occasion. A fourteen-year-old Elizabeth Taylor was at the party, and in 1975 Taylor told David Frost about the silence that fell when Como stood up to sing "Happy Birthday." Perry ended with "Happy Birthday dear LB, and fuck you," she said.[26] Taylor added that Como had "broken the sacred bond and had told the old man what everybody else in their hearts was dying to tell him.... It was one of the happiest moments of my life and I was only fourteen."[27]

L.B. Mayer was the inventor of the star system in Hollywood. By 1948, he was past his peak of influence, but he was still a maker and breaker of careers. Como's "tribute," if it really happened, would have meant certain death to his career in Hollywood. It may also have resulted in two of his songs being cut from the film. Taylor's account of the incident is first-hand although others who knew Perry most of his life professed no knowledge of it. And it was out of character. Como was generally a placid individual who didn't look for public conflict. "I won't allow myself to get angry in front of a group of people," he told Michael Parkinson in 1977, adding that issues still needed to be dealt with, but in private not public.[28]

Whether Como's outburst at the party was an exception to his rule or a calculated move to ensure the end of his MGM contract will never be known. In the light of what was to come, it was irrelevant. While Perry Como's name would occasionally get mentioned in connection with a big screen role, he never appeared in another film.[29] He had no need. Within two weeks of *Words and Music*'s appearing on the big screen in Radio City, America saw the face of Perry Como on a much smaller screen for the first time. That smaller screen—television—would prove more powerful than all the Hollywood movie moguls put together.

Chapter 5

The Supper Club

PERRY COMO'S ABORTIVE FILM CAREER was in complete contrast to his meteoric rise as a singer. "Till the End of Time" had established him as the hottest new singer in the business in 1945. He had recorded the song as virtually his last professional engagement before filming *Doll Face*, and when Como returned from Hollywood in October 1945, he picked up where he had left off in the summer. RCA wasted no time in getting him back into the recording studios and his first session came on Saturday, October 13, with another lined up four days later.

Top of the slate was the hit song from his film *Doll Face*. "(A Hubba-Hubba-Hubba) Dig You Later" could not have been more different from "Till the End of Time," either in style or in the strictly time-limited nature of its appeal. "Hubba-Hubba" was a nonsense song that made capital out of the American bombing of Japan that had brought World War II to its close. Its lyric now sounds insensitive and would certainly breach 21st century standards of political correctness. Yet, in its time, it was what the record-buying public wanted. *Billboard* said that, together with its flip side, "Here Comes Heaven Again" (also from *Doll Face*), the disc was "a double decker that is set to reap a fine collection of coins in the jukes." Using the odiously over-the-top language that characterized post-war reviews, the magazine said that "Hubba-Hubba" "socks for the entire expanse of the spinning" with Como "singing in a free and easy rhythmic manner [and digging] into the jive vernacular for a clever and toe-tapping hubba-hubba-hubba."[1] The disc reached #3 in the Billboard Best Seller chart in December 1945 and became Perry's second Gold disc.[2]

Como's two other recordings in October 1945 were "You Won't Be Satisfied (Until You Break My Heart)" and "I'm Always Chasing Rainbows," the latter from the Betty Grable picture *The Dolly Sisters*. "Rainbows" was an attempt to repeat the classics-to-pop magic that had been so successful on "Till the End of Time" and was another adaptation of a piece by Chopin, this time his "Fantasie Impromptu." The disc reached #5 in the Jukebox chart on its release in February 1946[3] despite *Billboard's* review saying that it was "a dirge."[4]

There was still time to squeeze one more Gold recording into 1945. That came from Perry's final session on December 18, 1945, when he revived a Russ Columbo song, "Prisoner of Love," that Columbo had co-written in 1931.[5] It was another dramatic piece in the style that had worked so well already, and again it required Como to sing at the limit of his vocal range. The session was produced by Eli Oberstein and Herb Hendler. Oberstein had recently returned to Victor as head of A&R, a job he had held in the thirties. He wasted no time in taking direct charge of RCA's biggest selling artist, although the relationship with Como got off to a testy beginning. Oberstein grew frustrated by Como's unwillingness to let his voice rip to its maximum power. To force his singer to project his voice, Oberstein positioned himself alongside Como and pulled the microphone further from his mouth at critical points in the song.[6] The results were faultless, although Como remained unimpressed by the producer's style. (When questioned about it in 1992, Como confirmed that events had happened as reported but said that it showed that some A&R men "didn't know anything about singing.")[7] *Billboard* said, "Como turns in some real pash piping to make this torchy plaint ring true once more."[8] And even Columbo's sister was moved to write to Perry. "I'm quite convinced that you're the only singer with my brother's vocal style and personality," she told him.[9] Like "Till the End of Time," the song topped all three of the Billboard charts, spending a total of 21 weeks there. It became Perry's third Gold record. RCA realized that they had found a winning formula and that the first evidence of it had been under their noses for some time. When they dug out Como's March 1945 recording of "Temptation" a year later, it immediately became Perry's fourth Gold record.

Como's hit stream in 1945 ran alongside a successful year as host of the *Chesterfield Supper Club*. Apart from his spell in Hollywood to film *Doll Face*, Como fronted the show every weekday evening throughout the year. The format remained unchanged, with Como sharing the microphone with Mary Ashworth and the Ted Steele Orchestra. Occasional guests included established names such as Louis Prima and Connee Boswell, plus newer names such as the King Cole Trio and Danish comedian Victor Borge. The 11:00 P.M. repeat proved unpopular with many of the guests, some of whom failed to turn up for the West Coast broadcast. Como was unfazed and tossed in an extra song or two to fill the gap.

Gradually, the components of what would become the first Perry Como television show began to fall into place in Perry's daily radio slot. The first piece was the association between Perry and his choral director, Ray Charles,[10] which started out on the night that President Roosevelt died suddenly in Warm Springs, Georgia. That evening, Perry broadcast a short tribute to FDR, supported by a WAVE (Women Accepted for Volunteer Emergency Service) choral group, with Charles acting as their conductor. Later, Art Lambert of the Satisfiers asked Charles to do some arrangements for them and by 1948, he had become a part of the regular team. Eventually, Charles' own group, the Ray Charles Singers, would become Como's resident group of backing singers on television, and Charles would remain at Como's side for the next 35 years.

A month after Como's first encounter with Ray Charles, a three-girl singing group from Milford, New Jersey, appeared as guests on the *Supper Club*. Bea, Geri and Margi Rosse—better known as the Fontane Sisters—had performed originally with their brother, Frank, a guitarist, until his death during World War II. The Fontanes became regular visitors to the *Supper Club* until they replaced the Satisfiers as the resident singers towards the end of 1948. Their partnership with Como extended to both records and television and had echoes of the hugely successful pairing of Bing Crosby with the Andrews Sisters. The Fontanes would go on to become big recording stars in their own right, initially with Perry on the RCA label before switching to Dot in 1954. When the Fontanes eventually left the Como shows that year, the Ray Charles Singers replaced them.

In December 1945, former Tommy Dorsey singer Jo Stafford joined the *Supper Club* team, fronting the show on Tuesdays and Thursdays while Como covered Mondays, Wednesdays and Fridays. Perry's move to a three-day week was not an indication of any

Always Buy Chesterfield! Perry with Jo Stafford and Arthur Godfrey in a late 1940s ad (courtesy Colleen Zwack).

fall in his popularity. Indeed it was anything but. When he looked back on his career, he always said that 1945 was the year in which he felt his career had truly taken off. He also singled out "Till the End of Time" as the single most important item. The critics and the public endorsed Como's view. During the *Supper Club* broadcast on New Year's Eve 1945, *Metronome* presented him with their Outstanding Achievement Award for popular singing during 1945. *Picture News* voted him the outstanding male vocalist of 1945 and the National Veterans of America chose him as their favorite singer.

Roselle Como's faith in her husband's talents had brought quicker rewards than either of them anticipated. By early 1946, they were in a position to trade up from their modest home in Queens to a prestigious Long Island location. They paid $35,000 for a house and three acres of land at Flower Hill. It was there that the Como family grew through the adoption of two more children, a daughter, Terri, in 1947 and a son, David, three years later. Not long after David's arrival, the Comos moved to a larger property on Cornwells Beach Road at Sands Point, Long Island. It remained their primary home until they left New York for Florida 20 years later.

Como experienced the same problems as everyone else when it came to fitting out a new home in the post-war years. Dorothy Kilgallen, writing in *The Lowell Sun*, said it took a month for Perry just to get a telephone installed.[11] His number was unlisted of course, a move that was as much a reflection of Como's concerns about his privacy as a mark of his star status. Throughout his career, Como displayed a commitment to separate totally his private and public lives. Jack Sher, writing in the *Los Angeles Times*, said that Como's new home was a haven from the pace of the city. He was, said Sher, "strictly a feet-in-the-fireplace fellow" and that once inside his new home, "callers from the city can't budge him."[12]

Sher's sympathetic portrayal of Como was one of the first to cast him as relaxed figure. Como himself put his easy-going nature down to his father. "He was a very relaxed man," he told Regis Philbin, "and I guess some of it rubbed off on me."[13] Como was happy to admit to being a laid-back character, but was less happy when people equated it with not caring. It was something Jack Sher's 1947 article hinted at when it described Como as an "admittedly lazy young guy with dark hair and sleepy brown eyes in a Rudolf Valentino face [who] has found a painless way to make money."[14] For a time, Como was happy to ride along with such a portrayal, but eventually he felt the need to set the record straight. "Inside, there's just as much going on as with anyone else," he said in 1973.[15] A few years later, he told the BBC's Michael Parkinson that the relaxed image was the result of hard work rather than a carefree outlook. "I rehearsed 7 days a week to the point where I felt I knew what I was doing and I could relax. It didn't mean that I didn't care. I assure you, I do care."[16]

Perry Como's work rate during the mid-forties was certainly not that of a lazy man. Between January 1946 and December 1947, he hosted 234 *Chesterfield Supper Clubs*, cut 66 songs for RCA–Victor, made two films and toured extensively throughout the Eastern Seaboard. It was hard work but the financial rewards were enormous. Jack Sher estimated that Como's 1947 earnings would be "close to $1,000,000."[17] This, at a time when the average American family income was $2,600 per annum, was a staggering sum.[18] Even Perry's immediate family found it hard to come to terms with the wealth that the young man from Canonsburg was acquiring. Perry told Sher that his mother thought he was rich when Ted Weems had paid him $100 per week. She would never comprehend the money that was now coming his way. If she asked how he was doing, he would just say, "I'm doing terrific, Mama." "You're gonna be a rich boy, some day," she told him. He already was.[19]

Late 1940s publicity shot.

A big slice of Como's income came from record sales. Whereas his first RCA contract in 1943 had been for 16 titles at $75 dollars a side, the extension he signed in 1947 gave him $300,000 for the same output.[20] Such were his sales that RCA designated the first week of September 1946 as "Perry Como Week." They announced that the company's Camden plant in New Jersey would press four million Como records during the week. It was, said *Billboard,* "the greatest number of recordings of a single artist produced in any similar period in the history of the disc business."[21] In the weeks leading up to Perry Como Week, RCA flooded the pages of *Billboard* with Como ads and announced that all of his singles for the label were being re-run "by popular demand."[22]

Personal appearances were another lucrative source of income. Como's heavy radio schedule limited his stage appearances but the few that he made swelled the coffers handsomely. In September 1946, he played a matinee and an evening performance at the 6000-seater New Haven Arena in Connecticut, receiving a one-off fee of $10,000.[23] The following year, during his summer break from radio in 1947, Como made a six-week tour of theatres in the Midwest, grossing $142,500 in his share of the take.[24] A four-week engagement at the New York Paramount brought him another $40,000, ten times what a similar stint there had given him just four years earlier.[25]

With income at that level, Como needed someone he could trust to handle his business affairs. He was no great businessman himself and indeed, David Como recalled that of his two parents, his mother was the more financially astute. His father's main concern, he said, was always to be seen to be "giving value to the fans."[26] In addition to Roselle, Como relied heavily on two sources of advice. One was Jack J. Katz, a partner in the New York law firm of Katz, Moselle & Schier. Katz and his partners served a strong show business client list that included Arthur Godfrey and Patti Page. Katz was Como's closest advisor for much of his career. Como's other source of advice was from his agents, Tommy Rockwell and subsequently, Larry Kanaga, of GAC.[27]

Como also needed someone to handle the day-to-day demands that came with his new-found stardom and during 1946, his brother-in-law, Dee Belline, started to fill that role. Belline was Roselle Como's younger brother and had been working as a mill-hand in Washington, Pennsylvania. His role with Perry was never precisely defined. Indeed there were those who thought that Belline was best placed to act as a bodyguard, his large mill-worker's hands making, in the words of comedian Jack E. Leonard, "an ideal man to be tail-gunner on a beer lorry."[28] Belline was sometimes described as Como's manager, a title that probably overstates his role. Nevertheless, Como relied heavily on him to keep his life organized and stress free.

Another key member of the Como team was Mickey Glass. He joined the Como organization in 1950, ostensibly to handle Como's growing involvement in music publishing. Glass's arrival coincided with the formation of Roncom Inc, a company named for Como's son Ronnie.[29] Initially, Roncom was the focus for Como's music publishing interests although in time, the company also took on the production responsibilities for Como's TV specials and all other related business affairs. Mickey Glass had worked for the Paramount Music Company as a song-plugger since the early thirties and had first come across Como in 1943.[30] Even as a fledgling balladeer, Como was a rich target for the song-pluggers and by the time his hit stream started, as many as 30 or 40 song-pluggers would vie for his attention. It was Dee Belline who suggested that they should bring Glass on board, and his role soon extended into handling marketing and publicity and any other day-to-day tasks that needed looking after. Eventually he took over from Belline as Como's general factotum. "He's my right arm," Como said in a 1992 interview.[31]

Belline and subsequently Glass helped enforce the iron curtain that Como placed between his public and private lives. It remained in place for the rest of his career and was non-negotiable. While never appearing to be reclusive, Como limited the occasions when he talked directly to the inquisitive media. When talk shows took a hold on television, Como refused all requests to appear on one until finally agreeing to meet the BBC's Michael Parkinson in London in 1977. Parkinson's well-researched interviews were often probing, but always respectful, and he succeeded in persuading a swarm of Hollywood greats into his studio. When Como finally made his way down the stairs of the BBC Television Theatre, it seemed he might break his own golden rule—until he answered Parkinson's first question. "My private life is my own," he said, firmly but with no hint of confrontation.[32]

Sands Point was Como's refuge. If any journalists ever managed to get through the door, they found a very ordinary, non-show business home. "My needs are very small," he said in 1992, and it was a comment that applied as much to the beginning of Como's career as to the end. His children were aware of course that their father was in show business but there was little evidence of it around the house. Como's interests mainly focused on his golf and television. He also loved to walk. Son David recalled one of his earliest memories as walking for three hours with his father from Port Washington to Great Neck and straying so far from home that they had to catch a cab back.[33] Como's friends were the people he met at the golf club or who supported him in his work. These, and not show business stars, were the visitors to the Como house. Nor was there much evidence around the house of who Perry was or what he did. "Perry," said Ray Charles in 1975, "doesn't save a thing. There's no ego, no 'Look what I've done.'"[34] Jack Sher's 1947 piece said that Perry would "not have a Perry Como record in the house."[35]

Although Long Island was now Perry's home, there was no way that the town of Canonsburg was about to relinquish its claim to its favorite son. It first honored him in 1946 and did so twice more over the next 50 years. The first event took place on September 14, 1946, when Perry was presented with the freedom of the town. During the celebrations, Third Street (where Perry had first worked in Steve Fragapane's barbershop) was renamed *Perry Como Avenue*. Perry and Roselle flew in from New York for the event and, accompanied by Perry's mother, Lucy, traveled in a motorcade from Allegheny County Airport. Schools and businesses declared the day a local holiday and a crowd gathered to watch the ceremonial change of street signs on the new Perry Como Avenue. That evening a 500-seat banquet was held at the State Armory in Como's honor.

Not surprisingly Como was uncomfortable with the honor, which he found both over-whelming and embarrassing. It would have offended too many people, his mother included, to allow any indication of his unease to appear during the day, but later he explained his sentiments to Roselle. "Changing the name of a street," he said. "That's something you do for a real hero, a guy who's really accomplished something. What did I do big? I'm nobody to yell about. And everybody I knew was acting so stiff. Like Mrs. So and So. She used to smack my behind when I was a kid, and there she was, trying to call me Mr. Como. I wanted to bawl."[36]

Professionally, 1946 and 1947 offered more of the same recipe that had worked so well in 1945. Perry continued to host the *Supper Club* three times a week and apart from a new bandleader—Lloyd Shaffer replaced Ted Steele late in 1945—its format was unaltered. The show had topped *Billboard's* 1945 poll as the nation's favorite 15-minute radio show. Still, the sponsor, Chesterfield, was always on the lookout for new gimmicks. That is why the *Supper Club*, on April 5, 1946, became the first commercial program to be broadcast entirely from the air. Perry and the cast boarded a 51-seat TWA Con-stellation Starliner that flew over New York while they performed. Como took it in his stride, despite a lack of fondness for flying. Chesterfield saw it as just a marketing ploy, although *Variety* thought it was a groundbreaking move. "It opens up a world of new possibilities for the reporting of news, sports, acts of God (floods), even wars," the mag-azine said.[37]

Como's hit records from 1945 guaranteed that 1946 would be another busy year for him in the recording studio. RCA ads for Como's records were regular features in the pages of *Billboard* throughout the year. Como had taken second place in *Billboard's* Favorite Male Singer Poll for 1945 (behind Crosby but ahead of Sinatra and Haymes) and the magazine featured him on its cover on March 16, 1946. Como was now being increasingly mentioned in the same breath as Crosby and Sinatra and the trio seemed to have put distance between themselves and the rest of the crooning pack. Coinciding with *Billboard's* feature, *Time* magazine ran a piece that compared the singing styles of the big three. It was strangely prophetic. Como, they said, stood somewhere between "The Groaner" (Crosby) and "The Voice." "He sings straighter than the slow-drag Sina-tra but with somewhat less ease than the Groaner," *Time* said, "but is less apt to break into 'Ave Maria' than either of his two main rivals [all three were Roman Catholics]. Something like the new nonsense song, 'One-zy, Two-zy I Love You-zy' is more his style. He sometimes sings 'Ah, Sweet Mystery of Life' to win the old folks, but in general he's a bobby-soxer's man."[38]

Time's comment was, at best, a backhanded compliment and was the first indica-tion that Como would find his vocal abilities understated by the critics. Over the extended lengths of their respective careers (51 years for Crosby, 59 for Sinatra and 61 for Como), Perry would prove to be a more technically reliable performer than either of his two counterparts. Como's commercial success during the fifties with a now derided series of TV-inspired novelty songs was such that his prowess as a balladeer *par excellence* is often overlooked. In 1946, all of Como's hit records, with the exception of "A-Hubba-Hubba-Hubba," had been straight ballads. His singing was a model of pitch, diction and breath control. When *Billboard* reviewed his March 1946 recording of "More Than You Know," Como, they said, "makes every word and every note of the verse and cho-rus count."[39] *Time's* assessment might have been a foretaste of critical opinion to come, but as an assessment of Perry Como in 1946, it was wide of the mark.

When *Billboard's* Como feature hit the newsstands, Perry was busy with Russ Case in RCA's Studio #2 in New York. There were four sessions during March 1946 and they were a look into the future for the record business. Until then, the output from all of Como's sessions for RCA had been a two-sided 78 rpm disc. Microgroove technology and the long-playing record (LP) were just around the corner but still not in commercial use in 1946. The only way an "album" could be put together was to sell three or four 78s in a bound set of sheaths. These sets, known as folios, were increasingly popular. Originally they were simply blank albums into which the distributor could insert whatever 78s he liked, but the idea of using a theme to link the records in the folio was catching on. By 1946, this trend had developed to the point where artists were going into studios to record six or eight titles with a folio set in mind. This in effect was the birth of the concept album, although it would not be until LPs became commonplace that the phrase gained any currency.

Perry Como's sessions in March 1946 were his first step towards a concept album. He recorded nine songs, six of which RCA released together with a folio set in mind. There was no overt theme (or indeed even a name) to the set and all that the songs had in common was that they were simple, old songs, simply sung. "Kentucky Babe" dated from 1896; the two most recent compositions were "You Must Have Been a Beautiful Baby" from 1938 and "Little Man You've Had a Busy Day" from 1934. Como's next visit to the studio in April 1946 had the Hit Parade more in mind. "They Say It's Wonderful" was an Irving Berlin song from the Broadway musical *Annie Get Your Gun* and reached #4 in the *Billboard* bestseller charts in June 1946. Once more, Perry found himself in a head-to-head with Sinatra and Crosby. This time, it was Sinatra who came out on top, his disc of the same song reaching #2 in the bestseller chart.[40]

Como's other song on the April session was a ballad called "Surrender." It sounded like a follow up to "Temptation" but was a more gentle composition, with none of the drama of its sound-alike companion. The song was a product of a new song-writing partnership between Bennie Benjamin and George David Weiss, whose other credits in 1946 included #1 hits with "Oh What It Seemed to Be" and "Rumors Are Flying." Como's reading brought out the tenderness of Bennie Benjamin's lyric and made the most of Russ Case's "slow and dreamy" arrangement.[41] "Surrender" charted in July 1946 and became Como's third record to top *Billboard's* bestseller chart.[42] It also reflected Como's growing business portfolio. By the time it hit the charts, Como was a partner in Santly-Joy Inc., the music publishing business responsible for the song as well as for Benjamin and Weiss's two other hits in 1946.[43]

After Perry's return from Hollywood in the summer of 1946, he was soon back at work with Russ Case, entering the Christmas market for the first time. Christmas in the 1940s was a simpler and less commercial holiday season than it is now, but Christmas records were already commonplace. The first Christmas singles dated from 1934.[44] The following year, Bing Crosby recorded "Silent Night" and by the time World War II arrived, Christmas records were an indelible part of the holiday season. The war itself gave the genre an added fillip, never more so than with Crosby's recording of "White Christmas." It became the biggest selling record of all time, although its success owed as much to its being a symbol of home for U.S. troops serving abroad as to Irving Berlin's sentimental portrayal of Christmas.

August in New York is hardly the time to get into the Christmas spirit, but for record companies needing to have discs in the shops by November, summer is often the prime time for Christmas recording.[45] The eight songs that Como recorded in August 1946 became *Perry Como Sings Merry Christmas Music,* a four-disc "Musical Smart Set." So began an association between Perry Como and the Christmas season that would endure and strengthen throughout the remainder of his career. Over the years, the songs provided the basis for a series of Como Christmas releases and re-issues until he re-recorded many of the titles in stereo in the late fifties.

The year 1947 brought more of the same for Como's ever-growing army of fans. His *Supper Club* broadcasts continued their regular pattern, although the Comos took a three-week holiday in Florida during February. Betty Hutton took over Como's hosting role while Perry and his family made a first visit to the state that would become their home in the 1970s. In June, Perry took a longer break from the show and set out on his first series of personal appearances since 1944. Four days after handing over the reins to Tex Beneke and the Glenn Miller Orchestra, Perry opened at the New York Paramount in a cine-variety show. His three-week stay at the Paramount was the prelude to a six-week tour which took in Cleveland and Boston, Steel Pier in Atlantic City, and the Chicago Theater before winding up with a five-day stint at the Meadowbrook Club in New Jersey. Como was by now such a big draw that in Chicago, the theater management forecasted that his week there would match the $90,000 weekly take from Frank Sinatra's week there the previous May. Como, despite being troubled during his stay by a tooth abscess, did not disappoint. *Variety* said "his singing technique, working sans tie in the last half of his routine, had youngsters squealing at the informality."[46]

One man who might have traded the informality for a little more energy was theatre manager Nat Platt. Como told Pete Martin in 1960 that Platt had proved a hard and unsympathetic taskmaster. With Como doing eight shows a day, the first starting at 8:15 A.M., his first morning found him in the dentist's chair at 7:00 having his tooth fixed. "Anyway, I'm up there on the stage doing the day's first show and my jaw is out to here. I'm in real bad shape. I hadn't been able to eat; I hadn't slept. I looked 80 years old. Nat walked in—I didn't know who he was—and said, 'For heaven's sake, can't you sing a little faster? I manage this theater and we've got to get people in and out of here. We have to have a certain turnover, you know, but you sing so slow, we'll never make it.'" Platt and Como went on to become good friends and three years later, Como was in Chicago again and looked him up. "'Come with me,' said Platt. He took me backstage where out front, Billy Eckstine was singing—'O-o-o-ollllldddddd man riiivvveeeer.' Platt said, 'I wanted you to see one who sings even slower than you do. I could run two pictures in the time it takes him to get through one chorus.'"[47]

The spell back on the road was a refreshing break for Perry from his weekly radio routine. When Perry returned to the *Supper Club* on September 8, 1947, *Variety* remarked on a difference in his performance. "He's looser and seemed to display more personality than in past performances. Not so much in his singing which has always been of the crack variety ... but more in his handling of lines."[48] It was a perceptive observation. Just as *Time* magazine had talked about the "straightness" of Perry's singing, the same characteristic had been there in his reading of lines. It had been part of the reason why his impact in films had not been great and it came through too in his handling of dialogue on radio. Como never revealed that he suffered from nerves, but nervousness may have contributed to his "straight" line readings in his early days. He was also an indecisive character and as such, not a great risk taker. It took time for his confidence to grow, but as it did, his looser, natural personality started to come through. It would be a critical factor in his success on television and for Perry, the ability to relax more during his performances was arriving just at the right time.

Aside from radio, Como's work schedule for the remaining months of 1947 was dominated by a heavy schedule for Victor. Another musicians' strike was in the offing. The issue was the same one that had caused the 1942–44 blackout: royalties. This time, Petrillo's *bête noire* was television and a worry that musicians would get no royalty stream from TV. Unlike the previous ban, however, the record companies saw this one coming and got busy stockpiling sides. Como recorded 28 titles in 14 sessions during the last three months of 1947 and was then absent from the studios until December the following year.

Como went into the sessions with a considerable tail wind behind him. He had been a fixture in the *Billboard* charts for most of the year with three major hits to his name: "Chi-Baba Chi Baba (My Bambino Go to Sleep)," "When You Were Sweet Sixteen" and "I Wonder Who's Kissing Her Now." Together, they occupied 49 weeks in the charts, taking the number #1, 2 and 3 slots respectively. "Chi-Baba" was a new song by Al Hoffman and Jerry Livingston, to a Mack David melody. In contrast, "When You Were Sweet Sixteen" was an old song, dating back to the last years of the 19th century and twice a hit for Al Jolson (in 1929 and again in 1947). The third song, "I Wonder Who's Kissing Her Now," was a throwback to Como's days with Ted Weems. Como had recorded the song with Weems in October 1939 but it gained a new lease on life from a 1947 film of the same name. Como re-recorded the song for RCA in May 1947 but Decca, who owned the Weems masters, reissued the Weems version in an effort to cash in on the film's release. The Decca version was first to the market and was listed in *Billboard's* charts for 11 weeks before the RCA version became available. From then on, *Billboard* listed both versions in one chart position.[49]

Como's stockpile of recordings sustained RCA through the 1948 strike and indeed beyond. The titles he recorded included a mixture of songs, some of which were in the vaults until the early fifties before seeing release. The biggest hit in the batch was a song of which his late father would doubtless have approved. "Because" was written in 1902 by Guy d'Hardelot and Edward Teschemacher and recorded in 1913 by Enrico Caruso, although it was another tenor, Richard Crooks, who first brought the song to the attention of the American public in the 1920s. Como's revival made the song an international hit, its soaring melody offering yet another opportunity for the dramatic vocals that had served him so well. Although the song peaked no higher than #4 in the *Billboard* bestseller chart, RCA gave it Gold record status.[50]

The Petrillo ban ended in December 1948, a month that would become a significant milestone in the career of Perry Como. On Christmas Eve, Perry's *Chesterfield Supper Club* began a three-week experimental run on the new medium of television. No one knew precisely what the impact of television would be. Its origins went back to the twenties but it was only after World War II concluded that it gained any real momentum. It cried out for a new generation of stars, performers who could exploit its informality, offer a friendly face and be welcome in the living rooms of America. Nobody became more welcome than Perry Como.

Chapter 6

First Contact

PERRY COMO NEEDED JUST 30 SECONDS and 23 words to demonstrate that he understood television. After Martin Block's opening announcement for the Christmas Eve
Supper Club on December 24, 1948, Perry stepped up to the microphone. The show was
Como's regular Friday *Supper Club* radio broadcast but on this occasion, a set of TV
cameras was trained on the stars. This televising of radio, known as simulcasting, had
been in use since March 1948. The radio performers made few, if any, concessions to
the new medium and Como appeared, just as he always had, with script in hand. In
these fledgling days of television, some seasoned radio performers carried on as though
there were no cameras present. Not Perry Como.

"Here it is, Christmas Eve," he said, "and a very exciting one for us because for
the first time, we are being televised." Then, looking straight at the camera, he added,
"Aren't we?" delivering the rhetorical question with a few seconds' pause, just enough
to create a visual impact.[1] The gesture was an instinctive recognition by Como that his
audience was now the camera. Its demands were small but they included recognition,
acknowledgement and a hint of emotion. The most successful television performers were
those who let the viewers in on their secrets. Expansive gestures were out. Television
needed only a nod, a wink here and there, a slight change to the facial expression. Viewers took to performers who were prepared to share their fun and fears and who had the
confidence to walk away from a script. "The race is to the quick-witted," said Alistair
Cooke, describing the early days of television in one of his transatlantic radio letters for
the BBC.[2]

The new stars of television would be those who could make themselves welcome
in people's homes. No one did it better than Perry Como. "His personality was such
that he wasn't intrusive," Ray Charles recalled. "You looked at him like a friend of the
family and that's how he was treated by audiences. His whole approach was very non-
threatening, which is one of the reasons men liked him as well as women."[3] Jazz critic
Gary Giddins picked up the same theme when he contributed to *TV Guide's* eulogy to
Como in 2001. "If you were going to invite a stranger into your living room in those
early days of television," he said, "Como was a good choice."[4]

Christmas 1948 was first contact time for Perry Como and his television audience.
In truth, the audience that day was a small one. At Christmas 1948, there were only
350,000 television sets in use in the United States. Television had reached 18 states and
there were 27 stations, but 75 percent of the sets were still around New York. Forty-
two hours of programming was on offer each week, mainly from 5:00 P.M. until 11.

Viewers paid $350 for a set and picked from 24 models available. With average annual salaries around $3000, television was undoubtedly a luxury item. When Perry took his bow, one in ten Americans had never seen a television set, leave alone watched a program. There were plenty of voices willing to say that the new medium was nothing more than a passing fancy.[5]

How wrong they were. Television had admittedly been slow to develop from the first NBC broadcasts in 1939, but that was due mainly to the hiatus caused by World War II. As America moved towards an affluent peace, television was one of the major beneficiaries. In 1946, the first hour-long musical variety show, *Hourglass,* aired on NBC. A year later, the *Kraft Television Theatre* became the first commercial television dramatic series (the first TV commercial, for Bulova watches, had appeared in 1941). In the same year, NBC and Kodak developed kinescopes, a primitive means of recording TV pictures direct from a screen. Viewed now, their quality is dire, but on the grainy, 12" black and white screen of an early TV set, few noticed. Kinescopes allowed networks to record live shows and repeat them later in different time zones. It was a massive breakthrough. Twice-nightly broadcasting to meet Eastern and Pacific time zones became a thing of the past.

By the end of 1949, there were two million television sets in the United States. The number quadrupled during 1950 and the following year, President Truman inaugurated the first coast-to-coast telecast. The charge was on. By 1953, 50 percent of Americans had regular access to a television set. In November 1953, RCA's electronic compatible color system made its debut via the *Colgate Comedy Hour* and a year later, RCA sold 5,000 color sets at $1,000 each. The first coast-to-coast national color telecast came on January 1, 1954. In 1956, CBS introduced videotape and by 1957, televisions were a feature in 41 million U.S. homes.[6]

Perry Como never pretended to have foreseen the unstoppable surge of television. "All of us were scared to death," he said in a 1994 interview. "It was a new thing."[7] When asked by another BBC interviewer, Chris Stuart, whether he had been aware of it as an intimate medium, Como said, "No. It wasn't really a conscious thing, but you can't act on TV. With me, what you see is what you get."[8] Although he conceded in an earlier TV interview that he had "always been aware that television was one on one,"[9] Como's immediate concerns were more practical. "It was the toughest job I'd ever had," he told Charles Dexter in 1955. "On camera, I suddenly found myself alone in the middle of a big stage, with no mike to lean on. I didn't know what to do with my hands. I held them out stiffly; I stuck them in my pockets. They were always getting in the way. And I had to make up, dress the part of a star. After the song ended, I had to read lines and talk. I thought I'd never make it."[10]

Como's debut year was also one that saw other significant players step up to the plate for the first time. In June, Ed Sullivan's *Toast of the Town Show* debuted, followed in September by Milton Berle's *Texaco Star Theatre.* BF Goodrich, the tire manufacturers who sponsored radio's *Burns & Allen Show,* took the show to TV that year, becoming one of 933 television sponsors during 1948. The figure was up 500 percent from the previous year. Meanwhile, surveys showed that 68 percent of viewers remembered the name of the sponsor for a program that they enjoyed.[11]

Simulcasts were destined for a short life. *Variety* quickly came to that conclusion. Reviewing Como's first televised *Supper Club,* they said the "badly spotted" cameras brought Como back into prominence too often and the floor mikes often hid his face. A simulcast, the journal said, was fundamentally flawed. "There is something disillusioning about watching a performer with a script in his hand."[12] Despite its reservations about the format, *Variety* had nothing but praise for the star. "Como, small-size," they said, "was king-size."[13] It was a telling assessment.

Perry's first two TV outings used his 7:00 p.m. broadcast for the TV simulcast. Despite its being the more reliable and predictable show, NBC soon changed to using the 11:00 p.m. broadcast for the TV version. The move puzzled some observers. "They didn't get on the air all the time," Perry's choral director, Ray Charles, recalled. Charles was by now working regularly with Como, handling the arrangements and conducting the backup singers, but he, like others, shared the frustration of TV's early days. "If the prize fights at Madison Square Garden, which were televised, ran over, the Como Show wouldn't get on the air at all," he said.[14]

By the time that Perry's third outing came around on January 14, 1949, *Variety* noticed a discernible shift. "Perry Como's television broadcasts have become in the few weeks since the first broadcast, almost models for similar shows," they said.[15] "In fact, the producers of the shows have gone from one extreme to another. Whereas the opening video—a radio simulcast presented the picture of tele lenses looking in on a regular broadcast, last Friday's performance was strictly a video show."[16] The journal attributed much of the difference to the appearance of Borrah Minnevitch's Rascals as the featured guests. The 7:00 p.m. radio-only show had, said *Variety*, been "a solid show," but much of the comedy from the Rascals was visual in nature. All that the radio audience had heard, said the reviewer, were "audience howls they couldn't understand." The repeat video performance, they said, "brought it all into focus." And just as the production of the show was developing, so too was the star. Como, said *Variety*, "is free and relaxed both vocally and otherwise; he looks good and the script and mike shortcomings so evident in the opening show have been cleaned up."[17] *Variety* signed off however with a cautionary word that radio was not dead just yet. "The show's producers must remember in handling guest acts that the larger audience is on radio," it said.[18]

The success of the television experiment was such that the Friday night *Supper Club* remained on TV screens until the end of the season in June 1949. In the meantime, Perry continued to offer up twice-nightly radio broadcasts on Mondays and Wednesdays, and his 7:00 p.m. Friday slot also remained sound only. Chesterfield continued to work imaginatively with NBC to keep the radio offering fresh. Early 1949 shows included an old time minstrel offering with Perry in the role of Interlocutor plus Martin Block and conductor Mitchell Ayres acting as End Men. On Good Friday, April 15, 1949, NBC broadcast the show live from Duke University in Durham, North Carolina. Perry's material included hymns such as "The Lord's Prayer" and "Holy, Holy, Holy," sung with the university choir. The trip to Durham continued Perry's association with Duke University that had started in 1945: Liggett and Myers, makers of Chesterfield cigarettes, had a production plant near the university. Como would retain the association well beyond his Chesterfield days. He became a major benefactor of Duke University Children's Hospital and remained so for the rest of his life.

Nobody was quite sounding the death-knell of network radio in 1949, but it was soon obvious that its days were numbered. By 1952, most of the established stars had moved to television, hastened by pressure from sponsors. The balance of power had shifted. Many performers, including Como, Bob Hope and Burns & Allen took the change in their stride although there were those who made an uncertain start. Both of Como's main crooning rivals, Bing Crosby and Frank Sinatra, fell into this latter category. "He [Como] came from this whole generation of crooners—Crosby and Sinatra," said Crosby's biographer, Gary Giddins, in 2001, "but he was the only one of them who figured out TV."[19]

Crosby made his TV debut five days before Como's, albeit in a pre-recorded film. (He sang "Silent Night" for the Philco Playhouse *A Christmas Carol* presentation on December 19, 1948). *Variety* reported during 1949 that Crosby was negotiating with CBS about a simulcast of his weekly radio show, but nothing developed. It was 1954 before a *Bing Crosby Show* appeared on TV.[20] Crosby never committed to a regular series of music shows for TV (the one-season sitcom *The Bing Crosby Show* in 1964–65 was a flop). Indeed, Como's singing idol clung to radio until the medium died beneath him. Bing's final sign-off on network radio came on November 2, 1962. Ten days later, national network radio closed down.[21]

Frank Sinatra took his first bow on television as a guest on a Bob Hope feature, *Star Spangled Review*, in May 1950. His debut revealed the same uncertainties that seemed to haunt Crosby. In its review, *Variety* said, "If TV is his oyster, Sinatra hasn't broken out of his shell."[22] Sinatra at this time was going through the lowest personal and professional period of his life, but was still a strong enough proposition for CBS to take a chance on him with a weekly variety show called *The Frank Sinatra Show*. The show aired in October 1950 and limped through its first season. When CBS programmed a second season directly against Milton Berle, Jack Gould in *The New York Times* noticed some improvement in Sinatra's performance. However, Gould prophetically warned Sinatra (and any other crooner who might venture into the variety show format) "the evening's honors were captured effortlessly and smoothly by another gentleman, Perry Como."[23]

It had taken Como only a matter of months to make television his personal domain. Jack Gould in the *New York Times* said the *Supper Club* broadcasts were "a model for the many producers of capsule music shows on video." Gould was in no doubt that most of the success was due to Como himself. Gould was no great fan of Como on radio, but on television, he said, "the baritone undeniably has a casual and likeable manner perfectly suited to the medium." He also added a significant note about the way Como treated the medium. "He does not take himself too seriously," said Gould.[24]

Not taking himself too seriously was just one of the characteristics that endeared Como to the early TV audience. His selflessness was another. "He had no vanity about having the guests have all the laughs," said critic Gary Giddins.[25] What's more, Como was having fun and wasn't afraid to show it. "I got a kick out of live television," he said in 1989. "The spontaneity was the fun of it."[26] In those early days, it was commonplace for a performer to find himself competing with crashing scenery and colliding cameras. When Como hosted Bing Crosby as his guest, the two crooners took turns in an Irish medley. As Crosby finished up a rousing "MacNamara's Band," Como moved into the soft lullaby, "Too-Ra-Loo-Ra-Loo-Ral," only to have a part of the set come crashing down, off camera but clearly audible. At first, Como carried on regardless, but, aware that everyone watching had heard what he heard, he stopped his song. "You couldn't do it in the other song, right?" he said to the off-screen stagehands. It was typical of Como's approach. Whatever happened while the cameras were running had to be integrated it into the show. There was no pretense, no attempt to make a clear mistake look like something that they had planned. It was fun for Como but fun for the audience too. When he reminisced for the BBC on his 80th birthday, he lamented the passing of live TV. "Taping took a lot of the fun out of it," he said.[27]

Live television would continue to be the norm for some time but Como's new season on radio that commenced in September 1949 offered Perry his first experience of recording a show. The first magnetic recording device, the Magnetophon, was a German invention of the 1930s. The machines found their way to the United States after

Perry, with Chesterfields in hand, at work on his CBS TV show, ca. 1952 (courtesy Colleen Zwack).

the war. Bing Crosby, seeing the potential for both business and personal gain, was the first to throw his weight behind the new technology. On the business side, he invested in the Ampex Corporation, which developed the recording machines (the tape used was a product of 3M, the Minnesota Mining Corporation).[28] Crosby's personal interest was to free himself from the demands of a live weekly radio schedule that had dominated his life since 1933. The major networks were unconvinced about the quality of recorded shows and Crosby took his new *Philco Radio Time* show to the fledgling broadcaster ABC.[29] Soon, all the major stations followed his lead. Como taped his first radio show on September 6, 1949, for broadcast two days later.

With Como such a success on TV, NBC decided to separate his radio and TV offerings. For the new 1949–50 season, it launched two new shows, although each retained the title of *The Chesterfield Supper Club*. Although Como's name did not feature, both shows were to all intents and purposes the first *Perry Como Shows*. Each one aired once a week for a half hour. Como's first radio show had Jane Powell and his megaphone mentor, Rudy Vallee, as guests. It included a mystery voice competition, a carry-over from Jo Stafford's *Supper Club* shows, which offered listeners the chance to phone in and win $1,000 if they named the voice correctly. The critics slated the phone-in competition—the mystery voice was in fact Vallee's, one of the guests on the show—but liked everything else. Como's performance, *Variety* said, indicated, "whatever type of assignment he might draw out of the new format won't easily stump his capabilities."[30] His singing was "smooth and clear" and his repertoire smartly included the *Billboard* #1 song of the month, "You're Breaking My Heart."[31] *Billboard's* Sam Chase was similarly effusive. "Como's voice and delivery," he wrote, "remains mellow and as appealing as any on the air."[32] Jane Powell and the vocals by the Fontane Sisters also scored well. Rudy Vallee's appearance offered the chance for some comedy on the theme of Como (as opposed to Crosby) becoming Vallee's crooning successor. The skit gave Perry a backdoor opening to plug Crosby's new radio show, now also sponsored by Chesterfield.

The following month, Como launched the TV version of the *Supper Club*. The first show went out on October 16, 1949, using a Sunday night slot at 8:00 p.m. Como's guest on the first show was Milton Berle, the show going head-to-head with Ed Sullivan's *Toast of the Town*. West Coast audiences saw the show two weeks later from a kinescope film of the live broadcast. *Variety* liked what it saw despite some "first-show traces."[33] The criticisms focused on an overly long comedy routine that they said gave the show a "too relaxed pace, occasionally sagging as a result."[34] Perry's singing, including a medley that was to become a request section of the show, attracted the by now usual plaudits. In time, the medley would grow into Como's trademark "Sing to Me, Mr. C" spot.

The reviewers also praised the greater emphasis on video production. It was less than a year since Como had debuted with a radio script in hand, but the new series now introduced some early television show settings. One featured the Fontane Sisters aboard a vintage car with Milton Berle dressed as a Texaco (his regular sponsor) mechanic underneath it while the girls sang "Get Out and Get Under." When Como and the Fontanes performed their new recording of "I Wanna Go Home (With You)," a semi-comedic song around the girls' rivalry to date Perry, the song faded out to Perry engaging with "an old crone selling flowers."[35] The following week, *Variety* liked the comedy pieces much more. They included a piece of pie-in-the-face slapstick comedy that "was startling because it was so unexpected of Como."[36] The same show also showed a willingness by the producers to poke fun at their own product. Surprisingly, Martin Block had appeared to be extremely nervous during his commercials in the opening show. When he appeared on screen a week later, six hands grabbed him to stop his hands from shaking.[37]

As the season progressed, the TV *Supper Clubs* continued to push the boundaries of the new medium. In November, Como welcomed the actor Raymond Massey as his guest on a show that coincided with the anniversary of the Gettysburg Address. Massey played Lincoln in a scene followed by one in which Como discusses the address with his "daughter" (played by a child actress). This in turn segued into a picture of the girl with Lincoln as he recalled and repeated his speech. The technique of integrating pictures from one scene to another was also used when Como sang a medley of college songs. As each member of the cast reminisced about his or her college days while Como sang, the technicians used shadow and double-exposure techniques to superimpose Como's image into the college scenes.

On November 27, 1949, Como's guest was Victor Borge. The show demonstrated Perry's growing confidence as both a light comedian and straight man. The scene with Borge involved the comedian giving Como a piano lesson. Seated at a piano directly across from the Dane, Como demonstrated excellent comedy timing and control in the face of Borge's quick and unpredictable humor. Later in the same show, Martin Block announced Perry to sing Frankie Laine's #1 hit, "Mule Train." What viewers thought would be a straight song turned into a delightful piece of comedy. Como appeared as an Italian farmer, dragging a pantomime horse. "You no wanna clippetty-clop?" said Como in a Chico Marx accent as the mule refused to move. The piece was the clearest example yet of Como's growing breadth and maturity as a performer.

By the close of the year, many of the ingredients that would make Perry Como one of the biggest television stars of the fifties were in place. He now had a regular musical director in the ample form of Mitchell Ayres. Ayres had taken over conducting responsibilities for the *Supper Club* radio shows in September 1948. His association with Como endured until 1964, Perry's weekly TV shows having ended the year before. Ayres also conducted most of Como's RCA sessions during the same period. Born in Milwaukee in 1910, Ayres (his birth name was Mitchell Agress) played violin in a local band before leaving to lead the Fashions in Music Orchestra. In the late forties, Ayres joined Columbia Records as an arranger and conductor, where he worked with Dinah Shore and Frank Sinatra. His primary musical relationship, however, was with singer Buddy Clark.[38] Clark was one of Como's major rivals in the late forties and scored three *Billboard* #1s before his untimely death in a plane crash in 1949. Michael Drury of *Collier's Magazine* later described Como's wooing of Ayres. "One day Ayres' phone rang and Como asked him if he would like to play golf on Saturday. Ayres said sure. He'd met Como a few times casually and he wondered, as any man would have, whether he was going to be offered a new job. Nothing whatever was said. They played golf. Ayres was not a talkative man but he was a little puzzled. Two weeks later, Como called again, suggesting another game. Again, the job was not mentioned. Como phoned a third time and Ayres, by now convinced that the singer just liked to play golf with him, was concentrating on getting out of a sand trap on the thirteenth hole when Como, standing on a grassy rise above him, said 'Hey, you want to be my musical conductor?' Ayres stopped, squinted up at him, and said 'Yeah.' Then he went back to the sand trap and finished the game."[39]

The Fontane Sisters were also regular members of the *Supper Club* team, both on television and radio. Like Ayres, they had joined the regular cast of the radio show for the 1948–49 season. The association moved from radio to records in December 1948 when they accompanied Como on the only disc that he made during the period of the Petrillo Ban. "N'yot N'yow (The Pussycat Song)" was a novelty tune, written by Dick Manning, who would later provide lyrics for Como on "Papa Loves Mambo" and "Hot Diggity." The song served more as a vehicle for the Fontanes than for Como and played heavily to the vocal interplay between the three sisters. As a vocal piece, it needed no orchestral backing and RCA was able to record it without breaching the Petrillo Ban. The session also utilized a four-man chorus plus a solitary ukulele, played by Jack Lathrope, a non–AFM member. The record was a modest success, reaching #20 in the *Billboard* chart early in 1949. More importantly, it served as a successful auditioning piece for the Como-Fontanes partnership.[40] They would go on to record 17 more titles together between 1949 and 1954, scoring several hits.

"N'yot N'yow" was Como's first venture into the RCA studios since December 1947. Once the major labels came to an agreement with Petrillo's AFM, however, Como picked up the production line once more. His first post-ban title was a tribute to the newly re-elected president, Harry S Truman. "Missouri Waltz" was the official state song of the president's home state and it featured in a special RCA tribute to the president on December 14, 1948, the day that the ban ended. Como recorded the song during that evening and by noon the following day, it was on sale on Broadway. It was the first commercial record to hit the streets after the end of the ban. Despite the race to get a record out for the president, the real competition was to capitalize on the other

Perry with the Fontane Sisters during an early *Supper Club* TV broadcast (courtesy Colleen Zwack).

song recorded at that evening session, "Far Away Places." Joan Whitney and Alex Kramer, who had scored well in 1947 with "Love Somebody" (a hit for Buddy Clark and Doris Day), were the writers. Como joined Bing Crosby, Margaret Whiting and Dinah Shore in taking the song into the *Billboard* charts. Despite an appropriately down-beat review from *Downbeat* ("'Places,' despite its popularity, is unappealing to these ears yet Perry makes it sound rather pretty with the soft intimacy of the Henri René fiddles"), Como's version scored well. Its chart entries were #6 in the bestseller listings and #4 on the disc jockey chart. Crosby and Whiting shared top spot with the song, each reaching #2 in the best seller charts, despite Crosby's being an *a capella* version, recorded before the end of the AFM ban.[41]

During 1949, Perry put in another ten sessions for RCA, recording 21 titles. The hits included "Forever and Ever," "'A' You're Adorable" and "A Dreamer's Holiday," which scored #3, #4 and #4 respectively in the *Billboard* bestseller charts.[42] Como's biggest record of the year, however, was the hit song from the show *South Pacific*. "Some Enchanted Evening" attracted all of the major vocal talents and Crosby, Sinatra, Jo Stafford and even a resurgent Al Jolson all had records out. This time, Como came out tops, producing an immaculate reading of a deceptively simple-sounding song. Aside from delivering his biggest hit of the year, the recording was also one of his finest vocal performances. The lilting tune that underpins the melody of the song can easily tempt a singer into allowing the vocal to be carried along with it. Even Crosby's recording falls into that trap at times. The song demands that the singer imposes the vocal over the melody, a task that Como achieves perfectly. Robert Jones, in his sleeve notes to a Como compilation in 1998, pointed out that Como's enunciation on words ending in m, n and ing—"room," "own," "evening"—was near flawless. "Few singers sang 'Some Enchanted Evening' as persuasively as Ezio Pinza," he wrote, referring to the star who put the song across on the Broadway stage. "Perry Como was one of the few."[43]

RCA's release of "Some Enchanted Evening," backed with another song from the same show, "Bali Ha'i," unwittingly pitched Como into the middle of the "Battle of the Speeds." The battle, a stand off between Columbia and RCA about the preferred format for the new microgroove records, began on June 21, 1948. At a press conference at the Waldorf Astoria, New York, Columbia launched its new "Long-Playing Microgroove Record"—LP, for short. The new disc promised up to 25 minutes of music on each side of a 12" disc, playing at a speed of 33 rpm. This was five or six times as much as on a standard 78. The LP also offered a price saving. Columbia's price tag was $4.85. To buy the equivalent amount of music on six 78s would cost $8.50.[44] At the press conference, a beaming Edward Wallerstein, Chief Operating Officer of Columbia Records, stood between a fifteen-inch stack of LP records and an eight-foot high stack of the same music on 78s.[45] Aside from the economy, the new microgroove records were made from vinylite, a non-breakable and silent surface material that offered superior sound to the gritty crackle of a 78.[46]

The critical factor in the success of the new format, however, was not the quality of the record but the availability of a machine that would play them. Columbia went to Philco for the solution. The first foray into the world of long-playing records, by RCA Victor in 1931, had failed partly because of the inadequacies of the associated hardware. This time, Columbia was able to market its LPs through Philco's "clam," a turntable, pick-up and tone arm combination in a Bakelite case with a lid that, in fact, closed like a clamshell. The new player retailed at $29.95, ready to plug into existing radios, television sets, or phonographs.[47]

Wallerstein realized that a critical success factor for the new LP was to get it adopted by the industry generally. He therefore encouraged other labels to use Columbia's new technology, but initially few did. Everyone was waiting for the response of Columbia's biggest rival, RCA Victor. Chairman David Sarnoff had nodded politely when given an advance demonstration of the Columbia product but immediately issued instructions to his engineers to come up with an alternative. The following year, RCA launched a 7" disc that played at 45 rpm, complete with its own rapid speed changer. Accounts varied as to whether the choice of speed was scientifically calculated or simply derived by deducting 33 from 78—a kind of mathematical nose thumbing to Columbia.[48]

RCA invested heavily in its new format and record changer, calling it the "the sensible, modern, inexpensive way to enjoy recorded music."[49] For popular songs, the distinction between a single LP and several auto-changed 45s was less of an issue, but for a lengthy classical piece, the LP was undeniably superior. RCA, with record sales falling and a sense of lethargy about its Victor subsidiary, pulled out all the stops.[50] In August 1949, *Downbeat* carried a report that suggested some desperation inside RCA. "Tip-off on the merchandising pressure Victor is putting behind its 45 rpm rapid change records is the fact that for the first time in its history, the company is allowing dealers 100 per cent returns until August 1," they said.[51]

RCA finally accepted the permanence of Columbia's LP format later the same year when it demonstrated a three-speed changer that it promised the market for the spring of 1950. RCA also announced that it would use LPs for its classical catalogue, but clung to 45s for popular material until 1952.[52]

What no one seemed to realize was that Columbia and RCA were fighting the wrong enemy. Victor's rapid changer 45s might be no match for the LP but they were dynamite against the old shellac 78s. The 45s—and their sibling, the extended play disc— soon became the industry standard for single releases, and the 78 rpm record was history well before the fifties were over.

With Como as RCA's main seller, it was inevitable that the company would throw his discs to the front of the battle with Columbia. Not only did RCA use the 45 rpm format for his new releases, they also saw an opportunity to repackage the back catalogue onto a series of 45s. "The timing for Perry couldn't have been better," wrote Como historian George Townsend. "The introduction of new songs on Perry's [television] shows where the audience could see and hear the performers added a completely new dimension to the marketing of popular music. Either by happenstance or by genius Perry found himself at the fore of this developing technology. Perry's newest pop songs were cleverly mixed with the older evergreens and RCA Victor were able to sell back catalogue recordings and new ones equally well in several different formats."[53] These new formats included not only the single 45 releases but also special 45-rpm extended play albums, box sets of the same and in due course, RCA's own 10" and 12" long play records.

Como was as oblivious to the war going on about speeds as he was to the type of material that came his way. It was testament to his vocal dexterity that, at the same session where he put down "Some Enchanted Evening," he also recorded the novelty tune "'A' You're Adorable" with the Fontane Sisters. This song was a model of perseverance by one of its writers, Buddy Kaye. Kaye had written the lyrics for Como's signature hit "Till the End of Time" in 1945. Kaye had peddled and pushed that song himself until Como took it on board. Convinced that he had found the formula for success, he dug out a song that he had written seven years earlier, based on the letters of the alphabet. Packing the sheet music in his briefcase, he flogged his way from publisher to publisher. "Who wants to hear a song about the alphabet?" was the standard response until he finally persuaded M-G-M Records to record the song just before the Petrillo Ban. The record came out a year later and Kaye found himself back on the road, badgering disc jockeys, record shops and department stores. Finally, he struck the jackpot when Como sang it on the *Supper Club*.[54] RCA slated it for Perry and the Fontanes, and Kaye chalked up another hit song.

By the end of 1949, two distinct sides to Perry Como as a disc performer had emerged. The differences were more to do with his choice of material rather than an ability to vary his singing style, although that too would soon arrive. RCA A&R director Joe Coida, writing in 1950, called Como "an artist and repertoire man's dream. We took him over to a little church on a Friday, and with 36 voices and an organ, made the most thrilling record of 'The Lord's Prayer' and 'Ave Maria' that I've ever heard. A few days later in our own studios on 24th Street, we recorded a bit of nonsense called 'Bibbidi-Bobbidi-Boo,' and still another lilting little Irish thing named 'Did Anyone Ever Tell You, Mrs. Murphy.'"[55] Such was Como's selling power that the products of both sessions appeared in the charts. The two religious songs were, not surprisingly, Christmas hits, and "Bibbidi-Bobbidi-Boo" reached the best seller #17 early in the following year.[56]

Despite Como's ongoing sales, his performance in the year-end polls was mixed. He gained top spot for the first time in the *Billboard* Disc Jockey Most Popular Male Vocalist Chart, pushing Bing Crosby into second place, but in the *Downbeat* Male Singer poll, Como trailed in seventh place, with Billy Eckstine top and Frankie Laine second.[57] The unseating of Crosby and the emergence of Eckstine and Laine were signs of a new day dawning in the singing business. Crosby's reign as the undisputed king was over; Sinatra looked like a busted flush. A new generation of singers was making the hits. Names such as Eckstine, Laine, Vic Damone, Eddie Fisher and Tony Bennett seemed set to be the stars of the new decade. Como, it seemed, had more in common with the Crosby-Sinatra generation than these new kids on the block. Most bets would have been on any of them to outsell him in the coming decade. It was testament to his versatility— and to the growing power of television—that Perry Como would make the fifties his own.

Chapter 7

Hoop-Dee-Doing It

I T HAS ALWAYS BEEN FASHIONABLE TO ascribe a label to a decade. Convention has it that the twenties "roared" and the sixties "swung." The fifties were simply "fabulous," and few people enjoyed a more fabulous time than Perry Como. The decade has become synonymous with U.S. affluence and prosperity, a decade when a nation that had secured freedom for the world in World War II returned home to enjoy the fruits of victory. "In the years following the traumatic experiences of the Depression and World War II, the American Dream was to exercise personal freedom not in social and political terms, but rather in economic ones," said David Halberstam in his book *The Fifties*.[1] "Eager to be part of the burgeoning middle class, young men and women opted for material well-being."[2] This clamor for economic advance created a decade when social convention dominated individuals' behavior. It influenced how they dressed, how they talked, which records they bought and whom they watched on television. The prevailing mood was one of non-challenging conformity. Perry Como—smart, clean-cut, friendly, successful— had all the right characteristics to become one of the decade's cultural icons.

Music in 1950, said Halberstam, "was still slow and saccharine, mirroring the generally bland popular taste."[3] Other writers have made similar assessments. Joshua Zeitz wrote that "light melodies, sweet lyrics, wholesome songs, innocent and inoffensive songs" were the hallmarks of fifties music.[4] The emergence of black rhythm and blues music would, by the middle of the decade, spawn rock 'n' roll (*Billboard* began charting the most popular "R&B" records during 1949), and with it, a challenge to the established order. As Zeitz points out however, "rock, despite its massive popularity, never displaced the softer variations on the pop song." It was not until the arrival of the Beatles in 1964 that Como and his ilk really felt the cold wind of change.

Arguably, decades and their characteristics have more to do with a nation's state of mind than the arithmetic symmetry of a calendar. Many Americans moved into what became the fifties mindset as early as 1948 with the emergence of a television-fueled consumerism at home and the first Cold War standoff in Berlin. Conversely, some have suggested that the succeeding decade did not really take on its "sixties" feel until 1963, when the assassination of a president, Civil Rights legislation and the beginnings of America's self-appointed role as the world's policeman ended the tranquil isolationism of Eisenhower's decade. The fifteen years between 1948 and 1963 fit more easily into the stereotype of fifties America than the digits on the calendar. The purity of the argument matters not to the story of Perry Como, but it is no coincidence that the period from 1948 to 1963 represented his halcyon years.

Even though American musical tastes in 1950 were much as they had been ten years before, there was still a demand in the music business for something fresh. New singers and new songs were just as much in demand as the new models of cars, refrigerators and televisions that took up so much of America's advertising space. The endurance, however, of the same musical styles that had dominated the forties lulled the major companies into a false sense of security. The results for 1947 only served to add to that sense of complacency. Record sales that year were the best ever, beating the previous best, which had come, surprisingly, as long ago as 1921.[5] Gross sales in 1947 reached $214 million with sales of record players reaching three and a half million. The big four labels alone issued over 300 million records, with another 75 million issued by other labels during the year.[6]

The momentum in the record business had come to a grinding halt with the Petrillo Ban in 1948, but most people in the business saw that as a temporary blip. All the major labels assumed that once they settled the dispute, sales would start to soar again. With the strikes looming, most companies did the same as RCA and began stockpiling recordings by their best-selling artists. The move enabled them to see out the Petrillo strike, but it meant that buyers were offered an 18-month shrink-wrapped diet, with little innovation or evolution in the music they heard. The result, wrote Russell Sanjek, was that what the major labels offered in 1949 was "too large an output, too startlingly alike."[7] When the results for the year came in, they showed sales of only $172 million, 20 percent down on 1947, despite the stimulus provided by Columbia and RCA's new format LPs and 45s.[8] RCA Victor felt the chill as keenly as any other label. The 1949 results made Victor's head of A&R, Eli Oberstein, one of the first casualties despite his being a major figure in the industry.[9] A collective leadership of product and merchandising heads replaced him, similar to that which had run the label twenty years before. They immediately set out looking for new talent and new sounds. One innovation was the "disk test," a series of countrywide auditions for up and coming singers and bands. The new leadership also refocused Victor's marketing and promotion and put more emphasis on the disc jockey community, a recognition that it was they who influenced 85 percent of all record sales.[10]

Perry Como was not immune to the dip in sales. Although he had enjoyed several major hits in 1949, his sales dropped to around 200–300,000, even on a good-selling single. "Such sales would be seventh heaven to many a singer, but they made Como think," Time magazine reported.[11] When RCA arranged for him to make a tour of their record distributors, their message struck home. Jukebox operators would come in, they told him, and listen to the introduction and a few bars of the record and use that to decide whether to stock it. The distributors said that what they needed were records with "short, loud intros and snappy tempos."[12] It was the opposite of what Como expected. His taste had always been for long intros, slow tempos and big finishes.[13] Although Como had already developed a reputation as a novelty song singer, none of the records that he had made so far had required him to vary his singing. "Bibbidi-Bobbidi-Boo" and "'A' You're Adorable" might have been novelty numbers but they were more like nursery rhymes than jump tunes. They were songs that Como could sing in his sleep. Now, he was being told that he needed something different. It wasn't a case of giving himself a total makeover, but he needed to find a way of matching the freshness of the new singers who were moving into his territory. Television was a major asset to him and the ability to plug his new songs week in, week out was something that most of his competitors did not have. All he needed was the material, and that meant putting more reliance on RCA's coterie of A&R men.

Como's relationship with the A&R community was not always an easy one, particularly when they came up with songs that Como didn't like and wouldn't sing. "I'd tell the A&R man, 'I can't sing that garbage,'" Como told Colin Escott in 1993, "and he'd say, 'Just do one take—one take for me.'"[14] In time, Como came to see that he needed to follow their guidance. He had already turned down several songs that became hits— "Shoo Fly Pie And Apple Pan Dowdy," which charted for Dinah Shore in 1946, would have been Como's first real novelty song, but he had said no.[15] He told his lawyer, Jack Katz, "If I ever say a song stinks, see that I record it,"[16] but he was slow to take the lesson on board. Years later, Como admitted that if he had been left to his own devices, many of his hits would have appeared in someone else's repertoire. During the BBC's *The Barber Comes to Town* feature in 1975, Como said, "Half of the gold records, I was asked to do—firmly."[17] Two years later, he told Michael Parkinson, "If I was gonna be the picker of songs, I'd still be cutting hair."[18]

The songs that worked best on television shared several characteristics: a catchy and memorable tune, an equally memorable title that featured regularly in the lyric and an arrangement that matched Como with a vocal chorus. It did not matter that Como's style was to do little more than move a cheek muscle while the chorus danced around him. The result was nevertheless a piece of active TV, a group of young people having fun and that served as much as anything to get the songs into the hearts of the viewers. From there, it was one small step to the record shop. The first record that Perry Como made during the fifties had all of these characteristics. It was also the first song that Como remembered describing as "garbage."

"Hoop-Dee-Doo" had a lyric by Frank Loesser of *Guys and Dolls* fame, set to a melody by Milton Delugg. Como recorded the song on March 16, 1950, with the Fontane Sisters and a 23-piece session band conducted by Mitchell Ayres. Charles Magnante's accordion playing dominated the arrangement, a reflection no doubt of Delugg's own affiliation with that instrument. Loesser's lyric, tightly packed into Delugg's polka rhythm, required Como to apply some new vocal techniques. The songs may have been novelty ditties but they were far from easy to sing. As Como historian George Townsend observed, "they required a remarkable talent to pull off; a comedic sense of timing, perfect breath control and the uncanny ability of Perry to smile with his voice. Perry was always able to draw a delicate balance between humor and good taste—with vocal twists and turns he was able to deliver with the musical equivalent of an acrobat."[19] Perry's rendition of "Hoop-Dee-Doo" is a perfect example of what Townsend meant. Como sings the song the way Fred Astaire performed a quickstep—light and nimble, always on his toes and landing smoothly and fleetingly on each note. Loesser's lyric talked about "hoop-dee-doing it tonight" without every revealing exactly what the "hoop-dee-doo" was. The record buyers didn't mind. Como's disc, despite competition from Russ Morgan, Kay Starr and Doris Day, took him back to the top spot in the *Billboard* charts in May 1950.[20]

"Hoop-Dee-Doo" marked the beginning of an eclectic year in the recording studio for Perry. His next two sessions in April and June produced four conventional ballad sides of which only "I Cross My Fingers" made any chart impact. In June, Como embarked upon three sessions at the Academy of Arts & Letters in New York for his first microgroove album. It had a religious theme but with RCA still clinging to its 45-rpm-only policy, the songs appeared on two 7" extended play discs. Como sang six spiritual songs during the three recording sessions and these were added to "The Lord's Prayer" and "Ave Maria" from 1949 to make two EPs—*Perry Como Sings His Favorite Songs of Worship* and *Songs of Faith*. Later when Como added some non–Christian songs in 1953, RCA released a 10" LP with the title *I Believe,* with a subtitle *Songs of All Faiths.*[21] Looking back in 1992, Como recalled it as being one of his greatest disappointments. "I thought the album would be the biggest thing I had ever done," he told Chris Stuart. "It bombed. The different faiths bit didn't work. People only wanted songs of their own faith."[22]

More sessions during August 1950 produced a further seven sides, including two new Christmas songs and two ballads from Irving Berlin's new musical *Call Me Madam.* Three more conventional pop offerings included a lilting number called "Patricia" that took Como back into the *Billboard* top ten during October 1950.[23] Como followed up immediately with his first commercial duet for RCA.[24] His vocal partner was Betty Hutton, fresh from her on-screen success in *Annie Get Your Gun.* Their A-side title was "A Bushel and a Peck," introduced in the Broadway production of *Guys and Dolls* by Como's Hollywood screen partner, Vivian Blaine. The flip side was a Cy Coben song, "She's a Lady." The public personas of the two could hardly have differed more. Hutton was a brash, loud, rootin'-tootin' comedienne to Como's sedate, gentle demeanor. This matching of opposites gave the record its appeal, although Como's studio duets never captured the informality that he displayed on television. His attempts to match Hutton's volume on the disc ("So where's your Como button!!??") sound forced and stilted and Perry Como the duettist sounds much more like the wooden actor from the Hollywood screen than the loose guy on TV. Nevertheless, the novelty behind the pairing was enough to make "Bushel" a top three hit.[25]

Como made three more visits to the RCA studios during 1950. He and the Fontanes returned to the score of *Call Me Madam* for "You're Just in Love" and "It's a Lovely Day Today," reaching #5 in the charts in December. In November, the Fontanes were again with him when he recorded "If Wishes Were Kisses," a Larry Stock–Milton Drake song and one of the first songs published by Como's new Roncom music publishing company. The song was never more than a filler, destined for a flip side release towards the end of 1951. The real interest at the evening session on November 28 was "If," an English song from 1934 that suddenly captured everyone's attention late in 1950. Apart from Perry, Dean Martin, Jo Stafford, Billy Eckstine and Vic Damone were among the singers who sought to make the song their own. It was a race that Como won, his version becoming his ninth Gold record and spending ten weeks on top of *Your Hit Parade,* as well as topping the *Cash Box, Variety* and *Billboard* charts. Como's vocal was immaculate, delivered with perfect diction and a lightness of touch that belied the song's range, until the final stanza when Perry let rip, sustaining a high finish through a booming brass and percussion crescendo.

When RCA released "If," they used a song that Como had recorded a week earlier for the flip side. "Zing-Zing, Zoom-Zoom" was in many respects a follow up to "Hoop-Dee-Doo," although for a trite novelty piece, it came with an impeccable pedigree. Its composer was Sigmund Romberg, a Broadway legend from his operettas that included *The Student Prince, The Desert Song* and *Rosalie* (with George Gershwin). Romberg himself took the baton at Como's December 5 session, one of his final conducting engagements before his death the following year. Whereas "Hoop-Dee-Doo" had been a polka, "Zing" was a waltz. Its lilting Viennese melody ideally suited a choral arrangement and meant that it was perfect for TV. Como had too much respect for Romberg to be critical of the song. When he sang it on television early in 1951, however, he looked embarrassed and uneasy. He misread the lyrics off his cue cards and, unusually for him, lost the meter for parts of the song. "You'd think after doing that song 20 times, I'd know the lyrics, wouldn't you?" he said to the audience, returning to the issue again as he

Como was always keen to try his hand with a musical instrument. His experiment with a trombone comes from mid–1950s television show (courtesy Colleen Zwack).

closed the show. "I have a few seconds left to apologize to Sigmund Romberg for fluffing 'Zing-Zing, Zoom-Zoom,'" he said.[26]

There was still time for Como to add one more genre to his list of 1950 recordings. On December 18, Como was back in Victor's Studio 2 in New York, along with the Western-Ayres (Mitchell Ayres in a Stetson) plus the Sons of the Pioneers. The latter were a cowboy-singing group formed in 1934 by Leonard Slye, Tim Spencer and Bob Nolan. Slye went on to achieve movie and television fame as Roy Rogers, while other members, including Lloyd Perryman, joined the group later in the thirties. The Sons of the Pioneers were already country music legends by the time they arrived in New York in December 1950 for a concert at Carnegie Hall. While in the city, they had TV appearances lined up with Steve Allen and Como, and RCA saw the opportunity to add a recording session with Perry to their itinerary.

Their appearance on the Como TV show was set for December 18, with the recording session arranged for the following day. Keen to get home a day early, the group asked Perry if they might do the session straight after the TV show. For their television appearance, the Sons of the Pioneers dressed in their usual western attire, while Perry was in his usual suit and tie. After the broadcast, the Pioneers headed straight to the RCA studios where they were rehearsing when Como arrived, slightly late. The Pioneers had changed back into their street clothes by now, but Como appeared in full western garb— bright cowboy suit, ten-gallon hat, spurs and chaps. "Oh, no, what happened to my cowboys?" said a stunned Perry.[27]

The joking over, Como and the group recorded two songs that evening. Cowboy songs had been a standard feature in Bing Crosby's repertoire since he starred with the Pioneers in *Rhythm on the Range* in 1936, but "You Don't Kno' What Lonesome Is ('Til You Get to Herdin' Cows)" and "Tumbling Tumbleweeds" were Como's only forays into the genre on disc. Perry's former Ted Weems colleague, Country Washburne, wrote "Lonesome"; "Tumbleweeds" came from the pen of one of the original Pioneers, Bob Nolan. Their version with Como was a virtual re-make of their 1934 original.

The TV Show on which the Pioneers joined Perry was now *The Perry Como Show,* which debuted in the fall of 1950 on NBC. Como's dual radio and TV schedule on *The Chesterfield Supper Club* had ended in the summer, although the final months of Como on radio had been part of a strong Chesterfield offering for the new decade. "Chesterfield's ABC" (Always Buy Chesterfield) had been a favorite marketing line for Chesterfield for some time. With Bing Crosby joining Como and Arthur Godfrey, L&M now had an alternative makeup to the "ABC," also read as "Arthur, Bing & Como," and the sponsor took every opportunity to group the three performers together.

In January 1950, Perry had hosted his radio show from Duke Indoor Stadium in Durham, North Carolina, with Bob Hope, Eddy Arnold and Arthur Godfrey as his guests. The show marked the opening of a new Liggett and Myers factory in the town, and 8,000 people crammed into the stadium to watch the broadcast. The following month, Mae West provided Como with an unlikely duet partner, managing to inject more than a hint of double-entendre into the innocence of "I Wanna Go Home with You." In March, Dorothy Lamour, the perpetual prey of Hope and Crosby in the *Road* films, made an appearance, performing a skit with Perry called "The Rut to Roaring Gulch." Later that month in Chicago, Como achieved one of his life's ambitions when he guested on *The Bing Crosby Show for Chesterfield,* joining his mentor in a duet on "A Dream Is a Wish Your Heart Makes," a song from Walt Disney's *Cinderella* that Como had recorded the previous fall. Como later told reporters, "I went out on stage and told the audience that I owed what success I had completely to a man I scarcely knew—Bing Crosby. It was corny but true. Bing walked onstage, kissed me and told the audience that it was just wonderful to have someone say thank you in public. We've been good friends ever since."[28]

Como's final radio show for Chesterfield aired on June 1, 1950. With a distinct end-of-semester air to the program, members of the cast got the chance to do what they had wanted to do all year. Martin Block and fellow announcer Tony Marvin sang a duet, and bandleader Mitchell Ayres joined Perry in a rendition of "It Isn't Fair." The show brought the curtain down not just on the season but also on Como's radio career.[29] He would make occasional guest appearances in the future, but from now on, Perry Como's future was indelibly on the small screen.

The television version of the *Chesterfield Supper Club* continued to go from strength to strength. Como's shows during January 1950 included a re-enactment of Christmas Day in the Como household, but with child actors playing the part of the Como children. A week later, on January 15, Como had the comedy team of Helene & Howard as his guests. *Variety* said that the show "improves constantly on the production end" and rated the show as "one of the best that the singer has hosted so far."[30] When Perry and Helene reprised Como and the Fontanes' "I Wanna Go Home with You," Helene finished the show by picking Perry up in a fireman's carry. "It was a rare bit, carried off nicely," said *Variety,* seemingly oblivious to the pun.[31]

As television continued to gain momentum, so too did the quality of Como's guest list. Burgess Meredith, Franchot Tone and Ethel Waters joined him in February, and in

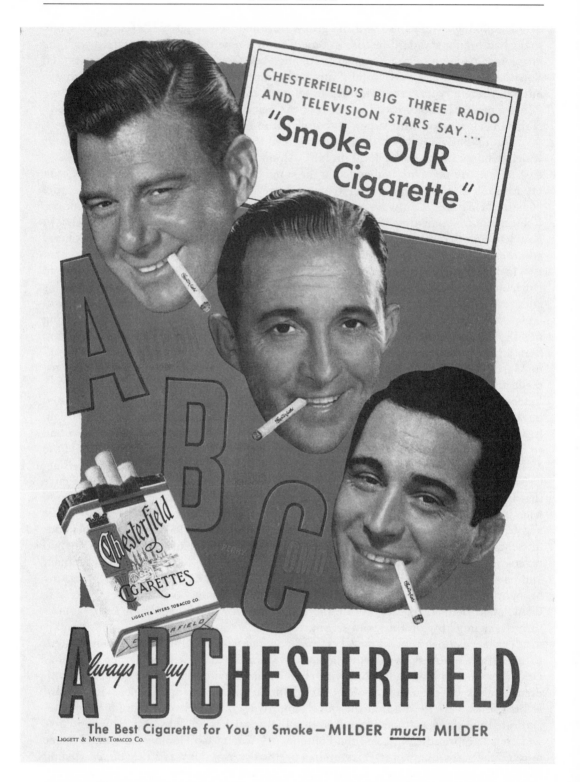

Chesterfield's alternative A-B-C: Arthur, Bing and Como. From the top, Arthur Godfrey, Bing Crosby and Perry.

March, the roster included Douglas Fairbanks Jr. and the Nat King Cole Trio. April saw Perry host Sigmund Romberg on the show, and he used the occasion to deliver a superb vocal on "Serenade" from Romberg's *The Student Prince*. It was a world away from "Zing-Zing, Zoom-Zoom." Bing Crosby, Chico Marx and the Mills Brothers also guested later in the series, and the only blot on a second successful season came when a throat ailment caused Perry to miss the final show on June 11.

As with the radio series, the June show was the last *Supper Club* that Perry would host. When Perry returned to the screen in October, the sponsor was still Chesterfield, but Como had switched his network allegiance to CBS. The new show represented both a step forward and a step back. For the first time, Perry's name featured ahead of the sponsor in what was now known as *The Perry Como Show*, but Perry found himself back in the thrice-weekly, 15-minute show routine of the old radio-only *Supper Clubs*. Regular Como team members Ray Charles, Mitchell Ayres and the Fontanes moved to CBS with Perry, with a guest appearing from time to time. The shows usually opened with Perry in front of the Mitchell Ayres orchestra, beneath a large Chesterfield banner.

Lee Cooley was the producer-director of the new show. Forty-year-old Cooley had entered television in its fledgling days before World War II but in 1940 had moved into advertising, believing that if he planned a career in television production, he needed to understand the industry from the perspective of the sponsors. When he took up the reins on the Como series, Cooley deliberately changed the way he presented Como. "I felt that no one had let him be himself," he said in 1956. "He was lost and the show was over-produced. The production became the star of the show. I went on the basis that the people made the show and that the backdrops and splendor were second to the human quality."[32] The result met with the critics' approval. *Variety* liked the new show, which they described as "a simple, straight and solid musical show." Como, they said, was "freed from any production folderol," allowing him to deliver three or four "pop tunes" during each quarter hour. This, they said, together with his "ingratiating personality" was more than enough to compensate for the "absence of any special video angles."

Commercials were of course an indelible part of any show on television and the Chesterfield spots on the Como show typically took up around a quarter of the planned airtime. The early shows opened with the Fontanes singing the Chesterfield "Sound Off" jingle, followed by announcer Dick Stark's pronouncement that it was time to "sound off for Chesterfield." Stark took over the announcing duties on the show at the start of Perry's second season in August 1951. He was already a doyen of television salesmen, known not only for selling Chesterfields but also for extolling the virtues of "Amm-i-dent" toothpaste on *Danger* and Camay Soap on radio's *Pepper Young's Family*. Stark's success, *Time* magazine said, owed much to his "averageness."[33] "He is of medium height, has thinning hair and a bland, open face that is naggingly familiar to people," the magazine said. Stark's accent too was "neutral," one that didn't identify readily with any part of the United States and didn't offend any regional prejudices. Retailers, said *Time*, want "a man like Stark who sounds as if he came from nowhere and every-where."[34]

The first signs that cigarette smoking might have dangerous health consequences were recognized in 1950, although it would still be some years before campaigns to ban tobacco advertising from television gained any momentum.[35] Nevertheless, Stark's scripts for Chesterfield took on an increasingly defensive tone. "Bi-monthly examinations show no known effects to the nose, throat and sinuses from smoking Chesterfields," he reas-suringly told viewers. Como too took his share of the marketing, performing most of his songs with a cigarette in his hand, although rarely putting it to his lips. His exhortations to viewers to "go out and buy a pack of Chesterfields" had the same casualness as his singing. "Tell 'em Como sent you," he would say.

Como breezed through 1951 in much the same manner as in 1950. His own show on TV moved into its second series and was welcomed back by *Variety*, who saw "the same informal, infectious atmosphere that characterized last year's sessions."[36] The guest list included names such as Patti Page, Nat King Cole, Les Paul and Mary Ford, and in November 1951, the show saw the television debut of country legend Hank Williams. *Variety* said that Williams "filled the bill excellently, complete with 10-gallon hat and sharp twangy vocalizing" and forecasted that he would become a "sock TV guest star."[37] Williams sang "Hey Good Lookin'" and the following week, Como reprised the song. Under a banner billing them as "Cactus Como and the 3 Skunkville Violets," Como sang the song with the Fontanes, looking somewhat incongruous in 10-gallon hat and lounge suit (Como had yet to adopt his fabled cardigans). Como and the sisters came up with a tongue-in-cheek rendition of the song and offered their on-screen apologies to Williams at the end of it. The 15-minute duration of the show meant that there was no time for an on-screen duet between Como and Williams, and the opportunity would not arise again. Just over a year later, Williams was found dead in his car at the age of 29.

Aside from his own shows, Como guested twice during the year on *The Frank Sinatra Show*, also on CBS-TV. Each time, Como shared the guest spot with Frankie Laine. In the first show, Sinatra and Como delivered a good comedy sketch that had Como as a working barber in his "Saturday job" when Sinatra drops in for a shave. Como handled the comedy with good aplomb and timing, including one moment of slapstick where he dropped a brush-load of shaving cream onto Sinatra to stop him singing. Como then delivered "If" from the barber's chair, with shaving mug and brush in hand before joining the host and Frankie Laine in a send-up of the Andrews Sisters. In what appeared to be a genuine surprise, the Sisters themselves appeared from the audience at the end of the sketch and set about the trio with their handbags. "The impact was terrif," said *Variety*.[38] Such was the success of the show that Como and Laine, plus the Andrews Sisters, reprised the performance in October, a month in which Como also filmed a cameo appearance in *The Fifth Freedom*, a Chesterfield film promoting cigarettes and the American way of life, in that order. Como joined fellow Chesterfield artists Bing Crosby and Arthur Godfrey in the film, singing "Bless This House." Also in October, Como opened the third game of the all–New York World Series between the Yankees and the Giants by singing the national anthem at the Giants' Polo Grounds home.

By the end of 1951, Perry Como had settled into a television routine. It was as a close as anyone in show business could have to a 9-to-5 job. Each morning, he would leave his home on Sands Point and drive into Manhattan. Some days he would head for the CBS studios on West 54th Street. If it was not a show day, he would head either for the RCA studios or for the Roncom offices at Radio City. "This business of being a singer is no different from working in a shoe factory," he told the *New York Times* in December 1951.[39] Como said he was happy with his life but added, "I could be just as happy doing a lot of other things as I am singing." The interview offered a perceptive insight, both into the man who had become such a star of television and into the production of the show itself. The man came across in simple terms. "I have no philosophy," said Perry. "I just like to be around people." His success was something that he appreciated but put down to good fortune. "I've never maliciously nudged anyone to get what I wanted," he said, "and I'm thankful for what I have. Whatever there is in my voice, I was born with. To sing the stuff I do, you don't need musical training."[40]

As to the show, Como admitted to more nerves than anyone would have guessed. When asked what he thought about while he was singing, Como said that the trick was to get the audience to believe that his focus was on the song. The truth however was that on any live show, the concern was more "with what comes next, not what is happening at the moment." When it came to his songs, Como said that on a live show, nobody would entrust the lyrics to 12 or 13 songs to memory. "Without this boy who stands right beside the camera and holds the cue card over his head, there'd be no music on television,"[41] he said. Como's card had the words to his songs written in large, black letters. If the song were a duet, his partner's lyrics would be written in red. Over time, Como became over-dependent on the cards. Stephen Pouliot, who directed several of Como's shows in the 1970s, said that a joke among the crew was that Perry almost needed a cue card that said, "Hello, I'm Perry Como."[42]

Como closed out the *New York Times* interview saying that his ambition was simply to "go on as long as I can and as long as I'm wanted, and then go out and have a ball." In a rare concession to his enjoyment of the spotlight, however, he added a note of caution. "I dread the day when nobody wants me on television, radio, or records," he said.[43] There was no hint at the end of 1951 that such a day was anywhere near, although Como—and RCA—had one nagging doubt. Since Como had topped the record charts with "If," he had not had another top ten hit. Apart from a duet with Eddie Fisher, the hottest property in the record business in 1952, the same pattern would repeat the following year. The slump would last until RCA found the song that they thought would take Perry back to the top. Their only problem was that their star refused to sing it.

Chapter 8

Don't Let the Stars
Get in Your Eyes

B Y THE TIME 1952 ARRIVED, the Comos lived in a comfortable, 12-room home in the village of Sands Point. The community covered 3000 acres at the tip of the Port Washington Peninsula as it overlooks Long Island Sound. The Como home, a white pebble-dashed structure set in three acres of land, was located close to the ocean and within a mile of Sands Point Golf Club. The Como household was marked by its ordinariness— "a thoroughly suburban life, about as glamorous as a plate of spaghetti," said one fifties feature on the family.[1]

The Comos' third child, David, arrived in 1950. At the time of the adoption, he was four years old. His baptismal name was Paul Vitali. Roselle added the name David and the child became David Paul Como. According to a 1956 magazine article, David's adoption took Perry slightly by surprise. "The boy," said *Collier's*, "entered Mrs. Como's heart at an adoption agency when he was about three and a half. There was, of course, much family discussion before the adoption, but Como had never actually seen the child until one day he came home and found him sitting on the front steps. 'Hi,' he said. 'What's your name?' The child told him, adding that his last name was Como. 'Is it?' Como asked. 'Well, do you know who I am?' 'Yes,' the little boy replied, 'you're my daddy.'"[2] Overlooking the element of poetic license, David Como later confirmed this account of his first meeting with his father to be broadly accurate, although his recollection was that he had asked Perry, "Are you my daddy?" Como's response had been to go and seek out Roselle before returning to say, "Yes, I am." It was, said David, some time before it dawned on him that this was a permanent home and not just another temporary fostering.[3]

When Como was asked in later life about his experience as a parent, his reply was always the same. "You need to talk to Mrs. Como," he told Phil Donahue in 1979. "The kids were her life—and still are." With Roselle's desire to stay out of the spotlight enduring throughout her life, there were few, if any, opportunities for interviewers to act on Perry's suggestion. If they had, they would have found Mrs. Como as difficult a nut to crack as her husband. Roselle and Perry shared the same philosophy about keeping their personal life private. In a rare 1950 article, Roselle was quick to dispel any sense of glamour about their lives. "Perry's and my closest friends are people you have never heard of," she said.[4]

David Como recalled that his mother was the disciplinarian in the household and administered any punishments that were needed "with her wooden spoon."[5] In the 1950 *Dell* magazine feature, Roselle had said that she took on the task of disciplining the children because Perry's time with them so was so limited. "I want those hours to be carefree," she said. David Como recalled that his father always backed up Roselle in any stance she might take, usually preceded by a discussion between the two of them in Italian, a language that the children did not speak. As well as Perry, Roselle, and their children, Roselle's mother also lived with the family on Long Island and looked after the children when their parents were away. Perry's own mother had also lived there briefly in the early fifties, but had been unable to settle, in part because most of the household chores were in the hands of a maid. "I like to work and cook in the kitchen," Mrs. Como said, "so I came home again."[6]

Roselle Como's hobbies included reading and painting, and in later life, her work was displayed in several exhibitions.[7] Perry's pastimes were more sports orientated, mainly golf. Neither son David nor Ray Charles recalled Perry as a great reader. David Como said that as he grew older, his father developed a liking for the Sherlock Holmes novels. Ray Charles said that Como's literary tastes did not extend much beyond golf magazines. When Como's TV team met regularly on Mondays to go through the first reading of that week's script, "we would all discuss what program ideas we had gotten from the Sunday *New York Times* and would ask Perry if he had seen any of these articles, to which he replied, 'Roselle reads the *Times*, I read the *Daily News*,'" said Charles.[8] Como's other great love was television. As an early TV pioneer, he took both a professional and personal interest in the medium and was quick with his opinions about what he saw.[9] *Time* magazine in 1959 said Como's main interest was "watching TV while sprawled on a couch in his den, writing congratulatory telegrams to TV comedians."[10]

Como was also a TV sports fan—his son David said that his father was "the kind of guy who would watch a baseball game from the beginning to the end"—but as a participant, Como's main hobby was golf. When the Comos moved to Long Island, Perry joined the Garden City Country Club, an exclusive establishment that dated back to 1916. Como was an accomplished player, regularly shooting scores in the mid–70s and attaining a handicap of five at his peak. His slow, smooth swing matched Como's effortless public persona, something that golf legend Sam Snead picked up on when he hosted Perry in a TV celebrity golf match in 1960. "You swing like you sing," he said, "never rushed."[11] Como's golfing ability was good enough to bring him the Garden City Club Championship in 1954.[12]

Golf never became quite so associated with Como's image as it did with Bing Crosby, although the link was strong enough for one manufacturer (MacGregor) to launch a "Perry Como Putter," complete with an autograph on every one. Golf was one of the few "private" elements of his life that he was willing to share with his public. Throughout the fifties, he appeared regularly in several national events, including the National Association of Songwriters' Championship, which he won twice. He was also a regular in the National Celebrities Golf Championship, plus other similar events.

As a game, golf is one of the great levelers. No matter what the wealth or celebrity of the player, the only way to maintain a handicap as low as Como's is to play regularly. There was no doubt that the golf bug had its teeth firmly into Perry's soul. When RCA sent him out on a two-week promotional tour in 1960, Como filled every free minute with a game of golf. In California, he managed to play 36 holes a day for each of three days. It was the same in Chicago and Cincinnati, and when the tour reached Philadelphia, Dick Kleiner, writing in the Uniontown *Morning Herald*, said, "he even got a police escort to take him to the links, squeezing in 18 holes between a luncheon and a late afternoon cocktail party."[13] Como's work ethic of course ensured that the golf did not get in the way of his main purpose. "Don't get the wrong impression," Kleiner wrote. "Perry didn't cut short any of his duties. In each city, he met the press, the record company distributors, and the sponsor's local brass. He toured plants, signed autographs, posed for pictures and made everybody feel good. That was the purpose of the jaunt."[14]

Many of Como's public golfing outings had a fund-raising element to them and were just one facet of a major contribution to charitable causes that Como made throughout his life. Much of the focus of Como's charitable efforts was on local establishments. After moving to Long Island, he established a link with the St. Francis Children's Hospital in Roslyn and supported their fund-raising over many years. Even in the 1980s, long after the Comos had made Florida their permanent home, Perry returned each year to play in the St. Francis Celebrity Golf Classic. "Perry is the spirit of the tournament," said Dr. Robert F. Vizza, the president and chief executive of the hospital in 1990. "You mention the St. Francis golf tournament and people say, 'Oh, that's the one with Perry Como.'"[15]

The Duke's University Children's Hospital in North Carolina was also a Como beneficiary for almost 50 years, but Perry was also keen to support causes that were close to his childhood home. In 1950, he returned to Canonsburg to present two personal checks totaling $35,000 to the Canonsburg General Hospital Building Fund.[16] Other gestures were often more spontaneous. In 1952, Como was honored at a formal dinner at the Statler Hotel in Washington, D.C. Press reports said Como had to splash out $350 for a tuxedo—the first one he had owned since his Ted Weems days. On the afternoon preceding the dinner, Como visited a local children's hospital and that night, as the dinner reached its conclusion, Como stripped out of his tux and auctioned it, raising $3000 for the hospital's polio fund.[17]

Charity and benefit performances were, by 1952, just about the only way that the Como fans could see their hero in the flesh other than by attending his TV show. His last tour in the States had been in the summer of 1947. Since then, his only stage appearances had been occasional one-off shows such as his February 1952 appearance at the Boston Opera House, raising funds for the Christopher Columbus Youth Center.

There were several reasons why Como turned his back on personal appearances, although lack of opportunity was certainly not one of them. *Downbeat* carried a report in 1949 that Como was seriously considering a lucrative offer from the London Palladium, which had succeeded in attracting many of his contemporaries.[18] The offer from the Palladium remained on the table and the New York Paramount mounted a similar pursuit, but all to no avail.[19] *Downbeat* reported in July 1952 that Como had planned to make a personal appearance tour during his summer break from TV but changed his mind at the last moment.[20] Even the new hot venue of Las Vegas could not tempt him, Como turning down a $70,000 offer for a two-week stint. "It's a fabulous sum for a night club to pay," said Perry. "But I'd be uncomfortable. It would make me nothing more than an expensive shill for a gambling joint."[21] It would be another 18 years before Perry overcame his ethical objections.

Como said later that the main reason why he turned down so many offers was lack of time. He told a TV interviewer in 1984 that the demands of this television show—39 weeks per year, and between 1951 and 1955, three times per week, plus his recording schedule meant there was no time for anything else. "When I was through with that, I was through. Not doing personal appearances was just a case of not having time. I was working seven days a week on TV," he said.[22]

Perry was a good standard amateur golfer, often playing in front of a gallery, as this late 1950s shot shows (courtesy Colleen Zwack).

There was no doubt too that live shows were hard work—Como's eight shows a day in Chicago in 1947 had been evidence of that. In an interview in 1950, Roselle Como was quick to point out that there was little glamour in touring. "In the beginning, we were excited when Perry got booked into big theaters like the Paramount and the Strand," she said. "For a while, I had stars in my eyes.... I wanted to go dancing, and

Perry and Roselle at the All-American Collegiate Golf Dinner at the Waldorf-Astoria in New York City, July 27, 1965 (courtesy Colleen Zwack).

see happy faces. After five shows a day, Perry could hardly walk, let alone dance, and the only happy face we ever laid eyes on belonged to the milkman. Perry met him every morning on the way home from work."[23]

Como finally succumbed to the pressure to perform live and agreed to headline a three-night GAC songfest in July 1954. He took top billing in an extravaganza that included other GAC luminaries such as Nat King Cole, Patti Page, Ray Anthony and Sarah Vaughan. First stop on July 23 was Detroit, followed by Chicago and Cleveland. Each show was staged outdoors in a sports arena. *Billboard* said that the Chicago event "came off like a World's Fair," with 75,000 people cramming into Soldier Field and traffic backed up for two miles.[24] Tickets prices ranged from $1.50 to $4.50. The Cleveland show was similar, although "only" 15,000 fans turned up at the 80,000 seat Municipal Stadium.

All three events suffered from a mismatch between the type of acts on view and the nature of the venues. *Billboard* said that in Chicago, the stage was still a "half a block" from the nearest seated fans, and the sound system delivered a massive echo problem. It was a similar situation in Cleveland, with Como and the cast appearing "in a boxing ring at second base."[25] None of the acts, with the possible exception of the Four Lads and Ray Anthony, recognized that an outdoor appearance required more than the normal amount of showmanship. Como got a "strong response" to his catalogue of hits, said *Billboard*, but "in a huge stadium, it takes more than a singer just standing at a microphone." "GAC Package Lays Egg in Cleve," was the journal's summation of the third night of the tour. Como nevertheless picked up $30,000 for his three nights' work. It would be 12 years before he next set foot on a live stage.

Como's success on television and records meant that he was easily able to sustain his $1 million annual income without the need to subject himself to the rigors of touring. Nevertheless, for all his success and development as a TV personality, he was a singer first and foremost, and a singer needed to sell records. Como's sales through 1951 were good, but the boost that songs like "Hoop-Dee-Doo" had given him seemed once more to have slowed. After his #1 with "If" in January 1951, Como had fared no better than #12 in the *Billboard* charts for the remainder of the year.

It was much the same story during 1952. Como's first disc of the year featured a coupling of two new ballads, "Please Mr. Sun" by Ray Getzov and Sid Frank, and "Tulips and Heather" by Milton Carson. When RCA found that Como's version of "Mr. Sun" was running a poor second to a version by the new heartthrob, Johnnie Ray, they flipped the disc and started plugging Carson's song. Como featured the tender, sweet ballad on his TV show, including one memorable rendition when a stagehand dropped a heavy piece of scenery just off camera. Como winced as the crash momentarily drowned him out, shrugged his shoulders and carried on. Both songs registered in the *Billboard* charts, but as hits go, they were never more than a pair of also-rans. With one exception, record sales for the remainder of 1952 went downhill from there. In January, Como had two RCA sessions in New York. The first, on January 29, produced two sides with the Fontanes, "Noodlin' Rag" and "Play Me a Hurtin' Tune." The songs were typical of the way Como's TV and disc repertoire with the Fontanes had developed, but despite considerable exposure on television, "Noodlin'" registered only a minor hit on the Disc Jockey charts. It made no impact whatsoever on the best sellers.

The session itself was more notable for the fact that it was Como's first involvement with musical director Hugo Winterhalter. Winterhalter had arrived at RCA in 1950 via MGM and Columbia records where he had developed a reputation as both an arranger-conductor for solo singers and a hit-maker in his own right. Once at RCA, he continued to plough both furrows, although his most significant association was the one that he formed with Eddie Fisher, the 21-year-old singer who rocketed to fame in 1949 on Eddie Cantor's radio show. Winterhalter shared the billing on Fisher's first six discs. By then, Fisher had established himself as the hottest disc property in the country with nine Top 10 records during 1952.

Fisher was a confessed admirer of Como and it made sense for RCA to pair the two of them on disc. The session, on May 13, 1952, had Mitchell Ayres, rather than Winterhalter, doing the conducting, with Dave Kapp in the control booth. Legend has it that it was this session where Como first discovered that Kapp, the man who had branded him a poor Crosby sound-alike when he heard him sing with Ted Weems, was now with RCA and had him thrown out of the studio. In truth, Kapp had already handled the A&R role on some previous sessions for Como. Less contentious is the suggestion that Como found Fisher a very difficult duet partner because of the latter's infamous difficulty in keeping to musical time. Colin Escott, who interviewed Como in 1993 for his notes to RCA's fiftieth anniversary CD set, said that "Perry liked Eddie on a personal level, but when it came to record, he found that Eddie skipped bars and sang out of meter. 'I heard him rehearsing and I thought "What the hell is that?" said Perry. I thought he was putting me on. Ray Charles, who conducted the chorus, came to me and whispered in my ear that I had to stand in front of him and cue him on the beat.'"[26] Ray Charles himself recalled that he had to perform the same role on many of Fisher's solo sessions.[27]

Kapp had slated two contrasting titles for the Como-Fisher duets. First cut was "Watermelon Weather," a new song by Hoagy Carmichael and Paul Francis Webster, which was the original A-side of the disc. For the flip side, Kapp went back to an older song, but one that had been written with a voice blend in mind. "Maybe" had been a #2 hit in 1940 for the Ink Spots, and it was soon apparent that this was still the more commercial song. Como and Fisher produced an excellent vocal blend, Como singing the melody and the lighter-voiced Fisher, despite his timing difficulties, handling the more challenging harmony. *Billboard* hailed the "fine blending of talent and beautiful matching in quality" of the two singers, and with strong RCA publicity, the disc hit #3 in the Disc Jockey chart.

Como's duets with Fisher were the high spot in an otherwise frustrating year. Ahead of the sessions with Fisher, Como had recorded another pair of ballads, "It's Easter Time" and the semi-inspirational "One Little Candle." The Easter song made no impact on disc although it served as a springtime opener for Como's Easter television shows down the years. "Candle" reached #18 in the Disc Jockey charts. The jockey charts were fine but the money came from sales and once again, Como was missing from the best seller listings.

After the duet session, the paths of Eddie Fisher and Perry Como continued in much the same direction as they had before. Fisher immediately went to the top of the *Billboard* charts with "Wish You Were Here" while Como struggled to find a way out of his slump. Indeed, none of the output from his next two sessions saw immediate release. In June 1952, RCA had tried to repeat the trick of pairing Perry with Betty Hutton but although they recorded two songs, neither was deemed suitable for release. Perry later recorded one of the titles, "To Know You (Is to Love You)" with the Fontane Sisters, which resulted in a minor but short-lived hit. Perry's next release was a re-issue of "One Little Candle" alongside "Childhood Is a Meadow," a song by Charles, Frederick and Jerry Tobias. It made no impact, nor did "My Love and Devotion," which was Perry's next release. This was another Milton Carson song, a follow up to "Tulips and Heather."

By now, Como's failure to register in the charts was becoming a real cause for concern. "My Love and Devotion" bore all the hallmarks of a classic Perry Como vocal performance—excellent diction, vocal power when it was needed and a tender reading of the lyric. Mitchell Ayres' backing was, as ever, sympathetic and unobtrusive. This was the kind of record that Como's fans had lapped up in the forties, but now the magic seemed to have gone. With only one significant hit in almost two years—and that a duet with the strongest property currently in the market—Como had to find the formula that had worked so well with songs like "Hoop-Dee-Doo" and needed to do it fast. In May 1952, he had celebrated his fortieth birthday and he was now competing with singers almost a generation younger. The record buyers were younger still. He needed to try something different.

The man who found the answer was RCA's head of country music, Steve Sholes. In the sixties, Sholes would be responsible for taking Como to Nashville, but his contribution to taking Perry out of his early 1950s slump came when he brought Como a song called "Don't Let the Stars Get in Your Eyes." It came from a young Texan music student called Winston L. Moore. He wrote the song for a local radio appearance and, thinking he needed a more overt country music name to go with a hillbilly song, billed himself as Slim Willet. Moore later recalled that after he recorded the song, half a dozen other country singers picked it up before Red Foley finally gained some success with it. The song still seemed destined for nothing more than the country charts—still, in the early fifties, a poor relation in the music business—until Como recorded it.

Sholes was convinced that the song would take Como back to the top. His problem was that Perry hated it. "I complained," Como said. "I told them 'the meter's wrong. I don't understand it.' They said to do just one take, so I did. Almost two million records later, I guess they were right."[28]

The song was certainly unusual in its construction. It was based on a Mexican ranchera rhythm, which is notoriously unpredictable. Ranchera rhythms can be in 3/4, 2/4 or 4/4 time, reflecting waltz, polka or bolero tempos. Don Tyler in his survey of *Hit Songs 1900–55: American Popular Music of the Pre-Rock Era* described the song as having its "chorus sung first, with two verses interspersed between choruses. Two chords, the tonic and the dominant seventh comprise the sparse harmonic scheme."[29] Even for a musically literate singer such as Como, it was a difficult tune to follow.

Not only was it a different type of song, but "Don't Let the Stars" was also the first time that Hugo Winterhalter took on the conducting as well as the production role with Como. His arrangement gave the song a "bounding beat and bleating brass" sound, sufficient to take it away from its hillbilly roots and create a mainstream pop feel.[30] Winterhalter conducted a nine-piece band, with Ray Charles leading a spin-off from his usual group of singers that took the name of the Ramblers. Charles had a major impact on the session. Como later said that even after he had overcome his objections to the song, he still found it a difficult one to sing. "It has an odd graduate measure," he said, "and I didn't think I could sing it. I had to have Ray Charles standing right in front of me so he could point when it was time for me to come in and when not to."[31]

RCA released "Don't Let the Stars Get in Your Eyes" in November 1952 and the impact was immediate. "This disking [stet], out for little more than a week, has met with an immediate favorable reaction," said *Billboard*. "Early reports indicate that the waxing will establish the tune in the pop field very rapidly and can be Como's biggest disk in some time."[32] The results were spectacular. Como's recording entered the *Billboard* charts in December 1952 and stayed there for 21 weeks. It topped all three regular *Billboard* listings, holding the #1 spot in the best seller chart for five weeks.[33] By the summer of 1953, the disc had sold over a million and a half copies, a staggering total when compared to the 200–300,000 sales normally expected of a pop hit.[34] If ever a song matched the formula that the nation's juke box operators had given to Perry, this was it. *Time* magazine was in no doubt that this was the key to its success, hailing its "blaring introduction and frantic Latin rhythm" as key. "The juke box operators ate it up," they said.[35]

"Don't Let the Stars Get in Your Eyes" meant that Perry Como rode into his tenth anniversary year as a solo performer on the crest of a giant wave. By the time the exact date came around in June 1953, Como had delivered three more top 10 discs. "Wild Horses" was a suitable anniversary piece, having a classical background like Perry's first major hit, "Till the End of Time." Robert Schumann's 19th century piece "Wilder Reiter" (The Wild Horseman) provided the basis for the melody and the idea for the lyric. That came from the pen of Johnny Burke, who with Jimmy Van Heusen was responsible for many of Bing Crosby's 1940s hits. Burke's work on "Wild Horses," however, used the pseudonym of K.C. Rogan. With its similar frantic style, *Downbeat* thought that "Wild Horses" was "a powerful follow-up to 'Don't Let the Stars Get in Your Eyes' and keeps Como assured of hit parade entry," which it duly provided, taking #7 spot in the best seller charts.

The winning team of Como, Winterhalter, the Ramblers and Dave Kapp stayed together for Como's next offering in March 1953. "Say You're Mine Again" was a new song by Charles Nathan and Dave Heisler and offered a sensible variation on the pace of the previous two hits. Kapp in particular recognized that once a hit stream was underway, the momentum behind it could often make a hit out of a disc that otherwise might fail. "Say You're Mine Again" was an example. *Billboard* in its review said, "Como could extend his string to three in a row very easily on this side. It's a lovely tune with an old-fashioned flavor, and the singer's performance is in the groove. Vocal backing by the Ramblers adds to the disc's power. This could easily be a big winner."[36] The disc duly delivered, taking #5 spot in the best seller chart during the spring of 1953, part of a 16-week stay in the charts.

As well as the anniversary of his solo debut, 1953 also marked Como's twentieth year as a professional singer and his twentieth wedding anniversary too. *Time, Newsweek* and *Billboard* all ran celebratory features on Como. The *Billboard* piece included an open letter to Perry from over 150 staff at RCA:

> Dear Perry—June 20th marked your 10th anniversary on the RCA Victor label. It's been a long time since your first record, "Goodbye Sue." These have been ten very happy years, not only because we have been especially proud to be associated with you, Perry, but because of the way all of us feel about working with you. We don't think there is a finer guy in the entire music industry, in the entire entertainment world—or anywhere else, for that matter.—With all our respect and deep affection....[37]

The signatories included Mannie Sachs, Vice-President and General Manager of the RCA Records Division, plus all of the A&R men and arrangers and conductors who had worked with Como. It was an unusual and heartfelt tribute from people who worked in an industry where nice guys often finished last. Perry Como seemed to be the exception to the rule. In a separate tribute in the same issue of *Billboard*, Mannie Sachs spelled out just how significant Como was to RCA. He had, said Sachs, chalked up 43 hits (defined as a disc selling more than 200,000 copies) over his 10 years with Victor. Seven of the discs had sold over one million, with "Don't Let the Stars Get in Your Eyes" being both the most recent and biggest seller.[38]

There was no better way to celebrate the anniversary than by coming up with another #1 hit and Como did exactly that in his session on May 19, 1953. This time, Henri René took the conductor's role with Hugo Winterhalter assuming the production responsibilities. Como had two songs slated for the session, "No Other Love" and "Keep It Gay," both from the new Rodgers and Hammerstein play, *Me and Juliet.* "No Other Love" was the big song from the show. In writing it, Richard Rodgers had stolen from himself, basing it on the melody "Beneath the Southern Cross" which he had written as the theme for the acclaimed 1952–53 TV series, *Victory at Sea.* He and Hammerstein then transformed the song for Broadway and the result was a soaring, dramatic ballad, similar in style to "If." The song demanded a full-voiced, high note ending that Como, singing at the very limit of his register, met head-on. It prompted critic Henry Pleasants to comment that Como was "so easy, so natural, so inevitable. Como sings so well that few notice how well he sings."[39] RCA rushed the record onto the market to meet the show's Broadway opening and *Billboard* was quick to predict another hit. "Looks like Como is off to the races on his fourth hit in a row," the review said.[40] The prediction was correct. "No Other Love" took top spot in the Disc Jockey chart and #2 in the best sellers during a 22-week stay in the charts. It was Como's second #1 inside six months.

Meanwhile, Como's third TV season for CBS had started on October 1, 1952, and ran through to the end of June 1953. Como devoted one of the shows during the final

Perry's TV show was also broadcast on radio during the 1953-54 season. This is the Mutual Broadcasting System publicity for the show (courtesy Colleen Zwack).

week to a celebration of his tenth anniversary, covering several of his major hits in a special show. The format through the season was the same as the previous year—three 15-minute shows each week, on Mondays, Wednesdays and Fridays—and the regular cast members remained unchanged. There was indeed no need to change—the show was by now commonly regarded as the best music show on TV and on the strength of his first season, Como had picked up a Michael award from the Academy of Radio and Television Arts and Sciences. It was Como's second such award, as prestigious then as the Emmy is now.[41]

Como's handling of his 15-minute show was now routine but a glimpse of his TV future came early in 1953 when NBC approached him to front a 60-minute "All Star Review" show. Perry would soon find himself in the middle of the Saturday night ratings battle with Jackie Gleason, but the experience of his hour debut suggested that there was still some work to do before he would be ready for that challenge. He was, said *Variety,* "an amiable tele personality and a top flight crooner, but the 60-minute load was too much for him to carry. Even with neat assists from guesters Patti Page, Joan Blondell and Ben Blue, the show added up to an erratic hour that hit some high points in between the lulls."[42]

Season Four of *The Perry Como Show* opened its doors in August 1953 and demonstrated that in five years, television had come full circle. Whereas Perry's TV debut in 1948 had been a radio show with the addition of cameras, his 1953–54 shows were television programs that were also broadcast on the radio. The difference from the early simulcasts was that now, different networks carried the audio and the video transmissions. CBS–TV still held Como's TV contract, but the sound version of the show came out on the Mutual radio network. It made little difference to the format or the content of the show, although Como in his words of welcome went out of his way to embrace his viewers "and those listening on radio." Once more, *Variety* welcomed Como's return to the screens. "Perry Como returned to his customary early evening, thrice-weekly spot on CBS–TV in top form. Como's vocal talents and likeable personality, with the backing of a couple of good choral groups, add up to one of the most consistently pleasing offerings on TV."[43]

Como's Christmas Day show offered a rare break with his policy of keeping his family out of the limelight. Son Ronnie and daughter Terri appeared among a group of children participating in "The Story of the First Christmas." That apart, the season passed predictably. At its end, in June 1954, Como finished with an 11.9 Nielsen rating, beating other 15-minute music shows such as Eddie Fisher (rating: 9) and Dinah Shore (8.7).[44] During the year, Perry had taken another shot at hosting an hour-long show in December 1953 when he starred in NBC's *Colgate Comedy Hour. Variety* again was lukewarm about his performance, liking his singing but being less taken with his role as host-comedian. Walter Ames, writing in the *Los Angeles Times*, felt the same and said that Como was "a bit too much at ease."[45] The gap between sustaining a show for 15 minutes and doing the same for an hour seemed to be a big one.

Both reviews singled out the fact that Como's songs were greeted by a "frenzied screaming from the teenage femme fan fringe that follows Como around."[46] This was particularly so when Perry featured "Pa-Paya Mama," the latest in his unbroken string of hits during 1953. Ames too disliked the "screeching of a bunch of Como-crazy bobby-soxers."[47] Perry also seemed unhappy with the screamers—it was an audience response that he had never liked since the day his father had fled from a theater, thinking that the screaming indicated hostility towards his son. During a commercial on the show, Como was heard to let the girl fans have a "kidding-in-earnest 'Oh, shut up.'"[48]

Unattractive to the critics though it was, there was nevertheless something remarkable about the fact that Perry Como was generating such a response. Towards the end of 1952, it seemed that his hit making days might be drawing to a close and that the focus of his recordings would henceforth be on easy listening albums. A year later, he had turned the world on its head. Perry Como had six successive hits during 1953 and easily topped the *Billboard* chart of charts for the year.[49] The turnaround showed not only the power of the small television screen, but also the chameleon-like qualities of the man from Canonsburg. No other singer could deliver such convincing vocal performances on such diverse material as "Don't Let the Stars Get in Your Eyes" and "No Other Love," yet Como took both of them to #1 within the space of six months. When he looked back on 1953, Perry Como must have thought that things couldn't get much better. How wrong he was.

Chapter 9

Old Silver Throat

AS PERRY COMO'S RECORDING OF "No Other Love" was climbing the charts, a young man called Elvis Aaron Presley walked into a recording studio in Memphis, Tennessee, and cut his first record. Within two years, Elvis would be the hottest property in the music business, heralding a revolution that for the first time created a generation gap in American music. Presley was 18 years old when he cut his first record, 20 when he signed with RCA Records and 21 when he had his first Gold record. Rock music was born, and the gap between it and the soft, sweet, and gentle era that had begotten singers like Perry Como was a chasm.

Como and his peers found themselves in a battle for survival, although for a time, none of them knew it. No one took rock seriously; no one gave it any longevity. It was just kids letting off steam. The early days of rock 'n' roll brought no sense of rebellion or challenge to the established order. When Elvis made his TV debut, the cameras shot him from the waist up, to protect the viewers from the sight of his below-the-waist gyrations. TV interviews with Elvis and the new pop stars who followed in his wake portrayed them as clean-cut young men, polite and respectful to their elders.

Perry Como was unquestionably one of the "elders"—indeed, he was old enough to be Elvis's father.[1] One magazine said that Como's years "were well distributed. His eyes are dark brown and look out with a contagious kindness. His hair has this year's charcoal gray color. His physique is inclined to be stocky when he follows his stomach's orders."[2] Como, in short, was moving gently towards middle age, and although that did not necessarily threaten his career, he was an unlikely bet to be the man who would swim most effectively against—and sometimes with—the tide of rock 'n' roll.

Yet that man he was. Between 1954 and 1959, Como produced another 27 hit records, including three #1 hits and seven more Top 10 successes. In contrast, many of his peers all but disappeared from the charts. Tony Bennett had eight hits during the period, Eddie Fisher seven (but none after 1954) and Vic Damone, two. Como's most resilient contemporaries were Nat King Cole, who managed 24 hits (mainly one or two week stays in the lower reaches) and a resurgent Frank Sinatra. Even "The Voice," arguably at the peak of his vocal powers, only managed 18 hits from 1954 to 1959, with only one #1 and five other Top 10 appearances.[3]

There is no question that it was television that set Como apart from the rest. His face was familiar in every home in America. To parents and grandparents, he was a friendly figure who offered no threat or offense. Grey Lockwood, who took over as director of Como's TV show in 1955, said that Como was "like the guy sitting next to you in the audience who gets up and fills the void when the star gets sick."[4] Kids grew up with Como always around, three times a week in the early fifties and from 1955 to the end of the decade, in the prime time Saturday night spot. Como might have been of their parents' generation, but he was like the friendly adult next door who wasn't mom or dad and who made you smile. Everybody liked him. Como himself was in no doubt that this was the critical factor in sustaining his success. "I'm convinced that it doesn't matter what you do, or even how you sing," he said in 1957. "People have to like you as a person first. If they like you, you're in. When they stop liking you, you're gone."[5] There was no doubt that Como passed the likeability test. By the middle of the fifties, he was receiving 2,500 fan letters every week, with fan clubs in every major city.[6] When NBC television decided they needed someone to lead their assault on the Saturday night ratings, Perry Como was their first call.

Como's 15-minute Chesterfield shows on CBS had entered their fifth season in August 1954. *Variety* said that the show was now "the best of the personality song shows," while acknowledging that the news that "Perry Como is a natural click before the TV cameras is now an old story."[7] The show ran its usual 39-week season, the only change to the regular line-up being the departure of the Fontane Sisters, who were replaced with an extended role for the Ray Charles Singers. The sisters' exit was non-contentious. Ray Charles said there was no acrimony between Como and the girls and put their departure down to their growing success as a stand-alone act. "They may have become too expensive for a supporting act," he said.[8]

Como hosted 126 15-minute shows during his fifth and final season for CBS. A weekly budget of $50,000 meant that guest appearances were still limited to around one show in three, and Como's final season visitors included the Mills Brothers, Al Hibbler and Kitty Kallen. In November 1954, the Como show was the top-rated multi-weekly program according to the Nielsen ratings, and Como emerged as the top male singer in *Billboard's* annual poll.

Rating performance was a primary driver of advertising revenue and dominated the thinking of the two leading networks, NBC and CBS. In the early days of television, NBC had gained the upper hand on their main rival by offering a blend of upscale quiz shows, live drama and sophisticated comedy. As television spread into more American homes, the nature of the audience changed. Merchandise oriented shows such as *The 64,000 Question* thrived, as did a new breed of show, the pre-recorded situation comedy. CBS chairman William Paley gambled on the latter, particularly one featuring a former B-movie star, Lucille Ball, and by the middle of the decade, the ratings battle had tipped in the favor of the Columbia network.

Another of Paley's gambles had been on Jackie Gleason, an amiable *bon vivant* who had made his first TV impact in *The Life of Riley* in 1949. The following year, the self-styled "Great One" hosted the *Cavalcade of Stars* variety hour on the now forgotten Dumont network. The show included music, dance and an increasingly popular series of short comedy sketches. Its impact was sufficient for Paley to woo Gleason and the show over to CBS in 1952. Renamed *The Jackie Gleason Show,* it soon became the second most popular show on television and dominated the Saturday evening schedule.

NBC needed a response. When they canvassed their leading sponsors as to the sales value of various stars, Como's name topped the list.[9] The first signs that they had their man came in February 1955 when they paid Como $25,000 for a 15-minute appearance in *Max Liebman presents "Variety."* Como's appearance, said *Variety,* broke the "stay on your own side of the street" approach that the major networks were taking when it came to their big stars guesting for the competition. Two months later, NBC announced

Perry with (left to right) Lee Cooley, the producer of the CBS *Perry Como Show*, and Ib Melchior, the director.

that Como had signed a 12-year contract to move from CBS. The deal was worth $15 million and was one of the biggest in television history. Tommy Rockwell, the agent who first brought him to New York in 1943, handled Como's input.[10] Press reports said that Como's new show would be an hour-long variety program, and was "tentatively" scheduled for Saturday nights, directly against the Gleason spot.[11] The show would have three new sponsors and would end Como's 11-year association with Chesterfield.

The final CBS *Perry Como Show* went on the air on June 24, 1955. While the last show of any series was always a time for some more-than-usually relaxed banter, Como's last appearance for Chesterfield broke new ground. Perry was almost hyperactive for much of the show, engaging for almost the entire 15 minutes in conversation with the off-screen technicians and bringing them one by one in front of the camera. Como himself took a turn at the camera for one scene, with the image of Mitchell Ayres appearing upside down on the screen as the apparent result. Como's songs included a perennial favorite, "It's a Big, Wide, Wonderful World" ("a little softer, eh, Mitch?" Como said two lines in) plus a reprise of his first solo disc, "Goodbye Sue." As the entire cast and crew gathered for a final send-off, Roselle Como made an unannounced walk-on that clearly took Perry by surprise. With a chorus of "Auld Lang Syne," the curtain came down on Perry Como and Chesterfield for the last time.

After a summer vacation in Canada, Como returned to New York to begin prepa-

Musical director Mitchell Ayres accompanied Perry in the move from CBS to NBC. This shot captures a television studio in July 1954 (courtesy Colleen Zwack).

rations for his new show, which was set to make its debut on September 17, 1955. NBC scheduled the show for 8:00–9:00 P.M. This was prime time Saturday evening viewing and had been the slot for the Gleason show. For 1955–56, though, CBS decided to split the Gleason hour into two parts. From 8:00 to 8:30, *The Stage Show* aired, produced by Gleason but featuring the Dorsey Brothers (Tommy and Jimmy) as hosts. Gleason made the occasional appearance before taking center stage at 8:30 in *The Honeymooners,* a sitcom that started life as one of the regular sketches in Gleason's hour-long show. Gleason played Ralph Kramden, a bus driver in the fictional Gotham Bus Company. Although now regarded as a TV classic, the series only ran for one season in stand-alone mode. From 1956, CBS returned to the one-hour format for the Gleason show, with *The Honeymooners* back inside the main show.

Crucially, the CBS makeover of the Gleason show gave Como a half-hour start on his rival. NBC also pulled out all the stops for their assault on Gleason. George McGar-rett, whose credits included the popular *Show of Shows*, came in as executive producer, with Grey Lockwood as director. Lee Cooley, who had produced and directed the 15-minute shows, was retained as producer, and to beef up the comedy elements of the show, NBC recruited Milton Berle's chief writer, Goodman ("Goody") Ace, to write Como's scripts. Mitchell Ayres and Ray Charles moved across with Como, and Frank Gallop arrived to take on the announcer's duties. In a modern television show, the announcer was almost an anachronism, but Gallop became a regular part of Como's show until the mid-sixties. An established radio announcer, Gallop also had television experience. His most significant TV work to date had been as host of *Lights Out,* a *Twilight Zone*–style suspense show during 1950–52. Gallop's booming voice and soulful demeanor were in sharp contrast to Como's loose, on-camera persona, and the apparent feuding and point-scoring nature of their relationship worked surprisingly well.

The show reportedly had a weekly budget of $80,000, of which $25,000 went straight to Como. There were six sponsors for the opening show and a long list of guests that included Rosemary Clooney and Frankie Laine, plus an array of cameos from names such as Julius La Rosa, Sid Caesar and Dodgers pitcher Don Newcombe. The show opened with an image of a night sky littered with stars as Como sang a snatch of his new TV theme "Dream Along with Me (I'm on My Way to a Star)." Broadcast live from the Century Theater in New York at 58th and 7th, the show also gave the impression of a more expansive set than on Perry's CBS show and left the viewer with a sense of a much bigger and more ambitious production.

Reviews overall were mixed, but as ever, Como's own performance scored well. His songs, ranging from the pseudo-rock 'n' roll "Tina Marie" to "Abide with Me," came across well and Jack Singer in *Billboard* said, "Como, in his usual, informal, relaxed manner, carried the show,"[12] adding that the whole thing had a "breezy, good-natured air about it."[13] J.P. Shanley in *The New York Times* agreed although he thought "when Mr. Como was off camera—or when he was struggling with the inferior comedy material at his disposal—the show faltered."[14] *Variety*, in a lengthy piece, liked Como's show-manship and Goodman Ace's writing and predicted that the show would translate into a "rousing Como-NBC victory 8 to 8:30"—but warned that the 8:30 to 9:00 Como-Gleason competition "looks pretty rough."

Much was made of the rivalry between Como and Gleason and it served both camps well to talk up a feud between the two stars. The reality was different. Como and Glea-son were near neighbors on Long Island and became good friends. Gleason would often call the Como home on Sunday mornings. "Hey silver throat," he would say, "I knocked your ass off last night."[15] If Como felt he had the edge, he would often respond in kind. It was a good-natured rivalry as illustrated by a story that Como told Colin Escott in 1993. Roselle's mother loved the Gleason show; although she spoke no English, she could still appreciate the physical comedy of "Jackie Glissi," as she called him. Como phoned Gleason and asked him to put in an appearance at the house. "I was worried he was gonna turn up naked with a lamp shade on his head," said Como. One morn-ing, however, at 9:00 A.M., Gleason knocked on the kitchen door and walked in. "Well, hello there, Mrs. Belline," he said. Como said that his mother-in-law thought she was dreaming as "Jackie Glissi" danced around the kitchen. Finally, Gleason said, "Well, Mrs. Belline, I have to get the Hell out of here. I have to work a show opposite this old muthafucker here." Mrs. Belline had no idea what Gleason was saying. Como said that he called Gleason later and said, "Anything you want, you got it."[16]

There was inevitably some tweaking needed before the Como show settled into a regular pattern. One change was to reduce the comedy in favor of more songs. "Ace thinks I'm the funniest guy in the world," Como told an interviewer in December 1955, "but I'm not, I'm a singer. So we made some changes and now I'm back doing more songs and less comedy."[17] Ray Charles later remembered that Ace had found Como's handling of the comedy scripts very frustrating. "Perry didn't understand the construction of a sentence," said Charles, "and that when you told a joke, the words had to be in a specific order or the joke didn't happen. They would write wonderful lines which would be on cue cards but Perry would switch the words around which often spoiled the joke." Ace would often confide his frustration in Charles, saying, "How come he never changes the words to any of the songs you give him?"[18] One consequence of the more-music, less-jokes format was the introduction of a three-song request medley by Como, for which Charles wrote an introductory piece called "We Get Letters, Letters, Stacks and Stacks of Letters." In time, the medley became the "Sing to Me, Mr. C" medley, a focal point of both the show and Como's enduring image.

CBS's decision to split the Gleason hour into two parts worked to Como's advantage. In December 1955, he outstripped Gleason in the ratings for the first time[19] and by February the following year, had established a clear lead. Como's first half hour rating led *The Stage Show* by 29.5 to 15.9; *The Honeymooners* just edged Como, 25.1 to 24.5. For the hour overall, Como was seven points ahead. Gleason conceded defeat to his rival.[20] "The mistake," he said, "was to let Perry Como get a half hour ahead of us. Como is a very tough man for anyone to beat."[21] Nevertheless, when the annual George Peabody Awards came round in April 1956, Como and Gleason shared the award for the best television program. "They have," said the Awards Committee, "split the television audience on Saturday evenings almost squarely down the middle."[22]

Como's television work had already had a big impact on Como's pop singles and with RCA's final acceptance of the inevitability of the 33-rpm popular LP, it also influenced his early album work. Aside from the Christmas and religious "albums," both of which had made their first appearances as sets of 78 or 45 rpm records, Como's first microgroove LP had appeared in 1952. Titled *TV Favorites,* the 10" disc (the first LPs were the same size as the standard 10" 78 to avoid the need for separate shelving displays in record stores) featured eight songs, all but one of which had been recorded in March 1952.[23]

The album cover showed an image of Como superimposed into an early 12" television set, with the added explanation, as though it were needed, "as sung by Perry Como on his Chesterfield TV show." In truth, the songs were not ones that Como featured regularly on TV. Most of them were drawn from Broadway shows and were more dramatic in nature than the type of material that Como slotted into his 15-minute TV spots. Mitchell Ayres' orchestrations were strings-based, in contrast to the rhythm section dominance of the TV accompaniment. The standout song on the album was "You'll Never Walk Alone" from the musical *Carousel,* which Como sang with great power and range. He continued to feature the song and to rise to its vocal challenges well into his seventies.

With LPs still a fringe market in the music business, it was three years before Como's next "pop" LP sessions. These took place over five dates in January and February 1955 and resulted in Como's first modern-sized 12" disc with the title *So Smooth.* The cover featured Como in a casual shirt and monogrammed cardigan, dress that has since become an indelible part of the Como image (although not until late in the decade did it displace Perry's suit and tie as his standard TV uniform). *So Smooth,* in the new format, had room for 12 songs, all of which were drawn from what is now known as the Great

American Song Book. Cole Porter, Rodgers and Hart and Harold Arlen were some of the featured composers and the arrangements, variously by Joe Lipman, Joe Reisman and Jack Andrews, were much closer to the style of Perry's TV work than his 1952 set. In particular, songs such as "I've Got the World on a String," "Breezin' Along with the Breeze" and "For Me and My Gal" gave prominence to Billy Rowland's piano playing and Terry Snyder's drums.[24]

The type of material used on *So Smooth* was the main ingredient for Como's "We Get Letters" medleys that Ray Charles put together for him for the new NBC television show. These in turn provided a basis for Como's next album sessions in June 1956 and February 1957. The result was *We Get Letters*, a 12" disc that came just too early to catch the increasing use of stereo sound. As with its predecessor, the album featured a casual Como on the cover, with samples of the letters and postcards that by now were flooding the request spot on the TV shows. Mitchell Ayres, as ever, provided the backing, this time with a smaller group that took the title "Como's Little Combo." The result gave even greater prominence to the rhythmic beat of Rowland and Snyder, although Ayres varied the instrumentation from track to track, with Tony Mottola's guitar replacing Rowland's piano on some tracks.

Jazz critic Will Friedwald described *We Get Letters* as "the one absolutely essential Como record," and rejoiced that the album took Como "away from the glee clubs and all the orchestra sections, except the rhythm, natch."[25] Certainly, the absence of any choral backing on the album gave it more of a jazz feel and it was the closest Como would ever come to a jazz album. Como was always quick to acknowledge that he had neither Crosby's natural sense of rhythm nor Sinatra's orchestrated ability to swing. "I'm not really a rhythm singer," he said in 1992.[26] Ray Charles concurred. "Perry was comfortable in a jazz setting," he said in 2007, "but couldn't swing. He was not a natural jazz singer."[27] Unquestionably, though, Como was a natural singer. It was a constant surprise that someone who produced so many technically perfect records "never had a singing lesson in his life."[28] Mel Tormé said that Como was "technically, one of the most immaculate singers in our business. Good intonation, warm delivery. He always does a beautiful job."[29]

More surprising still was the apparent lack of any need by Como to "vocalize," the preparatory running up and down of scales that most singers go through to keep the vocal cords loose. Not Como. "How can you just get out of bed and sing?" was a question that both Mitchell Ayres and Nick Perito often asked.[30] Sometimes Perry literally did just that, his normal routine being to take a nap before a show. "Sometimes I wake up in the middle of a song,"[31] he said, a joking acceptance of the somnambulant image that he portrayed, certainly in his later years. "I never have to worry about singing," Como said, frankly but with no hint of immodesty. "If I get enough rest, what comes out sounds okay."[32]

Despite the informality that Como brought to his singing, his preparation for a recording session was meticulous. Mitchell Ayres had been taken aback when he turned up for his first session with Como to find him there already, running through the arrangement with the orchestra.[33] Ayres later spoke of Como's "unremitting diligence to what he is doing."[34] Mickey Glass recalled that Como would invariably be at the recording studio early, looking at the songs and going over them with the orchestra, rather than preparing at home.[35] (Como commented in a TV interview in 1984 that he never sang at home.)[36] Once Como was familiar with the songs, he would take a close interest in the arrangements. "Mitch, I'm not sure that strings ought to come in here."[37] "Nick, do we need all those flutes?"[38] "Could we hear that one again? I'm sorry to be a nuisance but I didn't quite get it."[39] All were the kinds of interventions that Perry would offer during a session. As the rhythm section picked up the beat for an unissued take of Fats Waller's "Ain't Misbehavin'" in 1955, Perry told the band to "take it easy, uh fellas, the guitar, it's not their fault, you gotta get that guitar down a little bit, you know," before delivering a wonderfully relaxed vocal.

Once Como had decided on an approach to a song, he was ready to record it. A take was an attempt to deliver the finished product that Como had in mind, not a time for experimenting. Most of Como's sessions featured only two or three titles with only a handful of takes of each song. Como insisted on listening to the playback for each take and deciding what, if anything, he wanted to do differently in the next take. Differences between takes were, however, minimal, any changes in Como's phrasing arising from a re-working of the lyric rather than a change of intonation on the part of the singer. Yet for all the precision and attention to detail, the sessions were generally happy, laid back affairs. Although the recording industry had moved to tape in the late forties, discs were still generally the product of a live session, with the singer, chorus, orchestra and any other participants all in the studio together. Como made himself popular with the musicians by taking the sessions beyond their contracted end time, thus generating overtime payments. In time, the industry would move to an approach where singers would often cut the vocal with a small rhythm section, leaving the producer to embellish the recordings with strings, brass and other accompaniments later. Other singers would prefer to come in and add their vocals to a pre-recorded backing track. Como's preference was always to do the disc live.[40]

Como's increasing focus on TV-inspired LPs did not come at the expense of an ongoing assault on the singles charts. After his hit-streaming year of 1953, he had continued in the same vein with two more blockbusters during the first part of 1954. "Wanted," recorded four days after Christmas in 1953, was a new song by Lois Steele and Jack Fulton. Taking a police "Wanted" poster as its theme, the lyric cleverly built on the criminal-police link with phrases such as "hiding out," "a jury may find her guilty" and "a signed confession."[41] Como's voice floats gently over a lilting, rhythmic melody, combining "suave singing and a distinct tongue-in-cheek emotionalism. Como always knew how to smile with his voice and the smile is clearly audible here," Robert Jones wrote.[42] RCA played up the criminological links, promoting the disc with a "Wanted" poster of their own. "Watch for him," the poster said, "he's heading your way—North, South, East and West! Remember—Perry Como's WANTED!" The result was another Como blockbuster, topping all three *Billboard* charts and delivering another Gold record.

Perry's follow up continued the criminal theme with "Hit and Run Affair" that provided a modest hit before his next Gold record arrived in the form of "Papa Loves Mambo." The mambo craze had arrived in the United States from Cuba in 1947 when bandleader Perez Prado first introduced it at New York's Park Plaza Ballroom. By 1954, the Palladium Ballroom on Broadway had become the self-acclaimed "temple of mambo."[43] Such was the popularity of the dance that veteran songwriter Bix Reichner came up with the idea for a song with the title "Papa Loves Mambo." He approached Al Hoffman with the idea, who in turn took it to his regular partner, Dick Manning. Hoffman and Manning had already developed a reputation as novelty songwriters with hits such as "Gilly Gilly Ossenfeffer Katzenellen Bogen by the Sea." Manning and Hoffman worked through the night, struggling to fit a simple rhyme scheme to a complicated cha-cha-cha melody. The end product was a masterful example of the novelty song, its 113 words offering memorable rhymes and lots of repetition of the papa and mama theme.

Hoffman and Manning had started work on the song on Monday, August 23, 1954. By Tuesday afternoon, they were playing it back to Reichner and later that evening, giving a demo to publishers Shapiro-Bernstein. The next day, Al Gallico, general manager at Shapiro, took the song to Joe Carlton, head of A&R at RCA. "It's perfect for Como," said Carlton, who promptly handed it to arranger Joe Reisman, asking for a "spirited, raucous arrangement." Five days later, on Tuesday, August 31, 1954, Como arrived at Webster Hall in New York to record the song. When he saw it, he reaction was the same one he often gave to novelty material. "I'm not sure it's right for me," he said. With some persuasion from Carlton, Como entered into the spirit of the arrangement, tripping once or twice over the intricacies of the lyric but laughing along with Ray Charles at the choirmaster's hammy arrangement that mimicked Perez Prado's band-leading style.[44] Finally, Como and Carlton were happy with the recording although Perry was still not convinced that it was hit material. "I bet my friend Larry Kanaga (general sales and merchandising manager at RCA) $50 that the other side, 'The Things I Didn't Do' would be the hit," Como said. As soon as Kanaga played the demo to RCA's distributors, Como knew that he had lost his bet. When the disc went on sale in September 1954, it surged to a top four spot in all three *Billboard* charts and became a regular song on Como's final CBS-TV season.[45]

Over the next two years, Como produced six more Top 10 records. Ever since "Hoop-Dee-Doo," Como's uneasy association with novelty songs had brought him great commercial success, but between 1955 and 1958, Como took the genre to a new high— although some critics would say a new low. The mambo craze soon gave way to a generation raised on rock and once more, Perry Como was on the front line. If asked, "what was RCA's first rock 'n' roll record?" most people would reach for the chronology of

For many years during the 1950s, Perry's appeal spanned the generations. This late '50s shot shows him surrounded by a group of young female fans (courtesy Michael Dunnington).

Elvis's hits and pick the earliest. They would be wrong. The correct answer is "Ko-Ko-Mo (I Love You So)" by the cardigan crooner, Perry Como.[46]

"Ko-Ko-Mo" was written and recorded in late 1954 by the black R&B partnership of Gene Forrest and Eunice Levy. It was their first single, recorded in the basement of veteran black musician Jake Porter's residence and released on Porter's home label, Combo Records. No matter how good their recording was, there was no chance in the racial climate of 1955 that a black R&B pairing could take a song into the mainstream pop charts. "Ko-Ko-Mo" cried out for someone to record a cover version and make it a hit. It was a similar situation to "Don't Let the Stars Get in Your Eyes," which Como rescued from the country and western charts. On "Ko-Ko-Mo," he faced stiffer competition with the Crew-Cuts, the Hutton Sisters, Bill Darnell and Betty Clooney and Louis Armstrong (in an unlikely duet with Bing Crosby's son, Gary) all getting in on the act, but it was Como who came out tops. RCA marketed his disc with a two-page ad in *Billboard,* showing "Perry In Action on a Great Rock-and-Roll [sic] Record."[47] His version, recorded on January 4, 1955, reached #2 in the *Billboard* disc jockey chart, and #4 in the best sellers.

Despite the success of the record, RCA chose not to give Como's disc Gold record status, although it surely outsold some of the other discs that were thus honored. There is no evidence that Como had any direct bearing on the cold-shouldering that the disc received although one can imagine that producer Joe Carlton must have dragged a kicking and screaming Como to the recording microphone. With a raucous Joe Reisman arrangement that is noticeably more piercing than even Forrest and Levy's original, plus a choral backing that borders on the inane, "Ko-Ko-Mo" has few competitors for the dubious honor of being Como's worst recording. His discomfort is apparent throughout the vocal and in the final chorus, he badly loses both the rhythm and meter of the song.

Nobody cared. Ray Charles said that for everyone riding the Como bandwagon in the mid-fifties, it was a fun place to be. Nobody stopped to think about the artistic merit of the songs. Como too was smart enough to realize that he needed to embrace the new sound publicly. His guest list for the TV show included most of the new rock 'n' roll names, such as Fats Domino, Paul Anka, Fabian, Frankie Avalon and Bobby Rydell. When the Everly Brothers guested on the show, they found the experience a total contrast to the cold and unwelcoming atmosphere that they had encountered on other shows. "Perry Como was the first decent 'star' they met and he treated them kindly," wrote Consuelo Dodge.[48]

Como's flirtation with rock 'n' roll, however, was never more than a musical one-night stand. In 1960, he told journalist Pete Martin, "When I hear 'Hound Dog,' I have to vomit a little. If you're built the way I am, it's got to make you a little sick." Yet with a strange foresight into the way rock would etch itself into the country's soul, Como added the perceptive remark that "in 1970 or 1975, it will probably be a slightly ancient classic."[49] As Colin Escott pointed out, Como in the mid-fifties found material that "hinted broadly enough at rock 'n' roll to get played, but never so broadly as to alienate the long-time fans." It was, said Escott, "a skilled tightrope act."[50]

The next step along the rope took Perry to a song called "Tina Marie," a brainchild of Bob Merrill, who had written several of Perry's ballad hits. Joe Reisman once again brought the song to life with a toe-tapping arrangement. For a while, RCA hedged its bets, marketing the other side of the disc, a more conventional ballad called "Fooled," with equal prominence. *Billboard* called that song "an appealing ballad with rich sincerity and tenderness. The star is at his best with this type of romantic material and the disc is sure to sweep its full share of action." The review added dismissively, "The flip is 'Tina Marie.'"[51] Within two weeks of the review, however, it was clear that it was the flip side that the disc jockeys were playing, and "Tina Marie" reached #6 in the best sellers in August 1955.

RCA pulled the trick for the third time in January 1956 with "Juke Box Baby," written by Noel and Joe Sherman. The disc shamelessly ploughed the same furrow as its two predecessors, Reisman's arrangement paralleling "Tina Marie" with snatches of both that song and "Ko-Ko-Mo" appearing in the lyric. At the same session, Como recorded another creation from Al Hoffman and Dick Manning, "Hot Diggity (Dog-Ziggity-Boom)." This song was a more familiar novelty piece, again with a title built around popular parlance (similar to "A-Hubba-Hubba-Hubba" in 1945), and once more Joe Reisman came up with a vibrant arrangement that hinged on two virtuoso xylophone performances by Harry Breuer and Phil Krause.[52] Como capped his acrobatic vocal with a strangulated "Hot Dog!" to finish the song and it was soon apparent that it was a winner. After Perry gave it a trial run on TV, RCA pushed it as the A-side of the next single release, relegating "Juke Box Baby" to the flip. It was, wrote Colin Escott, another song that "made Perry wince" but by May 1956, it had winced its way to the top of the *Billboard* charts, where Como sat alongside Presley's "Heartbreak Hotel."[53]

The success of "Hot Diggity" coincided with the conclusion of Como's first series for NBC-TV. The series had gone well, with positive reviews and Como picking up his second successive Emmy award as best male singer on television. In ratings terms, however, the results fell short of what both CBS and the sponsors would have hoped for. Como had indeed won the battle with Gleason—just—but with rankings of #19 and #20 overall, the performance was not what either of the major networks was looking for from its two heavyweights. The network decided that their star crooner needed something new.

Chapter 10

Catch a Falling Star

SOMETHING NEW FOR *THE PERRY COMO SHOW* meant a new studio, color transmission and a different producer. All three changes were interconnected. NBC had first embraced color television in 1953 and a musical variety show such as Como's was an obvious priority for the upgrade. The change to color also required a move to a new studio, the newly refurbished Ziegfeld Theater on the northwest corner of 54th Street and 6th Avenue. The Ziegfeld was a legendary Broadway venue, built in 1927 and the original home for hit shows such as *Show Boat*. Showman Billy Rose bought the theater in 1944 before NBC acquired it for television use in 1955. Rose would occasionally appear during the filming of the Como show, sitting quietly in the balcony.[1]

Lee Cooley, who had carried the producer's role over from Como's Chesterfield days, had no color experience. That alone was a convenient reason for replacing him, without even citing the under-performance in the ratings. Cooley's replacement was Robert (Bob) Finkel, who moved from Los Angeles to New York to take on the role. Finkel, a former director with ABC Television and Revue Productions before joining NBC, had earned good reviews on some color specials on the West Coast. He was an obvious choice, even if he did live on the other side of the continent. On the face of it, there was also some synergy between Finkel and Grey Lockwood, who continued in the role of director. The two had been together in the class of 1940 at Carnegie Tech and were friends. Nevertheless, there was a sense that two into one would not go, at least in Finkel's mind. "I didn't have the heart to fire him," he said in an interview in 1997.[2]

Part of the reason why Finkel might have fired Lockwood was that his concept of the producer's role embraced some of the tasks that Lockwood carried out as director. The key thing for Finkel was to be close to the action—and to Como in particular. The set-up at the Ziegfeld, however, put the production booth on a different floor from the stage. To speak to Como, Finkel either needed to race up two flights of stairs or use a bullhorn microphone, which everyone could hear. Finkel did not like the first option and Como would not tolerate the second. The solution was a portable control booth, on rollers that could move around the various sets. Finkel worked from there and was always close to Como, and of course, to Lockwood too.

The production of a color show was far more complex than simply using different cameras. Things that had not been apparent in black and white now became significant. The cast's costumes needed to blend with Como's clothing and all that needed to integrate with the colors of the sets. These in turn needed to be carefully selected to reflect the mood of a particular part of the show—brighter colors for the expansive dance numbers and greater use of pastels for Como's ballads. All of which required a more closely integrated style of working from everyone on the production team. Finkel also believed however that the show needed other changes. He thought that the opening minutes of the previous season shows had been too soft, lacking impact and thus encouraging viewers to "shop around" other channels. From 1956, the show always opened with a lively production number, featuring Como, the Louis Da Pron Dancers and the Ray Charles Singers. Finkel also developed Perry's weekly request spot. He said later that he believed that it had helped Como further develop his on-screen persona. Even though Perry was already regarded as the epitome of relaxation, Finkel said that the request spot gave him even greater warmth and engagement with the audience.[3]

Bob Finkel was the first producer to give real thought to how Como's image should be portrayed on television. Ever since Como's TV debut, "relaxed" had been the word that appeared most frequently in Como's TV reviews, an image that grew naturally out of Como's own personality. In later years, Como usually dismissed questions about it with jokes like "I think I was born old"[4] or simply attributed his easy-going nature to his father. Beneath the relaxed exterior, though, there was a professional at work. In a more serious moment of reflection in 1977, Como told Michael Parkinson, "You can only relax if you know what you are doing. I rehearsed seven days a week to the point where I felt that I knew what I was doing and I could relax. It didn't mean I didn't care. I assure you, I do care."[5] Those who knew Perry well raise an eyebrow at the notion of him rehearsing seven days a week. "Not in your wildest dreams," said Ray Charles when told of the quote.[6] While Como might have exaggerated his diligence, there was no question that, at the peak of his career, he was a hard worker. Actress Jane Wyman

The Perry Como cardigan.

guested on the show and saw both sides of Como. "At rehearsal, Como looks like he's ready for a mortician," she said, "but at show time he comes on like a bat out of hell."[7]

The obvious route for Finkel was to build on the image of relaxation that sat so comfortably with Como. "We wanted to give the impression that Perry had just woken up to do the show," he said in 1997,[8] a fiction that was given literal meaning in one show when Como was shown asleep in the audience during one of the guest spots, bursting immediately into song when his neighbor nudged him in the ribs. Finkel also added a casualness to Como's demeanor. Until now, Perry had usually appeared in a lounge suit and tie, which in black and white always looked the same. Finkel was the first producer to cast his star in casual dress—the "Perry Como cardigan." With Como displaying a natural liking for bright colors, the change was perfectly timed for the growing number of color sets in the country.

Color images were one thing, but the quality of the dialogue given to Como and his interaction with his guests were other critical factors in creating the right image. Goodman Ace continued as the lead writer for the show, heading a strong team that included Jay Burton, Mort Green and George Foster. Ace was the key man, although Finkel found his way of working somewhat strange. Ace was not one for lengthy writers' conferences and indeed Finkel's first sight of the script each week came when Ace pushed it under the door of his Central Park apartment. Nor did Ace routinely attend rehearsals. When he did—on special request from Finkel—he turned his back on the performance, preferring to listen rather than watch, the mark of a writer who had grown up in radio rather than TV.[9] Finkel thought that Ace's writing was critical to the show's success and to developing the Como image. "There were very few sketches in the show," said Finkel, "and Perry's interaction with the guests was mainly as a twosome. It worked because the dialogue was so beautifully written."[10] Choice of guests was also critical. The show was so big that it could draw almost anyone that the team wanted, but Finkel vetted the list to make sure that those chosen were ones who could "function with Perry."[11] It's no surprise to see that a number of guests who met this criterion were featured time and again on the show.

Finkel said that he enjoyed his time working with Como—"anyone who worked with Perry fell in love with him"[12]—but also found him strangely insular. There were few, if any, one-to-one meetings with him. Most of their consultations took place, he said, "during the time it took Perry to enter the building from a side entrance in his inevitable coat and scarf (regardless of the temperature) and walk across the auditorium to the elevator."[13] Guests too found Como to be very business-like, with no interest in socializing. At times, he could be distant and a little cold. There was also no question as to who was in charge on the set. "Perry intimidated everyone," said Finkel. "People didn't fool around with him—they just did what they were supposed to do."[14] Dwight Hemion, who took on the director's role in 1961, remembered him as "a one-way kind of guy. If he liked things, he did them; if he didn't like them, he didn't."[15] Buz Kohan joined the writing team in 1963 and echoed the same sentiment. "Perry was definitely in charge," he said. "He didn't object to too much in the script, but there was no budging him when he took a view."[16]

The new season got off to slow start. *Variety* gave Finkel a "well done"[17] for the first show on September 15, but the *Daily Variety* called the show "uninspired, jerky [and] far off the high batting average and entertainment voltage that was generally maintained through Como's first season romp."[18] Even long time Como fan Jack Gould, writing in the *New York Times*, struggled to find any pluses with the opening show. By November, however, Finkel's changes were beginning to have an impact. Como's female alter ego, Dinah Shore, headed the guest list on November 17. (It was the start of an era of "guest-spot trading" that Como disliked, he having to guest on *The Dinah Shore Chevy Show* as a balancing trade.) Lily Pons and an 11-year-old Brenda Lee joined the guests, but the skill and thought that had gone into using them was apparent. *Variety* said, "It ain't who you got so much as how you use 'em and producer Robert Finkel, Como and head writer Goody Ace sure know how to use 'em. The point is this wasn't just a group of guest stars coming up for their turn at bat and bowing off, but a skillfully integrated show that makes use of their personalities."[19]

NBC continued to broadcast the show live on Saturday nights, both Como and Finkel being keen to retain the spontaneity that came with a live show, much of it from unpredictable circumstances. In December 1956, the guests included bandleader Guy Lombardo. "He'd gone upstairs," Como recalled, "thinking he had ten minutes to make a costume change. Nobody had told him that he had only three minutes. When he was through changing, he started down, only to get stuck in the elevator. In the meantime, I was standing before our TV cameras saying, 'Now, Guy ...' and there was no Guy. So I told our musical conductor, Mitchell Ayres, 'Mitch, you come up here and read Guy's lines.' Mitch read Guy's lines, and I called him Guy. We'd finished a few lines of script when in walked Guy, all flustered. He hurried over to me and rattled off his first line, and I had to tell him, 'We've already done that one.' He died. He didn't know what was going on. But the rest of us thought it pretty funny. Fortunately our viewers did too."[20] A similar situation arose later in the season when swimmer-turned-movie star Esther Williams was a guest. As soon as she appeared on camera, she accidentally tore off a piece of lace that was designed to camouflage her cleavage. Next, the lighting went askew, all of which caused so much amusement that the audience kept on laughing right through Como's romantic ballads. When the show ended, with Williams in a swimming pool that had been built on the set, Perry looked at the camera, said, "Goodnight folks," and jumped in, fully clothed.[21]

Some critics felt that it was the live nature of the show that gave it its edge over Gleason, who had returned to his one-hour format in direct competition with Perry. For the 1956–57 season, there was no question who was the winner of the Saturday night battle. When the ratings came in, Gleason had fallen to #29, whereas the Como show was up to #9. It was the beginning of the end for Gleason as a variety host and for the upcoming 1957–58 season, Como's Saturday night opponent would be another Perry— fictional lawyer *Perry Mason*.

The third season of *The Perry Como Show* on NBC opened on Saturday, September 14, 1957. The production and support team was unchanged, and even though it was reported that NBC had imposed a $7,500 ceiling on the fee for any one guest star during the season, the critics still forecasted even greater success. *Variety* said, "They're laying odds that this is the season when Perry Como will top the whole Nielsen parade in TV—a wager predicated on the fact that (1) The Como, now thoroughly vintaged, can do no wrong; (2) his competition (*Perry Mason*) is as yet an untested item, and (3) in the intramural sweepstakes and drastic overhaul of programming, there are no longer any 'soft spots' save perhaps for Saturday 8 to 9."[22] The *Daily Variety* made similar prophecies of success. "Como's own individualistic style," it said, "is naturally the hallmark of the show's high favor as it eases into its third season. The easy-does-it attitude, the unhurried pace, the warmth of the songs and riposte of his sallies with the guest talent have brought the show to its high estate and will keep it there."[23]

The show moved smoothly through its 39-week season, and although *Variety*'s predictions of top spot in the ratings proved over-ambitious, the show nevertheless finished a highly creditable eleventh overall, comfortably the most popular music variety show on the screens. Como himself narrowly missed a third consecutive *Emmy* for his performance. The only blot on the horizon for the show was Bob Finkel's decision to return to California at the end of his second season. Finkel's decision was based solely on personal circumstances—his main home was in Los Angeles and he didn't think it was practical to continue living and working 3,000 miles away.[24] Finkel's departure was the first of several of Como's regular team to conclude that the lights were brighter on the West Coast. Finkel's recollection in 2007 was that Perry was disappointed at his decision to leave but said nothing about it. He was, said Finkel, "not very verbal."[25] The two of them would work together again in the seventies but the coolness that greeted Finkel's departure would recur with other members of the team in the coming years.

Bob Finkel left *The Perry Como Show* at the peak of both its popularity and mar-

Singer Patti Page was a regular guest on Como's Chesterfield television show during the mid–1950s (courtesy Colleen Zwack).

ketability. Credit for its success was genuinely spread around the team, but Finkel did as much as anyone to convert Como's natural personality into a powerful media force. By the beginning of the 1958–59 season, he had created the *Perry Como Show* that became known and remembered around the world—a slick production, an informality of style, a genuinely relaxed host and good music. NBC soon discovered that they had a highly exportable product on their hands, with the BBC in Britain heading a stream of overseas networks that included Germany, Australia and Italy, who all signed up to take the show.

Como's third season for NBC wrapped up on June 7, 1958. Como's post-season schedule saw him attending a benefit for the St. Francis Cardiac Home for Children, playing some golf in the Pepsi Charity tournament (again on Long Island), and recording some sides for another album of faith songs. Their Roman Catholic faith was a major feature in both Perry and Roselle's lives, particularly Roselle. Ray Charles remembered her as a "serious Catholic" but saw Perry as being "more secular."[26] It was quite definitely a family tradition to attend church on Long Island every Sunday, although as with many things, Como was reluctant to talk publicly about his faith. "I don't like to talk about religion," he told Phil Donahue in 1979. "I'm just an ordinary Christian. If I am troubled, I go to my confessor."[27]

Aside from his charity work, the most public demonstration of Como's faith was an unusual relationship between him and a New York priest. Father Robert Perrella, often dubbed "Father Bob," met Como shortly after the singer arrived in New York in

1943. Perrella was a newly ordained priest, stationed at the Church of Saint Anthony of Padua in Greenwich Village. When asked by a superior to find some entertainment for an annual event that the church organized, Perrella remembered seeing Como at the Strand Theater on Broadway. He approached him at the one-room apartment at the Lexington Hotel, where the Comos were living. Perry agreed to perform at the benefit, "on one condition," recounted Perrella, "that you and me become friends."[28] They did. As a thank-you for that first appearance, Perrella gave Como a crucifix ring, which he regularly wore. For the next 20 years, Father Bob was a regular visitor to Como's dressing room.

Perrella's published account of his relationship with Como is strangely defensive and suggests that his role was as much that of companion and *factotum* as father confessor. When *Look Magazine* writer Joe McCarthy interviewed Como one Saturday night after the show, Perrella entertained the writer before Como, Mickey Glass and Dee Belline arrived. Perrella took on himself to offer some drinks and a free-flowing dinner with wine followed. When the feature appeared, Perrella was shocked to find himself described in the article as the "official bartender of the group."[29] Perrella accompanied Como on most of his trips out of New York during the fifties and was a regular at the Ziegfeld Theater during the rehearsals for the TV show. Sitting at the back of the theater, Perrella was the arbiter of taste in the show. When Sheree North appeared in a costume that offered "too great an expanse of carnal exposure," it was Father Bob who gave the thumbs down, much to Miss North's disgust.[30]

Como never talked about his relationship with Perrella, who was eventually transferred to a parish in upstate New York. When he left the city, his relationship with Como ended with some bitterness. According to Perrella, the transfer was sudden and the result of "sacerdotal jealousy and priestly venom" within the church.[31] He left without saying goodbye—to anyone, not just the Comos—before receiving a call from Dee Belline berating him for the manner of his departure. Perrella eventually spoke to Como and made an ill-timed request for a television set for his new rectory. Whether it was that or some other issue that caused the breach, Perrella purported not to know. Subsequent calls to Como, he said, were always blocked. When eventually he did get through, he was rebuffed. "Steel could not have been any more frigid," wrote Perrella.[32]

Perrella had certainly been as close to Como as anyone had for a long period of time. "I think Father Bob gave Perry a blessing before each show, because he was always in Perry's dressing room," recalled Ray Charles. "Or maybe Perry was confessing."[33] Charles certainly recalled Perrella's sudden disappearance from the scene and was not surprised by the priest's account of his split with Perry. "It's interesting to hear him describing Perry's dismissal of people," he wrote. "It was like an ice curtain came down.... He did the same thing with Mitch Ayres and to some extent with me, although I guess the ice curtain melted in my case."[34]

Perrella apart, the other most overt indication of the importance of religion to Perry Como came in the summer of 1958. Notwithstanding his international success through records and the export of the TV show, Como had never set foot outside the American continent. He and Roselle decided to rectify that with a silver wedding anniversary trip to Italy. Como had done some work for Boys Town in the United States and indirectly, some benefit work for its counterpart organization in Italy. When the Comos finally got around to making the trip—they had talked about it, said Como, for 10 years—Monsignor Carroll Abbey, who founded the Boys Town of Italy, made arrangements for the entire Como family to visit the Vatican while they were in Rome.

The Comos had been told that an audience with Pope Pius XII was possible during their stay, but were taken aback when they received a note on their arrival in Rome inviting them to an audience the following morning. "Nobody had told us we were going to have a private audience," Como told Pete Martin two years later. "We'd been told we were to have an audience, period. So we sat there, and our friend the monsignor kept saying, 'Don't worry.' 'But' we asked, 'what do we do?' 'Do nothing,' he said. 'When you see him, he'll take care of making you feel comfortable.' A door opened quietly, and two cardinals came through and knelt down. You're not a Catholic, so you won't understand this, but I was so stirred up I was about to jump right out through the window from which His Holiness blesses the crowds on St. Peter's Square. Then the Holy Father came in; we knelt, but he told us to stand, and he said, 'I know all about you and your NBC TV shows.'"[35] Como's account of the meeting with the Pope demonstrated not only the strength of his faith but also his genuine surprise at the extent of his own personal fame. Como's weekly television show had been on the air for some time in Italy, screened on Saturday evening right after the popular *Il Musichiere,* a musical quiz show that Como guested on while in Rome. (The show, conducted in Italian, demonstrated that Como could get by in his parents' native tongue but that he was quite definitely an American-Italian rather than *vice versa.*)

After a lengthy stay in Italy, Perry was back in New York by early September, working in RCA recording studio A. Since his flirtation with rock 'n' roll in 1955–56, Como and RCA had delivered a string of major hit records. None of them had quite the closeness to rock that "Ko-Ko-Mo" demonstrated, and as the label "novelty songs" implies, each had a structure and identity of its own. Como's detractors might argue that 1956–58 saw him record some of the tritest material of his career, but this ignores the strong fit between the songs and the production ideas behind the TV show. After the success of "Hot Diggity," Como's next disc was another two-sided winner. The A-side was "More," a lilting ballad (different from the film song of the same name that was part of Andy Williams' repertoire in the sixties). Its flip was "Glendora," a brassy, foot-tapping song about a guy who falls in love with a dummy in a department store window! "More" reached #4 in the bestseller chart, although "Glendora" received the same amount of attention from disc jockeys, with both sides of the disc reaching #8 in *Billboard's* Disc Jockey chart.[36] A pair of ballads followed, "Somebody up There Likes Me," which was a minor hit, coupled with Perry's TV theme, "Dream Along with Me (I'm on My Way to a Star)," followed in September 1956 by "Chincherinchee." Another novelty item, this song had a jungle theme, with an appropriate tom-tom beat to drive it along. It was perfect TV material for Perry and the Ray Charles Singers, although for once, the television exposure failed to turn the song into a chart hit.

Como was not absent long from the charts. In January 1957, the successful pairing of producer Joe Carlton and arranger Joe Reisman orchestrated five titles for Perry, over two sessions at RCA's Webster Hall studios on East 11th Street. Three of the titles, "Close," "I Accuse" and "I Have You to Thank" never saw release, but the remaining two were combined to generate yet another monster hit. The A-side was a song called "Round and Round," written by Joe Shapiro and Lou Stallman. Once more, RCA brought Como a song with an unusual construction, akin in many ways to a children's musical "round," where different voices sing the same lyric and melody, but beginning at different times ("Three Blind Mice" being perhaps the best known example).

The songwriters wrote the song in 45 minutes while riding the New York subway from the Brill Building to their homes in Sea Gate, Brooklyn. Stallman later described how the song had come about. "We took our seats on the train in Times Square," he said. "By the time we reached the first stop, we had the thought of those wheels going round. I had my guitar out, Joe had his pencil moving on his paper, and we were going from wheels to the sun to the moon to a ring, and what we didn't know at that time, to the biggest hit we had ever known. Forty-five minutes later, when we got off at our station, we were singing 'Round and Round.'"[37] The song was one that took longer to record than it did to write. Perry and the musicians experimented with different background sounds before settling on drummer Terry Snyder's wire brushes on his drum case. "We all thought it would be a hot one," Perry said later, "but if we handed it to an arranger, what could he arrange? There was really nothing there. I said why don't we do a row-row-row-your boat-thing? I started the beat on the piano, and that's what we came up with."[38]

"Round and Round" spent two weeks atop the *Billboard* charts, heading the Jockey, Best Seller and the new Top 100 listing. It reached #3 in the Juke Box chart, Como's final appearance in that listing, which was discontinued in June 1957. Although not recorded as having a chart impact in its own right, the B-side, "Mi Casa Su Casa" (another Al Hoffman—Dick Manning song), also claimed a place in Como folklore to the extent that it appeared (inaccurately) on a compilation LP of *Como's Golden Records* in 1958. It has been a regular member of any "Best Of" compilation ever since. Como made great play of "Round and Round" on television, with Grey Lockwood coming up with an imaginative routine in which Como, the Ray Charles Singers, the cue-card boys, and even a cameraman formed a rotating circle around Como, and he performed the song. With so much movement in the piece, Como lip-synched the vocal, but within seconds of the song beginning, he had made it clear to the viewers what was going on by mistiming his lip movement in an exaggerated manner.

More television-oriented songs followed during the rest of 1957, each with a record out featuring Como with his regular Ray Charles Singers. In June 1957, "The Girl with the Golden Braids" reached #15 in the *Billboard* Top 100, and later in the year, another double-sided disc, "Just Born (To Be Your Baby)" and "Ivy Rose," had a similar impact. "Ivy Rose" was described by one reviewer as a "corny waltz"[39] although the A-side, "Just Born" was as close as Perry had come to a rock 'n' roll song since "Juke Box Baby." With a high-pitched choral backing, the song required Perry to sing louder than normal and was one of the few occasions where he could be heard to come rhythmically unstuck.

Both of Como's summer 1957 releases were mere fillers as compared to his next single. It featured two songs, both from new song writing partnerships with strong futures ahead. The first song was "Catch a Falling Star," written by Lee Pockriss and Paul Vance. The pair would go to produce other notorious examples of novelty songs such as "Itsy Bitsy Teenie Weenie Yellow Polka Dot Bikini," but in 1957, they struggled to find a publisher for "Catch a Falling Star."[40] Eventually they did and the song soon came to Joe Carlton's attention. Its construction was similar to "Round and Round" and when Como recorded it on October 9, 1957, Joe Reisman's arrangement borrowed heavily from the year's earlier #1 hit and again featured Como singing a counterpoint with the Ray Charles Singers.

The other side of the disc was "Magic Moments," from the equally new writing team of Burt Bacharach and Hal David. Bacharach's unusual melodies had not found instant favor with the music publishers, but once he teamed with lyricist David, the pair struck gold immediately with "Magic Moments" and "The Story of My Life," two songs that together held the top spot in the British music charts for 10 weeks early in 1958. Como recorded "Magic Moments" on December 3, 1957, and as with "Catch a Falling Star," it was the only title put to tape at that session. Surviving outtakes demonstrate that Reisman and Carlton experimented with different configurations of Hal David's lyric, with over 20 takes being attempted during the afternoon session; it was take 8 that eventually provided the master for release.[41] As with previous releases, RCA kept its options open as to which side would be the driver of sales. *Billboard* thought that "Catch a Falling Star" was a "cute, rhythmic tune that is delivered with an approach similar to 'Round and Round,'" while also welcoming "Magic Moments" for its "shuffling melody and relaxed style. Either can step out," the magazine said.[42] In January, RCA seemed to come down on the side of the Bacharach and David song, with a full-page ad in *Billboard* telling of the "BIG COMO-TION" around "Magic Moments."[43] Como's own plugging of the songs was even-handed, featuring both of them several times on TV between January and March 1958. In chart terms, "Catch a Falling Star" came out just on top, hitting #1 in the *Billboard* Disc Jockey chart and #3 in the Best Seller. The best placing for "Magic Moments" was #4 in the Jockey chart. In England, these outcomes were reversed. "Magic Moments" topped the British chart on February 28, 1958, and stayed there for eight weeks, giving Como his biggest Transatlantic hit.[44]

"Catch a Falling Star" and "Magic Moments," released together as RCA single 47/20–7128, was a watershed for Perry Como in several ways. It was the last time that Perry Como would reach the #1 position in the U.S. charts, a position that he had occupied on 12 previous occasions. While "Catch a Falling Star" was the first of Perry's million-sellers to receive formal accreditation from the Recording Industry Association of America (RIAA) as a Gold record (indeed was the first such award by the RIAA to any performer), it was also Como's seventeenth and final Gold record for a single. In December 1958, Como became the first singer to receive the newly launched Grammy Award for the Best Male Vocal Performance of the year for "Catch a Falling Star." It would be Como's only Grammy other than a posthumous Lifetime Achievement Award in 2002. Despite the massive worldwide success of the two songs, they marked the end of Perry Como's time as a competitor for the top spots in the U.S. charts. His immediate follow up to "Catch a Falling Star" was "Kewpie Doll," a Sid Tepper–Roy Bennett composition about a fairground game of bell-ring. Ray Charles joined Como in an unbilled role as solo backing vocalist, with his Singers also providing their usual support.[45] "Kewpie Doll" reached #6 in the *Billboard* charts, with sales just short of the million mark. Como jokingly gave Ray Charles a Gold Record, but with a quarter piece missing. "Kewpie Doll" was Como's last Top 10 appearance for 11 years. Nevertheless, as his hits in the U.S. began to dry up, Como found that his records started to have more impact abroad. "Magic Moments" heralded a string of several Top 10 hits in the U.K., on the back of the by now enormous popularity generated by the BBC screenings of Como's television show.

The Perry Como Show rolled into its fourth Saturday night season on September 13, 1958. Clark Jones had replaced Bob Finkel in the mobile production booth, but that was the only change from the regular team. Como was by now synonymous with Saturday night on television and during the year, had recorded an album that took *Saturday Night with Mr. C* as its title. Como, it seemed, was a fixture in that slot and no one anticipated that a change was likely, until Kraft Cheese, and the biggest contract in television history, came calling.

Chapter 11

Perry Como's Kraft Music Hall

THERE WERE FEW NAMES BIGGER IN media sponsorship in the fifties than Kraft Foods. There were also few stars on television bigger than Perry Como and it was no surprise that when the two of them came together, the result was the biggest contract in television history. It was worth $25 million. News of the deal went public on March 5, 1959. Not only was the deal the biggest ever in television, it was groundbreaking in other ways too. The contract put Como, via his production company, Roncom, in complete control of the show. Under its terms, Roncom assumed responsibility for all programming matters and met all production costs, including guest star fees. The company also took responsibility for producing and funding Como's summer season replacement. With the new Kraft remit, Como significantly expanded Roncom. It remained wholly owned by the Como family but now operated through two subsidiaries. Roncom TV Inc. handled all television matters while the music publishing side of the business operated through Roncom Music Co. What had been a 33-person business grew to over 100 employees on the back of the Kraft deal.[1]

The contract ran for a two-year period and required Como to star in 66 shows over the term. The working title for the new show was *The Kraft Music Hall Presents Perry Como*. Perry did not disclose his own take from the $25 million, but *Time* magazine summarized it by saying, "Como will pay expenses out of the $25 million and keep what is left." *Time* also said he would "go on collecting $1.2 million yearly from NBC."[2] All of that was in addition to the separate, 10-year employment contract that Kraft also announced that Como had signed. He would, they said, work "as a consultant in areas unrelated to television."[3]

The signing of Como represented a move by Kraft to reclaim their position as the pre-eminent sponsor of music shows on television. *The Kraft Music Hall* on radio had been an American institution from its inception in 1933 until its demise in 1949. Its halcyon days undoubtedly coincided with Bing Crosby's period as host from 1935 to 1946. That 11-year period was the peak of Crosby's popularity and the Kraft brand gained enormously from its association with "The Groaner." After Crosby switched his allegiance to Philco and ABC in 1946 a succession of short-lived hosts took on the show. Al Jolson was the final custodian from 1947 to 1949, before Kraft decided to move all of its sponsorship money to television. Drama rather than music was the immediate beneficiary, the *Kraft Television Theater* opening in 1947 and staying on the air until 1958, when Kraft then decided to revive the Music Hall. Milton Berle, a TV giant of comedy rather than music, was a surprising choice as the first TV *Music Hall* host before Kraft secured Como's signature.

The move to Kraft meant two changes for the Como show. The first was the name. What had been *The Perry Como Show* now became *Perry Como's Kraft Music Hall*. The second change was more significant. Perry Como had been the king of Saturday night television since he left CBS in 1955 but the move to Kraft now took him to a Wednesday evening slot at 9:00 P.M. With hindsight, the move away from Saturday nights was a mistake and marked the beginning of the end of Como's pre-eminence on TV. Como's Wednesday ratings were good enough to sustain him for another four years, but he never recaptured the dominance that had turned Saturdays into "Saturday Night with Mr. C."

Through the spring of 1959, Como played out the remainder of his fourth NBC season. Lee Cooley returned briefly as producer for two shows while Clark Jones was indisposed, and the guest list for the shows maintained its "who's-who of showbiz" feel. The inclusion of some of Tin Pan Alley's finest songwriters, such as Oscar Hammerstein II, Yip Harburg and Dorothy Fields, gave a new angle to the guest list. When the season ended, the Como show stood at #23 in the ratings.

After a summer break overshadowed by the serious illness of his mother, Perry opened the doors of the *Kraft Music Hall* on Wednesday, September 30, 1959. Peggy King, Walter Brennan, the Everly Brothers and Maurice Gosfield ("Doberman" in the *Bilko* series) were Perry's first guests. All of Como's regular production team stayed with him for the new show, with the exception of head writer Goodman Ace. The series started sluggishly and *Variety* immediately remarked on Ace's absence. "That may yet prove to be the most significant difference for the future of the Como show," the review said.[4] "The show lacked the sparkle, the wit and the effortlessness that were consistent hallmarks of Como's shows in the past."[5] Jack Gould, writing in *The New York Times*, also found the show wanting. "A more able proprietor of the Hall would be hard to find," he wrote, "and in the coming weeks, he undoubtedly will put things in order. But last night, the familiar light touch simply wasn't there."[6]

As the season progressed, *Variety* continued to drop hints that the show needed to find another Goodman Ace, although Como's personality, plus some excellent guests, brought the new show back on to a stable course. "As an effortless host and comfortable crooner, Como is still top of the league," said *Variety* in December 1959. The show received a massive boost early in 1960 when Como and his singing idol, Bing Crosby, agreed to a guest swap. It was Como's only "trade" of the season and in January 1960, Como flew to Los Angeles to deliver the first part of the deal as a guest on Crosby's show. Crosby was there to meet him at the airport and over two days, 11–12 January 1960, the two singers plus three of Crosby's four sons taped a one-hour *Bing Crosby Show for Oldsmobile*.

The show aired on February 29. Crosby was by now the elder statesman of the music business, but a succession of singers who guested on his shows, including Sinatra and Dean Martin, all paid respectful homage to the man who, in Sinatra's words, was "the father of their careers." Crosby's writers came up with some clever dialogue that enabled Como to pay his dues while also having fun with his comatose image. As Crosby greeted him on a bare set, Como asked why there were no stools or chairs.

Bing: Anyway, I think you'll sing much better standing up.

Perry: You want me to sing much better?

Bing: Well, no, not too much—I trust you're not gonna be a show-off here tonight and sing much better than me.

Perry: Oh, I wouldn't do that—even if I could.

Finally, the pair moved into a medley of "Lazy" songs, hanging from a pair of sub-way straps. "Pairing Bing Crosby and Perry Como may not be change of pace casting," said *Variety*, "but the two stars are masters of the song craft and joined together for a consistently pleasing and of course, always relaxing musical session."[7]

Perry and Bing take a breather during rehearsals for Crosby's guest spot on the *Kraft Music Hall* in 1960.

Two weeks later, Crosby turned up as the guest on Como's Kraft Show in New York. Once more, the camaraderie between the two was apparent, Crosby opening the show instead of Como and singing Como's "Dream Along with Me" theme. When Como appeared at his side, Crosby enquired, "Are you in show business?" "Not for the past five minutes," said Como in reply. "The pair," said *Variety*, "had another ball as they cavorted through a repertoire a mile-wide."[8]

A feature of both shows was the making of a would-be Crosby-Como LP. Some viewers thought that the album was for real and eagerly awaited its appearance in stores. Copyright and permission issues precluded any such release, but the ruse made good television. It also gave Como the chance of a lifetime to sit on a stool and watch Crosby up close. At one point, as Bing launched into his familiar mannerisms while singing "Gigi," Como sat transfixed. "Now you can see why I took that style," he said to the camera, before picking up his own part of the medley. After the show, Crosby—never comfortable with any directly expressed praise or emotion—chided him for the remark. "Don't say those things," Crosby told him. Como continued to tell that story almost until he died and despite the admonition, the two singers parted as the best of friends, the Crosbys heading to Florida to stay in the Como's newly acquired second home there. Como never lost his admiration for Bing. When he began working in Las Vegas in the seventies, someone asked him how he killed the time between shows. "I put on some Crosby records to see if I'm doing it right," was his reply.[9]

The shows captured the two singers at the top of their form. By 1960, Crosby sometimes appeared bored, with the geniality that had sustained his image coming across as a little forced. With Como, he genuinely seemed to enjoy himself, displaying the naturalness that was the hallmark of his peak years. The two medleys each contained around 25 songs and ran over 10 minutes—two of the longest unbroken medleys ever seen on TV. It was no surprise that the shows achieved high ratings, the Crosby show capturing, remarkably, one viewer in three, according to the definitive *Trendex* ratings.

Guests of Crosby's caliber also added to the export value of Como's *Kraft Music Hall*. Como's primary audience outside the United States was Great Britain. As his hit-making potential tailed off in the U.S., it reached a new peak in England. The BBC had started broadcasting Como's NBC show on January 1, 1958, and it was no coincidence that his record of "Magic Moments" took up a two-month residence at the top of the British charts soon after. Como's next four novelty singles all scored heavily in Britain. "Love Makes the World Go Round," a trite piece with a banal "yeah-yeah" lyric, hit #6 in Britain while failing to make the top thirty at home. "Tomboy," a song etched onto a large wooden placard and sent to Como c/o his TV show by two firemen from "Firehouse 2, Miami, Florida," reached #10 in the U.K. (#29 in *Billboard*). The more serious "I Know" was a #13 hit in Britain but failed to score at home. Perhaps most surprising of all were the different results for "Delaware." Written by Irving Gordon, who had composed two of Como's hits with the Fontane Sisters, the song used puns based on the names of American states to tell its story. Driven along by a snare drum combination of Terry Snyder and Ted Sommer plus a chanting Ray Charles choral arrangement, the song reached #22 in the *Billboard* charts, but rocketed to #3 in Great Britain early in 1960.[10] His seventies hits apart, "Delaware" is for many people the best-remembered Perry Como hit in Britain. (Ray Charles said that when they arrived in Britain for the 1975 tour, BBC producer Yvonne Littlewood asked them to make sure they included "Delaware" in the act because of its popularity. Perry, said Ray, "could barely remember it.")[11]

The BBC screenings of *The Perry Como Show* used a kinescope film flown over from New York for the British transmission. Generally, the show in the U.K. ran a couple of weeks behind the U.S. version, to allow for the transatlantic trip and critically, for the editing out of the commercials and the gathering of copyright clearances. Both tasks fell to the young BBC associate producer Yvonne Littlewood. She recalled that permissions were generally straightforward, with most publishers being happy to agree to one exclusive showing with no additional royalty. Commercials, however, were a different matter. The BBC had been a publicly funded broadcaster since its founding in the 1920s, but by 1955, the U.K. had seen the arrival of commercial television as the first challenge to the BBC monopoly. The BBC's response to the competition was strong, although its status as an advertisement-free station was protected by a zeal that combined a dose of paranoia with an almost religious fervor. Littlewood's duties included the editing of the Como film from the States to remove all hints of product names or references. It was a significant task. The show that filled a one-hour spot in the American schedules ran to only 44 minutes with the advertising removed.

Prior to the Kraft contract, the editing out of commercials had been more straightforward. Como's NBC shows had several sponsors, and apart from an early roll call, they plugged their products through a series of self-contained commercial breaks. With the move back to a single sponsor, Como's shows regained some of the characteristics of the old Chesterfield shows, with the plugs for Kraft's cheeses and other food products very much an integral part of the show. Como's dialogue was sprinkled with references to his sponsor, just as he had never missed a chance in the old days to give a plug to Chesterfield. Littlewood's problems started right up front. The title of the show—*Perry Como's Kraft Music Hall*—was unacceptable to the BBC because of the work "Kraft" and had to become *Perry Como's Music Hall*. That meant some editing to the opening shots, and Frank Gallop's booming welcome announcement also had to go. The BBC encountered so much difficulty with the editing that Littlewood was eventually dispatched New York to try to persuade the Como team to use a more clearly demarcated approach to the commercials.

Yvonne Littlewood soon found herself with the chance to influence the Como show more directly. Como himself had hinted in an interview in February 1960 that he thought the format of the show was becoming stale. "We can't just keep on doing the same things over and over again," he told *Show Time*. "My set designers are going absolutely mad trying to think of new ideas and so are my writers. You list the guest stars for them and say 'Write something' and their eyes roll back in their heads."[12] Como went on to say that what he had in mind was to cut his shows down to around ten per year and "do some stuff out of the country."[13] There were plans, he said, to do something in London later in the year but "nothing definite yet."[14]

Virtually as Como spoke, a team from the BBC was in New York to discuss exactly that suggestion with NBC and Roncom. Como received a heavy volume of fan mail from Britain, and London was an obvious first choice for an on-location show. When they broached the idea with the BBC, the response was positive. A British-made production of such a prestigious show would be a considerable feather in the cap of the BBC at a time when British television still looked in awe at its American counterpart. BBC entertainment chiefs Ronnie Waldman and Bill Cotton arrived in New York on February 9, 1960, to discuss the idea. They returned home four days later with an agreement in principle that Como would fly to Britain on Easter Monday. He would film the show at several "typically British" locations, pulling the final production together at the BBC Television Center.

Como, apart from his cameo appearance on Italian TV in 1958, had never performed outside the United States. Despite Como's advocacy of the idea in the press, BBC chief Waldman reported that the star was "fairly nervous about the whole operation."[15] His nervousness however was nothing as compared to that of the BBC itself. "Operation Como" was the first time that the BBC had produced a show for an American network. As such, it faced a big technical challenge because the BBC was geared up to make programs on the British 405-line system. A show for the States had to be made in 525 lines and the BBC did not possess the means to produce a 525-line videotape.

Worst still, one of the BBC's U.K. commercial rivals, Associated Television (ATV), did. While NBC saw the solution as simple—contract with ATV to produce the show—BBC top brass would have none of it. "In view of the considerable impression made in the United States by ATV's mobile 525-line recording equipment, it is a matter of great importance that the impression made by BBC Television servicing and facilities in relation to "Operation Como" should be as good as possible. Much of the success of future activities in relation to overseas disposal of BBC produced programs will depend on the excellence of our handling of this very important project," said BBC Television Business Manager Ronnie Waldman in a memo to his staff.[16] Eventually, the BBC hired a Marconi unit to film the show in 525 lines while also making a 35mm tape-recording. Neither technology could handle color, so when transmitted back in the States, the show went out in black and white.

Como flew into London as planned on April 16, 1960. After completing customs procedures at London Airport, he re-boarded his plane, which then taxied to a spot in the maintenance area. There, the cameras and sound equipment were waiting to film Como's "arrival." Perry stayed in London for one week, spending his nights at the exclusive Dorchester Hotel and his days on location. He filmed with Margot Fonteyn outside the Royal Opera House in Covent Garden, then traveled to Woburn Abbey to meet the Duke of Bedford. He chatted with actor Ralph Richardson in Parliament Square and joined in an English pub sing-along with British stars Harry Secombe, Fenella Fielding and Russ Conway. Mitchell Ayres and Ray Charles accompanied him on

Perry in England, meeting the Duke of Bedford at Woburn Abbey, April 20, 1960, as part of the filming of Como's first U.K. show.

the trip, Ayres conducting the Eric Robinson Orchestra in support of Como and Charles directing the Beryl Stott Singers, augmented by two of Charles' regular singers who also made the trip across. Finally, Como and his team pulled the whole show together at the BBC Television Center on April 23, 1960.

Variety said that the show was a "travelog with style and taste,"[17] while *The New York Times* adopted a very British tone in its review. Como's "low-pressure style," it said, had made him very popular with British audiences, and "there was evidence of public enthusiasm on several occasions during the telecast."[18] Producer-director Clark Jones was similarly enthusiastic about the team's first experience of a TV show on the road. Writing to BBC chief Waldman on May 3, 1960, Jones said, "I don't think any of us expected to find anywhere the cooperation, patience, understanding, efficiency and downright ability we found in your organization."[19] The show was Como's first that was done on the road, setting a pattern that would become the norm for his seventies and eighties specials.

The BBC continued to import the Como show until June 1961, all the while constantly on the lookout for a homegrown star to host a similar show of the BBC's own. Liverpool-born singer Michael Holliday was the first to offer some of the relaxed Como image to a British-based show, and after his premature death in 1963, Irish singer Val Doonican picked up Como's mantle. Yvonne Littlewood produced some of the Doonican shows, as well as Como's further BBC appearances in the 1970s. She was in no doubt that the influence of the Como show continued to be felt in Britain long after it disappeared from the screens. Como's show, she said, was the first time anyone in Britain had seen made-for-TV ideas influencing on the production of a show. "Until then," she said, "the production ideas had come mainly from the theater or music hall.... Perry's distinctly new approach had a big influence on the style of shows built around a singer and particularly Val Doonican's early sixties shows."[20]

Perry Como wrapped up his first *Kraft Music Hall* season on June 1, 1960. As had become customary, the final show had a party atmosphere to it. Fred Danzig, writing for UPI, loved it. "Wednesday night's NBC-TV color show was a ball," he wrote. "It gave us more production and directorial daring, more spontaneity and clean fun than anything Perry has done since, well, last year's finale."[21] Danzig's enthusiasm was a backhanded reminder that *The Kraft Music Hall* had not met expectations. A final ranking of 29th in the ratings was scant return for the first half of Kraft's $25 million investment. It was no surprise to discover that the show was lined up for a major makeover before the next season began.

With Como's hit singles drying up, his visits to the recording studio were becoming fewer and further between. During 1959 he had however taken on two album projects. One was a new collection of Christmas recordings, giving a stereo treatment to many of the seasonal standards that he had first recorded in the mid-forties. Prior to that, Como recorded an album with the title *Como Swings*. Although the cover showed Como in golfing mode, the title referred to the style of the album, which some critics saw as a first attempt by Como to emulate the swing style of Sinatra's Capitol Records albums, beginning with *Songs for Swinging Lovers*. William Ruhlmann, writing on the *All Music Guide* website, observed "arrangers Joe Lipman and Jack Andrews wrote a bunch of charts that aped the sound Billy May got for Sinatra, full of blaring horn fanfares and loud percussion. Song after song features these aggressive orchestrations, which push Como to assert himself more than usual."[22]

Como Swings was a refreshing break from the TV-linked albums that had dominated his LP repertoire since 1955, and his next album project in the fall of 1960 was similar. For *Songs for the Young at Heart,* a concept album built around songs with the word "young" in the title, RCA assigned both a new arranger and a new production team to Como. The arranger was O.B. Masingill, who had previously worked with Roy Hamilton and the de John Sisters before joining RCA. The production team was Hugo (Peretti) and Luigi (Creatore), who had joined RCA after successful writing and production spells, first at Mercury and then at Roulette Records, which they owned.

Songs for the Young at Heart featured 12 songs, mainly of fifties vintage, including standards such as "Young at Heart," "Too Young" and "Hello Young Lovers." Masingill opted for a set of arrangements that excluded any strings, utilizing slightly muted horns to impose a lightly swinging style on the Mitchell Ayres Orchestra. A prominent chorus (seemingly under the direction of Ray Charles, although there is no credit given either on the album or the sessions sheets) sings along with Como. "The approach," wrote William Ruhlmann, "is more conducive to the singer, who turns in characteristically warm and easy interpretations."[23] Certainly, Como seemed more comfortable with the arrangements than had been the case on *Como Swings.* One song from the album, "Hello Young Lovers," became Como's regular opening song for his live shows from the seventies through to the end of his career.

By the time that Como started work on the *Songs for the Young at Heart* album, he had already returned to the TV screens for his second season for Kraft. The 1960–61 season also marked Como's sixth consecutive series of one-hour weekly shows. With the performance of the first season disappointing, change once again was afoot. Nick Vanoff replaced Clark Jones as producer and brought in Dwight Hemion as director. Gary Smith, who subsequently formed a production company with Hemion, also arrived to handle set design. Goodman Ace returned as head writer on a show that now moved to taped transmission rather than going out live. With Peter Gennaro working as choreographer and Peter Matz as the dance arranger, it was, said Ray Charles, "a truly all-star team."[24]

The change in the production team for the Como show was a bold one. Vanoff and Hemion had met each other when they worked together on the Steve Allen *Tonight Show* and had become good friends. Both were young. Vanoff, a Greek, was 31 years old when he took on the Como role and Hemion was 34. Vanoff had actually worked as a cue card boy on the Como show in 1954, but such was his talent that within four months the producer, Lee Cooley, made him an associate producer.

Unlike most of the people who worked with Como, the relationship between Perry and Vanoff, and between their families, did become a social one. Vanoff's widow, Felisa, described the relationship between Perry and her husband as "symbiotic," saying that Vanoff had looked on Como as a father figure.[25] The two families had also traditionally exchanged Christmas gifts, the Vanoffs giving the Comos a case of champagne and receiving a case of Chivas in return. When Vanoff finally summoned the courage to tell Como that his family did not drink Chivas, Perry replied "Thank God." The Comos, he said, did not drink champagne.[26] When Vanoff died at age 61 in 1991, Como flew unannounced to Los Angeles to sing "Ave Maria" at his funeral.

The Como show in 1960 was still working to the template created by Bob Finkel three years earlier and Dwight Hemion was in no doubt that the new team was brought in to give the show a re-fresh.[27] Much of the new look came, unsurprisingly, from set designer Gary Smith, although he was quick to credit Hemion with some of the ideas. One immediate impact that Hemion made on Smith was to encourage him to think of the set in terms of depth. "Traditional thinking," said Smith, "was to see television as across the front of you—from left to right."[28] Hemion, he said, saw it differently, believ-

The classic "Sing to me, Mr. C" set, as revamped by Gary Smith for the Kraft show 1961–63 (courtesy Colleen Zwack).

ing that going into the set was just as important. The impact of the change was immediately apparent.

Smith was the most proactive set designer ever to work with Como. He was 26 years old when he started working with Como but had sufficient confidence to design a set and encourage the rest of the team to fit songs to it rather than *vice versa*.[29] The result was that the visual image started to drive the show, rather than the music content. Smith was behind other changes too, not least of which was the re-design of the "Sing to Me, Mr. C" set for Como's weekly request medley. Smith came up with the idea of putting Como high on a pedestal made out of letters which when seen from above, spelled out "Mr. C" on the studio floor. As the scene opened, viewers saw Como walk onto the set and settle on a stool in front of a music stand. It was an image of a professional at work, concentrating on his music, rather than a performer in the spotlight. Each week, Como sang three songs, accompanied either by Tony Mottola's guitar or by Billy Rowland's piano. Como later told impressionist Rich Little that the thing he liked most about the set was the music stand. Como, said Little, told him that he couldn't possibly learn all the songs every week by heart, but he disliked reading lyrics from cue cards, which sometimes he couldn't see. The music stand was the perfect solution.[30] The only concession to any sense of imagery around the set was a thin vase containing a single red rose that stood at the base of the stand. It gave Vanoff a focal point for his cameras at the opening and closing of the medley. The red rose became a Como trademark and that too was Smith's idea, although he confessed in 2001 that he had "no idea" where it came from.[31] Como himself said that at first, the simplicity of the set surprised him. "The rose in the vase was the set designer's idea and it stuck," he told BBC radio host Pete Murray in 1973. "I thought it might be my last show; that we must be running out of money!"[32]

The first show of the new season went out on October 5, 1960, to good reviews. *Variety,* which had been harping about Ace's departure for most of the previous season, welcomed his return. The review also praised the quality of the writing from the team, which now included Selma Diamond, Frank Peppiatt and John Aylesworth, as well as Como veteran Jay Burton. The first show had a guest list that ran from the thirties to the sixties, placing diva Ethel Merman alongside pop stars Fabian and Frankie Avalon. *Variety* described the task of balancing the kids against the established stars as a "tightrope," which it said, the writers handled by "unobtrusively keeping Como on stage, as a kind of shadow guide."[33]

One week later Como, dashed off a by now rare single in the RCA studios before heading to a script conference in the Roncom offices. John P. Shanley of *The New York Times* was invited to sit in and was struck by the willingness of the participants—Vanoff, Hemion, Ace, Como and others—to challenge each other without any friction or rancor. Privately, Goodman Ace told Shanley that working with Como was easy because "Perry never gets excited or frantic."[34] Dwight Hemion, speaking in 2002, said that the key attribute to the show was what it had always been—"just Perry. He didn't push or try to be anything that he wasn't," he recalled.[35] But like others before him, Hemion was in no doubt as to who was in charge. When asked about Como's input to "directing" the show, he said it was "nothing—it didn't interest him." But talk about the "direction that the show would take" and that was different. "He set the scale for the show and created a team around him," said Hemion, while remaining "one of the kindest and most likeable men I've ever known."[36]

By the end of 1960, the Vanoff-Hemion changes to the show were clearly having an effect. When Bob Hope and Anne Bancroft joined the guests for the November 30 show,

Perry (right) as a Viennese-accented psychiatrist examining Bob Hope in the *Bob Hope Buick Show*, October 22, 1960 (courtesy Colleen Zwack).

Variety said that the show was unquestionably the best of the current season and ranked alongside any that he had done, "including the heyday of his Saturday nights."[37] The team maintained the pace and variety in the show through the early months of 1961, a varied and eclectic guest list helping to keep the show fresh and lively. Peggy Lee, Jimmy Durante, Harry Belafonte and the "other" Ray Charles, the black soul singer, all took turns alongside Como. Perry by now was also picking his songs mainly from the songbook of American standards, the novelty tunes seemingly having had their day.

On Friday, April 21, 1961, Como arrived at the Ziegfeld Theater to tape the show as usual. Final rehearsals were underway when the news came through that Lucia Como, Perry's mother, had died of a heart attack at her daughter's home in Canonsburg. Como finished the taping of the show and flew immediately to Pittsburgh. Mrs. Como had been ill for some time, losing a leg to diabetes complications two years previously. She was buried the following week alongside her husband. Andy Williams stood in for Como as the host of that week's show; Perry gave him a Jaguar convertible as a "thank you."[38]

Como returned to the show on May 10, 1961, and hosted five more shows before the season ended. Despite the positive reviews and upbeat feel to the show, the end-of-year ratings were disappointing. The Como show was out of the top 30 ratings for the first time since 1955–56. Perry continued to drop hints that he was tiring of the weekly format. In a *New York Times* interview in October 1960, he admitted that the ratings were a concern. "I don't look too far ahead," he said, "but I don't think I want to continue to do 33 shows every year." Como added, surprisingly, that he was considering a role in a film called *The St. Bernard Pass*. "It would be a change for me and I'm not sure about it. A lot will depend on how we go on television this year. I like to work one year at a time."[39] The film idea quickly vanished and Kraft announced that they had contracted with Roncom for Como to do another 33 shows during the 1961–62 season. It would be Como's thirteenth consecutive year as the host of a weekly TV show. The question was just how much longer he would go on.

Chapter 12

The Scene Changes

PERRY COMO SURPRISED EVERYONE BY hosting a further 66 weekly shows for Kraft between October 1961 and June 1963. His third season began on October 4, 1961, with no significant changes to either the show or the backroom team. Producer Nick Vanoff continued to look for ways to keep the show fresh and the first show of the new season took baseball as its theme. With the New York Yankees due up in the World Series the following week, Vanoff recruited Yankee hitters Roger Maris and Mickey Mantle to the guest list. Maris and Mantle had captured the public imagination all summer as they went head-to-head to capture Babe Ruth's home run record, Maris eventually passing the Yankees legend in the final game of the season.

Baseball apart, the rest of the show followed the by now predictable theme, which *Variety* saw as a virtue. "Como keeps sailing along in this time slot on a fixed course with no regard for transient fads, mercurial ratings or the shifting competition," the reviewer said.[1] Two weeks later, Como's guest list included his former colleagues from the Ted Weems days, who recreated their thirties act for the show. John P. Shanley in the *New York Times* said it was "wonderful nostalgia; altogether, this was an excellent show, written, directed, produced and performed by a group of unusually talented people."[2]

A key feature of Como's success had always been his cross-generational appeal, but there were signs during the third Kraft season that Como was re–focusing on his own age group for the core of his support. Three months shy of his fiftieth birthday, he became a grandfather for the first time as son Ronnie and daughter-in-law Melanie presented Perry and Roselle with a granddaughter. The baby was the first of 13 grandchildren. The following month, on March 28, 1962, Alice Faye headed the TV guest list. Faye, herself a recent grandmother, was making a show business comeback and joined grandpa Como in a celebration of ageism. *Variety* said it overstepped the mark. "The interminable quipping about the ancient age of the pair and their offspring's offspring had a viewer aching with rheumatic empathy every time one or other tried a giddy half kick," the magazine said.[3]

Despite the jokes about being a grandpa, Como was carrying his years well. His hair was still thick, albeit flecked with grey (a British music journal carried a story about Como's refusal to bow to NBC's request to dye out the grey), and apart from a few laugh-lines around his eyes, his face retained a youthful candor. In private, he wore glasses for reading, but he continued to appear on stage without them until he was into his seventies. As he grew older, Perry also found that he put weight on more easily, par-

A slightly plumper-looking Como during the final days of the *Kraft Music Hall* shows in 1963 (courtesy Bill Klages).

ticularly if he let loose with his love of pasta. "I tend to blow up a little," he said in 1975, but added that he could still "take off ten pounds without too much difficulty."[4] Apart from the occasional show where he looked a little plump, there was no significant change to the Perry Como that viewers saw each week from the man they had been used to since the mid–fifties.

One way that producer Nick Vanoff made sure that the show kept in touch with what else was happening in television was by raiding some of the rival shows for his guests. In January 1962, Vanoff created a *Bonanza* theme, as Lorne Greene and Dan Blocker, respectively Ben and "Hoss" Cartwright from the hit western show, came on board. Fred Gwynne, soon to become Hermann Munster but then one of the stars of *Car 54, Where Are You?* was the guest in March, and in May 1962, Dennis Weaver of *Gunsmoke* appeared. Goodman Ace picked up on Weaver's description of himself as "strictly a bathtub singer" to create a scene where he joined Perry in a medley of old-time hits, with both of them strumming guitars as they sat in bathtubs.

Despite Vanoff's innovative work, the Como show once again missed the top 30 ratings for the 1962 season. Yet another cowboy series, *Wagon Train*, took top spot. Como's final show of the season had its customary party atmosphere, buoyed by the news from Kraft that despite the continuing ratings battle, Como had signed for another 33 shows during 1962–63.

Como set about his fourth season for Kraft immediately, recording his Christmas 1962 and Easter 1963 specials before the month of June 1962 was out. When the regular weekly shows resumed in October 1962, Vanoff once again opened with a sporting theme. The guests on that show were that era's "Big Three" of golf: Jack Nicklaus, Arnold Palmer and Gary Player, who featured in scenes shot at Sands Point Golf Club on Long Island. Como was clearly indulging himself alongside the three greatest exponents of his favorite hobby. *Variety* thought that the show went too far. "These segments [i.e. the golf] were interesting to a point, humorous to a point and even entertaining to a point. But if the viewer didn't share the host's interest in golf—forget it."[5]

In December, the Como show moved to a location of a different sort. With the Cuban Missile Crisis dominating the news during the autumn of 1962, the United States had a significant body of troops stationed at the Guantánamo Naval Base in Cuba. American troops had remained there despite the Cuban revolution in 1959. Arriving on December 5, Como and an eight-member troupe gave ten shows for the sailors over the next three days, as well as recording segments of the weekly show for TV. The show echoed the front-line performances that show biz stars had delivered during World War

II and in Korea. Ray Charles, who accompanied Como on the trip, recalled "gun–toting Cubans" surrounding them at every opportunity.[6]

Despite the best efforts of the Como team, the show faced its biggest challenge yet during the 1962–63 season. On September 26, 1962, CBS premiered *The Beverly Hillbillies*, a sitcom about a backwoods family who strike gold on their land in the Ozarks and take up residence in a mansion in Beverly Hills. Despite the repetitive nature of its plots, the series shot straight to the top of the Nielsen ratings and stayed there. Its time slot—9:00 to 9:30 P.M. on Wednesdays—was directly against the Como show, which had no answer. Despite beefing up the quality of the guest list—forties tap dancer Eleanor Powell made her TV debut on the show in December, followed over successive weeks by big names such as Ethel Merman, Jane Powell, Ray Bolger, Lauren Bacall and Charlton Heston—there was no stemming the tide.

The news that Perry Como was bringing the curtain down on his weekly shows broke on February 21, 1963. Carrying the headline "Perry Como Plans Big Schedule Cut," Associated Press said that Como planned to do only a handful of shows during the next season. "I think I've had it," Como was quoted as saying. "Eight years of a weekly hour show is a long time. I'm tired and I think maybe they (the audience) are tired. I want to get off before it's too late."[7] Asked for a quote about *The Beverly Hillbillies*, Como said with a grin, "Every once in a while a 'Hillbillies' comes along—that's part of our business. But why did it have to happen to me?"[8]

Como's final weekly show came on June 12, 1963. It ended an unbroken spell of weekly television shows that stretched back to December 1948. Since 1955, Como had hosted a weekly one-hour show, which over the eight years tallied at 278 shows. Including the thrice-weekly Supper Clubs for Chesterfield in the early fifties, Como's total number of shows as star and host reached a staggering 1049. In a medium where familiarity fast bred contempt, the only other singer who came close to matching Como's longevity on the small screen was Dinah Shore. Her unbroken TV run started in 1951 and also ended in 1963. Como's mantle was to an extent picked up by Andy Williams on NBC, but while his show developed something of Como's reputation, it lasted only five seasons in its original form. No other musical performer came close to matching Como's durability on television or his influence on the development of the medium as a vehicle for musical variety.

Como told writer Colin Escott in 1993 that he thought the durability of the show came from the fact that he had become part of the family. "Television will do that," he said. "We tried to bring on guests that people wanted to see and we could tell from the letters what we meant to people."[9] Escott attributed Como's success to his rapport with his audience. "He didn't talk down to them. He was a good neighbor who dropped in once a week and didn't overstay his welcome," he wrote. "Quitting in '63 was a good move. Perry was inextricably linked to the '50s and if you reckon that the '50s really ended around 1964, then 1963 was the time to go. Six months after he did his last weekly show, the Beatles arrived. The turbulence of the mid–to-late '60s was on the horizon, and the '50s' quiet, buoyant optimism, which seemed to find its embodiment in Perry Como, forever disappeared."[10]

When Como announced the end of the weekly shows, Kraft Foods was quick to point out that they had a long-term contract with him. They were, they said, keen to see him host a "handful" of specials the following season.[11] Nevertheless, the demise of the weekly shows when taken alongside Como's almost total withdrawal from recording was an undeniable watershed in Como's career. His RCA sessions in March and May 1963 would be his last for almost two years, an unprecedented gap in the disc career of the man who had sold more records in the Fifties than any other singer bar Elvis Presley.[12]

Although Como's success as a singles artist had virtually disappeared, he found a new vein of success in the ever-growing LP market. After the experiment with the two theme-based albums in 1959 and 1960, Como's next two LP releases had reverted to the tried and tested TV-link formula. *Sing to Me, Mr. C,* which Como recorded over two sessions in May 1961, was the most direct lift from the TV show since *We Get Letters* in 1957. It was also the only time that Como recorded in the format of the TV request spot. With six medleys, each of three tracks, RCA marketed the album as containing "18 of your all-time favorites." The cover showed Como in a blue cardigan, seated on a white stool behind the music stand, the red rose prominent in the foreground.

The album also replicated the minimalist accompaniment of the TV spot. The songs ranged from Irving Berlin's 1921 composition "All by Myself" through to the contemporary "Portrait of My Love." Joe Lipman and Jack Andrews, who did much of the arranging for TV, also supplied the charts for the album. Mitchell Ayres conducted a full studio orchestra, with guitarist Tony Mottola prominent on many of the songs, as he was on TV. Como cruised effortlessly through the blend of ballads and light swing and rattled off the whole project in two sessions. *The Troy Record* said that the album was "the best recorded Como in a long time. Perry is relaxed, obviously enjoying himself and in fine voice."[13]

Como followed up with an album called *By Request.* Once more, the LP used a television trademark, the cover featuring a single rose in a white vase against a blue background. The oldest of the twelve songs featured on the album were "What's New" from 1939 and "I'll Remember April" from 1942. The rest of the album comprised newer songs such as "Maria" (from *West Side Story*), "My Favorite Things" (from *The Sound of Music*) and "Can't Help Falling in Love" (co–written for Elvis Presley's *Blue Hawaii* film by Hugo & Luigi and George Weiss, the composer of "Surrender" for Como back in the forties.) Como sang smoothly on all 12 titles, although the album lacked the change of pace that made the previous album of medleys such a standout collection.

In between the two albums, Como had twice teamed with Hugo & Luigi to attempt a return to the singles market. The first 45, "You're Following Me" in October 1961, was a Burt Bacharach–Bob Hilliard song, but despite a good fit to the early sixties pop sound, it made no impact. Then in February 1962, Como recorded "Caterina" and "The Island of Forgotten Lovers," the latter a ballad sung to a Hawaiian arrangement. "Caterina" received most of the attention. A bouncy, sing-along tune that had echoes of "Delaware" to it, the disc briefly took Como back into the *Billboard* Top 30. Like most of Como's recent singles, however, it was a bigger hit outside the United States. "The crazy thing about this song," recalled Maurice (Bugs) Bower, "is that we had a song, but we needed a title. We called it 'Caterina,' and it turned out to be perfect because the title doesn't have to translate overseas ... and we had this song, with the original title, in the Top Ten in almost every country in the world."[14] He might have added "except America," although the song nevertheless counted as a hit for Bower and his writing partner, Earl Shuman.

Como was back in the RCA studios over three days in September and October 1962 for his strangest and, with hindsight, most misconceived album. *Mr. President* featured Como, along with his TV regulars Kaye Ballard and Sandy Stewart, on the songs from the new Irving Berlin musical. The show was Berlin's first full score since *Call Me Madam* ten years previously, but ran for only 265 performances on Broadway. Como's album of the songs—the only time he covered a full show score—met with a similarly disappointing result. The highlight of the project for Como's choral associate, Ray Charles, was a meeting with Irving Berlin. He and Mitch Ayres watched the show ahead of Como's sessions. After the show, they visited Berlin in his hotel suite. Berlin told them that he was a regular viewer of Como on TV. "As we were leaving," said Charles, "he took me by the arm and said, 'You know, I used to write special material.' I didn't know whether to cry or just die right there—Irving Berlin knew what I did!"[15]

Como's 1963 sessions saw him working on one more album plus another novelty single. The album was *The Songs I Love,* which took Como's "Mr. C" set from the TV show as its cover. "It's a rare album cover that can win immediate identification without the picture of the artist on it, but the TV set pictured on this sleeve is as familiar to millions of Americans as their own living rooms," said Hugo & Luigi in their sleeve note.[16] The album featured 12 more ballads, mostly contemporary, with such big early sixties songs as "I Left My Heart in San Francisco" and Gordon Jenkins' anthem to approaching middle age, "This Is All I Ask." Sammy Cahn and Jimmy Van Heusen wrote a special title song for the album and the only exception to the "new" feel to the songs was the inclusion of Irving Berlin's "When I Lost You." This time, instead of focusing on Berlin's most recent work, Como went back to the year of his own birth, when Berlin composed his touching memorial to his first wife.

Como as ever sang beautifully on the March sessions, although the gentle, relaxed sound of his voice was yet again in stark contrast to one of the sides he recorded in May 1963. The session on May 1, 1963, was notable in several ways. Not only was it Como's final novelty single, it was also the last time that Mitchell Ayres would hoist the baton at a Como session. The main song was "I Love You (And Don't You Forget It)," which had lyrics by regular Como wordsmith Al Stillman, to a Henry Mancini melody. With a Hugo & Luigi arrangement built around a honky-tonk piano, the Ray Charles singers joined Como on the lyric that used the title of the song over twenty times during its 2½-minute duration. Como had lost none of his aplomb with material of this type and the single was a minor hit, making the *Billboard* chart in 39th position for one week in July 1963.[17]

With a schedule of monthly TV specials due to begin in Pittsburgh in October 1963, the Roncom production team showed only minimal change from the one that had wound up the weekly season. The most significant departure was that of producer Nick Vanoff to California; musically, the team of Como, Mitch Ayres and Ray Charles remained intact. From October 1963, however, Nick Perito joined the team as arranger for the TV shows. Perito's opportunity arose when Mitchell Ayres invited him to audition to replace the long-standing team of Joe Lipman and Jack Andrews. Perito got the job and appointed Torrie Zito, later famous for his work with Tony Bennett and Barbra Streisand, as his assistant. When the two found out that the role carried no screen credit, however, they almost quit before they had started. Ayres was sympathetic to their stance and they got their screen credits from the second show of the season.[18]

Perito, born in Denver in 1924, had come a long way since he had first witnessed the young Perry Como as a touring vocalist with the Ted Weems band. After studying at the Juilliard School of Music after the war, Perito settled in New York, making his living as a session man (he was an accordion player but also an accomplished pianist) and an arranger. He had first worked with Perry on the Chesterfield shows in 1950, playing the accordion for Perry's TV versions of "Hoop-Dee-Doo."[19] When Perito joined the Como team in 1963, there was no hint that he would soon succeed Mitchell Ayres as Perry's musical director.

The partnership between Como and Ayres was strong, as was their friendship. Ray

Charles said that socially, Ayres was "probably as close as anyone from show business to Como for 15 years."[20] Ayres, however, like everyone else, had a living to make. The drop in shows from thirty-three to seven in a season cut his workload and his income. Como was always slow to re–engage his staff at the end of the season and 1964 was no exception. Ayres found himself with no guaranteed work for the next TV season, and he was being wooed by Nick Vanoff to join him in Hollywood as the musical director of Vanoff's new variety show, *The Hollywood Palace*. With no word from Como about the future, Ayres agreed to take on the job. Vanoff apparently expected Ayres still to handle Como's occasional TV shows alongside his Hollywood commitments, but Como was unhappy. He did nothing to encourage Ayres to stay, although after he was gone, he said to Mickey Glass, "Why didn't he wait?"[21] Ray Charles saw in Ayres' departure another example of Como's "possessiveness" about his team.[22] BBC producer Yvonne Littlewood detected the same characteristic. She said that Como felt "betrayed" when Ayres—and indeed Vanoff—left for the West Coast.[23] (Sadly, Ayres' time in California was short. In 1969, he was killed by a car while crossing a street in Las Vegas.)

With Ayres gone, Como found himself with a ready-made replacement in the form of Nick Perito. The association lasted until Como's retirement in 1994. Perito later credited Ray Charles' influence as the decisive factor in getting the job. He and Charles were already close friends and together with Como, they forged a powerful musical partnership until Charles found himself on the wrong side of Como's "ice curtain" during the eighties.

Prior to Ayres' departure, Como's seven specials for Kraft during the 1963–64 season had gone well—at least from an entertainment perspective. Financially, they were a disaster. Roncom still bore all the production costs for the shows but, said Como, no one recognized that the financial side of taking a show on the road was a lot different from the costs of staging a weekly show in the same studio. "We lost several hundred thousand dollars," he said.[24] That first season of specials took Como to Pittsburgh, San Francisco, Dallas (a sensitive situation, only weeks after the assassination there of JFK), Burbank, New Orleans, Minneapolis and Chicago. The Burbank show in February 1964 saw Perry welcome Lena Horne and Dean Martin as guests, a show that Cecil Smith in the *Los Angeles Times* described as a "lollapalooza—one of the great delights of the season."[25] The shows fared no better in the ratings than the outgoing weekly show, although their touring nature brought added benefits for Kraft. *Variety,* in its review of the last of the season, said, "Whatever the rating score of these shows, Kraft is understood to be very happy with their promotional impact in each of the cities."[26]

Despite the good reviews for the first season of specials, the entertainment press continued to speculate about Como's retirement. At the end of another touring TV season in 1965, one headline suggested, "Como Taking Last Bow Tonight." Como, it said, had made no commitment for the next season and planned to call it a day.[27] The reports, as they had been with the weekly show, were premature. Moving the show to NBC's new studios in Brooklyn, Como hosted another 12 specials for Kraft over the next two years before ending his relationship with the food company. Ray Charles took over as producer for those last two seasons, with former director Clark Jones making a return to the show. The writing team remained strong and included Bill Angelos and Buz Kohan, who worked alongside Goodman Ace, a man who quit and returned more times to the show than anyone could count. "Goody leaves and always comes back," said Como in 1965. "He's a rich, grumpy old man."[28]

The Como specials continued to attract headline guests and generally played to good reviews. Lena Horne, Judy Garland, Bill Cosby, Liza Minnelli and Ella Fitzgerald

With Martha Raye on the *Kraft Music Hall* show of March 5, 1964, broadcast live from the Municipal Auditorium in New Orleans (courtesy Bill Klages).

all featured alongside Perry during 1966. Through it all, Como remained the same as he had always been—Mr. Relaxation. In November 1966, *Variety* said, "Como's sleepsville identification apparently rates as a strong point with the fans and is not to be toyed with."[29] The only show that failed to win the critics' plaudits was the special with Judy Garland. It was a partnership, said *Variety*, that ought to have worked but didn't. "There may be a germ of an idea in pitting Como, who is so casual a viewer expects him to topple over any minute, against Judy Garland, who projects with an undercurrent of frenetics that seem ever on the verge of explosion. The chemistry didn't work however."[30] Part of the reason may have been Miss Garland's unpredictability. Nick Perito recalled how he, Ray Charles and Perry had their first meeting with Garland a week before the show. "Perry asked if she would like a Tanqueray Gin on the rocks (his favorite drink at the time), only for her to decline. Opening up a black brief-case that contained two glasses and a bottle of vodka, she said, 'I brought my own.'"[31] When show day arrived (it went out live), Judy stayed in her dressing room. Nothing could persuade her to come on the set until Como himself went in to speak to her. To everyone's surprise, she emerged and gave a stunning performance. Three years later, she was gone, the victim of an accidental overdose.

With the Como shows now based back in New York, Perry and Roselle were split-ting their time equally between their home on Long Island and their second home in

Florida. They first acquired a home in the sunshine state in 1959, although they had been regular visitors since the forties. Initially, they spent time in rented property at Fort Myers on the Gulf Coast. After visiting friends in Palm Beach, however, they heard about the small island colony at Jupiter, 15 miles to the north. They purchased their first home there after a chance encounter with its owners while walking on the beach. That home, on Ocean Drive, faced directly onto the Atlantic. It was the first of several properties that the Comos bought and sold in the area. David Como recalled that his parents tired of the ocean side of Jupiter because of the surf and salt from the Atlantic and bought five lots of land in nearby Tequesta, with a river frontage. There they built a grand home on Yacht Club Point, making that their permanent home and selling their Sands Point property. There were more house moves to come, with the Comos eventually returning to a more modest seafront home on Lighthouse Drive in Jupiter, but with a second house nearby that they used to accommodate family and other visitors.

Perry Como never explained his absence from the recording studios between May 1963 and February 1965. When he did finally return, it was with a change of scene. As he walked out of the RCA studios on May 1, 1963, Perry Como had probably never heard of an English group called the Beatles. Within 12 months, however, they had changed the face of popular music like nothing before or since. In April 1964, the *Billboard* Hot 100 contained 12 Beatles records, including the top five places. Everything had changed. "Instead of twenty artists selling, say, a million records each, from the sixties on it became a matter of a single artist selling 20 million records while the other nineteen went unrecorded or got dumped into the cutout bins," wrote Will Friedwald.[32]

Tony Bennett in his autobiography said that although he had survived the first wave of rock—the Presley phenomenon—"relatively unscathed," the impact of the Beatles was much greater. "Rock music had become big business," he said, and his record company, Columbia, "jumped on the bandwagon." It meant that artists like Bennett, Barbra Streisand and Johnny Mathis lost out to "bands called the Byrds and Paul Revere and The Raiders."[33] Even Frank Sinatra, who by the mid–sixties had become the dominant male singer in the business, seemed fazed by the musical revolution. "One hand acts as if it doesn't know what the other is doing," wrote Will Friedwald about Sinatra's behavior in 1965. "One grabs for the same audience that is buying his daughter's records and making her a platinum pop star; the other pats himself on the back for having the panache and the forbearance to do it *his* way all these years."[34]

Como seemed content to allow the waters to flow over him. With his TV profile seemingly winding down and the music business in flux, there was little motivation to try to swim against the tide. One man who saw things differently, though, was Steve Sholes, now head of A&R at RCA Records. Sholes had known Como since the early fifties, when as RCA's head of country music he had persuaded Como to record "Don't Let the Stars Get in Your Eyes." Now, his vision was once more to take Perry down the road of country music, but this time in a much more significant way. Sholes, in tandem with guitarist and producer Chet Atkins, had been one of the architects of RCA's "Nashville sound" Studio B when it opened in 1957. The studio became the home of many of America's top C&W acts, including Jim Reeves, Eddy Arnold, Hank Snow and Don Gibson, and was also Elvis Presley's RCA base. Atkins sat in as the producer on many of those sessions, as well as churning out his own string of guitar records. Together with Owen Bradley (who produced many of Patsy Cline's hit records), Atkins created a smoother country style and took the music to the point where mainstream pop performers could embrace it.

Como already knew Atkins, who, together with piano player Floyd Cramer and

Perry's first visit to Nashville in 1965 teamed him with RCA producer Chet Atkins (left) (courtesy Colleen Zwack).

saxophonist Boots Randolph, had participated in a Florida golf tournament that Como promoted in 1962. Doubtless, that familiarity helped Perry overcome his unease about working with a group of musicians that at best he knew by name only, and in a totally unfamiliar studio setting. When he arrived in Nashville early in February 1965 to prepare for four days of recording sessions, Como made the trip without any of his regular musical entourage. Walking into the Nashville studio for the first time, he found a near-empty room with only a handful of musicians as compared to the full orchestra that he was used to in New York. Mitchell Ayres always had the arrangements ready in Perry's key, but in Nashville, nothing was laid down. "I looked over to see the arrangements and all is I see is "I-IV-V-II," he told Colin Escott. "I say, 'what's this?' and they say 'that's the arrangement.' It was just a chord sequence, and they'd change the key and make up the arrangement as they went along."[35]

Chet Atkins took responsibility for the sessions and Anita Kerr handled the arrangements. Kerr had joined Atkins as his A&R assistant at RCA in 1961, but was already a Nashville legend in her own right. When her singing group backed Red Foley on his hit "Our Lady of Fatima," Decca A&R man Paul Cohen labeled her group as "The Anita Kerr Singers." It stuck and over the next ten years, the group did as much as anyone in developing the Nashville sound. At their early sixties peak, the Anita Kerr Singers graced one-quarter of all the records that came out of Nashville's studios.[36] By the time that the chance to work with Perry came around, Kerr had relinquished her executive role at RCA, returning to working solely with her singers. She was, of course, familiar with Como's style and with the Ray Charles Singers. "I knew how different the Anita Kerr Singers' style was from Ray Charles," she said, "in fact, entirely different."[37] For one thing, the Kerr singers were fewer in a number—four as opposed to the 8 or 12 singers that Charles used. A bigger difference, however, was their approach. "When Perry came back after the first date," said Charles, "he handed me a piece of paper and said, 'Anita sent you a copy of the group part.' It was a piece of paper with the lyrics on. The Nashville singers were able to fake parts from a lyric sheet. We couldn't have done that in New York."[38] For Atkins and Kerr, the critical thing was not to try and change the way Perry sang. "He didn't have to change his style," said Kerr. "That was the idea. Perry Como, singing his usual style with a Nashville musical background."[39]

Como took to Nashville as if he had been recording there all his life. Kerr found him "relaxed, pleasant and quite at home," although as ever, there was little social interaction between him and the musicians. The title of the album was *The Scene Changes,* with the subtitle *Perry Goes to Nashville.* Atkins came up with a blend of songs, mixing new material such as "Stand Beside Me" and "My Own Peculiar Way," with more established country songs such as "Funny How Time Slips Away" and "I Really Don't Want to Know." RCA issued another of the new songs, "Dream On (Little Dreamer)," as a single that to everyone's surprise reached #25 in the *Billboard* charts during a six-week stay in May and June 1965.[40] The album was a gem, Como in excellent voice and the sound engineering superb. It also benefited from Sholes' insistence that Como go to Nashville. While other singers such as Vic Damone, Frank Sinatra, Dean Martin, and even Bing Crosby were importing country and western arrangers around this time, Como's *The Scene Changes* was perhaps the only album by a mainstream vocalist to capture the Nashville sound. Reviewer Morgan Ames summed it up: "Como fits himself perfectly into the groove. He carefully takes on the Nashville flavor and inflections without warping his own style a bit. All this is done, of course, with his usual ease, as though it required no effort at all. If you want an example of the best that Nashville can do, why settle for less than this album?"[41]

Como returned to Nashville in June 1965 and recorded seven more sides with the Anita Kerr Singers. What looked like the beginnings of a solid musical partnership, however, never came to pass. The planned follow-up album to *The Scene Changes* was never completed and of the seven tracks that Como recorded with Kerr, only two, "Summer Wind" and "Oowee Oowee," saw release as a single late in 1965. The rest remained unreleased for 40 years. By the end of the year, Anita Kerr's career had taken a change of course with a move to Hollywood, and subsequently to Switzerland. She would never record with Como again.

The Scene Changes brought Perry Como back to life as a recording artist. During December 1965 and February–March 1966, he was back in the RCA studios in New York for the first of a dozen albums that he would record with Nick Perito over the next twenty years. Once again, the project placed Como in a different musical setting. On *Lightly Latin,* Perry Como embraced the bossa nova, recording twelve songs by Latin composers. The music of Antonio Carlos Jobim dominated the album, which also offered a home for Como's Latin treatment of Johnny Mandel's "The Shadow of Your Smile" plus his first Lennon and McCartney song, "Yesterday." RCA's marketing described the album as "a perfect matching of man to music" and with Como singing at his softest throughout the sessions, the statement was directly on the mark. *Lightly Latin* provided further proof that Como's vocal skills were undiminished, although once again it proved to be Como's one and only venture into a new genre.

Despite the quality of *The Scene Changes* and *Lightly Latin,* Perry Como in 1966 was a declining force in the music business. His TV contract with Kraft had one more year to run but when it expired, Como's only other TV shows in 1967 and 1968 were his annual Christmas shows. He continued to record, completing three more albums between 1966 and the middle of 1968, including an album of Italian love songs that Como flew to Rome to record in May 1966. He also rode along on a batch of ill-fitting singles that went nowhere. In England, the popularity that Como had enjoyed just a few years before seemed almost to disappear overnight. Most of his RCA albums were deleted and by the time he recorded "Look to Your Heart" in 1968 (the album that Nick Perito thought was his best ever), Decca Records, who distributed RCA in the U.K., decided that a U.K. release was not worthwhile. "Whatever happened to Perry Como?" was the question for a while, but soon it seemed that nobody cared.

Nor seemingly did Perry. He spent most of his time in Florida, walking, fishing, golfing and supervising the construction of a new home. He seemed content. Nevertheless, he was still a performer at heart. Deep down, a flame was still burning. It seemed, however, that as the ultimate symbol of fifties America, he would be one of the highest profile casualties of the sixties revolution. Como still had his fan base and still received fan mail, but most people would have subscribed to a view that his best days were yester. Then a song called "It's Impossible" changed Perry Como's life once more.

Chapter 13

It's Impossible

THE 48 DAYS FROM MAY 5 TO JUNE 22, 1970, transformed Perry Como from a retired Floridian into an international superstar once more. No one saw it coming, least of all Mr. C. The recording work that he had always been able to fall back on had now become no more than an occasional return to the RCA studios. Indeed, before the company scheduled a session in New York in May 1970, his previous session had been almost a year ago, in June 1969. That session had not been a productive one and none of the three titles he recorded that day ever saw release. His last set of issued recordings had come in the autumn of 1968 from a visit to Nashville, where he recorded two songs for release as a single. The titles were "Seattle," based on the instrumental theme used in the TV series *Here Come the Brides,* and "Sunshine Wine." "Seattle" was a bright, perky number, with a brassy arrangement by Bill McElhiney that gave the song a different sound from Como's previous Nashville outings. "Sunshine Wine" was written by Cindy Walker, whose many credits included the Roy Orbison hit "Dream Baby (How Long Must I Dream)" and Jim Reeves' "Distant Drums." With the TV series driving it along, "Seattle" was a minor hit for Como, reaching #38 in the *Billboard* Hot 100. It also served as the title track for a June 1969 album that pulled together an eclectic mix of Como's late sixties recordings.

The October '68 session was one of several that RCA labeled as "Nashville," after his first visit there in 1965. Whether Como actually traveled to Nashville for the sessions is unclear. It seems unlikely that he would have flown to Nashville on October 10, 1968, to record just two sides, particularly when he was in the RCA studios in New York just three days earlier. More likely is that Chet Atkins put together the backing tracks in Nashville, with Como over-dubbing his vocals in New York. "Seattle" brought Perry his first modest success with a single since "Dream On" in 1965. In between, he had recorded a handful of other singles that made little commercial impact. These included two pleasant but relatively weak Christmas songs, two gentle ballads called "What Love Is Made Of" and "A World of Love" plus such ill-fitting up-tempo songs as "Stop! And Think It Over" and "Another Go Round." All the sessions were stop-start affairs, with a number of other titles recorded but never released. Andy Wiswell, recently arrived at RCA from Capitol Records, had taken over the production responsibilities for Como's New York sessions, and while Perry seemed comfortable with his album work with Wiswell, the attempts to find a hit single looked like he was pursuing a lost cause.

When Como arrived at RCA's Studio A in New York on May 5, 1970, it was with neither enthusiasm nor expectation. He had five songs lined up for him over the next two days, but what greeted him was an unfamiliar environment. The studio was the same but none of the musicians contracted for the session had been there during his great days in the fifties, nor had he worked with either the producer, Ernie Altschuler, or the arranger, Marty Manning, before. Altschuler had recently arrived at RCA as Division Vice President and Executive Artists and Repertoire Producer from Columbia Records where he had enjoyed a long and successful career, working alongside Tony Bennett, Ray Conniff and Johnny Mathis. When Columbia sold its soul to rock, he sought pastures new. Altschuler tempted Manning to make the move with him. Manning was a highly respected musician who had won a Grammy in 1962 for his arrangement of Tony Bennett's "I Left My Heart in San Francisco." His new career at RCA was destined to be cut short by his sudden death in 1971.

The five songs slated for Como included a new piece by Neil Sedaka and Howard Greenfield called "Love Is Spreading over the World." The song's strongest feature was that it was overtly contemporary, with its hippy-esque pleas for love and brotherhood playing to a strong beat. It required Como to sing in an unusual, clipped style that sounded neither convincing nor comfortable. RCA nevertheless released the song immediately as a single to tie in with Como's upcoming Las Vegas debut, where Perry featured it in his stage act. The flip side to the single was "Don't Leave Me," a Harry Nilsson song that required Como to insert some "oh-ohhs" into his singing. Despite Perry's vocal versatility, neither song suited his natural style.

The first of the three remaining titles was "Turn Around," a different song from "Turnaround" that Como had recorded in 1968; the 1970 song never saw release. "Long Life, Lots of Happiness," Como's second song on the May 5 session, was never more than a B-side record. As the afternoon wore on, Como came to the third song lined up for that day.

"It's Impossible" was an anachronism. The song was a ballad, with a simple love message that might have been at home in the forties. What made it different was Sid Wayne's lyric, written to a melody by the prolific Mexican composer Canache Armando Manzanero. Wayne's lyric cleverly crafted the song's title into a repetitive phrase that provided the "hook" that all successful singles need. Manning's arrangement too was a blend of old and new. He mixed a predominant strings section with a Fender and conga drum beat to create a sound that was sympathetic to the song's message, but undeniably modern. Often with singers of Como's vintage, the record company would add the words "Newly Recorded" to new records to distinguish them from back catalogue reissues. With "It's Impossible," there was no need. The recording doffed its hat to the principles of the forties but was undeniably a seventies creation. It was perfect for Como.

When Perry first heard the song, he thought it pleasant but not much more. "The funny thing is when I first heard the tune, I wasn't really choked up about it, but Ernie Altschuler insisted I record it," he later told George Simon. "Then it began to grow on me and so the next week, I went back in the studio and did just one more take to the orchestra track. And you know, to this day, I'm not sure which one of my takes they released."[1] Como's memory let him down slightly because the gap between takes was one day rather than a week. Both takes were ultimately released, the "alternate" appearing on a 1992 CD compilation. The mystery as to which take was used for the single was never officially resolved, although it is almost certain that it was the second take. Como's vocal on the alternate is more tentative and is that of a singer feeling his way with a new song. It is inconceivable that Como could have recorded the hit take with such confidence and then gone back the following day to produce a version so obviously lacking in familiarity.

When the single appeared in November 1970, it broke all the established rules in the music business. RCA saw most of Como's value as being in his back catalogue and their promotion of his new material was minimal. Como himself sang the song only once on TV before it became a hit (*The Flip Wilson Show* in October 1970). That a sentimental ballad could challenge George Harrison, Elton John and Santana for a place in the charts seemed, well, impossible. Yet from the minute that people started hearing the song, things began to happen. Como's first indication that he had something came from his family. "My daughter was the first one to say 'Boy, that's really good.' I couldn't figure out why. But the kids in our neighborhood came out and said 'Well, we're finally glad you made it to our list.' I didn't know what they were talking about. They have all kind of Top 40s. How they grabbed onto this is a little beyond me."[2] Later, Como rationalized the record's success as due to the "simplicity" both of the song and his vocal, which was classic Como. His diction and tender reading of the lyric are perfect and his vocal range and breath control undiminished.

The song entered the U.S. charts in December 1970 and gave Como his first top ten hit since 1958. In England, the impact was even greater. When the press began to carry stories of Perry Como's return to the U.S. charts, a bandwagon started to roll. Britain's *New Musical Express* reviewed the disc in December and said, "'It's Impossible'? No, it's not, even for 58 year-old Perry. This beautiful ballad could be the surprise hit of 1971. It has everything."[3] The disc entered the U.K. charts on the strength of pre-release sales alone, a phenomenon normally reserved for the Beatles. It peaked at #2, with George Harrison's "My Sweet Lord" the only thing that stood between Como and his first #1 hit since "Magic Moments." "It's Impossible" became a standard, recorded by many of Como's peers, and a hit around the world. Como seldom made a live appearance without bowing to the clamor to feature the song.

"It's Impossible" complemented the second element of Como's resurgence that had begun seven weeks after his recording session in May 1970. On June 22, 1970, he opened a three-week season at the International Hotel, Las Vegas. The notion of Como appearing live at the nation's undisputed gambling capital was almost as unlikely as a return to the Top Ten in the charts. His last nightclub appearance had been at the Meadowbrook Club in New Jersey in 1947, 23 years before. Between 1954 and 1966, Como did not appear before a live audience in any setting other than the small studio audience who watched the broadcast of his weekly TV show. The first signs of a re-awakening of interest in performing live had come after Como returned from Italy in 1966 and agreed to an eight-week summer tour of the various state fairs throughout the Midwest and Canada. Playing venues such as the Allentown Fair in Pennsylvania, the Wisconsin Fair in Milwaukee and the Kansas State Fair in Topeka, the dates were significant only in that they re-acquainted Como with the stage.

The calls from Las Vegas had continued to come Como's way ever since he had first turned down the chance to appear there in 1953. During the sixties, Vegas continued to grow and to broaden its appeal, away from the seediness that was often associated with its gambling roots. New hotels sprang up all the time and in 1969, the International Hotel opened its doors. Barbra Streisand played its opening night, followed by 58 consecutive sold-out shows by Elvis Presley. When the International offered Como $100,000 per week for a two-shows-a-night, three-week contract, it was too good to turn down. (One newspaper article in 1972 made the point that Como's earnings were exactly $99,250 more than his first nightclub appearance at the Copacabana in 1943.[4])

Como was nervous about the opening. As one way of easing his nerves, Nick Perito and Ray Charles threw themselves into the challenge of getting an act together with a program of songs that they knew Como liked. Ray Charles also wrote a special piece of material called "I Can Almost Read Your Mind." The song put into words what Como thought his audience might be thinking, poking gentle fun at virtually every aspect of his own image. Charles later explained that the idea for the song came from "If They Could See Me Now," the Dorothy Fields–Cy Coleman hit from *Sweet Charity*. Charles' original plan was to use the same melody and put his Como-words to it. He called Fields, who said the idea was fine so long as Como sang a chorus of the original lyric first. "That was no good," said Charles, so instead he "wrote the song upside down. Where the original melody went up, I went down."[5] Como loved it, not just the re-working of the melody but the pulling apart of his own image. The song became a standard for most of his live appearances right through until his final appearance in Ireland in 1994.

Perito recalled that Como had his own technique for dealing with the Las Vegas audiences, who had a reputation for boisterousness. "If on a given night he felt there was too much noise in the room, instead of singing louder, he would do just the opposite and sing softer," Perito wrote. "At first, I thought this was a bad idea, but I soon learned that his theory worked perfectly. At every performance, he, together with the Ray Charles Singers, would stand at the very front of the stage and sing a lovely ballad without microphones. Naturally, the orchestra had to play very softly behind them. The effect was fantastic."[6] Como's repertoire included old favorites such as "Without a Song" and "Prisoner of Love" alongside newer material such as "If I Had a Hammer" and Harry Nilsson's "Everybody's Talkin.'" Como even included a "Sing to Me, Mr. C" medley which pulled his 1945 hit "When You Were Sweet Sixteen" alongside Jimmy Webb's contemporary "Didn't We?" Como sang the latter with just Perito's piano to accompany him, a setting that offers no hiding place for a singer. His vocals, night after night, were immaculate. Como ended his act with a rousing "You'll Never Walk Alone," and apart from taking an additional breath in the penultimate line, there was no hint of any diminution of his vocal range. John L. Scott in *The Los Angeles Times* said, "You could shut your eyes and revert to those 'good old days' when Como, Sinatra and Crosby dominated the popular vocal scene."[7]

Como's opening night drew a strong celebrity presence to the 1,500 strong audience, with Bob Hope, Andy Williams, Ray Bolger and the Mills Brothers among those present. One backstage visitor during Como's stay was Elvis Presley. He and Como were still RCA's top two selling recording stars. Both Charles and Perito said Elvis, free from his entourage of sycophants and hangers-on, was a "charming, humble and courteous young man"[8] who was "very much in awe of Perry."[9] Mickey Glass's recollection, however, was of a stranger side to Presley. "He just sat there and stared at us for a while and that was it," he said.[10]

The buzz that Como got from performing for a live audience quickly cast away his nerves. "After his first song, he realized that he was starting out on a new live-performance career," Nick Perito wrote. "People of all ages packed the showroom night after night and he was a smash."[11] Como said later that he had enjoyed Vegas, to a point. "I enjoyed the first show, but not the second. Singing at 2:00 in the morning is not for me," he told Phil Donahue in 1979.[12] Nevertheless, Mickey Glass said that Como had liked the whole experience, playing golf during the day, gambling a little (unless he started winning, in which case a crowd would gather), and taking a nap between shows. It wasn't hard work, said Glass, and of course, the money was very good.[13]

Perry's first live album that captured his Las Vegas debut in 1970.

Como returned to Vegas for another three-week season in November 1970, by which time it was apparent that "It's Impossible" had indeed done the impossible. RCA, who had released a live album of Como's first Vegas show, was keen to have a studio album to which they could attach the hit single. With Como tied to Nevada for three weeks, there was no chance of putting some album sessions together in New York until December at the earliest, so the showroom at the International Hotel doubled as a recording studio. There, Como recorded nine contemporary titles including "Snowbird," George Harrison's "Something" and the Carpenters' hit "We've Only Just Begun" to join the *It's Impossible* album.

Don Costa, best known for his arrangements for Frank Sinatra, was a long-time friend of Nick Perito and had produced the Las Vegas live album. He took the same role for the November sessions, with Perito conducting. Although the album was put together hurriedly, it showed that Como was able to adjust his style to contemporary songs as he doffed his cap to the Carpenters, Simon & Garfunkel and the Beatles. One British review of the LP, which was a big seller on both sides of the Atlantic, said, "This is a GREAT album for those who like relaxed, happy singing by a truly excellent singer, albeit he has been off the scene for so long."[14]

The RCA recording executives realized that if Como was not to be a one-hit-wonder, at least in this phase of his career, they needed a follow up to "It's Impossible." The song they chose was "I Think of You," a Rod McKuen lyric to a Francis Lai melody. As with "Impossible," Como had two stabs at the song, recording it first in New York in January 1971 before over-dubbing a second vocal in Hollywood the following month. Now with a greater expectation of some chart success, Como also began work straight away on the *I Think of You* album, continuing his association with Don Costa and again tiptoeing through the contemporary song catalogue. "I Think of You" didn't quite repeat the success of "It's Impossible," but it reached #53 in the U.S. charts and #14 in England. When the *I Think of You* album appeared, Morgan Ames in *High Fidelity* not only praised a fine collection of recordings but also observed that Como had grown with his resurgence. "He's taken on some difficult songs here (all sensitive and fitting to his style, as usual) such as 'Where Do I Begin' and 'For All We Know' (the new one, not the standard), and 'Yesterday I Heard the Rain,'" the reviewer added. "Mr. Como's intonation and phrasing are warm and burnished. It all sounds as effortless as ever. Paul Simon's 'Bridge over Troubled Water' takes on new maturity and comfort in Mr. Como's reading."[15]

Ames' observations were perceptive, as were those of Greer Johnson in the sleeve note to the album. Both talked about a "new Perry Como." The concept was more than just a marketing line. By 1970, many of Como's singing peers were still struggling to come to terms with the new music scene that had developed in the Beatles' wake. Frank Sinatra, Tony Bennett, Johnny Mathis *et al.* all visited the same material as Como for early seventies albums, but few adjusted their vocal style the way Como did. This flexibility was the same that had allowed Perry to find an accommodation with the novelty material of the fifties. Again, Como recognized that he needed to change both the way he sang and what he sang. In the era of syncopation and swing that dominated pre-rock music, most singers had learned to sing slightly behind the beat. The technique sat at the heart of Bing Crosby's style and most singers copied it. When Frank Sinatra developed an alternative style, one element of it was to sing on the beat, leading the orchestra rather than following it. Now in the seventies, the construction of songs was markedly different from the pre-rock days, with Latin and Cuban rhythms a strong influence. New singers were pitching their vocals slightly ahead of the beat and it was this technique that Como took on board, most evidently in some of the songs he recorded for his *And I Love You So* album in 1973. Of his peers, only Andy Williams made a similar adjustment. The approach of others, including both Sinatra and a still active Crosby, attempted to retrofit the new songs into the vocal styles with which they had grown up. As a result, contemporary material seldom sat comfortably with them.

The resurgence of Perry Como was especially strong in Great Britain. Ever since his visit in 1960, the BBC had harbored hopes that Como might return to make a show purely for British consumption. His return to the charts provided the perfect opportunity. Jack Katz negotiated a deal with the BBC and Como duly flew to London in May 1971.[16] There, he filmed an appearance on the BBC TV pop music show *Top of the Pops*, before recording a one-hour special for the network. The show went out in Britain on May 19, 1971, with the BBC filming a separate Christmas ending to the show for a festive season repeat.

By the time Christmas came around, however, Como's thoughts were a million miles away from his spring visit to London. On his return from England, he had taken a couple of months off from his heaviest work schedule for some years before heading to Las Vegas in July for another three-week stint. There, a kidney stone attack interrupted Como's generally robust good health and saw him admitted to the Sunshine Hospital in Vegas on August 2. It caused him to miss the last week of his engagement at the International Hotel. The problem resolved, Como headed to Lake Tahoe, making his debut at Harrah's on August 19 and playing there for two weeks.

Como's next stop was California to film a Christmas show for NBC. *Perry Como's Winter Show* would be his first holiday special for three years. With Art Carney and Mitzi Gaynor lined up as guests, filming was set for October 9–11 at NBC's Burbank studios. It turned out to be one of the most catastrophic times of Como's life. Buz Kohan, who was one of the writers on the show, described what happened. "There was a scene where Perry was walking between two rectangular columns lying on the floor, and they were supposed to come together to form a single path. What happened next is subject to debate but the result was the columns came together on cue, perhaps too soon for Perry to clear them, and he was caught in between them and tripped and injured his leg quite seriously."[17]

For producer Bob Finkel, the accident was an unhappy return to working with Perry. After the fall, Finkel accompanied Como to a local hospital, where x-rays apparently showed no serious damage. With his leg in a makeshift cast, Como returned to the set the next day and completed the taping of the show, albeit with some imaginative scene changes that disguised his loss of mobility. By then, Como's knee had swollen to twice its normal size. Perry immediately chartered a plane home to Florida where he was admitted to the Good Samaritan Hospital in West Palm Beach. Doctors there discovered that Como's knee was broken in a complex and serious way. He spent the next eight months with his leg in a cast. "I almost went out of my mind," Como said in November 1972. "What the hell can you do for eight months in a cast? I watched television. I mean everything—*Guiding Light, General Hospital, As the World Turns*, all those goodies. I was like that comedian who said he was so hung up on TV that he watched the test patterns when the station went off the air. I even watched that little dot that disappears when you turn off the set."[18]

Aside from Como's physical discomfort, the accident also had an unpleasant aftertaste. Como sued NBC for $1 million damages. When the case came to court, Bob Finkel was called to give evidence. He testified that Como had been told to make sure that he was in a certain spot. He had not been on his mark and the injury was the result.[19] When Como heard about the testimony, he called Finkel and accused him of telling untruths. Finkel said that he had described the event as he had seen it, but Como was unhappy. By then, the two of them had worked together on two more shows, but Como did not speak to Bob Finkel for another 15 years. (When he did, it was at the funeral of Nick Vanoff in 1991. Como's presence at the ceremony in Los Angeles was unexpected, but when he saw Finkel in the congregation Como came up and "started speaking as though nothing had ever happened.")[20] Como's case against NBC rumbled through the court system until a superior court in California finally awarded Perry damages of $257,509 in November 1977.

Como's convalescence put his comeback firmly on hold. A three-week booking in Las Vegas for November 1971 had to be cancelled, with Ann-Margret taking Como's place. It was July 1972 before Perry was fit to resume performing. Como's period of incapacity was a frustrating one, for both him and his family. Golf was impossible and fishing was severely curtailed. "I could swing myself into the boat at normal tide; at low tide, forget it," he said.[21] Son David recalled that Como hated being housebound and with Roselle looking after Perry 24 hours a day, it was a difficult time for everyone.[22] When Como finally had the cast removed from his leg, he was horrified by what he saw. His leg, he said, looked "like a water pipe—and my legs have always looked like they were put on backwards."[23] So began an equally long and boring period of rehabilitation.

Despite the pleas of some booking agents who wanted to see Perry on stage with a cane, Como waited until he had most of his normal mobility before returning to the stage. The accident had done nothing to dim his renewed zeal for live performing and he returned to the renamed Hilton Hotel in Vegas for a three-week stint in July and August 1972. When he did, the ill luck and acrimony that had dogged him for the past nine months seemed to continue. As part of a revised act for Como's return, Ray Charles put together a medley of songs written by female writers for the Ray Charles Singers' solo spot in the show. One of the songs was "Wanted," one of Como's major hits, written by Lois Steele. Como accused Charles of doing his song and insisted that he take it out of the medley. Charles had to write a new closing number, and have it orchestrated and choreographed in no time at all. Como also took issue with the marquee outside the hotel that gave billing to Charles' Singers as well as Como. In a rare display of temper, Como fired his long-time choral director. The estrangement lasted for some weeks until a mystified Charles wrote to Como seeking an explanation, at which point Como called him and the two resumed their vocal partnership.[24] Charles was sympathetic in his recollection of the incident. "He was still suffering from the fall," he said.[25]

The reviews for Como's return to the stage were as though he had never been away. He followed up his stint in Vegas with a three-week engagement at Harrah's at Lake Tahoe and took on two TV commitments before the end of 1972, including another *Perry Como Winter Show*. CBS screened the show, which took sixth place in the Nielsen ratings for the first week of December, with an audience share of 42 percent. Bob Finkel was the executive producer of the show (this was before he was called to give evidence about Perry's fall), although many of the plaudits went to the writing team of Saul Turtlebaub and Bernie Ornstein. *Variety* said, "All of the festivities were permeated with that ingratiating warmth that the star projects so effortlessly. The hour had a brisk pace despite Como's casualness and got exceptional mileage out of the set, which served as a teaser at the outset of the hour then, by the magic of editing, progressed by sections from a bare stage to a completely believable town for the unique finale under the closing credit crawl."[26]

Perry Como's career was back on two of the three fronts that he had opened up since "It's Impossible." Strangely, the one dimension of his career that he could have sustained from a wheelchair—recording—remained untouched. By the time he and the family spent Christmas 1972 in Lake Tahoe, Como playing a two-week Christmas–New Year season, he had not ventured into a recording studio for 18 months. A call from Chet Atkins took Como back to Nashville. Atkins told Perry that he had a song that thought he should hear. Its title was "And I Love You So."

Chapter 14

The Barber Comes to Town

WHEN CHET ATKINS HEARD *TAPESTRY*, the debut album of a young singer-songwriter called Don McLean, one song leapt out. Atkins called Perry Como and told him that he had a song that he thought was ideally suited. McLean had written the song in 1969, two years before another of his songs, "American Pie," catapulted him to stardom. "American Pie" was an enigmatic mix of autobiography and eulogy (to Buddy Holly). It became a rock anthem. "And I Love You So" was a complete contrast. With a similar message to "It's Impossible," it was a conventional love song, written with four verses and a chorus that repeated twice. Like "Wind Beneath My Wings" which Como would come to late in his career, "And I Love You So" was a song just waiting for the right singer to make it a hit.

Como first recorded Don McLean's ballad on January 17, 1973, in Nashville, redubbing his vocal two days later for the version that RCA released on a single. The recording was one of 12 that Como made during a week in the Nashville studios, working on each of five consecutive days. As on previous visits, Chet Atkins produced the sessions, with Cam Mullins arranging and conducting. Mullins had worked with Como in 1965, playing in the brass section on Como's first Nashville sessions. The 12 titles that Como recorded that week were intended for an album that would take *And I Love You So* as the title.

The planned album was similar in concept to *The Scene Changes* with many new and unfamiliar songs, although musically, it lacked the simplicity that Atkins and Anita Kerr had brought to the 1965 LP. When the album did eventually appear, it was much different from the one that Atkins had in mind. The reason was that RCA quickly realized that "And I Love You So" was set to do what "It's Impossible" had done two years before. With the likelihood of another massive Como hit, their thinking changed and Como returned to Nashville in March to record six more titles. This time the songs were well known, most of them already hits by other artists. By including them in the album at the expense of some of the less familiar titles, RCA strengthened its mainstream pop credentials. It was the same formula that had worked so well with the *It's Impossible* album in 1971.

"And I Love You So" entered the U.S. charts in May 1973, reaching #29 in the all-songs listings, but topping the easy listening charts. In England, the impact was once again measurably greater. There, the single reached #3 in the British chart. Once again, Britain was Como-mad. It prompted RCA to pull another song, "For the Good Times," from the album as a follow-up single. That song also scored in the Top 10, reaching #7.[1]

In Australia, where "It's Impossible" had been only a minor hit, the two singles reached #2 and #5 respectively. With releases in France, Germany and Japan, plus a specially recorded version in Spanish, "And I Love You So" became a worldwide hit.

The *And I Love You So* album appeared later in the year. The additional titles that Como recorded included "Killing Me Softly with His (Her) Song" (a song about the impact that a Don McLean concert had on folk singer Lori Lieberman). Roberta Flack had made the song a hit. Como also offered his versions of the Carpenters' "Sing," Dawn's "Tie a Yellow Ribbon" and Bread's "Aubrey." The four new songs included "I Want to Give," which RCA released in England as the third single to come from the album, reaching #31 in the chart. Como was by now one of the most popular artists in Great Britain, as three hit singles from the same ten-song album demonstrated.

Perry Como was a 61-year-old grandfather who was outperforming names such as Donny Osmond and David Bowie. How did he do it? Morgan Ames, reviewing *And I Love You So* for *High Fidelity,* said that Como succeeded with contemporary songs because "he chooses extremely well and appears to like what he sings."[2] Ames also added that an equally important factor was that "Como has always been inordinately true to his material," contrasting Perry with other singers who "put style ahead of song.... One cannot be stylish with today's songs. Como has no fixed style. That is his style."[3] Another frequent question was what motivated Como to keep going? A British newspaper ran a headline *Como at 60: The Old Master of Pop.* In it, Como was quoted as saying that what kept him going was emotion. "You've no idea of the charge I get, knowing that people like my work enough to buy the records and put them in the charts."[4] The RIAA eventually certified *And I Love You So* as a Gold album in 1976, although its sales were into millions long before. Its success gave Como a renewed interest in recording. "There were eight years where I didn't record hardly at all," he told a BBC interviewer in December 1973. "I was doing other things. I forgot the most important thing—and I think recording is the most important thing."[5]

Yet despite his best intentions, "And I Love You So" was the last time that Perry Como climbed to the summit of the recording mountain. A follow up session to the album in Nashville in August 1973 proved abortive. Of seven titles recorded, only two saw release. "Walk Right Back," Como's U.S. follow-up single to "And I Love You So," was an odd choice and made no impact. The song had been a hit for the Everly Brothers in 1961, but Como's version was a poor cover, with Perry sounding tired and lethargic. His U.K. slipstream was strong enough to take it to #33 in the charts over there, but most observers felt that Como had missed an opportunity. When he arrived in London in November 1973 to promote the single, Pete Murray was one of several interviewers who politely raised an eyebrow. "I have the final say," said Perry. "I liked it because it was happy. I was getting into a groove with soft material. This is a little more up-tempo."[6] It was neither a convincing description of the disc nor Como's rationale for choosing it. If Como had indeed had the final say, "Walk Right Back" was yet another example of why he should have stuck to singing and trusted others to pick his songs.

Como's winter trip to London combined the promotion of the single with a guest spot on a special hosted by Julie Andrews featuring the popular *Sesame Street* characters. Since his leg injury in 1971, Como had taken a long time to recover fully his mobility. Many of his spots in his previous outing, *Cole Porter in Paris,* showed him sitting down. The show aired in January 1973 but Como was then absent from the screens until his *Sesame Street* appearance in November. A third *Perry Como Winter Show* took sixth place in the Nielsen ratings for its week in December, although *Variety* saw little merit

With Julie Andrews for the TV special *Julie on Sesame Street* shown on November 23, 1973.

in the show. "With tight money and the energy crisis, one wonders why CBS and Kraft didn't simply run last year's Perry Como Christmas Show," it said.[7] It took Perry Como two years to regain fully the momentum behind his career after his accident. It was no surprise. Aside from the physical problems he encountered, he was in his sixties and had re-set his lifestyle for a gradual slide into retirement. Then, seemingly from nowhere, he was selling four million records a year and found himself in greater demand than any time since his weekly TV days had ended.

There was no doubt too that his accident had aged him. In an interview with *Stereo Review Magazine* in 1974, Como complained about getting old. "I don't mind being 62, I just don't like to look and feel 62," he said.[8] Interviewer Robert Windeler added that Como had never felt his age until the accident in 1971. The wiry Italian hair was still thick and a little longer but what had once been a steely grey was largely white. His features, which had always been sharp and Roman, now took on a more avuncular appearance. Yet, despite passing 40 years in the business, Como was not ready to quit. Indeed, his rediscovered love of performing motivated him to find ways of turning the aging process to his advantage. Rather than seek to deny the inevitable, Como incorporated it into his act and his persona. "The legs go first," became a standard line as Como sat on his trademark stool; then he would pause and say, "Well, second."

Como entered 1974 with a heavy workload ahead of him. After the abortive sessions in Nashville the previous year, Perry started 1974 with two recording sessions in New York. Ultimately, they would lead to an album simply called *Perry*. The project sought to bring some of the flavor of Nashville to New York, although its producer, Pete Spargo (another debutante with Como), had a background in jazz and Latin arrangements. Como recorded four titles for the album in January, returning to New York for two more sessions in late April and early May when he added the six more songs that made up the 10-track LP. The album was a mix of material and styles. Overt country songs such as "Behind Closed Doors" and "The Most Beautiful Girl," both Charlie Rich covers, sat alongside contemporary material such as "The Way We Were," a song that fitted Como like a glove, and "You Are the Sunshine of My Life." Como also included an updated arrangement of his 1946 hit, "Temptation." Reviewer Peter Reilly picked "I Don't Know What He Told You" as the standout song on the album. Como had attempted it twice previously in Nashville under the title "He Couldn't Love You More." Now, with a gentle Latin beat, Como produced the definitive version. "The singing of it is so masterfully relaxed, the dramatic punches so underplayed, and the mood so much more a wistful regret than whining complaint," Reilly wrote, contrasting Como's delivery with "the teary breast beating" that some of his peers would have given it.[9]

On television, Como's resurgence brought him his first term sponsorship deal since his Kraft contract ended in 1967. Early in 1974, Como signed with General Telephone & Electronics (GTE), plus their lighting subsidiary GTE Sylvania, to do six specials over two years, a deal that Como subsequently extended. The shows all continued the travel theme that had been a part of Como's Kraft specials in 1964–65, with the first show, *The Perry Como Sunshine Show*, going out over Easter 1974. That show re-acquainted Perry with Nick Vanoff, whose direction and production was hailed by *Variety* as "an example of how it's done at its best."[10] John J. O'Connor, writing in *The New York Times*, compared Como with the recently "un-retired" Frank Sinatra, saying that Como had "survived with physique and voice considerably more intact."[11]

Como's shows with GTE over the next two years included a *Perry Como's Summer of '74*, a *Springtime Special* in 1975, *Perry Como's Christmas in Mexico* (1975) and *Perry Como's Hawaiian Holiday* (1976). Como also combined his fondness for Nashville with his TV work, using the city as the venue for *Como Country: Perry and his Nashville Friends*, for which the guest list read like a who's-who of country music. Reviews and ratings for the GTE shows were good. The first show in 1974 had topped the Nielsen ratings for the week that it was aired, and *Christmas in Mexico* captured 47 percent of the viewing audience. It was also the top rated music show for all of 1975.[12] *Variety* said that the show "was exceptional, a visual and aural treat."[13] Highlighting the work of producer Bob Banner, the magazine said that its "outstanding achievement ... was maintaining the authentic Mexican flavor throughout."[14]

Como had begun working with Bob Banner earlier in 1975 on his *Lake Tahoe Holiday Special* and continued to work with him until 1982. Banner introduced Como to his associate Stephen Pouliot later that year and with Banner as executive producer, Pouliot filled a variety of writing, directing and producing roles on the Como specials during the Banner years. Pouliot recalled that he and Banner "always tried to bring the feeling of a big screen musical to the small screen."[15] The production of the shows was an expansive—and expensive—affair. Typically, each of the shows ran to a budget of around half a million dollars, including Como's fee. Local promotional deals from airlines, hotels and local tourist boards offset some of the costs. Como was treated like a global ambassador when he arrived at a location, with a tour of the area and often a civic reception.[16]

Pouliot's recollection was that Perry was not particularly interested in seeing the sights, but went along anyway. Cecil Smith, interviewing Como for a *Los Angeles Times* piece in 1976, said that Como "crosses the street with reluctance," while Bob Banner described Como as an "at home kinda guy who liked to fish and eat at Denny's."[17] He took little interest, said Banner, in where he was, relying on Mickey Glass to accompany him and make sure he caught the right plane to the right place. Even then, there were some surprises. Banner said that during the filming of the 1975 Christmas special in Santa Fe, New Mexico, Como mistook the location for Mexico, telling Glass that he "needed to get this bag fixed when we get back to the States."[18] Nevertheless, Como said in a press interview that he enjoyed the location work and the travel, telling Cecil Smith of the *Los Angeles Times* that he was looking forward to his upcoming trip to Hawaii because he had never been before.[19] "People stare at me and say 'You've never been to Hawaii?' I tell them that I'm from Pittsburgh, but it doesn't seem to help," said Como.[20] He went on to say he was enjoying his current batch of traveling shows because they weren't rushed. Banner's use of a 16mm portable camera brought a flexibility that Como said you "didn't get with tape" and he thought that the production maximized the impact of the backdrops without the shows "ever looking like travelogues."[21]

Como's mid-seventies shows introduced him to a new generation of guest stars. During his weekly heyday, his guests had largely been his show business contemporaries, plus the occasional new rock 'n' roll name. Now, his lists included emerging talent such as Rich Little, the Carpenters and Olivia Newton-John, alongside more established names such as Ann-Margret and Petula Clark. Stephen Pouliot recalled that finding guests for the specials was not as easy as filling Como's roster had been in the fifties. Many of the people he approached, he said, were unwilling to appear because Como had refused guest spots on their shows. Como's elder statesman image was also a turn-off for some guests that he targeted. One pop singer with a reputation built on songs of protest and challenge laughed out loud at the idea when Pouliot called, before saying "No."[22]

Rich Little did two shows with Como in 1974 and 1976. He was typical of the new generation of stars who approached the shows with a mixture of awe and trepidation, but soon found that Como put the newcomers at ease. "Everyone liked him and found the set very relaxed. When Perry entered a room, people approached him easily, in contrast to the Sinatras and Crosbys of this world where they were in awe and tended to hold back."[23] As an impressionist, Little studied Como closely for his act. Perry, he said, loved the impression although he complained that Little's mimic of his singing voice was "too nasal." As well as mimicking Como's voice, Little also looked for other mannerisms that Como displayed. He was, said Little, "a toucher—constantly fidgeting with his face or his guest's clothes."[24]

Although Como's American renaissance was remarkable, his resurgence in England was even more so. The strength of his comeback there was directly proportional to the extent of his disappearance after the BBC stopped taking his weekly shows. When Como hit the charts again, a generation of British listeners had never heard of him. The British music press found that the best way of describing him was as "the Andy Williams of the late '50s,"[25] a curious juxtaposition of master and apprentice. Nevertheless, the effect was to bring a new band of younger fans to Como's door, alongside those who had been Como fans since the fifties.

There had been talk of Como returning to Britain for some live appearances ever since his BBC special in 1971. Finally, Como committed to a British stage appearance that came in May 1974. Perry flew to London to top the bill at a *Stars in a Gala Mid-*

night Charity Show at the London Palladium. The show raised money for the Variety Club's children's charities. Como delivered his Las Vegas act, updated to include some of the songs from his new *Perry* album. The reviews were outstanding. James Green in the *London Evening News* described Perry's performance as "superbly professional."[26] Brian Mulligan in *Music Week* said, "It was the sheer professionalism of his performance that sticks in the mind, the impeccable phrasing, the tonal purity contrasted with an unexpected robustness, and the ease and assurance with which he hit and held the high notes."[27] Como opened the show so late that he said "Good Morning" rather than "Good Evening" when he walked out on stage. He left at 3:00 A.M., saying he had stayed awake long enough. Touched by the warmth of the ovation, however, he hinted at a longer return the following year.[28]

The promised tour of Britain materialized in the spring of 1975. Before then, Como crossed the Atlantic once more to top the bill at the annual Royal Variety Performance in November 1974. The show was a British institution, with stars again performing for charity. Ray Charles and Nick Perito made the trip with Como. *The Stage* said, "Perry's warm, caressing baritone brought a wonderful evening to a gorgeous close."[29] Charles and Perito stood alongside Perry as the members of the cast each shook the hand of Queen Elizabeth the Queen Mother. Ray Charles recalled her somewhat surprised comment to Perry that "they [the audience] know all your songs!"[30]

Como's concert tour of Britain began on April 2, 1975. It was his first sustained tour of one-night stands since the Ted Weems days. All 53,000 seats for the 19 concerts sold out well in advance, some venues such as Southport on England's northwest coast selling out within hours of the tickets going on sale. K-Tel released a special compilation of *Perry Como's 40 Greatest Hits* to tie in with the tour, which went straight to the top of the British album charts. Many of Como's fans said the tour was a 30-year dream come true. Como played three theatres in London, the Theatre Royal at Drury Lane, the Royal Festival Hall and the Palladium, doing two shows a night at each, as he also did in Birmingham. Other cities on the tour included Bristol, Manchester, Glasgow and Edinburgh. Nick Perito conducted a British band who toured with them, and Ray Charles directed the Tony Mansell Singers. Charles also took the role of stand-in for Perry during the rehearsal at each venue. It was not a new thing, said Como. "Ray has been taking over for me at rehearsals for so long, he's beginning to look like me," he told one interviewer.[31] In fact, Charles had filled the role ever since the second series of Como's weekly TV show in the fifties.[32] Charles explained in a BBC documentary that it wasn't just a case of Como taking it easy. By sitting in the audience, he said, Como was able to see the show the way the paying customers did. Charles said that he didn't try to sound like Perry but that he had been with him for so long that he knew the volume and timing that Como would bring to each song.[33]

The reaction of the British audiences exceeded Como's wildest imaginings. "I never *dreamed* it would be like this," he said to interviewer Benny Green the day after the tour ended. "It's been just one big love affair."[34] The *Daily Mirror* captured the mood of the audiences in its report on Como's Southport concert. At the end of the show, it said, "he leaves the stage and moves down to shake hands with the front row. A wave of women flows towards him as he drowns in their delight. They shower him with gifts of flowers and sweets. They try to kiss him. Or just touch him."[35] The same scenes were repeated at every venue, but one show stood out in everyone's memory. When Como appeared at the Kelvin Hall in Glasgow, it was, he said, "the wildest thing I had ever seen, like a frenzy. Men and women, young and old. Men jumping up on stage and hugging me."[36] Both Charles and Perito also singled out Glasgow in their remembrances.

In England, introductions all around. Left to right: Sir Bernard Delfont, Queen Elizabeth the Queen Mother, Nick Perito, Ray Charles, and Perry Como November 18, 1974.

Charles said that the security in Glasgow had been in the hands of "four old men,"[37] which was why one man had managed to get all the way onto the stage. "After a lot of hugs and humorous exchanges," Perito wrote, "Perry managed to get him off the stage, much to the audience's delight."[38] BBC cameras captured Como on stage at the end of show, a tartan scarf around his neck and tam o'shanter hat on his head, mobbed by a crowd that had invaded the stage. When Como emerged, he had a glass of whisky in his hand, drinking a toast to his audience with an expression on his face that was a mixture of bewilderment and sheer joy.

Despite promises to tour again in the U.K., Como never did. A tour in the late eighties was briefly advertised but then withdrawn. Workload and demands from elsewhere were part of the reason, although there was a sense that Como also wanted to preserve the unique memory of his 1975 experience. "These are beautiful moments in our business," he told Benny Green, saying that when he got home, he was not going to speak to anyone for a week so that he could just savor the memory. "In fact, I may never work again," he said, a little tongue-in-cheek.

When Como did return to work, it was a season at the Hilton in Vegas

Perry at his concert in Bristol in the U.K., April 1975 (courtesy Michael Dunnington).

followed by two weeks at Harrah's at Lake Tahoe. Como stayed on in the resort to film *Perry Como's Lake Tahoe Holiday,* with Bob Hope, Anne Murray and tennis star Billie Jean King among the guests. Other sports stars also featured in a show that offered a demonstration of sporting skills, set in the context of a turn-of-the-century picnic. Como sang "The Way We Were" as a backdrop to a scene where he played an old-fashioned tennis match against King. Como's last commitment of the year took him to Mexico to film his Christmas show.

The year 1976 opened in similar vein. His trip to Hawaii came in January, followed by a week in New Orleans for *Perry Como's Spring in New Orleans.* Dick Van Dyke and Leslie Uggams joined Como in a show that gave him the opportunity to add two New Orleans songs, "Way Down Yonder in New Orleans" and "Do You Know What It Means to Miss New Orleans," to his library. The show ended with Como playing the part of King Bacchus VIII in the annual Mardi Gras parade. From there, he flew to Australia and opened a two-week tour at the Sydney Opera House. The tour went on to play the Hordern Pavilion in Sydney and venues in Brisbane, Melbourne, Adelaide and

Perth. Como was forced this time to make the trip without Ray Charles, who was recovering from heart surgery, but Nick Perito, as ever, was at his side. "A great promoter named Pat Condon booked Perry on a tour in Australia," Perito wrote. "We played all the major cities with a local choir and orchestra. The concerts were enthusiastically received everywhere. Again, all the ladies swooned over Perry. Performing a concert in the famed opera house in Sydney was very interesting. The structure is impressive but the acoustics were not what we had hoped for, but Perry still managed to please all of his adoring fans."[39] The Australian press was as enthusiastic as the British press had been a year before. "He fulfilled every expectation," said the *Sydney Morning Herald*. "The voice sounded undiminished, the style was easy, the songs well-remembered, the personality more than nice and the jokes bleached."[40]

Como returned home at the end of May 1976 and began preparations for his first U.S. tour since 1966. In July, he played a week at the Arie Crown Theatre in Chicago, followed by a week at the Westbury Music Fair on Long Island and a week at the Valley Forge Fair in Devon, Pennsylvania. Como's earnings were reportedly $200,000 per week for the tour.[41] At Westbury, John S. Wilson in *The New York Times* said that Como's return to his former base on Long Island was "like a homecoming."[42] Como reminisced with his audience and told stories about the barber business. "A man could starve to death cutting hair," he said, to which one wag in the audience shouted, "Not my barber." "Mr. Como," said Wilson, "flickered an eyebrow in recognition of the riposte and went on to his next song."[43] When he sang, Wilson said, "he occasionally opens up and goes after the big notes on songs such as 'Without a Song.' There is no uncertainty, no hesitation. He hits the notes clearly and fully."[44]

Perry as King Bacchus in the Mardi Gras parade in New Orleans, February 29, 1976.

There was barely time for Como to draw breath between the close of his music fair tour and his next stint in Las Vegas. He opened at the Hilton on August 30 and played ten nights. Ahead of the live dates, he filmed *Perry Como, Las Vegas Style*, the latest of his TV specials, which went out on September 11, 1976. Como taped the show at the Hilton. It is the only film of Como on stage in Vegas. His guests included Ann-Margret and Rich Little, who sang a duet medley of Como's hits with Perry, Little providing a different celebrity voice for each song.

A brief interlude fishing in Florida soon gave way to another trip. Early in November 1976, he flew to Austria to tape *Perry Como's Christmas in Austria* on locations in Vienna, Salzburg, Dienten, and Arnsdorf. For the show, Como added some Austrian-linked songs to his repertoire, including "The Sound of Music" and a delightful "Happy Wanderer." He closed the show by singing "Silent Night," filmed in a church next to the house where the carol was written. *Variety* enthused about the show, saying, "No major performer on U.S. TV seems more compatible with the mood and music of the holiday season. His performance was the icing on a confection that was by far the most imaginative special of this TV season's Christmas efforts."[45] The show won the prestigious Peabody Award in March 1977.

Despite the heavy touring and TV schedule, Como still managed to fit some recording time into his diary, although the results were generally disappointing. "It's Impossible" and "And I Love You So" were tough acts to follow, and most of Como's recording activity between 1975 and the end of the decade seemed shrouded in doubt and uncertainty. Many of his recordings remained unissued, suggesting either unhappiness with the choice of material or Como's reading of it. He had returned to Nashville in January 1975 to begin work on another album with Chet Atkins, with the working title *World of Dreams*. Written by British comedian-crooner Des O'Connor, the proposed title song was released in the spring of 1975 as a single. The primary target was the British market, tying in with Como's British tour and O'Connor's profile there. That it flopped so badly was a mark of the inadequacy of both the song and Como's performance. Como's tour created such an impact that even the most moderately commercial disc would have swept into the charts. "World of Dreams," however, was an unobtrusive song, with neither the lyric nor the melody especially memorable. Press coverage implied that O'Connor had written the song with Como in mind, and indeed, Roncom was listed as the publisher, although there were other indications that the song had been around for a while. O'Connor himself had featured a song with the same title as early as 1971 in a U.S. TV show that was part of Kraft's summer replacement season.

Como's singing on "World of Dreams" and the rest of the material that he recorded that year in Nashville suggested, almost for the first time ever, a lack of vocal confidence. If he was uncertain, it was probably a reflection of the material he was given rather than any signs of doubt about his vocal prowess. Those present at his live shows continued to be amazed by the quality and resilience of his voice. Ray Charles said that in all the years that he stood in the wings watching Perry sing, he never detected any deterioration.[46] Yet on record, and to an extent on TV, Como started to sound a little different. He had always liked to sing softly, but on several occasions—and his recording of "World of Dreams" is a prime example—the result was a thinner, more emaciated vocal than Como's usual warm, velvet sound.

When "World of Dreams" flopped, Chet Atkins was forced to rethink the album concept behind it. He had picked several contemporary songs for Como's January 1975 sessions for an album similar to *And I Love You So*. "Wonderful Baby," a Don McLean hit, was an example and had been the "B" side to "World of Dreams." The change of plan meant that songs such as the Craig Doerge–Judy Henske composition, "Yellow Beach Umbrella," never saw release. When the album did finally appear, its title track was "Just Out of Reach," an old song that Patsy Cline had recorded back in 1958. Como recorded it during a set of May–June 1975 sessions, multi-tracking on the vocal to provide in effect his own vocal chorus. The single sneaked into the C&W charts in the United States at #100[47] but overall, it was Como's most disappointing result from Nashville. He never recorded there again.

After the disappointment of the Nashville album, Como once again seemed to stand back from the recording element of his career. In 1976, he spent only one day in a recording studio. That session came on August 11 when he recorded five titles in New York. Only two saw eventual release on a back-to-back single. The titles were "Lovers, Kids and Fools," a Marvin Hamlisch–Paul Williams song, and "My Days of Loving You," an Italian song with English lyrics by Tony Romeo.[48] Both of the released takes sounded like work in progress, although "Lovers, Kids and Fools" was a complex song that Como might have made it into something with further time and attention. Como's next significant recording work came in June 1977 and took place in England. Tommy Loftus, the RCA representative in London who had done much to create Como's recording popularity there earlier in the decade, came up with the idea for an album of songs by British writers. The summer of 1977 was awash with patriotic fervor with HM Queen Elizabeth II celebrating her silver jubilee. Loftus thought that an album of homegrown songs, none previously recorded by Perry, would fit the country's mood. *The Best of British* was the result. Back home, where the United States had just celebrated its bicentennial of freedom from "British tyranny," an album of British songs could hardly have been less appropriate. The album thus became *Where You're Concerned*, using some of the London tracks alongside some additional material that Como recorded in October 1977. These included a cover of the Debbie Boone hit "You Light Up My Life" and "Feelings," a "woah-woah-woah" song that is often used as a parody of the insipid soft-rock songs of the period. The October session, believed to have taken place in California, featured arrangements by Nick Perito, with an uncredited choral backing that had the characteristics of Ray Charles' work. The results were Como's best vocal performances on record since 1974.

Loftus's thinking behind the *Best of British* album was to try and recapture some of the magic of Como's 1975 tour. The sessions featured many of the same personnel with Nick Perito conducting a British orchestra and Ray Charles again directing the Tony Mansell Singers. The songs were a mixed bag of new, old and ancient. The best tracks on the album were undoubtedly the standards—Charlie Chaplin's "Smile" and Ray Noble's "The Very Thought of You" especially. The ancient included the traditional air "Greensleeves," and the new included such ephemeral pop tunes as "There's a Kind of Hush (All over the World)" and "The Other Man's Grass Is Always Greener." Como's vocals were again diffident and overall the album lacked variety and a change of pace. Ironically, Perry's most convincing vocal came on "Where You're Concerned," one of the two non–British titles recorded during the session for release as an American single. If Como was running out of steam in the recording studio, no one would have been surprised. He was 65 years old and had climbed every recording mountain several times over. Nevertheless, the failure to find a successful follow-up to "And I Love You So" at a time when Perry's popularity was at its highest for almost 20 years was one of the few missed opportunities of his career.

The ups and downs of the recording business did not appear to bother him greatly as he headed to his sixty-fifth birthday celebrations in May 1977. Since his recovery from his broken knee, his life and career had settled into a regular pattern of summer touring, three or four TV specials per year and the occasional record date. He spent more of his leisure time on his boat in Florida and rather less on the golf course, his game never having recovered after his leg injury. Inevitably, interviewers asked him whether he had any plans to retire. His reply was always the same. "As long as I can keep pulling myself together, I'll want to keep working. Singers are like comics, they never retire unless they have to."[49]

Perry on the golf course in 1974. His game never fully recovered from the leg injury that he suffered three years earlier, as his expression perhaps shows! (courtesy Colleen Zwack).

Indeed as Perry Como approached the end of his fifth decade as a professional singer, retirement never seemed further away. He continued to find ways of re-inventing himself, taking on new challenges on stage, television and on record, all of which would take his career through its sixth decade and into a seventh. For Perry Como, the next stop would be Japan.

Chapter 15

Charisma in Slow Motion

PERRY COMO APPROACHED OLD AGE WITH the same grace that had carried him through the first 40 years of his career. He joked in a 1984 TV interview that there were three stages to life—"adolescence, middle age and 'gee, you look good.'"[1] And he did. Apart from a little weight gain in the late seventies that temporarily gave his face a cherubic appearance, he looked much the same as he had done ten years before. His only real concession to age was that his glasses were now *de rigueur* for any occasion.

Inevitably, the questions that came his way when he consented to a TV interview focused on how he retained his generally healthy demeanor, how his voice sounded so good and whether he had any plans to retire. He handled them with the same aplomb each time they came up. He put his youthful oldness down to regular exercise—mainly walking and fishing, with a little golf thrown in—and said, as he had always done before, that as long as he felt healthy, his singing just came naturally. As to retirement, he had no such thoughts. He told Bob Protzman of the *Detroit Free Press*, "I'm just taking it a little easier, doing a little more of what I've wanted to do for years—a little fishing, a little golfing. But I do one or two shows a year, and every couple of years I get a little fidgety and go on a six-to-eight week tour, or as long as I hold up. I like to do that once in a while just to keep in touch."[2]

Como had been following the routine that he described to Protzman since the late seventies. Although he regarded himself as just "keeping in touch," he was still keen to break new ground if the opportunity arose—as it did in 1979. Promoters Yoshiko and Tadao (Terry) Terajima of Pacific Enterprises came up with a proposal for Perry to do a six-concert tour of Japan. Western music was enjoying a considerable revival in Japan during the seventies and it had become a regular tour spot for singers of Como's ilk. Frank Sinatra was already a regular visitor (and indeed would give his last full public performance there in 1994).

To the suggestion that he might add a concert tour of Japan to his itinerary, Perry gave his usual cautious response. "I was a little taken aback," he said during his final visit there, some years later. "I was hesitant about coming. I didn't realize that our shows came here. I said 'Why would I want to go to Japan? They won't know who I am.'"[3] The reaction, from a man who despite his international fame was little traveled, was unsurprising. Japan, he said, "seemed a long way from Florida." To Como's mind, the differences in language and culture were massive obstacles. He had no appreciation of his own popularity in Japan, but the tour promoters assured him that he would be warmly received and that his shows would sell out. Both their prophecies proved to be correct.

Como arrived in Tokyo in April 1979 to give six concerts over ten days. His regular traveling companions, Nick Perito and Ray Charles, made the trip accompanied by a group of six female singers. As was the norm with Como's tours, the promoters contracted with local musicians to provide the orchestra. For the Japanese trips, the contract went to the Tokyo-based Sharps and Flats Orchestra. Nick Perito had directed local bands before but had no experience of Japanese musicianship. He was nervous, although his friend Don Costa, who had used local musicians on a recent tour with Frank Sinatra, told him not to worry. Nevertheless, when Perito opened the first rehearsal, he was alarmed to see "a trombone player pull out an instrument that looked like a reject from some Midwestern college marching band."[4] As rehearsals progressed, Perito's fears grew. After four or five numbers, he called a time out, but while he took a break, the band stayed in the rehearsal room. Perito returned 30 minutes later, this time with Perry. He found the band still working on some of the numbers. Having told Perry that he had some doubts, Perito was nonplussed when the orchestra struck up the first song, note perfect. Como, he said, looked at him with a raised eyebrow. What Perito was discovering was that the Japanese work ethic was such that the band would practice on its own for as long as it took to be on top of every number.[5]

From then on, the tour ran smoothly. Como kept the same song selections as for his live appearances in the States, blending old favorites such as "Without a Song" and "Temptation" with newer material such as "The Way We Were" and Neil Diamond's hit "Beautiful Noise." Concessions to his setting included a Japanese folk song, "Sakura," plus long forgotten numbers from his back catalogue such as "The Rose Tattoo" that had been big in Japan. As in Britain in 1975, Como was overwhelmed by the audience response. During his Sun Plaza Hall concert in Tokyo, he had to stop several times as fans approached the stage with garlands of flowers. Perry graciously received and acknowledged each one. "This doesn't usually happen to me," he told the audience. The success of the tour was such that Como returned several times during the eighties. He played the Tokyo Music Festival in 1981, and the following year, he put together a Christmas tour of Japan and the Philippines.

The Japanese trips fitted in to the year-by-year work pattern that Como described in the Bob Protzman interview. Typically, he would do two television specials, one for Easter and one for Christmas, with a summer tour in between. The occasional recording date still cropped up here and there, plus regular appearances at charity events, usually built around golf. He spent the rest of his time enjoying the Florida sun. The focus of his U.S. tours was usually the music fairs in the Midwest but in 1978, he headed west and played four July nights at the Greek Theater in Los Angeles. (He curtailed his planned weeklong engagement as he took longer than expected to recover from dental problems.) Harvey Siders in the *Los Angeles Times* said that Como's LA appearances were "as regular as clockwork," the last having been exactly 40 years before with the Weems Band. "Those four decades have not diminished the voice, the looks or the personality of 'Mr. Mellow,' who is now 66," Siders wrote. "The phrasing, the silken tenor, the casual approach to lyrics are still intact, as are the boyish charm and the infectious laugh. As soon as Como opened his mouth for 'Hello Young Lovers,' the old trademark was evident. He is still nonchalance personified, charisma in slow motion."[6]

More of the same came in 1979, albeit with the Japanese trip thrown in as an extra. On his return, Como played a series of venues in the Midwest. On both his 1978 and 1979 tours, an up and coming comedian called Jay Leno opened the shows for Perry. "The great thing for me was that Perry was always very down to earth. It was like being with an uncle or a relative or someone who just happened to sing for a living. There was never a show business connotation to it. He enjoys his fame, he'd stop and sign autographs but he never took it very seriously," said Leno.[7]

By the time Como's sixth decade as a performer dawned in 1980, he was 67 years old. Harvey Siders' and Jay Leno's observations both bore out the fact that Como was growing old in a happy and graceful manner. He seemed comfortable with the grandfatherly image, happy to poke fun at himself and indeed, content to let the years show. It was an uncommon characteristic in an industry known for its perpetual search for the fountain of youth. Como also displayed a greater willingness, as the years passed, to talk about himself. As he toured the various cities in the United States, local television stations persuaded him to drop in for the occasional daytime TV interview.

For most of his career, Como had steered well clear of the TV chat show.[8] His first experience of one had come in London in 1977 when he agreed to a one-hour guest spot on BBC Television's *Parkinson* show. A significant factor in persuading Como to do the show had been Bing Crosby, who had made two appearances with Parkinson and was able to assure Como that it would be a professional rather than a personally prying interview. Ironically, Como's appearance on the show came just weeks after Crosby's sudden death on a golf course in Spain. Como used the show to pay tribute to his friend and mentor. When Parkinson, an avowed Sinatra aficionado, asked Como just how significant Crosby had been, Perry's answers provided the most forthright moments of an otherwise bland show. "From the '30s to the '50s, he was the most influential singer," Perry said. "Frank has made a fine reputation, but no one has been able to sustain it like Bing." Como also alluded to the complexities of Crosby's character. "He was a hard man to know," he said. "He didn't make friends easily; he had a lot of acquaintances, not many friends. But when he made a friendship, he did everything he could to keep it."[9]

Part of Como's reluctance to appear on a chat show came from his ongoing refusal to allow the media into his off-stage life. It sat alongside a genuinely held belief, however, that he also had nothing to say. Musician-turned-journalist Benny Green had interviewed Como for the 1975 BBC feature *The Barber Comes to Town*. "Como cannot agree that there is anything very interesting about him," Green wrote later. "He insists that apart from his singing, he is a perfectly ordinary fellow."[10] Green, a hardened show business veteran often given to a cynical tone, went on to say that "Como's modesty is utterly genuine; he is not one of those bores who wait to be cajoled into backing modestly into the limelight."[11]

Not surprisingly then, Como's appearances on U.S. shows such as *Donahue* in 1979, followed by the *Today Show, Good Company (Minneapolis)* and *AM Cleveland,* revealed no deep insight into the man behind the voice. He was happy to talk about his father, his childhood and his early days in the barber business, but other than that, he had little to say. When asked about his ambitions in 1984, he shrugged his shoulders and said, "Play golf a little better, live a little longer, keep singing as long as I can."[12] When Bing Crosby had told Barbara Walters in one of his last interviews that he thought he was an average guy who sang adequately but had no great philosophy or opinions, her reaction had been incredulous. When Como painted much the same picture of himself, however, it seemed to fit. It was as it had always been: with Perry Como, what you saw was what you got.

By 1980, ABC held exclusive rights to Como on TV. All of his shows by now were filmed on location with a strong sense of a musical travelogue about them. His Easter shows included *Perry Como's Bahamas Holiday* (1980), *Spring in San Francisco* (1981) and *Easter in Guadalajara* (1982). They were light affairs, with one or two big name guests and a coterie of more local performers. John J. O'Connor in the *New York Times* said of Como's 1981 visit to San Francisco, "As usual, the guests wander to several colorful locations ... and all the while, it's sing, sing, sing."[13] More and more, however, the focus of Como's TV work—and indeed his television image—built on his association with the Christmas season. After Crosby's death, Como picked up the Mr. Christmas mantle. "Now that Bing is gone, Christmas belongs to Perry Como," wrote Tom Shales in the *Washington Post*.[14] Como's Christmas shows kept the "Christmas around the world" theme that he had started earlier in the seventies. In 1978 and 1979, he visited Colonial Williamsburg and New Mexico respectively. The 1978 show, *Perry Como's Early American Christmas,* featured one of the last TV appearances by the all–American cowboy, John Wayne. Wayne was already in the final stages of the cancer that would kill him the following year, and the Bob Banner production team arranged early morning filming sessions that suited him best. One morning, an ill and tetchy Wayne took exception to the fact that his call was for 8:00 but Perry's not until 9:30. When Wayne berated Como for several minutes over his late appearance, Perry just looked up at him ("He was about nine feet tall," Como said). Finally Wayne ran out of steam and said to Como, "Aren't you gonna say anything?" to which Como replied, "You're a pain in the ass." Whatever Perry's intention with this remark, it defused the situation and Wayne, along with everyone else on the set, broke up.[15]

From 1980, Como took his Christmas show abroad, adding luggage tags for Holy Land (1980), Montreal (1981), Paris (1982) and London (1984). The one exception to the pattern was Como's 1983 Christmas show that he filmed in New York. It gave Como an opportunity to pay a nostalgic visit to Studio 54, by then a discothèque but once the TV studio that had been home for his Kraft shows. Producer Jeff Margolis grabbed the chance to re-create Como's trademark "Sing to Me, Mr. C" set, complete with music stand, single rose and solitary guitarist. Como sang "White Christmas" there in what *Variety* called an "understated tribute to Bing Crosby."[16]

Despite a predictable pattern and heavy dosages of sweetness and light, Como's Christmas shows generally received good reviews. The Bob Banner–Stephen Pouliot production team regarded the 1980 show from the Holy Land as the best of the shows they did with Como, Perry delivering an "absolutely outstanding" version of "Bless This House."[17] *Variety* said in 1981, "The holiday specials starring Perry Como have become a stand-out example of good taste, good music and what, for want of a better description, is best described as the proper Christmas mood."[18] In 1982, reviewing *Perry Como's Christmas in Paris,* the magazine said that the show was "a study in class" and that Como "reasserted his place at the top of the Christmas spec ladder."[19]

As Como's Parisian Christmas outing aired in the States, Perry was bringing the year to a close with *Perry Como's Christmas Special* tour of the Far East. It was the first time that Como had taken a Christmas show on the road. It brought the curtain down on an otherwise quiet year. Como had not toured in the States during the summer and his two TV outings apart, the highlight of the year came at the White House in March 1982. President Reagan invited Como and Frank Sinatra to perform a double act in honor of the Italian president, Sandro Pertini. With Reagan as a charming host, Como and Sinatra clearly enjoyed each other's company, rattling through a series of your-turn, my-turn solos before combining on a couple of duets. As dictated by their personalities, it was Sinatra who hogged center stage although in the vocal department, there was little doubt that it was the pipes of the man from Canonsburg that were holding up the better. The two singers repeated their performance in February 1983 when the Reagans played host to Queen Elizabeth II in California. The concert took place on the M*A*S*H

John Wayne (left) and Diana Canova join Perry on his 1978 Christmas special from Williamsburg.

soundstage at 20th Century-Fox studios in Hollywood, scene of most of Como's brief movie appearances. Once more, Como stole the vocal honors, although both singers lost out to the incessant noise of pouring rain on the tin roof of the soundstage.[20]

The trip to Hollywood marked the beginning of Como's golden anniversary year. April saw the fiftieth anniversary of Como's debut as a professional singer; June 1983 brought around the fortieth anniversary of Como's association with RCA. In July he and Roselle celebrated their fiftieth wedding anniversary with a gathering of their three children and 12 grandchildren at their new summer home in Saluda, North Carolina. The Comos had purchased land there in 1977 and two years later, had commissioned the building of a summer home as a refuge from the Florida heat.[21]

Although Como's relationship with RCA was cooling by the time the anniversary came around, top brass from the company hosted a fortieth anniversary salute to Como at New York's Rockefeller Center Rainbow Grill on June 21, 1983. Despite the stop-start nature of Perry's recording activity during the late seventies, some measure of consistency had returned in 1980 when Como began working with producer Mike Berniker. Berniker was an experienced and respected producer who had worked with Barbra Streisand and Brenda Lee, as well as building a reputation for producing top quality cast albums of Broadway shows.

Como's rolling contract with RCA had reached a breakpoint in 1979 and Perry seemed surprised that the company wanted to extend it for another ten years. "I told them 'you must be crazy. I'll be in a wheelchair ten years from now,'" Como told Bill Kaufman of the *Los Angeles Times*.[22] Nevertheless, the contract provided the impetus for Como to head to New York in April 1980 for a series of sessions in RCA's studios C and D. The resulting album, simply titled *Perry Como*, featured ten contemporary songs. Two show songs stood out from the rest. "Not While I'm Around" was a Stephen Sondheim composition for the 1978 musical *Sweeney Todd*. "The Colors of My Life" came from the 1980 show *Barnum*. Como sang with greater authority on the sessions than on any of his recent recordings. *High Fidelity* magazine said that Como sounded "mellow and endlessly smooth."[23]

Later that year, Mike Berniker was on hand to capture Perry's live show at the Mill Run Theatre, Niles, Illinois, over three nights in July 1980. The resulting album—*Perry Como Live on Tour*—offered a demonstration of how Como's act had developed since his previous live album from Vegas, ten years before. The basic structure was the same, with a lively opener, some ballads, a hits medley and some evergreens along the way, but much of the material had changed since 1970. "It's Impossible" and "And I Love You So" were shoe-ins for any concert, while some of the new material included "Beautiful Noise" and "You Needed Me," a song that Como had recorded in 1978.

The album captured Como in terrific vocal form, suggesting that he sang with greater freedom on the stage than he now did in the recording studio. John S. Wilson in *High Fidelity* was effusive in his praise. Although his comment that Como's voice was "richer, fuller, and more controlled than [it was] thirty years ago" was surely an exaggeration, his comment that Como's ability to project his voice as on "Temptation" "does not just come from a good microphone" was perceptive. "Experience is a wonderful thing when the instrument stays in shape," he wrote.[24] Wilson also added an interesting comparison with the aging Sinatra, saying that the huskiness that started to cloud Como's voice at the *end* of his show was similar to that heard from Sinatra at the *start* of a show. "Como never quite achieved the adulation of Crosby or Sinatra," Wilson wrote, "but perhaps he has found a way to grow older more gracefully."[25]

RCA released another "new" Como album in time for Christmas 1982, although it featured only one new recording: "I Wish It Could Be Christmas Forever," a Nick Perito melody with lyrics by Richard B. Matheson. Como used the song for the first time in his 1981 Christmas special, from which RCA lifted a recording for a new compilation of Christmas songs, plus a Christmas single. Around the same time, Como recorded eight new songs for an album whose working title was *Goodbye for Now,* a Stephen Sondheim song from the motion picture *Reds.* The remaining titles were again contemporary ballads. With eight new recordings to hand, RCA needed two more to make up the now standard ten for an album. They found one in an unreleased track from 1978, "You Are So Beautiful." The remaining track was a strange choice. RCA reached all the way back to the *Mr. President* album from 1962 for "Is She the Only Girl in the World."[26] Como explained the choice in a press interview: "There was one song I didn't think fit. My grandson had an old song 'Is She the Only Girl in the World' on one of his tapes. We put that track on this album right after 'You Are So Beautiful.' They were sung 15 or 18 years apart, but they don't sound very different to me."[27]

Despite the public face that Como put on the album, its production was not a happy experience. Both Nick Perito and Ray Charles were involved in the sessions but felt marginalized by Berniker. "He found us irrelevant," said Charles. "My recollection is that Perry was not very happy at this date. I seem to recall a dark, gloomy studio and one of the few times that Perry recorded to a track."[28] Yet despite Como's apparent unease, some of the vocals that he produced were the best since his *And I Love You So* sessions almost ten years before. On "What's One More Time," Como sang with great authority and the power and precision of his vocal matched the great ballad performances of the late forties. With unfamiliar, contemporary material, Como at age 70 demonstrated once again that he had the ability to meet any vocal challenge that a composer might give him. RCA held the finished product over for 12 months prior to release. When it appeared, the title went to another song on it, *So It Goes.* With the release of the album tying in with the fortieth anniversary of Perry with RCA, *Goodbye for Now* would perhaps have been an inappropriate and inaccurate indication of retirement.

RCA's celebration of their 40 years with Como in June 1983 was a grand affair. RCA Chairman and Chief Executive Thornton T. Bradshaw said, "RCA is honored by its long association with one of the most gifted gentlemen in the entertainment business."[29] RCA Records President Robert D. Summer told the gathering that Como had accumulated sales of more than 100,000,000 records but added, "The numbers don't begin to tell the real story of Perry's music. Through the years, his music has become part of the fabric of our times, giving us moments that evoke memories of the best times of our lives."[30] President Reagan and Governor Cuomo both sent letters of congratulation, and Mayor Koch proclaimed the entire week as "Perry Como Week" in New York City. Marvin Hamlisch wrote a special song to mark the anniversary and RCA pressed a special album, *40 Golden Years,* of Como's hits and favorites for those attending the event.

Como appeared to be genuinely touched by the plaudits, thanking RCA and the media for its generosity. "Did I really sell 100,000,000 records?" he asked incredulously. Despite the bonhomie of the event, however, Como's mind was already calculating the value of his record sales to RCA and comparing it to the inscribed Timex watch that Bradshaw had presented to him. When Perry gently made his displeasure known, Bradshaw said he could go out and buy any watch he liked and charge it to RCA. Como duly purchased a $25,000 Presidential Rolex and had it engraved exactly as the Timex had been.[31]

Despite his extended contract with RCA, Como was feeling increasingly uncomfortable in the new world of digital recording. He felt that the people he was working with at RCA did not understand him or his music.[32] There would be only more session at the RCA New York studios that he had graced for so long. That came in October 1983, when he teamed up once more with Mike Berniker to record two songs for release as a single. Both songs came from the Jerry Herman musical *La Cage aux Folles*. The A-side of the single, "The Best of Times," resonated with Perry and he immediately built it into his stage act. It was an up-tempo number that featured Perry with the Ray Charles Singers—also with him for the last time on disc. The flip side was a ballad, "Song on the Sand." Como's vocal on the latter was particularly impressive, his voice showing both richness and range. The single once again proved especially popular in Britain, where it crept briefly into the lower reaches of the Top 50, prompting RCA to compile an album around it. Time was when Como would have offered some new recordings on the back of the single. Now, RCA was content to put out some fifties and sixties reissues alongside the two new single tracks.

By the time 1984 opened, Perry Como was no longer a cross-generational performer. In January 1984, he found himself with Dallas Cowboys coach Tom Landry, tennis player John McEnroe and a host of other celebrities as a recipient of a *Dull Life-style Award* from International Dull Folks Unlimited.[33] A better-known send up of Como's somnambulant image came on an SCTV sketch where Eugene Levy offered a caricature of Perry carrying on singing as he gradually lapsed into a comatose state. Como told the press that he got a little tired of some of the jokes but "I was amused by the skit on SCTV. The producer sent me a tape and said that they meant it to be in the spirit of fun. I play it for my kids, just for laughs."[34] Producer Stephen Pouliot, however, saw Como's reaction to the skit in private. "He did not smile once and obviously did not like it," he said.[35]

While the skit was a caricature, it seemed that as Como grew older, he relaxed even more. Before any live show, he always took a nap in his dressing room, in his underwear. Mickey Glass would wake him and help him dress just before he was due on stage. With minimal interest now in rehearsing, Como relied more and more on cue cards. The combination of having just woken up and being unfamiliar with the material would spell disaster for many performers, but with Perry, it enabled him to come across as a benign, slightly mesmerized old gent. Nick Perito's role on stage now combined orchestral direction with piano playing and he was seldom more than a yard or two from his master. For the remaining few years of Como's career, Perito was as much an on-stage butler to Perry as musical director.

As Como's velocity on stage receded, his itinerary nevertheless grew. He had not toured the United States in 1983, but made up for it the following summer, making over 40 concert appearances in nine locations during July and August. A bout with a bronchial virus laid him low for a spell just before the tour, but by the time he arrived at the Valley Forge Music Fair, he was in good form. When Stephen X. Rea asked him about how he got by without any nerves, Como told him, "Oh, don't believe that. Everybody's nervous. And I think you have to earn the right to be relaxed. I get nervous, sure. I get excited. When they say, 'You're not nervous,' that's nonsense. There is no such a thing."[36]

The year 1985 brought more of the same, Como heading west to begin a tour that required 54 performances in 15 cities. When asked about the infrequency of his visits to California, Como told Jack Hawn of the *Los Angeles Times* that he had "nothing against performing on the West Coast, but I live back East and after six, seven or eight weeks of concerts there, I'm ready to quit. So this year, I said, let's go the other way."[37] Como, said Hawn, was happy to "cruise along, throttle at half-speed, feeling fine and enjoying life."[38] Gerald Nachman in San Francisco remarked on the way Como constantly turned tedium to this advantage. "In an era of flash and fizzle, Como is an unfizzy, laid-back throwback, the Classic Coke of singers," he wrote. "He made a career out of not moving a muscle, which became a trait, then a trademark, then a shtick (no Como impression is complete without a yawn), and now a way of life. He was always the nice guy who finished, if not first, a respectable third, behind Crosby and Sinatra. It is hard to get excited about this most unexciting of performers, yet you can hear him all night and not get bored."[39]

Ray Charles, as ever, accompanied Perry on the 1985 tour but it proved to be the final time they would work together. The tour had originally been planned to end in Atlantic City in August. Having checked with Mickey Glass that Como would not need him after that engagement, Charles had booked a special anniversary holiday with his wife. When Glass told him that Perry had added a series of one-nighters on to the tour, Charles reminded him that Como already knew that he was planning to take a holiday, one that he could not change. No words were spoken but Como seemingly regarded it as a slight. With echoes of the way other professional relationships had ended earlier in his career, Como and Charles never worked together again. They did not speak for two years. Finally, when Como arrived in Washington in 1987 to receive a Kennedy Center Honor (an annual ceremony where Charles acted as the musical consultant), their paths crossed again. The choirmaster saw his former boss at the supper that followed the show and decided to approach him. Roselle Como noticed him first and said, "Daddy, look who's here!"[40] Perry turned and hugged Ray. Charles congratulated him on the honor and Como responded by saying, "You had a lot to do with it."[41] Although the friendship was restored, their professional partnership remained in abeyance. Twenty years on, Charles' loyalty and affection for Como was undimmed despite the unsatisfactory ending to a 35-year association.

Como closed out 1985 with a Christmas TV show from Hawaii. His original plan had been to take the show to Rome but security worries about transatlantic flights caused the change. For the 1984 show, in London, Como had broken with his own tradition and closed the show with "O Holy Night" instead of the customary "Ave Maria." "I caught hell for it," Como said two years later.[42] In Hawaii, Como reverted to his usual format. Buz Kohan, a veteran from the Kraft shows in the sixties, returned as writer and Dick Williams, brother of Andy, took over the Ray Charles role. Burt Reynolds and Marie Osmond were the big name stars recruited for the show. *Perry Como's Christmas in Hawaii* aired on ABC on Saturday, December 14, at 10:00 P.M. The week before Christmas had been the regular air spot for the Como festive show since the early seventies. By the time Christmas 1986 came around, CBS told Como that they planned to keep his show (recorded in San Antonio, Texas) in a Saturday 10:00 P.M. spot, but that it would go out a week earlier, on December 6. Como was unhappy but so late in the day, there was little he could do about it. When discussions opened with ABC regarding a show for 1987, however, Como said that he wanted a weekday spot at 9:00 P.M., believing that most of his audience would be in bed by 10:00 on a Saturday. ABC held firm and offered the same slot. Como walked away. "Sad holiday tidings for the Poli-Grip generation. For the first time since the Civil War, Perry Como won't have a Christmas show this year," one Florida journalist wrote.[43] "I hated to do it," Como told *Dallas Morning News* TV critic Ed Bark, "but I just kind of felt that we were throwing our show away Saturday night at 10. That's kind of late. The last two years, it was like we weren't even on. It looked like a Secret Service show."[44]

Como's performance in the San Antonio show seemed to suggest that Como was

Perry with choral director with Ray Charles during a 1970s tour. Their professional relationship came to a surprising end in 1985 (courtesy Colleen Zwack).

perhaps coming to the end of a long road. Ed Bark writing in the *Dallas Morning Herald* said, "Perry's 75-year-old singing voice has faded to a wibbly-wobbly condition. It's evident at the start of the show when he shucks the usual lip syncing, goes it *au naturel* and struggles through 'Joy to the World.'"[45] Dick Williams wrote some special lyrics for the show. He recalled that the cast rehearsed at great length at the Waldorf in New York before heading to Texas. Perry he said "had great difficulty in learning these [lyrics], or indeed anything new at that time."[46] Even the ever-loyal Nick Perito noticed a difference in the way Como approached the show. The director for the show was Bob Wynn, who was working with Como for the first time. His task, wrote Perito, was difficult "because Perry at this point in his professional career, was ambivalent about any and all things connected with rehearsing. He was never angry or disrespectful to anyone, but it was clear that he felt we all knew what we were doing and everything would be fine."[47]

It looked as though the scheduling dispute with ABC would be the final curtain on a 38-year television career as well as bringing to an end a run of 33 consecutive Christmas specials for Perry. With his seventy-fifth birthday just around the corner, it seemed that he might finally swap his microphone for his fishing rod full-time. But anyone who believed that reckoned without the resilience of the barber from Canonsburg. There were still some songs waiting to be sung.

Chapter 16

Final Curtain

IN MAY 1987, PERRY COMO CELEBRATED his seventy-fifth birthday. The days when a young barber had put down his shears and joined Freddie Carlone's band were a lifetime ago. Yet despite the end of his television career, Mr. C was not ready to quit just yet. To prove the point, he flew to California to record a new album. The venue was unusual. Apart from an odd session on the West Coast in the late seventies, all of Como's previous RCA recordings had been in New York or Nashville. For his new album, Perry spent two days at the Evergreen Studios in Burbank, California, close to the home of Nick Perito.

Perry Como Today was Como's 31st album[1] and his final set of studio recordings. Although the disc was an RCA release under Como's ongoing contract, the ownership of the label had changed since Perry's last outing in 1983. A series of acquisitions and mergers between 1983 and 1986 moved RCA Victor into the hands of the Bertelsmann Music Group (BMG).[2] The change had little direct impact on Como, but equally did nothing to halt the growing distance between him and the label that he had served for 44 years. The decision to record the album in California was no doubt a reflection of Como's unhappiness with the atmosphere that he had found in New York during his sessions there a few years before.

Nick Perito played the dominant role in getting the 1987 session underway. He arranged and conducted all of the material, writing one new Hawaiian song that Como included, and took on the role of producer for the album. Together with Como, he came up with song selections that contained a fifty-year blend of material. Two Rodgers and Hart ballads from the thirties were set alongside several more contemporary, up-tempo songs. The results were good. Como had recorded both of the Rodgers and Hart songs before but "My Heart Stood Still," 1987 style, compared well with his previous version from 35 years before. The newer songs included Burt Bacharach and Carole Bayer Sager's "That's What Friends Are For," which Como had attempted previously in an abortive session in the late seventies. Perry also got around to recording "Bless the Beasts and the Children," a 1971 song that he had featured on TV during his Easter specials. The outstanding song on the album, however, was "Wind Beneath My Wings," written by Jeff Silbar and Larry Henley in 1982. As with Don McLean's "And I Love You So," Silbar and Henry's song had "hit" written all over it and was just waiting for a singer to pick it up. It was the song that Como had been looking for in the late seventies when his recording momentum was still strong, but it came to him ten years too late.

Como's recording of "Wind Beneath My Wings" was as good as any record he had

162

made since "It's Impossible." The song, a reflective love ballad, had a lyric that was ideally suited to a singer of his vintage, although its melodic range was testing for a septuagenarian. Perry, however, proved that his voice could still soar and sustain a high note as he comfortably coped with a towering chorus that flew, both lyrically and musically, "higher than an eagle." When Perito and Como listened to the playback, both felt that the song was hit material for Perry but were unable to persuade the new masters at RCA to release it as a single.[3] Two years later, Bette Midler recorded the song for the soundtrack of the film *Beaches* and made it into a worldwide hit. At the 1990 Grammys, Silbar and Henry walked off with the award for Song of the Year, while Midler picked up the Record of the Year award.[4]

Perry Como—Today was a pleasant album and Como sang as well as, if not better than, on any session since 1973. For his "Best of Times" session in 1983, Como had dropped his key by a half tone. It gave him a new resonance in his lower register and his voice gained greater authority with it. Good singing, though, was no longer enough to sell Perry Como records. Como himself knew that. In an interview with *The Los Angeles Times* in 1985, he said, "I'm recording less and less. It's a waste of time to record now. I don't think the kids are buying it and I don't think the elderly people go into the stores. There's no way of plugging one unless you do a video and I can't see myself doing one of those."[5] It proved to be a self-fulfilling prophecy. With little advance promotion, the album crept quietly into the stores. It was the first and only new Como recording issued in the format of compact disc, although a conventional 12" vinyl record appeared too. Reviews were disappointing. "There's a better way to thank Como for the memories than adding this one to the collection," said Roger Piantadosi in the *Washington Post*.[6]

Como's RCA contract ran until 1989 but when it expired, neither Como nor BMG seemed interested in a further extension. It was unsurprising. Como by then was 77 and from Bertelsmann's perspective, his greatest value was in his back catalogue. There was one brief attempt by RCA engineer John Schneider to lure Perry back into the studios in the early nineties, as his fiftieth anniversary with RCA approached, but it came to naught.[7] RCA instead settled for a three–CD set of recordings dating from the forties through to the 1987 session. The set marked "two special anniversaries," with Como's sixtieth year of show business coinciding with the 50-year RCA landmark. Como seemed pleased with the set and did some limited marketing of it on TV and radio.

With his ABC-TV deal having folded in 1986, Como was a free agent on television and record for the first time since 1943. For most of the intervening years, the news that Perry Como was available would have prompted a stampede for his services. No more. Nobody would have been surprised if Perry had retreated to his boat and his lady in Jupiter and called it a day. What's more, there would soon be the first real indication that the Comos were no more immune from the ravages of time than anyone else was. In May 1988, just as Perry and Roselle were planning their fifty-fifth wedding anniversary celebration, the couple were attending the annual Duke Children's Classic Golf Tournament in Durham, North Carolina, when Roselle suffered chest pains. Tests revealed that she was suffering from coronary heart disease and angina pectoris. On May 26, she underwent a quadruple heart by-pass at the Duke Hospital in Durham, returning home to Florida a week later to recuperate.[8] There seemed more reason than ever for Perry to end his days on the road.

Perry Como had, however, never been a predictable individual and once again showed that leopards do not change their spots. Within weeks of Roselle's discharge from hospital, Perry was in Boston for a TV appearance with John Williams and the

Boston Pops Orchestra. Filmed in Symphony Hall, Boston, the show was a half hour tribute to Bing Crosby. Nick Perito recalled that Como was apprehensive about singing with such a large orchestra, fearing that they would be unable to play softly enough for him. John Williams asked Perito to re-score Como's Crosby medley for the full orchestra, which Williams conducted perfectly. When Como got back to the hotel after the show, the first thing he did was to call Williams and tell him how pleased he had been with the whole experience.[9] Apart from his usual Crosby medley that was now a regular part of his touring show, Como also sang "Wind Beneath My Wings" as part of the tribute, black and white footage of the two singers together on TV providing the backdrop as Como sang about his "hero." Cassie Miller, one of the backup singers, recalled watching the video through a crack in the door at the run-through before the taping. She felt a hand on her shoulder. "I sure loved that man," said Como as he watched the old film of him singing with his idol.[10]

In 1989 Perry resumed his summer touring, again focusing on the music fairs in the Midwest and starting at the Westbury Fair on July 5. From there, he moved on to Connecticut, where Regis Philbin caught up with him for an interview for *Live with Regis and Kathie Lee* for ABC-TV. Next stop was Hyannis before the Como road show rolled on through New York, New Jersey, Pennsylvania, Michigan, Ohio, Indiana, winding up in St. Louis, Missouri. Most of the dates were one-nighters, played to what Mark Taylor in the *Merriville Post-Tribune* called a "graying, bifocaled audience."[11] Como, he said, strolled onto the stage in a black tuxedo, "exuding the calm charm that won him the nickname of the most relaxed man in show business."[12] In October, Como flew to Japan to appear with opera star Plácido Domingo at a Friendship Concert in the Yokohama Arena. Former president Ronald Reagan was among an audience of 10,000 for a show that raised $1 million for Reagan's Presidential Library Foundation.

The New Year took Como into his seventh decade as an entertainer and, fittingly, opened with his induction into the Academy of Television Arts & Sciences Hall of Fame. The ceremony took place on January 7, 1990, at the 20th Century-Fox Studios in Los Angeles. A frail-looking Milton Berle delivered the tribute to Perry, introducing an ailing Frank Sinatra ("I swallowed a shot glass") who presented the award. Como delivered a short thank-you speech, modestly and with an

Frank Sinatra and Perry clown for the cameras at the Hall of Fame show, broadcast on January 24, 1990 (courtesy Colleen Zwack).

air of bemusement. The inductions were shown on the Fox network on TV two weeks later.

Charitable appearances still marked a regular part of Como's itinerary, all handled in a quiet, understated way. In March 1990 Perry appeared on the Sammy Davis Jr. Variety Club Telethon in St. Louis. Davis and Como had fallen out in the mid-sixties when Sammy had pulled out of a Como special at the last minute.[13] Producer Bob Wynn recalled that when he first approached Perry about doing the telethon, his initial negative response was full of expletives. Before the show took place, however, news emerged that Davis was suffering from terminal cancer and would be unable to act as host. Como, said Wynn, immediately agreed to step in and host the show, as he did in each of the following two years. "He did not claim a single dime in expenses," said Wynn.[14]

In May 1990, Como made his regular appearance at the Duke Children's Classic Celebrity Golf Tournament. Como had been involved in establishing the event in 1974, acting as honorary chairman and persuading a raft of personalities to make an appearance. By 1990, the Duke Children's Classic was able to boast a roster that included names such as Frank Sinatra, Bob Hope, Arnold Palmer and former president Gerald Ford. The Liggett Group, still owners of the Chesterfield brand, were also regular sponsors, continuing an association that dated back to Como's radio days on the *Supper Club* in the forties. As well as playing in the event, Como gave a small, private performance each year at the gala dinner that followed. In 1982, the university had established the Perry Como Fund for Children and in 1990, Duke dedicated three pediatric inpatient units of the Children's Hospital as the Roselle and Perry Como Pavilion, "in honor of their longtime friendship and devotion."[15] Perry, said the 1990 event brochure, "works tirelessly and elegantly to bring warmth and joy to this event."[16]

Como followed up his appearance in the Duke event with another regular charity spot, the St. Francis Celebrity Golf Classic on Long Island. Accompanied by his grandson, Chris, Como found time to talk to Diane Ketcham of the *New York Times,* who also checked out some of the locals who remembered the days when Perry was a resident. One lady recalled seeing Perry driving around town in a gray Cadillac with the license plate PC–42. "He always waved to me," she said. Another local recalled the time he heard Perry curse on a golf course, with as much surprise as if he had just been told that the moon was indeed made of green cheese. Como told Ketcham that he still got recognized wherever he went, although sometimes, the comments surprised him. "I was at the grocery store in Florida pushing one of those carts," he said, "and this woman comes up to me and starts staring and staring. I thought she was ill, so I said, 'Are you having a problem?' and she said, 'I thought you were dead.'"[17]

Como was very much alive and returned to Long Island in December 1990, bringing *The Perry Como Christmas Show* to the Westbury Music Fair. It was the first time that Perry had undertaken a winter tour in the United States, but with no network prepared to offer him an acceptable slot for a TV special, it was his way of sustaining his association with the Christmas season. The show toured familiar venues such as Valley Forge, the Niagara Falls Convention Center, Shea's Buffalo Theater and the Landmark Theater in Syracuse. The tour ended close to home in Miami Beach on December 22. Ray Boyce, reviewing the show in Syracuse, summed it up with three words—"Como! Supremo! Fineto! There has been much ado concerning Frank Sinatra's 75th birthday," he added. "Justifiably, to be sure. But Como's is a longer career; he's had more million-sellers and No. 1 hits than Sinatra; and has had more success and longevity in his radio and TV endeavors. This is not meant to disparage Sinatra, a monumental talent, but rather to remind one of Como's credentials, which are not all that shabby."[18] Como repeated the Christmas tour twice more in 1991 and 1992. The itinerary was largely the same as in 1990, with a few additions, and by 1992, the tour took up the whole of the month of December.

Christmas shows apart, Como's other appearances during 1991 and 1992 had been restricted to the occasional charity benefit or private function. In March 1991, Nick Vanoff, who had produced Como's weekly show in the sixties, died in Los Angeles at the age of 61. Como surprised everyone by flying to California for the funeral where he wanted to sing "Ave Maria." Nick Perito fashioned another reunion with Ray Charles before the service and the trio who had worked together for so long went to the church beforehand to plan the spot where Perry could sing. Charles suggested that the most appropriate place would be for Perry to stand next to the piano. Perry agreed. When the service got underway, Como suddenly turned to Perito and said, "Where are the words?" Perito was taken aback that Como no longer knew the words to the song he had always regarded as his favorite and one that he had sung countless times. He handed over the sheet music that he was playing from and accompanied Como by ear.[19]

Como had of course always been reliant on cue cards, but now he seemed to have great difficulty in remembering the words to virtually any of his songs. In May 1992, he agreed to perform at the National Memorial Day Concert on the West Lawn of the Capitol Building in Washington. With the concert aired live on PBS-TV, it was an audacious step for a singer who a week earlier had celebrated his eightieth birthday. To overcome Como's problems remembering words—he was due to sing "No Other Love," a song that no one could remember him singing live before—a lectern was provided for Como to have the words in front of him. Freed from the uncertainty, Como delivered a stunning vocal performance of a song that had been a test for his vocal range when he had recorded it almost 40 years before.

When his Christmas tour concluded once more back in Florida, Perry invited his touring cast to join him for a Christmas celebration at his home. Comedian-juggler Jack Swersie, who had opened the show each year, sensed that the demands of winter touring were getting to be too much. "In 1992, Perry was starting to feel tired and sick again," he wrote. "Everyone on the tour just kind of knew that it would be the last time that Perry would want to subject himself to a winter tour, or any tour for that matter. There was talk of a Japanese tour and a possible spring and summer tour, but most of us saw the writing on the wall. We could certainly understand why Perry wouldn't want to continue at that pace."[20]

Swersie's recollections also provided a rare glimpse of life inside the Como home on Lighthouse Drive. The full tour complement had traveled to Jupiter inside the tour bus that had ferried them around the northern states. "What a sight it must have been as twenty or so people poured out of the bus parked in front of Perry's suburban home." Swersie wrote. "I'm sure his neighbors got a kick out of that. Perry's wife, Roselle, welcomed all of us with open arms and snacks and drinks were served. Roselle showed us around their beautiful and unpretentious house, and Perry took us out to his backyard to show us his dock and boat. I was really impressed with how humble his home was. Nothing ostentatious. Everything was very modest. Don't get me wrong, his home was beautiful and everything in it was first-class, but nothing was overdone or too showy. A true reflection of the modest man himself and his classy wife, Roselle. In his den, nicely framed gold records hung on the walls along with various plaques and awards that he had been presented with over his long and successful years as a crooner. In his backyard Perry had a putting green where he practiced his golf swing, a small built-in swimming pool, and a dock where his fishing boat floated."[21]

Despite Swersie's feelings that Perry was ready to quit, Como responded enthusiastically to Terry Terajima's proposal that he make one final visit to Japan. In February 1993, Perry, Nick Perito and a backing group of eight girl singers flew to Tokyo for a three-concert farewell tour. Opening dates were at the Okura and Capitol hotels in Tokyo, with a full concert taking place at the NHK Hall in Tokyo on March 8, 1993. In a TV interview before the show, Como was more open than usual. When asked the inevitable question about how he was still able to sing at the age of 80, he pointed to the sky. "The Man upstairs will tell me, the Good Lord will tell me one day 'You're finished.' Till he tells me that, I'll keep on singing."[22]

The show itself offered nothing to indicate that such a moment was nigh. The television presentation showed Como laughing and joking backstage as he waited for

Perry performs in Japan, March 1993.

the orchestra to play out his hits medley as an overture. When the medley moved into "It's Impossible," Como shuffled quietly onto the stage, shielding his eyes to the spotlight and looking slightly embarrassed at the reception he received. The tux sagged a little over a shrinking frame and a lectern held his music and lyrics. Yet when he sang, the voice gave no concession to age. Como moved quickly into three of his standard opening numbers, "Sitting on Top of the World," "Where or When" and "Hello Young Lovers." Each was delivered with the same vigor that Como had shown back on his Vegas debut in 1970. His voice was clear and strong and he coped easily with the high finish that each song demanded. As the show progressed, Como lost his way musically a couple of times but overall, his performance mocked the fact that his eighty-first birthday was just around the corner.

As Swersie had predicted, there was to be no Christmas tour in 1993, but Perry surprised everyone by announcing that he would be returning to TV in 1994 with a Christmas special. Perry revealed that he would fly to Dublin, Ireland, in January 1994 to record the show, under a deal with PBS who would air the show in December 1994. A separate deal with Teal Records also provided for the show to be recorded for both CD and video release around the world. Como it seemed was turning the clock back at least ten years and there were those who wondered if this might be a bridge too far. They were right. When Como arrived at an icy Dublin Airport on Wednesday, January 12, 1994, he put on his overcoat in the airport and never took it off. His week's schedule was demanding—local TV and radio, some location shooting around Dublin and then the TV recording before a live audience at Dublin's cavernous Point Theatre on Friday, Jan-

Perry finds his namesake's barber shop in Dublin in January 1994.

uary 21. The show was also marketed as stand-alone concert, with fans paying up to $50 for a seat.

The decision to forsake the Florida sun for the cold climes of Ireland was looking like a mistake almost from the word go. On Saturday, January 15, Perry appeared on *Kenny Live*, Ireland's top TV talk show. Despite the heat of the studio lights, Como insisted on wearing his camelhair overcoat throughout the interview. As the interview progressed, Como came across as forgetful and at times, confused, mixing up his three children with his 13 grandchildren. It was some relief when Kenny revealed the "surprise" of Nick Perito sitting at a piano across the studio. Perry went into autopilot, delivering croaky but passable renditions of "How to Handle a Woman" and "It Could Happen to You" and recovering enough composure to remind his host to "plug the show."[23] Como's son David, who accompanied him on the trip, missed the *Kenny Show*, but was with his father before and after. He recalled him being cold and dry-throated throughout.[24] Despite feeling ill, Como worked through the week, doing some location shots around Dublin and recording vocal snippets for the show. By Friday, the day of the concert and TV recording, Como was still no warmer and by then, his dry throat had developed into a cold.

The concert was a sell-out, with many of Como's British fans making the trip across the Irish Sea for a surprising opportunity to see Como in person one more time. The show however was fully scripted, meaning that Como needed to read from large cue cards at the foot of the stage, both for the words to his songs and his linking dialogue. Cue cards in a brightly lit TV studio are one thing, but in a darkened concert hall, Perry had not got beyond the first sentence of his welcoming dialogue before stopping and telling producer Bob Wynn, "I can't read in the dark." Como's opening song—"I Can Almost Read Your Mind"—had gone over well, with Como sounding in good voice after making a gladiatorial-style entrance through the auditorium. Once he was required to follow a script, however, the show started to come apart at the seams. Wynn's call of "Cut" was the first of many before the evening was out. Nevertheless, when the interval came around, the show was only marginally off schedule. Como had been a little croaky but the audience (which included Irish president Mary Robinson and other VIPs) was in good spirits and seemed happy just to have him there.

Around nine o'clock, Perry announced a 15-minute interval "to rest my aching limbs" and headed off to his dressing room. As the barrooms throughout the Point filled up, there was no hint of the drama to come. The audience, orchestra and choir were all back in their seats after the break as scheduled. Como failed to appear. Thirty, 40, 50 minutes went by but no Perry. Rumors started to fly and then a slow handclap took up before Perry's Irish guest star, Twink (Adele King), appeared on stage. Perry, she said,

The authors meet Perry, January 21, 1994. Left to right: Perry, Joe Lynch (leader of the Artane Boys Band), George O'Reilly (Irish impresario), Ken Crossland and Malcolm Macfarlane (authors' photograph).

had a cold and felt that his performance was not giving the audience what they were entitled to hear. He had asked that they do the rest of the show without him.

The audience reaction was one of disbelief. It was as if they had been granted an audience with the Pope and then been offered Father O'Malley. Twink said that she would try and persuade Perry to return but in the meantime, there was little else to do but proceed with the parts of the show that did not need the presence of the star. While Twink, Nick Perito and the cast filmed these one after the other, the audience muttered and shuffled in their seats. By 10 P.M., any semblance of this being a regular concert had disappeared and one by one, the audience was beginning to do the same.

Producer Bob Wynn recalled that he had gone into Como's dressing room during the interval and found him stripped to his underwear, sweating and whispering, "I can't go back." Wynn told him that if he didn't, they would face hefty legal claims, but he left without knowing whether Perry would change his mind. A half hour later, a message reached him that Perry was in the wings. "Has he got his clothes on?" Wynn asked the messenger before dashing off to speak to Como. "I think I can do it," Como said. "I think you can do it, too," Wynn told him.[25] Moments later, Como was back on stage. "I have a cold," he told the audience as he took the mike, "and my throat has gone. But I'll give it one more try and if it doesn't come out right, I know you'll forgive me." The cheering almost raised the roof of the theatre.

After the show, Como confided in his son that he had prayed during the interval. "If You'll let me go out there and You'll let me finish, I'll never sing professionally again," Como had said to his Lord.[26] His prayer was answered. For the next 30 minutes, something allowed Como to roll back the years and summon his slaves of the lamp—the velvet tone, his immaculate diction and breath control, and a soaring range to his voice. He sang "And I Love You So" with such force that the audience cheered him on every high note. "Wind Beneath My Wings" got the same treatment, then "Father of Girls" and "It's Impossible." Como himself was visibly moved at the audience response. "When you did that," he told them, referring to the cheering, "no one ever did that for me before." By 11:00 P.M., Como was finally running on empty but Twink and the company carried him through a medley of Irish and Christmas tunes, sustaining the show to its conclusion. By 11:30, it was finally over.

The reviews the morning after were harsh. "Twink saves the day on Perry's big night," said the *Irish Examiner*.[27] "Perry's so sore at letting fans down," said another.[28] The *Irish Times* was kinder. "A great singer hits mark," Gerry Colgan wrote.[29] A phone-in to *Talk Radio* was, according to its host Des Cahill, "pretty evenly divided." Como was clearly upset and went on radio to apologize "for letting people down" before flying home. He offered a refund from his own pocket to anyone who wanted one. It was the only time in 60 years that Perry Como had felt the need to offer anyone their money back.

Perry Como's Irish Christmas aired on PBS in December 1994 and was released on videotape and CD the following year. The final product was a production triumph for Bob Wynn who told his team that he alone would handle the editing.[30] Apart from one impossible continuity challenge—Como had pulled off his bow tie after his reappearance—the show in its final form contained little indication of the drama of the night. Reviews were good and a tribute to Wynn's editing. John Voorhees in the *Seattle Times* said Como was "as relaxed as ever"[31] while Beverley Beckham for the *Boston Herald* said that Como was "back where he belongs, in our homes, crooning just for us."[32] The show also enjoyed some commercial success through the CD and videotape sales, plus frequent re-running on syndicated TV. Nick Perito, however, was sad that such a show should become his master's last hurrah. "It was not one of Como's better performances," he wrote, "but it was the most widely viewed show of his entire career."[33]

Perry Como was true to the pledge that he had made in his dressing room at the Point Theater. In November 1994, he appeared on *Regis & Kathie Lee Live* to promote the Christmas show, delivering an impromptu rendition of "It Could Happen to You." The following spring, he made his final appearance at the Duke Children's Classic gala, singing a handful of songs, but there were no more concerts, no more TV shows. There was still a demand for Como—Mickey Glass said in 2005 that he had been offered $1 million for Perry to play seven nights on an East Coast tour later in 1994, but Como had refused.[34] "Mickey, I'm 82. How many other singers are still doing this stuff at 82?"

The Good Lord, it seemed, was finally telling him that it was time to stop. Perry Como was listening.

Chapter 17

You Are Never
Far Away from Me

Perry Como died peacefully in his sleep on May 12, 2001, six days short of his eighty-ninth birthday. Since his retirement in 1994, he had lived quietly at his home in Jupiter, Florida, largely out of public view. He suffered increasingly from Alzheimer's disease, the first manifestations of which might have contributed to the confusion he had shown during his TV interview in Dublin in 1994.

In 1998, Perry and Roselle celebrated their sixty-fifth wedding anniversary. Two weeks later, on August 12, 1998, Roselle suffered a massive heart attack. She was rushed to the local hospital but died later in the day. She was buried at the Riverside Memorial Park in nearby Tequesta. Nick Perito wrote that after Roselle's death, Como "seemed to give up his desire to live."[1]

In 1999, Como's home town of Canonsburg marked his eighty-seventh birthday with the unveiling of a life-size statue. Como was too ill to attend the ceremony and was represented by his daughter-in-law, Melanie, and some of his grandchildren. His three surviving siblings were also present. "It is a tremendous honor," Melanie Como told the crowd. "I assure you Dad is here in his spirit."[2] Nick Perito also attended. "Thank God we were born at a time when we've all been able to appreciate the talent and the soul of this wonderful human being, Perry Como," he said.[3]

In October 2000, Como was rushed to Jupiter Medical Center complaining of light-headedness and shortage of breath, but was well enough to return home after a four-day stay. By the spring of 2001, however, it was clear that the end was near. Perito flew to Jupiter to say his good-byes. "Even though he was practically comatose at that time, his medical attendants were surprised at how he'd perk up whenever I came to see him," Perito wrote. "Acting as if nothing was wrong, I said things like, 'Hey, Big Daddy, we have a big summer tour all booked, and I brought down some new songs that I know you're anxious to learn.' Upon hearing my voice, he would open his eyes, give me a big smile and pretend to listen to my silly comments reminding him of all the laughs and fun times we shared in the previous 36-plus years. I spent the better part of three days with him. The last morning I was there, we exchanged hugs and I tearfully said good-bye. I knew the end was near."[4]

Como's son David saw his father for the last time early in May 2001. "He knew who I was and we had a nice chat," he said.[5] Como's daughter, Terri, told the press that

Perry's statue in Canonsburg, which was unveiled on May 15, 1999 (authors' photograph).

The graves of Perry and Roselle in Riverside Cemetery, Jupiter, Florida (courtesy Matthew Long).

on his last day, May 12, her father "spent two beautiful hours with me and my grandson, Holden. We shared ice cream. It was a wonderful moment for us."[6]

Perry Como was buried alongside his wife of 65 years on May 18, 2001. Four hundred mourners attended the funeral service and heard Como's recording of "You Are Never Far Away from Me." "This," said Como's daughter, "was Dad's last show."[7] Obituaries and tributes appeared around the world and told the rags to riches life story of a first generation Italian-American. None told the story as simply as the man himself. "I was a barber. Since then, I've been a singer. That's it."[8]

⟨ Appendix A ⟩

Perry Como on Record

This discography shows all of the commercial recordings made by Perry Como from 1936 to 1994, including live concerts that were recorded for commercial release, together with a listing of the primary single and album releases by RCA Records.

We are grateful to George Townsend of Nova Scotia for his help and for the use of his comprehensive web site at www.kokomo.ca. which provides extensive details of all of Perry Como's record and CD releases.

RECORDINGS BY DATE OF SESSION

The Ted Weems Orchestra, Featuring Perry Como— Decca Records, 1936–1941

1936

May 15	You Can't Pull the Wool Over My Eyes / Lazy Weather *(with whistling by Elmo Tanner)*
Aug. 6	Until Today / Fooled by the Moon / Knock, Knock, Who's There? *(with Red Ingle)*
Sept. 27	Picture Me Without You *(with whistling by Elmo Tanner)* / Rainbow on the River *(with whistling by Elmo Tanner)* / Darling, Not Without You / (Trouble Ends) Out Where the Blue Begins

1938

Feb. 22	A Gypsy Told Me / Sunday in the Park / Goodnight, Sweet Dreams, Goodnight
Feb. 23	A Shack in the Back of the Hills / In My Little Red Book *(with whistling by Elmo Tanner)*
Aug. 23	Simple and Sweet / Ribbons and Roses

1939

March 10	Ad-De-Day (the Song of the Cuban Money Divers)
March 11	Class Will Tell
Oct. 4	Goody Goodbye / Two Blind Loves / That Old Gang of Mine
Oct. 5	I Wonder Who's Kissing Her Now? / On the Island of Catalina

1941

Jan. 27	May I Never Love Again
Jan. 28	It All Comes Back to Me Now / Rose of the Rockies *(with whistling by Elmo Tanner)*
Dec. 9	Angeline / Having a Lonely Time / Ollie Ollie Out's in Free / Deep in the Heart of Texas

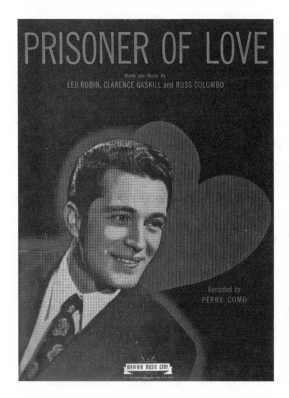

Above and opposite: Perry Como was a regular feature on sheet music copy in the 1940s, often on songs that he never sang! He did, however, sing all the songs shown here—including "Goodbye Sue," his first RCA recording, and "I Can Almost Read Your Mind," which Ray Charles wrote for Perry's 1970 Vegas debut (courtesy Colleen Zwack).

Perry Como on RCA Records, 1943–1987

1943

•Recorded during the American Federation of Musicians (AFM) recording ban. Vocal with mixed chorus only

June 20	Goodbye Sue / There'll Soon Be a Rainbow / Secretly *(unreleased)*
Dec. 1	Have I Stayed Away Too Long? / I've Had This Feeling Before

1944

Feb. 8	Long Ago (and Far Away) / I Love You
June 27	Lili Marlene / First Class Private Mary Brown

•With orchestra conducted by Lew Martin

Dec. 8	More and More / I Dream of You (More Than You Dream I Do) / I Wish We Didn't Have to Say Goodnight
Dec. 11	I'm Confessin' (That I Love You)

1945

•With orchestra conducted by Ted Steele

March 27	I Love You Truly / I'll Always Be with You / Temptation

•With orchestra conducted by Russ Case

May 19	I'm Gonna Love That Gal (Like She's Never Been Loved Before) / If I Loved You
July 3	(Did You Ever Get) That Feeling in the Moonlight / Till the End of Time
Oct. 13	(A Hubba-Hubba-Hubba) Dig You Later (*with The Satisfiers*)
Oct. 17	Here Comes Heaven (Again) / I'm Always Chasing Rainbows *(with The Satisfiers)* / You Won't Be Satisfied (Until You Break My Heart) *(with The Satisfiers)*
Dec. 18	All Through the Day / Prisoner of Love

1946

March 12	Little Man You've Had a Busy Day *(with The Satisfiers)* / More Than You Know
March 14	Kentucky Babe / A Garden in the Rain *(both with The Satisfiers)*
March 19	Blue Skies / My Blue Heaven *(with The Satisfiers)*
March 21	You Must Have Been a Beautiful Baby *(with The Satisfiers)* / If You Were the Only Girl (in the World) / Girl of My Dreams
April 2	Surrender / They Say It's Wonderful
July 15	One More Vote *(with The Satisfiers)* / If I'm Lucky

•*August 1–22, 1946 with orchestra conducted by Russ Case*[1]
Aug. 1	Winter Wonderland *(with The Satisfiers)* / Santa Claus Is Comin' to Town
Aug. 6	I'll Be Home for Christmas / That Christmas Feeling

•*With organ and choir conducted by Russ Case*
Aug. 20	Silent Night / O Come All Ye Faithful (Adeste Fideles) / O Little Town of Bethlehem

•*With orchestra conducted by Russ Case*
Aug. 22	Jingle Bells

•*With orchestra conducted by Lloyd Shaffer*
Oct. 17	That's the Beginning of the End / Sonata
Dec. 12	What Am I Gonna Do About You? / I Gotta Gal I Love (in North and South Dakota) *(with The Satisfiers)*
Dec. 19	That's Where I Came In / I Want to Thank Your Folks

1947

Jan. 23	Easter Parade / (The) Song of Songs
April 10	Chi-Baba, Chi-Baba (My Bambino Go to Sleep) *(with The Satisfiers)* / When You Were Sweet Sixteen *(with The Satisfiers)*
May 29	I Wonder Who's Kissing Her Now? / When Tonight Is Just a Memory *(with Helen Carroll and The Satisfiers)*
July 10	Carolina Moon / White Christmas

•*With orchestra conducted by Russ Case*
July 11	Body and Soul
July 28	So Far / A Fellow Needs a Girl
Sept. 25	When Your Hair Has Turned to Silver (I Will Love You Just the Same) / What'll I Do? / If We Can't Be the Same Old Sweethearts (We'll Just Be the Same Old Friends)
Sept. 30	When Day Is Done / Love Me or Leave Me *(with The Satisfiers)*
Oct. 7	Two Loves Have I / I Never Loved Anyone
Oct. 14	I've Got a Feelin' I'm Fallin' *(with The Satisfiers)* / Pianissimo
Oct. 16	You Can Do No Wrong / Better Luck Next Time
Oct. 21	Love of My Life / It Only Happens When I Dance with You
Nov. 4	My Melancholy Baby / Roses of Picardy
Nov. 11	When Is Sometime? / Laroo Laroo Lilli Bolero
Nov. 20	Oh, How I Miss You Tonight / For You
Nov. 25	When You're Smiling *(with The Satisfiers)*
Dec. 2	If You Had All the World and Its Gold *(with The Mariners)* / Because
Dec. 4	Marcheta
Dec. 9	There Must Be a Way / Haunted Heart
Dec. 30	Every Time I Meet You / Rambling Rose *(with The Satisfiers)* / By the Way

1948

•*With The Fontane Sisters*
Dec. 2	N'yot N'yow (the Pussycat Song)

•*With chorus and orchestra conducted by Henri René*
Dec. 14	Far Away Places / Missouri Waltz
Dec. 17	Blue Room
Dec. 23	With a Song in My Heart

1949

•*With chorus and orchestra conducted by Mitchell Ayres*
Jan. 13	I Don't See Me in Your Eyes Anymore / Forever and Ever
March 1	'A'—You're Adorable *(with The Fontane Sisters)* / Some Enchanted Evening / Bali Ha'i
May 3	Two Little New Little Blue Little Eyes / Give Me Your Hand
May 24	Just One Way to Say I Love You / Let's Take an Old-Fashioned Walk
July 7	I Wish I Had a Record (Of the Promises You Made) / The Meadows of Heaven

Aug. 11   A Dreamer's Holiday *(with The Fontane Sisters* / I Wanna Go Home (with You) *(with The Fontane Sisters)*

♦*With choir and organ directed by Mitchell Ayres*
Sept. 30   Ave Maria / The Lord's Prayer

♦*With chorus and orchestra conducted by Mitchell Ayres*
Oct. 3   Hush Little Darlin' *(with The Fontane Sisters)* / A Dream Is a Wish Your Heart Makes
Nov. 7   Bibbidi-Bobbidi-Boo (the Magic Song) *(with The Fontane Sisters)*
Dec. 1   Please Believe Me / Did Anyone Ever Tell You Mrs. Murphy? / My Child *(unreleased)*

1950

March 16   On the Outgoing Tide / Hoop-Dee-Doo *(with The Fontane Sisters)*
Apr. 3   Let's Go to Church (Next Sunday Morning) / If You Were Only Mine
June 15   If You Were My Girl / I Cross My Fingers *(with The Fontane Sisters)*

♦*With mixed chorus and women's choir and the St. Patrick's Cathedral Boys Choir, conducted by Mitchell Ayres with organ accompaniment*
June 26/29 Bless This House / (The) Rosary / Rock of Ages / Mother Dear, O Pray for Me / Holy God We Praise Thy Name / Prayer of Thanksgiving

♦*With orchestra and chorus conducted by Mitchell Ayres*
Aug. 10   Patricia / Watchin' the Trains Go By
Aug. 15   There Is No Christmas Like a Home Christmas / (The) Christmas Symphony
Aug. 31   The Best Thing for You / So Long Sally / Marrying for Love

♦*With orchestra conducted by Mitchell Ayres*
Sept. 12   A Bushel and a Peck / She's a Lady *(both with Betty Hutton)*
Sept. 26   It's a Lovely Day Today / You're Just in Love (I Wonder Why) *(both with The Fontane Sisters)*
Nov. 28   If Wishes Were Kisses *(with The Fontane Sisters)* / If

♦*With orchestra and chorus conducted by the composer Sigmund Romberg*
Dec. 5   Zing Zing—Zoom Zoom / Black Moonlight

♦*With the Western-Ayres (Mitchell Ayres) and The Sons of the Pioneers*
Dec. 18   Tumbling Tumbleweeds / You Don't Kno' What Lonesome Is ('Til You Get to Herdin' Cows)

1951

♦*With Mitchell Ayres and His Orchestra*
Jan. 11   Without a Song / More Than You Know / It's Only a Paper Moon *(unreleased)* / Me and My Shadow *(unreleased)* / That Old Gang of Mine
Jan. 16   It's Only a Paper Moon *(unreleased)* / Me and My Shadow *(unreleased)*
Feb. 1   It's Only a Paper Moon / Me and My Shadow / I Found a Million Dollar Baby (in a Five and Ten Cent Store)
March 20   Hello, Young Lovers *(unreleased)* / We Kiss in a Shadow *(unreleased)*
March 27   Hello, Young Lovers / We Kiss in a Shadow / You'll Never Walk Alone *(unreleased)*
May 15   There's a Big Blue Cloud (Next to Heaven) / There's No Boat Like a Rowboat *(with The Fontane Sisters)*
June 26   Surprising / Cara Cara Bella Bella
Aug. 28   Rollin' Stone *(with The Fontane Sisters)* / With All My Heart and Soul / Cold, Cold Heart *(unreleased)*
Sept. 18   It's Beginning to Look Like Christmas *(with The Fontane Sisters)* / Here's to My Lady
Dec. 18   Tulips and Heather / Please Mr. Sun

1952

Jan. 29   Noodlin' Rag / Play Me a Hurtin' Tune *(both with The Fontane Sisters)*
Jan. 31   It's Easter Time *(unreleased)* / One Little Candle

♦*With orchestra and chorus conducted by Mitchell Ayres[2]*
March 4   Over the Rainbow *(with Sally Sweetland)* / I Concentrate on You / It's Easter Time
March 11   If There Is Someone Lovelier Than You / My Heart Stood Still *(unreleased)* / Summertime *(with Sally Sweetland)* / While We're Young *(unreleased)* / You'll Never Walk Alone *(test only)* / Nobody *(test only)*
March 13   My Heart Stood Still / While We're Young / You'll Never Walk Alone

♦*With Mitchell Ayres and His Orchestra*
April 1   Lonesome, That's All / Why Did You Leave Me?
April 10   When You Come to the End of the Day / Childhood Is a Meadow
May 13   Watermelon Weather / Maybe *(both with Eddie Fisher)*
June 19   To Know You (Is to Love You) / The Last Straw *(both with Betty Hutton; both unreleased)*
July 15   The Ruby and the Pearl / What More Is There to Say? *(unreleased)*

With Mitchell Ayres and His Orchestra and the Ray Charles Singers
July 17   Sweethearts Holiday / My Love and Devotion / You Are Never Far Away from Me *(unreleased)*

With Mitchell Ayres and His Orchestra
Sept. 9   To Know You (Is to Love You) *(with The Fontane Sisters)* / My Lady Loves to Dance

With Hugo Winterhalter's Orchestra and The Ramblers
Nov. 4   Don't Let the Stars Get in Your Eyes / Lies

1953

With Hugo Winterhalter's Orchestra and Chorus
Jan. 6   Wild Horses / I Confess

With Hugo Winterhalter's Orchestra
March 28   Say You're Mine Again *(with The Ramblers)* / My One and Only Heart

May 5–June 22, 1953, with Mitchell Ayres and His Orchestra[3]
May 5   The Christmas Song *(with The Ray Charles Singers)* / C-H-R-I-S-T-M-A-S

With Mitchell Ayres and His Orchestra and Chorus
May 18   (The) First Christmas *(this song is believed to have been recorded in 1949-50. The date shown here refers to its remastering by RCA. Exact recording date is unknown)*

With Henri René's Orchestra and Chorus
May 19   No Other Love / Keep It Gay

With Mitchell Ayres and His Orchestra and Chorus
May 21   Frosty the Snowman / I Saw Mommy Kissing Santa Claus / Rudolph the Red-Nosed Reindeer
May 26   The Twelve Days of Christmas / Joy to the World / God Rest Ye Merry, Gentlemen

With String Ensemble directed by Mitchell Ayres
June 22   'Twas the Night Before Christmas

With Hugo Winterhalter's Orchestra and Chorus
Aug. 19   Idle Gossip / You Alone (Solo Tu) / Pa-paya Mama

September 24–November 23, 1953, with orchestra and chorus under the direction of Hugo Winterhalter[4]
Sept. 24   I Believe (unreleased) / Onward Christian Soldiers

With orchestra under the direction of Mitchell Ayres and chorus under the direction of Ray Charles
Sept. 29   Act of Contrition / Nearer My God to Thee / Abide with Me / Goodnight Sweet Jesus

With Mitchell Ayres and His Orchestra
Nov. 17   Eli Eli / Kol Nidrei *(first part)*
Nov. 23   I Believe / Kol Nidrei *(completed)*

With Hugo Winterhalter's Orchestra and Chorus
Nov. 29   I'll Love Nobody Else but You *(unreleased)*
Dec. 29   Wanted / I'll Love Nobody Else but You *(unreleased)* / Look out the Window (And See How I'm Standing in the Rain) / Hit and Run Affair

1954

Jan. 2   Door of Dreams *(unreleased)* / There Never Was a Night So Beautiful

With Mitchell Ayres and His Orchestra (not confirmed) and The Ames Brothers
July 14   One More Time / Hopelessly *(both unreleased)*

With Mitchell Ayres and His Orchestra and The Ray Charles Chorus
Aug. 31   The Things I Didn't Do / Papa Loves Mambo
Sept. 2   The Things I Didn't Do / Door of Dreams / Don't Ask Me Why *(all unreleased)*

With Mitchell Ayres and His Orchestra
Nov. 16   Silk Stockings / (There's No Place Like) Home for the Holidays *(with The Ray Charles Singers)*

1955

With Mitchell Ayres and His Orchestra and the Ray Charles Singers
Jan. 4   Ko-Ko-Mo (I Love You So) / You'll Always Be My Lifetime Sweetheart

January 20–February 17, 1955, with Mitchell Ayres and His Orchestra and the Ray Charles Singers[5]
Jan. 20   It's the Talk of the Town *(unreleased)* / My Funny Valentine / As Time Goes By / I've Got the World on a String / Ain't Misbehavin' *(unreleased)* / You Do Something to Me
Jan. 25   It Happened in Monterey / I Gotta Right to Sing the Blues / Breezin' Along with the Breeze
Feb. 8   It's a Good Day / When You're Away *(unreleased)* / For Me and My Gal / Nobody
Feb. 17   One for My Baby (And One More for the Road) / In the Still of the Night / It's the Talk of the Town / Trees *(unreleased)*

•*With Mitchell Ayres and His Orchestra and the Ray Charles Singers*
Feb. 22   Door of Dreams / Maderia (*unreleased*)
April 28   Chee Chee-Oo Chee (Sang the Little Bird) / Two Lost Souls (*both with Jaye P. Morgan*)
June 21   Fooled / (The) Rose Tattoo (*unreleased*) / Tina Marie
Sept. 27   (The) Rose Tattoo[6] / All at Once You Love Her

1956

Feb. 2   Juke Box Baby / Hot Diggity (Dog Ziggity Boom)
May 8   More / Glendora
June 7   Dream Along with Me (I'm on My Way to a Star) / Somebody up There Likes Me

•*With Mitchell Ayres' Orchestra*
June 13   Try a Little Tenderness / Say It Isn't So (*unreleased*) / Unchained Melody

•*June 18, 1956–February 19, 1957, with Mitchell Ayres' Orchestra*[7]
June 18   Somebody Loves Me / They Can't Take That Away from Me / S'posin' / It's Been a Long,
             Long Time (*unreleased*) / If I Could Be with You (One Hour Tonight)

•*With Mitchell Ayres' Orchestra and the Ray Charles Singers*
Sept. 6   Moonlight Love / Chincherinchee

1957

Jan. 8   Close (*unreleased*) / Mi Casa, Su Casa (My House Is Your House)
Jan. 15   I Accuse (*unreleased*) / Round and Round / I Have You to Thank (*unreleased*)

•*With Mitchell Ayres and His Orchestra*
Feb. 12   That's What I Like / South of the Border (Down Mexico Way) / I Had the Craziest Dream /
             Angry / Swingin' Down the Lane
Feb. 19   It's Easy to Remember / 'Deed I Do / Honey, Honey (Bless Your Heart) / Sleepy Time Gal

•*With Mitchell Ayres' Orchestra and Chorus*
April 9   The Girl with the Golden Braids / My Little Baby

•*With Mitchell Ayres' Orchestra and the Ray Charles Singers*
July 1   Just Born (to Be your Baby) / Sad and Lonely (*unreleased*) / Dancin'
July 2   Ivy Rose / Heartaches for Sale (*unreleased*) / Marchin' Along to the Blues
Oct. 9   Catch a Falling Star
Dec. 3   Magic Moments

1958

•*February 12–March 12, 1958, with Mitchell Ayres' Orchestra and the Ray Charles Singers*[8]
Feb. 12   Little Man You've Had a Busy Day (*take 1—not known which take used*) / Almost Like Being
             in Love (*take 4 partially completed*) / (The) Whiffenpoof Song
Feb. 13   Almost Like Being in Love (*take 4 completed*) / Vaya Con Dios (May God Be with You) /
             Love Letters
Feb. 19   It Had to Be You / Gypsy in My Soul / Ac-Cent-Tchu-Ate the Positive
Feb. 20   When I Fall in Love / Red Sails in the Sunset / Little Man You've Had a Busy Day (*take 9—not
             known which take used*)
March 4   Dance Only with Me / Moon Talk (*unreleased*) / Kewpie Doll (*unreleased*) / Beats There a
             Heart So True (*unreleased*)
March 5   I May Be Wrong / Between the Devil and the Deep Blue Sea / Begin the Beguine (*unreleased*)
March 6   Moon Talk (*not included in album*) / You Made Me Love You / It Could Happen to You /
             Twilight on the Trail / Like Someone in Love
March 11   Kewpie Doll (*not included in album*) / Birth of the Blues
March 12   Beats There a Heart So True (*unreleased*) / Come Rain or Come Shine / Dream Along with Me
             (I'm on My Way to a Star) / You Are Never Far Away from Me

•*April 30–June 23, 1958, with Mitchell Ayres' Orchestra and the Ray Charles Singers*[9]
April 30   Only One / Whither Thou Goest
May 1   I May Never Pass This Way Again / Prayer for Peace
May 29   Beats There a Heart So True / Sow the Seeds of Happiness (*both unreleased*)
June 5   Beats There a Heart So True / Sow the Seeds of Happiness (*unreleased*)
June 18   No Well on Earth / In the Garden / All Through the Night
June 19   When You Come to the End of the Day / May the Good Lord Bless and Keep You / Scarlet
             Ribbons
June 23   A Still Small Voice / He's Got the Whole World in His Hands

•*With Mitchell Ayres' Orchestra and the Ray Charles Singers*
Sept. 5   If and When / Love Makes the World Go 'Round (*both unreleased*)

Sept. 16	If and When (unreleased) / Love Makes the World Go 'Round / Mandolins in the Moonlight
Dec. 17	Bella Bella Sue / Trouble Comes *(unreleased)* / Tell Her of My Love, Paloma *(unreleased)*

1959

Jan. 29	Tomboy / Kiss Me and Kiss Me and Kiss Me

•April 9–May 21, 1959, with Mitchell Ayres' Orchestra[10]

April 9	St. Louis Blues / I've Got You Under My Skin
April 16	Donkey Serenade / Honey, Honey (Bless Your Heart) / Let a Smile Be Your Umbrella
April 23	Dear Hearts and Gentle People / You Came a Long Way from St. Louis / (Get Your Kicks On) Route 66
May 14	You Are in Love / I Know *(with The Ray Charles Singers)*
May 21	Begin the Beguine / Mood Indigo / To Know You (Is to Love You) *(with Ray Charles)* / Linda

•July 13–15, 1959, with Mitchell Ayres' Orchestra and the Ray Charles Singers[11]

July 13	Here We Come a Caroling / We Wish You a Merry Christmas *(a-cappella medley with the Ray Charles Singers)* / O Holy Night / The Story of the First Christmas
July 14	Winter Wonderland / Santa Claus Is Comin' to Town / God Rest Ye Merry, Gentlemen
July 15	(There's No Place Like) Home for the Holidays / White Christmas / (The) Christmas Song (Merry Christmas to You) / Silent Night

•With Mitchell Ayres' Orchestra and the Male Voices of the Robert Shaw Chorale

Oct. 26	Ave Maria (Schubert) / (The) Lord's Prayer

•With Mitchell Ayres' Orchestra and the Ray Charles Singers

Dec. 28	I Know What God Is / I Can't Remember *(unreleased)* / Delaware / Mandolino *(unreleased)*

1960

Oct. 13	Gone Is My Love / Make Someone Happy

•October 25–November 15, 1960. With Mitchell Ayres' Orchestra[12]

Oct. 25	You Make Me Feel So Young
Oct. 26	Too Young / Hello, Young Lovers / While We're Young / Young at Heart
Nov. 2	Especially for the Young / Young Love / I Was Young and Foolish / Too Young to Go Steady
Nov. 15	When You and I Were Young, Maggie / When Hearts Are Young / Like Young

1961

•May 15 & 17, 1961, with Mitchell Ayres' Orchestra, Tony Mottola on guitar and The Ray Charles Singers[13]

May 15	Medley: Say It Isn't So; Blue Skies; Here's That Rainy Day / Medley: All by Myself; I've Grown Accustomed to Her Face; So in Love / It All Depends on You *(unreleased)*
May 17	Medley: Thank Heaven for Little Girls; You Were Meant for Me; A Fellow Needs a Girl / Medley: You Alone (Solo Tu); I'm Gonna Sit Right Down and Write Myself a Letter; A Portrait of My Love / Medley: All I Do Is Dream of You; Gigi; The Way You Look Tonight / You Are Never Far Away from Me (Theme) / Back in Your Own Backyard *(unreleased)* / Medley: Smile; How Deep Is the Ocean?; This Nearly Was Mine

•With Mitchell Ayres' Orchestra and The Ray Charles Singers

Oct. 18	You're Following Me

1962

Feb. 14	(The) Island of Forgotten Lovers / Caterina

•June 8–26, 1962, with Mitchell Ayres' Orchestra and The Ray Charles Singers[14]

June 8	Moonglow and Theme from "Picnic" / Maria / Lollipops and Roses / The Sweetest Sounds
June 14	My Favorite Things / Once Upon a Time / What's New? *(unreleased)* / The Bells of St. Mary's
June 21	Moon River / I'll Remember April
June 26	What's New? / Can't Help Falling in Love / Somebody Cares / More Than Likely

•September 30–October 2, 1962, with Mitchell Ayres' Orchestra and The Ray Charles Singers[15]

Sept. 30	It Gets Lonely in the White House / In Our Hide-Away *(with Sandy Stewart)*
Oct. 1	Pigtails and Freckles / Is She the Only Girl in the World / I'm Gonna Get Him *(with Sandy Stewart)*
Oct. 2	Glad to Be Home / Empty Pockets Filled with Love / This Is a Great Country *(with Sandy Stewart & Kaye Ballard)*

1963

•March 18–26, 1963, with Mitchell Ayres' Orchestra and The Ray Charles Singers[16]

March 18	Carnival / When I Lost You / I Left My Heart in San Francisco / Fly Me to the Moon *(1st version—not known which one used)*

March 19   Days of Wine and Roses / This Is All I Ask / I Wanna Be Around *(1st version—not known which one used)*
March 25   The Hawaiian Wedding Song / Slightly out of Tune / I Wanna Be Around *(2nd version—not known which one used)*
March 26   The Songs I Love / Fly Me to the Moon *(2nd version—not known which one used)* / My Coloring Book / What Kind of Fool Am I?

•*With Mitchell Ayres' Orchestra and The Ray Charles Singers*
May 1   One More Mountain / (I Love You) Don't You Forget It

1965

•*February 9–June 23, 1965, with The Anita Kerr Quartet*[17]
Feb. 9   My Own Peculiar Way / Give Myself a Party / Gringo's Guitar / Funny How Time Slips Away / I Really Don't Want to Know
Feb. 10   Where Does a Little Tear Come From? / A Hatchet, a Hammer, a Bucket of Nails / Dream On Little Dreamer / That Ain't All / Stand Beside Me *(all unreleased)*
Feb. 11   Where Does a Little Tear Come From? *(unreleased)* / A Hatchet, a Hammer, a Bucket of Nails / Dream On Little Dreamer / That Ain't All
Feb. 12   Where Does a Little Tear Come From? / Stand Beside Me / Here Comes My Baby / Sweet Adorable You
June 22   Roamin' Through the Countryside / Bye, Bye Little Girl / Bummin' Around / Oowee, Oowee *(unreleased)*
June 23   Oowee, Oowee / (The) Summer Wind / Meet Me at the Altar / Beady Eyed Buzzard

•*Orchestra conducted by Nick Perito with the Ray Charles Singers*
Nov. 12   Meet Me at the Altar / Bye, Bye Little Girl

•*December 29, 1965–March 1, 1966, with Orchestra conducted by Nick Perito with the Ray Charles Singers*[18]
Dec. 29   Happiness Comes, Happiness Goes / How Insensitive / Perhaps, Perhaps, Perhaps *(not included in album)*/ Coo Coo Roo Coo Coo Paloma
Dec. 30   Baia *(unreleased)* / Quiet Nights of Quiet Stars / Little Boat *(not included in album)* / Pardon My English *(not included in album)*

1966

Feb. 22   The Shadow of Your Smile / Stay with Me *(unreleased)* / Once I Loved *(unreleased)*
Feb. 25   Baia *(unreleased)* / Meditation / And Roses and Roses
Feb. 28   Manhã de Carnaval / Yesterday / Dindi
March 1   Stay with Me / Once I Loved

•*May 9–19, 1966, with orchestra conducted by Nick Perito with The Allesandro Allessandroni Singers under the direction of Ray Charles*[19]
May 9   Forget Domani / Santa Lucia *(unreleased)*
May 11   Santa Lucia / Un Giorno Dopo l'Altro (One Day Is Like Another) *(unreleased)* / Love Theme from "La Strada" (Traveling Down a Lonely Road)
May 13   O Marenariello / Arrivederci Roma (Goodbye to Rome*) (unreleased)*
May 16   Cominciamo Ad Amarci *(unreleased)* / Un Giorno Dopo l'Altro (One Day Is Like Another) *(unreleased)*
May 17   Anema E Core / Souvenir d'Italie *(unreleased)*
May 18   Arrivederci Roma (Goodbye to Rome) / Oh Marie
May 19   Cominciamo Ad Amarci / Souvenir d'Italie / Toselli's Serenade (Dreams and Memories) / E Lei (to You)

1967

•*Orchestra conducted by Nick Perito with The Ray Charles Singers*
Jan. 12   A World of Love (That I Found in Your Arms) *(unreleased)* / Stop! And Think It Over *(unreleased)*
Feb. 15   How Beautiful the World Can Be / Stop! And Think It Over / What Love Is Made Of *(unreleased)*
June 1   A World of Love (That I Found in Your Arms) / What Love Is Made Of / I Looked Back
June 2   Happiness Comes, Happiness Goes / Happy Together *(unreleased)* / That's All This Old World Needs *(unreleased)*
July 28   Happy Man / He Who Loves / Another Go Around *(all unreleased)*
Aug. 3   He Who Loves *(unreleased)* / Another Go Around

•*Arranged and conducted by Cam Mullins*
Aug. 22   You Made It That Way (Watermelon Summer) / That's All This Old World Needs / Deep in Your Heart

◆*Arranged and conducted by Bill McElhiney*
Aug. 24   Love Is a Christmas Rose / Christmas Bells (in the Steeple) / Nobody but You / Hearts Will Be
            Hearts / Happy Man
◆*Orchestra conducted by Nick Perito with The Ray Charles Singers*
Dec. 29   (The) Father of Girls / How to Handle a Woman *(unreleased)* / Somebody Makes It So

1968

◆*June 5–19, 1968, with orchestra conducted by Nick Perito, with The Ray Charles Singers*[20]
June 5   Together Forever *(not included in album)* / When You're in Love / You're Nearer
June 7   In These Crazy Times / How to Handle a Woman / Turnaround *(not included in album)*
June 12   Look to Your Heart / Try to Remember / My Cup Runneth Over
June 19   Somebody Somewhere *(unconfirmed recording)* / People *(unconfirmed recording)* / Love in a
            Home / Sunrise, Sunset / (The) Father of Girls

◆*July 9–August 6, 1968 with orchestra conducted by Nick Perito with The Ray Charles Singers*[21]
July 9   Have Yourself a Merry Little Christmas / (The) Little Drummer Boy *(both unreleased)*
July 12   Do You Hear What I Hear? / O Holy Night / Silver Bells *(all unreleased)*
July 17   Have Yourself a Merry Little Christmas / (The) Little Drummer Boy / Ave Maria *(all unreleased)*
July 23   There Is No Christmas Like a Home Christmas / Carol Medley: Caroling, Caroling—The First
            Noël—Hark! The Herald Angels Sing—Silent Night *(all unreleased)*

Aug. 1   Have Yourself a Merry Little Christmas / Silver Bells / Ave Maria / Carol Medley: Caroling,
            Caroling—The First Noël—Hark! The Herald Angels Sing—Silent Night
Aug. 3   (The) Little Drummer Boy / Do You Hear What I Hear? / O Holy Night / There Is No Christ-
            mas Like a Home Christmas
Aug. 6   Some Children See Him / Christmas Eve / Toyland / Christ Is Born

◆Orchestra conducted by Nick Perito
Oct. 7   I Want That Girl *(unreleased)* / Buongiorno Teresa / That's Me *(unreleased)*

◆Arranged and conducted by Bill McElhiney
Oct. 10   Sunshine Wine / Seattle

1969

◆Orchestra conducted by Nick Perito
June 25   Summer Me, Winter Me / A Love to Wear / That's Me *(all unreleased)*

1970

◆Orchestra conducted by Marty Manning
May 5   Love Is Spreading over the World / Long Life, Lots of Happiness / It's Impossible[22] *(take 1+)*
May 6   Don't Leave Me / Turn Around *(unreleased)* / It's Impossible *(take 2)*

*◆June 25–27, 1970 with orchestra conducted by Nick Perito with vocal accompaniment by The Doodletown
  Pipers[23]*
            I've Got You Under My Skin / Hello Young Lovers *(Medley)* / Everybody's Talkin' / If I Had a
            Hammer / Without a Song / I Can Almost Read Your Mind / Prisoner of Love / (The)
            Father of Girls / Love Is Spreading over the World; / When You Were Sweet Sixteen /
            Didn't We? / Oh Marenariello *(Medley)* / It's a Good Day / You'll Never Walk Alone

◆November 23–25, 1970 with orchestra conducted by Nick Perito[24]
Nov 23   Raindrops Keep Fallin' on My Head / Something / Snowbird
Nov 24   A House Is Not a Home / Everybody Is Looking for an Answer / El Condor Pasa
Nov 25   (They Long to Be) Close to You / I Think I Love You / We've Only Just Begun

1971

◆January 14–April 30, 1971. Sessions arranged and conducted by Don Costa with The Ray Charles Singers[25]
Jan. 14   I Think of You *(take 1+) (unreleased)* / Someone Who Cares *(unreleased)*
Feb. 10   I Think of You *(take 1+, overdubbed)*
April 26   Yesterday I Heard the Rain / My Days of Loving You / Someone Who Cares *(unreleased)*
April 27   If / For All We Know / Where Do I Begin
April 28   Dream Baby *(unreleased)*
April 29   Someone Who Cares / Dream Baby / Me and You and a Dog Named Boo
April 30   Put Your Hand in the Hand / Bridge over Troubled Water

1973

◆January 15th–April 4th, 1973. Sessions arranged and conducted by Cam Mullins[26]
Jan. 15   I Want to Give / Reach out Your Hand *(both unreleased)*
Jan. 16   If I Had Never Loved You *(unreleased)* / Take a Look at Me *(unreleased)* / It All Seems to Fall
            into Line / Without Your Love *(unreleased)* / He Couldn't Love You More *(unreleased)*
Jan. 17   It Was Such a Good Day / And I Love You So / Take Me Home / Love Looks So Good on
            You / I Thought About You *(all unreleased)*
Jan. 18   Reach Out Your Hand / Take Me Home *(both unreleased)*
Jan. 19   I Want to Give / And I Love You So / Love Looks So Good on You / I Thought About You
March 26   Tie a Yellow Ribbon 'Round the Ole Oak Tree / Sing / For the Good Times *(all unreleased)*
March 27   Killing Me Softly with Her Song / Aubrey / I Believe in Music *(all unreleased)*
April 4   Tie a Yellow Ribbon 'Round the Ole Oak Tree / Sing / For the Good Times / Killing Me
            Softly with Her Song / Aubrey / I Believe in Music

◆Arranged and conducted by Cam Mullins
May 18   Take a Look at Me / If I Had Never Loved You / Without Your Love / He Couldn't Love You
            More *(all unreleased)*
June 4   Ahora Que Soy Libre (I Want to Give) / Yo Te Quiero Asi (And I Love You So)

◆Arranged and conducted by Bill McElhiney
Aug. 7   Welcome Home / Walk Right Back / Somehow *(all unreleased)*
Aug. 8   Woman of the World / I'll Take My Chances with You / Turn the World Around *(all unreleased)*
Aug. 9   Love Don't Care (Where It Grows) *(unreleased)*
Aug. 17   Walk Right Back / Somehow *(unreleased)* / I'll Take My Chances with You *(unreleased)* / Love
            Don't Care (Where It Grows)

1974

•*Arranged and conducted by Nick Perito with the Ray Charles Singers*[27]
Jan. 4   The Hands of Time / Beyond Tomorrow
Jan. 7   I Don't Know What He Told You / Weave Me the Sunshine / Harmony *(unreleased)*
April 29   Temptation / You Are the Sunshine of My Life / That's You
May 1   The Way We Were / The Most Beautiful Girl / Behind Closed Doors

•*Conducted by Anthony Bowles and Alan Doggett with The London Boys Choir*
Aug. 7   Christmas Dream

1975

•*January 7–June 6, 1975. Arranged and conducted by Cam Mullins, vocal accompaniment by The Nashville Sounds*[28]
Jan. 7   Wonderful Baby / World of Dreams / Love Put a Song in My Heart *(all unreleased)*
Jan. 8   Yellow Beach Umbrella / Wrong Rainbow / Let It Be Love / Loving Her Was Easier (Than Anything I'll Ever Do Again) *(all unreleased)*
Jan. 9   Let's Do It Again / Tomorrow's Good Old Days / A Point of View / Here, There and Everywhere / Good Friends and Fireplaces *(all unreleased)*
Jan. 16   Then You Can Tell Me Goodbye / The Grass Keeps Right on Growin' *(both unreleased)*
Jan. 22   World of Dreams *(not included in album)* / Love Put a Song in My Heart / Yellow Beach Umbrella *(unreleased)* / Wonderful Baby *(not included in album)*
Jan. 27   Let It Be Love / Loving Her Was Easier (Than Anything I'll Ever Do Again) / Let's Do It Again / Here, There and Everywhere
May 6   Yellow Beach Umbrella / I've Loved You All over the World / Wrong Rainbow *(all unreleased)*
May 27   Let Me Call You Baby Tonight *(unreleased* / Then You Can Tell Me Goodbye / Make Love to Life *(unreleased)* / Just out of Reach *(unreleased)*
May 28   The Grass Keeps Right on Growin'
June 6   Let Me Call You Baby Tonight / Make Love to Life / Just out of Reach / The Grass Keeps Right on Growin'

•*Arranged and conducted by Cam Mullins, vocal accompaniment by The Nashville Sounds*
Oct. 1   I've Loved You All over the World / Wrong Rainbow *(both unreleased)*
Oct. 15   I've Loved You All over the World / Wrong Rainbow *(both unreleased)*

1976

•*Produced and arranged by Bob Mersey*
Aug. 11   Lovers, Kids and Fools / My Days of Loving You (Anima Mia) / Everything *(unreleased)* / Coming Back for More *(unreleased)* / Yes, No, Maybe! *(unreleased)*

1977

•*Recording details not known*
Feb. 3   Marie / That's What Friends Are for *(both unreleased)*

•*June 6–10, 1977. Sessions conducted by Nick Perito with The Tony Mansell Singers under the direction of Ray Charles*[29]
             Greensleeves / My Kind of Girl / The Very Thought of You / A Nightingale Sang in Berkeley Square / Someday I'll Find You / Michelle / We'll Meet Again / There's a Kind of Hush (All over the World) / Smile / The Other Man's Grass Is Always Greener / Where Is Love? / Where You're Concerned / Girl You Make It Happen *(note: the last 2 tracks were not included in the album)*

•*Arranged and conducted by Nick Perito*
Oct. 5   You Light up My Life / Feelings / When I Need You

1978

Jan. 17   Marie *(unreleased)*
Dec. 10/11   To Make You Smile Again *(unreleased)* / When I Wanted You / You Are So Beautiful / Forever / Rosemary Blue *(unreleased)*

1980

•*April 8–17, 1980 Arranged and conducted by Byron Olsen*[30]
             Not While I'm Around / Regrets / When / There'll Never Be Another Night Like This / Love / When She Smiles / (The) Colors of My Life / Save Me the Dance / Someone Is Waiting / You Are My World

•*July 29–31, 1980. Arranged and conducted by Nick Perito with vocal arrangements by Ray Charles*[31]
             Where or When / Beautiful Noise / You Needed Me / Temptation / Bing Crosby medley (Blue

Skies—But Beautiful—Dear Hearts and Gentle People—Sweet Leilani—Ac-Cent-Tchu-Ate the Positive—Swinging on a Star—Pennies from Heaven—Too-Ra-Loo-Ra-Lo-Ral—White Christmas—In the Cool, Cool, Cool of the Evening) / I Can Almost Read Your Mind / Perry Como medley ('Till the End of Time—Catch a Falling Star—Round and Round—Don't Let the Stars Get in Your Eyes) / You'll Never Walk Alone / You Are Never Far Away from Me (theme) / Encore: (Oh Marie—It Could Happen to You—And I Love You So—It's Impossible—Send in the Clowns)

1981

•*Arranged and conducted by Nick Perito*
Oct.   I Wish It Could Be Christmas Forever

•*December 1981–1982 Arranged and conducted by Nick Perito and Byron Olsen*[32]
What's One More Time / So It Goes / Here Comes That Song Again / Goodbye for Now (Love Theme from 'Reds') / (The) Second Time / Jason / As My Love for You / Fancy Dancer

1983

•*Arranged and conducted by Nick Perito with the Ray Charles Singers*
Oct. 17/18   (The) Best of Times / Song on the Sand (La Da Da Da)

1987

•*Arranged, conducted and produced by Nick Perito*[33]
Feb. 2/3   Making Love to You / Sing Along with Me / Tonight I Celebrate My Love for You / Butterfly (I'll Set You Free) / Bless the Beasts and the Children / That's What Friends Are For / (The) Wind Beneath My Wings / I'm Dreaming of Hawaii / You're Nearer / My Heart Stood Still / Do You Remember Me? / (The) Best of Times

Perry Como for Teal Entertainment

1994

•*January 21, 1994. Arranged and conducted by Nick Perito, with the RTE Concert Orchestra, leader Michael Healy.*[34]
A Little Bit of Heaven / I Can Almost Read Your Mind / Happy Holiday /We Need a Little Christmas / Medley (It's Beginning to Look Like Christmas; Have Yourself a Merry Little Christmas; Bless This House) / Little Drummer Boy / Medley (And I Love You So; Catch a Falling Star; Round and Round; Hot Diggity (Dog Ziggity Boom); Don't Let the Stars Get in Your Eyes) / Too-Ra-Loo-Ra-Loo-Ral *(with Twink)* / (The) Father of Girls / Christ Is Born *(with the Boys of The Glasnevin Music Society)* / Medley (If You're Irish; When Irish Eyes Are Smiling *[with Twink])* / Medley with Twink (Sing Along with Me; Santa Claus Is Comin' to Town; White Christmas; Jingle Bells) / The Wind Beneath My Wings / Medley (O Little Town of Bethlehem; Hark! The Herald Angels Sing; Silent Night; O Come All Ye Faithful) / Toyland / I Wish It Could Be Christmas Forever / We Wish You a Merry Christmas / Ave Maria

ISSUED RECORDINGS BY CATALOG NUMBER

Decca Records

Decca Records issued the following 78s of Ted Weems and his Orchestra that featured vocals by Perry Como. (Titles are provided only for the sides including a Como vocal. "[Non-Como]" indicates a side without a Como vocal.)

Catalog #	Title
820	You Can't Pull the Wool Over My Eyes / [non–Como]
822	Lazy Weather / [non–Como]
885	Knock, Knock, Who's There?
895	Until Today / [non–Como]
921	Fooled by the Moon / [non–Como]
958	Picture Me Without You / [non–Como]
959	Darling, Not Without You / (Trouble Ends) Out Where the Blue Begins

Catalog #	Title
969	Rainbow on the River / [non–Como]
1964	Sunday in the Park / [non–Como]
1695	A Gypsy Told Me / In My Little Red Book
1704	Goodnight, Sweet Dreams, Goodnight / [non–Como]
1705	A Shack in The Back of the Hills / [non–Como]
2019	Simple and Sweet / [non–Como]
2041	Ribbons and Roses / [non–Como]
2365	Ad-de-Day / Class Will Tell
2794	Goody Goodbye / Two Blind Loves
2829	That Old Gang of Mine / [non–Como]
2919	I Wonder Who's Kissing Her Now / On the Island of Catalina
3627	It All Comes Back to Me Now / May I Never Love Again
3628	Rose of the Rockies / [non–Como]
4131	Angeline / Having a Lonely Time
4138	Deep in the Heart of Texas / Ollie Ollie Out's in Free

RCA Records

RCA Victor issued the following Perry Como singles and long playing albums (excluding reissues and compilations) in the USA.

Until the mid–1950s, 78 rpm records were the primary format for these releases, although from 1949 onwards, some singles were simultaneously released on 45 rpm discs. These discs bore the same catalogue number for both formats, with the prefix "20" denoting a 78 and "47" denoting a 45. Prior to this use of dual formats, all 78s bore the "20" prefix and after the release of the final 78 in 1958, all 45s continued to bear the prefix "47" until 1969.

RCA Singles

Catalog #	Title
1538	Goodbye Sue / There'll Soon Be a Rainbow
1548	Have I Stayed Away Too Long? / I've Had This Feeling Before (But Never Like This)
1569	Long Ago (and Far Away) / I Love You
1592	Lili Marlene / First Class Private Mary Brown
1629	I Dream of You (More Than You Dream I Do) / I'm Confessin' (That I Love You)
1630	More and More / I Wish We Didn't Have to Say Goodnight
1658	I'll Always Be with You / Temptation
1676	I'm Gonna Love That Gal (Like She's Never Been Loved Before) / If I Loved You
1709	(Did You Ever Get) That Feeling in the Moonlight / 'Till the End of Time
1750	(A Hubba, Hubba, Hubba) Dig You Later / Here Comes Heaven (Again)
1788	I'm Always Chasing Rainbows / You Won't Be Satisfied (Until You Break My Heart)
1814	All Through the Day / Prisoner of Love
1857	If You Were the Only Girl (in the World) / They Say It's Wonderful
1877	More Than You Know / Surrender
1916	A Garden in the Rain / You Must Have Been a Beautiful Baby
1917	Blue Skies / Girl of My Dreams
1918	Little Man You've Had a Busy Day / Kentucky Babe
1945	One More Vote (One More Kiss) / If I'm Lucky
1968	Winter Wonderland / That Christmas Feelin'
1969	Santa Claus Is Comin' to Town / I'll Be Home for Christmas
1970	O Little Town of Bethlehem / Silent Night [35]
1971	O Come all Ye Faithful (Adeste Fideles) / Jingle Bells
2033	That's the Beginning of the End / Sonata
2103	What Am I Gonna Do About You? / I Gotta Gal I Love (in North and South Dakota)
2117	That's Where I Came In / I Want To Thank Your Folks
2142	Easter Parade / (The) Song of Songs
2259	Chi-Baba, Chi-Baba (My Bambino Go to Sleep) / When You Were Sweet Sixteen
2315	I Wonder Who's Kissing Her Now / When Tonight Is Just a Memory
2402	So Far / A Fellow Needs a Girl
2545	Two Loves Have I / I Never Loved Anyone
2593	I've Got a Feelin' I'm Fallin' / Pianissimo
2653	If You Had All the World and Its Gold / Because
2660	When Day Is Done / When Your Hair Has Turned to Silver (I Will Love You Just the Same)

Catalog #	Title
2661	Carolina Moon / Body and Soul
2662	What'll I Do? / Love Me or Leave Me
2663	If We Can't Be the Same Old Sweethearts (We'll Just Be the Same Old Friends) / I'm Always Chasing Rainbows
2713	Haunted Heart / Carolina Moon
2734	When Your Hair Has Turned to Silver (I Will Love You Just the Same) / Laroo Laroo Lilli Bolero
2784	You Can Do No Wrong / Love of My Life
2824	I Love You Truly / Lili Marlene
2888	Better Luck Next Time / It Only Happens When I Dance with You
2947	There Must Be a Way / Rambling Rose
3066	My Melancholy Baby / When You're Smiling (the Whole World Smiles with You)
3099	For You / By the Way
3288	Roses of Picardy / N'Yot, N'Yow (the Pussycat Song)
3316	Far Away Places / Missouri Waltz
3329	Blue Room / With a Song in My Heart
3347	Forever and Ever / I Don't See Me in Your Eyes Anymore
3381	"A" You're Adorable / When Is Sometime?
3402	Some Enchanted Evening / Bali Ha'i
3455	Every Time I Meet You / Two Little New Little Blue Little Eyes
3469	(Just One Way to Say) I Love You / Let's Take an Old-Fashioned Walk
3521	Give Me Your Hand / I Wish I Had a Record (of the Promises You Made)
3543	(A) Dreamer's Holiday / (The) Meadows of Heaven
3586	I Wanna Go Home (With You) / Hush Little Darlin'
3607	Bibbidi-Bobbidi-Boo (the Magic Song) / A Dream Is a Wish Your Heart Makes
3684	Please Believe Me / Did Anyone Ever Tell You, Mrs. Murphy?
3747[36]	Hoop-Dee-Doo / On the Outgoing Tide
3763	If You Were Only Mine / Let's Go to Church (Next Sunday Morning)
3846	If You Were My Girl / I Cross My Fingers
3850	Bless This House / (The) Rosary
3851	Mother Dear, O Pray For Me / Holy God, We Praise Thy Name
3852	Rock of Ages / Prayer of Thanksgiving
3905	Patricia / Watchin' the Trains Go By
3922	(The) Best Thing for You (Would Be Me) / Marrying for Love
3930	A Bushel and a Peck / She's a Lady
3931	So Long Sally / Marcheta
3933	There Is No Christmas Like a Home Christmas / (The) Christmas Symphony
3945	It's a Lovely Day Today / You're Just in Love (I Wonder Why)
3997	If / Zing Zing—Zoom Zoom
4033	Without a Song / More Than You Know
4034	It's Only a Paper Moon / Me and My Shadow
4035	That Old Gang of Mine / I Found a Million Dollar Baby (in a Five and Ten Cent Store)
4081	Tumbling Tumbleweeds / You Don't Kno' What Lonesome Is ('Til You Get to Herdin' Cows)
4112	Hello, Young Lovers / We Kiss in a Shadow
4158	There's a Big Blue Cloud (Next to Heaven) / There's No Boat Like a Rowboat
4203	Surprisin' / Cara Cara Bella Bella
4269	Rollin' Stone / With All My Heart and Soul
4314	It's Beginning to Look Like Christmas / There Is No Christmas Like a Home Christmas
4344	If Wishes Were Kisses / Here's to My Lady
4445	Oh! How I Miss You Tonight / A Garden in the Rain
4453	Tulips and Heather / Please Mr. Sun
4527	Over the Rainbow / You'll Never Walk Alone
4529	If There Is Someone Lovelier Than You / My Heart Stood Still
4542	Noodlin' Rag / Play Me a Hurtin' Tune
4631	It's Easter Time / One Little Candle
4687	Lonesome, That's All / Why Did You Leave Me?
4707	Childhood Is a Meadow / One Little Candle
4744	Watermelon Weather / Maybe
4877	Sweethearts Holiday / My Love and Devotion
4959	To Know You (Is to Love You) / My Lady Loves to Dance
5064	Don't Let the Stars Get in Your Eyes / Lies
5152	Wild Horses / I Confess
5277	Say You're Mine Again / My One and Only Heart
5317	No Other Love / Keep It Gay
5447	You Alone (Solo Tu) / Pa-Paya Mama

Catalog #	Title
5647	Wanted / Look Out the Window (and See How I'm Standing in the Rain)
5749	Hit and Run Affair / There Never Was a Night So Beautiful
5857	Papa Loves Mambo / The Things I Didn't Do
5950	(There's No Place Like) Home For the Holidays / Silk Stockings
5994	Ko-Ko-Mo (I Love You So) / You'll Always Be My Lifetime Sweetheart
6059	Nobody / Door of Dreams
6137	Chee Chee-Oo Chee (Sang the Little Bird) / Two Lost Souls
6192	Fooled / Tina Marie
6294	(The) Rose Tattoo / All at Once You Love Her
6427	Hot Diggity (Dog Ziggity Boom) / Juke Box Baby
6554	More / Glendora
6590	Dream Along with Me (I'm on My Way to a Star) / Somebody up There Likes Me
6670	Moonlight Love / Chincherinchee
6815	Round and Round / Mi Casa, Su Casa (My House Is Your House)
6904	(The) Girl with the Golden Braids / My Little Baby
6991	Dancin' / Marchin' Along to the Blues
7050	Just Born (To Be Your Baby) / Ivy Rose
7128	Catch a Falling Star / Magic Moments
7202[37]	Kewpie Doll / Dance Only with Me
7274	Moon Talk / Beats There a Heart So True
7353	Love Makes the World Go 'Round / Mandolins in the Moonlight
7464	Tomboy / Kiss Me and Kiss Me and Kiss Me
7541	You Are in Love / I Know
7628	I May Never Pass This Way Again / A Still Small Voice
7650	Ave Maria / (The) Lord's Prayer
7670	I Know What God Is / Delaware
7812	Gone Is My Love / Make Someone Happy
7962	You're Following Me / Especially For the Young
8004	Caterina / (The) Island of Forgotten Lovers
8186	(I Love You) Don't You Forget It / One More Mountain
8518	You Came a Long Way from St. Louis / (Get Your Kicks On) Route 66
8533	Dream On Little Dreamer / My Own Peculiar Way
8636	(The) Summer Wind / Oowee, Oowee
8722	Meet Me at the Altar / Bye, Bye Little Girl
8823	Coo Coo Roo Coo Coo Paloma / Stay with Me
8945	Forget Domani / Un Giorno Dopo L'altro (One Day Is Like Another)
9165	How Beautiful the World Can Be / Stop! And Think It Over
9262	A World of Love (That I Found in Your Arms) / I Looked Back
9352	Too Young / Young Love
9356	What Love Is Made of / You Made It That Way (Watermelon Summer)
9367	Love Is a Christmas Rose / Christmas Bells (in the Steeple)
9448	(The) Father of Girls / Somebody Makes It So
9533	Another Go Around / Happy Man (If I Ever Find the Time)
9683	There Is No Christmas Like a Home Christmas / Christmas Eve
9722	Seattle / Sunshine Wine
74-0193	Happiness Comes, Happiness Goes / That's All This Old World Needs
74-0356	Love Is Spreading Over the World / Don't Leave Me
74-0387	It's Impossible / Long Life, Lots of Happiness
74-0444	I Think of You / El Condor Pasa
74-0518	Yesterday I Heard the Rain / My Days of Loving You
74-0906	And I Love You So / Love Looks So Good on You
74-9151	Yo Te Quiero asi (And I Love You So) / Ahora Que Soy Libre (I Want to Give)
APB0-0096	Walk Right Back / Love Don't Care (Where It Grows)
APB0-0225	Beyond Tomorrow / It All Seems to Fall into Line
APB0-0274	I Don't Know What He Told You / Weave Me the Sunshine
PB-9147	Greensleeves / We'll Meet again
PB-10045	Temptation / In These Crazy Times
PB-10122	Christmas Dream / Christ is Born
PB-10257	World of Dreams / Wonderful Baby
PB-10402	Just Out of Reach / Love Put a Song in My Heart
PB-10604	Then You Can Tell Me Goodbye / The Grass Keeps Right on Growin'
PB-10894	Lovers, Kids and Fools / My Days of Loving You (Anima Mia)
PB-11185	Where You're Concerned / Girl You Make It Happen
PB-11434	When I Wanted You / Forever
PB-12028	(The) Colors of My Life / Someone Is Waiting

Catalog #	Title
PB-12088	Not While I'm Around / When
PB-12146	Regrets / You Are My World
PB-13069	Goodbye For Now / Jason
PB-13307	I Wish It Could Be Christmas Forever / Toyland
PB-13453	So It Goes / Fancy Dancer
PB-13613	(The) Second Time / As My Love for You
PB-13690	(The) Best of Times / Song on the Sand (La Da Da Da)

Long-Playing Records: 10-inch

This listing shows all the main catalogue LPs issued by RCA Victor in the USA. Albums marked with * were compilations rather than specially recorded albums, but are included because they were issued in RCA's main catalogue of Como releases.

Catalog #	Title
LPM-3013	TV Favorites
LPM-3023	Perry Como Sings Merry Christmas Music
LPM-3035*	A Sentimental Date with Perry Como
LPM-3044*	Supper Club Favorites
LPM-3124*	Perry Como Sings the Hits From Broadway Shows
LPM-3133	Around the Christmas Tree
LPM-3188	I Believe
LPM-3224*	Como's Golden Records

Long-Playing Records: 12-inch

Catalog #	Title
LPM-1085	So Smooth
LPM-1172*	I Believe
LPM-1176*	Relaxing with Perry Como
LPM-1177*	A Sentimental Date with Perry Como
LPM-1191*	Perry Como Sings the Song Hits from Broadway Shows
LPM-1243	Perry Como Sings Merry Christmas Music
LPM-1463	We Get Letters
LPM-1885	When You Come to the End of the Day
LSP-1971	Saturday Night with Mr. C
LSP-1981	Como's Golden Records
LSP-2010	Como Swings
LSP-2066	Season's Greetings
LSP-2343	For the Young at Heart
LSP-2390	Sing to Me, Mr. C
LSP-2567	By Request
LSP-2630	The Best of Irving Berlin's Songs From *Mr. President*
LSP-2708	The Songs I Love
LSP-3396	The Scene Changes
LSP-3552	Lightly Latin
LSP-3608	Perry Como in Italy
LSP-4016	The Perry Como Christmas Album
LSP-4052	Look to Your Heart
LSP-4183	Seattle
LSPX-1001	In Person at the International Hotel, Las Vegas
LSP-4473	It's Impossible
LSP-4539	I Think of You
APLI-0100	And I Love You So
CPLI-0585	Perry
APLI-0863	Just Out of Reach
AFLI-2641	Where You're Concerned
AFLI-3629	Perry Como
AQLI-3826	Perry Como Live on Tour
AYLI-4526	I Wish It Could Be Christmas Forever
AFLI-4272	So It Goes
6368-1-R	Perry Como Today

$$\boxed{\text{Appendix B}}$$

Perry Como on Television, 1948–1995

The details of the 1948 to June 24, 1955, shows have mainly been assembled from newspapers through the Newspaper Archive (www.newspaperarchive.com) and inevitably are somewhat incomplete. Information regarding subsequent shows has largely been obtained from the Perry Como Collection, American Music Research Center, University of Colorado, Boulder. The songs performed by Perry Como on each show are shown in *italics*.

NBC Television—The Chesterfield Supper Club—Series 1

Most shows featured the orchestra conducted by Mitchell Ayres plus the Fontane Sisters. Announcer—Martin Block

Air dates

December 24 & 31, 1948. The guests on December 24 are the St. Peter of Alcantra boys' choir.
January 7, 14, 21 & 28, 1949. Guests on January 14 are Borrah Minnevitch's Harmonica Rascals.
February 4/11/18/25, 1949
March 4/11/18/25, 1949. The guest on March 11 is Tony Pastor.
April 1/8/15/22/29, 1949. The guests on April 15 are the Duke University Choir. *Prayer Perfect, The Lord's Prayer, Holy, Holy, Holy, Morning Prayer* and *May the Good Lord Bless You and Keep You.*
May 6/13/20/27, 1949. The guests on May 20 are the Mills Brothers.
June 3/10, 1949

NBC Television—The Chesterfield Supper Club—Series 2

Most shows featured the orchestra conducted by Mitchell Ayres plus the Fontane Sisters. Announcer—Martin Block

Air dates

October 16, 1949. Guest: Milton Berle. *Fiddle Dee Dee (with the Fontane Sisters)—Just One Way to Say I Love You—I Wanna Go Home (With You) (with the Fontane Sisters)*
October 23, 1949. Guest: Jesus Maria San Roma. *I Like to Work in a Travel Bureau (with the Fontane Sisters)*
October 30, 1949
November 6/13/20/27, 1949. Guests: Peggy Ann Ellis and comedian Phil Foster (13), Raymond Massey *Dear Hearts and Gentle People (with the Fontane Sisters)—Till the End of Time—I Wanna Go Home (With You) (with the Fontane Sisters)—(The) Sweetheart of Sigma Chi—Hail to Thee, Our Alma Mater (With Cast)* [20], Patti Page and Victor Borge *When You're Smiling (with the Fontane Sisters)—Because—Mule Train (comedy version)—Be the Good Lord Willing* (27)
December 4/11/18/25, 1949. Guests: Jerry Colonna and Karen Tedder (4), Borrah Minnevitch's Harmonica Rascals (featuring Johnny Puleo) *Bibbidi-Bobbidi-Boo (The Magic Song) (with the Fontane Sisters)—I Can*

Dream, Can't I?—(A) Dreamer's Holiday (with the Fontane Sisters) (18) and Robert Q. Lewis and Eddy Arnold (25)

January 1/8/15/22/29, 1950. Guests include Sister Rosetta Tharpe (January 1), the dance team of Mata & Hari plus Nancy Andrews (8), Jean Carroll and Helene & Howard, *I Wanna Go Home (With You)* (15) Hoagy Carmichael (22) and Charles Boyer (29)

February 5/12/26, 1950. Guests include Burgess Meredith, Franchot Tone and Ethel Waters (5), Marion Hutton and Jack Douglas (26)

March 5/12/19/26, 1950. Guests include Wally Cox, *Rag Mop—Black Moonlight* (5), Gertrude Niesen (12), Douglas Fairbanks Jr. (19) and Nat King Cole & His Trio (26)

April 2/9/16/23/30, 1950. Guests include Joan Blondell (2), Sigmund Romberg—*Serenade* from *The Student Prince* (9), Morey Amsterdam (16), William Bendix (23) and Eddy Arnold and Arnold Stang (30)

May 7/14/21/28, 1950. Guests include Jack Carson (7), Sir Cedric Hardwicke (14), Chico Marx (21) and the Mills Brothers (28)

June 4/11, 1950

CBS Television—The Perry Como Show—Series 1

Most shows featured the orchestra conducted by Mitchell Ayres plus the Fontane Sisters and the Ray Charles Singers. Announcer—Dick Stark

Air dates

October 2/4/6/9/11/13/16/18/20/23/25/27/30, 1950. The Paulette Sisters are the guests on October 2—songs *Patricia—I Cross My Fingers (with the Fontane Sisters)—Bless This House (with the Ray Charles Singers)*. The guest on October 9, 11 & 16 is Mindy Carson).

November 1/3/6/8/10/13/15/17/20/22/24/27/29, 1950. Mindy Carson is the guest on November 1/8/15/22 & 29. The guest on November 6 is Jimmy Dorsey.

December 1/4/6/8/11/13/15/18/20/22/25/27/29, 1950. Guests include trombonist Buddy Morrow (4), guitarist Tony Mottola and Mindy Carson (6), The Little Singers of Paris (15) and Mindy Carson (13, 20 & 27).

January 1/3/5/8/10/12/15/17/19/22/24/26/29/31, 1951. Guests include Mindy Carson (3rd) and Teresa Brewer (19th & 26th). On January 29, Perry sings *Get out Those Old Records* and *Blue Room*.

February 2/5/7/9/12/14/16/19/21/23/26/28, 1951. Guests include Kay Starr (2), Rosemary Clooney (7), Teresa Brewer (9 & 12), Texas Jim Robertson (19) and The Larks (14). Songs (14) *You and Your Beautiful Eyes (with the Fontane Sisters)—Me and My Shadow—Zing Zing Zoom Zoom)*

March 2/5/7/9/12/14/16/19/21/23/26/28/30, 1951. Guests include Jim Robertson (5), King Cole Trio (9), Peggy Lee (16), Margaret Whiting (26), Rosemary Clooney (28) and Helen O'Connell (30).

April 2/4/6/9/11/13/16/18/20/23/25/27/30, 1951. Guests include Patti Page (4), Duke University Men's Glee Club (9), Toni Arden (11), Les Paul & Mary Ford (18) and the Ames Brothers (25).

May 2/4/7/9/11/14/16/18/21/23/25/28/30, 1951. Guests include Mindy Carson (2 & 30) and Nat King Cole (21).

June 1/4/6/8/11/13/15/18/20/22/25/27/29, 1951. Guests include Mindy Carson (20) and Eileen Barton (27).

CBS Television—The Perry Como Show—Series 2

Most shows featured the orchestra conducted by Mitchell Ayres plus the Fontane Sisters and the Ray Charles Singers. Announcer—Dick Stark.
Perry and the Fontane Sisters open most shows by singing "Sound Off," the Chesterfield theme song

Air dates

August 27/29/31, September 3/5/7/10/12/14/17/19/21/24/26/28, 1951. Guests include Sally Sweetland (3), Les Paul & Mary Ford (5), Sarah Vaughan (19) and Nat King Cole (28). Songs (August 27) *In the Cool, Cool, Cool of the Evening (with the Fontane Sisters)—Surprisin'—Black Moonlight.*

October 1/3/5/8/10/12/15/17/19/22/24/26/29/31, 1951. Guests include Nat King Cole (5), Ralph Marterie (10), Peggy Lee (17) and the Mills Brothers (22).

November 2/5/7/9/12/14/16/19/21/23/26/28/30, 1951. Guests include Tommy Edwards (7) and Hank Williams (14). Songs *(14) Sin—A Fine Romance (with the Fontane Sisters)—That Old Gang of Mine—(21) Hey Good Lookin'* (with the Fontane Sisters)—*A Garden in the Rain—Tulips and Heather*

December 3/5/7/10/12/14/17/19/21/24/26/28/31, 1951. Guests include Sarah Vaughan (19).

January 2/4/7/9/11/14/16/18/21/23/25/28/30, 1952 (guests include Tommy Edwards (2), Pee Wee King (16), Johnnie Ray (18) and Buddy Morrow (23) *songs (16) Shrimp Boat)*

February 1/4/6/8/11/13/15/18/20/22/25/27/29, 1952. Guests include Vera Lynn (6th), Johnnie Ray (25th) and Margaret Whiting (29th). (Exact date not confirmed) *Noodlin' Rag* (with the Fontane Sisters)—*At Last—Why Did You Leave Me?*

March 3/5/7/10/12/14/17/19/21/24/26/28/31, 1952. Guests include Hank Snow (5th). Songs *Silver and Gold (with* the Fontane Sisters)—Tell Me Why—Angela Mia, Margaret Whiting (7th), Nat King Cole (17th), Ray Charles Chorus (19th), Lefty Frizzell (26th) and Rosemary Clooney (31st). Other songs (precise date unknown) Be My Life's Companion (with the Fontane Sisters)—Only Forever—I Concentrate on You (show with Joni James as guest)—exact date not confirmed) What's New?—String Along with Me (With the Fontane Sisters)—Over the Rainbow

April 2/4/7/9/11/14/16/18/21/23/25/28, 1952. Guests include Frank Sinatra (4), Rosemary Clooney (7) and the Duke University Men's Glee Club (14).

May 2/5/7/9/12/14/16/19/21/23/26/28/30, 1952. Guests include Ella Mae Morse (19th).

June 2/4/6/9/11/13/16/18/20/23/25/27/30, 1952. Guests include The Jerry Murad Harmonicats (25th).

July 2/4/7/9/11, 1952. Guests include The Mills Brothers (2).

CBS Television—The Perry Como Show—Series 3

Most shows featured the orchestra conducted by Mitchell Ayres plus the Fontane Sisters and the Ray Charles Singers. Announcer—Dick Stark.

Air dates

August 25/27/29, 1952. Guests include Helen O'Connell (29)—songs (25) Maybe (with the Fontane Sisters)—Somewhere Along The Way—My Love and Devotion.

September 1/3/5/8/10/12/15/17/19/22/24/26/29, 1952. Guests include Robert Whalen (17) and Georgia Gibbs (24).

October 1/3/6/8/10/13/15/17/20/22/24/27/29/31, 1952. Guests include Mary Small (15 & 22).

November 3/5/7/10/12/14/17/19/21/24/26/28, 1952. Guests include Teresa Brewer (5 & 12) and Eileen Barton (26).

December 1/3/5/8/10/12/15/17/19/22/24/26/29/31, 1952. Guests include Eddy Arnold (10) and Jimmy Boyd (8—songs I'm Never Satisfied—Yours—Pennies from Heaven, 15, 22 & 29) (precise date unknown) songs: Because You're Mine—Winter Wonderland (with the Fontane Sisters)—When Your Lover Has Gone, (show with Peggy Lee as guest—some time before Dec. 24) Keep It a Secret—Santa Claus Is Comin' to Town (with the Fontane Sisters)—Don't Let the Stars Get in Your Eyes), songs (24)—The Story of the First Christmas including Perry singing O Come All Ye Faithful and Silent Night—Ave Maria) (26 or earlier) It's Nice to Be Nice—That Old Feeling—I Went to Your Wedding

January 2/5/7/9/12/14/16/19/21/23/26/28/30, 1953. Guests include Teresa Brewer (14).

February 2/4/6/9/11/13/16/18/20/23/25/27, 1953. Guests include The Four Aces (9) and Karen Chandler (18).

March 9/11/13/16/18/20/23/25/27/30, 1953. Guests include Julius La Rosa (13 & 20).

April 1/3/6/8/10/13/15/20/22/24/27/29, 1953. Guests include Duke University Glee Club (1) and Karen Chandler (8).

May 1/4/6/8/11/13/15/18/20/22/25/27/29, 1953. Guests include Joni James (1) and Al Martino (11)—songs (11) Ain't Misbehavin'—Don't Take Your Love from Me—Begin the Beguine.

June 1/3/5/8/10/12/15/17/19/22/24/26/29, 1953

July 1/3, 1953

CBS Television—The Perry Como Show—Series 4

Most shows featured the orchestra conducted by Mitchell Ayres plus the Fontane Sisters and the Ray Charles Singers. Announcer—Dick Stark.

Air dates

August 24/26/28/31, 1953—songs (24) Crazy Man Crazy—P.S. I Love You—Linger Awhile (with the Fontane Sisters)—No Other Love

September 2/4/7/9/11/14/16/18/21/23/25/28/30, 1953. Guests include Nat King Cole (28)—songs (2nd) You, You, You (with the Fontane Sisters)—Imagination—No Other Love (early September) Would You Like to Take a Walk (with the Fontane Sisters)—Crying in the Chapel—September Song (11th) Hi Lili, Hi Lo—La Vie En Rose—I Love Paris (precise date unknown)—Wrap Your Troubles In Dreams—Because You're Mine—In the Still of the Night (precise date unknown) Pa-paya Mama—You'll Always Be My Love—I Love Paris (precise date unknown) When My Dreamboat Comes Home—Vaya Con Dios (May God Be with You)—You Alone (Solo Tu)

October 2/5/7/9/12/14/16/19/21/23/26/28/30, 1953.

November 2/4/6/9/11/13/16/18/20/23/25/27/30, 1953. Guests include Helen O'Connell (23).

December 2/4/7/9/11/14/16/18/21/23/25/28/30, 1953. Guests include Ronald and Terri Como (25)—songs The Story of the First Christmas (includes Perry singing: O Come All Ye Faithful—Silent Night)—The Lord's Prayer.

January 1/4/6/8/11/13/15/18/20/22/25/27/29, 1954—songs (27) Way Down Yonder in New Orleans (with the Fontane Sisters)—Tenderly—Stranger in Paradise

February 1/3/5/8/10/12/15/17/19/22/24/26, 1954. Guests include the Cornell University Glee Club (26).

March 15/17/19/22/24/26/29/31, 1954. Guests include Joni James.
April 2/5/7/9/12/14/16/19/21/23/26/28/30, 1954
May 3/5/7/10/12/14/17/19/21/24/26/28/31, 1954. Guests include Teresa Brewer (5).
June 2/4/7/9/11/14/16/18/21/23/25, 1954. Guests include Ben Hogan (14) and Ray Anthony (16).

CBS Television—The Perry Como Show—Series 5

Most shows featured the orchestra conducted by Mitchell Ayres and the Ray Charles Singers. Announcer—Dick Stark.

Air dates

August 23/25/27/30, 1954—songs (23) *It's a Good Day—If You Love Me*
September 1/3/6/8/10/13/15/17/20/22/24/27/29, 1954. Guests include the Mills Brothers (15) and Kitty Kallen (10 & 22)—songs (precise date unknown) *Sway—A Fellow Needs a Girl—Papa Loves Mambo*
October 1/4/6/8/11/13/15/18/20/22/25/27/29, 1954. Guests include June Valli (20) and Peggy Lee (date unknown)—songs (precise date unknown) *Sway—Someone to Watch over Me—Papa Loves Mambo*
November 1/3/5/8/10/12/15/17/19/22/24/26/29, 1954. Guests include Kitty Kallen (15).
December 1/3/6/8/10/13/15/17/20/22/24/27/29/31, 1954. Guests include Teresa Brewer (8th) and Sarah Vaughan (15).
January 3/5/7/10/12/14/17/19/21/24/26/28/31, 1955. Guests include Joan Weber (12).
February 2/4/7/9/11/14/16/18/21/23/25, 1955. Guests include Eddy Arnold (2).
March 14/16/18/21/23/25/28/30, 1955. Guests include Frankie Frisch (25).
April 1/4/6/8/11/13/15/18/20/22/25/27/29, 1955. Guests include the Mills Brothers (6), Wynne Miller (18) and Duke University Glee Club (29).
May 2/4/6/9/11/13/16/18/20/23/25/27/30, 1955. Guests include Al Hibbler (4 & 11), Jaye P Morgan (16) and Georgia Gibbs (18).
June 1/3/6/8/10/13/15/17/20/22/24, 1955. Guests include Julius La Rosa (22)—songs (10) *For Me and My Girl—Darling, Je Vous Aime Beaucoup—If There is Someone Lovelier Than You*, (24) *It's a Big Wide Wonderful World—Goodbye Sue—Beyond the Blue Horizon* (Perry runs the cameras while The Ray Charles Singers sing)—*Auld Lang Syne* (with cast and crew)

NBC Television—The Perry Como Show—Series 1

All shows featured orchestra conducted by Mitchell Ayres plus the Ray Charles Singers and the Louis DaPron Dancers. Announcer: Frank Gallop. Perry introduces all programs by singing a snatch of "Dream Along with Me"

Show #1—Air date: September 17, 1955

Guests: Julius La Rosa, Rosemary Clooney, Dave Barry, Marion Lorne, Don Newcombe, Sid Caesar, Nanette Fabray, Carl Reiner, Howard Morris and Frankie Laine
Unchained Melody—That's My Desire (snatch only)—Mule Train (snatch only)—Learning the Blues (with Frankie Laine)—Too Marvelous for Words (with Rosemary Clooney)—Tina Marie—Dear Perry Medley (Hard to Get—Over the Rainbow)—Abide with Me

Show #2—Air date: September 24, 1955

Guests: Patti Page, Archie Moore, Peter Lawford and Jean Carroll
Rock Around the Clock—It's De-Lovely (with Patti Page & Peter Lawford)—I Concentrate on You—Dear Perry Medley (The Longest Walk—It's the Talk of the Town)—Heart (with Patti Page & Peter Lawford)—Kol Nidre

Show #3—Air date: October 1, 1955

Guests: Yvonne De Carlo, Tab Hunter, Joan Collins, Georgia Gibbs and Buddy Hackett
It's A Good Day—Dear Perry Medley (Wake the Town and Tell the People—When Your Hair Has Turned to Silver—If There is Someone Lovelier Than You)—Without a Song—Rock of Ages

Show #4—Air date: October 8, 1955

Guests: Gale Storm, Marion Lorne, Gino Prato and Paul Winchell
Tina Marie—Where or When—In the Still of the Night—Oh Marie—Dear Perry Medley (Love is a Many Splendored Thing—You Made Me Love You—For Me and My Gal)—Yellow Rose of Texas

Show #5—Air date: October 15, 1955

Guests: Peggy Lee and Lorraine Prato
I Want You to Be My Baby—More Than You Know—I Gotta Right to Sing the Blues—Manana (parody with Peggy Lee)—Dear Perry medley (Girl of My Dreams—If I Loved You)—Autumn in New York

Show #6—Air date: October 22, 1955

Guests: Fred Allen, Hal March, Aldo Ray, Joey Bishop and Jaye P. Morgan
It's a Big, Wide, Wonderful World—Suddenly There's a Valley—Love and Marriage (with Jaye P. Morgan)—All At Once You Know—How Deep Is the Ocean (snatch only)—Dear Perry medley (Try a Little Tenderness—The Bible Tells Me So—Night and Day)—Temptation

Show #7—Air date: October 29, 1955

Guests: Connie Russell, Arnold Stang, Dunninger, George Prentice and The Four Lads
Great Day—Song of Songs—Come Rain or Come Shine—Dear Perry medley (When You Were Sweet Sixteen—Ko-Ko-Mo)—The Skeleton in the Closet (with Connie Russell)—He

Show #8—Air date: November 5, 1955

Guests: Julius La Rosa, Jean Simmons, Stubby Kaye, Arnold Stang, The Rudells, Johnny Puleo and his Harmonica Gang
My Bonnie Lassie—Autumn Leaves—One for My Baby—Dear Perry medley (I Wonder Who's Kissing Her Now—On the Atchison, Topeka and the Sante Fe—No Other Love)—Play a Simple Melody (with Julius La Rosa)—Black Moonlight

Show #9—Air date: November 12, 1955

Guests: Dorothy Kirsten, Richard Egan, Roger (Droodles) Price, The Acromaniacs and Gino Prato
You've Got to Be a Football Hero—Love Is a Many Splendored Thing—All at Once You Know—They Didn't Believe Me (with Dorothy Kirsten)—Dear Perry Medley (I'm Thru with Love—You Do Something to Me—Don't Let the Stars Get in Your Eyes)—You'll Never Walk Alone

Show #10—Air date: November 19, 1955

Guests: Robert Merrill, Buster Crabbe, Dave Barry and Rosemary Clooney
Hallelujah—Moments to Remember—Dear Perry Medley (Oh, How I Miss You Tonight—Same Old Saturday Night—Someone to Watch over Me)—Begin the Beguine—Bless This House

Show #11—Air date: November 26, 1955

Guests: Arnold Stang, Barry Gordon, Paul Sydell & Suzy, The Mills Brothers and Debra Paget
Pepper Hot Baby—Only You—I'll Never Stop Loving You—Medley with Mills Brothers (Basin Street Blues—Dinah—Lazy River)—Dear Perry Medley (S'posin'—If You Love Me)—One Little Candle

Show #12—Air date: December 3, 1955

Guests: Steve Allen, Arnold Stang, Ivy Glee Club and Gloria De Haven
(There's No Place Like) Home for the Holidays—C'est La Vie—Sixteen Tons—Dear Perry Medley (For You—By the Light of the Silvery Moon—You'll Always Be My Lifetime Sweetheart—Old Devil Moon)—The Rosary

Show #13—Air date: December 10, 1955

Guests: Polly Bergen, Gertrude Berg, Morty Gunty, Francis Brunn and Pierre Aumont
It's Beginning to Look Like Christmas—All at Once You Know—Some Enchanted Evening—Dear Perry Medley (Love and Marriage—Embraceable You—Rudolph, the Red-Nosed Reindeer)—Holy God, We Praise Thy Name—Now the Day Is Over

Show #14—Air date: December 17, 1955

Guests: Kirk Douglas, June Valli, Arnold Stang, Ruth Gilbert and The Treniers
Jingle Bells—The Christmas Song—Memories Are Made of This—Dear Perry Medley (Shadow Waltz—Memories of You—Hello Young Lovers)—The Lord's Prayer

Show #15—Air date: December 24, 1955

Guests: The Vienna Boys' Choir, Barry Gordon and Roger Ray
Carols Medley (Deck the Halls—God Rest Ye Merry, Gentlemen—Joy to the World)—White Christmas—Silver Bells (with Barry Gordon)—The Story of the First Christmas—Ave Maria

Show #16—Air date: December 31, 1955

Guests: Julie London and Buddy Hackett
It's a Grand Night for Singing—A Woman in Love—Birth of the Blues—Dear Perry Medley (Rock Around the Clock—Melody of Love—Cherry Pink and Apple Blossom White—Unchained Melody)—Auld Lang Syne

Show #17—Air date: January 7, 1956

Guests: Patti Page, Max Baer, Mickey Walker, Jimmy Braddock, Rocky Graziano, Jay Lawrence and Wassan Troupe
Zip-A-Dee-Doo-Dah—A Woman in Love—Sixteen Tons—Dear Perry Medley (It's the Talk of the Town—You Do Something to Me—In the Still of the Night)—When You Come to the End of the Day

Show #18—Air date: January 14, 1956

Guests: Kay Starr, The Four Stanley Boys, Larry Storch, The Shyrettos, Barry Gordon, Dinah Shore and Ezio Pinza
Button up Your Overcoat—Autumn Leaves—Memories Are Made of This—Wrap Your Troubles in Dreams (with Kay Starr)—Dear Perry Medley (I've Got the World on a String—The Very Thought of You)—He

Show #19—Air date: January 21, 1956

Guests: Keenan Wynn, Ernest Borgnine, Abe Weiler, Willie Mosconi, Vivian Blaine and The Four Lads
When You're Smiling—No Arms Can Ever Hold You—Dear Perry Medley (I Wonder What's Become of Sally—While We're Young)—Nobody

Show #20—Air date: January 28, 1956

Guests: Julius La Rosa, Gale Storm, Buddy Hackett, Tuesday Weld, David Winters, Aura Vainio and Matt Mattox
Dungaree Doll—June In January—Dear Perry Medley (The Tender Trap—I Hadn't Anyone 'Till You—Wanted)—I Believe

Show #21—Air date: February 4, 1956

Guests: Tom Ewell, Farley Granger, Patrice Munsel, Don Cherry and The U.S. Navy Drill Team
Lullaby of Broadway—Are You Satisfied? (with Patrice Munsel)—Eighteen Holes (with Farley Granger and Don Cherry)—Dear Perry Medley (Breezin' Along with the Breeze—I Wonder)—The Way You Look Tonight

Show #22—Air date: February 11, 1956

Guests: Johnnie Ray, Rhonda Fleming, Alene Dalton, The Dream Weavers, The George Wright Trio, Harriet Van Horne and Cyril Ritchard
The Rock and Roll Waltz—Young at Heart—My Funny Valentine—Dear Perry Medley (Dear Old Girl—I Want a Girl—When Your Hair Has Turned to Silver)—I Love You (Porter)

Show #23—Air date: February 18, 1956

Guests: The Platters, Henry Fonda, Vera-Ellen, Ann Francis and Paul Winchell & Jerry Mahoney
Ac-Cen-Tchu-Ate The Positive—Juke Box Baby—The Soft Shoe Song (with Vera-Ellen)—Dear Perry Medley (It's Been a Long, Long Time—The Night Is Young and You're So Beautiful)—Hot Diggity (Dog Ziggity Boom)

Show #24—Air date: February 25, 1956

Guests: Andy Devine, Jane Russell, Bobby Van, Buddy Hackett, Elaine Lynn and Lilli Palmer
Hoop-Dee-Doo—Band of Gold—Little Child (with Elaine Lynn)—Dear Perry Medley (I Found a Million Dollar Baby—Stardust)—Peace of Mind

Show #25—Air date: March 3, 1956

Guests: Jaye P. Morgan, Dennis Day, Rochester and the U.S. Coast Guard Academy Glee Club
Jeepers Creepers—No, Not Much—Because—The Waiter, the Porter and the Upstairs Maid (with cast)—Dear Perry Medley (It's Only a Paper Moon—If I Had My Way—Little Man, You've Had a Busy Day)—Hot Diggity (Dog Ziggity Boom)

Show #26—Air date: March 10, 1956

Guests: Dinah Shore, Rock Hudson, The All American Basket Ball Team, Louis Jordan and his Tympany Five
Juke Box Baby—You Made Me Love You—It Happened in Monterey—You're Getting to Be a Habit with Me

(with Dinah Shore)—Dear Perry Medley (Somebody Loves Me—You're Mine, You—Lover, Come Back to Me)—When You're Away

Show #27—Air date: March 17, 1956

Guests: Imogene Coca, Eddie Fisher, Pat O'Brien, Bob Hope (by split screen) and Governor George Foss (South Dakota)
McNamara's Band—Maybe (with Eddie Fisher)—Till the End of Time—Dear Perry Medley (Did Your Mother Come from Ireland?—My Wild Irish Rose)—Now the Day Is Over—Goodnight, Sweet Jesus

Show #28—Air date: March 24, 1956

Guests: Ann Blyth, Basil Rathbone and Buddy Hackett
When The Red, Red Robin Comes Bob-Bob-Bobbin' Along—Eleventh Hour Melody—It Could Happen to You—Carolina in the Morning (with Ann Blyth)—Dear Perry Medley (The Object of My Affection—They Say It's Wonderful—The Touch of Your Lips)—Hot Diggity (Dog Ziggity Boom)

Show #29—Air date: March 31, 1956

Guests: Robert Cummings, Patrice Munsel, Alene Dalton, Johnny Puleo & His Harmonica Gang
Love Is Sweeping The Country—No Well on Earth—Thou Swell (duet with Patrice Munsel)—Dear Perry Medley (Swingin' Down the Lane—Always—It's Easter Time)—The Lord's Prayer

Show #30—Air date: April 7, 1956

Guests: Dennis O'Keefe, Jackie Miles, Dick Hyman and Shelley Winters
Juke Box Baby—No, Not Much—Stairway to the Stars—Dear Perry Medley (In a Little Spanish Town—I'm in the Mood for Love—Once in a While)—Prisoner of Love

Show #31—Air date: April 14, 1956

Guests: Tennessee Ernie Ford, Phil Foster, Ginger Rogers and Duke University Glee Club
When the Saints Go Marching In—A Tear Fell—April in Paris—Medley with Ginger Rogers & Tennessee Ernie Ford (They Can't Take That Away from Me—Cheek to Cheek)—Dear Perry Medley (It's a Lovely Day Today— When I Grow Too Old to Dream—Trees)

Show #32—Air date: April 21, 1956

Guests: Peggy Lee, Mark Stevens, Rudy Cardenas and Jack E. Leonard
Blue Suede Shoes—Isn't It Romantic—Two Sleepy People (with Peggy Lee)—I've Got You Under My Skin— Dear Perry Medley (They Can't Take That Away from Me—Say It Isn't So—There Never Was a Night So Beautiful)—Hot Diggity (Dog Ziggity Boom)

Show #33—Air date: April 28, 1956

Guests: Louis Armstrong, Patti Page, Alan King and The Golden Kids
I'm an Old Cowhand—Do You Ever Think of Me? (with Patti Page)—Red Sails in The Sunset—Ko-Ko-Mo (with Louis Armstrong)—Dear Perry Medley (Don't Blame Me—Home)—Twilight on the Trail

Show #34—Air date: May 5, 1956

Guests: George Gobel, Philip Maero and Dorothy Shay
Get Happy—Isn't It Romantic—Feudin' and Fightin' (with George Gobel & Dorothy Shay)—My Heart Stood Still—Dear Perry Medley (Little White Lies—I'll Be Seeing You—You Go to My Head)—The Rosary

Show #35—Air date: May 12, 1956

Guests: The Mills Brothers, Eydie Gorme, Alene Dalton and Buddy Hackett
Alexander's Ragtime Band—Medley with the Mills Brothers (Down By the Old Mill Stream—Paper Doll—Tiger Rag)—Moonglow—Dear Perry Medley (Can You Find It in Your Heart—Don't Blame Me—My Mother's Eyes)—In the Summertime

Show #36—Air date: May 19, 1956

Guests: Ronald Reagan, Dolores Gray, Jay Lawrence and Lonnie Donegan
Hi Lili, Hi Lo—Like Someone in Love—Where or When—Dear Perry Medley (If I Could Be with You—I'm Confessin' (That I Love You)—All the Things You Are)—Give Us This Day

Show #37—Air date: May 26, 1956

Guests: Clifford Guest, Ozzie & Harriet, The Carl Perkins Trio and General Omar Bradley
Put on Your Old Grey Bonnet—It's Easy to Remember—I Can't Give You Anything but Love (with Ozzie & Harriet)—Oh, How I Miss You Tonight—Glendora—Dear Perry Medley (You Must Have Been a Beautiful Baby—Try a Little Tenderness—Out of Nowhere)—More

Show #38—Air date: June 2, 1956

Guests: Dick Powell, Dana Wynter, Jackie Miles and Cathy Carr
June Is Bustin' out All Over—Hello Young Lovers—Medley with Dick Powell (Just a Gigolo—In the Shadows—I Only Have Eyes for You—Shuffle Off to Buffalo)—Standing on The Corner—Dear Perry Medley (Love Is Just Around the Corner—Without a Word of Warning—I Concentrate on You)—Hot Diggity (Dog Ziggity Boom)

Show #39—Air date: June 9, 1956

Guests: Kim Novak, Patti Page, Mickey Mantle and Buddy Hackett
In the Good Old Summertime—If You Love Me—Without a Song—Dear Perry Medley (To Love Again—On the Sunny Side of the Street—La Vie En Rose—To Love Again [Reprise])—You Are Never Far Away from Me

NBC Television—The Perry Como Show—Series 2

All shows featured orchestra conducted by Mitchell Ayres plus the Ray Charles Singers and the Louis DaPron Dancers. Announcer: Frank Gallop. Perry introduces all programs by singing a snatch of "Dream Along With Me"

Show #1—Air date: September 15, 1956

Guests: Sal Mineo, Patience & Prudence, Robert Sarnoff, Buddy Hackett and Irene Dunne
Whatever Will Be, Will Be—On the Street Where You Live—Somebody Loves Me—Dear Perry Medley (Say It Isn't So—Tangerine)—Medley with Irene Dunne (Smoke Gets in Your Eyes—Why Do I Love You?)—Somebody up There Likes Me

Show #2—Air date: September 22, 1956

Guests: Natalie Wood, Martha Davis & Spouse, Tab Hunter and The Seven Ashtons
Hound Dog—Moonlight Becomes You—Allegheny Moon—I'm Gonna Sit Right Down and Write Myself a Letter (with Martha Davis & Spouse)—Dear Perry Medley (The Nearness of You—Night and Day)—Give Us This Day—If I Could Be with You

Show #3—Air date: September 29, 1956

Guests: William Holden, Jan Peerce, Dave Barry, Julius La Rosa and Jeanne Crain
Big D—Too Marvelous for Words—Medley with Jeanne Crain (It's a Grand Night for Singing—If I Had You—Honey)—Canadian Sunset—Dear Perry Medley (Too Young—Almost Like Being in Love—If There Is Someone Lovelier Than You)—A House with Love in It

Show #4—Air date: October 6, 1956

Guests: Kathryn Grayson, Walter Winchell, Paul Douglas, Robert Lamouret and Rudy Cardenas.
With a Little Bit of Luck—True Love—Ain't We Got Fun (with Kathryn Grayson)—Chincherinchee—Dear Perry Medley (I Don't Want to Walk Without You, Baby—It's Been a Long, Long Time—I'll Never Smile Again)

Show #5—Air date: October 13, 1956

Guests: Ray Bolger, Yogi Berra, Guy Madison, Rudy Cardenas, the De Castro Sisters and Jo Stafford
Buckle Down, Winsocki—Medley with Jo Stafford (I'll Be Seeing You—Temptation)—Autumn in New York—Dear Perry Medley (Sweetheart of Sigma Chi—Down the Old Ox Road—The Whiffenpoof Song)—Now the Day Is Over

Show #6—Air date: October 20, 1956

Guests: Lita Baron, Pearl Bailey, Robert Lamouret and Rory Calhoun
The Trolley Song—Tonight You Belong to Me—Moonlight Love—Tired (with Pearl Bailey)—Dear Perry Medley (Tumbling Tumbleweeds—I'm an Old Cowhand—Little Man You've Had a Busy Day)—Only One

Show #7—Air date: October 27, 1956

Guests: Sheree North, Frankie Laine, Robert Lamouret and 9-year-old Brenda Lee

Get Me to the Church on Time—Two Different Worlds—Swinging on a Star (with Brenda Lee)—No Other Love—Dear Perry Medley (S'posin'—Ain't Misbehavin'—Whither Thou Goest)—Chincherinchee

Show #8—Air date: November 3, 1956

Guests: Nat King Cole, Giselle MacKenzie, Robert Lamouret and George De Witt
There's a Great Day Coming Manana—Blueberry Hill—Without a Song—Canadian Sunset (with Giselle MacKenzie & Nat King Cole)—Dear Perry Medley (Oh, How I Miss You Tonight—When My Dreamboat Comes In—While We're Young)—Count Your Blessings Instead of Sheep

Show #9—Air date: November 10, 1956

Guests: Bob Hope, Glenn Derringer, Robert Lamouret and Yvonne De Carlo
Another Openin,' Another Show—True Love—Autumn Leaves—Dear Perry Medley (Lonesome, That's All—That's What I Like—Old Devil Moon)—May the Good Lord Bless and Keep You

Show #10—Air date: November 17, 1956

Guests: Brenda Lee, Glenn Derringer, Robert Lamouret, Lily Pons and Dinah Shore
(There's No Place Like) Home for the Holidays—Cindy—You Must Have Been a Beautiful Baby (with Dinah Shore)—Life Is Just a Bowl of Cherries (with Brenda Lee)—J'Attendrai (with Lily Pons)—Dear Perry Medley (When Your Hair Has Turned to Silver)—Bless This House

Show #11—Air date: November 24, 1956

Guests: Roy Rogers, Dale Evans, The Rogers children, Gene Sheldon and Martha Davis & Spouse
Dear Hearts and Gentle People—Love Me Tender—Western Medley (Wagon Wheels [with Roy Rogers & Dale Evans]—Home on the Range—Happy Trails [with Roy Rogers & Dale Evans])—Black Moonlight—I'm Sitting on Top of the World (with Martha Davis & Spouse)—Dear Perry Medley (Love Is the Sweetest Thing—It Had to Be You—Love Letters)—When You Come to the End of the Day

Show #12—Air date: December 1, 1956

Guests: Nat King Cole, Carol Channing, Isaac Stern, Robert Lamouret and Red Skelton
Stanley Steamer—If (with Carol Channing)—Cuba (with Nat King Cole)—Two Different Worlds—Dear Perry Medley (I'd Love to Live in Loveland—Lady Be Good—The More I See You)—It's Beginning to Look Like Christmas

Show #13—Air date: December 8, 1956

Guests: Guy Lombardo (and Band), Kenny Gardner, Carmen Lombardo, Pearl Bailey, Billy Barty and Spike Jones
You Gotta Be a Football Hero—Hey, Jealous Lover—You'll Never Walk Alone—Seems Like Old Times (with Kenny Gardner and Carmen Lombardo)—Dear Perry Medley (Memory Lane—I Had the Craziest Dream—I've Got You Under My Skin)—Miami Shore

Show #14—Air date: December 15, 1956

Guests: Groucho Marx, Melinda Marx, Jo Stafford, Gina Lollobrigida, Johnnie Ray and Robert Sarnoff
Miami—Cindy—Oh Marie (with Gina Lollobrigida)—The Money Tree (with Jo Stafford and Johnnie Ray)—You're Just in Love (with Melinda Marx)—Dear Perry Medley (Someone to Watch over Me—It All Depends on You—When Day Is Done)

Show #15—Air date: December 22, 1956

Guests: Rosemary Clooney, Gail Clooney, Robert Lamouret, Glenn Derringer and Bishop Fulton J. Sheen.
Christmas Songs Medley (Jingle Bells—Santa Claus Is Comin' to Town—Happy Holiday)—Carols Medley with guests (Joy to the World—God Rest Ye Merry, Gentlemen—It Came Upon a Midnight Clear—Deck the Halls)—The Story of the First Christmas—Ave Maria

Show #16—Air date: December 29, 1956

Guests: Teresa Brewer, Louis Armstrong and Red Buttons
It's a Grand Night for Singing—Mutual Admiration Society (with Teresa Brewer)—True Love—Heart (with Red Buttons)—Medley of 1956 hits with guests (Memories Are Made of This—Love Me Tender—Ivory Tower—Moonglow—Whatever Will Be, Will Be—Blueberry Hill—Canadian Sunset—Hound Dog)

Show #17—Air date: January 5, 1957

Guests: Walter Pidgeon, Gertrude Berg, Brenda Lee, The Tokayers and Johnny Puleo & His Harmonica Gang

Be a Clown—Singing the Blues—Mr. Wonderful (with Gertrude Berg and Walter Pidgeon)—Gonna Get Along Without Ya Now (with Brenda Lee)—Temptation—Dear Perry Medley (I'm Yours—Little White Lies—Long Ago)—You Are Never Far Away from Me

Show #18—Air date: January 12, 1957

Guests: Patti Page, Robert Lamouret, Jerry Lewis, Jackie Robinson and the Four Aces
There'll Be a Hot Time in the Old Town Tonight—Because—I Wonder (with Patti Page)—Dear Perry Medley (Imagination—Angry—If You Are but a Dream)—That Old Feeling

Show #19—Air date: January 19, 1957

Guests: George Gobel, The Mills Brothers, Jeff Chandler and John Scott Trotter
Heigh Ho—Whistle While You Work—When You Wish upon a Star—Lazy River (with Jeff Chandler, George Gobel and Ray Charles)—Dear Perry Medley (Guilty—Paper Moon—If I Loved You)

Show #20—Air date: January 26, 1957

Guests: Edie Adams, Peter Palmer, Joey Bishop and Helen Traubel
Chattanooga Choo-Choo—True Love—Namely You (with Peter Palmer)—Carolina in the Morning (with Helen Traubel)—I Don't Know Why (with Helen Traubel)—Dear Perry Medley (Everything I Have Is Yours—Sweet Lorraine—The Thrill Is Gone)—Over the Rainbow

Show #21—Air date: February 2, 1957

Guests: Fats Domino, Teresa Brewer, The Four Lads and Tab Hunter
Minnie the Mermaid—More Than You Know—My Heart Stood Still—When You and I Were Young Maggie Blues (with Polly Bergen)—Dear Perry Medley (I've Grown Accustomed to Her Face—The Best Things in Life Are Free—Ballerina)—Round and Round

Show #22—Air date: February 9, 1957

Guests: Myrna Loy, Jackie Cooper, Tommy Noonan, Cleo, Lord Flea & Group
There's No Business Like Show Business—Moonlight Gambler—Run, Run, Run (with Lord Flea & Group)—Mi Casa, Su Casa—When My Sugar Walks Down the Street (with Jackie Cooper)—Mr. Gallagher & Mr. Shean (with Jackie Cooper)—Say It With Music (with Jackie Cooper)—Dear Perry Medley (Beloved—Lifetime Sweetheart—You Alone)—Calypso Style Nights (with entire cast)

Show #23—Air date: February 16, 1957

Guests: Ginger Rogers, Vic Damone and Mickey & Sylvia
Wringle Wrangle—The Eyes Of Texas—Blow Gabriel Blow—Trust In Me—Manhattan (with Ginger Rogers)—Round and Round—Dear Perry Medley (Forgive Me—'Deed I Do—I Love You—Good Night Sweet Jesus)

Show #24—Air date: February 23, 1957

Guests: Ernie Kovacs, Tony Bennett and the Andrews Sisters
Chantez, Chantez—Where or When—Rum and Coca Cola (with The Andrews Sisters)—Scarlet Ribbons—Dear Perry Medley (A Friend of Yours—Come Rain or Come Shine)—The Rosary

Show #25—Air date: March 9, 1957

Guests: Ethel Merman, Jack Carter and the Mills Brothers
It's a Good Day—It Could Happen to You—Mutual Admiration Society (with Ethel Merman)—Without You (with Ethel Merman & Jack Carter)—The Banana Boat Song—Lazy River (with The Mills Brothers)—Dear Perry Medley (The Very Thought of You—Breezin' Along with the Breeze—Hello Young Lovers)—Round and Round

Show #26—Air date: March 16, 1957

Guests: Dana Andrews, Georgie Kaye and Esther Williams
McNamara's Band—Love Me Tender—School Days—I Gotta Right to Sing the Blues—Medley with Esther Williams (Row, Row, Row—On a Slow Boat to China)—Dear Perry Medley (Did Your Mother Come from Ireland?—Peg O' My Heart—My Wild Irish Rose)—I Believe

Show #27—Air date: March 23, 1957

Guests: Ed Wynn, Robert Strom, Benny Goodman & Trio, Andy Williams and Anna Maria Alberghetti

Keep Your Sunny Side Up—O Sole Mio (with Anna Maria Alberghetti)—One Fine Day (with Anna Maria Alberghetti & Ed Wynn)—Marianne—Dear Perry Medley (Sunday, Monday or Always—Swingin' Down the Lane—Dancing in the Dark)—Sing, Sing, Sing (with entire cast)

Show #28—Air date: March 30, 1957

Guests: Rowan & Martin, Julius La Rosa and Hedy Lamarr
Hi Neighbor—It Might as Well Be Spring—April in Paris—Chantez, Chantez (with Hedy Lamarr & Julius La Rosa)—Dear Perry Medley (It Must Be True—S'posin—I May Be Wrong—Love Letters)—Round and Round

Show #29—Air date: April 6, 1957

Guests: Jack Palance & Teresa Brewer
When You're Smiling—How Deep is the Ocean?—How Could You Believe Me (with Teresa Brewer)—Brahms' Lullaby (with Jack Palance)—Song of Songs—Dear Perry Medley (Say It Isn't So—When the Red, Red Robin Comes Bob-Bob-Bobbin' Along—Easy to Love)—Now the Day Is Over

Show #30—Air date: April 13, 1957

Guests: Gale Storm, Roger Williams, the Fontane Sisters and The Diamonds
Come Josephine in My Flying Machine—When I Fall in Love—Begin the Beguine—Dear Perry Medley (Don't Worry 'Bout Me—You Turned the Tables on Me—All at Once You Love Her)—You're Just in Love (with the Fontane Sisters)

Perry applauds a guest's performance on his television show, ca. 1957.

Show #31—Air date: April 20, 1957

Guests: Arlene Dahl and Pat Boone
It's a Star Time—So In Love—Round and Round—Medley with Pat Boone (Tutti Frutti—I Almost Lost My Mind—My One and Only Heart)—Oh, You Beautiful Doll (with Arlene Dahl & Pat Boone)—Dear Perry Medley (Peter Cottontail—Did You Ever See a Dream Walking?—Easter Parade)—The Lord's Prayer

Show #32—Air date: April 27, 1957

Guests: Red Buttons, Peggy King and Frankie Laine
I Feel a Song Coming On—It Could Happen to You—Mangos—That Old Gang of Mine (with Red Buttons)—April Showers (with Peggy King)—Marianne (with guests)—Dear Perry Medley (Marrying for Love—Tina Marie—The Night Is Young and You're So Beautiful)—You Are Never Far Away from Me

Show #33—Air date: May 4, 1957

Guests: Patti Page, Buddy Hackett and Gene Autry
New York medley (New York, New York—Sidewalks of New York—Lullaby of Broadway)—Around the World—Home on the Range (with Patti Page)—Birth of the Blues—A Good Old-fashioned Hoedown (with guests)—Dear Perry medley (It's a Lovely Day Today—When I Grow Too Old to Dream—All or Nothing at All)—The Gal with the Golden Braids

Show #34—Air date: May 11, 1957

Guests: Liberace, George Liberace, Jean Fenn and the Wiere Brothers
Come to the Fair—My Little Baby—The Old Piano Roll Blues (with Liberace)—Without a Song—Dear Perry Medley (Try a Little Tenderness—Little Old Lady—My Mother's Eyes)—Mother Dear, O Pray for Me

Show #35—Air date: May 18, 1957

Guests: Janice Paige, Lou Carter and Joey Bishop
Flying Down to Rio—Love Letters in the Sand—I Caught a Cold in My Heart—Some Enchanted Evening— Dear Perry Medley (You Do Something to Me—Ain't Misbehavin'—With My Eyes Wide Open I'm Dreaming)—The Girl with the Golden Braids

Show #36—Air date: May 25, 1957

Guests: Jo Stafford, Jackie Miles and Fats Domino
Toot, Toot, Tootsie—So Rare—Blue Tail Fly/He's Gone Away (with Jo Stafford, Perry on guitar also)—With a Song in My Heart—Dear Perry Medley (Stay As Sweet As You Are—Nice Work If You Can Get It—All the Things You Are)—Let the Rest of the World Go By (single chorus, Dean Martin joins in a snatch)

Show #37—Air date: June 1, 1957

Guests: Patrice Munsel, Jack Carter, Vaughn Monroe and The Goofers
June Is Bustin' out All Over—In the Cool, Cool, Cool of the Evening (with Patrice Munsel)—My Little Baby— Medley with Jack Carter (Partnership—Love and Marriage—Straw Hat and Cane—Nature Boy—After the Lights Go Down Low—All Shook Up—Racing with the Moon)—Dear Perry Medley (S'Wonderful—June Night—Love Walked In)—In the Good Old Summertime

Show #38—Air date: June 8, 1957

Guests: Ethel Merman, Ed Wynn and The Four Lads
God's Country—Summertime—Anything You Can Do (with Ethel Merman)—The World Is Waiting for the Sunrise/Tea for Two (with Ed Wynn)—Medley with The Four Lads (Down by the Old Mill Stream—Sweet Adeline—Down by the Station)—Dear Perry Medley (Night and Day)—The Girl with the Golden Braids

NBC Television—The Perry Como Show—Series 3

All shows featured orchestra conducted by Mitchell Ayres plus the Ray Charles Singers.
Announcer: Frank Gallop. Perry introduced all shows by singing a snatch of "Dream Along With Me"

Show #1—Air date: September 14, 1957

Guests: Ginger Rogers, Lou Carter and George Sanders
Hallelujah—Around the World—In the Still of the Night—Dear Perry Medley (Angry—It's Easy to Remember—'Deed I Do)—Whither Thou Goest

Show #2—Air date: September 21, 1957

Guests: Ginger Rogers, Jack Carter and Johnny Mercer
When You're Smiling—Tammy—One for My Baby—Glow Worm (with Johnny Mercer)—Ivy Rose—Dear Perry Medley (It's Not for Me to Say—I'm Gonna Sit Right Down and Write Myself a Letter)—Medley with guests (Como sings: Too Marvelous for Words—Lazy Bones—That Old Black Magic—Come Rain or Come Shine—Laura—Dream—One for My Baby—On the Atchison, Topeka & the Santa Fe)—Just Born (to Be Your Baby)

Show #3—Air date: September 28, 1957

Guests: Pearl Bailey, Julie Wilson, Irene Dunne, Kukla & Ollie
Love Is Sweeping the Country—It Could Happen to You—Gone Fishin' (with Pearl Bailey)—Getting to Know You (with Irene Dunne and Kukla & Ollie)—Dear Perry Medley (Swingin' Down the Lane—Somebody Loves Me—They Can't Take That Away from Me—Autumn Leaves)—Kol Nidre

Show #4—Air date: October 5, 1957

Guests: Ethel Merman, Kukla & Ollie and Garry Moore
Zip-A-Dee-Doo-Dah—An Affair to Remember—You're Just in Love (with Ethel Merman)—There's No Business Like Show Business (with Ethel Merman & Kukla & Ollie)—You Can't Please All the People (with Garry Moore)—Autumn in New York—Dear Perry Medley (South of the Border—Honey, Honey—Dancing in the Dark)—Holy God We Praise Thy Name

Show #5—Air date: October 12, 1957

Guests: Red Buttons, Miyoshi Umeki, Miiko Taka and Ann Sothern
Great Day—Temptation—Just Born (to Be Your Baby)—I'm Gonna Sit Right Down and Write Myself a Letter (with Ann Sothern)—Top Banana—Dear Perry Medley (Let a Smile Be Your Umbrella—I've Grown Accustomed to Her Face—The Way You Look Tonight)—Ivy Rose

Show #6—Air date: October 19, 1957

Guests: Tony Bennett, Jackie Miles, Edie Adams, Diana Dors and the Benny Goodman Trio
It's a Big Wide Wonderful World—Tammy—Medley with Diana Dors (I Love You—Smile, Darn You Smile—Me and My Shadow—Dinah)—Old Devil Moon—Dear Perry Medley (You'll Never Know—That's What I Like—No Other Love)—Sing, Sing, Sing (with all guests)

Show #7—Air date: October 26, 1957

Guests: Roy Rogers, Dale Evans, Ernie Kovacs and Edie Adams
Hooray for Hollywood—Fascination—Love and Marriage (with Roy Rogers and Dale Evans)—Melodie D'Amour—Dear Perry Medley (Say It Isn't So—Back in Your Own Back Yard—September Song)—Hoe Down (with Roy Rogers, Dale Evans and Ernie Kovacs)

Show #8—Air date: November 2, 1957

Guests: Ed Wynn, Sal Mineo and Dorothy Collins
Ducky Day (special lyrics)—Till—Let's Take a Walk Around The Block (with Dorothy Collins)—Dear Perry Medley (My Melancholy Baby—Oh. How I Miss You Tonight—Sleepy Time Gal)—I May Never Pass This Way Again

Show #9—Air date: November 9, 1957

Guests: Johnny Mathis, Dean Martin, Betty Walker, Peter Lind Hayes and Mary Healy
Brazil—April Love—Dear Perry Medley (Angry—What Is This Thing Called Love)—Oh, Marie (with Dean Martin via split screen)—Ivy Rose

Show #10—Air date: November 23, 1957

Guests: Pearl Bailey, Red Barber, Jackie Cooper and The Four Lads
(There's No Place Like) Home for the Holidays—Medley with guests (Down by the Station—Sweet Adeline—Bill Bailey, Won't You Please Come Home)—My Heart Reminds Me—Bye Bye Blues (with Jackie Cooper)—Honeycomb—Dearie (with Pearl Bailey)—Dear Perry Medley (You Must Have Been a Beautiful Baby—Love Letters)—Deep in the Heart of Texas (with Debbie Dixon)—Bless This House

Show #11—Air date: November 30, 1957

Guests: Ginger Rogers, Gertrude Berg and Johnny Puleo and his Harmonica Gang plus walk-on by Jerry Lewis for MDA.
Fine and Dandy—Chances Are—While We're Young—The Peanut Vendor (with Johnny Puleo)—Once In Love With Amy (with Ginger Rogers)—Dear Perry medley (You Make Me Feel So Young—A Fellow Needs a Girl—Between the Devil and The Deep Blue Sea)—One Little Candle

Show #12—Air date: December 7, 1957

Guests: Ethel Merman, Red Buttons, The Everly Brothers and the Look All-America Football Team
All American Girl—All the Way—When the Red, Red Robin Comes Bob-Bob-Bobbin' Along (with Ethel Merman)—Dear Perry medley (I Never Knew—It Had to Be You)—Strange Things Are Happening (with Ethel Merman and Red Buttons)—Count Your Blessings Instead of Sheep

Show #13—Air date: December 14, 1957

Guests: Janis Paige, George Sanders, Johnny Mathis and Lou Carter
Chicago—April Love—Winter Wonderland (with Janis Paige)—You'll Never Walk Alone—Dear Perry Medley (Santa Claus Is Comin' to Town—There's No Christmas Like a Home Christmas—Jingle Bells)—It's Beginning to Look Like Christmas (with guests)

Show #14—Air date: December 21, 1957

Guests: The McGuire Sisters, Kukla & Ollie, and The Marquis Family
Christmas Opening Medley—Christmas Carols medley with guests—The Story of the First Christmas—Ave Maria

Show #15—Air date: December 28, 1957

Guests: Kay Thompson, Helen Traubel and The Look TV Award guests
Good News—Catch a Falling Star—Dear Perry Medley with Kay Thompson and Helen Traubel (Perry sings: Honeycomb—Fascination—Love Letters in the Sand—Marianne—Tammy—Round and Round)—Auld Lang Syne

Show #16—Air date: January 4, 1958

Guests: Mary Healy and Peter Lind Hayes, Roger Williams, Jimmy Dean and The Vagabonds
That's Entertainment—Magic Moments—Country Style (with Jimmy Dean)—Dear Perry medley (I May Be Wrong—I Surrender Dear—All or Nothing at All)—I May Never Pass This Way Again

Show #17—Air date: January 11, 1958

Guests: Pearl Bailey, Ginger Rogers and Jack Carter
Liechtensteiner Polka—All the Way—There'll Be Some Changes Made (with Pearl Bailey)—If—Medley with guests (There's No Business Like Show Business—Swanee—Some of These Days—If You Knew Susie)—Dear Perry Medley (Can't We Talk It Over—But Beautiful—Don't Let the Stars Get in Your Eyes)—May the Good Lord Bless and Keep You

Show #18—Air date: January 18, 1958

Guests: Ginger Rogers, Tony Bennett and Buddy Hackett
From This Moment On—Why Don't They Understand—Say It with Music medley with guests (Alexander's Ragtime Band—Say It Isn't So—Easter Parade—White Christmas—They Say That Falling in Love Is Wonderful—You're Just in Love—Play a Simple Melody)—Dear Perry medley (If I Could Be with You [One Hour Tonight]—You Call It Madness—Gypsy in My Soul)—Catch a Falling Star

Show #19—Air date: January 25, 1958

Guests: Peggy Lee, Pat Boone and John Bubbles
At the Hop—It Could Happen to You—Sing a Song of Sunbeams (with Peggy Lee)—A Shine on Your Shoes (with Pat Boone)—I Gotta Right to Sing the Blues—Dear Perry medley (Try a Little Tenderness—I Found a Million Dollar Baby (in a Five and Ten Cent Store)—All the Things You Are)—Medley with Pat Boone, Peggy Lee & John Bubbles (Get Out Those Old Records—Golden Earrings—Taking a Chance on Love—April Love—When You Were Sweet Sixteen—Manana—It Ain't Necessarily So—"A" You're Adorable—Lover—Way Down Yonder in New Orleans)—Magic Moments

Show #20—Air date: February 1, 1958

Guests: Judy Holliday, George Hamilton IV, Mike Nichols & Elaine May
The Ferryboat Serenade—I Concentrate on You—The Party's Over (with Judy Holliday)—Sugartime—Dear Perry medley (Little Man You've Had a Busy Day—Almost Like Being in Love—The Whiffenpoof Song)—In the Garden

Show #21—Air date: February 8, 1958

Guests: Julius La Rosa, Joey Bishop and the Mary Kaye Trio
Hot Diggity (Dog Ziggity Boom)—Like Someone in Love—Sail Along, Silv'ry Moon (with Julius La Rosa)—In the Still of The Night—Dear Perry medley (Glory of Love—S'posin'—Vaya Con Dios)—Catch a Falling Star

Show #22—Air date: February 15, 1958

Guests: Pearl Bailey, Kay Starr, Eddie Fisher and the Mary Kaye Trio
Whistle While You Work—When I Fall in Love—Medley with Eddie Fisher (I Love You—Three Little Words—I Love You Truly—One Dozen Roses)—My Man (with Pearl Bailey)—Dear Perry medley (Who's Sorry Now?—So in Love—You'll Always Be My Lifetime Sweetheart)—Side by Side (with Kay Starr via split screen)—Mother Dear, O Pray for Me

Show #23—Air date: February 22, 1958

Guests: Kay Thompson, Teresa Brewer and the Four Lads
Strike up the Band—Medley with Teresa Brewer (Hit the Road to Dreamland—Baby Face—Kentucky Babe—His Rocking Horse Ran Away—Brahms Lullaby)—Magic Moments—I Love a Violin (with Teresa Brewer and Kay Thompson)—Dear Perry Medley (What'll I Do—You and the Night and the Music)

Show #24—Air date: March 1, 1958

Guests: Kate Smith, The Goofers and Rowan & Martin
Miami—Belonging to Someone—Moon Medley with Kate Smith (Moon Song—It's Only a Paper Moon—Sleepy Time Down South—Moonglow—When the Moon Comes over the Mountain)—Birth of the Blues—Dear Perry medley (I'm Nobody's Baby—Someone to Watch over Me—South of the Border)—I May Never Pass This Way Again

Show #25—Air date: March 8, 1958

Guests: Judy Holliday, Jimmy Dean, The Baird Puppets and Frankie Avalon
You—Love Me Again—To Know You Is to Love You (with Judy Holliday)—Medley with Jimmy Dean (I'm an Old Cowhand—Tumbling Tumbleweeds)—Black Moonlight—Dear Perry medley (Just in Time—Speak to Me of Love)—Sweet Hour of Prayer

Show #26—Air date: March 15, 1958

Guests: Maureen O'Hara, the McGuire Sisters and Jack Carter
It's a Great Day for the Irish (with guests)—Sugartime (with the McGuire Sisters)—Catch a Falling Star—Medley with guests (Did Your Mother Come from Ireland?—Too-Ra-Loo-Ra-Loo-Ral—Dear Old Donegal—When Irish Eyes Are Smiling—McNamara's Band)

Show #27—Air date: March 29, 1958

Guests: Frankie Laine, Teresa Brewer and Count Basie's Band (with Joe Williams)
Come to the Fair—Where or When—When the Red, Red Robin Comes Bob-Bob-Bobbin' Along (with Teresa Brewer)—Let's All Sing Like the Birdies Sing (with Teresa Brewer)—Dance Only with Me—All Right OK, You Win (with Count Basie)—Dear Perry medley (I May Be Wrong—I'm Confessin' (That I Love You)—I Love You)—Kewpie Doll

Show #28—Air date: April 5, 1958

Guests: Hedda Hopper, Alan King and Eddie Hodges
It's Easter Time—Between the Devil and the Deep Blue Sea—I Concentrate on You—Dear Perry Medley (Easter Sunday—Easter Parade)—Cinderella Waltz—The Lord's Prayer

Show #29—Air date: April 12, 1958

Guests: Bob Hope, Carol Channing and Johnny Puleo & his Harmonica Gang
In Acapulco—Tequila—Gigi—Cecilia (with Carol Channing)—Medley with Bob Hope (Nothing in Common—I Know That You Know—Somewhere You're Gonna Find Your Little Bluebird)—Dear Perry medley (Who's Sorry Now—Too Young—Ac-Cent-Tchu-Ate The Positive)—All Through the Night

Show #30—Air date: April 19, 1958

Guests: Shirley Booth, George Sanders and Marge & Gower Champion
Take Me Out to the Ball Game—So In Love—Return to Me—Happy Habit (with Shirley Booth)—Dear Perry medley (Louise—If I Loved You)—Look Who's Dancin' (with guests)—Kewpie Doll

Show #31—Air date: April 26, 1958

Guests: Pearl Bailey, Lily Pons and Gertrude Molly Berg
The Latin Quarter—Chanson D'Amour—Watchin' the Trains Go By (with Pearl Bailey)—Chattanooga Choo-Choo (with Pearl Bailey)—Darling, Je Vous Aime Beaucoup (with Lily Pons)—Dance Only with Me—Happy to Make Your Acquaintance (with guests)—Dear Perry medley (Blue Skies—I've Got You Under My Skin)—When You Come to the End of the Day

Show #32—Air date: May 3, 1958

Guests: Eve Arden, Bob & Ray, Rosemary June and Tennessee Ernie Ford
A Romantic Guy I—Just One of Those Things—Drop That Name (with Eve Arden)—Summertime—Don't Be Ashamed of Your Age (with Tennessee Ernie Ford)—Dear Perry medley (You Are Never Far Away from Me—Dream Along with Me—Where the Blue of the Night [with Bing Crosby—on tape])

Show #33—Air date: May 10, 1958

Guests: Johnny Mathis, Rusty Hamer, Sherry Jackson and Rowan & Martin
Oklahoma—A Very Precious Love—Over the Rainbow—Witch Doctor (with Rusty Hamer & Sherry Jack-

son)—Dear Perry medley (My Mother's Eyes—Mother [with Rusty Hamer & Sherry Jackson]—No Well on Earth)—Mother Dear, O Pray for Me

Show #34—Air date: May 17, 1958

Guests: Jack Carter, Sally Ann Howes, Andy Davies, The Baird Puppets and the Mills Brothers
Honolulu/Hawaiian War Chant/On The Beach At Waikiki (with guests)—Return to Me—Let's Call the Whole Thing Off (with Sally Ann Howes)—Kewpie Doll—Dear Perry medley (Easy Street—When I Fall in Love—It Had to Be You)—Softly and Tenderly

Show #35—Air date: May 24, 1958

Guests: Jane Wyman, Art Carney, Dean Martin, Don Ameche and the McGuire Sisters
The Trolley Song—This Nearly Was Mine—In the Cool, Cool, Cool of the Evening (with Jane Wyman)—Witch Doctor—Prayer for Peace—Zing a Little Zong (with guests)—Return to Me (with Dean Martin)

Show #36—Air date: May 31, 1958

Guests: Patti Page, Dave Barry, Eddie Hodges and Poodle Symphony
June Is Bustin' out All Over—Thank Heaven for Little Girls/I Want a Girl, Just Like the Girl (That Married Dear Old Dad) (with Eddie Hodges)—The Birth of the Blues—All I Have to Do Is Dream/Dream (with Patti Page)—Dear Perry medley (Gypsy in My Soul—You Made Me Love You—Ac-Cent-Tchu-Ate The Positive)—Softly and Tenderly

Show #37—Air date: June 7, 1958

Guests: Bob Crosby, Tony Curtis, Eydie Gorme, Richard Rodgers and Paul Anka
Good News—True Love—Sugar Moon/By the Light of the Silvery Moon (with Eydie Gorme)—Padre—Medley of Richard Rodgers songs (If I Loved You—Oh, What a Beautiful Mornin'—A Fellow Needs a Girl—My Funny Valentine—Lover—Hello, Young Lovers—Falling in Love with Love—The Most Beautiful Girl in the World—It's a Grand Night for Singing—Oklahoma—With a Song in My Heart—Manhattan—There is Nothin' Like a Dame—It's Easy to Remember—Some Enchanted Evening—Mountain Greenery—It Might As Well Be Spring—No Other Love—You'll Never Walk Alone)

NBC Television—The Perry Como Show—Series 4

All shows featured orchestra conducted by Mitchell Ayres plus the Ray Charles Singers.
Announcer: Frank Gallop. Perry introduced all shows by singing a snatch of "Dream Along With Me"

Show #1—Air date: September 13, 1958

Guests: Maureen O'Hara, Jimmy Van Heusen and Robert Preston. Several musicians make walk-on appearances: Tony Pastor; Buddy Morrow; Ray McKinley; Red Nichols and Russ Morgan
Volare—Another Op'nin, Another Show—Without a Song—Saturday Night With Mr. C medley (Moonlight Becomes You—I Thought About You)—Jimmy Van Heusen medley (Imagination—Sunday, Monday or Always—Road to Morocco (parody)—Aren't You Glad You're You (with Maureen O'Hara)—Like Someone in Love—Life Is So Peculiar—I Could Have Told You—The Tender Trap—Swinging on a Star (with Maureen O'Hara)—All the Way—Love and Marriage (with Maureen O'Hara)—Now the Day Is Over

Show #2—Air date: September 20, 1958

Guests: Tommy Sands, Vivian Blaine, Don Wilson, The Raiders and Thelma Ritter
He's Got the Whole World in His Hands—Medley with Vivian Blaine (I Wish We Didn't Have to Say Goodnight—If I'm Lucky—Dig You Later [A Hubba, Hubba, Hubba])—Moon Talk—There'll Be a Hot Time in the Old Town Tonight (with the whole cast)—The History of the World (with the whole cast)—Nobody—Waitin' for the Robert E. Lee (with the whole cast)—Kol Nidre

Show #3—Air date: September 27, 1958

Guests: Ann Sheridan, Ray Walston, the Everly Brothers and Arthur Schwartz
Love Makes the World Go 'Round—Begin the Beguine—Saturday Night with Mr. C. medley (Something to Remember You By—A Shine on Your Shoes)—Arthur Schwartz medley (Something to Remember You By—Haunted Heart—Look Who's Dancin'—Alone Together—If There Is Someone Lovelier Than You—That's Entertainment (with the whole cast))—Mandolins in the Moonlight

Show #4—Air date: October 4, 1958

Guests: Ann Jeffreys, Robert Sterling, Richard Hayman and Jackie Dennis

Tea for Two—Night and Day—Enjoy Yourself (with Ann Jeffreys and Robert Sterling)—Saturday Night with Mr. C medley (Embraceable You—Arrivederci Roma)—When It's Springtime in the Rockies (with Richard Hayman)—Enjoy Yourself (reprise—with entire company)—All Through the Night

Show #5—Air date: October 11, 1958

Guests: Shirley Booth, Lucho Gatica, Johnny Mercer and Dale Robertson
Everybody Loves a Lover—Come to Me, Bend to Me—Saturday Night with Mr. C. medley (Autumn in New York—'Deed I Do—So in Love)—Whoopee Ti Ai Yo / I'm an Old Cowhand (with entire cast plus Johnny Mercer)—El Rancho Grande (with Lucho Gatica)—Home on the Range—Twilight on the Trail—Goodnight Ladies (with entire cast)

Show #6—Air date: October 18, 1958

Guests: Eydie Gorme, Ralph Bellamy, Gretchen Wyler, Robin Luke and Jule Styne
Mandolins in the Moonlight—It's All in the Game—Love Makes the World Go Round—Jule Styne medley (That's What I Like—I've Heard That Song Before—Sunday—Just in Time—Let It Snow, Let It Snow, Let It Snow [with Eydie Gorme]—I'll Walk Alone—I Still Get Jealous [with Robin Luke]—It's Been a Long, Long Time [with Gretchen Wyler]—It's Magic—Papa, Won't You Dance with Me [with whole cast])

Show #7—Air date: October 25, 1958

Guests: Lena Horne, Janis Paige, David Wayne and Jimmy McHugh
The Birth of the Blues—It's All Right with Me (with Lena Horne)—The End—Saturday Night with Mr. C medley (Don't Blame Me—A Lovely Way to Spend an Evening)—Jimmy McHugh medley (When My Sugar Walks Down the Street—I Couldn't Sleep a Wink Last Night—I Can't Give You Anything but Love—You're a Sweetheart—Where Are You?—Cuban Love Song—I'm in the Mood for Love)—I Feel a Song Coming On (with entire cast)—Thank You for a Lovely Evening

Show #8—Air date: November 1, 1958

Guests: Judy Holliday, The Dunhills, Kukla & Ollie, and Jane Morgan
That Old Black Magic—Non Dimenticar—Medley with Judy Holliday (Row, Row, Row Your Boat—Three Blind Mice—Frere Jacques—Swanee River—Humoresque—My One and Only Heart—You're Just in Love—Play a Simple Melody)—Shine on Harvest Moon (with Kukla & Ollie)—Saturday Night with Mr. C. medley (Love Letters—Autumn Leaves—Gypsy in My Soul)—Cecilia (with Jane Morgan and The Dunhills)—Softly and Tenderly

Show #9—Air date: November 8, 1958

Guests: Edgar Bergen, Burl Ives, Ann Miller plus Ferrante & Teicher
I'm Sitting on Top of the World—There Goes My Heart—Only One—Folksong Medley (On Top of Old Smokey [with cast]—Blue Tail Fly [with cast]—Red River Valley—Down in the Valley [with Burl Ives]—Polly-Wolly Doodle [with Edgar Bergen]—She'll Be Coming Round the Mountain [with cast])

Show #10—Air date: November 15, 1958

Guests: Sally Ann Howes, Gisele MacKenzie, The Buffalo Bills and Richard Adler
It All Depends on You—When the World Was Young—I Could Have Danced All Night—If You Were the Only Girl in the World (with The Buffalo Bills)—Mandolins in the Moonlight—Richard Adler medley (Rags to Riches—Everybody Loves a Lover (with Gisele MacKenzie)—Hey There—Heart (with entire cast))—When You Come to the End of the Day

Show #11—Air date: November 22, 1958

Guests: Dorothy Collins, Vera-Ellen, Harry Warren and Jimmie Rodgers
(There's No Place Like) Home for the Holidays—Here's to My Lady—Love Is a Simple Thing (with Dorothy Collins)—I'll String Along with You—Harry Warren medley (I Found a Million Dollar Baby—Shadow Waltz—Zing a Little Zong (with Dorothy Collins)—You Must Have Been a Beautiful Baby—The More I See You—That's Amore (with Vera-Ellen)—You'll Never Know—Lullaby of Broadway (with whole cast))—Bless This House

Show #12—Air date: November 29, 1958

Guests: Ethel Merman, Conway Twitty, Hugh Martin, Ralph Blane plus Marge & Gower Champion
It's a Good Day—I Concentrate on You—Scarlet Ribbons—The Girl Next Door—Martin and Blane medley (Buckle Down Winsocki [with Hugh Martin and Ralph Blane]—Love—Skip to My Lou [with Conway Twitty]—The Girl Next Door—The Trolley Song [with cast])

Show #13—Air date: December 6, 1958

Guests: Pier Angeli, Andy Griffith, Helen O'Connell and The Look All-America Football Team

It's Beginning to Look Like Christmas—Medley with Pier Angeli (Funiculi Funicula—Santa Lucia—Funiculi Funicula)—Scarlet Ribbons—Love Makes the World Go Round (with The Look All-America Football Team)—College medley with guests (Mr. Touchdown—The Sweetheart of Sigma Chi—Down the Old Ox Road—The Whiffenpoof Song—You Gotta To Be a Football Hero)—When You Come to the End of the Day

Show #14—Air date: December 13, 1958

Guests: Kate Smith, Joey Bishop, Harry Ruby and Andy Williams

Button Up Your Overcoat—The Christmas Song—Jingle Bell Rock (with Andy Williams & Kate Smith)—Old Devil Moon—Three Little Words—Harry Ruby medley with Kate Smith, Andy Williams and Joey Bishop (Perry's contribution: Who's Sorry Now? [with Harry Ruby]—Thinking of You)—Give Me the Simple Life—When You Come to the End of the Day

Show #15—Air date: December 20, 1958

Guests: Ann Blyth plus Kukla & Ollie.

Happy Holiday—There's No Christmas Like a Home Christmas—White Christmas (with Ann Blyth)—Carols medley with guests (It Came Upon a Midnight Clear—God Rest Ye Merry, Gentlemen—Joy to the World—We Wish You a Merry Christmas)—Winter Wonderland (with Ann Blyth)—The Story of the First Christmas—Ave Maria

Show #16—Air date: December 27, 1958

Guests: Art Carney, Steve Lawrence, Alcetty, Dolores Hawkins and Joe Bushkin

It's a Grand Night for Singing—Oh, How I Miss You Tonight—You Tell Me Your Dream (with Art Carney)—Medley of 1958 hits (Volare—Witch Doctor—Sail Along Silv'ry Moon—Return to Me—Bird Dog [with Art Carney]—Catch a Falling Star—He's Got the Whole World in His Hands [with whole cast])—Auld Lang Syne (with whole cast)

Show #17—Air date: January 3, 1959

Guests: Louis Jourdan, Peggy King, The Teddy Bears (with Phil Spector), Harold Arlen and Eddie Foy Jr.

Ac-Cent-Tchu-Ate The Positive—Come Rain or Come Shine—Medley with Louis Jourdan (Gigi—Give Me the Simple Life—Lazy River)—One for My Baby—Harold Arlen Medley (Get Happy [with Harold Arlen]—Between the Devil and the Deep Blue Sea—I've Got the World on a String—I Gotta Right to Sing the Blues—That Old Black Magic—Let's Take a Walk [with Peggy King]—Over the Rainbow—I Love a Parade [with entire cast])—When You Come to the End of the Day

Show #18—Air date: January 10, 1959

Guests: Jane Wyman, Rosemary Clooney, Claudio Villa and the Kingston Trio

I've Got My Love to Keep Me Warm—If You Were the Only Girl in the World (with Rosemary Clooney)—On a Slow Boat to China (with Rosemary Clooney)—It's a Perfect Relationship (with Jane Wyman)—Sunshine Cake (with Jane Wyman & Rosemary Clooney)—You Do Something to Me—When I Fall in Love—Tomboy (with Rosemary Clooney & Jane Wyman)—Whither Thou Goest

Show #19—Air date: January 17, 1959

Guests: Nat King Cole, Eddie Foy Jr., Dick Van Dyke, Rosemary June and the McGuire Sisters

St. Louis Blues—A Fellow Needs a Girl—In the Still of the Night—My Happiness (with Rosemary June)—Breezin' Along with the Breeze—Prisoner of Love—Hot Diggity (Dog Ziggity Boom) (with cast)—When You Come to the End of the Day

Show #20—Air date: January 24, 1959

Guests: Kay Starr, Cornelia Otis Skinner, Sammy Cahn and John Bubbles

South of the Border—Song of Songs—Smoke Gets in Your Eyes—It's Been a Long, Long Time—Sammy Cahn medley (To Love and Be Loved—I've Heard That Song Before—Love and Marriage—Be My Love—It's Magic—Let it Snow, Let It Snow, Let It Snow [with Sammy Cahn & Kay Starr]—All the Way)—When You Come to the End of the Day

Show #21—Air date: January 31, 1959

Guests: Tab Hunter and Patti Page plus Rowan & Martin

Tomboy—Always—That's My Desire—Don't Fence Me In (with Patti Page)—Saturday Night with Mr. C. medley

(Angry—It's the Talk of the Town—The Night is Young and You're So Beautiful)—Four Way Stretch (with guests)—A Still Small Voice—When You Come to the End of the Day

Show #22—Air date: February 7, 1959

Guests: Connie Francis, Charlton Heston, Sid Gould, Al Hoffman, Bernice Massey, Dick Manning, Mickey Glass and the Mills Brothers

Honey, Honey—Where or When—Kiss Me and Kiss Me and Kiss Me—Cielito Lindo (with The Mills Brothers)—Little Man You've Had a Busy Day—Hoffman & Manning medley (Hot Diggity [Dog Ziggity Boom]) [with Al Hoffman & Dick Manning]—Are You Really Mine?—Mairzy Doats [with Charlton Heston & Connie Francis]—I Apologize—Chi-Baba, Chi-Baba (with The Mills Brothers)—Ivy Rose—Fascination—Papa Loves Mambo [with guests])

Show #23—Air date: February 14, 1959

Guests: Tony Bennett, Lorin Hollander, Sammy Fain and Patrice Munsel

Love Is Sweeping the Country—When You Were Sweet Sixteen—I Love You—Let a Smile Be Your Umbrella—Sammy Fain medley (Dear Hearts and Gentle People [with guests]—Secret Love—When I Take My Sugar to Tea [with Tony Bennett]—That Old Gang of Mine [with Patrice Munsel]—Love Is a Many Splendored Thing—Are You Having Any Fun?)—No Well on Earth

Show #24—Air date: February 21, 1959

Guests: Gary Cooper, Lena Horne and Margaret Ann & The Jada Quartet

Hallelujah—More Than You Know—Jada—All I Do Is Dream of You—I've Grown Accustomed to Her Face—Napoleon (with Lena Horne)—Life is Just a Bowl of Cherries (with Lena Horne)

Show #25—Air date: February 28, 1959

Guests: Gene Barry, Lorin Hollander, Kitza and Paul Anka

An Affair to Remember—My Heart Stood Still—Tomboy—When the Red, Red Robin Comes Bob-Bob-Bobbin' Along (with Gene Barry)—Saturday Night with Mr. C. medley (I May Be Wrong—It Could Happen to You—All or Nothing at All)—Love is Just Around the Corner

Show #26—Air date: March 7, 1959

Guests: Eve Arden, Max Bygraves and Ronnie Burns

The Donkey Serenade—Way Back Home (with Eve Arden)—George's Welcome—Saturday Night with Mr. C. medley (Them There Eyes—How About Me?—I've Got You Under My Skin)—My Heart Stood Still—I Wonder Who's Kissing Her Now (with Max Bygraves)—One Little Candle

Show #27—Air date: March 14, 1959

Guests: Ida Lupino, Howard Duff, June Valli and Margaret Ann & The Jada Quartet

It's a Great Day for the Irish—McNamara's Band—True Love—Did Your Mother Come from Ireland?—Peg O' My Heart—When Irish Eyes Are Smiling—Saturday Night with Mr. C. medley (I'm Sitting on Top of the World—Five Foot Two, Eyes of Blue—It All Depends on You)—Sonny Boy—Life Is Just a Bowl of Cherries (with June Valli & The Jada Quartet)—You're the Cream in My Coffee (with June Valli)—The Birth of the Blues

Show #28—Air date: March 21, 1959

Guests: Nanette Fabray, Billy Rose and the Everly Brothers

Great Day—Trees—Spring Is Here—Saturday Night with Mr. C. medley (Back in Your Own Backyard—Barney Google—It Happened in Monterey—The Night is Young and You're So Beautiful—Without a Song)—To Love and Be Loved

Show #29—Air date: March 28, 1959

Guests: Dorothy Collins, Lorin Hollander and The Students of the Ballet Theatre School

It's Easter Time—Easter Parade—Gigi—Everything Happens to Me (with Dorothy Collins)—Tip-toe Through the Tulips—When the Red, Red, Robin Comes Bob-Bob-Bobbin' Along (with Dorothy Collins)—When It's Springtime in the Rockies (with whole cast)

Show #30—Air date: April 4, 1959

Guests: Maureen O'Hara, Don Ameche, Dave King and Fabian

St. Louis Blues—A Very Precious Love—I Gotta Right to Sing the Blues—It Had to Be You—Someone to Watch Over Me—Between the Devil and the Deep Blue Sea—Vaya Con Dios

Show #31—Air date: April 11, 1959

Guests: Kathryn Grayson, Frankie Laine, Buddy Hackett and Oscar Hammerstein II
All Right, OK, You Win—I Concentrate on You—April in Paris—It Might As Well Be Spring—Oscar Hammerstein medley (Rose Marie—The Desert Song—Make Believe—The Song is You—The Last Time I Saw Paris—Oklahoma [with guests])—You Are Never Far Away from Me

Show #32—Air date: April 18, 1959

Guests: Julie London, Art Wall, Bobby Darin and Lou Carter
Take Me out to the Ball Game—I'll Never Smile Again—This Nearly Was Mine—Medley with Lou Carter & his Orchestra (Perry contributes: Split Your Sandwich with a Stranger—Selfish—If I Had a Nose Full of Nickels—What's a Matter with Me? [with Bobby Darin])—When You Come to the End of the Day

Show #33—Air date: April 25, 1959

Guests: Eydie Gorme, Fernandel, E. Y. Harburg and Julius La Rosa
Stardust—Let a Smile Be Your Umbrella—Turn Me Loose (with Eydie Gorme)—With a Song in My Heart—Brother, Can You Spare a Dime—E. Y. Harburg medley (We're Off to See the Wizard—April in Paris—How Are Things in Glocca Morra?—Old Devil Moon—It's Only a Paper Moon [with Eydie Gorme]—Over the Rainbow—There's a Great Day Comin' Manana [with guests])

Show #34—Air date: May 2, 1959

Guests: Hermione Gingold, Jane Morgan, The Four Freshmen and Johnny Burke
Too Marvelous for Words—They Didn't Believe Me—Red Sails in the Sunset—Pennies from Heaven—Johnny Burke Medley (Annie Doesn't Live Here Anymore—What's New?—I've Got a Pocketful of Dreams [with Jane Morgan]—Sunday, Monday or Always—Wild Horses—Aren't You Glad You're You [with Jane Morgan]—Swinging on a Star [with whole cast])

Show #35—Air date: May 9, 1959

Guests: Carol Haney, Don Ameche, Jackie Miles and Joni James
Jeepers, Creepers—While We're Young—South Rampart Street Parade—Saturday Night with Mr. C. medley (You Made Me Love You—S'posin'—Our Love Is Here to Stay)—No Well on Earth

Show #36—Air date: May 16, 1959

Guests: Dave King, Kay Starr, Enzo Stuarti, Dick Hills, Sid Green and Howard Dietz
A Shine on Your Shoes—If There Is Someone Lovelier Than You—You and the Night and the Music—Howard Dietz Medley (I Guess I'll Have To Change My Plan—Something to Remember You By [with Kay Starr]—I See Your Face Before Me—Dancing in the Dark—That's Entertainment [with the whole cast])

Show #37—Air date: May 23, 1959

Guests: Gisele MacKenzie, Bob Williams & dog, Carol Hughes and Dorothy Fields
Dear Hearts and Gentle People—Don't Take Your Love from Me—Have You Ever Been Lonely (with Gisele MacKenzie)—The Test of Time—The Way You Look Tonight—Dorothy Fields Medley (Exactly Like You—Lovely to Look At—A Fine Romance [with Gisele Mackenzie]—Love Is the Reason [with Carol Hughes]—I'm in The Mood for Love—I Feel a Song Coming On [with the whole cast])

Show #38—Air date: May 30, 1959

Guests: Andy Griffith, David Lawrence, Betty Johnson and Nacio Herb Brown
You Are in Love—Gigi—I Know—Temptation—Nacio Herb Brown medley (You Were Meant for Me—All I Do Is Dream of You—You're an Old Smoothie [with Betty Johnson]—Alone—Pagan Love Song [with Betty Johnson]—Paradise—You Are My Lucky Star—Singin' in the Rain [with guests])

Show #39—Air date: June 6, 1959

Guests: Tony Bennett, Teresa Brewer and The Four Lads
When You're Smiling—I've Got You Under My Skin—My Melancholy Baby—You Came a Long Way from St. Louis—Say One for Me

NBC Television—The Kraft Music Hall—Series 1

All shows featured orchestra conducted by Mitchell Ayres plus the Ray Charles Singers. Announcer: Frank Gallop.

Show #1—Air date: September 30, 1959

Guests: The Everly Brothers, Peggy King, Walter Brennan, Jack Cole, The Pitch Hikers, Maurice Gosfield ("Doberman" in the Bilko series) and Bing Crosby (on record)
Dream Along with Me—Where or When—How High the Moon (snatch only)—Somebody Else Is Taking My Place ('duet' with Bing Crosby record)—In the Evening By the Moonlight (with The Pitch Hikers)—Waiting for the Robert E. Lee (snatch only—with The Pitch Hikers)—Unchained Melody—Put Your Arms Around Me, Honey—Cavalcade spot (Dig You Later (A Hubba-Hubba-Hubba)—Don't Let the Stars Get in Your Eyes—Hot Diggity (Dog Ziggity Boom)—Catch a Falling Star—Prisoner of Love)

Show #2—Air date: October 7, 1959

Guests: Dorothy Collins, John Payne, Ivo Robic & Petite Michele
Let a Smile Be Your Umbrella—St. Louis Blues—Getting to Know You (with Petite Michele)—Schnitzelbank (with guests)—Just a Cottage Small (by a Waterfall)—Till There Was You—Everything I Love—John Payne medley (Carolina in the Morning—Ragtime Cowboy Joe [with Petite Michele & John Payne]—You Say the Sweetest Things Baby [with Dorothy Collins]—You'll Never Know—It Happened in Sun Valley [with guests]—Goodbye Broadway, Hello France [with guests]—America I Love You [with guests])

Show #3—Air date: October 14, 1959

Guests: Phil Harris, Carol Haney, Dick Clark, Santo & Johnny
The Lonesome Road—Together, Wherever We Go (with guests—includes a snatch of "Dream Along with Me")—Is It True What They Say About Dixie (with Phil Harris)—Not One Minute More—Smile—So in Love—Minstrel Show medley (Row, Row, Row [with Phil Harris]—Nobody [with Phil Harris]—Waiting for the Robert E. Lee [with guests])—When You Come to the End of the Day

Show #4—Air date: October 21, 1959

Guests: Nat King Cole, Rosemary Clooney, Gail Davis, Frank Barnes and Rin Tin Tin
The Donkey Serenade—Autumn In New York—Medley with Rosemary Clooney (Makin' Whoopee—The Glory of Love—The Blue Room—Blue Moon—I Let a Song Go out of My Heart—Don't Get Around Much Anymore—Blue Skies—Just One of Those Things—I've Got You Under My Skin—I Get a Kick Out Of You—You're Just in Love)—Life Is Just a Bowl of Cherries (with Rosemary Clooney & Nat King Cole)—Ac-Cent-Tchu-Ate the Positive (with Rosemary Clooney & Nat King Cole)—It Had To Be You—All or Nothing at All—Campfire medley (The Old Chisholm Trail [with guests]—Red River Valley [with Rosemary Clooney]—I'm an Old Cowhand [with Rosemary Clooney]—Tumbling Tumbleweeds [with guests]—Twilight on the Trail—Git Along Little Dogies [with guests])—When You Come to the End of the Day

Show #5—Air date: October 28, 1959

Guests: Teresa Brewer, Buddy Hackett, The Lennon Sisters and Paul O'Keefe.
It's a Good Night—In the Still of the Night—Skeleton in the Closet (with Teresa Brewer)—Pennies from Heaven—Pennsylvania Polka (with The Lennon Sisters)—You Do Something to Me—You Made Me Love You—That Old Black Magic—Dry Bones (with Paul O'Keefe & The Lennon Sisters)—Autumn Leaves (with The Lennon Sisters)—This Ole House (with guests)—You Are Never Far Away from Me

Show #6—Air date: November 11, 1959

Guests: Janis Paige, Frankie Vaughan, The Bilko Platoon and the Anna Sokolov Dancers
It's a Big Wide Wonderful World—The Birth of the Blues—Everybody Loves a Lover (with Frankie Vaughan)—Begin the Beguine—Dear Perry medley (I'm a Fool to Want You—The Night is Young and You're So Beautiful)—Soldier medley (Oh, How I Hate to Get Up in the Morning—My Buddy—This is the Army [with guests])—I May Never Pass This Way Again

Show #7—Air date: November 18, 1959

Guests: Benny Goodman, Connie Francis and Celeste Holm
Sing, Sing, Sing—I've Got You Under My Skin—And That's Jazz—Come Rain or Come Shine—"Deed I Do—That Old Feeling—Swing—Let's Dance—The Music Goes Round and Round—Oh, Johnny—Heartaches—A Still Small Voice—Rudolph the Red-Nosed Reindeer

Show #8—Air date: November 25, 1959

Guests: Dave King, The Lennon Sisters, Rod Lauren and Lorin Hollander.
Opening medley ((There's No Place Like) Home for the Holidays—I Concentrate on You—Diane—Peg O' My Heart—I'll Take You Home Again Kathleen—No Other Love—Step Right into the Kitchen—(There's No Place Like) Home for The Holidays—Bless This House)—Too Marvelous for Words (with The Lennon Sisters)—A Little Street Where Old Friends Meet (with The Lennon Sisters)

Show #9—Air date: December 2, 1959

Guests: Dolores Gray, Joe Bushkin and Andy Griffith.
I've Got You Under My Skin—A Still Small Voice—That Old Feeling—Sing, Sing, Sing—I Love You—Dear Perry medley (Only Forever—Dear Hearts and Gentle People—I Love You [Porter])

Show #10—Air date: December 9, 1959

Guests: Tommy Sands, Sandra Church, Allen & Rossi and The Look All-America Football team
You Gotta Be a Football Hero—Dream—Song of Songs—Let Me Entertain You (with Sandra Church)—Seven Little Girls Sitting in the Back Seat—College medley (The Sweetheart of Sigma Chi—The Whiffenpoof Song—You Gotta Be a Football Hero [with guests])—Now the Day Is Over

Show #11—Air date: December 16, 1959

Guests: Maurice Evans, Jane Morgan and the Wiere Brothers.
A Foggy Day—Night and Day—Mack Gordon medley with Jane Morgan (Stay As Sweet As You Are—You Make Me Feel So Young—Time on My Hands—Chattanooga Choo-Choo—You'll Never Know)—It's Beginning to Look Like Christmas—Here We Come A-Caroling—Santa Claus is Comin' to Town—White Christmas—English Music Hall Spot (Let's All Go Down the Strand—Underneath the Arches [with the Wiere Brothers]—I've Got a Lovely Bunch Of Coconuts [with Maurice Evans])—It's Beginning to Look Like Christmas (reprise—with entire cast)

Show #12—Air date: December 23, 1959

Guests: Shari Lewis and Bob Williams & his dog (Louie)
Happy Holiday—Jingle Bells—There's No Christmas Like a Home Christmas—Christmas Carols medley with Shari Lewis (Here We Come A-Caroling—It Came Upon a Midnight Clear—God Rest Ye Merry, Gentlemen—Deck The Halls—Joy to the World—We Wish You a Merry Christmas)—Ave Maria

Show #13—Air date: December 30, 1959

Guests: Maureen O'Hara, Cliff Norton, Jonah Jones & Group and Imogene Coca.
I'm Sitting on Top of the World—Little Man You've Had a Busy Day—Auld Lang Syne—Jimmy Valentine

Show #14—Air date: January 6, 1960

Guests: Kay Starr, Paul Anka, Peter Gennaro, Wisa d'Orso and Buddy Hackett.
Delaware—The Sound of Music—Black Moonlight—Ain't Nobody's Business But My Own (with Kay Starr)—Dear Perry medley (Love Is Just Around the Corner—Try a Little Tenderness—Angry)—Delaware (reprise with guests)—I Know What God Is

Show #15—Air date: January 20, 1960

Guests: Lena Horne, Corbett Monica and Robert Horton.
(Get Your Kicks on) Route 66 (with guests)—I'll String Along with You—Schizo Square Dance (with Robert Horton)—Old Devil Moon—Between the Devil And the Deep Blue Sea—Birdland Medley with Lena Horne (Bob White—Cuckoo in the Clock—Yellow Bird—Listen to the Mockin' Bird—When the Red, Red, Robin Comes Bob-Bob-Bobbin' Along)—The Village of St. Bernadette

Show #16—Air date: January 27, 1960

Guests: Patti Page, Don Adams, Eddie Hodges and The Erroll Garner Trio.
Acapulco (with guests)—June in January—Small Fry (with Eddie Hodges)—Jerome Kern medley with guests (They Didn't Believe Me—Long Ago (and Far Away)—All Through the Day—Smoke Gets in Your Eyes—The Way You Look Tonight—Who)—You Are Never Far Away from Me

Show #17—Air date: February 3, 1960

Guests: Birgit Nilsson, Kaye Ballard, Jaye P. Morgan and Carol Haney
Girls (with guests)—A Fellow Needs a Girl—Down by the Old Mill Stream (with Carol Haney, Kaye Ballard & Jaye P. Morgan)—It All Depends on You—Eternally—Merry Widow medley with guests (Maxim's—I Love You So—Romance—Girls, Girls, Girls)—When You Come to The End of the Day

Show #18—Air date: February 10, 1960

Guests: Raymond Massey, Taina Elg, Dorothy Collins and the Kingston Trio.
Love Is Sweeping the Country—Be My Love—Blue Tail Fly (with Raymond Massey)—My Funny Valentine—

Medley with Dorothy Collins (Love Is The Sweetest Thing—Love Is a Many Splendored Thing—Love Is a Simple Thing—Love Is the Reason)—Calypso Carnival medley with guests (Matilda—Matilda [reprise])—It Had to Be You—Beyond the Sea

Show #19—Air date: February 17, 1960

Guests: Jose Ferrer, Senor Wences, Frank D'Rone and Patrice Munsel
Where or When—Delaware (with Jose Ferrer and Patrice Munsel)—That's What I Like—Alexander's Ragtime Band—Granada—Lady of Spain (with guests)—When You Come to the End of the Day

Show #20—Air date: February 24, 1960

Guests: Anne Bancroft, Bert Lahr, Kay Starr and the Mills Brothers.
That's Entertainment (with entire cast)—Smile—Sleepy Time Gal (with The Mills Brothers)—So in Love—Opus One (with Kay Starr & The Mills Brothers)—Oh, Marie (with Anne Bancroft)—Funiculi, Funicula (with Anne Bancroft)—When You Come to the End of the Day

Show #21—Air date: March 2, 1960

Guests: Theodore Bikel, Nancy Walker, Pat Benton, Carol Lawrence and Robert Morse.
Hi Neighbor (with guests)—My Favorite Things—I Gotta Right to Sing the Blues—Molly Malone (with Theodore Bikel)—All Night Supermarket / Hi Neighbor (with entire cast)—You Are Never Far Away from Me

Show #22—Air date: March 9, 1960

Guests: Gisele MacKenzie, Bob Denver, Frankie Avalon and Margaret Ann & The Jadas.
To Know You Is to Love You—Come to Me, Bend to Me—You'll Never Walk Alone—By the Light of the Silvery Moon (with Frankie Avalon)—Medley with Gisele MacKenzie (Winnipeg—Way Down Yonder in New Orleans—Tramp, Tramp, Tramp—Peg O' My Heart—All the Way—Delaware—Oklahoma)—They Can't Take That Away from Me—When You Were Sweet Sixteen—That Old Black Magic

Show #23—Air date: March 16, 1960

Guests: Bing Crosby, Genevieve and Peter Gennaro
Medley with Bing Crosby (In the Cool, Cool, Cool of the Evening—On Behalf of the Visiting Firemen—In the Cool, Cool, Cool of the Evening [reprise])—Old Songs medley with Bing Crosby (Yes! We Have No Bananas—The Aba Daba Honeymoon—Barney Google—Collegiate—C-o-n-s-t-a-n-t-i-n-o-p-l-e—Crazy Words, Crazy Tune (Vo-Do-De-O-Do)—It Ain't Gonna Rain No Mo'—I Scream, You Scream, We All Scream for Ice Cream—Mr. Gallagher & Mr. Shean)—C'est Si Bon (with Genevieve)—Too-Ra-Loo-Ra-Loo-Ral (with Bing Crosby)—'First LP' medley with Bing Crosby (I Hear Music—Oh, How I Hate To Get Up in the Morning—Blue Skies—Breezin' Along with the Breeze—Let's Get Away from It All—Back in Your Own Backyard—Mountain Greenery—Aren't You Glad You're You?—When My Sugar Walks Down the Street—My Blue Heaven—Moonlight Bay—Dream Along with Me—Let's Put Out the Lights and Go to Sleep (Parody)—On Behalf of the Visiting Firemen (reprise)—In the Cool, Cool, Cool of the Evening (reprise)—I Hear Music (reprise))

Show #24—Air date: March 23, 1960

Guests: Martyn Green, Don Adams, Steve Lawrence and Eydie Gorme.
It's a Big Wide Wonderful World—Beyond the Sea—Eternally—Almost Like Being in Love—Green Room medley with guests (Stranger in Paradise—The Song Is You—Of Thee I Sing)—I Know What God Is

Show #25—Air date: March 30, 1960

Guests: Jane Morgan, Peter Lawford, Ann Thomas, Elaine Dunn and the Four Lads.
County Fair (with guests)—C'est Magnifique—Relax-ay-voo (with Jane Morgan)—Down by the Riverside (with The Four Lads)—Without a Song—It Could Happen to You—South of the Border—Hayride medley with guests (Goin' on a Hayride—Let's All Sing Like the Birdies Sing—The Band Played On—Daisy Bell—The Man on the Flying Trapeze—After the Ball—Let Me Call You Sweetheart—The Sidewalks of New York—School Days—Goodnight Ladies)—When You Come to the End of the Day

Show #26—Air date: April 6, 1960

Guests: Eve Arden, The Piero Brothers and Sarah Vaughan plus Allen & Rossi.
Take Me out to the Ball Game—Play Ball—All of Me—More Than You Know—We Get Letters medley (When You're Smiling—Hello, Young Lovers)—In the Garden

Show #27—Air date: April 13, 1960

Guests: Dorothy Collins, The Lennon Sisters, Bill Baird Puppets, Arnold Palmer and Johnny Puleo & His Harmonica Gang
It's Easter Time (with guests)—Easter Parade (with guests)—Young at Heart—My Favorite Things (with Dorothy Collins and The Lennon Sisters)—The Wizard of Oz (with guests)—Ave Maria

Show #28—Air date: April 27, 1960

Guests: Sir Ralph Richardson, Dame Margot Fonteyn, Harry Secombe, Fenella Fielding, Russ Conway and the Duke of Bedford
Gypsy in My Soul—Blue Skies—I Love You (Porter)—Cruising Down the River (with Harry Secombe, Fenella Fielding & Russ Conway [piano])—Where or When—When I Fall in Love—I'm Sitting on Top of the World—Delaware (snatch) (with British choir under the direction of Ray Charles)—Now Is the Hour

Show #29—Air date: May 4, 1960

Guests: Kay Starr, Neile Adams, Steve McQueen and the Wiere Brothers.
Be a Clown (with guests)—Smile—Smiles—You're My Sugar (with Kay Starr)—Here's to My Lady—No Well on Earth—When You Come to the End of the Day

Show #30—Air date: May 11, 1960

Guests: Genevieve, Johnny Carson, Toni Arden and Roger Williams.
Alexander's Ragtime Band (with guests)—How Deep Is the Ocean?—Play a Simple Melody (with Genevieve)—Cheek to Cheek—Irving Berlin medley with guests (Blue Skies—You're Just in Love (with Toni Arden)—White Christmas (with Toni Arden)—Say It Isn't So—Always—God Bless America)

Show #31—Air date: May 18, 1960

Guests: Edie Adams, Ray Walston, Della Reese and Jose Greco.
It's a Good Day—Greenfields—The Old Lamplighter—How About You? (with Edie Adams)—Manhattan—When You Come to the End of the Day

Show #32—Air date: May 25, 1960

Guests: Carol Lawrence, Genevieve, Don Adams and the Crosby Brothers.
Lucky Day (with guests)—It Had to Be You—All or Nothing at All—Medley with Crosby Brothers (Zing a Little Zong—Mam'selle—Dinah)—You Turned the Tables on Me—Country Style (with guests)—When You Come to the End of the Day—Where the Blue of the Night

Show #33—Air date: June 1, 1960

Guests: David McLean and Donald Stewart
June Is Bustin' out All Over (with Ray Charles)—It's Easy to Remember—My Melancholy Baby—You Are Never Far Away from Me (with cast)

NBC Television—The Kraft Music Hall—Series 2

All shows featured orchestra conducted by Mitchell Ayres plus the Ray Charles Singers.
Announcer: Frank Gallop.

Show #1—Air date: October 5, 1960

Guests: Ethel Merman, Shelley Berman, Frankie Avalon and Fabian
Taking a Chance on Love—I Didn't Mean Me—Alexander's Ragtime Band—It's a Lonesome Old Town—Together Wherever We Go—Autumn in New York—Medley with Ethel Merman (I Got Rhythm—You're Just in Love [with Ethel Merman]—Everything's Coming up Roses—I Get a Kick Out of You—There's No Business Like Show Business—I Got Rhythm [with Ethel Merman])—Saturday Afternoon Before the Game (with Frankie Avalon and Fabian)—Sing to Me Mr. C medley (Back in Your Own Backyard—But Beautiful—So in Love)—Inchworm (with Shelley Berman)—You're the Top (with Ethel Merman)

Show #2—Air date: October 12, 1960

Guests: Sid Caesar, Renee Taylor and Bobby Rydell
Are You Having Any Fun?—Unchained Melody—Mack the Knife (with Bobby Rydell)—Sing to Me Mr. C medley (Just in Time—I've Grown Accustomed to Her Face—All or Nothing at All)

Show #3—Air date: October 19, 1960

Guests: Keely Smith and Jack Paar
You Do Something to Me—Bluebird of Happiness—Let a Smile Be Your Umbrella—On the Sunny Side of the Street—Smile—When You're Smiling—My Mammy—Ain't We Got Fun (with Keely Smith)—Gigi—Sing to Me, Mr. C medley ('Deed I Do—Just Friends—I Concentrate on You)

Show #4—Air date: October 26, 1960

Guests: Andy Williams, Jane Powell and Thelma Ritter.
The Lonesome Road—I Gotta Right to Sing The Blues—Sentimental Journey—Boo-Hoo, You've Got Me Cryin' for You—I Got a Gal in Kalamazoo—Begin the Beguine—Sing, Sing, Sing—Big Noise—Sweet Lorraine—Thank Heaven for Little Girls—Easy to Love

Show #5—Air date: November 2, 1960

Guests: Rosemary Clooney, Casey Stengel, Elroy Face, Hal Smith & Ginny Tiu
A Shine on Your Shoes—St. Louis Blues—Brahms Lullaby—Rock-A-Bye Your Baby (with Rosemary Clooney)—I Love You (Porter)—If I Could Be with You—Can't We Talk It Over—Love Letters

Show #6—Air date: November 9, 1960

Guests: Ginger Rogers, Renee Taylor, Alan King and Della Reese
Clap Yo' Hands—Talking with Your Hands—Clap Yo' Hands (with guests)—Without a Song—Medley with Ginger Rogers (I Won't Dance—Cheek to Cheek—The Continental—Ballerina—Mexican Hat Dance—The Continental—That's a Plenty—The Man on the Flying Trapeze)—Make Someone Happy—Gone Is My Love—Bill Bailey, Won't You Please Come Home (with Della Reese)

Show #7—Air date: November 23, 1960

Guests: Tommy Sands, Renee Taylor, The Crosby Brothers, The Lennon Sisters and Frank Gorshin
In the Cool, Cool, Cool of the Evening (with entire cast)—(There's No Place Like) Home for The Holidays—I'm an Old Cowhand (with The Crosby Brothers)—Dream (with The Crosby Brothers, The Lennon Sisters and Tommy Sands)—Keep-A-Hoppin' (with The Crosby Brothers, The Lennon Sisters and Tommy Sands)—(There's No Place Like) Home for The Holidays—Home—Nancy (with Tommy Sands)—Bless This House

Show #8—Air date: November 30, 1960

Guests: Bob Hope, Milt Kamen, Peter Gennaro and Anne Bancroft.
Ac-Cent-Tchu-Ate the Positive—Sing to Me Mr. C medley (Georgia on My Mind—Ev'rything I Love)—Volare (with Anne Bancroft)—Medley with Bob Hope (People Will Say We're in Love—I Remember It Well—Baby, It's Cold Outside—How About You?—Why Do I Love You?—There is Nothin' Like a Dame)—Two Sleepy People (parody with Bob Hope & Anne Bancroft)

Show #9—Air date: December 7, 1960

Guests: Juliet Prowse, Steve Lawrence, Milt Kamen and The Kingston Trio.
Round and Round—Tonight—Violets for Your Furs—Western Medley with Steve Lawrence and The Kingston Trio (Legend of Wyatt Earp—Ballad of Paladin—Bat Masterson Theme—Bonanza—Maverick)—Sing to Me Mr. C medley (Nice 'N Easy—The Very Thought of You—Old Devil Moon)—Medley with Steve Lawrence (Way Back Home—A Little Street Where Old Friends Meet—Gary, Indiana—Avalon—Carolina in the Morning—Sleepy Time Down South—Dear Hearts and Gentle People)

Show #10—Air date: December 14, 1960

Guests: Betty Grable, Brook Benton, Renee Taylor, Joey Heatherton, Bea Arthur, Milt Kamen and Brenda Lee
It's Beginning to Look Like Christmas—The Christmas Song—Harry James medley with Betty Grable (Music Makers—I've Heard That Song Before—I Had the Craziest Dream—Trumpet Blues—Ciribiribin)—What I'll Do—They Can't Take That Away from Me—This Nearly Was Mine—In the Garden

Show #11—Air date: December 21, 1960

Guests: Chet Huntley, Ginny Tiu, Virginia O'Hanlon Douglas and Peter Gennaro
We Wish You a Merry Christmas—Do-Re-Mi (with Ginny Tiu)—White Christmas—Christmas Carols medley (God Rest Ye Merry, Gentlemen—Deck the Halls—O Holy Night—Joy to the World—We Wish You a Merry Christmas)—The Story of the First Christmas—Ave Maria

Show #12—Air date: December 28, 1960

Guests: Connie Francis, Milt Kamen, Renee Taylor and Kay Thompson.

Fine and Dandy—When Your Lover Has Gone (with Milt Kamen)—Isle of Capri (with Milt Kamen)—Whispering (with Kay Thompson)—The Anniversary Waltz (with Connie Francis)—Almost Like Being in Love—When I Fall in Love—Make Someone Happy—1960 medley with guests (Itsy Bitsy Teenie Weenie Yellow Polka Dot Bikini—My Heart Has a Mind of Its Own—Are You Lonesome Tonight?—You Got What It Takes—Alley-Oop—Catch a Falling Star—Greenfields—The Twist)—Auld Lang Syne (with entire cast)

Show #13—Air date: January 4, 1961

Guests: Bobby Rydell, Alan King, Yvonne Lime, Ronnie Burns and Elizabeth Seal.
One O'Clock Jump—You'll Never Walk Alone—Don't Go to Strangers—S'posin'—Yesterdays—Popeye The Sailor Man—Quick Draw McGraw—Woody Woodpecker—Mickey Mouse

Show #14—Air date: January 18, 1961

Guests: Gwen Verdon, George Gobel and Paul Anka.
Flamboyenco (with George Gobel and Gwen Verdon)—Little White Duck (with George Gobel)—Alone Together—Blue Moon (with Paul Anka)—Medley with guests (My Home Town—The Moonlight is Bright Tonight)—Sing to Me Mr. C. medley (All by Myself—There Never Was a Night So Beautiful—When I Grow Too Old to Dream)—Flamboyenco (with Gwen Verdon and George Gobel)—You Don't Want My Love (with George Gobel)—The Moonlight is Bright Tonight (with all guests)—I Feel a Song Coming On

Show #15—Air date: January 25, 1961

Guests: Peggy Lee, Peter Gennaro, Joey Heatherton, Bea Arthur and Shelley Berman
A Foggy Day (with guests)—Medley with Peggy Lee (Song of Songs—Fever—It's Too Darn Hot—Heat Wave—Steam Heat—You're the Top—Indian Love Call—I Get a Kick Out of You—Strike up the Band—Fever)—Sing to Me Mr. C medley (How About Me—Too Marvelous for Words—All the Things You Are)—St Louis Blues—The Birth of the Blues

Show #16—Air date: February 1, 1961

Guests: Harry Belafonte, Bea Arthur, Joey Heatherton and Buddy Hackett.
Why Can't a Woman Be More Like a Man (with Harry Belafonte and Buddy Hackett)—The Whiffenpoof Song—Tammy

Show #17—Air date: February 8, 1961

Guests: Eydie Gorme, Andre Previn, Joey Heatherton, Renee Taylor and Sammy Cahn.
In the Still of The Night—Like Young—Especially for the Young—You Make Me Feel So Young—Sing to Me Mr. C. medley (Bei Mir Bist Du Schon—I've Heard That Song Before)—Five Minutes More (with Sammy Cahn)—Medley with Eydie Gorme (It's Magic—All the Way—It's Magic)—Papa, Won't You Dance with Me (with guests)—High Hopes (with entire cast)

Show #18—Air date: February 15, 1961

Guests: Nancy Walker, The Limelighters and Caterina Valente.
Walk It Off (with guests)—My Funny Valentine—Medley with Caterina Valente using various languages (Delaware—Hot Diggity (Dog Ziggity Boom)—Dream Along with Me—Catch a Falling Star—Hoop-Dee-Doo)—Sing to Me, Mr. C medley (Oh, How I Miss You Tonight—It All Depends on You—Here's That Rainy Day)

Show #19—Air date: February 22, 1961

Guests: Anne Bancroft, Ray Charles (who sings "Georgia On My Mind"), Renee Taylor and Jimmy Durante
Love and Marriage—You Gotta Start off Each Day with a Song (with Jimmy Durante)—Bill Bailey, Won't You Please Come Home (with Jimmy Durante and Anne Bancroft)—Young at Heart—It's Delightful to Be Married—Medley with Anne Bancroft (It's Nice to Have a Man Around the House—The Glory of Love—It Could Happen to You—The Glory of Love—Tea for Two)—You Are Never Far Away from Me—Goodnight Song (with Jimmy Durante and Anne Bancroft)

Show #20—Air date: March 1, 1961

Guests: Janet Blair plus Mike Nichols & Elaine May.
Lets Face the Music and Dance—Over the Rainbow—Sing to Me Mr. C medley (Try a Little Tenderness—Angry—The Night Is Young and You're So Beautiful)—Medley with Janet Blair (Short'nin' Bread—I Wonder What's Become of Sally—Shine on Harvest Moon—Pennies from Heaven—It's a Big Wide Wonderful World—Why Do I Love You—Varsity Drag—Witchcraft)

Show #21—Air date: March 8, 1961

Guests: George Sanders and Judy Holliday
*I'm Beginning to See the Light—Sing to Me, Mr. S (Perry sings to George Sanders)—That Old Black Magic—
Sing to Me, Mr. C medley (Without a Word of Warning—It's Only a Paper Moon—The Way You Look
Tonight)—Goodnight medley with guests (May the Good Lord Bless and Keep You—When the Moon Comes
over the Mountain—You Are Never Far Away from Me—Happy Trails to You [with guests])*

Show #22—Air date: March 15, 1961

Guests: Don Ameche and Frances Langford.
*We Aren't Gonna Have a Home—Prisoner of Love—Too Young to Go Steady—Too Young—Hello, Young
Lovers—St. Patrick's Day medley with guests (Dear Old Donegal—When Irish Eyes Are Smiling—H-A-R-
R-I-G-A-N—Sweet Rosie O'Grady—McNamara's Band—Kerry Dancers—It's a Great Day for the Irish)—
Too-Ra-Loo-Ra-Loo-Ral (with whole cast)*

Show #23—Air date: March 22, 1961

Guests: Martha Raye, Ginny Tiu and Julie Newmar
*Here's to My Lady—The Lady's in Love with You—A Fellow Needs a Girl—Boy Song medley with guests (Mr.
Paganini—Davy Crockett—Ragtime Cowboy Joe—Little Sir Echo—Popeye the Sailor Man—Christopher
Columbus—Stout-Hearted Men)*

Show #24—Air date: March 29, 1961

Guests: Dorothy Collins, Gaudsmith Brothers, Lorin Hollander, The Lennon Sisters and Peter Gennaro
*Peter Cottontail—It's Easter Time—Flowers medley with Dorothy Collins (The Flowers That Bloom—Tip Toe
Through the Tulips—I'll Be with You in Apple Blossom Time—Cherry Pink & Apple Blossom White—
Artificial Flowers)—Begin the Beguine—Rain medley with guests (If You Didn't Have Rain—Singin' in the
Rain—Pennies from Heaven)—The Lord's Prayer*

Show #25—Air date: April 5, 1961

Guests: Caterina Valente, Bobby Rydell, Don Adams and Peter Gennaro
*Come to the Fair / It's a Grand Night for Singing (with guests)—No Other Love—Medley with Caterina Valente
(El Sombrero—Sweet Little Mountain Bird—El Sombrero)—Sing to Me, Mr. C medley (You Alone—Swingin'
Down the Lane—Portrait of My Love)—Tea for Two (with guests)*

Show #26—Air date: April 19, 1961

Guests: Martha Raye, Gary Player and Milburn Stone.
*My Blue Heaven (with Martha Raye)—Turn Back the Pages—That's Entertainment—That Old Feeling—Radio
Themes medley with Martha Raye (Someday I'll Find You—The Perfect Song—Wave the Flag for Hudson
High—Toselli's Serenade—Little Orphan Annie—Love in Bloom—Smoke Rings—Manhattan Merry-Go-
Round)—You Were Meant for Me—My Ideal—When Your Lover Has Gone*

Show #27—Air date: April 26, 1961

Guests: Jane Morgan, Paul Lynde, Alan King, Solange & Charles
*Bonjour Paree—Latin Quarter—If You Love Me—April in Paris—Chantez medley with guests (C'est Si Bon
[with Jane Morgan]—I Love Paris [with Jane Morgan]—Bonjour Paree [with guests])*

Show #28—Air date: May 10, 1961

Guests: Jack E. Leonard, Marion Marlowe, Paul Lynde and Paul Anka.
*Back in Your Own Backyard—Red Sails in the Sunset—Sing to Me, Mr. C medley (It's Been a Long, Long
Time—Angry—Here's That Rainy Day)—Tonight on Broadway medley with guests (Make Someone Happy—
The Sound of Music [with Marion Marlowe]—Hey, Look Me Over [with all guests])*

Show #29—Air date: May 17, 1961

Guests: Don Ameche, Frances Langford, Paul Lynde and the West Points Cadets Glee Club
*Stout-Hearted Men / Sound Off (with West Points Cadets Glee Club)—Medley with Frances Langford (You
Are My Lucky Star—I've Got a Feelin' You're Foolin'—True Love)—If I Loved You—Till We Meet Again
(with West Point Cadets Glee Club)—Now the Day is Over (with West Point Cadets Glee Club)*

Show #30—Air date: May 24, 1961

Guests: Martha Raye, George Gobel, Paul Lynde and Johnny Puleo and his Harmonica Gang

*Chicago—Medley with Martha Raye (On Behalf of the Visiting Firemen—Bye, Bye, Blackbird—If I Had You—
After You've Gone—Somebody Loves Me—I'm Following You—Bye, Bye, Blackbird)—Sing to Me, Mr. C
medley (Oh, How I Miss You Tonight—Heartaches)—Bands medley with guests (The Waltz You Saved For
Me—Auld Lang Syne—Boo Hoo [with Martha Raye & George Gobel]—Heartaches [with Martha Raye])*

Show #31—Air date: May 31, 1961

Guests: Audrey Meadows, Cliff Arquette, Paul Lynde, Seth Edwards and Brenda Lee
*Let a Smile Be Your Umbrella—School Medley with Brenda Lee (Teach Me Tonight—An Apple for the Teacher—
C-o-n-s-t-a-n-t-i-n-o-p-l-e—Istanbul—In a Little Red School House)—Come to Me, Bend to Me—Sing to Me,
Mr. C medley (How Deep is The Ocean—All by Myself—Portrait of My Love)—Square Dance medley with
guests (Don't Let the Stars Get in Your Eyes—Temptation)*

Show #32—Air date: June 7, 1961

Guests: Paul Lynde and Perry's own production staff.
The Party's Over—Begin the Beguine—I've Grown Accustomed to Her Face

NBC Television—The Kraft Music Hall—Series 3

*All shows featured orchestra conducted by Mitchell Ayres plus the Ray Charles Singers and the Peter
Gennaro Dancers.*
Announcer: Frank Gallop

Show #1—Air date: October 4, 1961

Guests: Mickey Mantle, Roger Maris, Fran Jeffries and Buddy Hackett
*Let Me Entertain You—Take Me Out to the Ball Game (with Buddy Hackett)—Medley with Fran Jeffries (It
Might As Well Be Spring—You'll Never Know—Little White Lies)—This Nearly Was Mine—I'm Gonna Sit
Right Down and Write Myself a Letter—Thank Heaven for Little Girls*

Show #2—Air date: October 11, 1961

Guests: Kaye Ballard, Don Adams, Jack Duffy, Caterina Valente, Sandy Stewart and Paul Lynde.
*Dancing on the Ceiling—You're Following Me (with Caterina Valente)—Climb Ev'ry Mountain—I Never Knew—
Gigi—The Way You Look Tonight—In the Garden*

Show #3—Air date: October 18, 1961

Guests: Martha Raye, Rita Moreno, Kaye Ballard, Sandy Stewart, Ted Weems, Country Washburn, Red Ingle,
   Parker Gibbs, Elmo Tanner and Paul Lynde
*All by Myself /You're Following Me (with guests)—I Wonder Who's Kissing Her Now—The One I Love—A
Fellow Needs a Girl—You're Following Me (with guests)*

Show #4—Air date: October 25, 1961

Guests: Tony Bennett, Kaye Ballard, Sandy Stewart, Jack Duffy and Paul Lynde
*Ma Blushin' Rosie—Ev'rything Is Rosy Now—That Old Black Magic—Pennsylvania medley with guests (Six-
teen Tons—Beautiful Dreamer—De Camptown Races)*

Show #5—Air date: November 1, 1961

Guests: Shirley Booth, Gloria De Haven, Sandy Stewart, Jack Duffy, Paul Lynde and Kaye Ballard.
*Lady Be Good—You're Following Me (with Gloria De Haven)—Autumn Leaves—Sing to Me, Mr. C medley
(You're Nobody 'Til Somebody Loves You—Smile—Perhaps, Perhaps, Perhaps)—Missouri medley with guests
(St. Louis Blues—Meet Me in St. Louis, Louis)*

Show #6—Air date: November 8, 1961

Guests: Betty Hutton, Tom Bosley, Paul Lynde, Kaye Ballard, Sandy Stewart and Jack Duffy
*Five Foot Two, Eyes of Blue—The Sound of Music—Sing to Me, Mr. C medley (Say It Isn't So—Blue Skies—
My Buddy)—New York medley (Will You Love Me in December—Love and Marriage—Dancing in the
Dark—Almost Like Being in Love—It's Only a Paper Moon—Lullaby of Broadway—Home Sweet Home)*

Show #7—Air date: November 15, 1961

Guests: Rudy Vallee, Tommy Sands and Nancy Sinatra.

Medley with guests (Life Is Just a Bowl of Cherries—My Time Is Your Time—The Whiffenpoof Song)—Alone Together—Louisiana medley with cast (Basin Street Blues—He's Got the Whole World in His Hands—Jambalaya—Way Down Yonder in New Orleans)

Show #8—Air date: November 22, 1961

Guests: Gwen Verdon, Dorothy Collins, Paul Lynde and the Kane Triplets.
(There's No Place Like) Home for The Holidays—(Howdy Neighbor) Happy Harvest (with Gwen Verdon & Dorothy Collins)—Inchworm (with the Kane Triplets)—Home—Medley with guests (Down in the Valley [with Dorothy Collins]—Ol' Macdonald [parody with cast])—Bless This House

Show #9—Air date: December 6, 1961

Guests: George Sanders, Sandy Stewart, Kaye Ballard, Paul Lynde, Don Adams and Jack Duffy
It's Beginning to Look Like Christmas—If There Is Someone Lovelier Than You—Medley of Children's' Christmas songs with George Sanders (I Saw Mommy Kissing Santa Claus—Santa Claus Is Comin' To Town—All I Want for Christmas Is My Two Front Teeth—Rudolph The Red-Nosed Reindeer—The Teddy Bear's Picnic)—Texas medley with guests (San Antonio Rose—Home on the Range)—The Rosary

Show #10—Air date: December 20, 1961

Guests: Kaye Ballard, Sandy Stewart, Ken Kealy and Tom Tichenor and his puppets
The Christmas Song—Christmas Carols medley (God Rest Ye Merry, Gentlemen—O Holy Night—We Wish You A Merry Christmas)—The Story of the First Christmas—Ave Maria

Show #11—Air date: December 27, 1961

Guests: Caterina Valente, Peter Gennaro and Silvio Francesco.
Hoop-Dee-Doo—Moon River—Twelfth Street Rag (with Caterina Valente and Silvio Francesco)—Huntley-Brinkley medley with guests (Make Someone Happy)—Auld Lang Syne

Show #12—Air date: January 3, 1962

Guests: Lorne Greene, Dan Blocker, Sandy Stewart, Kaye Ballard and Jack Duffy
Bonanza (with Lorne Greene & Dan Blocker)—Twilight on the Trail—Bye, Bye, Blackbird—Here's That Rainy Day—New Jersey medley with cast (I'll Never Smile Again—I Feel a Song Coming On—I'm in the Mood For Love)

Show #13—Air date: January 10, 1962

Guests: Juliet Prowse, Art Linkletter and the usual KMH players
Hey Mr. Banjo—A Little Bitty Tear—I Gotta Right to Sing the Blues—Don't Take Your Love from Me—What's New—Indiana medley with cast (Begin the Beguine—(Back Home Again in) Indiana—Rockin' Chair

Show #14—Air date: January 17, 1962

Guests: Polly Bergen and the usual KMH players
It's a Good Day—No Other Love—Always—You Make Me Feel So Young—My Heart Tells Me—Washington State medley with cast (Please—See You in Seattle)—The Party's Over (with Polly Bergen)

Show #15—Air date: January 31, 1962

Guests: Lena Horne and George Burns
On the Street Where You Live—My Favorite Things—My Baby Just Cares for Me—If You Were the Only Girl in the World—Birdland medley with guests (Bob White [parody]—Cuckoo in the Clock—Yellow Bird—Listen to the Mockin' Bird—When the Red, Red, Robin Comes Bob-Bob-Bobbin' Along)—You Are Never Far Away from Me (with Lena Horne & George Burns)

Show #16—Air date: February 7, 1962

Guests: Barrie Chase and the usual KMH players
The New Ashmolean Marching Society—Till the End of Time—You Were Meant for Me—Too-Ra-Loo-Ra-Loo-Ral—S'Posin'—Massachusetts medley with cast (Old Cape Cod—Maria—America)—Cheek to Cheek

Show #17—Air date: February 14, 1962

Guests: Dorothy Collins, Lorin Hollander and the usual KMH players
My Funny Valentine—Hooray for Love—In the Wee Small Hours of the Morning—When Your Lover Has Gone—I Love You—Hello, Young Lovers—I Love You Truly—Blissful Love medley with cast (Ma Blushin' Rosie)

Show #18—Air date: February 21, 1962

Guests: Johnny Carson and the usual KMH players
Something's Gotta Give—In the Still of the Night—Virginia medley with cast (Shenandoah—I'll Take You Home Again, Kathleen—Dixie)

Show #19—Air date: March 7, 1962

Guests: Carol Lawrence, Don Herbert and the usual KMH players.
Happy Jose—Some Enchanted Evening—It Might As Well Be Spring—Too Marvelous for Words—Love Letters—Minnesota medley with cast (In the Shade of the Old Apple Tree—From the Land of the Sky Blue Water)—Caterina

Show #20—Air date: March 14, 1962

Guests: Joe E. Ross, Fred Gwynne, Hawaiian Room Group and the usual KMH players.
Dear Old Donegal—It's a Great Day for the Irish—Maria—Danny Boy—H-A-R-R-I-G-A-N—How Are Things in Glocca Morra?—Hawaii medley with cast (Hawaiian Wedding Song—Aloha Oe)—Island of Forgotten Lovers

Show #21—Air date: March 21, 1962

Guests: Anna Maria Alberghetti, Dee Erickson and the usual KMH players
This Ole House—Spring is Here—It's a Big Wide Wonderful World (with Anna Maria Alberghetti)—Straight Down the Middle (with Paul Lynde, Don Adams & Jack Duffy)—While We're Young—It Could Happen to You—Lollipops and Roses—The Meaning of Spring medley with cast (A Young Man's Fancy)

Show #22—Air date: March 28, 1962

Guests: Alice Faye and the usual KMH players
If I Could Be with You—You Make Me Feel So Young (with Alice Faye)—Caterina—Medley with Alice Faye (You Can't Have Everything—When I'm with You—You Turned the Tables on Me—Never in a Million Years—I've Got My Love to Keep Me Warm—You're a Sweetheart—Alexander's Ragtime Band—You'll Never Know—The Little Things in Texas—Goodnight My Love)—Arizona medley with cast (Along the Navajo Trail)—I'm Glad That I'm Not Young Anymore (with Alice Faye)

Show #23—Air date: April 4, 1962

Guests: Anne Bancroft and the usual KMH players.
Dear Hearts and Gentle People—Unchained Melody—My Melancholy Baby—Just in Time—Moon River—Illinois medley with cast (Sleepy Time Gal—Battle Hymn of the Republic)

Show #24—Air date: April 18, 1962

Guests: Jane Morgan, Kukla & Ollie, and the St. Monica Children's Choir of NYC
It's Easter Time (Ray Charles Singers sing "Easter Parade" in counterpoint)—This Old Man—Thank Heaven for Little Girls—Children's Songs medley with guests (Bibbidi-Bobbidi-Boo—Hi-Lili, Hi Lo—When You Wish Upon a Star—Follow the Yellow Brick Road—We're off to See the Wizard)—The Lord's Prayer

Show #25—Air date: May 2, 1962

Guests: Lola Albright, Eddie Arcaro, Sammy Renick and the usual KMH players
Caterina—When Your Lover Has Gone—A Good Man Is Hard to Find (with Lola Albright)—Two Different Worlds—It's Been a Long, Long Time—But Beautiful—Kentucky medley with KMH players (Kentucky Babe—My Old Kentucky Home)

Show #26—Air date: May 9, 1962

Guests: Caterina Valente, Peter Gennaro and the usual KMH players
A Couple of Song and Dance Men (with Caterina Valente)—Climb Ev'ry Mountain—Yours (with Caterina Valente)—Here's to My Lady—I Want a Girl—No Well on Earth—North Carolina medley with KMH players (On Top of Old Smokey—Carolina Moon)—Caterina

Show #27—Air date: May 16, 1962

Guests: Dennis Weaver and the usual KMH players
Too Darn Hot—Colonel Bogey—Mad Dogs and Englishmen—The Sweetest Sounds—Bathtub medley with Dennis Weaver (Singin' In the Bathtub—Moonlight Bay—Row, Row, Row Your Boat—Row, Row, Row)—

Someone to Watch Over Me—For Me and My Gal—Here's That Rainy Day—Maine medley with the KMH players (Blow Ye Winds—Rock-A-Bye Baby)

Show #28—Air date: May 23, 1962
Guests: Anne Bancroft and the usual KMH players (except Paul Lynde)
When The Beach Umbrellas Bloom—Back in Your Own Backyard (with Anne Bancroft)—Moonglow—Michigan medley with KMH players (The Sweetheart of Sigma Chi—I Want to Go Back to Michigan)

Show #29—Air date: May 30, 1962
Guests: Jack E. Leonard, Dorothy Collins and the usual KMH players (except Paul Lynde)
This Could Be the Start of Something Big (with guests)—That Old Black Magic—Lollipops and Roses—'Deed I Do—My Buddy—Rhode Island medley with KMH players (Mary's a Grand Old Name—It's a Grand Old Flag)—Jumpin' at the Woodside (with cast)

Show #30—Air date: June 6, 1962
Guests: The KMH players except Paul Lynde
Everything's Coming up Roses—You Are Never Far Away from Me—When I Fall In Love

NBC Television—The Kraft Music Hall—Series 4
All shows featured orchestra conducted by Mitchell Ayres plus the Ray Charles Singers.
The other regulars, namely Peter Gennaro and his dancers, plus the Music Hall Players (Don Adams, Sandy Stewart, Jack Duffy, Kaye Ballard) all continue with Pierre Olaf being welcomed to their ranks. Announcer: Frank Gallop

Show #1—Air date: October 3, 1962
Guests: Arnold Palmer, Gary Player and Jack Nicklaus
Dream Along with Me—I Left My Heart in San Francisco—Fly Me to the Moon—Consider Yourself (with the KMH players)—In Other Words—What's New

Show #2—Air date: October 10, 1962
Guests: Anne Bancroft
Yesterdays—At the Moving Picture Ball—Yesterdays (reprise)—I Remember It Well (with Anne Bancroft)—Jeannine—Dardanella—Beloved—Movie Tonight

Show #3—Air date: October 17, 1962
Guests: Lena Horne, Charlie Byrd, Stan Getz and Carol Haney
It's All Right with Me (with guests)—So in Love—It Happened in Monterey (with Stan Getz and Charlie Byrd)—More Than Likely—Medley with Ray Charles Singers (Autumn Leaves—'Tis Autumn—Autumn in New York)—It's All Right with Me (reprise with guests)

Show #4—Air date: October 31, 1962
Guests: Terry-Thomas and Bobby Van
Hail the Music Hall—Moonglow—Ballin' the Jack (with Terry-Thomas)—In Our Hide-Away (with Sandy Stewart)—The Sweetheart of Sigma Chi—All American Girl—The Whiffenpoof Song—College medley with cast (Talk—Army Fight Song—Navy Fight Song—Far Above Cayuga's Waters—Talk)

Show #5—Air date: November 7, 1962
Guests: Bob Cummings
Is She the Only Girl in the World—Can't Help Falling in Love—Mr. President medley (It Gets Lonely in the White House—The First Lady (with Kaye Ballard)—In Our Hide-Away [with Sandy Stewart]—Glad to Be Home—I'm Gonna Get Him [with Sandy Stewart]—Pigtails and Freckles—This is a Great Country [with Kaye Ballard & Sandy Stewart])

Show #6—Air date: November 14, 1962
Guests: Dorothy Provine
Wrap Your Troubles in Dreams—Charleston (with Dorothy Provine)—Street of Dreams—Desafinado—Songs of the Twenties medley with Dorothy Provine (Crazy Words, Crazy Tune—When the Pussy Willow Whis-

pers to the Catnip—Barney Google—Blah, Blah, Blah—If I Give up the Clarinet—Crazy Rhythm)—When I Lost You—Empty Pockets—But Beautiful—Oklahoma medley with KMH Players (The Object of My Affection—Swing Low, Sweet Chariot)

Show #7—Air date: November 21, 1962

Guests: Thomas Mitchell
(There's No Place Like) Home for The Holidays—Our Town—Home—Sweet Adeline (with Don Adams & Jack Duffy)—Band Concert medley with KMH Players (Till Tomorrow—76 Trombones)—Bless This House

Show #8—Air date: November 28, 1962

Guests: George Sanders and Damita Jo
(Get Your Kicks on) Route 66—Once Upon a Time—My Favorite Things—You're Nobody 'Til Somebody Loves You—Smile—I Wish You Love

Show #9—Air date: December 5, 1962

Guests: Johnny Mercer, Bill Hinnant and Carol Lawrence
Sing with Me, Mr. C (with Johnny Mercer & Carol Lawrence)—Skip to My Lou (parody—with Johnny Mercer & Carol Lawrence)—Food medley (parody versions of many songs—with Johnny Mercer & Carol Lawrence)—Come Rain or Come Shine—I've Heard That Song Before (with Johnny Mercer)—Gonna Get a Girl / Shall We Dance (with Johnny Mercer and Carol Lawrence)—Here's to My Lady—Too Marvelous for Words—Moon River—Georgia medley with entire cast (Georgia on My Mind—Atlanta, GA—Uncle Remus Said—Georgia on My Mind [reprise])—Hit the Road to Dreamland (with Johnny Mercer and Carol Lawrence)

Show #10—Air date: December 12, 1962

Guests: Dorothy Collins, Senor Wences and Jean Carroll
Gonna Raise a Ruckus Tonight—I Left My Heart in San Francisco—Make Someone Happy—I've Grown Accustomed to Her Face—Caterina (with cast and audience)—White Christmas (with entire company)

Show #11—Air date: December 19, 1962

Guests: Burr Tillstrom Puppets & Roselle Como
Jingle Bells—Let's Trim the Christmas Tree—We Wish You a Merry Christmas—White Christmas—Christmas Carols medley with company (God Rest Ye Merry, Gentlemen—O Holy Night—We Wish You a Merry Christmas)—The Story of the First Christmas—Ave Maria

Show #12—Air date: December 26, 1962

Guests: Eleanor Powell, Caterina Valente and Roger Williams
I've Got You Under My Skin—Is She the Only Girl in the World—More Than Likely—'Deed I Do—Maria—Eleanor Powell medley with guests (Broadway Rhythm—Lady Be Good—I've Got a Feelin' You're Foolin'—Rosalie—You Are My Lucky Star)

Show #13—Air date: January 2, 1963

Guests: Ethel Merman, Luis Bonfa and George Kirby
Happy New Year—Speak Low—Whispering (with Ethel Merman and Sandy Stewart)—Carnival—1962 album medley (If Ever I Would Leave You)

Show #14—Air date: January 9, 1963

Guests: Peter Ustinov and Jane Powell
Alexander's Ragtime Band—Muskrat Ramble—Gigi—Empty Pockets (with Jane Powell)—Pigtails and Freckles—All by Myself—Somebody Cares—Opera medley with cast (I Am Sick and Tired—Is There a Barber Worthy Of Me—I Am the Barber—We'll Leave You Now)—Goodnight Sweet Jesus

Show #15—Air date: January 23, 1963

Guests: Ray Bolger and Lauren Bacall
Crossword Baby Blues / Gonna Build A Mountain (with entire company)—Once In Love with Amy (with Ray Bolger and Lauren Bacall)—Alone Together—If I Only Had a Brain (with Ray Bolger, Lauren Bacall and Sandy Stewart)—We're Off to See the Wizard (with Ray Bolger, Lauren Bacall and Sandy Stewart)—The Sound of Music—Back in Your Own Backyard—When I Fall in Love—Ohio medley with KMH Players (Paper Doll—Beautiful Ohio)—Once in Love with Amy (with entire company)

Show #16—Air date: January 30, 1963

Guests: Erroll Garner, Charlton Heston and Phyllis McGuire
Merry Widow Waltz—Here's That Rainy Day—Misty (with Phyllis McGuire and Erroll Garner)—Tonight on Broadway medley with cast (The Sweetest Sounds—Climb Ev'ry Mountain)

Show #17—Air date: February 6, 1963

Guests: Peter Lind Hayes, Anita Bryant and Mary Healy
Blame It on the Bossa Nova—This Is All I Ask—Stardust—Cuddle up a Little Closer—Who—Smoke Gets In Your Eyes—California medley with entire cast (I Left My Heart in San Francisco—California, Here I Come)

Show #18—Air date: February 20, 1963

Guests: Eleanor Powell, Hugh Downs and Johnny Puleo and his Harmonica Gang
Put on a Happy Face—Smile—The Whiffenpoof Song—Oh, Promise Me—Yankee Doodle Dandy

Show #19—Air date: February 27, 1963

Guests: Patrice Munsel, Frank Gorshin and The Baird Puppets
Opening medley (Walk It Off—Colonel Bogey—Take It Easy)—If Ever I Would Leave You—In Other Words—I Wanna Be Around—You Alone—Florida medley with entire company (Moon Over Miami—Swanee River)

Show #20—Air date: March 6, 1963

Guests: Joanie Sommers, Gene Sheldon, Charlie Manna and The Four Step Brothers
Breezin' Along with the Breeze—Just in Time (with Joanie Sommers—in various arrangements)

Show #21—Air date: March 20, 1963

Guests: Dorothy Provine, Ginny Tiu and Dick Shawn
What Kind of Fool Am I (with guests)—Unchained Melody—Don't Kid Around with Kids—Tonight on Broadway medley with entire company (The Sound of Music—Pigtails and Freckles—Do-Re-Mi)

Perry ca. 1963—smooth and relaxed as ever.

Show #22—Air date: March 27, 1963

Guests: Carol Lawrence, Ray Eberle & The Modernaires, Wynne Miller and the Tex Beneke-led Glenn Miller Orchestra
Oh I Can't Sit Down—Days of Wine and Roses—Walk Right In (with Carol Lawrence)—Carnival—You Make Me Feel So Young (with Ray Eberle)—Danny Boy (with Tex Beneke)—In the Garden (with Wynne Miller)

Show #23—Air date: April 3, 1963

Guests: Caterina Valente, Ken Murray and George Kirby
This Is All I Ask—To Be a Performer—Whispering (with Caterina Valente)—I Left My Heart in San Francisco—They Can't Take That Away from Me—Try a Little Tenderness—Mood Indigo

Show #24—Air date: April 10, 1963

Guests: Lorin Hollander and Carl Ballantine
It's Easter Time—Easter Parade—Once Upon a Time—My Heart Sings—My Favorite Things—When the Red, Red Robin Comes Bob-Bob-Bobbin' Along—I'll Remember April—The Lord's Prayer

Show #25—Air date: April 24, 1963

Guests: Ken Murray, Peggy March and The Kessler Twins

Who Will Buy—Gigi—Around the World medley with The Kessler Twins (I Wish You Love—Mack the Knife—Cuando Calienta El Sol—Desafinado—Arrivederci Roma)—Days of Wine and Roses—I Wanna Be Around—Love Letters—When You Come to the End of the Day

Show #26—Air date: May 1, 1963

Guests: Allan Sherman, Connie Stevens and Mickey Rooney
On the First Warm Day—If There Is Someone Lovelier Than You—It's Easy to Remember—Walkin' My Baby Back Home—But Beautiful—Hootenanny medley with cast (This Land Is Your Land—Shenandoah—Cottonfields)

Show #27—Air date: May 8, 1963

Guests: Peter Nero, Jack E. Leonard, Dorothy Collins and the Bentleyville Little Leaguers
Lawrence of Arabia medley—In the Still of the Night—Waltz medley with Dorothy Collins and Peter Nero (True Love—Gravy Waltz—It's a Big Wide Wonderful World)—My Mother's Eyes—I Want a Girl Just Like the Girl That Married Dear Old Dad—No Well on Earth—(I Love You) Don't You Forget It

Show #28—Air date: May 22, 1963

Guests: Jimmy Durante, Eddie Jackson, Sonny King and Jane Powell
(I Love You) Don't You Forget It—One More Mountain—First You Tip Your Hat-Ta (with Jimmy Durante)—Out of the Night—Only Forever—Heartaches—Chicago medley with entire company (Angry—Careless [with Jane Powell]—Chicago [with cast])

Show #29—Air date: June 5, 1963

Guests: Barbara Cook, Elaine Dunn and Peter Ustinov
The Glory of Love—Love Is a Many Splendored Thing—Oh Promise Me—I Love You Truly—All Over the World—Love Makes the World Go 'Round—Around the World—(I Love You) Don't You Forget It—Love and Marriage—Ave Maria

Show #30—Air date: June 12, 1963

Guests: Jane Magruder and Perry's usual support staff
Begin the Beguine—One More Mountain—Missouri Waltz—When You Were Sweet Sixteen—Love Is the Reason—Dream—This Land Is Your Land—Aria from La Traviata—Song and Dance Man—I Left My Heart in San Francisco—This Is All I Ask

NBC Television—The Kraft Music Hall—Series 5

All shows featured orchestra conducted by Mitchell Ayres plus the Ray Charles Singers.
Announcer: Frank Gallop

Show #1—Air date: October 3, 1963

Guests: June Allyson, George Burns, Cyd Charisse, James Mitchell and Allan Sherman
Back in Your Own Backyard—Medley with George Burns (Red Rose Rag—The Doogies on the Street—Yankee Doodle Blues—Ain't Misbehavin'—Monkey Rag)—Where or When—Medley with June Allyson (Thou Swell—There's a Small Hotel—The Blue Room—The Best Things in Life Are Free)—Rag Mop (with guests)—I Wanna Be Around—This Is All I Ask—When You Come to the End of the Day

Show #2—Air date: November 21, 1963

Guests: Victor Borge, Nanette Fabray and Jose Greco
San Francisco—Medley with Nanette Fabray (Round and Round—Catch a Falling Star—Hot Diggity (Dog Ziggity Boom))—No Other Love (with Victor Borge)—But Beautiful—You Do Something to Me—I Left My Heart in San Francisco—Bless This House

Show #3—Air date: January 23, 1964

Guests: Jimmy Durante, Dorothy Provine, Russ Tamblyn and The Texas Boys' Choir
Don't Fence Me In / The Chisholm Trail (with The Texas Boys' Choir)—Tumbling Tumbleweeds—South of the Border—There, I've Said It Again—So in Love—S'Posin'—Inchworm (with The Texas Boys' Choir)—Making Whoopee / The Glory of Love (with Jimmy Durante)—One Little Candle

Show #4—Air date: February 13, 1964

Guests: Lena Horne and Dean Martin

Hello Dolly—Hello Dolly (parody, with Lena Horne & Dean Martin)—Valentine medley with Dean Martin & Lena Horne (When You Were Sweet Sixteen—Love Is the Reason—Guys & Dolls)—Sentimental Journey (single chorus only)—Ohio (with Dean Martin)—Pennsylvania Polka—Sentimental Journey (with Dean Martin)—Star medley with Lena Horne (I've Told Every Little Star—I Only Have Eyes for You—About a Quarter to Nine—Twinkle, Twinkle, Little Star—When You Wish Upon a Star—You Are My Lucky Star)—My Favorite Things—Almost Like Being in Love—I Love You (Porter)—Rhythm Medley with Dean Martin and Lena Horne (A Doodling Song—Lazy Bones—The Anniversary Song—Fascinatin' Rhythm [snatch only])—When You Come to the End of the Day

Show #5—Air date: March 5, 1964

Guests: Mickey Rooney, Martha Raye, Al Hirt, Lee Becker Theodore and Jacques d'Amboise

Basin Street Blues—South Rampart Street Parade (with guests)—Brush Up Your Shakespeare (with Mickey Rooney)—River medley with Martha Raye (Moon River—River, Stay Away from My Door—Lazy River—Down by the Riverside—Ol' Man River)—Sleepy Time Down South (with Al Hirt)—'Deed I Do—Here's That Rainy Day—Now You Has Jazz (with guests)—Way Down Yonder in New Orleans

Show #6—Air date: April 9, 1964

Guests: Keely Smith, Bob Newhart, Peter Nero, University of Minnesota Men's Glee Club and the University of Minnesota Pom Pom Girls

Hello Dolly—Indian medley with Keely Smith (Cherokee—Totem Tom Tom—From the Land of the Sky Blue Water—Indian Love Call)—Maria (with University of Minnesota Men's Glee Club)—Little Brown Jug (with University of Minnesota Men's Glee Club)—I've Grown Accustomed to Her Face—Only Forever—I Concentrate on You—College Songs medley (Como content unknown)

Show #7—Air date: May 21, 1964

Guests: Roberta Peters, Jack E. Leonard and The Four Step Brothers

Chicago—Medley with Roberta Peters (True Love—La Ci Darem La Mano)—I Wanna Hold Your Hand (with Roberta Peters and Jack E. Leonard)—In the Still of the Night—Don't Let the Rain Come Down (with Ray Charles)—Medley (Call Me Irresponsible—Angry—This Is All I Ask)

NBC Television—The Kraft Music Hall—Series 6

*All shows featured orchestra conducted by Nick Perito plus the Ray Charles Singers.
Announcer: Frank Gallop*

Show #1—Air date: October 29, 1964

Guests: Anne Bancroft, Stanley Holloway, Victor Borge, Leonid Hambro and Michigan University Glee Club

The Song of the Open Road—People—Everybody Loves Somebody—On the Street Where You Live—Santa Lucia (with Anne Bancroft)—With a Little Bit of Luck (with Stanley Holloway and Anne Bancroft)—A Taste of Honey (with University of Michigan Glee Club)

Show #2—Air date: December 17, 1964

Guests: Roberta Peters, Burr Tillstrom and the Sistine Chapel Choir

O, Come All Ye Faithful—Silent Night—White Christmas (with Roberta Peters)—Ave Maria—It's Beginning to Look Like Christmas—The Sound of Music—Twelve Days of Christmas (with Burr Tillstrom as Kukla and Ollie)

Show #3—Air date: January 7, 1965

Guests: Dean Martin, Carol Lawrence and Guy Marks

If I Had a Hammer—Who Can I Turn To?—Medley with Dean Martin and Carol Lawrence (This Little Piggy Went to Market—Bye, Bye, Baby)—Medley (How About Me?—All by Myself—Dear Heart)

Show #4—Air date: February 4, 1965

Guests: Danny Thomas, Shirley Jones and The Marquis Chimps

St. Louis Blues—Somebody, Somewhere—Lida Rose (with Shirley Jones)—Medley (There Will Never Be Another You—I've Grown Accustomed to Her Face)

Stanley Holloway (center) and Anne Bancroft are Perry's guests on the *Kraft Music Hall* of October 29, 1964, broadcast live from Detroit (courtesy Bill Klages).

Show #5—Air date: March 4, 1965

Guests: Lena Horne, Peter Nero, Johnny Puleo and His Harmonica Gang plus The Wellesley Chapel Choir
Nat King Cole medley with Lena Horne (Somewhere Along the Way—It's Only a Paper Moon—The Christmas Song—Mona Lisa—Ramblin' Rose)—Gypsy in My Soul—Here's That Rainy Day—Medley with Lena Horne (Old Cape Cod—Moonlight in Vermont—Massachusetts)—My Favorite Things (with Wellesley Chapel Choir)—Johnny One-Note (with Lena Horne)

Show #6—Air date: April 8, 1965

Guests: Al Hirt, Connie Stevens, Woody Allen, Kathy Jean Keene and Rosarian Academy Choir
On a Wonderful Day Like Today—Ebb Tide—Medley with Connie Stevens and Al Hirt (Jeepers Creepers—Them There Eyes)—Medley (Dream on, Little Dreamer—Gigi)—Oh God of Loveliness (with Rosarian Academy Choir)

Show #7—Air date: May 27, 1965

Guests: Richard Chamberlain, Diahann Carroll and The New Christy Minstrels
My Kind of Town—Who Can I Turn To?—Whispering (with Diahann Carroll)—The River (with the New Christy Minstrels)—Medley (Dream on, Little Dreamer—A Hatchet, a Hammer, a Bucket of Nails)—Medley (Here Comes the Showboat—The Thousand Island Song—Canadian Sunset—Chicago)

NBC Television—The Kraft Music Hall—Series 7

All shows featured orchestra conducted by Nick Perito plus the Ray Charles Singers.
Announcer: Frank Gallop

Show #1—Air date: October 18, 1965

Guests: Nancy Ames, Ginger Rogers and Lena Horne
Try to Remember—The Music Goes Round and Round—Pennies from Heaven—Jeepers, Creepers—I'll Never Smile Again—Two Sleepy People—I Feel a Song Coming On—Medley with Nancy Ames (Zip-a-Dee-Doo-Dah—Almost Like Being in Love—Till the End of Time—It's All Right with Me—In the Cool, Cool, Cool of the Evening—Goodnight, Irene)—It's a Good Day—Walk Right In (with Nancy Ames)—Medley (People—Yesterday)

Show #2—Air date: November 22, 1965

Guests: Bobby Vinton, Gertrude Berg and The Lennon Sisters
Autumn in New York—Love in a Home—Melodie D'Amour (with The Lennon Sisters)—If the Rain's Gotta Fall (with Bobby Vinton and The Lennon Sisters)—Sunrise, Sunset (with Gertrude Berg)—Medley (They Didn't Believe Me—On a Clear Day—A Taste of Honey)—Bless This House

Show #3—Air date: December 20, 1965

Guests: Roberta Peters, Jackie Vernon and The Muppets
The Christmas Song—We Wish You a Merry Christmas—Christmas Is a Birthday (with Roberta Peters)—God Rest Ye Merry, Gentlemen—Oh Bambino—O Holy Night—Joy to the World—Ave Maria—Nativity Story (O Come All Ye Faithful)

Show #4—Air date: January 24, 1966

Guests: Lena Horne, Patty Duke, Tony Mottola and Norm Crosby
Western medley with Lena Horne—Downtown (with Patty Duke)—Marriage tunes medley with Lena Horne

Show #5—Air date: February 28, 1966

Guests: Judy Garland and Bill Cosby
Medley with Judy Garland (If You Feel Like Singing, Sing—It's a Grand Night for Singing)—This Is All I Ask—Medley with Judy Garland (Bye, Bye, Blues—My Honey's Lovin' Arms—For Me and My Gal)—Medley (But Beautiful—Make Someone Happy—Coo Coo Roo Coo Coo Paloma)—Side by Side (with Judy Garland & Bill Cosby)

Show #6—Air date: March 28, 1966

Guests: Tommy Steele, Liza Minnelli and Burr Tillstrom
Spring, Spring, Spring—I Love You (Porter)—Medley with Liza Minnelli (Yellow Bird—When the Red, Red Robin Comes Bob-Bob-Bobbin' Along)—Young at Heart (with Burr Tillstrom as Kukla and Ollie)—Spring Is Here—Hey Mister Banjo (with Tommy Steele)—New Sun in the Sky (with Liza Minnelli & Tommy Steele)—Medley (Dream—A Very Precious Love—Easter Parade)

Show #7—Air date: April 25, 1966

Guests: Caterina Valente, Ella Fitzgerald, John Davidson, Jack Burns and Avery Schreiber
Turn Around—Santa Lucia (with Caterina Valente)—A-Tisket, A-Tasket (with Ella Fitzgerald)—Medley (And Roses and Roses—Stay with Me—Baia)—Avalon (with Caterina Valente, Ella Fitzgerald & John Davidson)

NBC Television—The Kraft Music Hall—Series 8

All shows featured orchestra conducted by Nick Perito plus the Ray Charles Singers.

Show #1—Air date: November 21, 1966

Guests: Angela Lansbury, Bob Newhart and The Young Americans
If I Had a Hammer—What the World Needs Now (with The Young Americans)—Medley with Angela Lansbury (Wouldn't It Be Loverly?—A Lovely Way to Spend an Evening)—Medley (Cominciamo Ad Amarci—Souvenir D'Italie)—Bless This House

Show #2—Air date: December 19, 1966

Guests: Anna Moffo, Senor Wences, Jerry Stiller and Anne Meara
It's Beginning to Look Like Christmas—Santa Claus is Comin' To Town—The Twelve Days of Christmas—O Bambino (with Anna Moffo)—God Rest Ye Merry, Gentlemen—O Tannebaum (with Anna Moffo)—O Holy Night—Toyland—Ave Maria

Show #3—Air date: January 25, 1967

Guests: Eddy Arnold, Nancy Ames, Chet Atkins and Tony Hendra and Nick Ullett
When You're Smiling (plus reprise with guests)—Country & Western medley with guests (Dream on, Little Dreamer—Here Comes My Baby—Sweet Adorable You [with Nancy Ames]—Where Does a Little Tear Come From—That Ain't All)—I've Grown Accustomed to Her Face—You Do Something to Me—You Are Never Far Away from Me

Show #4—Air date: February 22, 1967

Guests: Frances Langford, Jack Burns, Avery Schreiber and Frank Gallop
True Love (with Frances Langford)—Walking Happy—Without a Song

Show #5—Air date: March 20, 1967

Guests: Connie Stevens, Woody Allen and Frank Gallop
Happy Easter (with Connie Stevens and Woody Allen)—I Love You—Play a Simple Melody (with Woody Allen)—Gonna Get Along Without You Now (with Connie Stevens)—Thoroughly Modern Millie (with Connie Stevens and Woody Allen)—Medley (Yesterday—Red Roses for a Blue Lady—Vaya Con Dios)—Medley with Connie Stevens and Woody Allen (It Might As Well Be Spring—Spring Is Here—It Happens Every Spring)—It's Easter Time—The Lord's Prayer

Show #6—Air date: April 17, 1967

Guests: Nancy Wilson, George Carlin and Joyce Cuoco
A Taste of Honey—Stop and Think It Over—Medley with Nancy Wilson (Feelin' Groovy—Breezin' Along with the Breeze)—Medley (How Beautiful the World Can Be—Dindi)—Pennies from Heaven

Show #7—Air date: May 22, 1967

Guests: Monique Leyrac, Oscar Peterson, The Craddock Family (Kenny, Tommy, Bonnie, Timmy, Phillip) and Don Rice
Medley (It's Nice to Be Nice to Your Neighbor—Hi, Neighbor—South of the Border—Come to the Fair)—I Concentrate on You—Canadian Sunset (with Monique Leyrac)—Medley (Catch a Falling Star—When You Were Sweet Sixteen—Stop and Think It Over)

Specials

The Perry Como Holiday Special—Air date: November 30, 1967

Guests: Dan Rowan and Dick Martin, Bobbie Gentry, Jefferson Airplane and Sergio Mendes' Brasil '66
Medley (Love in a Home—How to Handle a Woman—(The) Father of Girls)—Going out of My Head—Talk to the Animals (with Bobbie Gentry)—Oh, Marie (with Brasil '66)—Feelin' Groovy (The 59th Street Bridge Song)—Chickasaw County Child—(Get Your Kicks on) Route 66—Christmas Bells—O Come All Ye Faithful

The Perry Como Holiday Special—Air Date December 1, 1968

Guests: Don Adams, Carol Burnett and The Young Americans
Medley with guests (In These Crazy Times—Try to Remember—The Happy Time)—Sears, Roebuck song (with The Young Americans)—Yesterday (brief snatch)—In the Evening by the Moonlight—Medley with Carol Burnett (Missouri Waltz—Moonlight Bay—Under the Bamboo Tree)—Little Green Apples—You're Nearer—In These Crazy Times (reprise)—You Are Never Far Away from Me

The Many Moods of Perry Como—Air Date February 22, 1970

Guests: Bob Hope, Bobby Sherman, Nancy Sinatra, John Harlan and Flip Wilson
Everybody's Talkin'—The Mood I'm In—Seattle—I Love You—Didn't We?—Thanks for the Memory

Perry Como—In Person (BBC-TV)—Air date: May 19, 1971 (U.K.)

The Way You Look Tonight—Where or When—I Think of You—Magic Moments—Catch a Falling Star—Round and Round—Don't Let the Stars Get in Your Eyes—I Can Almost Read Your Mind—Without a Song—(The) Father of Girls—Love Is Spreading over the World—(They Long to Be) Close to You—When You Were Sweet Sixteen—Here's That Rainy Day—O Marenariello—It's a Good Day—It's Impossible—I May Never Pass This Way Again

Perry Como's Christmas Show—Air date: December 9, 1971

Guests: Art Carney, The Establishment and Mitzi Gaynor
I Can Almost Read Your Mind (with Mitzi Gaynor and Art Carney)—Winter Is (with Art Carney and Mitzi Gaynor)—(Where Do I Begin) Love Story—Button up Your Overcoat (with Mitzi Gaynor)—If—For All We Know—Put Your Hand in the Hand (with The Establishment)—Christmas Waltz—Christ Is Born

Perry Como—In Person (BBC-TV)—Air date: December 26, 1971 (U.K.)
[edited version of May 19, 1971 show with "O Holy Night" added]

The Way You Look Tonight—Where or When—Magic Moments—Catch a Falling Star—Round and Round—Don't Let the Stars Get in Your Eyes—Without a Song—(The) Father of Girls—Love Is Spreading over the World—(They Long to Be) Close to You—When You Were Sweet Sixteen—Here's That Rainy Day—O Marenariello—It's a Good Day—It's Impossible—O Holy Night

The Perry Como Winter Show—Air date: December 4, 1972

Guests: Joey Heatherton, The Muppets and Art Carney
Winter Wonderland—Make Your Own Kind of Music—Song Sung Blue (with Joey Heatherton)—A House Is Not a Home—Goin' up the Mountain (with Joey Heatherton)—It's Beginning to Look Like Christmas—Let It Snow! Let It Snow! Let It Snow!—You've Got a Friend—Keep It Down—You Are Never Far Away from Me

The Perry Como Winter Show—Air date: December 10, 1973

Guests: Jack Burns and Avery Schreiber, The Establishment and Sally Struthers
A Time to Be Jolly—Deck the Halls (with cast)—Three O'Clock in the Morning—When Winter Comes (with Sally Struthers)—And I Love You So—The Christmas Song (with The Establishment)—The Hands of Time—Show Me Where The Good Times Are (with cast)—Harmony

The Perry Como Sunshine Show—Air date: April 10, 1974

Guests: Debbie Reynolds, Donny and Marie Osmond
Strike up the Band—Before the Parade Passes By—Easter Parade—You Are My Sunshine—You Are the Sunshine of My Life (with Donny and Marie Osmond)—The Way We Were—Five Foot Two, Eyes Of Blue (snatch)—Medley with Debbie Reynolds (S'Wonderful—I'm Sitting on Top of The World—Then I'll Be Happy—Ain't We Got Fun?)—The Way We Were (reprise)—Sing to Me, Mr. C Medley (The Most Beautiful Girl in the World—I Don't Know What He Told You)—Country Sunshine (with Donny and Marie Osmond)—Mountain Dew (with Donny and Marie Osmond)—Tie a Yellow Ribbon—The Lord's Prayer

Perry Como's Summer of '74—Air date: September 12, 1974

Guests: Paul Lynde, Michele Lee and Jimmy Walker
Summertime—I Can See Clearly Now (with cast)—Souvenir D'Italie—My Heart Stood Still (with Michele Lee)—How Little We Know (with Michele Lee)—Medley (Behind Closed Doors—For the Good Times—Temptation)—(The) Father of Girls—America The Beautiful

Perry Como's Christmas Show—Air date: December 17, 1974

Guests: Peggy Fleming, Rich Little and The Carpenters
Have Yourself a Merry Little Christmas—The Christmas Waltz (with Peggy Fleming)—All in the Family (theme—with Rich Little)—It's Beginning to Look Like Christmas—Christmas Dream—Sleep Well, Little Children (with Karen Carpenter)—This Is That Time of Year (with cast)—Medley with The Carpenters ((They Long to Be) Close to You—We've Only Just Begun—Yesterday Once More)—The Story of the First Christmas (O Little Town of Bethlehem—The First Noel—Hark! The Herald Angels Sing—O Come All Ye Faithful—We Three Kings—Silent Night—O Holy Night)

Como Country: Perry and his Nashville Friends—Air date: February 17, 1975

Guests: Chet Atkins, Boots Randolph, Floyd Cramer, Loretta Lynn, Donna Fargo, Minnie Pearl, Charlie Pride, Charlie Rich, Danny David and the Nashville Brass
Country Is (with cast)—Take Me Home, Country Roads—Behind Closed Doors (with Charlie Rich)—Kiss an Angel Good Morning (with Charlie Rich and Charlie Pride)—Oh, Lonesome Me (with Chet Atkins, Floyd Cramer and Boots Randolph)—I'm So Lonesome I Could Cry—Son of a Gun (with cast)—Gospel Medley (He's Got the Whole World in His Hands—Old Time Religion—Put Your Hand in the Hand [with cast])—Green, Green Grass of Home—You Are Never Far Away from Me (snatch only)

Perry Como's Springtime Special—Air date: March 27, 1975

Guests: Olivia Newton-John, Pat Boone and family plus Bob Newhart

Spring, Spring, Spring—Let's Take a Walk Around the Block—Medley with Pat Boone (Flyin' Machine—Up, Up and Away—Breezin' Along with the Breeze)—Walking Happy (with cast)—Laughter in the Rain (with Olivia Newton-John)—Caterina—Here, There, and Everywhere—Ave Maria—World of Dreams—Sing—You've Got a Friend—It's Easter Time (with Pat Boone and Olivia Newton-John)—Easter Parade (with Olivia Newton-John)

Perry Como's Lake Tahoe Holiday— Air date: October 28, 1975

Guests: Bob Hope, Anne Murray, Billie Jean King, Sandra Palmer, Suzy Chaffee, Robin Alaway, Tina Trefarthen & Desiree Vanessen

Temptation—The Grass Keeps Right On Growin'—Medley with Anne Murray (Chi-Baba, Chi-Baba—Catch a Falling Star—Don't Let the Stars Get in Your Eyes)—The Way We Were—Just Out of Reach—Something—On a Wonderful Day Like Today—I Love

The Barber Comes to Town (BBC2-TV)—Air date: December 14, 1975 (U.K.)

I've Got You Under My Skin—Hello, Young Lovers—For the Good Times—You Are the Sunshine of My Life—Without a Song—(The) Father of Girls—Temptation—Magic Moments—Catch a Falling Star—Round and Round—Don't Let the Stars Get in Your Eyes—I Can Almost Read Your Mind—It's Impossible—Put Your Hand in the Hand—And I Love You So—You Are Never Far Away from Me

The smiling Mr. C, ca. 1970.

Perry Como's Christmas in Mexico— Air date: December 15, 1975

Guests: Vikki Carr, Captain and Tennille, Ballet Folklorico, Zavala Brothers and Sisters, Armando Manzanero and the Zavala Children's Choir

Medley with Zavala Children's Choir (Happy Holiday—Sing)—Wonderful, Wonderful Day (with Zavalas Brothers and Sisters)—Wonderful, Wonderful Day (reprise—with Captain and Tennille and Zavalas Brothers and Sisters)—Yesterday I Heard the Rain (snatch only) (with Armando Manzanero)—It's Impossible (with Armando Manzanero)—Eres Tu (with Armando Manzanero and Zavalas Brothers and Sisters)—Solamente Una Vez (with Vikki Carr)—Christ Is Born—Christmas Medley with Vikki Carr and Captain and Tennille (Silent Night—Hark! The Herald Angels Sing)—Ave Maria (with Zavala Children's Choir)

Perry Como's Hawaiian Holiday—Air date: February 22, 1976

Guests: Petula Clark, George Carlin, Tavana, and Don Ho

Next Door to Paradise—Tiny Bubbles (with Don Ho)—One Paddle, Two Paddle (with Petula Clark and George Carlin)—Octopus' Garden (with Petula Clark and George Carlin)—Medley with Petula Clark (Pearly Shells—Beautiful Hawaii)—Love Put a Song in My Heart—Blue Hawaii (with Petula Clark, George Carlin, Tavana, and Don Ho)—You'll Never Go Home (with Petula Clark, George Carlin, and Don Ho)—The Hawaiian Wedding Song—Medley (Sweet Leilani—Now Is the Hour)

Perry Como's Spring in New Orleans—Air date: April 7, 1976

Guests: Leslie Uggams, Dick Van Dyke, Louis Cottrell Heritage Hall Band and the Southern University Marching Band.

Basin Street Blues (with guests)—Way Down Yonder in New Orleans (with guests)—Who Will Buy?—There's a Parade (with Dick Van Dyke)—If—You've Got a Friend (with Leslie Uggams)—Sleepy Time Down South—When the Saints Go Marching In (with Dick Van Dyke & Leslie Uggams)—If I Ruled the World—I Believe in Music—Do You Know What It Means to Miss New Orleans?

Perry with holiday beauties on *The Perry Como Winter Show*, December 10, 1973.

Perry Como in Australia (Channel ATN7)—Air date not confirmed—May 1976

Perry's concert at the Horden Pavilion in Sydney on May 5, 1976 was recorded for later transmission

Perry Como, Las Vegas Style—Air date: September 11, 1976

Guests: Ann-Margret, Rich Little, Bare Touch of Vegas and Los Pampas
Where or When (snatch only)—Hello, Young Lovers—I Write the Songs—Medley with Rich Little (snatches of "A" You're Adorable—Hot Diggity [Dog Ziggity Boom]—Papa Loves Mambo—You're Just in Love)—It Might As Well Be Spring (with Ann-Margret)—Feelings—Oh Marie—Bridge Over Troubled Water—Careers (with Rich Little and Ann-Margret)—Thank Heaven for Little Girls

Perry Como's Christmas in Austria—Air date: December 13, 1976

Guests: Sid Caesar, Senta Berger, Vienna Boys Choir, Salzburger Marionette Theater, Karl Schranz and the Vienna Waltz Champions
Christmas Is My Time of Year—The Shopping Song (with Sid Caesar)—The Sound of Music—Do-Re-Mi—Edelweiss—I'm in Love with Vienna—O Tannenbaum (with Vienna Boys Choir)—Christ Is Born (with Vienna Boys Choir)—The Happy Wanderer—Austrian Christmas Carol (with Senta Berger and Karl Schranz)—Silent Night—O Holy Night

Perry Como's Music from Hollywood—Air date: March 28, 1977

Guests: Shirley Jones, Hal Linden, Henry Mancini and Sandy Duncan
If I Had a Talking Picture of You—Hooray for Hollywood (plus reprise with guests)—(Where Do I Begin) Love Story—Days of Wine and Roses—Medley (Smile—They Can't Take That Away from Me—Temptation)—Academy Awards medley with guests (Perry's contribution: You'll Never Know—In the Cool, Cool, Cool of the Evening [with Shirley Jones]—Buttons and Bows [with Sandy Duncan]—Raindrops Keep Fallin' on My Head [with Hal Linden]—The Way You Look Tonight—Moon River—On the Atchison, Topeka and the Santa Fe [with guests])—The Way We Were

Perry's Olde English Christmas in London—Air date: December 14, 1977

Guests: Petula Clark, Gemma Craven, John Curry and Leo Sayer

Give Me an Old Fashioned Christmas Card—Christmas Medley (The Holly and the Ivy (with Gemma Craven); I Saw Three Ships (with Cast); Joy to the World! (with Cast); We Wish You a Merry Christmas (with Cast)— Greensleeves)—Medley with Petula Clark (Where Is Love?—There's a Kind of Hush—Where Is Love? (Reprise) (with Petula Clark))—Toyland—When I Need You (with Leo Sayer)—Hot Diggity (Dog Ziggity Boom) (snatch only)—The Story of the First Christmas (O, Little Town of Bethlehem—O, Come All Ye Faithful)—Silent Night—Ave Maria (NOTE: The version shown on BBC-TV in the U.K. included a medley (Here's to My Lady; My Kind of Girl). In its place in the USA broadcast was 'Toyland.'

Perry Como's Easter by the Sea—Air date: March 22, 1978

Guests: Debby Boone and Kenny Rogers

Beautiful Noise (With Debby Boone And Kenny Rogers)—Bless the Beasts and the Children—Far Away Places— Whale of a Tale (With Kenny Rogers And United States Navy Sea Chanters)—This Is All I Ask—Where You're Concerned (With Debby Boone)—You Light up My Life (With Debby Boone)—The Lord's Prayer

Perry Como's Early American Christmas—Air date: December 13, 1978

Guests: John Wayne, Diana Canova, Eugene Fodor, and Miss America (Kylene Barker)

The Twelve Days of Christmas—Little Drummer Boy—It Couldn't Please Me More (with Diana Canova)— (There's No Place Like) Home for The Holidays—Try to Remember (with Diana Canova)—Tavern carols with John Wayne and locals (Boar's Head Carol—Here We Come a Wassailing—I Saw Three Ships—We Wish You a Merry Christmas)—Ave Maria

Perry Como's Springtime Special—Air date: April 9, 1979

Guests: Pam Dawber, Bernadette Peters, Garry Owens, Vicky Lawrence, The Stardust Ballroom Champion Dancers and The St. Sophia Choir

It's Easter Time (plus reprise with Pam Dawber and Bernadette Peters)—It's Hollywood (with Pam Dawber and Bernadette Peters)—You Are So Beautiful—Wherever We Go (With Bernadette Peters)—You Needed Me (with Pam Dawber)—Dear Hearts and Gentle People (with Pam Dawber)—I Love to Dance Like They Used to Dance—If (with Bernadette Peters)—It's a Lovely Day Today (with Bernadette Peters)—On a Wonderful Day Like Today (with Pam Dawber & Bernadette Peters)—The Lord's Prayer

Perry Como in Tokyo: Concert at Sun Plaza Hall (April 22, 1979)— Air date on Japanese TV not confirmed

Hello Young Lovers—The Way You Look Tonight—The Way We Were—Beautiful Noise—You Light up My Life—Temptation—Without a Song—'Deed I Do—Medley (Till the End of Time; Catch a Falling Star; Round and Round; Don't Let the Stars Get in Your Eyes)—Feelings—You Are the Sunshine of My Life—Medley (If (David Gates); It's Impossible; Oh Marie)—You'll Never Walk Alone—Sakura—And I Love You So

Perry Como's Christmas in New Mexico—Air date: December 14, 1979

Guests: Anne Murray, Greer Garson, Joyce DeWitt and Buffy Sainte-Marie

On the Atchison, Topeka and the Santa Fe (with cast—including snatches of: White Christmas; Down by the Station)—Silver Bells—Why Do They Call It Chilli? (with Anne Murray and locals)—Up, up and Away (with Anne Murray)—Christ Is Born—Vamos Todas A Belen (with Joyce DeWitt)—We Wish You a Merry Christmas (with Cast)—Until It's Time for You to Go (with Buffy Sainte-Marie)—O Holy Night

Perry Como's Bahamas Holiday—Air date: May 21, 1980

Guests: Loretta Swit, The Captain and Toni Tennille, Blind Blake Hayes, The Royal Bahamas Police Marching Band and Bill Bonaparte

It's Better in the Bahamas (with Loretta Swit and Toni Tennille)—You Make Me Feel So Young—Ballymena (with Toni Tennille)—Love Alone Caused King Edward to Leave The Throne (with Loretta Swit and Blind Blake Hayes)—When I Fall in Love—It Could Happen to You—Sloop John B—Aubrey—The Mail Boats Are Coming (with cast)—Rushing Through the Crowd (with The Captain & Toni Tennille plus chorus)—I Want to Give (Ahora Que Soy Libre)

Perry Como's Christmas in The Holy Land—Air date: December 13, 1980

Guests: Richard Chamberlain, Ilanit and Shalom '80

The Holy City—I Wonder as I Wander—Tradition (with Ilanit)—Ave Maria—Medley with Ilanit and Shalom '80 (Chiribim—Hava Nagila)—The Lord's Prayer—Bless This House—The Story of the First Christmas (O, Come All Ye Faithful—Silent Night)—Christ Is Born

Perry Como's Spring in San Francisco—Air date: May 10, 1981

Guests: Larry Gatlin, The Gatlin Brothers, The Breeze Brothers, Cheryl Ladd and Jim Plunkett

It's a Miracle—San Francisco—The Crookedest Street (with Cheryl Ladd)—Send in the Clowns—That's the Way the Fortune Cookie Crumbles (with Cheryl Ladd)—Not While I'm Around—All the Gold in California (with The Gatlin Brothers)—The Colors of My Life—Hoop-Dee-Doo (with Cheryl Ladd)—I Left My Heart in San Francisco

Perry Como's French Canadian Christmas—Air date: December 12, 1981

Guests: Debby Boone, Diane Tell, Andre Gagnon and Dorothy Hamill

He is Born—Angels We Have Heard on High—Do You Hear What I Hear—One Little Word, Marry (with Debby Boone)—Wonderful, Wonderful Day (with Debby Boone)—I Wish It Could Be Christmas Forever— C'est Si Bon (with Diane Tell)—C'est Magnifique (with Diane Tell)—White Christmas (with Andre Gagnon— piano)—Christ Is Born—Deck the Halls—Away in a Manger (with Debby Boone)—O Come All Ye Faithful (with entire cast)—O Holy Night

Perry Como's Easter in Guadalajara—Air date: April 3, 1982

Guests: Mariachis Los Corporales, Ballet Folklorico Mariachis, Charo, Jose Placio, Pedrito Fernandez and Ann Jillian

It's Easter Time—There's a New World Coming (with cast)—Yesterday I Heard the Rain—Coo Coo Roo Coo Coo Paloma (with Ann Jillian)—El Rancho Grande (with Pedrito Fernandez & Charo)—Bless the Beasts and the Children—Easter Parade (with Ann Jillian)—Goodbye for Now (Love Theme from 'Reds')—We'll Meet Again (with Charo on guitar)—The Lord's Prayer

Concert at NHK Hall in Tokyo (December 19, 1982)—Japanese TV air date not confirmed

Medley (I've Got You Under My Skin; Hello Young Lovers)—Something—And I Love You So—Perry Como hits Medley (Till the End of Time; Catch a Falling Star; Round and Round; Don't Let the Stars Get in Your Eyes)—Feelings—(The) Rose Tattoo—Bing Crosby Medley (Blue Skies; But Beautiful; Dear Hearts and Gentle People; Sweet Leilani; Ac-Cent-Tchu-Ate the Positive; Swinging on a Star; Pennies from Heaven; Too-Ra-Loo-Ra-Loo-Ral; White Christmas; In the Cool, Cool, Cool of the Evening)—Medley (It's Been a Long, Long Time; It's Impossible)—You'll Never Walk Alone—Sakura—Christmas Medley (Silver Bells; I Wish It Could Be Christmas Forever; We Wish You a Merry Christmas)—We'll Meet Again (snatch only)

Perry Como's Christmas in Paris—Air date: December 18, 1982

Guests: Angie Dickinson, Line Renaud, Pierre Cardin, Jairo, Andre Tahon Puppets, Paradis Latin performers and the Boys Choir of Notre Dame

I Wish It Could Be Christmas Forever—I Love Paris / Pigalle—Medley with Angie Dickinson (It's Beginning to Look Like Christmas—Deck the Halls)—Christ Is Born—(The) Twelve Days of Christmas (parody—with Angie Dickinson))—Mona Lisa—Chantez, Chantez (with Line Renaud)—Medley with cast (Perry's Contributions: Noel Nouvelet; Silent Night; The First Noel; We Wish You a Merry Christmas)—Ave Maria

Perry Como's Christmas in New York—Air date: December 17, 1983

Guests: Sarah Litzsinger, Michele Lee, Peppercorn Choir, UN International School Fifth Grade Choir and St. Patrick's Cathedral Choir

Medley (Perry's Contributions: Happy Holiday; New York, New York (and reprise))—Have Yourself a Merry Little Christmas—The Best of Times (with Michele Lee)—Christ Is Born—Talk to the Animals (with Sarah Litzsinger)—The Greatest Love of All—Catch a Falling Star (incorporated with footage from a Perry Como TV Show—circa 1957-1958)—White Christmas—I Wish It Could Be Christmas Forever (with cast)—Ave Maria

Perry Como's Christmas in England—Air date: December 15, 1984

Guests: Ann-Margret, the Cambridge Buskers and London Folk

Happy Holiday—London Is London (with Ann-Margret)—It's the Most Wonderful Time of the Year—Thank You Very Much (with Ann-Margret)—(The) Best of Times (with Ann-Margret)—Santa Lucia (with Ann-Margret)—I Saw Three Ships (with cast)—I Wish It Could Be Christmas Forever (with Ann-Margret)—Silver Bells—Who Wants to Be a Millionaire? (with Ann-Margret)—Medley with Ann-Margret and local choir (Away in a Manger; It Came Upon a Midnight Clear)—Christ Is Born—O Holy Night

Perry Como's Christmas in Hawaii—Air date: December 14, 1985

Guests: Marie Osmond, Burt Reynolds, Tihati Dancers, Kamehameha Choir, The Hawaii Young Singers and Hualani's Pipers

Happy Holiday—It's Christmas in Hawaii (I'm Dreaming of Hawaii)—Medley with Marie Osmond (Sleigh

Ride—Jesus Was Born Today—Mele Kalikimaka)—Medley with Burt Reynolds (In the Cool, Cool, Cool of the Evening—How About You?—Don't Fence Me In)—Deck the Halls (with The Hawaii Young Singers)—Silent Night (with The Hawaii Young Singers)—Far Away Places (with Marie Osmond)—Santa Claus Is Comin' to Town—I Just Called to Say I Love You (with Marie Osmond)—Medley (The First Noel—O Holy Night)—Ave Maria (with Kamehameha Choir)

The Perry Como Christmas Special—Air date: December 6, 1986
Guests: George Strait, Julia Migenes-Johnson, Angie Dickinson, San Antonio Symphony Orchestra & Master Singers, Fifth Army Band & Air Force Band of the West, Mayor Henry Cisneros
Jesus Was Born Today—Joy to the World—Deep in the Heart of Texas (snatch only)—Sing (with Angie Dickinson)—Do You Hear What I Hear?—Bless the Beasts and the Children—Ave Maria (with Julia Migenes-Johnson)—We Wish You a Merry Christmas (with cast)—Silent Night (with Julia Migenes-Johnson)—We Need a Little Christmas—White Christmas—O, Come All Ye Faithful—O Holy Night

Perry Como in Japan (Japanese TV)—Air date: March 1993
I'm Sitting on Top of the World—Hello, Young Lovers—Where or When—And I Love You So—Temptation—The Rose Tattoo—That's What Friends Are For—(The) Father of Girls—Bing Crosby medley (Blue Skies—Dear Hearts and Gentle People—Ac-Cent-Tchu-Ate the Positive—Swinging on a Star—Pennies from Heaven—Too-Ra-Loo-Ra-Loo-Ral—White Christmas—In the Cool, Cool, Cool of the Evening)—It's Been a Long, Long Time—Almost Like Being in Love—Sakura—The Way You Look Tonight—Jingle Bells—The Wind Beneath My Wings—We'll Meet Again—It's Impossible—Always

Perry Como's Irish Christmas—Air date: December 1994
Guests: Twink, The Glasnevin Music Society, The Boys Of The Palestrina Choir, The Artane Boys Band and the RTE Concert Orchestra
A Little Bit of Heaven—I Can Almost Read Your Mind—Happy Holiday—We Need a Little Christmas—It's Beginning to Look Like Christmas—Have Yourself a Merry Little Christmas—Bless This House—Little Drummer Boy—And I Love You So—Catch a Falling Star—Round and Round—Hot Diggity (Dog Ziggity Boom)—Don't Let the Stars Get in Your Eyes—Too-Ra-Loo-Ra-Loo-Ral (with Twink)—Christ Is Born—It's the Time of Year—Santa Claus is Comin' to Town (with Twink)—White Christmas (with Twink)—Jingle Bells (with Twink)—Irish medley with Twink (If You're Irish—When Irish Eyes Are Smiling)—The Wind Beneath My Wings—Carols medley with Twink (O, Little Town Of Bethlehem—Hark! The Herald Angels Sing—Silent Night—O Come All Ye Faithful)—Toyland—I Wish It Could Be Christmas Forever—We Wish You a Merry Christmas—Ave Maria

Guest Appearances

Texaco Star Theatre (NBC-TV)—Air date: December 27, 1949
   The Lord's Prayer—Silent Night
Arthur Godfrey & Friends (NBC-TV)—Air date: March 29, 1950
Arthur Godfrey & Friends (NBC-TV)—Air date: April 5, 1950
Treasury Open House—Air date: June 2, 1950
The Toast Of The Town (CBS-TV)—Air date: July 9, 1950
Texaco Star Theatre (NBC-TV)—Air date: January 9, 1951
Texaco Star Theatre (NBC-TV)—Air date: January 16, 1951
The Frank Sinatra Show (CBS-TV)—Air date: March 3, 1951
   Como, Sinatra & Laine (special material, with Frank Sinatra and Frankie Laine)—If
The Frank Sinatra Show (CBS-TV)—Air date: October 9, 1951
   Heart And Soul—Sound Off! For Chesterfield (Snatch)
The U.S. Royal Showcase (NBC-TV)—Air date: February 23, 1952
New York Cardiac Hospital Telethon—Air date: March 14/15, 1952
Strike It Rich (CBS-TV)—Air date: December 17, 1952
The Stork Club (CBS-TV)—Air date: January 10, 1953
   Don't Let the Stars Get in Your Eyes
All-Star Revue (NBC-TV)—Air date: February 14, 1953
   Don't Let the Stars Get in Your Eyes—Temptation (A-Cappella) (snatch)—You'll Never Walk Alone—I Confess (on record) (snatch)—Side by Side (with Patti Page)—Wild Horses—When Day Is Done

Arthur Godfrey & Friends (CBS-TV)—Air date: May 13, 1953

The Colgate Comedy Hour (NBC-TV)—Air date: December 13, 1953
  Pa-Paya Mama—I Believe—You Alone

Stars On Parade—Air date: January 16, 1954

Dateline (NBC-TV)—Air date: December 13, 1954

Max Liebman Presents "Variety" (NBC-TV)—Air date: January 30, 1955
  Papa Loves Mambo—You'll Always Be My Lifetime Sweetheart—Kokomo—Peace of Mind

The Oldsmobile Show (NBC-TV)—Air date: November 2, 1955

The Dinah Shore Chevy Show (NBC-TV)—Air date: January 17, 1956
  You Must Have Been a Beautiful Baby (with Dinah Shore)

The Big Surprise (NBC-TV)—Air date: February 18, 1956

The Walter Winchell Show (NBC-TV)—Air date: October 5, 1956
  Lullaby of Broadway—Moonlight Love

The Bob Hope Chevy Show (NBC-TV)—Air date: November 18, 1956
  Chincherinchee

The Ed Sullivan Show (CBS-TV)—Air date: December 30, 1956

The Dinah Shore Chevy Show (NBC-TV)—Air date: January 13, 1957
  I Concentrate on You—I'm Following You (with Dinah Shore)—Medley with Dinah Shore (Partners; You
    Were Meant for Me; Pretty Baby; Jealous; For Me and My Gal)—Chantez, Chantez (reprise) (with cast)

Il Musichiere (Italian TV)—Air date: September 14, 1958
  Oh, Marie

Some Of Manie's Friends (NBC-TV)—Air date: March 3, 1959
  No Other Love

Pontiac Star Parade (NBC-TV)—Air date: March 24, 1959
  When You Come to the End of the Day—Gypsy in My Soul—I Love You—Oklahoma—Getting to Know
    You—Begin the Beguine—You Are Never Far Away from Me

Sunday Showcase—Air date: November 29, 1959

The Bing Crosby Show (ABC-TV)—Air date: February 29, 1960
  Sing, Sing, Sing (with Bing Crosby & The Crosby Brothers)—Zing a Little Zong (with Bing Crosby)—Lazy
    medley with Bing Crosby (Lazy—Gone Fishin'—Lazy Afternoon—Hoop-Dee-Doo)—Getting To Know
    You (with Bing Crosby, Elaine Dunn & Sandy Stewart)—A Couple of Song and Dance Men (with Bing
    Crosby, Elaine Dunn & Sandy Stewart)—Chevalier medley with Bing Crosby (Mimi—Louise—Valentine—
    Thank Heaven for Little Girls)—First LP medley with Bing Crosby (Sing, Sing, Sing—Dinah—Ida, Sweet
    As Apple Cider—I Could Write a Book—I Guess I'll Have to Change My Plan—Dream Along with Me—
    Get Happy—Mr. Meadowlark—I Whistle a Happy Tune—Manhattan—Hit the Road to Dreamland—Show
    Me the Way to Go Home—Two Sleepy People (Parody))

Perry Como in London (BBC-TV)—Air date: April 16, 1960
  Interviewed by John Timpson in conjunction with the recording of Perry Como's Kraft Music Hall in Lon-
    don.

Celebrity Golf—Air date: October 9, 1960
  On this show, Perry plays a round of golf with golfer/host Sam Snead

The Bob Hope Buick Show "Potomac Madness" (NBC-TV)—Air date: October 22, 1960
  I May Be Wrong—Playing Politics (With Bob Hope And Ginger Rogers)—It Could Happen to You—Where
    Else, but the USA!

Emmy Awards Show (NBC-TV)—Air date: May 22, 1962

The Danny Thomas Show (NBC-TV)—Air date: February 14, 1965

Land of 12 Tribes—Air date: January 29, 1967

The Bob Hope Show "Shoot-In At NBC" (NBC-TV)—Air date: November 8, 1967
  Unbilled cameo appearance only

Ethel Kennedy's Telethon—Air date: February 11, 1968

Rowan & Martin's "Laugh-In" (NBC-TV)—Air date: November 25, 1968

Rowan & Martin's "Laugh-In" (NBC-TV)—Air date: January 13, 1969

The Carol Burnett Show (CBS-TV)—Air date: January 20, 1969
  Sunshine Wine—Here's That Rainy Day—Brotherhood of Man (with Carol Burnett)

Academy Of Professional Sports (NBC-TV)—Air date: February 19, 1969

Rowan & Martin's "Laugh-In" (NBC-TV)—Air date: March 24, 1969

Rowan & Martin's "Laugh-In" (NBC-TV)—Air date: July 7, 1969

The Hollywood Palace (ABC-TV)—Air date: December 20, 1969
Guests: Diahann Carroll, Shecky Greene, Edward Vilella, Burr Tillstrom with Kukla and Ollie
(There's No Place Like) Home for The Holidays—Love in a Home—Put a Little Love in Your Heart (with Diahann Carroll)—Christmas Eve—The First Noel—Hark! The Herald Angels Sing—O Holy Night—Christ Is Born—Silver Bells (with Diahann Carroll)

Rowan & Martin's "Laugh-In" (NBC-TV)—Air date: February 16, 1970

The Bob Hope Show (NBC-TV)—Air date: March 18, 1970
(The) Father of Girls—Prisoner of Love (Snatch)

Jimmy Durante Presents The Lennon Sisters (ABC-TV)—Air date: March 28, 1970
Little Green Apples—Song Title Medley with The Lennon Sisters (snatches of) Memories—Old Spinning Wheel—Sunny—I'll Never Fall in Love Again (2 versions)—If I Had My Way—Bewitched, Bothered and Bewildered)—Duet with Jimmy Durante—Dear Hearts and Gentle People (with cast)

The Flip Wilson Show (NBC-TV)—Air date: October 8, 1970
I've Got You Under My Skin—Hello, Young Lovers—Medley with Flip Wilson (Don't Let the Stars Get in Your Eyes—When You Were Sweet Sixteen—Papa Loves Mambo—Prisoner of Love—Catch a Falling Star)— It's Impossible

This Is Tom Jones (ABC-TV)—Air date: November 6, 1970
(The) Father of Girls—The Men in My Little Girl's Life (with Patti Deutsch)—Beady Eyed Buzzard— Wand'rin' Star (with Tom Jones & Debbie Reynolds)

The Pearl Bailey Show (ABC-TV)—Air date: February 27, 1971
It's Impossible—Something (with Pearl Bailey)—You Stepped Out of a Dream

The Doris Mary Anne Kappelhoff Special (CBS-TV)—Air date: March 14, 1971
Didn't We—Medley with Doris Day (When You Were Sweet Sixteen—Everybody Loves a Lover—Meditation— Quiet Nights of Quiet Stars—Summertime—If I Had My Life to Live Over—Let Me Call You Sweetheart)

Top of The Pops (BBC-TV)—Air date: May 6, 1971 (U.K.)
I Think of You

This Is Your Life (re Pat Boone)—Air date: September 26, 1971

Zenith Presents a Salute to Television's 25th Anniversary (ABC-TV)—Air date: September 10, 1972

Cole Porter in Paris (NBC-TV)—Air date: January 17, 1973
I've Got You Under My Skin (snatch)—Let's Do It (Let's Fall in Love) (with Diahann Carroll and Connie Stevens)—You Do Something to Me—Night and Day—I Concentrate on You—Well, Did You Evah? (with Louis Jourdan)—In the Still of the Night—We Open in Venice (with Diahann Carroll, Connie Stevens and Louis Jourdan)—So in Love—Were Thine That Special Face—Brush up Your Shakespeare (with Diahann Carroll, Connie Stevens and Louis Jourdan)—So in Love (reprise) (with Diahann Carroll, Connie Stevens and Louis Jourdan)—I Love Paris—Medley (You'd Be So Nice to Come Home To; I Love You)—Begin the Beguine

Julie on Sesame Street (ABC-TV)—Air date: November 23, 1973
And I Love You So—Sing/Song Medley with Julie Andrews (Perry's contributions: Sing—And the Angels Sing—I Feel a Song Coming On—Singin' in the Rain—There Goes That Song Again—Look What They've Done to My Song—Singing the Blues—It's a Grand Night for Singing—If You Feel Like Singing, Sing!— The Donkey Serenade—The Song Is You—Make Your Own Kind of Music—Killing Me Softly with Her Song—Without a Song—Let Me Sing and I'm Happy—Sing [reprise])—Picture a World (with Julie Andrews and The Muppets)

Top of the Pops (BBC1 TV)—Air date: 1973 (U.K.)
For The Good Times

The Royal Variety Performance (BBC1 TV)—Air date: November 24, 1974 (U.K.)
The Way You Look Tonight—Where or When—For the Good Times—Temptation—It's Impossible—Medley (Magic Moments—Catch a Falling Star—Round and Round—Don't Let the Stars Get in Your Eyes)—Without a Song—And I Love You So

Jerry Lewis Telethon against Muscular Dystrophy—Air date: September 5, 1976

Ann-Margret—Rhinestone Cowgirl (NBC-TV)—Air date: April 26, 1977
And I Love You So (with Chet Atkins)—Medley of Country Songs with Ann-Margret

The Parkinson Show (BBC-TV)—Air date: November 26, 1977 (U.K.)
The Very Thought of You—Where Is Love?—We'll Meet Again—It's Impossible

The Bob Hope All Star Christmas Comedy Special (NBC-TV)—Air date: December 19, 1977
You Light up My Life—Prisoner of Love (Snatch)—It's Impossible (A-Cappella) (snatch)

Christmas With Nationwide: Journey To Bethlehem (BBC-TV)—Air date: December 21, 1977 (U.K.)
Glyn Worsnip reports from Hever Castle and Chiddingstone on the making of Perry Como's Olde English Christmas In London.

Queen Elizabeth Welcoming Party—February 27, 1983—news reports shown on subsequent days
Perry is seen with Frank Sinatra meeting the British Queen in Hollywood.

Today (NBC-TV)—Air date: July 5, 1983

Bob Hope's Salute to NASA (NBC-TV)—Air date: September 19, 1983

Annual Emmy Awards—Air date: September 25, 1983
Perry is honored with a special tribute to his 50 years in show-business. Then, he reads out the nominations for, and winner of the 'Outstanding Variety, Music Or Comedy Program'

The Kennedy Center Honors Show (CBS-TV)—Air date: December 27, 1983
Young at Heart

The Arlene Herson Show—Air date: June 6, 1984

Good Company (Minneapolis TV)—Air date: June 19, 1984
Perry is heard rehearsing snatches of: Blue Skies—White Christmas

AM Cleveland—Air date: July 31, 1984
Snatches heard of: I Love to Dance Like They Used to Dance—White Christmas—In the Cool, Cool, Cool of the Evening

Life Styles (Regis Philbin interviews Perry)—Air date: August, 1984

Val Doonican's Very Special Christmas (BBC-TV)—Air date: December 24, 1984 (U.K.)
Includes interview with Perry in conjunction with 'Perry Como's Christmas In England.'

Duke Children's Classic (ESPN)—Air date: May, 1986
You Are So Beautiful to Me

The Kennedy Center Honors Show (CBS-TV)—Air date: December 30, 1987

Evening at Pops (PBS-TV)—Air date: August 14, 1988
Where the Blue of the Night—Blue Skies—But Beautiful—Dear Hearts and Gentle People—Ac-Cent-Tchu-Ate the Positive—Swinging on a Star—Pennies from Heaven—Too-Ra-Loo-Ra-Loo-Ral—White Christmas—In the Cool, Cool, Cool of the Evening—The Wind Beneath Your Wings

Duke Children's Classic (ESPN)—Air date: May 15, 1989
I'm Sitting on Top of the World (with special lyrics)

Live With Regis & Kathie Lee (ABC-TV)—Air date: July 7, 1989

Gala Concert for President Ronald Reagan—Friendship Concert in Yokohama, Japan on October 22, 1989—Air date not confirmed
And I Love You So—That's What Friends Are For—Sing (with Yuzo Kayama)—You Are My Sunshine (with Plácido Domingo, Yuzo Kayama and the Harlem Boys Choir).

Academy of Television Arts & Sciences Hall of Fame (Fox-TV)—Air date: January 24, 1990

Sammy Davis Jr. Variety Club Telethon (St. Louis TV)—Air date: March 3–4, 1990

Live With Regis & Kathie Lee (ABC-TV)—Air date: December 5, 1990
And I Love You So (with Regis Philbin)—It's Impossible (with Regis Philbin)

Sinatra 75: The Best Is Yet to Come—Air date: December 16, 1990

Sammy Davis Jr. Variety Club Telethon (St. Louis TV)—Air date: March 2/3, 1991

Hard Copy—Air date: June 14, 1991

This Morning (CBS-TV)—Air date: December 20, 1991

Sammy Davis Jr. Variety Club Telethon (KMOV-TV)—Air date: March 7/8, 1992

National Memorial Day Concert (PBS-TV)—Air date: May 24, 1992
No Other Love—For Me and My Gal—We'll Meet Again

Kenny Live (RTE-TV)—Air date: January 15, 1994
It Could Happen to You—How to Handle a Woman

Sammy Davis Jr. Variety Club Telethon (KMOV-TV)—Air date: March 5/6, 1994

Live With Regis & Kathie Lee (ABC-TV)—Air date: November 15, 1994
It Could Happen to You

Duke Children's Classic—May, 1995—Air date not confirmed
Where or When—And I Love You So—The Wind Beneath My Wings—Almost Like Being in Love

Appendix C

Perry Como Year by Year

1912

May 12, Sunday. Pierino Ronald Como is born at 227 Franklin Avenue (later numbered 527) in Canonsburg, Pennsylvania. He is the seventh child of ten children born to his Italian immigrant parents, Pietro and Lucia Como, and the first to be a citizen of the U.S. by birth. He is soon known as "Perry."

1913

March 10, Monday. Perry is baptized at the Church of the Immaculate Conception in Washington, Pennsylvania. The baptismal records indicate that he was born on May 12, 1912 (not May 18 as usually quoted), and that he is named Perino Petrum. His father's name is given as Petro Como and his mother's as Lucia Travoglini. His sponsors are Gaetano Morietta and A. Jimeo. All spellings are as stated in the original records and may be incorrect in some instances. (Also, Jimeo should probably be Timeo.)

1918

Fall (undated). Perry would probably have started attending the nearby First Ward School on Franklin Avenue. A 1924 survey of schools shows that the First Ward School consists predominantly of Italian and Polish pupils and has 18 different nationalities attending it.

1920

January 23, Friday. The United States Census shows the Como family at 220 Franklin Avenue, Canonsburg, Pennsylvania, and confirms that they arrived in the United States in 1910. The house at 220 Franklin Avenue is later renumbered as 530. Pietro is shown as "Peter," his wife as "Lucy." Peter is a tanner at Standard Tinplate Corporation and daughter Giuseppina (known as Josephine) works at a paper mill. Peter is shown as being able to read and write but not his wife. Other children at home are Dominick, Perry and Vincent (sic—this should be daughter Venzie). In addition the census shows two "roomers," Louis (30) and James Rainaldi (23), both from Italy, who work at the tinplate mill. The population of Canonsburg in 1920 was 10,632.

September 18, Saturday. Albert Como is born to Pietro and Lucia Como.

1923

March 4, Sunday. Gene Francisco Como is born to Pietro and Lucia Como.

July 9, Monday. The *Daily Notes* newspaper in Canonsburg gives details of pupils who are being promoted to B-6–A class. Perry's name is among them.

Perry Como begins work at a shop at 214 Third Street in Canonsburg as an apprentice to a barber called Stefano ("Steve") Fragapane (age 40, from Italy). He works before school every morning and after school until 7:30 P.M. He receives 50 cents per week.

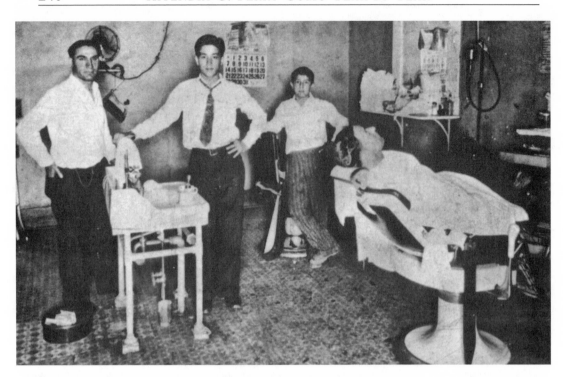

Perry is the young man with the tie next to the sink. The location is thought to be Vincent's barbershop in Canonsburg, Pennsylvania (courtesy Jim Herron, Canonsburg historian).

1926

Perry Como runs his own two-chair barber shop at the Greek Coffee House at 520 Blaine as an after-school money maker. Eventually he builds up a good business and is said to be earning $125 per week. He begins to gain local recognition as a singer by performing at the local chapter of the Sons of Italy and other fraternal organizations, wedding receptions and other functions. He learns to read music and plays both organ and baritone horn in the Canonsburg Italian Band.

Fall (undated). Perry would probably have entered Canonsburg High School. He had probably given up the Greek Coffee House shop by then.

1930

April 22, Tuesday. The United States Census shows the Como family at 530 Franklin Avenue, Canonsburg. Children at home are Dominick (30—now a laborer at the tin mill), Perry (17—a barber), Venzie, Albert and Jean (sic—it should have been Gene, a son not a daughter). There is also a boarder, Louie Rivaldi (age 40, from Italy, who works at the tin mill). Perry had left Canonsburg High School earlier without graduating. The population of Canonsburg in 1930 was 12,559. At some stage, Perry works as a barber in Tardio's Sanitary Barber Shop, 39 East Pike Street, Canonsburg.

In his spare time, Perry is part of an act called "Perry & Lou—The Comedy Boys." Perry is the straight man who sings and plays guitar while his colleague, Lou (surname thought to be Marchione; Perry said McHugh), is the comedian, using broken English as his trademark.

1931

September 2, Wednesday. Bing Crosby makes his first nationwide radio broadcast to great acclaim. Russ Columbo is also prominent on radio at this time.

1932

At some stage, Perry closes his shop in Canonsburg and goes to run the barber shop with his uncle at the Hotel Conneaut at Conneaut, near Meadville in Pennsylvania.

Perry is thought to have occasionally sung with Ernie Palmquist's Victor Recording Orchestra at weekends at Idora Park, in Youngstown, Ohio. He is also said to have sung over the radio station WNBO of Washington, Pennsylvania, which was run by John Brownlee Spriggs.

August 5, Friday. Freddie Carlone and his orchestra appear on the same bill as Duke Ellington and his orchestra at the Dreamland Ballroom in Conneaut Lake Park, Pennsylvania. It is possible that Perry Como attended this show.

1933

Early in the year, Perry is encouraged to audition for the 13-piece Freddy Carlone band in Cleveland. A week later he is offered a job with the band at $28 per week.

March 2–3, Thursday–Friday. The band plays at the Mayflower Hotel in Washington, D.C., at a family party for Elliot Roosevelt, son of the President.

March 4, Saturday. The band is one of several playing at President Roosevelt's Inaugural Ball in Washington, D.C.

March 12, Sunday. President Roosevelt makes the first of his "fireside chats" to a radio audience of sixty million people.

March–December. The band plays at various locations including the Palisades, McKeesport, Pennsylvania; Mapleview Park, Canonsburg; the Coliseum, Ceres Park, New York; Oil City, Pennsylvania; and the Seneca Pavilion in Olean, New York State. Perry is prominently advertised.

July 31, Monday. Perry marries his childhood sweetheart, Roselle Bellino, in front of a Justice of the Peace in Meadville, Pennsylvania.

1934

May–November. The Carlone band entertains at many venues including Elberta Beach, near Elyria, Ohio; Enna Jettick Park Pavilion at Owasco Lake, near Auburn, Syracuse; Kennywood Park in Monessen (near Pittsburgh); Olentangy Park, Columbus, Ohio; Italian Hall, Monessen, Pennsylvania; and the Coliseum, Ceres, New York.

August 15, Wednesday (8:00–8:30 P.M. and 10:00–10:15 P.M.). Freddy Carlone's orchestra broadcasts on station KQV in Pennsylvania.

September 2, Sunday. Russ Columbo dies following a bizarre shooting accident.

November. The band broadcasts direct from the "400" Club in Pittsburgh over radio station KDKA.

1935

June 29, Saturday. Commencing at 9 P.M., the Freddy Carlone band appears at the Village Casino ballroom at Bemus Point, New York. The entrance fee is $1 a couple.

July (undated). The Carlone orchestra plays a 3-week engagement at the Abraham Lincoln Hotel in Springfield, Illinois.

July 21, Sunday (9:00 P.M.–1:00 A.M.). The Carlone orchestra appears at Eldora Park, Charleroi, Pennsylvania, under the auspices of the Trianon Club.

> The outstanding feature of the band, and one whose fan mail proclaims him as one of the country's best baritones, is Perry Como, the Canonsburg boy, whose mellow voice rivals the most famous in the world [*Daily Independent,* Monessen, Pennsylvania, July 17].

July 29–August 4, Monday–Sunday. Freddie Carlone's orchestra entertains at Enna Jettick Park on Owasco Lake, near Auburn, Syracuse "with Perry Como—Celebrated Baritone."

December. Como tours with the Carlone band for nearly three years through Pennsylvania, West Virginia, and Ohio until one night in a gambling casino in Warren, Ohio, he strikes lucky. Band leader Ted Weems happens to be there. Perry joins the Ted Weems Band and earns $50 per week. His first performance is said to be at the Palmer House in Chicago. With the Weems Band he tours and is listed as "vocalist" on records for the Decca label, as well as making many radio appearances. The band's evening performances at major hotels are often carried by the local radio stations.

1936

April. The Ted Weems orchestra makes regular broadcasts on many evenings over station WGN.

April 12, Sunday (11:30–noon). The Ted Weems orchestra broadcasts on the Mutual network.

May 15, Friday. In Chicago, Perry records "You Can't Pull the Wool over My Eyes" and "Lazy Weather" with Ted Weems and His Orchestra.

June (undated). The Weems aggregate plays a short season at the Empire Room, Palmer House Hotel, in Chicago.

Perry (front row, third from left) with the Freddy Carlone band.

June 15, Monday (7:00–7:30 P.M.). The Ted Weems orchestra takes over as the musical support on the *Fibber McGee & Molly* show broadcast from Chicago on the NBC network. This episode is titled *Weems Welcomed to Wistful Vista.* The orchestra continues on the weekly show without a break until April 26, 1937.

July 27, Monday (6:00–6:30 P.M.). The *Fibber McGee & Molly* show comes from the Radioland Auditorium at the Great Lakes Exposition in Cleveland. An audience of 15,000 watches the show being broadcast. The episode is titled "McGees at the Great Lakes Expo."

August 6, Thursday. In Chicago, Perry records three more songs with Ted Weems. On one song—"Knock! Knock! Who's There?"—he is joined by Red Ingle and the song enjoys a modest chart success.

September 3, Thursday. Ted Weems and his band play a short season at the Trianon Ballroom in Chicago and broadcast nightly on radio.

September 17, Thursday (9:00 P.M.–1:00 A.M.). The band plays the Coliseum ballroom in Greensburg.

September 18, Friday (9:00 P.M.–1:00 A.M.). The Weems band is at Idora Park, Youngstown, Ohio.

September 27, Sunday. Further recording session with Ted Weems in Chicago.

November 3, Tuesday (10:30 P.M.). In Chicago, the band is featured in the "Portraits of Harmony" radio program over station WJZ.

December 25, Friday. The Ted Weems orchestra opens at the Trianon Ballroom in Chicago.

1937

February 10, Wednesday. On the band's nightly 15-minute broadcast from the Trianon, Perry sings "Old Fashioned Swing," "When My Dreamboat Comes Home" and "Goodnight My Love."

March 30, Tuesday (9:00 pm.–1:00 A.M.). Ted Weems and his orchestra entertain at the Coliseum, Greensburg.

April 26, Monday (8:00–8:30 P.M.). *Fibber McGee & Molly* show—"Preparing to Leave for Hollywood." As usual, the Ted Weems orchestra provides the musical support on the broadcast from the Trianon Ballroom, Chicago, on the Red Network of NBC. The show is sponsored by Johnson's Wax. Perry sings "There's Something in the Air." Following the show, Fibber and Molly leave for Hollywood where they are to appear in a film called *This Way, Please.* During the 1936-7 radio season, the *Fibber McGee & Molly* show has reached 19th position in the Hooper ratings with a rating of 13.0. Eddie Cantor's show is top with 29.1.

May 2, Sunday. Ted Weems and his orchestra return to the radio waves on W-G-N Mutual.

May 24/31, Mondays (6:00 P.M.). The Weems band takes over from Horace Heidt's Brigadiers on CBS radio so that the Heidt band can have a vacation.

June 6/13/20/27, Sundays (1:30–2:00 P.M.). The Ted Weems orchestra's weekly radio show on the Mutual network.

June 23, Wednesday. Ted Weems brings his band to entertain at Eweco Park, Oshkosh, Appleton, Wisconsin.

July 5, Monday. The Weems band entertains at Sunset Park, Johnstown, Pennsylvania.

July 19, Monday (8:00–8:30 P.M.). The Weems band returns to the *Fibber McGee & Molly* show in Chicago on NBC radio after playing the Cleveland Exposition. The episode is titled "Homecoming Program." They continue on the weekly program until January 10, 1938. The band is thought to have played a season at the Palmer House Hotel, Chicago, and no doubt its performances will have been featured on radio as well.

July 31, Saturday. The band plays at Eweco Park, Oshkosh, Appleton, Wisconsin.

August 5, Thursday. The orchestra plays at Waverly Beach, Menasha, Wisconsin.

August 25, Wednesday. The band plays a one-night engagement at the Oasis Ballroom, Michigan City, Indiana.

August 27, Friday. Ted Weems inaugurates a new radio series on WGN Mutual.

September 5–November 21, Sundays (1:30–2:00 P.M.). The Ted Weems orchestra's weekly radio show on the Mutual network.

October 10, Sunday. The Ted Weems orchestra plays the Trianon Ballroom in Chicago.

October 29, Friday. The orchestra plays a season at the Trianon in Chicago. Performances are nightly except Mondays. Their performances are broadcast frequently on WGN.

November 28, Sunday (noon–12:15 P.M.). Perry has his first solo broadcast program on the Chicago station WMAQ and continues on each Sunday at the earlier time of 10:45 A.M. until January 9, 1938.

1938

January 7–13, Friday–Thursday. The Weems band appears at the Chicago Theatre in Chicago.

January 9, Sunday (10:45 A.M.). Perry's final solo broadcast on WMAQ.

January 10, Monday (8:00–8:30 P.M.). Ted Weems and his band make their last appearance on the *Fibber McGee & Molly* show before embarking on a theatre tour. The show is entitled *Getting the Laundry Done*. During the 1937-8 radio season, the show has a Hooper rating of 14.8, putting it in 15th position. Edgar Bergen's show was top with an incredible 39.4.

January 14–February 17. The Weems band's tour takes in venues in Detroit, Pittsburgh, Washington, D.C., Philadelphia and Baltimore.

February 22–23, Tuesday–Wednesday. In New York, Perry records a number of songs with Ted Weems & his orchestra.

March 5, Saturday. The band opens at the Trianon in Chicago.

March 6, Sunday. Ted Weems returns to the Mutual Broadcasting System with a matinee broadcast.

April 3, Sunday. Ted Weems takes over from Henry Busse on the NBC-Red Network.

April 26, Tuesday (6:30–6:45 P.M.). Perry commences solo radio broadcasts on Tuesdays and Thursdays until July 3 over station WCFL.

June 22, Wednesday. The band plays at a ball in the Trianon Ballroom, Chicago. The event is associated with the mayoralty race.

August 6, Saturday. The band plays an engagement at Santa Catalina Island, California. During this period on the West Coast, the band broadcasts frequently. Much publicity is given to Elmo Tanner, the whistler with the band.

August 23, Tuesday. In Los Angeles, Perry records "Simple and Sweet" and "Ribbons and Roses" with Ted Weems.

September 14, Wednesday. The band plays at the Cocoanut Grove near Manteca, California.

November (undated). The Ted Weems orchestra films a short contribution to *Swing, Sister, Swing* for Universal. The film stars Ken Murray and Johnny Downs.

December 2, Friday. The band furnishes the music for the San Mateo Junior College Jaycee Night at the St. Francis Hotel, San Mateo.

December 16, Friday. *Swing, Sister, Swing* is released by Universal.

1939

January 8, Sunday. The Weems band stops for a short while at Ogden, Utah, en route from San Francisco to engagements in Salt Lake City, Denver and Kansas City.

January 20–26, Friday–Thursday. The band plays a week at the Chicago Theater in Chicago having returned from a six-month tour. Press comments state, "The featured entertainers are Perry Como, ballad singer; Country Washburne, Red Ingle, Parker Gibbs, and Orm Downes, novelty comedian; Elmo Tanner."

January 22, Sunday (6:30 P.M.). Ted Weems and the orchestra appear on the *Bandwagon* radio program.

February 1, Wednesday. The band is appearing at a theater in Indianapolis. During a break between shows, Elmo Tanner slips out and marries Eleanor Jones.

February. The Weems band plays at the Stanley Theatre in Pittsburgh before moving on to the Palace Theatre in Cleveland. Then they play at the Trianon, Huntington and the Broadway Ballroom, Glassport, Pennsylvania before going on to play a short season at the Palmer House, Chicago.

March 5, Sunday (6:30–7:00 P.M.). The band broadcasts on the *Show-of-the-Week* program on the Mutual network.

March 10–11, Friday–Saturday. In New York, Perry records "Ad-de-Dey" and "Class Will Tell" with Ted Weems.

March 13, Monday. The Ted Weems orchestra appears at the Liberty Theatre in Zanesville, Ohio.

April 10, Monday. The band plays at the Nitingale Ballroom, north of Kaukauna, Wisconsin.

June 18–August 5. The band plays a season at the Casino Ballroom, Santa Catalina, California. The band broadcasts frequently from the venue.

September 26, Tuesday. The Weems orchestra gives two shows at the Cathedral Theatre, New Castle, Pennsylvania.

September 27, Wednesday. The band plays at the Palisades in McKeesport, Monessen, Pennsylvania.

October 4–5, Wednesday–Thursday. Perry records five songs with Ted Weems in New York including "I Wonder Who's Kissing Her Now" which is reissued in 1947 and reaches No. 5 in the charts.

November. The Weems band plays at the Earle Theatre in Philadelphia; at the Victory Ball held at the WCHS auditorium in Charleston, West Virginia; and four shows at the Liberty Theatre in Zanesville, Ohio, as part of a cine-variety offering.

November 17–23, Friday–Thursday. Ted Weems and his orchestra are this week's headliners at the Chicago Theater.

1940

January 15, Monday. Ronald Como is born to Perry and Roselle in the Passavant Memorial Hospital, Chicago. Perry is working in Chicago with the Ted Weems orchestra when their son Ronnie is born.

January 28, Sunday. The Weems band is playing a season at the Edgewater Beach Hotel in Chicago (5:30–6:00 P.M.). A new radio program called *Beat the Band* makes its formal debut on the NBC radio network and is heard coast-to-coast. Ted Weems and his 14-piece orchestra, joined by Perry Como, Elmo "The Whistling Troubadour" Tanner, Marvel Maxwell, Parker Gibbs and Country Washburne provide the musical content. Perry sings "At the Balalaika." The *Beat the Band* show continues at weekly intervals until February 23, 1941, and is occasionally broadcast from remote locations where the band is working at the time.

February 5, Monday. The band plays at the Municipal Auditorium in St. Louis.

April 26, Friday (9:00 P.M.–1:00 A.M.). The Ted Weems band plays at the Junior Prom in Iowa City.

May 1, Wednesday. The band plays at the Sunset Ballroom at Clearfield, Pennsylvania.

May 6–8, Monday–Wednesday. The Weems band appears at Fort Wayne, Indiana.

May 19, Sunday (4:30–5:00 P.M.). Another *Beat The Band* show is broadcast. This time the show comes from Marshaltown, Iowa, as a feature of the Tail Corn Exposition.

June 8–14, Saturday–Friday. The band plays at Cedar Point Hotel on Lake Erie, Sandusky, Ohio.

June 30, Sunday (5:30–6:00 P.M.). Another *Beat the Band* show is broadcast. The program originates from the Meadowbrook Country Club, St. Louis. The first tune is "Manhattan Moon and You."

July 9, Tuesday. The band performs at Lakeside Park, Denver.

July 14, Sunday (5:30–6:00 P.M.). Another *Beat the Band* show is broadcast. The program originates from El Patio Ballroom, Lakeside Park, Denver. The first tune is "It Seems Like a Month of Sundays."

July 28, Sunday (5:30–6:00 P.M.). Another *Beat the Band* show is broadcast. The program originates from the Hotel Mayflower, Akron, Ohio. The first tune is "Toot That Trumpet." Perry sings "It's a Lovely Day Tomorrow."

August 6, Tuesday. The band puts on a show at Turnpike, Lincoln, Nebraska, which includes a reproduction of the *Beat the Band* show with audience participation.

October (undated). The Weems aggregation plays a short season at the Edgewater Beach hotel in Chicago.

October 13, Sunday (5:30–6:00 P.M.). Another *Beat the Band* show is broadcast. Ted Weems and the orchestra play at the Armory in Gary, Indiana.

October 16, Wednesday. All men aged 21 to 36 years of age are required to register for the draft.

November 20, Wednesday. The band plays at the Foundation Ball, University of Minnesota, Minneapolis.

1941

January 1, Wednesday. A dispute by the National Broadcasters' Association with ASCAP over royalties begins and removes the incentive for recording as radio networks are not licensed to play ASCAP material. When ASCAP announced it was going to hold back on a new license for 1941, the radio networks simply announced the formation of their own organization—BMI, Broadcasting Music Inc., which would look after the work of people who were not ASCAP members. As a result the Weems band can only play BMI tunes on the radio but can still play ASCAP songs in the theatre. The dispute lasts until October.

January 5, Sunday. Weems presents a matinee stage show at the Riverside Theatre in Milwaukee (5:30–6:00 P.M.). Another *Beat the Band* show is broadcast. The program originates from the Wisconsin Roof Ballroom, Milwaukee, Wisconsin.

January 27–28, Monday–Tuesday. In New York, Perry records three songs with the Ted Weems Orchestra.

February 2, Sunday (5:30–6:00 P.M.). Another *Beat the Band* show is broadcast. The Weems band is thought to be in Columbus, Ohio.

February 13, Thursday. The Weems band plays at the Kiwanis Youth Lodge charity dance at Lincoln Field House in Wisconsin Rapids. During the evening, Weems and Perry are interviewed in a special broadcast over station WFHR and later the band is heard over the air waves directly from the dance.

February 20, Thursday. The band plays at Danceland, Coe College, Cosmos, Iowa.

February 23, Sunday (6:30–7:00 P.M.). The final *Beat the Band* radio show with the Ted Weems orchestra is broadcast. The ASCAP ban is making it difficult for the program to continue.

February 25–September. The Weems band tours and among the venues played are the Coliseum, Oelwein, Iowa; the Crystal Palace in Michigan; the Roosevelt Hotel in New Orleans; the Shubert Theater, Cincinnati; the Radio Center, Huntington, Charleston, West Virginia; the Sikeston Armory, Sikeston, Missouri; El Patio Ballroom, Lakeside Park, Denver; the Peabody in Memphis; Hollywood Park, Calvary, Wisconsin; the Minnesota State Fair in St. Paul; the State Theatre in Uniontown, Pennsylvania; the Cedar Point Hotel on Lake Erie, Sandusky, Ohio; and the Shubert Theater, Cincinnati.

September 28, Sunday. The band plays at Sweet's Dancery in Oakland, California.

December 9, Tuesday. Another recording session with Ted Weems, this time in Los Angeles. Perry's version of 'Deep in the Heart of Texas' enjoys a modest chart success.

1942

January 6, Tuesday. Ted Weems brings his orchestra to the Liberty Theatre in Warren, Pennsylvania, for afternoon and evening performances.

February (undated). Universal Pictures release a 20-minute film short called *Swing Frolic* which features the Weems band.

February 7, Saturday. Ted Weems and his orchestra are performing at the Palace in Fort Wayne.

April 2, Thursday. The band plays a one-night engagement at a theater in Uniontown, Pennsylvania. After the show, they ride a West Penn Railways Company trolley to Connellsville where they catch a train for Cleveland.

April (undated). The band is thought to have played a short season at the Blackhawk in Chicago.

April 21, Tuesday. Ted Weems and his orchestra are at the Sheboygan Theatre, Wisconsin, for one day only.

May 26, Tuesday. The band plays one night at the Oasis in Valparaiso, Indiana.

September (undated). Frank Sinatra is released from his contract with Tommy Dorsey to begin his solo career.

October 20, Tuesday (6:30 P.M.). The band broadcasts from Camp Claiborne, Alexandria, Iowa, on the NBC-Blue network. The program is sponsored by the Coca Cola company.

December 1, Tuesday. Ted Weems announces that the band's current engagement in Memphis, which finishes on December 3, will be their last for the duration of the war. He and most of the band will be joining the Merchant Marine and will be stationed at Merchant Marine Basic Training School at San Mateo Point on December 20. Perry decides to await being drafted and as a married man with a child, he is some way down the priority list.

December 13, Sunday (7:30–8:00 P.M.). The Weems band appears on the Fitch *Bandwagon* show on NBC and makes its farewells to the public.

December 24, Thursday. Perry spends Christmas Eve in Chicago alone. He later describes it as the worst Christmas Eve he had ever spent.

December 30, Wednesday. Frank Sinatra makes his first solo appearance at the Paramount in New York alongside the premiere of the film Star Spangled Rhythm. The era of the bobbysoxers begins.

1943

Perry decides to return to Canonsburg, his family, and his barbering. Before he has time to resume his business, however, Tommy Rockwell of the Rockwell-O'Keefe Agency (who had been managing the Weems band) contacts him. Como accepts his offer after receiving assurances that he will be able to live in one place (in this case, New York) for a length of time.

March 12, Friday (6:45–7:00 P.M.). Perry is featured in a CBS radio program.

March 27, Saturday (6:45–7:00 P.M.). Perry is featured in a CBS program *Perry Como Gives the Song*.

April 4 (week beginning). Perry takes part in a *Treasury Star Parade* broadcast (Program #177) called "The Music of Irving Berlin." This is in support of the Second War Loan and the program has been transcribed in advance.

April 12, Monday (4:30–4:45 P.M.). Perry begins a regular series of broadcasts following the news at 4:30 P.M. on the CBS network called *Columbia Presents Perry Como*. This commences on a sustaining basis (i.e. without a sponsor) and is heard each day from Monday to Friday until August. He is supported by the Raymond Scott orchestra which includes Tony Mottola on guitar. The announcer is Warren Sweeney. The theme song is "For a Little While." The show is heard on the West Coast at 1:30 P.M.

June 10–August 19. Perry opens at the Copacabana night club in New York for what was intended to be a 2-week engagement but which is substantially extended due to his success at the venue. Although he is advertised to appear at the Copacabana until August, it is probable that he had to restrict his later appearances to the 2 A.M. show because of his other commitments.

June 17, Thursday. After listening to a demo submitted by Tommy Rockwell, RCA Victor offer Perry a recording contract and he signs for them on this date.

June 20, Sunday (11:30 A.M.–11:45 P.M.). Records three songs at RCA Victor Studio 2, New York City. The American Federation of Musicians (AFM) has imposed a recording ban and Perry's singing is supported by a mixed vocal chorus only. One song, "Goodbye Sue," backed with "There'll Soon Be a Rainbow," enjoys some success reaching No. 18 in the Billboard listings.

July 23–August 26, Friday–Thursday. Appears at the Strand Theatre at Broadway at 47th Street with Carmen Cavallaro and Connie Haines as part of a cine-variety show. He is described in the advertising as "The new CBS singing sensation."

July 29, Thursday. It is announced that Perry has signed a term contract with 20th Century–Fox calling for two pictures a year for seven years on an optional basis. If he works he will draw $1,010,000 for 108 weeks' work. He starts at $25,000 per film and graduates up to $125,000 a movie.

August (undated). Perry's daily radio show is now broadcast Tuesdays to Fridays.

September 9–October 6. Entertains at the Copacabana night club again for some weeks. He and his wife and child live in a small apartment in Long Island City, Queens. After the 2:30 A.M. show at the Copacabana, he takes the subway home.

October. His radio show is now broadcast between 4:45 and 5 P.M. Tuesdays to Fridays on the East Coast and 1:45–2:00 P.M. on the West Coast.

November 24, Wednesday. *Variety* carries a note about a possible new radio program for Perry. He also had plans to appear at the Stanley Theatre in Pittsburgh but these are frustrated by problems with his dental work (which it is assumed was being undertaken in readiness for his movie career).

December 1, Wednesday. Records "Have I Stayed Away Too Long?" and "I've Had This Feeling Before" with a mixed chorus at RCA Victor Studio 2, New York City. The AFM recording ban is still in place. The songs make little impact.

December 10, Friday. Perry ends his current series of radio shows.

December 21–23, Tuesday–Thursday. Perry appears at the Palace Theater in Columbus with the Tony Pastor orchestra.

December 24–29, Friday–Wednesday. Perry and the Tony Pastor orchestra move on to the Palace Theater in Cleveland.

1944

January 9, Sunday (7:15–7:30 P.M.). Appears in *Columbia Presents Perry Como* on CBS radio. The show is broadcast through WABC in New York and continues until June 11.

January 18, Tuesday. Perry flies to Hollywood for screen tests.

February 3–March 16. Undertakes an engagement at the Versailles Club on East Fiftieth St. in New York.

February 8, Tuesday. Another recording session at the RCA Victor Studio in New York supported by only a mixed chorus. Perry sings "Long Ago (And Far Away)" and "I Love You." Both songs reach the hit parade.

February 13, Sunday. Takes part in the "Stars for Victory" show at the Waldorf-Astoria in support of the 4th War Loan. Glenn Miller and Xavier Cugat are also on the bill.

March 4, Saturday (7:30 P.M.). Helps launch the new *Music America Loves Best* series on the Blue

Network of NBC through station WJZ. He co-stars with Jeanette MacDonald. Jay Blackton leads the orchestra.

March 13, Monday (starting at 8 P.M.). Is one of the stars appearing in *Show of Shows* at Madison Square Garden for the Emergency Committee to Save the Jewish People of Europe. Others appearing are Gracie Fields, the Andrews Sisters, Milton Berle and Jerry Lester.

March 20, Monday. Perry reports to 20th Century–Fox in Hollywood to film *Something for the Boys*. The film stars Carmen Miranda, Michael O'Shea, Vivian Blaine and Phil Silvers. Perry plays a soldier and sings "I Wish We Didn't Have to Say Goodnight" and "In the Middle of Nowhere." The film is directed by Lewis Seiler.

April 5, Wednesday. Records a *Mail Call* broadcast. Meanwhile, *Variety* magazine mentions that Perry is now in Hollywood making a picture and that he has been classified 1-A for military service. He does not get called up however and it is assumed that he received a deferment as did others such as Roy Rogers.

June 27, Tuesday. Back in New York, Perry is in RCA Victor Studio 1 for yet another session with only a mixed vocal chorus in support. He records "Lili Marlene" and "First Class Private Mary Brown."

July 14–August 8, Friday–Wednesday. Perry stars at the Paramount Theatre in New York in a cine-variety show alongside the film *And the Angels Sing* starring Dorothy Lamour. He is reported to receive $4,000 per week for his services.

July 26, Wednesday. *Variety* suggests that Perry and Jackie Gleason are to be teamed together for films and radio.

July 31, Monday (11:30 P.M.–midnight). Perry guests on the premiere edition of *For the Record*, a radio program which was transcribed by NBC and was designed to be put on V-Disc for the forces overseas. He is described as "a sensational young baritone" and he goes on to sing "Goodbye Sue." Other featured artists are Benny Goodman and His V-Disc All-Stars, Carmen Miranda and Mildred Bailey.

August 4, Friday (10:30–11:00 P.M.). Guests on *The Stage Door Canteen* CBS radio program with Franchot Tone.

September 27–October 5, Wednesday–Tuesday. Appears at the Chicago Theater in Chicago.

October 17–19, Tuesday–Thursday. Appears at the Palace Theater in Columbus, Ohio. He is accompanied by the Clyde Lucas orchestra.

October 26–November 2, Friday–Thursday. Appears at the RKO Theater in Boston as part of a cine-variety presentation.

November 1, Wednesday. Perry's film *Something for the Boys* with Carmen Miranda, Michael O'Shea, Vivian Blaine and Phil Silvers is released.

Around that time, recalled Madaline Mazza, another Como niece in Canonsburg, Como's father went to the movies to see his son act in either "Something for the Boys" or "Doll Face"—she can't remember which.

"My grandfather saw Perry kiss the girl in the movie and he walked out. He said, 'Is that how he's making his money?' He just thought that was terrible. You see, Perry was married" [Jonathan D. Silver and Mark Belko, *Pittsburgh Post-Gazette*, May 13, 2001].

November 9–15, Thursday. Perry appears in a cine-variety presentation at the Palace Theater in Cleveland with the Clyde Lucas orchestra.

November 24–30, Friday–Thursday. Appears at the Capitol Theater in Washington, D.C.

December 1–3, Friday–Sunday. Appears at the State Theatre, Hartford, Connecticut.

December 8, Friday. Records three songs at RCA Victor Studio 1, New York City, with an orchestra conducted by Lew Martin. One song—"I Dream of You (More Than You Dream I Do)"—reaches the No. 10 spot in the charts.

December 11, Monday. Records "I'm Confessin' (That I Love You)" with an orchestra conducted by Lew Martin. This song also registers in the *Billboard* charts. Also on December 11, Perry begins his long association with the Liggett and Myers Tobacco Company and its *Chesterfield Supper Club* series on NBC Radio through station WEAF (7:00–7:15 P.M.). He is accompanied by vocalist Mary Ashworth and Ted Steele's orchestra. The show has to be repeated at 11 P.M. for the West Coast audiences. Perry and Mary Ashworth present the show on every week night until July 1945.

1945

March 27, Tuesday (9:00 A.M.–1:00 P.M.). Recording session at RCA Victor Studio 2, New York City with an orchestra conducted by Ted Steele. Perry sings three songs including "Temptation" which reaches No. 15 in the charts.

March 30, Friday. Perry has traveled to Durham, North Carolina, to sing with the Duke University Glee Club of 125 voices on the *Chesterfield Supper Club* show. *Variety* magazine points out that it is cheaper for Como to travel to Durham rather than transport the choral group to New York. It is possible that the connection has stemmed from Liggett and Myers' factories in the area. Perry forges links with Duke University that continue for virtually the rest of his life.

April 8, Sunday (3:30–4:00 P.M.). Guests on the *Music America Loves* program on NBC Radio with Beatrice Lillie and the Art Tatum Trio.

April 12, Thursday. 3:35 P.M. President Franklin Delano Roosevelt dies suddenly in Warm Springs at the age of sixty-three. Vice President Harry S Truman is sworn in as president at 7:09 P.M. During his radio show that evening, Perry is joined by the WAVE choral group "The Singing Platoon" which is conducted by Ray Charles, who later works with Perry for many years.

May 19, Saturday. Perry records "If I Loved You" and "I'm Gonna Love That Gal" with an orchestra led by Russ Case at Lottos Club. The first song is a hit and reaches the No. 3 spot in the charts.

July 3, Tuesday (1:30–4:45 P.M.). Another recording session with Russ Case at Lottos Club. Perry records "(Did You Ever Get) That Feeling in the Moonlight" with the Satisfiers and then "Till the End of Time." The song becomes Perry's first No. 1 hit and his first Gold record.

July 5, Thursday (9:00–10:00 P.M.). Perry guests on *The Kraft Music Hall* on NBC and sings "If I Loved You." The host is Edward Everett Horton and other guests are Les Tremayne and Hildegarde. Music is provided by Raymond Paige and his orchestra.

July 8, Sunday (12:10 A.M.). Perry's father, Pietro Como, dies of a heart attack at the age of 68 in the family home at 504 Giffen Avenue, Canonsburg. Perry flies to Canonsburg the same day. Pietro is said to be survived by his wife and seven children (Mrs. Bessie D'Emilio, Mrs. Josephine Campana, Mrs. Venzie Jakubetz [all of Canonsburg], Dominick [of Los Angeles], Perry [of New York], Pfc. Albert Como and S/Sgt Gene Como [both overseas]). There is also a brother, Falco Como [of 348 Euclid Avenue, Canonsburg] and a sister living in Italy.

July 10, Tuesday. Press reports state that Perry is unable to appear on the *Chesterfield Supper Club* show because of illness. Marion Hutton deputizes for him and Frank Sinatra is the guest. Perry was in fact attending the funeral of his father in Canonsburg. Services are held at the family home and then at the Greenside United Presbyterian Church. Pietro is buried in Oak Spring cemetery. Pietro was originally of the Roman Catholic faith but lapsed following an accident at work when he lost his sight in one eye.

July–August (undated). Films *Doll Face* for 20th Century–Fox in Hollywood with Vivian Blaine, Dennis O'Keefe and Carmen Miranda. Perry sings "Red Hot and Beautiful," "Here Comes Heaven Again," "Somebody's Walking in My Dream" and "(A Hubba-Hubba-Hubba) Dig You Later" in the film which is directed by Lewis Seiler.

October (various) (7:00–7:15 P.M.). Perry returns to host further *Chesterfield Supper Club* shows on October 1 and every week night on NBC Radio. He is accompanied by Lloyd Shaffer and his orchestra plus the Satisfiers. The show continues to be repeated at 11 P.M. for the West Coast audiences.

October 7, Sunday (5:00–6:00 P.M.). Perry appears in *Parade of Stars* on NBC Radio. The program is designed to give listeners a preview of the winter schedule on NBC and many other stars take part.

October 13, Saturday. Back in RCA Victor Studio 2 in New York City, Perry records "(A Hubba-Hubba-Hubba) Dig You Later" with the Satisfiers and Russ Case's orchestra. It is another top ten hit.

October 14, Sunday (3:30–4:00 P.M.). Perry guests on the Tommy Dorsey Matinee radio show on NBC.

October 17, Wednesday. Another recording session with Russ Case's orchestra. Three songs are laid down including "I'm Always Chasing Rainbows" which reaches No. 5 in the hit parade.

November 9, Friday. Perry and Frank Sinatra appear in a special program of entertainment at the Manhattan Center to benefit the Italian Relief Charities.

November 11, Sunday (10:00–11:00 P.M.). Perry appears in a radio show called *The Victory Bond Hour* on the Mutual Broadcasting System.

November 20, Tuesday. Frank Sinatra is unable to perform at the Paramount Theater because of laryngitis and Perry substitutes for him in the last three performances of the day.

December 11, Tuesday (7:00–7:15 P.M.). Jo Stafford joins the *Chesterfield Supper Club* team on NBC Radio. She hosts the show on Tuesdays and Thursdays each week with Perry hosting on Mondays, Wednesdays and Fridays. Perry broadcasts the show from the East Coast until April 1946 when he has to be in Hollywood to make a film.

December 16, Sunday (4:00–5:00 P.M.). Guests on *The Philco Radio Hall of Fame* on the ABC network with Paul Whiteman and his orchestra, Glenn Riggs (announcer), Martha Tilton and Judy Canova.

December 18, Tuesday (1:30–4:45 P.M.). Records "All Through the Day" and "Prisoner of Love"" in RCA Victor Studio 2 with Russ Case's orchestra. The latter song becomes Perry's second No. 1 hit.

December 30, Sunday. Perry and Jo Stafford are crowned King and Queen of the Lake Placid Winter Carnival in ceremonies conducted by Lowell Thomas in the Lake Placid Olympic Arena.

December 31, Monday (7:00–7:15 P.M.). Perry and Jo Stafford join forces to present the *Chesterfield Supper Club* show from the Lake Placid Olympic Arena in New York State. During the broadcast, *Metronome* magazine present Perry with their Outstanding Achievement Award in the popular singing class for 1945.

1946

January 11, Friday. Perry is named outstanding male vocalist of 1945 by *Picture News* magazine.

January 30, Wednesday. Perry is in Washington, D.C., to help the March of Dimes campaign which aims to fight polio.

February 16, Saturday. The Comos have recently bought a house and three acres of land on Long Island for $35,000. Press coverage is seen about Perry eventually wrangling a telephone at his new home. Subsequent comment suggests that he is finding it difficult to obtain furniture for the house because of post-war shortages.

February 21, Thursday (9:00–9:30 P.M.). Perry guests on *The Andre Kostelanetz Show* on CBS radio.

March 12, Tuesday. Recording session with Russ Case's orchestra in RCA Victor Studio 2 in New York. Perry sings "Little Man You've Had a Busy Day" (with the Satisfiers) and "More Than You Know."

March 14, Thursday. Another recording session. Songs recorded are "Kentucky Babe" and "A Garden in the Rain" (with the Satisfiers).

March 19, Tuesday. Records "Blue Skies" and "My Blue Heaven" with the Russ Case Orchestra. The second song is not released.

March 21, Thursday. Another session in RCA Studio 2 with Russ Case at which three tracks are recorded.

March 30, Saturday. Perry's recording of "Prisoner of Love" enters the *Billboard* charts on its way to the No. 1 position.

April 2, Tuesday. Perry records "Surrender" and "They Say It's Wonderful" with the Russ Case orchestra.

April 5, Friday (7:00–7:15 P.M.). Perry hosts the *Chesterfield Supper Club* show on NBC Radio. The guests are Jo Stafford and the Art Van Damme Quintet. The show is broadcast from a TWA Constellation airplane 20,000 feet above New York City and has to be repeated for the West Coast audiences at 11 P.M.

April 6, Saturday. Flies to Hollywood to make his next film which is provisionally called *That's For Me*. The title changes to *If I'm Lucky* in due course. Continues his radio work but switches to Tuesdays and Thursdays. Roselle and son Ronnie are with him and Bing Crosby helps enroll the son in St. John's Parochial School in Hollywood which Bing's children attend.

April 8–June. Films *If I'm Lucky* for 20th Century–Fox in Hollywood. Perry has a starring role as a vocalist in Harry James' band who is maneuvered into politics by a conniving manager. The film also stars Vivian Blaine, Phil Silvers, Harry James and Carmen Miranda. Lewis Seiler is the director.

April 9, Tuesday (4:00–4:15 P.M.). Perry hosts the *Chesterfield Supper Club* show on NBC Radio from Hollywood. The show has to be repeated at 7 P.M. for the West Coast audiences. He is accompanied by Lloyd Shaffer and his orchestra. Paula Kelly and the Modernaires are regulars on the show while it is broadcast from Hollywood.

April 14, Sunday (starting at 8:30 P.M.). Perry appears in *A Night of Stars* in the Civic Auditorium, San Francisco, with Kay Kyser, Ella Mae Morse, Ish Kabibble, Lena Horne and Sonny Tufts (m.c.).

April 19, Friday. Takes part in the radio "Cancer Drive Program" with Bob Hope, Ginny Simms, Frank Sinatra, and Bing Crosby.

April 23, Tuesday. It is announced that Perry and Roselle have "adopted" a nine year old Belgian war orphan whose parents were mown down by a Nazi machine gun. This was not a formal adoption.

May 24, Friday. Press reports state that Perry is on the mend after an operation to remove an infected cyst which threatened the sight of his left eye. He has to miss three days of shooting of *If I'm Lucky*. Earlier reports had indicated that he was allergic to the hot lights in the film studio and that he was receiving antibiotic shots to counter the problem.

June 7, Friday. Press reports indicate that Perry is again having eye problems with the hot lights in the film studio and is once more receiving antibiotic shots.

June 14, Friday. RCA Victor announces that they have signed Perry for another five years.

June 24, Monday (7:00–7:15 P.M.). Back in New York, Perry reverts to a Monday-Wednesday-Friday pattern of hosting the *Chesterfield Supper Club* show on NBC Radio. He is accompanied by Lloyd Shaffer and his orchestra. Jo Stafford goes back to presenting the shows on Tuesday and Thursdays. The show has to be repeated at 10 P.M. for the West Coast audiences.

July 15, Monday. In New York, Perry records two songs from *If I'm Lucky*, the title song and "One More Vote." He is again accompanied by the Russ Case orchestra. He is still having problems with his eye.

August 1, Thursday. Commences recording sessions for an RCA Victor Musical Smart Set to be called *Perry Como Sings Merry Christmas Music*.

August (undated). Perry buys into the Santly-Joy music publishing firm.

September 2, Monday. This week is designated as Perry Como Week by record shops all over the United States. The film *If I'm Lucky* is released.

September 8, Sunday. Perry gives two shows in the New Haven Arena. He is accompanied by Lloyd Shaffer and his orchestra. He receives $10,000 for his services. This is one of the highest fees paid for such an event.

September 14, Saturday. Perry is in Canonsburg to see the name of Third Street changed to Perry Como Avenue. He is honored at a testimonial banquet at the State Armory in Canonsburg.

October 1, Tuesday. Guests on *The American Veterans Committee Salutes Al Jolson* with Al Jolson himself, Bob Hope, Dinah Shore, Frank Sinatra, Eddie Cantor, George Jessel, Hildegarde, George Burns, Gracie Allen and Martha Raye. The program originates from Hollywood while the banquet in honor of Jolson originates from New York. Perry (in New York) mentions this tribute as being on the ABC net although it was on Mutual.

October 17, Thursday. Perry records "That's the Beginning of the End" and "Sonata" in New York with backing from the Lloyd Shaffer orchestra. "Sonata" reaches the No. 9 position in the charts.

November 12, Tuesday. Perry appears at the United Jewish Appeal at Madison Square Garden with others such as Mickey Rooney, Milton Berle, Kate Smith and Sophie Tucker.

December 12, Thursday. Another recording session with Lloyd Shaffer. The songs recorded are "What Am I Gonna Do About You?" and "I Gotta Gal I Love (In North and South Dakota)."

December 19, Thursday. In RCA Victor Studio 2 in New York City, Perry records "That's Where I Came In" and "I Want to Thank Your Folks" with the orchestra conducted by Lloyd Shaffer.

Despite the competition of Sinatra, Bing Crosby and Dick Haymes, Como holds a high place in popularity polls. In *Billboard*'s first annual music-record poll (1946) Como's recording of "Prisoner of Love" proved to have made the most sales in that year and Como himself was voted the "top selling" male singer. He was also third in *Billboard*'s 1945 GI poll of favorites among male singers. In the annual poll by *Down Beat*, Frank Sinatra is voted top male singer of 1946. Bing Crosby is second with Perry third.

1947

Perry continues to host *Chesterfield Supper Club* shows on NBC Radio. He is accompanied by Lloyd Shaffer and his orchestra, Helen Carroll and the Satisfiers.

April 10, Thursday. Perry records "Chi-Baba, Chi-Baba (My Bambino Go to Sleep)" and "When You Were Sweet Sixteen" accompanied by an orchestra conducted by Lloyd Shaffer with the Satisfiers.

May 29, Thursday. Another recording session at RCA Victor Studio 2, New York City. Perry sings "When Tonight Is Just a Memory" and "I Wonder Who's Kissing Her Now." Lloyd Shaffer's orchestra and Helen Carroll and the Satisfiers provide the backing.

June 10–July 3, Tuesday–Thursday. Stars at the New York Paramount alongside the film *Dear Ruth* featuring William Holden and Joan Caulfield. He is supported by the Lloyd Shaffer orchestra plus Helen Carroll and the Satisfiers.

July 17–23, Thursday–Wednesday. Perry performs at the Palace Theatre in Cleveland for a week.

July 27–August 2, Sunday–Saturday. Perry's tour brings him to the Boston Theatre in Boston for a week.

July 28, Monday. Another recording session at the RCA Victor Studio in New York with the Russ Case orchestra. Perry sings "So Far" and "A Fellow Needs a Girl."

August 2, Saturday. Perry's 1939 recording of "I Wonder Who's Kissing Her Now" with the Ted Weems orchestra enters the charts and eventually reaches the No. 2 spot.

August 7–10, Thursday–Sunday. Appears at the Steel Pier in Atlantic City giving 22 performances in the short time he is there.

August 15–21, Friday–Thursday. Stars at the Chicago Theater in Chicago alongside the film *Cynthia*.

August (undated). Signs a non-cancellable 24-month contract with Chesterfield.

August 26–31, Tuesday–Sunday. Undertakes a singing engagement at the Meadowbrook club in Cedar Grove, New Jersey, with Sam Donahue and his orchestra.

September (various dates) (7:00–7:15 P.M.). Perry returns to host further *Chesterfield Supper Club* shows on NBC Radio until June 1948. He is accompanied by Lloyd Shaffer and his orchestra plus Helen Carroll and the Satisfiers.

September 25, Thursday. Back in the recording studio, Perry records three songs with Russ Case and his orchestra.

October 28, Tuesday. Perry sings at the *Cavalcade of Stars* event at Madison Square Garden together with Frank Sinatra, Vaughn Monroe and Buddy Clark among others. The show is a benefit for the Musicians Emergency Fund.

Perry starts a more intensive recording schedule as a strike of the Petrillo-led American Federation of Musicians is scheduled for January 1.

November 4, Tuesday (11 A.M.). Perry guests on *The Arthur Godfrey Show* on NBC Radio.

November 17, Monday. Perry appears at the United Jewish Appeal's 14th annual *Night of Stars* benefit show at Madison Square Garden.

Actor Adolphe Menjou (left) guests on Perry's radio show in the late '40s (courtesy Colleen Zwack).

December (undated). Perry guests on the *Jubilee* radio program with the Duke Ellington orchestra, Art Tatum and Louis Armstrong.

December 29, Monday, starting at midnight. Perry guests on *The Duke Ellington Show* on station WMCA. This is the premiere of the series and others taking part include Tommy Dorsey, Lena Horne and Vaughn Monroe.

1948

January (various dates) (7:00–7:15 P.M.). Perry hosts further *Chesterfield Supper Club* shows on NBC Radio. The show continues to be repeated for the West Coast audiences at 11 P.M. Perry misses one broadcast in early January when he is trapped at the Port Washington railroad station by heavy snowstorms. Mel Torme deputizes for him.

January 24, Saturday. Press reports indicate that Perry has suffered a broken rib after slipping on the ice in front of his Long Island home. It is not known whether he missed any shows.

April–July 14. Films *Words and Music* at MGM in Hollywood. Perry records six songs for the soundtrack with Allyn McLerie and chorus but three of them are not used. He continues with his radio broadcasts but switches to Tuesdays and Thursdays. Jo Stafford takes over Perry's rota. Perry pays all of the expenses involved in bringing the orchestra and cast of the show to Hollywood with him.

May (undated). Perry terminates his contract with 20th Century–Fox.

May 11, Tuesday (7:00–7:30 P.M.). Perry is a guest on the *Bob Hope Show* on NBC radio with Dean Cromwell and Virginia Maxey. Les Brown & His Band of Renown provides the music.

Left to right: Orchestra leader Lloyd Shaffer, Perry, Lizabeth Scott and Ben Grauer at the *Supper Club* (courtesy Colleen Zwack).

June (undated). The Comos adopt an 11-month-old baby girl.

June 3, Thursday (5:00–5:15 P.M.). Hosts his last *Chesterfield Supper Club* show on NBC Radio before his summer break. Sammy Kaye takes over.

September 27, Monday (7:00–7:15 P.M.). Perry returns to host the *Chesterfield Supper Club* show on NBC Radio on his old Monday-Wednesday-Friday rota with his new singing trio, the Fontane Sisters (Bea, Geri and Margi Rosse from New Milford, New Jersey), and a new orchestra leader called Mitchell Ayres. Martin Block returns as announcer. The show has to be repeated at 11 P.M. for the West Coast audiences. Jo Stafford takes the Tuesday shows again and Peggy Lee and Dave Barbour come in on Thursdays.

November 15, Monday. Perry is one of many stars appearing in the United Jewish Appeal's fifteenth annual *Night of Stars* benefit show at Madison Square Garden. Others performing include Milton Berle, Connee Boswell, Vic Damone and Marlene Dietrich.

December 2, Thursday. Back in RCA Victor Studio 2 in New York City, Perry records "N'yot N'yow (The Pussycat Song)" with the Fontane Sisters. The AFM strike is still preventing musicians' working in the recording studio.

December 14, Tuesday (3:00–6:00 P.M., 7:30–10:00 P.M.). The AFM strike has finally ended and Perry records two songs—"Far Away Places" and "Missouri Waltz"—with a chorus and orchestra conducted by Henri René. The first song reaches the No. 4 position in the charts.

December 24, Friday (7:00–7:15 P.M.). Perry's *Chesterfield Supper Club* show begins an experimental 3-week run on NBC-TV.

1949

January 7, Friday (7:00–7:15 P.M.). Perry hosts a further *Chesterfield Supper Club* show on NBC-TV. It is decided to televise the show at the later time of 11 P.M. from now on as this doubles up with the later radio broadcast for the West Coast. The show is basically a simulcast of Perry's popular radio show and makes few concessions to the new medium. Cameras are simply brought into the radio studio and Como and his guests are seen in front of a radio microphone, with scripts and music stands in full view. In succeeding months this is gradually modified, with simple backdrops and props being added. The basic format remains Perry's easygoing crooning, often of his latest hit record, with interludes by regulars the Fontane Sisters and assorted guest stars.

March 19, Saturday. Perry's recording of "Forever and Ever" enters the charts and eventually reaches the No. 2 spot.

April 9, Saturday. Perry's recording of "'A' You're Adorable" enters the *Billboard* charts on its way to the No. 1 position.

April 30, Saturday. Perry's recording of "Some Enchanted Evening" enters the *Billboard* charts on its way to the No. 1 position.

June 10, Friday (7:00–7:15 P.M.). Perry's final *Chesterfield Supper Club* shows of the season on NBC Radio and NBC-TV. Bill Lawrence takes over his time slot during the summer.

September 8, Thursday (10:00–10:30 P.M.). The *Chesterfield Supper Club* show becomes a half-hour weekly program on NBC Radio. Perry is supported by the Mitchell Ayres orchestra and the Fontane Sisters. The guests are Jane Powell and Rudy Vallee. The show is now recorded in advance. It continues until June 1, 1950.

October 8, Saturday. Perry's recording of "A Dreamer's Holiday" enters the charts and eventually reaches the No. 3 spot.

October 16, Sunday (8:00–8:30 P.M.). Perry returns to NBC-TV to host the *Chesterfield Supper Club* show. This time it is a half-hour show on a weekly basis. Mitchell Ayres and his orchestra and the Fontane Sisters are also in support. The show is in direct competition with Ed Sullivan's *Toast of the Town* program and continues until June 11, 1950. West Coast audiences see the show two weeks later via Kinescope.

December 27, Tuesday (8:00–9:00 P.M.). Perry guests on the *Texaco Star Theatre* on NBC-TV. He closes the show by singing "The Lord's Prayer" and "Silent Night." Hank Ladd is the m.c. deputizing for Milton Berle.

During the year, Perry was seen in a 19-minute film short called *It's in the Groove*, which also featured Guy Lombardo and Ella Fitzgerald in a look at the recording industry.

Subsequent statistical analysis by Joel Whitburn indicates that Perry was the fifth most successful recording artist of the 1940s. Bing Crosby was in first place.

Perry and Roselle are thought to have adopted a three and a half year old boy named David during the year.

1950

January 26, Thursday (10:00–11:00 P.M.). Perry hosts a special extended edition of the *Chesterfield Supper Club* on NBC Radio from the Duke Indoor Stadium in Durham, North Carolina. The guests are Bob Hope, Eddy Arnold and Arthur Godfrey. The show celebrates the opening of the new Chesterfield factory in Durham and the audience in the stadium is thought to number 8,000.

March 29, Wednesday. Attends the convention of the National Association of Tobacco Distributors in Chicago and guests on Bing Crosby's radio show for Chesterfield in the Civic Opera House with Arthur Godfrey. The show is taped and then broadcast on April 5 (7:00–8:00 P.M.). Perry appears on *Arthur Godfrey & Friends* on NBC-TV. Other guests are Bill Lawrence and the Chordettes.

June 1, Thursday (10:00–10:30 P.M.). The final *Chesterfield Supper Club* show of the season is aired on NBC Radio.

June 11, Sunday (8:00–8:30 P.M.). Perry's final *Chesterfield Supper Club* show for NBC-TV. He switches to CBS-TV starting on October 2 with the same sponsor. Press reports state that due to a throat affliction, Perry was unable to wind up his radio and TV series for NBC.

July 9, Sunday (8:00–9:00 P.M.). Perry is the guest host on *Toast of the Town* on CBS-TV. The guests are the Fontane Sisters, John Sebastian Sr., Toni Harper, Chris Nelson and Dick Buckley. Ray Bloch's orchestra provides the musical accompaniment.

July 16, Sunday. Perry is in Canonsburg and he presents a gift of $35,000 to the Canonsburg General Hospital Building Fund.

October 2, Monday (7:45–8:00 P.M.). Perry launches a new show on CBS-TV. This is a 15-minute show aptly titled *The Perry Como Show* following the CBS news on Mondays, Wednesdays and Fridays. It continues (with summer breaks) until June 24, 1955. The Fontane Sisters and the Ray Charles Singers are regulars on the show and Mitchell Ayres and his orchestra provide the musical backing. The announcer is Durward Kirby. Lee Cooley is the producer-director.

October 21, Saturday. Perry's recording with Betty Hutton of "A Bushel and a Peck" enters the charts and eventually reaches the No. 3 spot.

Perry and the Fontane Sisters take the Chesterfield advertising a step too far! (courtesy Colleen Zwack).

November 19, Sunday (6:00–7:30 P.M.). Perry is a guest on the NBC radio program *The Big Show* with Tallulah Bankhead, Eddie Cantor, Jimmy Durante, Bob Hope, Ray Middleton, Mindy Carson and Jose Ferrer. The show is broadcast from the Rockefeller Center Theatre in New York.

December 9, Saturday. Perry's recording of "You're Just in Love" enters the charts and eventually reaches the No. 5 spot.

1951

January 9, Tuesday (8:00–9:00 P.M.). Perry deputizes for Milton Berle as m.c. on the *Texaco Star Theatre* TV show on NBC. The guests are Bert Lahr, the Fontane Sisters and Louis Jordan.

January 13, Saturday. Perry's recording of "If" enters the *Billboard* charts on its way to the No. 1 position.

January 16, Tuesday (8:00–9:00 P.M.). Perry again deputizes for Milton Berle as m.c. on the *Texaco Star Theatre* TV show on NBC. The guest is Mindy Carson.

March 3, Saturday (8:00–8:30 P.M.). Perry guests on *Bulova Presents the Frank Sinatra Show* on CBS-TV with Frankie Laine and June Hutton. The Andrews Sisters make a walk-on appearance to confront Sinatra, Como and Laine, who are imitating them. Axel Stordahl directs the orchestra.

May 7, Monday. The Academy of Radio and Television Arts and Sciences awards Perry a "Michael" as best male vocalist.

June 29, Friday (7:45–8:00 P.M.). *The Perry Como Show* on CBS-TV is the last before Perry's summer break.

June 2–3, Saturday–Sunday. Plays in the National Celebrities Golf Tournament at the Army-Navy Country Club in Washington, D.C. Dagmar acts as his caddy. Perry has rounds of 86 and 81 for a total of 167 which puts him in fourth position in the Celebrities Division. Others taking part include Tony Martin, Gordon MacRae and Don Ameche.

August 27, Monday (7:45–8:00 P.M.). Returns to his TV show on CBS with the Fontane Sisters, the Ray Charles Singers and the Mitchell Ayres Orchestra. Dick Stark is the announcer and the producer is Lee Cooley. There are now 13 million homes with a TV set in the United States.

October 6, Saturday. Perry sings the National Anthem before the World Series game between the New York Giants and the New York Yankees at the Polo Grounds, New York.

October 9, Tuesday (8:00–9:00 P.M.). Perry guests on *The Frank Sinatra Show* on CBS-TV with Frankie Laine, the Andrews Sisters and Broderick Crawford. Axel Stordahl directs the orchestra.

October (undated). Perry films a cameo appearance in *The Fifth Freedom*, an advertising film made by Chesterfield Cigarettes, and sings "Bless This House." Bing Crosby, Bob Hope and Arthur Godfrey have short spots in the film too.

1952

February 17, Sunday. Perry flies to Boston to be present at ceremonies in which Archbishop Cushing dedicates the Perry Como Gymnasium in the Christopher Columbus Youth Center. Perry helped raise the money to build the center. Later, Perry performs in a charity show at the Boston Opera House.

March 4/11/13. Records his first 10" LP Album *TV Favorites* during three sessions at the Manhattan Center, New York City, with Mitchell Ayres' orchestra and chorus. Sally Sweetland joins Perry for "Over the Rainbow" and "Summertime."

April 30, Wednesday. Perry hosts a special show for the Chesterfield employees at Duke Indoor Stadium, Durham, with guests Edgar Bergen and Peggy Lee. The Fontane Sisters and the Mitchell Ayres orchestra also take part. Rosemary Clooney and Eddie Fisher with the Russ Case orchestra deputize for Perry on his TV show.

May 5, Monday. The Academy of Radio and Television Arts and Sciences awards Perry his second "Michael" as best male vocalist.

May 13, Tuesday. Records "Watermelon Weather" and "Maybe" with Eddie Fisher at the Manhattan Center. As usual, the musical backing is provided by Mitchell Ayres and his orchestra. "Maybe" reaches the No. 3 spot in the charts.

July 11, Friday (7:45–8:00 P.M.). Perry makes his last appearance on his TV show for six weeks.

August 25, Monday (7:45–8:00 P.M.). Returns to his TV show on CBS with the Fontane Sisters, the Ray Charles Singers and the Mitchell Ayres Orchestra. Dick Stark is the announcer and the producer is Lee Cooley. Ib Melchior is the director.

September 13, Saturday. Perry is made a Knight Commander of the Holy Sepulchre at St. Patrick's Cathedral in New York. Others honored at the same ceremony are Bishop Fulton Sheen, William Gargan, U.S. Attorney General James P. McGranery and John T. Grealis. The ceremony is conducted by Cardinal Spellman.

December 6, Saturday. Perry's recording of "Don't Let the Stars Get in Your Eyes" enters the *Billboard* charts on its way to the No. 1 position. It also reaches the top spot in the U.K.

1953

January 10, Saturday (7:00–7:30 P.M.). A party is thrown for Perry at the Stork Club and the proceedings are televised on CBS-TV. Guests include the Fontane Sisters, Teresa Brewer, Buddy Hackett and Terry Snyder. Sherman Billingsley is the host.

February 14, Saturday (8:00–9:00 P.M.). Stars in the NBC-TV program *All-Star Revue*. The guests include Joan Blondell, Patti Page and Ben Blue.

April 4, Saturday. Perry's recording of "Say You're Mine Again" enters the charts and eventually reaches the No. 3 spot.

April 17, Friday. Perry is in Durham, North Carolina, to entertain the local merchants.

June 16, Tuesday. Perry receives the Interfaith Award at the Interfaith Night Parade at Baltimore's Memorial Stadium. This is awarded for "his unselfish devotion, his humanitarian endeavors and wholehearted service in the advancement of the principles of Interfaith." A crowd of 25,000 watches the proceedings. Earlier in the day at a luncheon with the acting mayor, he receives the key to the city before going on to a cocktail reception for record dealers and disk jockeys.

July 3, Friday (7:45–8:00 P.M.). Perry's last TV show until the end of August. Helen O'Connell and Bob Eberly take over his spot.

July 4, Saturday. *Billboard* magazine devotes a special section to Perry to celebrate his tenth anniversary as an RCA Victor recording artist.

August 24, Monday (7:45–8:00 P.M.). Returns to his TV show on CBS. The show is said to become the first radio–TV simulcast as the audio is broadcast through the Mutual network. In fact, a similar

U.S. Open Golf Champion Ben Hogan (right) was a Como TV guest during 1953 (courtesy Colleen Zwack).

practice had been followed in 1948 with the NBC show but this is the first time that the audio and video are split between networks. Chesterfield continues to sponsor the show. Dick Stark is the announcer; Mitchell Ayres and his orchestra, the Fontane Sisters and the Ray Charles Singers are in support. Lee Cooley continues as producer, Ib Melchior as director.

December 13, Sunday (8:00–9:00 P.M.). Perry is the guest host on *The Colgate Comedy Hour* on NBC-TV. Other guests are Martha Raye, Ben Blue and the Fontane Sisters.

1954

June (various dates) (7:45–8:00 P.M.). *The Perry Como Show* on CBS-TV closes the season with an 11.9 Nielsen rating which beats other 15-minute shows such as Eddie Fisher (rating 9) and Dinah Shore (rating 8.7). The Ray Anthony orchestra takes over Perry's time slot for the summer. The Fontane Sisters do not return to the show in August.

July 23, Friday. Perry headlines *Star Night* at a Detroit venue. Other stars taking part include Nat King Cole, Patti Page, Ray Anthony, Julius La Rosa, the Four Lads and Sarah Vaughan.

July 24, Saturday. Perry headlines *Star Night* at Soldier Field in Chicago. The crowd is put at 40,000.

July 25, Sunday. Perry headlines *Star Night* in the Municipal Stadium in Cleveland. He receives $30,000 for his three nights' work.

August 23, Monday (7:45–8:00 P.M.). Returns to his CBS-TV show. Chesterfield continues as sponsor. Mitchell Ayres and the orchestra and the Ray Charles Singers provide support. Lee Cooley is producer-director. Dick Stark continues as announcer. West Coast viewers see the show a week later.

September 29, Wednesday. Perry sings "The Star Spangled Banner" at the first game in the World Series between the Cleveland Indians and the New York Giants at the Polo Grounds.

October 2, Saturday. Perry's recording of "Papa Loves Mambo" enters the charts and eventually reaches the No. 4 spot.

1955

January 20, Thursday. Commences recording sessions for a new album called *So Smooth* at Webster Hall. He is supported by the Mitchell Ayres orchestra and the Ray Charles Singers.

January 30, Sunday (7:30–9:00 P.M.). Guests on *Max Liebman Presents "Variety"* with Kitty Kallen and Buddy Hackett in color on NBC-TV. Perry is paid $25,000 for his 15-minute appearance. One of the songs he sings is "Peace of Mind" which is published by his own sheet music company.

March 7, Monday. Perry wins the Emmy for best male singer. He is not present at the awards ceremony as he is holidaying in Palm Springs. Dinah Shore wins the Emmy for best female singer.

March 31, Thursday. Signs a 12-year contract with NBC-TV for a reported $15M. It is announced that he will leave CBS on July 1. This will also mark the end of his sponsorship by Chesterfield.

June 24, Friday (7:45–8:00 P.M.). The last *Perry Como Show* on CBS-TV. Roselle Como makes a walk-on appearance at the end. Chesterfield gives Perry all the musical arrangements used during their 11 year relationship as a parting gift. The show is produced and directed by Lee Cooley.

September 17, Saturday (8:00–9:00 P.M.). Perry hosts *The Perry Como Show* on NBC-TV from the Century Theater in New York at 58th and 7th. The guests include Julius La Rosa, Rosemary Clooney and Frankie Laine. Mitchell Ayres and his orchestra, the Ray Charles Singers, the Louis DaPron Dancers and Frank Gallop (announcer) provide support. The head writer is Goodman Ace who used to write for Milton Berle. Lee Cooley is the producer and Grey Lockwood is the director for most of the shows in the series. The reviews are good. The first show has six sponsors: Kleenex, Dormeyer, Gold Seal, Noxzema, Armour and Toni. The show occupies part of the same time slot as the top-rated Jackie Gleason program, *The Honeymooners*, which is transmitted from 8:30 to 9:00 P.M., and the shows compete for the Saturday night top rating throughout the season. It is said that the Como show has a weekly budget of $80,000 with $25,000 of this going to Perry.

November 2, Wednesday (8:30–9:00 P.M.). Guests on a special Oldsmobile NBC-TV show with Patti Page. The program highlights the '56 Oldsmobile models.

1956

January 17, Tuesday (8:00–9:00 P.M.). Guests on *The Chevy Show* with Dinah Shore, Gisele MacKenzie and Stubby Kaye. The director-producer is Bob Banner and the show is written and staged by Don McGuire.

February 2, Thursday. Recording session at Webster Hall, New York City, with Mitchell Ayres' orchestra and the Ray Charles Singers. Perry records "Juke Box Baby" and "Hot Diggity (Dog Ziggity Boom)." The latter song reaches the No. 1 position in the charts and in the U.K. it gets to the No. 4 spot.

February 18, Saturday (7:30–8:00 P.M.). Makes a guest appearance on the game show *The Big Surprise* on NBC-TV. Also, Perry hosts *The Perry Como Show* on NBC-TV (8:00–9:00 P.M.). The guests include the Platters, Henry Fonda, Vera Ellen, Ann Francis and Paul Winchell. Jackie Gleason switches his half-hour show from 8:30 to 8:00 P.M. to meet the competition from Perry.

March 17, Saturday (9:00–10:30 P.M.). The Emmy Awards ceremony is televised. Perry again wins the Emmy for best male singer. He also wins the Emmy for best M.C. or program host (male or female). His show is unsuccessfully nominated for best music series and best variety series.

April 10, Tuesday. Perry and Jackie Gleason share the prestigious Peabody Award for the best radio and TV programs of 1955. The awards have been given since 1940 and the awards program is administered by the University of Georgia. The awards are announced at a luncheon of the Radio and Television Executives Society of New York.

June 9, Saturday (8:00–9:00 P.M.). Perry hosts *The Perry Como Show* on NBC-TV. It is the last show of the season. During the 1955-56 season, the show is placed at 19th in the ratings with *The Honeymooners* in 20th position. The top show of the season was *The $64,000 Question*. There are now 34.9 million households with a TV in the United States.

June 18, Monday. Perry records a number of tracks for his forthcoming album "We Get Letters" at RCA Victor Studio 2 in New York City.

September 15, Saturday (8:00–9:00 P.M.). Perry hosts *The Perry Como Show* in color on NBC-TV. The show comes from the newly opened Ziegfeld Theater, New York, Manhattan, located on the southwest corner of 54th Street and 6th Avenue (or the Avenue of the Americas, as it is also known). Mitchell Ayres and his orchestra, the Ray Charles Singers and Frank Gallop continue in their usual roles. Each show has a budget of $108,000. Grey Lockwood continues as director with Bob Finkel coming in as producer. The writers are Goodman Ace, Jay Burton, Mort Green and George Foster.

October 5, Friday (8:30–9:00 P.M.). Perry guests on the Walter Winchell Show on NBC-TV and sings "Lullaby of Broadway" and "Moonlight Love." Other guests include Sammy Davis Jr., Lisa Kirk, Lola Fisher and Martha Raye.

November 18, Sunday. Guests on *The Bob Hope Chevy Show* on NBC-TV with Julie London, Steve Allen, Milton Berle and Joan Davis. Les Brown leads the orchestra.

December 30, Sunday (8:00–9:00 P.M.). Guests on *The Ed Sullivan Show* with Sid Caesar and Bishop Sheen as the *Look* magazine awards for 1956 are presented.

1957

January 13, Sunday (9:00–10:00 P.M.). Perry guests on *The Chevy Show* hosted by Dinah Shore on NBC-TV.

January 15, Tuesday (2:00–7:00 P.M.). Records "Round and Round" and two other songs with Mitchell Ayres' orchestra and the Ray Charles Singers at Webster Hall. Perry's recording of "Round and Round" reaches the No. 1 position in the charts.

June 8, Saturday (8:00–9:00 P.M.). Perry hosts the last *Perry Como Show* of the season on NBC-TV. During the season, Perry's show is placed 9th overall in the Nielsen ratings with *The Jackie Gleason Show* down at 29th place. The top show is *I Love Lucy*. There are 38.9 million homes with a TV set and on average 12.6 million tune in to Perry.

August 28. Joseph Tito, a salesman of religious candles, is sent to a mental hospital after making a telephone call threatening Perry's three children with death. Mrs. Como recognized his voice on the phone and called the police.

September 14, Saturday (8:00–9:00 P.M.). Perry returns to host *The Perry Como Show* on NBC-TV. It is stated that the producers will not pay more than $7500 for a guest star during the series. As always, this is a Roncom Productions show and it continues to be directed by Grey Lockwood and produced by Bob Finkel. The writers are Goodman Ace, Jay Burton, Mort Green and George Foster.

October 9, Wednesday. Records "Catch a Falling Star" at RCA Victor Studio A, 24th Street, New York. The song reaches the No. 1 position in the charts in the U.S. and the U.K.

December 3, Tuesday. Records "Magic Moments" at RCA Victor Studio A, 24th Street, New York. The song reaches No. 4 in the U.S. charts and hits the No. 1 spot in the U.K.

During the year, Perry was honored by the Friars' Club at their "Man of the Year" testimonial dinner in the Grand Ballroom of the Waldorf-Astoria.

1958

February 12, Wednesday. Commences recording sessions for his first stereophonic album, *Saturday Night with Mr. C*, at RCA Victor Studio A with Mitchell Ayres and the orchestra plus the Ray Charles Singers.

March 14, Friday. "Catch a Falling Star" is certified as a Gold record by the Recording Industry Association of America (RIAA). This is the first award made by the RIAA and signifies sales over 1 million.

April 15, Tuesday (10:00–11:30 P.M.). The annual Emmy Awards ceremony is televised. Perry has been nominated for an Emmy for best continuing performance (male) in a series but does not win.

April 30, Wednesday. The first recording session for a new concept album, *When You Come to the End of the Day*, with the Mitchell Ayres orchestra and the Ray Charles Singers.

June 7, Saturday (8:00–9:00 P.M.). Perry hosts his final *Perry Como Show* of the season on NBC-TV. Bob Crosby is Perry's summer replacement. During the 1957-58 season, Perry's show is placed at 11th in the ratings overall. The top show is *Gunsmoke*. There are now 41.9 million homes with a TV set in the United States.

July (undated). It is reported that Perry has leased office space at 405 Park Avenue for himself and for Roncom Productions, Inc.

July 10, Thursday. Perry and his wife plus their three children arrive in Rome, Italy, to a riotous welcome at the airport.

July 12, Saturday. Perry and his wife plus their three children have a special audience with Pope Pius XII in the Vatican City.

July–August. On holiday in Italy, although he does not visit Palena. Films a guest appearance on *Il Musichiere*, an Italian TV show, during his stay. Perry is interviewed by Mario Riva and Perry responds in Italian, albeit somewhat haltingly. He is given a guitar which he tunes and then sings "Oh, Marie," also in Italian. The show airs on September 14.

September 13, Saturday (8:00–9:00 P.M.). Perry returns to host *The Perry Como Show* on NBC-TV. Mitchell Ayres, Ray Charles and Frank Gallop continue in support. The series is produced by Roncom Productions, the director-producer is Clark Jones and the writers are Goodman Ace, Jay Burton, Mort Green and George Foster.

1959

January 16, Friday. Perry and Kim Novak visit Dwight D. Eisenhower, the President of the United States, at the White House in Washington. Perry presents the President with honorary membership of the Variety Clubs of America.

March 3, Tuesday (7:30–9:00 P.M.). Perry hosts the New York segment of *Some of Manie's Friends*, a tribute on NBC-TV to the late Manie Sachs of RCA Victor and latterly a vice president at NBC. Dinah Shore hosts the Hollywood portion of the show. Stars taking part include Nat King Cole, Rosemary Clooney, Eddie Fisher, Bob Hope, Harry James, Frank Sinatra, Kay Starr, Jane Wyman, Vaughn Monroe, Jack Webb, Sid Caesar and Tony Martin. Bob Finkel is the producer-director.

March 5, Thursday. Perry signs a television contract calling for $25 million over a two-year period. The deal, described as the biggest in the history of show business, gives the exclusive services of Perry to the Kraft Foods Co, for a total of 66 color TV shows on Kraft's Wednesday 9 to 10 P.M. hour. Under the terms of the contract, Perry's personal corporation, Roncom, Inc., will produce all of the shows out of the $25 million. That includes production costs and the hiring of guest stars. The amount of money that Como personally will get of out of the deal is not disclosed.

March 24, Tuesday (8:00–9:00 P.M.). Stars in the *Pontiac Star Parade* NBC-TV show titled "A Visit to Broadway." The show has been taped during the day. Perry drops in on a number of Broadway stars including Juanita Hall, Gertrude Molly Berg, Sir Cedric Hardwicke, Francis Nuyen, Cyril Ritchard and Claudette Colbert. Clark Jones is producer-director and the writers are Goodman Ace, Mort Green, George Foster and Jay Burton.

April 9, Thursday. Perry begins recording sessions for his *Como Swings* album at RCA Victor Studio A, 24th Street, New York City. Mitchell Ayres leads the orchestra.

June 6, Saturday (8:00–9:00 P.M.). Perry hosts *The Perry Como Show* on NBC-TV. This is the final show of the season. The guests include Tony Bennett, Teresa Brewer and the Four Lads. During the 1958-59 season, Perry's show is placed at 23rd in the ratings overall. The top show is again *Gunsmoke*.

July 13, Monday (10:00 A.M.–2:30 P.M.). Starts recording the *Season's Greetings from Perry Como* album at Webster Hall with Mitchell Ayres' orchestra and the Ray Charles Singers.

July 26, Sunday. Perry's mother is in Mercy Hospital, Pittsburgh, in a serious condition after an operation. Perry is at her bedside.

August 7, Friday. Mrs. Lucia Como, Perry's mother, has a leg amputated. She has been suffering from diabetes for many years. Perry is still at her bedside. On August 12, the limb which had been amputated is interred in the grave purchased for Mrs. Como's eventual use.

September 30, Wednesday (9:00–10:00 P.M.). Perry hosts the first of the weekly series *Perry Como's Kraft Music Hall* on NBC-TV. Clark Jones continues as producer-director. The writers are Herbert Baker with Billy Friedberg and Will Glickman.

November 29, Sunday. Appears in *Sunday Showcase* which features the First Annual Grammy Awards for 1958. Receives a Grammy for best vocal performance, male, for "Catch a Falling Star."

December 28, Monday (9:00 A.M.–1:30 P.M.). Records "Delaware" and other songs at Webster Hall. "Delaware" is a success in the U.K., reaching No. 3 in the charts, but can only manage a lowly 22nd spot in the U.S.

Subsequent statistical analysis by Joel Whitburn indicates that Perry was the second most successful recording artist of the 1950s. Elvis Presley was in first place.

1960

January 11–12, Monday–Tuesday. In Los Angeles, tapes a guest appearance on *The Bing Crosby Show* with Bing Crosby, the Crosby Brothers, Elaine Dunn, and Sandy Stewart. The show is transmitted by ABC-TV on February 29.

February 29, Monday (8:30–9:30 P.M.). The taped *Bing Crosby Show* is transmitted by ABC-TV with Perry Como as the principal guest. Vic Schoen is the music director and William O. Harbach is producer-director. The Trendex ratings go to an incredible thirty-three.

April 16, Saturday. Perry arrives at London Airport en route to tape a Kraft Music Hall show in London. Dee Belline accompanies him. After he has cleared customs, special arrangements are made to film Perry's apparent "arrival" in the BOAC maintenance area. He stays at the Dorchester during his time in London.

April 20, Wednesday. Perry and his crew are at Woburn Abbey where they film for 3 hours with the Duke of Bedford. The Duke decides to close Woburn to the public for the day, leading to adverse comments in the press.

April 23, Saturday. Perry tapes part of his Kraft show at the BBC's Shepherd's Bush studio. Eric Robinson conducts the orchestra and Mitchell Ayres acts as musical director. Ray Charles leads the Beryl Stott Singers (which are augmented by two Americans) and Yvonne Littlewood is the producer. Bill Cotton Jr. supervises the production.

June 1, Wednesday (9:00–10:00 P.M.). Hosts *Perry Como's Kraft Music Hall* on NBC-TV. This is the final show of the season. Perry introduces David McLean who will be filling part of Perry's time slot during the summer in a Western called *Tate*. Perry's company, Roncom Productions, has produced the shows which will fill his hour during his vacation. The other show is called *Happy* and is about the thoughts of a talking baby. During the 1959-60 season, Perry's show is placed at 29th in the ratings overall. The top show is again *Gunsmoke*.

October 5, Wednesday (9:00–10:00 P.M.). Returns to host *Perry Como's Kraft Music Hall* on NBC-TV. Goodman Ace returns as chief writer in a move to bolster the show's falling ratings. The show is taped in advance during the season, usually on the preceding Friday. Dwight Hemion is the director and Nick Vanoff is the producer. Mitchell Ayres continues as music director and Ray Charles as choral director. Ed Herlihy is the announcer.

October 9, Sunday (5:00 P.M.). The *Celebrity Golf* program features Perry playing Sam Snead over 9 holes at Lakeside Golf Club, Hollywood. Perry, with a handicap of 6, loses to Sam but wins $1750 for St. Francis Hospital because of the number of pars he achieves. Harry Von Zell is the host. Norman Z. McLeod is the director. The executive producer is Norman Blackburn.

October 22, Saturday (8:30–9:30 P.M.). Perry appears on *The Bob Hope Buick Show* on NBC-TV which is a political satire called "Potomac Madness" with Ginger Rogers. This is described as an original musical comedy for TV. Hope and Como play presidential candidates while Ginger Rogers plays the richest woman in the world, who hungers for governmental power. Jack Shea is the director.

October 25, Tuesday. Commences recording sessions for the album *For the Young At Heart* at Webster Hall. The album is produced by the team of Hugo & Luigi.

Perry checks his music, rehearsing for a "Sing to Me, Mr. C" medley (courtesy Colleen Zwack).

1961

April 9, Sunday. Kraft Foods complete arrangements with Perry for the continuation of his program for another year. The show is now seen over 154 stations on the NBC network.

April 21, Friday. Perry's mother, Lucia Como, dies at 3:10 P.M. at the age of 78 in her daughter's home in Canonsburg. She had been living with her daughter, Mrs. Steve Jakubetz, at 455 Woodland Rd. for several years. Lucia had been seriously ill for six months and was bedfast since suffering a heart attack five weeks before. She was a member of St. Patrick's Roman Catholic Church. She was survived by three daughters: Bessie, wife of Joseph D'Emilio; Josephine, wife of Guy Campana; and Venzie, wife of Steve Jakubetz, all of Canonsburg. There were four surviving sons: Perry; Dominick, of San Antonio, Texas; Albert of Hempstead, New York; and Gene of Moninger. Lucia had 27 grandchildren and 19 great-grandchildren. Perry hears the news while taping his TV show for the following Wednesday. He flies to Pittsburgh as soon as the taping is completed.

April 25, Tuesday. Perry's mother is buried at Oak Springs Cemetery in Canonsburg alongside her husband after a Solemn High Mass of Requiem in St. Patrick Roman Catholic Church.

May 3, Wednesday (9:00–10:00 P.M.). Andy Williams hosts *Perry Como's Kraft Music Hall* on NBC-TV in the absence of Perry who has been attending his mother's funeral. Perry gives Andy a new Jaguar convertible to thank him for stepping in at short notice.

May 15/17, Monday/Wednesday. Records his album *Sing to Me, Mr. C* with Mitchell Ayres' orchestra, Tony Mottola on guitar and the Ray Charles Singers at RCA Victor Studio A, 24th Street, New York City. This is another Hugo & Luigi production.

May 22, Monday. Tapes his Kraft show "live" at the Arie Crown Theatre, McCormick Place in Chicago where Perry is entertaining the National Restaurants Association.

June 7, Wednesday (9:00–10:00 P.M.). Hosts *Perry Como's Kraft Music Hall* on NBC-TV. This is the final show of the season. During the 1960-61 season, Perry's show is not in the top 30 shows for the first time since 1955-56. The top show is again *Gunsmoke.*

June (various). Tapes three *Perry Como's Kraft Music Hall* shows for use in the 1962-63 season.

June 28, Wednesday. In New York, Perry gives evidence for 28 minutes to the Federal Communications Commission investigation into bad programming. "All you have to do is flip the little dial and it's over," he tells the commission.

August 11, Friday. Ronald Como weds Melanie Adams at Sacred Heart Roman Catholic Church on the University of Notre Dame campus. It is reported that Ronald is a senior geology major and will be a Senator at Notre Dame next month. The bride was Miss Elkhart in state beauty pageants in 1960 and 1961. Perry is in attendance.

October 4, Wednesday (9:00–10:00 P.M.). Returns as host of *Perry Como's Kraft Music Hall* on NBC-TV. The series is produced by Roncom Productions; directed by Dwight Hemion; produced by Nick Vanoff; written by Goodman Ace, Selma Diamond, Jay Burton, Frank Peppiatt and John Aylesworth. Mitchell Ayres continues to lead the orchestra with the Ray Charles Singers and the Peter Gennaro Dancers as regulars.

1962

May 22, Tuesday (10:00–11:30 P.M.). Perry appears on the Emmy Awards program on NBC-TV. He has been nominated for an Emmy for outstanding performance in a variety or musical program but does not win.

June (undated). Perry signs to do another 33 shows for Kraft in the fall.

June 6, Wednesday (9:00–10:00 P.M.). Hosts *Perry Como's Kraft Music Hall* on NBC-TV. This is the last show of the season and as is customary, all of Perry's regular team star on the show. During the 1961-62 season, Perry's show is again not placed in the top 30 shows. The top show is *Wagon Train.*

June 8, 14, 21, 26. Records songs for an album *By Request* with Mitchell Ayres' orchestra and the Ray Charles Singers at Webster Hall. This is another Hugo & Luigi production.

September 30, Sunday. Perry commences recording songs from the new Irving Berlin Broadway show *Mr. President.* The facilities of Webster Hall in New York City are utilized with musical support from the Mitchell Ayres' orchestra and the Ray Charles Singers. Kaye Ballard and Sandy Stewart also record contributions for the album. Hugo & Luigi are the producers. (Note: The show *Mr. President* ran for 265 performances from Oct 20, 1962 through June 8, 1963, thanks mainly to its advance sales. It starred Nanette Fabray and Robert Ryan. It was savaged by the critics.)

October 3, Wednesday (9:00–10:00 P.M.). *Perry Como's Kraft Music Hall* is shown on NBC-TV. The regulars, namely Mitchell Ayres' orchestra, the Ray Charles Singers, Peter Gennaro and his dancers, plus the Music Hall Players (Don Adams, Sandy Stewart, Jack Duffy, Kaye Ballard) all continue and Pierre Olaf joins their ranks. The series is produced by Roncom Productions; directed by Dwight Hemion; produced by Nick Vanoff; written by Goodman Ace, Selma Diamond, Jay Burton, Frank Peppiatt and John Aylesworth.

November 22–25, Thursday–Sunday. The inaugural Perry Como Invitational Golf Tournament for Amateurs takes place at St. Lucie Country Club, Florida.

December 4, Tuesday. Perry and an 8-member troupe leave Idlewild Airport, New York, to fly to Cuba where they are going to entertain the troops at Guantánamo Naval Base.

December 5, Wednesday. Perry and his troupe put on ten shows for the troops at Guantánamo Naval Base who made up the front line in the recent Cuban crisis. Some of the performances are filmed and included in the next Music Hall show.

1963

March 12, Tuesday. The RIAA certifies Perry's album *Season's Greetings from Perry Como* as a Gold album. This recognizes $1 million in sales based on the manufacturer's wholesale price.

March 18, Monday. Commences recording songs for his album *The Songs I Love* with Mitchell Ayres' orchestra and the Ray Charles Singers at Webster Hall. Hugo & Luigi are the producers. This is their last album with Perry.

May 22, Wednesday (8:00–9:00 P.M.). *Perry Como's Kraft Music Hall* is broadcast live from Chicago where Perry is entertaining the National Restaurant Association Convention. The guests include Jimmy Durante and Jane Powell.

June 12, Wednesday (9:00–10:00 P.M.). *Perry Como's Kraft Music Hall* is shown on NBC-TV. The guests include Jane Magruder, and Perry's usual support staff is also featured. This is the last of Perry's weekly hour-long shows after eight years. During the 1962-63 season, Perry's show has not featured in the top 30 shows. The top show is *The Beverly Hillbillies.*

October 3, Thursday (10:00–11:00 P.M.). Hosts *Perry Como's Kraft Music Hall* live from Pittsburgh's Civic Arena, Pennsylvania. Mitchell Ayres and his orchestra and the Ray Charles Singers continue in support. Perry later says that his agreement to do these shows from various locations across the United States was not a wise decision in financial terms as he was bearing the cost and they proved more expensive than anticipated. The show is produced by Roncom Productions; directed by Dwight Hemion; produced by Marlo Lewis; written by Herb Sargent, Art Baer, Ben Joelson, Bill Angelos and Buz Kohan.

November 21, Thursday (10:00–11:00 P.M.). Hosts *Perry Como's Kraft Music Hall* live from San Francisco's War Memorial Opera House. The show is produced by Roncom Productions; directed by Dwight Hemion; produced by Marlo Lewis; written by Herb Sargent, Art Baer, Ben Joelson, Bill Joelson, Bill Angelos and Buz Kohan.

November 28–December 1, Thursday–Sunday. Hosts the Perry Como Amateur Invitational Golf Tournament at Port St. Lucie, Florida.

1964

January 23, Thursday. Hosts *Perry Como's Kraft Music Hall* from the State Fair Music Hall in Dallas, Texas.

February 13, Thursday (10:00–11:00 P.M.). Hosts *Perry Como's Kraft Music Hall* live from NBC Studio 4, Burbank, California.

March 5, Thursday (10:00–11:00 P.M.). Hosts *Perry Como's Kraft Music Hall* live from the Municipal Auditorium in New Orleans.

April 9, Thursday (10:00–11:00 P.M.). Hosts *Perry Como's Kraft Music Hall* live from the Northrup Auditorium at the University of Minnesota in Minneapolis.

May 21, Thursday (10:00–11:00 P.M.). Hosts *Perry Como's Kraft Music Hall* from Chicago. This was probably the last time that Mitchell Ayres conducted the orchestra for Perry.

October 29, Thursday (10:00–11:00 P.M.). Hosts *Perry Como's Kraft Music Hall* live from Cobo Hall in Detroit. Nick Perito is the music director on the show for the first time. The show is produced by Roncom Productions; directed by Dwight Hemion; produced by Marlo Lewis; written by Goodman Ace, Bill Angelos and Buz Kohan.

November 6, Friday. For a forthcoming show, Perry tapes a scene featuring the Sistine Chapel Choir in Vatican City in Rome. During the visit to Italy, filming of Perry's traditional narration of the Nativity is done at Ostia Antica.

December 17, Thursday (10:00–11:00 P.M.). Hosts *Perry Como's Kraft Music Hall* which has been taped in Rome, Italy.

1965

January 7, Thursday (10:00–11:00 P.M.). Hosts *Perry Como's Kraft Music Hall* from Burbank.

February 4, Thursday (10:00–11:00 P.M.). Hosts *Perry Como's Kraft Music Hall* from the Kiel Auditorium in St. Louis.

February 9–12, Tuesday–Friday. Perry records a new album called *The Scene Changes* in RCA Victor's "Nashville Sound" Studios, Nashville, Tennessee. He is accompanied by the Anita Kerr Quartet.

February 14, Sunday (7:30–8:30 P.M.). Guests on *The Danny Thomas Show* on NBC-TV.

March 4, Thursday (10:00–11:00 P.M.). Hosts *Perry Como's Kraft Music Hall* live from the War Memorial Auditorium in Boston.

April 8, Thursday (10:00–11:00 P.M.). Hosts *Perry Como's Kraft Music Hall* from Miami Beach in Florida.

May 27, Thursday (10:00–11:00 P.M.). Hosts *Perry Como's Kraft Music Hall.* The guests are Richard Chamberlain, Diahann Carroll and the New Christy Minstrels. The show has been taped before a convention audience of 5,000 in the McCormick Place auditorium in Chicago.

October 18, Monday (8:00–9:00 P.M.). Hosts *Perry Como's Kraft Music Hall* from Brooklyn, New York, on NBC-TV. The show is produced by Roncom Productions; directed by Clark Jones; produced by Ray Charles; written by Goodman Ace, Bill Angelos and Buz Kohan.

November 22, Monday (8:00–9:00 P.M.). Hosts *Perry Como's Kraft Music Hall* from Brooklyn, New York.

December 20, Monday (8:00–9:00 P.M.). Hosts *Perry Como's Kraft Music Hall* from Brooklyn, New York.

December 29, Wednesday. Perry commences recording sessions for a new album to be called *Lightly Latin*. He uses RCA Victor's Studio A, New York City, and he is accompanied by an orchestra conducted by Nick Perito and by the Ray Charles Singers.

1966

January 24, Monday (9:00–10:00 P.M.). Hosts *Perry Como's Kraft Music Hall* from Brooklyn, New York.

February 15, Tuesday. Perry receives the Club of Champions Medal for 1965, the highest award conferred by the Catholic Youth Organization. Cardinal Spellman makes the presentation to Perry at a $50-a-plate benefit dinner at the Americana Hotel in New York attended by over 2,000 people.

February 28, Monday (9:00–10:00 P.M.). Hosts *Perry Como's Kraft Music Hall* from Brooklyn, New York.

March 28, Monday (9:00–10:00 P.M.). Hosts *Perry Como's Kraft Music Hall* from Brooklyn, New York.

April 25, Monday (9:00–10:00 P.M.). Hosts *Perry Como's Kraft Music Hall* from Brooklyn, New York.

May 9, Monday. Commences recording sessions for the album *Perry Como in Italy* at RCA Italiana Studios, Rome, Italy. The sessions are produced by Andy Wiswell and arranged and conducted by Nick Perito with the Allesandro Allessandroni Singers under the direction of Ray Charles.

August 9/11/13, Tuesday/Thursday/Saturday. Entertains at the Allentown Fair in Pennsylvania. He becomes an "Ambassador Extraordinaire" when he is presented with the special 100,000 Pennsylvanians' Award.

August 15–20, Monday–Saturday. Entertains at the Wisconsin State Fair in Milwaukee.

August 22–27, Monday–Saturday. Headlines the grandstand show at the Central Canada Exhibition in Ottawa, Canada.

August 29–31, Monday–Wednesday. Entertains at the Ohio State Fair at Columbus, Ohio.

September 7, Wednesday. Entertains at Omaha in a pre-centennial event.

September 10–13, Saturday–Tuesday. Entertains at the Kansas State Fair in Topeka.

October 27, Thursday. The RIAA certifies Perry's album *Perry Como Sings Merry Christmas Music* as a Gold album. This is awarded for $1 million in sales based on the manufacturer's wholesale price.

November 21, Monday (9:00–10:00 P.M.). Hosts *Perry Como's Kraft Music Hall* from Brooklyn, New York.

December 19, Monday (9:00–10:00 P.M.). Hosts *Perry Como's Kraft Music Hall* from Brooklyn, New York.

1967

January 25, Wednesday (9:00–10:00 P.M.). Hosts *Perry Como's Kraft Music Hall* from Brooklyn, New York, on NBC-TV. The show is produced by Roncom Productions; directed by Clark Jones; produced by Ray Charles; written by Goodman Ace, Bill Angelos and Buz Kohan.

February 22, Wednesday (9:00–10:00 P.M.). Hosts *Perry Como's Kraft Music Hall* from Brooklyn, New York.

March 20, Monday (9:00–10:00 P.M.). Hosts *Perry Como's Kraft Music Hall* from Brooklyn, New York.

April 17, Monday (9:00–10:00 P.M.). Hosts *Perry Como's Kraft Music Hall* from Brooklyn, New York. There had been a danger of an AFTRA strike and although there had been enough time to tape the show after the strike was called off, Perry and his guests decide to do the show "live."

May 22, Monday (9:00–10:00 P.M.). Hosts *Perry Como's Kraft Music Hall* on NBC-TV from Brooklyn, New York. This is the last show of the season.

August 22/24, Tuesday/Thursday. Perry returns to RCA's "Nashville Sound" Studios, Nashville, Tennessee, to cut a number of tracks. The sessions are produced by Chet Atkins and Andy Wiswell. The musical backing is arranged and conducted by Cam Mullins.

November 30, Thursday (7:30–8:30 P.M.). The *Perry Como Holiday Special* is shown on NBC-TV. It had been taped during October.

1968

February 11, Sunday. Performs in Ethel Kennedy's Telethon at the Lisner Auditorium in Washington, D.C. This is a benefit for Washington's Junior Village. Rose Kennedy offers to donate $500 if Perry will cut Robert Kennedy's hair.

June 5/7/12/19. Recording sessions at Webster Hall for an album called *Look to Your Heart*. This is produced by Andy Wiswell, arranged and conducted by Nick Perito with the Ray Charles Singers.

July 9, Tuesday. Commences recording *The Perry Como Christmas Album* at Webster Hall. The orchestra is conducted by Nick Perito and the Ray Charles Singers are also in support.

August 17, Saturday. Therese Como marries Paul Thibadeau at Our Lady of Fatima Church in Manor Haven, New York.

December 1, Sunday (10:00–11:00 P.M.). Hosts *The Perry Como Show* on NBC-TV.

1969

January 6–10, Monday–Friday. Tapes an appearance on *The Carol Burnett Show*.

January 13, Monday. Perry is seen on the *Rowan & Martin's Laugh-In* show aired today on NBC-TV.

February 19, Wednesday (10:00–11:00 P.M.). Hosts the "Academy of Professional Sports" show live on NBC-TV from the Burbank studios. Presenters include Jack Benny, Kim Novak and Danny Kaye.

March 24, Monday. Perry is seen on the *Rowan & Martin's Laugh-In* show aired today on NBC-TV.

September 5, Friday. Mitchell Ayres (age fifty-eight), who worked with Perry for many years, is struck by a car in Las Vegas and killed.

November 30, Sunday. Perry tapes a *Hollywood Palace* show which is transmitted on December 20.

1970

January 15, Thursday. Moves into his house at Tequesta, near Palm Beach. He also has houses at Jupiter and Port St. Lucie. The Sands Point house has been sold.

January 18–20, Sunday–Tuesday. Appears in a TV special titled *The Many Moods of Perry Como*. The actual taping is done on January 20 in Studio 2, NBC Color City, 3000 W. Alameda Ave., Burbank, California, starting at 8 P.M. The show is transmitted on February 22.

January 25, Sunday. Tapes an appearance on a TV show with Jimmy Durante which is shown on March 28.

March 18, Wednesday (9:00–10:00 P.M.). Guests on *The Bob Hope Show* on NBC-TV with Barbara Eden, Billy Casper and Tony Curtis.

May 5, Tuesday (1:30–4:30 P.M.). Records a number of tracks including "It's Impossible." The facilities of RCA Victor's Studio A in New York City are used. The orchestra is conducted by Marty Manning. "It's Impossible" reaches the No. 10 spot in the U.S. and hits the No. 4 position in the U.K. It is Perry's first Top 20 chart success in the U.S. for twelve years.

June 22, Monday. Opens at the International Hotel in Las Vegas for a 3-week season. His wife, Roselle, does not attend the opening night as she is too nervous. Perry, too, admits to nerves. He is said to have been paid $100,000 per week. He is a sell-out throughout his run. Among the celebrities at his first night are Bob Hope, Andy Williams, Pat Boone, Jack E. Leonard, Dorothy Lamour and the Mills Brothers. Perry is supported by an orchestra conducted by Nick Perito with vocal accompaniment by the Doodletown Pipers. Ray Charles writes some special material for Perry for the show which he continues to use at his live concerts until his final outing in 1994.

June 25–27, Thursday–Saturday. Perry's performances at the International Hotel are recorded for issue on a new album called *Perry Como in Person*.

September 29, Tuesday. Tapes an appearance on the *Flip Wilson Show* which is shown on October 8.

October 3–4, Saturday–Sunday. Tapes an appearance on a TV special with Tom Jones which is shown on November 6.

November 10–30, Tuesday–Monday. Undertakes another 3-week season at the International Hotel, Las Vegas, appearing twice nightly. He is reported to receive $125,000 per week. The Doodletown Pipers and comedian Billy Baxter provide support.

November 23–25, Monday–Wednesday. Recording sessions at the International Hotel, Las Vegas, with an orchestra conducted by Nick Perito. The sessions were in response to his surprise hit "It's Impossible" recorded the previous May in New York. Don Costa was brought in for production of these sessions, excluding the title track of course, and recordings were made using the facilities at the hotel. These were Don Costa's first recordings with Perry and the project was quickly folded into sessions for Perry's follow-up album *I Think of You* which was recorded more conventionally in New York but still prior to final release of the "It's Impossible" album.

1971

January 18–22, Monday–Friday. Tapes an appearance with Doris Day on a TV show called *The Doris Mary Anne Kappelhoff Special* which is shown on March 14.

February 21, Sunday. Tapes an appearance on *The Pearl Bailey Show* at the Hollywood Palace Theatre which is shown on February 27.

May 5, Wednesday. Records an appearance on *Top of the Pops* for BBC-TV at Television Centre in London. He receives a fee of £150.

May 12, Wednesday. Tapes a TV special in London at the BBC Studios, Shepherd's Bush, with the Mike Sammes Singers and the Gillian Lynne Dancers. John Benson conducts the orchestra. Ray Charles is credited as choral director and program assistant with Nick Perito credited as personal accompanist and music associate. The show is produced by Yvonne Littlewood and overseen by Ronnie Hazelhurst. An extra song, "O Holy Night," is taped and included in an edited version of the program which is shown at 8:15 P.M. on December 26, 1971, on BBC2 as *Perry Como Christmas Edition.*

July 19–August 8, Monday–Sunday. Headlines a show at the International Hotel, Las Vegas. He is supported by the Establishment. Due to kidney stone problems, Perry cannot complete the final week of the engagement and Bill Cosby takes over. Perry is admitted to the Sunshine Hospital on August 2 but is discharged after a few days.

August 19, Thursday. Opens at the South Shore Room at Harrah's, Lake Tahoe. He is again supported by the Establishment and by Foster Brooks. Nick Perito is the musical director. The show closes on September 1.

October 9–11, Saturday–Monday. Tapes his Christmas show in California and suffers a compound fracture to his left knee when the stage shifts. He finishes the taping of his show with his leg in a cast and on his return to Florida, he is admitted to the Good Samaritan Hospital in West Palm Beach. Perry sues NBC for $1 million in damages and the case is eventually settled in November 1977.

November 9–30, Tuesday–Tuesday. Perry is billed to appear at the Hilton in Las Vegas but he cannot fulfill the engagement due to his knee problems. Ann-Margret takes his place.

December 9, Thursday (8:00–9:00 P.M.). *Perry Como's Winter Show* is transmitted on NBC-TV. The director is Marty Pasetta and the producer is Bob Finkel. The writers are Bill Angelos, Buz Kohan, Ann Elder and Jerry Mayer. The show is sponsored by Kraft.

1972

Perry spends several months with his leg in a heavy plaster cast and then has his knee put in a metal brace. He has to use a wheelchair. He becomes very restless at home only being able to fish with difficulty.

July 20–August 3, Thursday–Thursday. Perry appears for a 2-week season at the Showroom Internationale at the Hilton Hotel in Las Vegas. The Ray Charles Singers provide support.

August 8, Tuesday. Flies to Los Angeles to tape an appearance on a show called *Zenith Presents a Salute to Television's 25th Anniversary.* The program is shown on September 10.

August 13–30, Sunday–Wednesday. Performs twice nightly at Harrah's at Lake Tahoe. He is supported by comedian Foster Brooks and the Ray Charles Singers. Nick Perito is the musical director.

September 11–15, 22–24. Perry tapes an appearance on an NBC-TV show called *Cole Porter in Paris* which is shown on January 17, 1973.

October 20–22, Friday–Sunday. Tapes his Christmas Special in California. The program is transmitted on December 4. The sponsor is Kraft Foods and the executive producer is Bob Finkel. John Moffitt is the director. The producer-writers are Saul Turteltaub and Bernie Orenstein. The show is in sixth place in the weekly Nielsen ratings with a rating of 30.1 and an audience share of 42.

December 22–January 4, 1973. Perry appears at the South Shore Room at Harrah's Lake Tahoe. He is supported by comedian Foster Brooks and the Ray Charles Singers. Nick Perito is the musical director. Perry's three children and their children join him and Roselle for Christmas in Tahoe.

1973

January 15, Monday. Perry returns to Nashville to start recording a large number of tracks over several months, only ten of which are actually released within an album eventually called *And I Love You So.* Some of the others are issued as singles, but many remain unreleased. The single release of *And I Love You So* reaches only a No. 29 spot in the U.S. charts but in the U.K. it soars to the No. 3 position. The album reaches the No. 1 spot in the U.K. charts.

October 27–30, Saturday–Tuesday. Perry tapes a TV special with Julie Andrews and the Muppets at the Elstree Studios in Borehamwood in the U.K. which is transmitted on November 23. Gary Smith and Dwight Hemion are the producers; Dwight Hemion is also the director. Ian Fraser is the music supervisor and arranger; Jack Parnell conducts the orchestra. This is an ATV Color Production, sponsored by GTE.

November 10–11, Saturday–Sunday. Tapes his Christmas show in California. The show is transmitted on December 10. The director is Tony Charmoli, the producer is Bob Finkel and the musical director is Nick Perito. The writers are Bob Wells, Johnny Bradford and Lorne Michaels. As usual this is a Roncom Production. The show places sixth in the Nielsen ratings for the week.

1974

January 4, Friday. Perry returns to New York to record his first country flavored album named simply *Perry*, albeit with a gentle pop mix, in the traditional New York City environment. The facilities of RCA Victor's Studio "C" are used. Nick Perito arranges the music and conducts the orchestra. The Ray Charles Singers provide support.

March 30–April 1, Saturday–Monday. Tapes a TV special called *The Perry Como Sunshine Show* in Hollywood which is shown on April 10. The show is produced and directed by Nick Vanoff. The writers are Frank Peppiatt, John Aylesworth and Jay Burton.

May 9, Thursday. Stars in a Gala Midnight Charity Show at the London Palladium in the U.K.

September 1–4, Sunday–Wednesday. Tapes a TV special called *Perry Como's Summer of '74* which is shown on September 12. The show is one of six to be sponsored by General Telephone & Electronics (GTE) at a reported figure of $500,000 per show.

November 18, Monday (8:00 P.M.). In the U.K., Perry tops the bill at the 45th Royal Performance in aid of the Entertainment Artistes Benevolent fund at the London Palladium in the presence of Queen Elizabeth the Queen Mother.

December 7–10, Saturday–Tuesday. Tapes his Christmas show with Peggy Fleming, Rich Little and the Carpenters. The show is transmitted on December 17. The producer-director is Nick Vanoff. GTE is the sponsor.

1975

January 7, Tuesday. Commences recording sessions for a new album (which is eventually named *Just Out of Reach*) at RCA's "Nashville Sound" Studios, Nashville, Tennessee. The session is arranged and conducted by Cam Mullins. The producer is Chet Atkins and the vocal accompaniment is by the Nashville Sounds. This is Perry's last album with Chet Atkins and there seems to have been an element of experimentation as many tracks are recorded and never released.

February 6, Thursday. Tapes a TV special, *Como Country: Perry and his Nashville Friends* "live" at the Grand Ole Opry in Nashville. The special is directed by Walter C. Miller and airs on February 17. The producer is Joseph Cates.

March 16–18. Sunday–Tuesday. Tapes *Perry Como's Springtime Special* which airs on CBS-TV on March 27. Rehearsals are held at the NBC Studios in Los Angeles and the show is taped at station KTTV.

April 2, Wednesday. Commences his 19-concert tour of England with a performance at the Winter Gardens, Bournemouth. He is supported by the Wedgewoods and comedian Ted Rogers. During the tour, the BBC films a documentary and Perry, Nick Perito and Ray Charles are interviewed by Benny Green. Extracts from Perry's concert at the Theatre Royal are used. The 90 minute documentary is called *The Barber Comes to Town* and is much acclaimed.

April 3, Thursday. Gives a concert at Colston Hall, Bristol.

April 4, Friday. Leaves his hotel in Bristol and is briefly interviewed by Harlech TV. The Free Trade Hall in Manchester is the next venue on Perry's concert tour.

April 5, Saturday (6 and 8:30 P.M.). Appears at the Royal Festival Hall in London.

April 6, Sunday (6 and 8:30 P.M.). Gives two performances at the London Palladium.

April 8, Tuesday (6 and 9 P.M.). Appears at the Odeon in New Street, Birmingham.

April 9, Wednesday. At the Southport Theatre in Southport.

April 10, Thursday. Appears at Kelvin Hall, Glasgow. Gives an interview to Radio Clyde while he is in Glasgow.

April 11, Friday. Perry gives a concert at Usher Hall in Edinburgh.

Perry on stage in the early 1970s.

April 13, Sunday (6 and 8:30 P.M.). Completes his U.K. tour with concerts at the Theatre Royal, Drury Lane, London. The BBC films the performance for its documentary. After the show, Perry is presented with a Platinum record for the *And I Love You So* LP.

April 14, Monday. Benny Green interviews Perry in his hotel room for the BBC documentary. Perry receives a fee of £2140.

July 25–August 7, Friday–Thursday. Appears at the Hilton International Hotel in Las Vegas. Said to be paid $125,000 per week.

September (undated). Plays a season at Harrah's, Lake Tahoe.

September 15–25, Monday–Thursday. Tapes a TV special called *Perry Como's Lake Tahoe Holiday* which airs on October 28. The program contains extracts from Perry's performances at Harrah's. The producers are Bob Banner and Dick Foster. Sterling Johnson is the director. GTE is the sponsor.

October 25, Saturday. A compilation album of Perry's songs called *40 Greatest Hits* enters the U.K. album charts and eventually reaches the top position.

October 30–November 10, Thursday–Monday. Tapes his Christmas show in Mexico City. The show airs on December 15. This is a Roncom production in association with Bob Banner Associates and Televisa, directed by Sterling Johnson. Nick Perito is the musical director, the co-producer is Stephen Pouliot and Jerry Winnick is the writer. The sponsor is GTE. This is Perry's last show under his CBS contract and he returns to NBC.

December 14, Sunday (7:25–8:40 P.M.). The BBC's documentary *The Barber Comes to Town* airs on BBC2-TV. The producer is Yvonne Littlewood.

1976

January 12–20, Monday–Tuesday. Tapes a TV special called *Perry Como's Hawaiian Holiday* in Hawaii which is shown on NBC-TV on February 22. Bob Banner is executive producer, Dick Foster is producer and director and the writer is Nick Castle Jr. Ray Charles provides choral supervision and special material with Nick Perito arranging and conducting. The sponsor is GTE.

February 24–29, Tuesday–Sunday. Tapes a TV special called *Perry Como's Spring in New Orleans* which is shown on April 7. The writer is Alan Baker, Ray Charles provides choral supervision and special material and the music is arranged and conducted by Nick Perito. The executive producer is Bob Banner and the sponsor is GTE.

April 25, Sunday. Flies to Australia for a concert tour. Ray Charles cannot accompany him as he has had to undergo heart bypass surgery.

May 1, Saturday. Opens his tour with a concert at Sydney Opera House.

May 4–5, Tuesday–Wednesday. Gives concerts at the Hordern Pavilion in Sydney.

May 6–7, Thursday–Friday. Appears at the Festival Hall, Brisbane.

May 9–11, Sunday–Tuesday. The tour moves on to the Festival Hall in Melbourne.

May 12 and 14, Wednesday and Friday. Gives concerts at the Apollo Stadium in Adelaide.

May 16, Sunday. Completes his tour of Australia with a concert at the Entertainment Centre in Perth.

July 12–17, Monday–Saturday. Performs at the Arie Crown Theatre, McCormick Place, Chicago. He is supported by Roy Prophet (a musician and comedian) and by the Establishment. Said to be paid $200,000 per week on his tour.

July 19–25, Monday–Sunday. Gives eight performances at the Westbury Music Fair, Long Island. This is a theatre in the round with a revolving stage.

July 26–August 1, Monday–Sunday. Performs at the Valley Forge Music Fair in Devon, Pennsylvania. This is another theatre in the round with a revolving stage.

August 24–26, Tuesday–Thursday. Tapes a TV special called *Perry Como, Las Vegas Style* in the Las Vegas Hilton showroom. This is shown on NBC-TV on September 11. The show is produced by Stephen Pouliot and directed by Kip Walton. The executive producer is Bob Banner. The musical director is Nick Perito and choral supervision and special material is by Ray Charles.

August 30–September 8, Monday–Wednesday. Performs at the Hilton in Las Vegas.

September 5, Sunday. Appears in the *Jerry Lewis Telethon against Muscular Dystrophy* at the Sahara Hotel in Las Vegas. During the show, Frank Sinatra brings Dean Martin on stage for a reunion with Jerry Lewis.

November (undated). Perry is in Austria taping his Christmas show. Visits Vienna, Salzburg, Dienten and Arnsdorf. Sings "Silent Night" in Arnsdorf where it was written. The show is transmitted on December 13 on NBC-TV. The executive producer is Bob Banner and the show is directed and written by Stephen Pouliot. The sponsor is GTE.

November 24, Wednesday. The RIAA certifies Perry's album *And I Love You So* as a Gold album. The award is now given for sales of 500,000 copies in addition to reaching $1 million in sales.

December 23, Thursday. Perry is awarded a Gold record for *And I Love You So*.

1977

February 3, Thursday. Perry records several tracks at an undisclosed site in California, three of which appear in his 1978 American release compilation album *Where You're Concerned*.

March 18, Friday. In Los Angeles, tapes the final part of a TV special called *Perry Como's Music from Hollywood*. The show airs on March 28. The producer-director is Bob Henry, George Yanok is the writer, and Nick Perito is music director with Ray Charles providing special material and choral direction. The executive producer is Bob Banner. This is a joint production of Roncom Productions, Inc., and Bob Henry Productions. The sponsor is GTE.

April 19, Tuesday. *Perry Como's Christmas in Austria* wins the Peabody Award.

April 26, Tuesday (9:00–10:00 P.M.). Perry's guest appearance in *Ann-Margret—Rhinestone Cowgirl* is shown on NBC-TV. The show has been taped in Opryland's Grand Ole Opry in Nashville, Tennessee. The show is produced by Dwight Hemion and Gary Smith. Buz Kohan is the writer.

May 8, Sunday. Duke University awards an honorary doctorate to Perry. He is made a Doctor of Humane Letters.

June 6–7, Monday–Tuesday. Recording sessions at Number One Studio, Olympic, Barnes in England. for an album called *The Best of British*. The orchestra is directed by Nick Perito and the Tony Mansell Singers are under the direction of Ray Charles.

July 25, Monday. Commences a 6-week concert tour taking in Buffalo (New York), Toronto, the Garden State Theatre in New Jersey, the Shady Grove Summer Theatre in Maryland, the Springfield Theatre in Massachusetts and then on to arenas in Pittsburgh and Warwick, Rhode Island. Kelly Monteith and Good Stuff provide support.

October 14, Friday. Bing Crosby dies on a golf course in Spain. Perry says, "I'm lucky that there was a Bing Crosby. If it hadn't been for Bing I'd probably still be cutting hair."

October (undated). Tapes a TV special called *Olde English Christmas in London* in England at locations such as Hever Castle in Kent and Harrod's in London. The show airs on ABC-TV on December 14. During his stay in the U.K., a reception is held at the Cafe Royal to launch Perry's album *The Best of British*.

October 29, Saturday. Tapes an appearance on the *Parkinson* show for BBC-TV. He is paid a fee of £500. The show is broadcast on November 26. This is said to be Perry's first appearance on a chat show and he uses it to gently plug his new album, *The Best of British*.

November 1, Tuesday. After a 5-year legal battle, Perry is awarded $257,509 in damages for the injury he suffered in 1971 when filming his Christmas show.

December 5–7, Monday–Wednesday. Tapes a guest appearance on *The Bob Hope All Star Christmas Comedy Special*. The show is transmitted on December 19.

1978

February 27–March 2, Monday–Thursday. Tapes a TV special called *Perry Como's Easter by the Sea* at Sea World in San Diego, California. Stephen Pouliot is the producer with Bob Banner acting as executive producer. ABC-TV broadcasts the show on March 22.

July 19–22, Wednesday–Saturday. Appears at the Greek Theatre in Los Angeles. Perry's appearances were due to start on July 16 but were put back to July 19 because he had undergone recent oral surgery. Skip Stephenson provides comedy support.

August 13, Sunday. Appears at the Front Row Theatre in Highland Heights, Ohio, for what should be a week's season. Has to postpone his last four concerts because of a sore throat. The Front Row Theater was a 3000-seat theater in the round with a revolving stage.

August 21–26, Monday–Friday. Perry appears at the Coliseum in Colonie, New York.

September (undated). Appears at Westbury Music Fair, Long Island.

September 5, Tuesday. In New York, Perry is presented with a Gold record by RCA for his album *And I Love You So* recognizing the sales of 500,000 copies.

September 7–10, Thursday–Sunday. Performs at the Front Row Theatre in Highland Heights, Ohio.

September 11–12, Monday–Tuesday. An interview with Perry is shown on *Good Morning, America* spread over two mornings.

September 17, Sunday. The annual Emmy Awards presentation. *Perry Como's Easter by the Sea* is unsuccessfully nominated for outstanding achievement in tape sound mixing with sound mixers Larry Stephens, Thomas J. Huth, Ron Bryan, Eric Levinson and Grover B. Helsley named.

November (undated). In Williamsburg, Virginia, Perry tapes a TV special called *Perry Como's Early American Christmas*. The executive producer is Bob Banner. Jeff Margolis is the director. The show airs on December 13 and is placed in the top 20 in the weekly Nielsen tables.

1979

January 12, Friday. Perry is honored with a special American Musical Award of Merit at the sixth annual American Music Awards ceremony at Santa Monica, California. He is not present to receive the award.

March (undated). Tapes a TV show in Hollywood called *Perry Como's Springtime Special* which airs on ABC-TV on April 9. The show is produced by Stephen Pouliot with Russ Petranto acting as director. The writers are Harry Crane and Stephen Pouliot. Nick Perito is music director with Ray Charles providing special material and giving choral direction. The executive producer is Bob Banner. The show is sponsored by Kentucky Fried Chicken.

April (various). Plays six concerts in ten days in Japan including Osaka (April 20) and Sun Plaza Hall in Tokyo (April 22).

July 16–22, Monday–Sunday. Appears at the Mill Run Theatre in Niles, Illinois. The concerts are completely sold out. Jay Leno is the opening act. While there, he tapes an appearance on *The Phil Donahue Show* which is shown in September.

August 17–18, Friday–Saturday. Entertains at the Merriweather Post Pavilion, Columbia, Maryland.

August 26, Sunday. Appears at the Dick Clark Westchester Theatre in Tarrytown.

August 27, Monday. Appears at the Frederic R. Mann Music Center in Philadelphia. Jay Leno again provides the comedy support.

September 9, Sunday. The annual Emmy Awards ceremony. *Perry Como's Early American Christmas* is unsuccessfully nominated for outstanding achievement in tape sound mixing with Gordon Klimuck (sound mixer) and Thomas J. Huth (sound mixer) named.

October 26–November 2, Friday–Friday. Tapes a TV special in Santa Fe called *Perry Como's Christmas in New Mexico*. The executive producer is Bob Banner. The show airs on December 14 on ABC-TV.

1980

January 26–February 6, Saturday–Wednesday. Tapes a TV special in Nassau in the Bahamas. The executive producer is Bob Banner. *Perry Como's Bahamas Holiday* is shown on ABC-TV on May 21. The show is written and produced by Stephen Pouliot; directed by Sterling Johnson, with Bob Banner as executive producer. Ray Charles provides special material and choral supervision and Nick Perito is musical director. The show is a joint production of Roncom Productions and Bob Banner Associates.

April 8–17, Tuesday–Thursday. During this period, Perry records the tracks for an album simply called *Perry Como* at RCA Studios C and D in New York. Byron Olsen conducts the orchestra. The sessions are produced by Mike Berniker.

July (undated). Starts a concert tour in Detroit, Michigan. Jay Leno opens each show to warm up the audience.

July 29–31, Tuesday–Thursday. At the Mill Run Theatre in Niles, Illinois, Perry's performances are recorded for an album called *Perry Como Live on Tour*. The producer of the album is Mike Berniker. The orchestra is led by Nick Perito and the vocal arrangements are by Ray Charles.

August 4–9, Monday–Friday. Appears at the Garden State Arts Centre in Holmdel, New Jersey.

August 19–24, Tuesday–Sunday. Entertains at the Front Row Theatre, near Cleveland, Ohio.

September 7. The annual Emmy Awards presentation takes place. *Perry Como's Christmas in New Mexico* is unsuccessfully nominated for outstanding video tape editing for a limited series or a special with Marco Zappia (editor) named.

November (undated). Spends two weeks in Israel taping his Christmas special. Locations used include Tel Aviv, Jerusalem and Bethlehem. *Perry Como's Christmas in the Holy Land* is shown on ABC-TV on December 13. The director is Sterling Johnson and Stephen Pouliot is writer and producer. Nick Perito is the musical director and Ray Charles provides original music. The executive producer is Bob Banner.

1981

April 2–7, Thursday–Tuesday. Tapes a TV special in San Francisco. *Perry Como's Spring in San Francisco* is shown on ABC-TV on May 10. The show is produced by Stephen Pouliot and directed by Sterling Johnson. Harry Crane and Stephen Pouliot are the writers. Ray Charles provides special musical material and choral supervision; Nick Perito is musical director. The executive producer is Bob Banner. This is a Roncom Production in association with Bob Banner Associates.

September 13. The annual Emmy Awards show is televised and *Perry Como's Christmas in the Holy Land* wins an Emmy for outstanding video tape editing for a limited series or a special with Marco Zappia (video tape editor) and Branda S. Miller (film editor) being named. The show is also unsuccessfully nominated for outstanding achievement in music direction with Nick Perito (music director and arranger) highlighted and for outstanding achievement in music and lyrics with Ray Charles (composer and lyricist) named for the song "The City of Tradition." *Perry Como's Spring in San Francisco* is unsuccessfully nominated for outstanding achievement in tape sound mixing with tape sound mixers Jerry Clemans, Ed Greene and Phillip Seretti named.

October 14–19, Wednesday–Monday. Tapes a TV special in Montreal and Quebec, Canada. *Perry Como's French Canadian Christmas* is shown on ABC-TV on December 12. This is a Roncom production in association with Bob Banner Associates, directed by Jeff Margolis. Stephen Pouliot is the writer-producer. Bob Banner is executive producer. Ray Charles provides special material and choral supervision. Nick Perito is the musical director. The sponsors are Canon and American Greetings. The show is nominated for an Emmy for video editing.

December 28, Monday. Album sessions for *So It Goes* are recorded at RCA Studios C and D, New York, on this day and other unknown days. The music is arranged and conducted by Nick Perito and Byron Olsen. The producer is Mike Berniker.

1982

March (undated). Tapes a TV special in Guadalajara, Mexico. *Perry Como's Easter in Guadalajara* is shown on ABC-TV on April 3. The show is written and produced by Stephen Pouliot with Jeff Margolis directing. Bob Banner is executive producer; Ray Charles provides choral supervision and special material, and Nick Perito is musical director. Certain costs are covered by the Mexican National Tourism Council and the Jalisco State Office of Tourism. The show is a joint production of Roncom Productions and Bob Banner Associates. The sponsor is Kraft.

March 25, Thursday. Perry and Frank Sinatra entertain together for 50 minutes at a White House dinner given by President Reagan honoring the Italian president Sandro Pertini.

September 19. The annual Emmy Awards presentation. *Perry Como's Easter in Guadalajara* wins the Emmy for outstanding achievement in tape sound mixing with sound mixers Chris Haire, Richard Masci, and Doug Nelson named. *Perry Como's French-Canadian Christmas* is unsuccessfully nominated for outstanding video tape editing for a limited series or a special with Pam Marshall (editor) named.

November (undated). Tapes his Christmas special in Paris, France. *Perry Como's Christmas in Paris* is shown on ABC-TV on December 18. This is a Roncom Production with Bob Banner Associates, directed by Kip Walton and produced by Stephen Pouliot. The writers are Phil Kellard and Stephen Pouliot. Nick Perito is musical director.

November 19, Friday. The RIAA certifies the *Perry Como Christmas Album* as a Gold album as it has sold more than 500,000 copies in addition to reaching $1 million in sales.

December. Perry is back in Japan and undertakes an 8-concert tour playing locations such as Tokyo, Osaka, Fukuwoka, Nagoya and Yokohama.

1983

February 27, Sunday. Perry, Frank Sinatra, George Burns and Dionne Warwick entertain at a dinner for Queen Elizabeth II of Great Britain on the M*A*S*H soundstage at the 20th Century–Fox studios in Hollywood.

June 21, Tuesday. RCA throws a party for Perry at the Rainbow Grill in New York to celebrate his 40 years with the company and his 50 years in show business. Marvin Hamlisch entertains.

June 23, Thursday. Roselle's brother, Dee, dies. He has been Perry's personal manager. Mickey Glass takes over his role.

July 5, Tuesday. Perry is interviewed by Brian Gumble on the *Today* show on NBC-TV. Further portions of the interview are shown on July 6 and 7.

July 31, Sunday. Perry and Roselle celebrate their Golden Wedding Anniversary at their mountain home in Saluda, North Carolina. Their children and 12 grandchildren are with them.

September 25, Sunday. Perry is honored with a special tribute to his 50 years in show-business at the annual Emmy Awards at the Pasadena Civic Auditorium. *Perry Como's Christmas in Paris* show is nominated unsuccessfully for outstanding achievement in music direction with Nick Perito (music director and principal arranger) and Jon Charles (principal arranger) named.

December 4, Sunday. Appears in the Kennedy Center Honors Show at the Opera House, Washington, D.C. President and Nancy Reagan are present. Frank Sinatra and James Stewart are honored. Walter Cronkite is the host. The show is aired on CBS-TV on December 27.

December 17, Saturday (10:00–11:00 P.M.). *Perry Como's Christmas in New York* is shown on ABC-TV. The show is supplied by Jeff Margolis Productions and Roncom Productions. The producer-director is Jeff Margolis and the writer is Rod Warren. The show reaches 11th place in the ratings with a 20.4 figure with 17.1 million people watching it.

1984

May 26, Saturday. Commences his 50th anniversary tour at the Sun City Arizona Dome but due to a bronchial virus he cannot complete the show. Is taken to hospital and then flown to Duke University for treatment there. Has to cancel three weeks' performances at various venues.

June 6, Wednesday. Interviewed on *The Arlene Herson Show*, a syndicated cable television program.
June 19, Tuesday. Interviewed on *Good Company*, a Minneapolis TV show.
June 20–24, Wednesday–Sunday. Appears at the Carlton Celebrity Room in Minneapolis.
July 6–7, Friday–Saturday. Appears at the Premier Center, Detroit.
July 16–21, Monday–Saturday. Appears at the South Shore Music Circus.
July 23, Monday. Perry entertains at the Saratoga Springs Performing Arts Center.
July 24, Tuesday. Performs at the Arena in Binghamton, New York.
July 25, Wednesday. Appears at the Concord Hotel resort in Monticello, New York.
July 27–29, Friday–Sunday. Appears at the Front Row Theatre in Elyria, Ohio.
August 2–5, Thursday–Sunday. Appears at the Arie Crown Memorial Theatre in Chicago.
August 7–18, Tuesday–Saturday. Appears at the Westbury Music Fair, Westbury, Long Island.
August (undated). Interviewed by Regis Philbin on his *Life Styles* program.
August 21–26, Tuesday–Sunday. Plays nine sold-out engagements at Valley Forge Music Fair in Devon, Pennsylvania.
October (undated). Tapes his Christmas special in London with Ann-Margret as the principal guest. *Perry Como's Christmas in England* is shown on ABC-TV on December 15. The show is supplied by Jeff Margolis Productions and Roncom Productions. Jeff Margolis is producer-director, the writer is Rod Warren and Nick Perito is the musical director. The show is placed at #32 in the weekly Nielsen ratings with a 16 rating and a 29 audience share. *Dynasty* was the top show with a rating of 26.5 and an audience share of 39.

Perry signs autographs for his fans in London, October 1984 (courtesy Michael Dunnington).

1985

July 18–21, Thursday–Sunday. Commences his summer tour with a performance at the Paramount Theatre in Seattle. During his tour he gives 54 performances in 15 cities including Las Vegas and Atlantic City.
July (undated). Appears at Portland, Oregon.
July 25, Thursday. Appears at the Orpheum, San Francisco, giving 8 performances during his booking there.
August 1, Friday. Sings to an audience of 8,500 at the Pacific Ampitheater, Costa Mesa, California.
August 2–3, Saturday–Sunday. Entertains at the Greek Theatre, Catalina.
August 13–18, Tuesday–Sunday. Performs at the Fox Theatre, Atlanta, Georgia. The concert is sponsored by Bailey's Irish Cream.
August 21–27, Wednesday–Tuesday. Performs at Resorts International, Atlantic City, New Jersey.
August 28–29, Wednesday–Thursday. Finger Lakes Performing Arts Center in Canandaigua, New York, is the next venue on the tour.
August 31–September 1, Saturday–Sunday. Appears at the Melody Tent in Hyannis, Cape Cod.
September 12, Thursday. Sings at the Holiday Star Theatre, Merriville, Indiana.

October 3, Thursday. Takes part in the Gala Italiana, a fund-raiser for Childhelp USA at the Beverly Hilton. Perry receives a lifetime achievement award.

November 1–7, Friday–Thursday. Tapes his Christmas special in Hawaii. It was originally planned to record this in Italy but this was changed because of security concerns. *Perry Como's Christmas in Hawaii* is shown on ABC-TV on December 14. The suppliers are Roncom Productions and Don Mischer Productions. Don Mischer is the producer-director and David J. Goldberg is the co-producer. The writer is Buz Kohan and the music director is Nick Perito. Dick Williams (Andy's brother) provides special musical material, replacing Ray Charles. The executive producer is Bob Banner. The sponsor is Folgers Coffee. The show places 43rd in the week's TV ratings.

1986

May 9–11, Friday–Sunday. Appears at Resorts International Casino Hotel, Atlantic City.

September 15–21, Monday–Sunday. Appears at the Westbury Music Fair, Long Island.

September 23–27, Tuesday–Saturday. Appears at the Valley Forge Music Fair in Devon, Pennsylvania.

November 1–5, Saturday–Wednesday. Tapes his Christmas show in San Antonio, Texas. *The Perry Como Christmas Show* airs on ABC-TV on December 6. The show is supplied by Roncom Productions and Mellodan Productions. Bob Wynn is the producer and director with Jim McGinn doing the writing. Nick Perito is the musical director and Dick Williams (Andy's brother) is choral director. The show is in 50th place in the weekly Nielsen ratings. *The Cosby Show* is top.

1987

February 2–3, Monday–Tuesday. In the Evergreen Studios in Burbank, California, Perry records tracks for an album called *Perry Como Today*. The music is arranged and conducted by Nick Perito. The album is co-produced by Roncom Productions but, in fact, paid for by the RCA label, which is now part of BMG Music.

July 19–20, Sunday–Monday. Entertains at Wolf Trap, Vienna, Virginia.

July 21, Tuesday. Appears at the Warwick Music Theatre in Providence, Rhode Island.

July 22–23, Wednesday–Thursday. Entertains at South Shore Music Circus in Cohasset, Massachusetts.

July 25–26, Saturday–Sunday. Appears at the Westbury Music Fair, Long Island.

July 31–August 1, Friday–Saturday. Entertains at the Front Row Theatre, Highland Heights, Ohio.

August 7–9, Friday–Sunday. Entertains at the Holiday Star Theatre, Merriville, Indiana.

October 24, Saturday. Perry and the composer-conductor Henry Mancini are given "lifetime achievement" awards at the annual dinner of the National Italian American Foundation at the Washington Hilton. Among those gathered to do them honor are the actresses Angie Dickinson and Polly Bergen.

December 6, Sunday. Is one of several receiving the Kennedy Center Honor from President Reagan at the White House in Washington, D.C. Bette Davis, choreographer Alwin Nikolais, Nathan Milstein, and Sammy Davis Jr. are similarly honored. Later, the Honors show takes place at the John F. Kennedy Center for the Performing Arts with President and Nancy Reagan in attendance. Walter Cronkite is the host and Don Ameche introduces the tribute to Perry. The show is produced by Kennedy Center Television Productions, Inc.; directed by Dwight Hemion; and produced by George Stevens, Jr. and Nick Vanoff. The show airs on CBS-TV on December 30.

1988

May (undated) At the Duke Children's Classic Celebrity Golf Tournament at Duke Golf Course in Durham, North Carolina. During the event, Roselle Como suffers chest pains and she undergoes tests which reveal that she has coronary disease and angina pectoris.

May 26, Thursday. Roselle undergoes a quadruple heart bypass operation in the Heart Center at Duke Hospital in Durham.

July/August (undated). Sings with John Williams and the Boston Pops Orchestra and presents his Bing Crosby medley. The show is aired as *Evening at Pops* on TV in various locations starting on August 14.

October 6–9, Thursday–Sunday. Entertains at the Opera House at Bally's Grand in Atlantic City, New Jersey. Rita Rudner is in support.

October 11, Tuesday. Appears on *Live with Regis and Kathie Lee*.

December 12, Monday. Perry executes what is stated to be his Last Will and Testament. Roselle and his son Ronald are appointed as co–Personal Representatives. Most of his estate is left to his wife, Roselle, with provisions made for his grandchildren. If Roselle should not survive him, he leaves $1 million to be split equally between his grandchildren with the remainder to be split between his descendants per stirpes.

1989

July 5–6, Wednesday–Thursday. Opens his concert tour at Westbury Music Fair.

July 7, Friday. Appears at the Oakdale Music Theatre in Wallingford, Connecticut. An interview with Perry is shown on *Live with Regis and Kathie Lee* on ABC-TV.

July 8, Saturday. Appears at the Cape Cod Melody Tent in Hyannis, Massachusetts.

July 9, Sunday. Entertains at the Saratoga Performing Arts Center, New York.

July 11, Tuesday. Entertains at Finger Lakes Performing Arts Center, Canandaigua, New York State.

July 13–14, Thursday–Friday. Appears at the Garden State Arts Center, Holmdel, New Jersey.

July 15–16, Saturday–Sunday. Entertains at the Valley Forge Music Fair in Devon, Pennsylvania.

July 18, Tuesday. Entertains at the Meadowbrook Music Festival in Rochester, Michigan.

July 19, Wednesday. Entertains at the Front Row Theatre, Highland Heights, Cleveland, Ohio.

July 20, Thursday. Perry moves on to Riverbend, Cincinnati, Ohio.

July 21, Friday. Entertains at Deer Creek Amphitheatre, Indianapolis, Indiana.

July 22–23, Saturday–Sunday. Entertains at the Star Plaza Theatre, Merriville, Indiana.

July 25–27, Tuesday–Thursday. Entertains at the Fox Theatre in St. Louis.

September 17, Sunday. Perry sings at the Good Shepherd Celebrity Classic dinner show in Pennsylvania.

October 22, Sunday. Perry joins Plácido Domingo, the Harlem Boys Choir and Japanese crooner Yuzo Kayama to entertain at a Friendship Concert in the Yokohama Arena, Yokohama, Japan attended by former U.S. president Ronald Reagan and his wife. A crowd of 10,000 watches the proceedings and raises almost $1 million for Mr. Reagan's Presidential Library. Both Perry and Plácido Domingo have been flown in especially for the concert.

1990

January 7, Sunday. Is one of seven inducted into the Academy of Television Arts and Sciences Hall of Fame at the 20th Century–Fox Studios in Los Angeles. Perry's life story in brief is narrated by Milton Berle who hosts Perry's induction. Frank Sinatra presents Perry with the award. Fred Astaire, Barbara Walters and Carroll O'Connor are also inducted. The proceedings are shown on the Fox network on January 24.

March 3–4, Saturday–Sunday (10:30 P.M.–5:30 P.M.). Hosts the Sammy Davis Jr. Variety Club Telethon at the Adam's Mark Hotel in St. Louis. Sammy cannot be there as he has been hospitalized with cancer. Bob Wynn is the producer.

April 24, Tuesday. Perry and Roselle are in Durham, North Carolina, and are honored at the dedication dinner for the Roselle and Perry Como Pavilion of the Children's Medical and Surgical Center. This comprises three inpatient units.

November 24–25, Saturday–Sunday. *The Perry Como Christmas Show* is presented at the Front Row Theatre, Highland Heights, Ohio. Nick Perito leads the orchestra and the Caroling Party Singers provide support during the tour. Jack Swersie makes his debut with the tour as a comedy juggler.

November 27–29, Tuesday–Thursday. *The Perry Como Christmas Show* is presented at the Valley Forge Music Fair in Devon, Pennsylvania.

November 30–December 3, Friday–Monday. *The Perry Como Christmas Show* is presented at the Westbury Music Fair on Long Island. On December 4, Perry records an interview for *Live with Regis and Kathie Lee* on ABC-TV which is shown on December 5.

December (undated). *The Perry Como Christmas Show* is presented at the Niagara Falls Convention Center.

December 9–10, Saturday–Sunday. *The Perry Como Christmas Show* is at Shea's Buffalo Theatre.

December 11–12, Tuesday–Wednesday. *The Perry Como Christmas Show* is presented at the Landmark Theatre, Syracuse. Jack Swersie provides the comedy support.

December 14–15, Friday–Saturday. *The Perry Como Christmas Show* is presented at Syria Mosque in Pittsburgh.

December 17–19, Monday–Wednesday. *The Perry Como Christmas Show* is at the Riverside Theatre, Milwaukee.

December 21–22, Friday–Saturday. *The Perry Como Christmas Show* is presented at the Sunrise Musical Theatre, Miami Beach. The show is completely sold out both days.

1991

March 2–3, Saturday–Sunday. Again hosts the Sammy Davis Jr. Variety Club Telethon at the Adam's Mark Hotel in St. Louis. Bob Wynn is the producer.

June 11, Tuesday. Entertains at a benefit dinner at Bel Age Hotel's Rooftop Atrium in West Hollywood for singer John Gary who is suffering with inoperable cancer. Other stars at the event include Esther Williams, Eddie Fisher, Red Buttons, Barbara Eden, Liza Minnelli, Johnny Mathis, Rich Little and many others. The fund raiser takes place in Bel Air, West Hollywood, at the Bel Age Hotel and the cost of admission is $5000 per couple. Press reports indicate that Perry gets stuck in an elevator for an hour with Milton Berle, Mel Tormé and Jerry Vale.

June 14, Friday. Perry is featured on the television program *Hard Copy* hosted by Terry Murphy. His career is briefly profiled with archive footage and an interview which had been recorded at the John Gary Fundraiser earlier that week is shown. When Perry was asked by a female reporter how long he had been married, he asked her how old she was. She said she was 28 and with a comically vacant glance, Perry said, "As Bob Hope says, I have a chicken that old!" Further on in the interview while recalling his weekly TV show years, Perry recalled what his "ratings war" buddy Jackie Gleason had said when asked how he wanted to be remembered: "I just want to be remembered!" Perry obviously liked the idea of that.

September 29, Sunday. Headlines the Good Shepherd Celebrity Classic benefit show in Allentown, Pennsylvania.

November 22–24, Friday–Sunday. *Perry Como's Holiday Show* is at Star Plaza Theatre, Merriville, Indiana.

November 25, Monday. *Perry Como's Holiday Show* is at the Fox Theatre in St. Louis.

November 27, Wednesday. Perry is presented with the St. Louis Variety Club's "Champion for Kids" Award following his work on the Sammy Davis Jr. telethon in March.

December 2, Monday. *Perry Como's Holiday Show* is due to be presented at Illinois State University's Braden Auditorium but has to be cancelled at the last moment because of illness. It is re-scheduled for January 6.

December 4, Wednesday. *Perry Como's Holiday Show* is due to be presented at A. J. Palumbo Center on the Duquesne University campus in Pittsburgh but Perry has to cancel as he has the flu. The show is re-scheduled for December 16.

December 5, Thursday. *Perry Como's Holiday Show* at the Valley Forge Music Fair in Devon, Pennsylvania. Jack Swersie provides the comedy support.

December 7–8, Saturday–Sunday. *Perry Como's Holiday Show* is presented at the Eastman Theatre, Rochester.

December 13, Friday. *Perry Como's Holiday Show* is at the Worcester Centrum in Massachusetts. The crowd is estimated at 10,000.

December 15, Sunday. *Perry Como's Holiday Show* moves on to the Hersheypark Arena in Hershey.

December 16, Monday. *Perry Como's Holiday Show* is presented at the A. J. Palumbo Center in Pittsburgh.

December (undated). *Perry Como's Holiday Show* is presented at Ruth Eckerd Hall, Clearwater, Florida.

December 19, Thursday. *Perry Como's Holiday Show* moves on to the Ocean Center in Daytona Beach, Florida.

December 21–22, Saturday–Sunday. *Perry Como's Holiday Show* is at Sunrise Musical Theatre in Miami Beach.

December 27–29, Friday–Sunday. *Perry Como's Holiday Show* is presented at the Trump Castle Casino Resort, Atlantic City.

1992

January 6. *Perry Como's Holiday Show* is presented at Illinois State University's Braden Auditorium.

March 7–8, Saturday–Sunday (10:30–5:30 P.M.). Entertains at the Sammy Davis Jr. Memorial Variety Club Telethon at the Adam's Mark Hotel in St. Louis, Missouri. Bob Wynn is the producer.

May 24, Sunday. Sings "No Other Love" at the National Memorial Day Concert on the West Lawn of the Capitol Building in Washington, D.C. Perry continues by singing "For Me and My Gal" and gets the audience joining in too. Perry closes his musical offering with "We'll Meet Again." Others featured are Ossie Davis (who acted as host), Mel Tormé, Leslie Uggams, Roger Williams, Richard Thomas and General Colin Powell. The event takes place in pouring rain and is aired live on PBS-TV at 7:30 P.M.

November 29, Sunday. *Perry Como's Holiday Show* starts its tour at the Patriot Center on the George Mason University campus in Washington, D.C.

November 30, Monday. *Perry Como's Holiday Show* is presented in the Baltimore Arena, Baltimore.

December 2, Wednesday. *Perry Como's Holiday Show* is at the Knickerbocker Arena, Albany, New York.

December 4–5, Friday–Saturday. Providence, Rhode Island, is the location for *Perry Como's Holiday Show*.

December 6, Sunday. *Perry Como's Holiday Show* moves on to the Hartford Civic Center, Connecticut.

December 8, Tuesday. *Perry Como's Holiday Show* is at Portland, Maine.

December 9, Wednesday. The Municipal Auditorium in Lowell, Massachusetts, is the venue for *Perry Como's Holiday Show.*

December 11, Friday. *Perry Como's Holiday Show* is at the Convention Center, Niagara Falls, New York. Perry stays at the nearby Radisson Hotel.

December 12, Saturday. *Perry Como's Holiday Show* is presented at the Landmark Theatre, Syracuse. Nick Perito leads the orchestra; the Perry Como Holiday Singers and Jack Swersie provide support.

December 13, Sunday. *Perry Como's Holiday Show* moves on to Poughkeepsie, New York.

December 16–18, Wednesday–Friday. *Perry Como's Holiday Show* is at the Westbury Music Fair.

December 20–21, Sunday–Monday. *Perry Como's Holiday Show* is at the Valley Forge Music Fair in Devon, Pennsylvania. The shows are completely sold out.

December 23, Wednesday. *Perry Como's Holiday Show* is at the West Palm Beach Auditorium.

December 26, Saturday. *Perry Como's Holiday Show* appears in Miami, Florida.

December 27, Sunday. Perry puts on his *Holiday Show* at the Jacksonville Coliseum in Florida.

December 28, Monday. *Perry Como's Holiday Show* moves on to Tampa, Florida.

December 29, Tuesday. *Perry Como's Holiday Show* is at the Orlando Arena, Orlando, Florida.

1993

March 8, Monday. Gives a concert at NHK Hall in Tokyo, Japan. Perry is accompanied by a Japanese orchestra (conducted by Nick Perito) and an unidentified group of female singers. It is thought that this is the last of a three-concert farewell tour.

1994

January 15, Saturday (9:20 P.M.). Appears on *Kenny Live* on RTE1-TV in Dublin, Ireland.

January 21, Friday. Perry tapes *Perry Como's Irish Christmas Show* at The Point in Dublin before a crowd of 4,000. Irish star Twink offers support and Nick Perito leads the RTE Concert Orchestra. The show is produced and directed by Bob Wynn. Nick Perito is the musical director and Dick Williams is choral director.

November 15, Thursday. Appears on the *Live with Regis and Kathie Lee* program and discusses his television special and live concert in Dublin, Ireland. Perry sings "It Could Happen to You" accompanied by Nick Perito.

December (various dates). *Perry Como's Irish Christmas* airs on PBS-TV.

1995

May 20–21, Saturday–Sunday. Perry is at the Duke Children's Classic Celebrity Golf Tournament at the Croasdaile Country Club golf course in Durham, North Carolina. He performs a selection of his classic songs for the Duke Children's Classic Celebrity Show at Cameron Stadium.

1996

May 18–19, Saturday–Sunday. Perry is unable to attend the Duke Children's Classic Celebrity Golf Tournament in Durham, North Carolina, for the first time in many years. Pat Boone acts as m.c.

September 24, Tuesday. Perry executes his Last Will and Testament which revokes all earlier wills. Roselle and his son Ronald are appointed as co–Personal Representatives. He leaves the bulk of his estate to Roselle with provision made for his grandchildren. If Roselle should not survive him, he leaves his estate to his descendants per stirpes.

1998

July 31, Friday. Perry and Roselle celebrate their 65th wedding anniversary.

August 12, Tuesday. Roselle suffers a heart attack and although she is rushed to Jupiter hospital, she dies the same day. She was 86 although her obituaries give her age as 84.

August 14, Thursday. Roselle is buried at a private ceremony in Jupiter, Florida, after a private funeral service attended by 60 family members and friends at St. Jude Roman Catholic Church.

1999

May 15, Saturday. For his 87th birthday, a life-size statue of Perry Como is dedicated in his hometown of Canonsburg, Pennsylvania.

2000

October (undated). Perry is rushed to the emergency room at Jupiter Medical Center after a spell of light-headedness and shortage of breath. He spends four days in the hospital before returning home.

December 22, Friday. A special biography is broadcast on A&E in the U.S. about Perry Como. The show runs for 50 minutes approximately and is called *The Singing Barber*. The show is updated after Perry passes away.

2001

May 12, Saturday. Perry dies in his sleep on his eighty-ninth birthday (according to his baptism certificate) at his home in Jupiter of natural causes. He is with his caregiver and simply closes his eyes while sitting in a chair in his bedroom.

May 18, Friday. Perry's funeral takes place at St. Edward Catholic Church in Palm Beach. Four hundred mourners are present. Perry is buried in Riverside Cemetery in Jupiter, Florida.

Chapter Notes

Introduction

1. "The Crooner, R.I.P.," by William F. Buckley, *National Review Online*, May 18, 2001.
2. *Ibid.*
3. Joel Whitburn, *Joel Whitburn Presents a Century of Pop Music* (Menomonee Falls, WI: Record Research, 2003).
4. *Christmas at the Hollywood Palace*, American Public Television, 2004.
5. "The Crooner, R. I. P."
6. "The Man Who Created Casual," by Richard Cook, *New Statesman*, April 2000.
7. Chart definition extends to any record reaching the Top 100.

Chapter 1

1. Church records relating to Como's baptism show his date of birth as May 12, 1912. The house in which he was born was later renumbered 527 Franklin Avenue.
2. *www.abruzzo2000.com*. Many archaeological findings show that the place was inhabited since prehistory. There is no certain information for the Roman period, but there is evidence of a Lombard presence, after the fall of the Roman empire, in the many names left in the area and in the cult of Sant'Angelo, the patron saint of these German tribes. The first news of medieval settlements dates back to the 11th century, when the center was a checkpoint on the road connecting Chieti to the monastery of Valva, and from the *Chronicon Vulturnensis* we know it consisted of 11 "villas" (a Latin term meaning an agricultural community): Castello Alberico, Pizzo Inferiore and Pizzo Superiore, Castelcieco, Pietrabbondante, Valle della Terra, Forca di Palena, Villa Sant'Egidio, Malvicino, Villa San Cristanziano and Lettopalena. In this period the castle was built by the Maneri family, lords also of Pacentro. Then in the 14th and 15th century it was ruled by the Orsini family, later on by the powerful Caldora, who made Palena an administrative center for the rich Maiella pastures. In 1447 a census was made in the Sangro Valley, and Palena had a count of 824 inhabitants. The last medieval lords were the d'Aquino. There were two terrible earthquakes in 1456 and 1706. The Second World War caused massive destruction in the area, and now only ruins of the 11th century castle, the bell tower of the parish church and the fine chiesa del Rosario are left as memories of the rich past.
3. Chuck Willis, *Destination America* (London: DK Publishing, 2005). U.S. immigration policy was to impose strict health checks on newly arrived immigrants, as well as to look for any evidence of previous crimes or misdemeanors.
4. Gene Como, author interview, September 4, 2007.
5. Ellis Island immigration record, *www.ellisisland.com*.
6. Gene Como, author interview.
7. Ken White, Archives & Records Center, Diocese of Pittsburgh, by email to author July 10, 2007.
8. Many commentators over the years have taken the family of thirteen as a statement of fact. Como's youngest brother, Gene (author interview), also referred to being one of thirteen children, but there was duplication in the names of three of the offspring quoted.
9. Perry's mother, Lucy, interviewed for the *San Antonio Light*, May 12, 1957, confirmed that Perry was one of seven children who survived to adulthood. "He was the middle one. We had four boys and three girls."
10. *Arlene Herson Show*, syndicated television, June 6, 1984. As late as 1984, Perry was happy to engage in a discussion that suggested he was the seventh son of a seventh son.
11. Gina Nestor, Canonsburg historian, compiler of high school graduation lists.
12. Perry Como interviewed by Michael Parkinson, *Parkinson*, BBC TV, November 26, 1977.
13. Perry Como interview by Brian Gumble, *Today*, NBC-TV, shown July 5, 6, and 7, 1983.
14. *Ibid.*
15. *The Barber Comes to Town*, BBC2 Television, December 14, 1975.
16. Gene Como, author interview.
17. Nick Tosches, *Dino: Living High in the Dirty Business of Dreams* (London: Secker and Warburg, 1992). Dean Martin's father, Gaetano Crocetti, was a barber in Steubenville, Ohio, about 35 miles from Canonsburg.
18. Judy Flanders, *Montreal Sun*, December 11, 1981.

19. *The Barber Comes to Town.*

20. *Observer-Reporter*, Washington PA, March 21, 2004.

21. *Arlene Herson Show.*

22. Perry struggled in TV interviews to remember the surname of his erstwhile partner, sometimes referring to him as "McHugh."

23. *Arlene Herson Show.*

24. Unpublished song, lyrics taken from *Parkinson* interview.

25. *Parkinson.*

26. As with her husband's birth, there is a discrepancy between the commonly accepted date of Roselle's birth and that shown in church records. The latter indicate that she was born on May 11, 1912, and show her family name as "Bellino." The 1920 and 1930 U.S. Census details show similar information although the family name in the 1920 survey is shown as "Ballino." It is not known when the family adopted the spelling of "Belline." As to her year of birth, Como said in a newspaper interview in 1983 (*Peoria Journal Star*, July 23) that Roselle had initially believed that she was born in 1912 until a passport application revealed that she was two years younger than she thought. The 1920 (January) Census shows her as age 7, however, and the 1930 (April) equivalent has her as 17. Her headstone shows her year of birth as 1914.

27. There is some conjecture about the nature of Perry's move to Meadville. Once Como's fame was established, many articles about him made reference only to his having gone to Cleveland for a vacation early in 1933 and stated that his audition with the Carlone band came about almost as a chance encounter during that vacation. More contemporary reports provide references to Como's leaving Canonsburg, although again there is variation. The *Nebraska State Journal* (October 24, 1943) carried a story that Como's barbering destination after leaving Canonsburg was Youngstown, Ohio.

A locally published book, *The Ghosts of Hotel Conneaut and Conneaut Lake Park* by Carrie Andra Pavlik, contains reference to Como working as a barber in the hotel, a fact confirmed by Pavlik in email to the present authors: "It's true. He worked as a barber in one of the hotels. They would call him 'the singing barber' because he would sing as he cut hair! I'm not sure, but I think he performed at The Beach Club in the Park as well." Local Conneaut historian Mike Costello is less certain. "Could be an urban legend. But people tell this story like it is gospel" (email to authors).

28. Radio interview with David Jacobs, BBC Radio 2, December 1994.

29. *Ibid.*

30. Colin Escott, *Roadkill on the Three-Chord Highway: Art and Trash in American Popular Music* (London: Routledge, 2002).

31. "Perry Como Tells His Secret of Happy Living to Joseph Kaye," *Coronet*, date unknown.

32. *Arlene Herson Show.*

33. Roy Hemming and David Hajdu, *Discovering Great Singers of Classic Pop* (New York: Newmarket, 1991).

34. Bing Crosby interviewed by Michael Parkinson, *Parkinson*, BBC TV, 1972.

35. *Daily Independent*, Monessen, PA, November 19, 1934.

36. *Ibid.*

37. R. David Heileman, writing about John Mensinger, *Sun Newspapers*, October 18, 2001.

38. Gene Como, author interview.

39. *Daily Notes*, Canonsburg, PA, April 5, 1933.

40. The Crystal Slipper later changed its name to the Trianon Ballroom, emulating a similarly named establishment in Chicago.

41. *Daily Independent*, July 17, 1935. There is some doubt as to the accuracy of this report—Carlone's band was regarded very much as a Midwest territory band, and whether they ever spread their bookings as far as Texas is doubtful.

42. *Parkinson.*

43. David Jacobs interview.

44. Hemming and Hadju.

45. George T. Simon and Friends, *The Best of the Music Makers* (Garden City, NY: Doubleday, 1979).

46. Rudy Vallee quoted by Henry Pleasants, *The Great American Popular Singers* (London: Victor Gollancz, 1974).

47. *Ibid.*

48. *The Barber Comes to Town.*

49. *Daily Notes*, July 16, 1934.

50. *A Tribute to Bing Crosby*—Perry Como with John Williams and the Boston Pops Orchestra, PBS-TV, August 14, 1988.

51. *Parkinson.*

52. Heileman, *Sun Newspapers.*

53. *Arlene Herson Show.*

54. Perry Como interviewed by Ken Barnes at a function in London, *The Song Stylists*, BBC Radio2, December 17, 1973.

55. *Daily Independent*, November 23, 1934.

56. Perry also said that he briefly considered calling himself "Pete Como." U.S. Army Reserve radio interview, December 1976.

Chapter 2

1. Joel Whitburn, *Pop Memories 1890–1954: The History of American Popular Music* (Menomonee Falls, WI: Record Research, 1986).

2. University of Memphis research.

3. George T. Simon, *The Big Bands* (New York: Macmillan, 1967).

4. *The Barber Comes to Town.*

5. Simon, *The Big Bands.*

6. Frankie Laine and Joseph Laredo, *That Lucky Old Son: The Autobiography of Frankie Laine* (New York: Pathfinder, 1993).

7. Cub Koda, All Music Guide as quoted on www.mmguide.musicmatch.com.

8. Later known as Marilyn Maxwell at the behest of MGM chief Louis B. Mayer, who insisted that she use her middle name of Marilyn in place of Marvel.

9. *The Barber Comes to Town.*

10. Ted Weems quoted in *Reader's Digest Music Guide* 1962.

11. Pleasants, *The Great American Popular Singers.*

12. By the end of the 1930s, Crosby had lost most the range that was such a characteristic of his voice through that decade. In 1960, he guested on Como's TV show and at the end of a medley, Como hit and sustained the high note at the end of his TV theme song, "Dream Along with Me," with consummate ease. "Man," said Crosby, "you can still soar, can't you?"

13. Bing Crosby interviewed by Joe Franklin on Franklin's television show in New York, December 3, 1976.

14. *The Barber Comes to Town.*

15. Decca Records was formed in the United Kingdom in 1929 by Edward Lewis. For a full history of the circumstances leading to the formation of Decca Records in the United States and the recruitment of Jack Kapp from Brunswick Records, see Gary Giddins, *Bing Crosby: A Pocketful of Dreams* (Boston: Little, Brown, 2001).

16. Colin Escott, *Yesterday and Today*, booklet accompanying RCA boxed CD set, 1993.

17. Colin Escott tells the Dave Kapp story in his *Roadkill on the Three-Chord Highway*. He bases the story on an interview that Como gave him in 1993 and cites the session where Como recorded "Don't Let the Stars Get in Your Eyes" as the one where the altercation with Kapp occurred. Ray Charles was also present at the session but had no recollection of a public standoff between Como and Kapp.

18. Ted Weems, *Reader's Digest Music Guide* 1962.

19. Nick Perito, *I Just Happened to Be There* (Philadelphia: Xlibris, 2004).

20. Crosby sang the same song on his *Kraft Music Hall* radio show around this time and demonstrates the gap that still existed between him and the next generation of singers, as typified by Como.

21. Perry Como interviewed by Phil Donahue on his syndicated television show *Donahue*, September 10, 1979.

22. *Variety*, January 31, 1940.

23. The show returned during 1943–44, with Hildegarde as host.

24. Escott, *Roadkill on the Three-Chord Highway.*

25. "Como Now Rivals Crosby and Sinatra with Juke-Box Fans," *Sunday Times*, Cumberland, MD, September 1, 1946.

26. "Olly olly oxen free" was often used in games such as hide-and-seek to indicate that it was safe for the child hiding to come out into the open.

27. Will Friedwald, *Sinatra: The Song Is You* (New York: Da Capo, 1997).

28. The Clarification Directive issued on July 27, 1942, stated that the order of priority for being drafted was (a) single men with no dependents—1A; (b) single men with financial dependents and employed in non-essential industries—3A; (c) single men with financial dependents and employed in essential industries—3B; (d) married men, maintaining bona-fide family relationships, with no children and in non-essential industries—3A; (e) married men, maintaining bona-fide family relationships, with no children and in essential industries—3B; (f) married men, maintaining bona-fide family relationships, with children and in non-essential industries—3A; (g) married men, maintaining bona-fide family relationships, with children and in essential industries—3B.

29. U.S. Army Reserve radio interview, December 1976.

Chapter 3

1. Simon, *The Big Bands.*

2. Perry Como interviewed by Chris Stuart, BBC Radio 2, broadcast May 18, 1992.

3. Escott, *Yesterday and Today.*

4. *Donahue.*

5. Ray Charles, email to authors, March 6, 2008.

6. Como interview by Chris Stuart.

7. *Variety*, April 14, 1943.

8. *Variety*, January 12, 1944.

9. *New York World-Telegram*, July 1943.

10. *Variety*, June 16, 1943.

11. "I Call on Perry Como," by Pete Martin, *Saturday Evening Post*, January 1960.

12. *Newsweek*, June 29, 1953.

13. Geoffrey C. Ward, *Jazz: A History of America's Music* (New York: Alfred A. Knopf, 2000).

14. Escott, *Yesterday and Today.*

15. *Billboard*, March 16, 1946.

16. *Billboard*, August 24, 1946.

17. *New York Times*, August 29, 1943.

18. *Variety*, January 24, 1944.

19. *Variety*, July 19, 1944.

20. L&M owned the Chesterfield brand from 1911 to 1998. Altria, the parent company of Philip Morris, Inc., now owns it.

21. Chesterfield advertising ca. 1918.

22. David Como, author interview, September 17, 2007.

23. Radio Hall of Fame, *www.radiohof.org.*

24. Como interview by David Jacobs.

25. *Variety*, December 13, 1944.

26. The original "Gold" record awards were presented to artists by their own record companies to publicize the achievement of 1,000,000 sales. The first of these was awarded by RCA to Glenn Miller in February 1942, celebrating 1,200,000 sales of "Chattanooga Choo Choo." The first official designation of a "Gold" record by the Recording Industry Association of America (RIAA) was established for singles in 1958, and the RIAA also trademarked the term "Gold Award" in the United States. On March 14, 1958, the RIAA certified Perry Como's hit single "Catch a Falling Star" as its first ever Gold record for sales of over one million. In the United States, the RIAA awards certification is based on the number of albums and singles sold through retail and other ancillary markets. Certification is not automatic; for an award to be made, the record label must pay a fee to have the sales of the recording audited. The audit is conducted against unit shipments (most often an artists' royalty statement is used), which includes albums sold directly to retailers and one-stops, direct to consumer sales (music clubs and mail order) and other outlets. Shipments that could potentially be returned to the label cannot be counted. (Recording Industry Association of America, *www.riaa.com*).

27. From audio tape recording made by Bing Crosby fan John Joyce at the opening night of Crosby's 1976 season at the London Palladium. The show over-ran and some songs, including "Temptation," were cut from subsequent shows.

28. *A Perry Como Discography and CD Companion*, http://kokomo.ca.

29. Joel Whitburn, *Billboard Pop Hits 1940–1954* (Menomonee Falls, WI: Record Research, 1994).

30. *Ibid.*

31. *Billboard*, July 28, 1945.

32. *Time*, March 18, 1946.

Chapter 4

1. *Parkinson.*

2. *Today.*

3. *The Barber Comes to Town.*
4. Ray Charles, author interview, September 20, 2007.
5. *The Barber Comes to Town.*
6. *Parkinson.*
7. *A Perry Como Album* (Dell Magazines, 1950).
8. *Ibid.*
9. *Variety*, November 8, 1944.
10. *New York Times*, November 30, 1944.
11. *New York Times*, March 28, 1946.
12. *A Perry Como Album.*
13. Harrison Carroll's syndicated column from Hollywood, as seen in *The Era*, Bradford, PA, May 24, 1946.
14. *Daily News*, Greensboro KY, June 1, 1946.
15. William Self, who produced a 1957 Christmas special with Sinatra and Crosby, told of the difficulties in recording the two stars together because of Sinatra's preference for singing live in the evening, and Crosby's desire to lip-sync to a track he had recorded first thing in the morning. *Happy Holiday with Bing and Frank*, Hart Sharp Video, 2003.
16. *New York Times*, September 20, 1946.
17. *Washington Post*, October 18, 1946.
18. *Los Angeles Times*, September 21, 1946.
19. "He Got Rich Quick," by Jack Sher, *Los Angeles Times*, March 23, 1947.
20. *Ibid.*
21. *A Perry Como Album.*
22. Edith Gwynn's syndicated column as reproduced in the *Pottstown Mercury*, Pottstown, PA, April 29, 1948.
23. *Words and Music*, WarnerVideo, 2007.
24. *Los Angeles Times*, January 15, 1949.
25. *New York Times*, December 10, 1948.
26. Elizabeth Taylor talking to David Frost on an American TV show as reproduced by Anne Edwards, *Judy Garland* (London: Constable, 1975). Miss Taylor's use of the word "fuck" was bleeped out in the television interview.
27. *Ibid.*
28. *Parkinson.*
29. Hedda Hopper in her syndicated column of August 27, 1948, said that Perry was to star alongside Judy Garland in the forthcoming MGM picture *Annie Get Your Gun*. She was incorrect. Louella Parsons' syndicated newspaper column suggested in October 1952 that Perry was being considered for the role of Russ Columbo in a biopic of the dead crooner. The film was never made. Also John P. Shanley, in the *New York Times* of October 16, 1960, quoted Como as saying that he was considering taking a starring role as a monk in a film to be called *The Saint Bernard Pass* that would be set in a monastery in Switzerland. Nothing came of this either.

Chapter 5

1. *Billboard*, November 24, 1945.
2. *Time*, March 18, 1946.
3. Whitburn, *Billboard Pop Hits 1940–1954.* "I'm Always Chasing Rainbows" reached #7 in the *Billboard* best seller chart.
4. *Billboard*, January 12, 1946.
5. Columbo wrote the melody with Clarence Gaskill. Lyrics were written by Leo Robin.
6. *The First Thirty Years*, booklet accompanying RCA boxed set, 1973.
7. Como interview by Chris Stuart.
8. *Billboard*, March 16, 1946.
9. *A Perry Como Album.*
10. Often referring to himself as "the other Ray Charles," Charles Raymond ("Chuck") Offenberg was born in Chicago on September 13, 1918. He worked in radio and on Broadway during the war, changing his name to "Ray Charles" in 1944, ten years before a black rhythm and blues singer called Ray Charles Robinson also took the name "Ray Charles."
11. *The Lowell Sun*, February 16, 1946.
12. "He Got Rich Quick."
13. *Regis & Kathy Live*, 1984.
14. "He Got Rich Quick."
15. *Open House*, BBC Radio 2, October 26, 1973. Perry Como interviewed by Pete Murray.
16. *Parkinson.*
17. "He Got Rich Quick."
18. *Current Population Reports—Consumer Income*, U.S. Department of Commerce, March 2, 1948. The report estimated that average income for a white family was $2,718 and for a black family $1,538. Computed average for all races was $2,621. Only 1.4 percent of families reported an income in excess of $10,000.
19. "He Got Rich Quick."
20. *Ibid.*
21. *Billboard*, September 7, 1946.
22. *Billboard*, August 17, 1946.
23. *Billboard*, September 1946.
24. *Variety*, August 27, 1947.
25. *Ibid.*
26. David Como, author interview.
27. *Variety*, August 27, 1947.
28. Buz Kohan, author interview, June 19, 2007.
29. Mickey Glass, interview by Larry Trompeter and Colleen Zwack, American Music Research Center, Music Library, University of Colorado (UCL) at Boulder, May 18, 2005.
30. *Ibid.*
31. Como interview by Chris Stuart.
32. *Parkinson.*
33. David Como, author interview.
34. *The Barber Comes to Town.*
35. "He Got Rich Quick."
36. *A Perry Como Album.*
37. *Variety*, April 10, 1946.
38. *Time*, March 18, 1946.
39. *Billboard*, June 15, 1946.
40. Whitburn, *Billboard Pop Hits 1940–1954.*
41. *Billboard*, June 15, 1946.
42. Whitburn, *Billboard Pop Hits 1940–1954.*
43. Jack O'Brian, syndicated column in *Iowa Press Citizen*, August 9, 1946.
44. "Winter Wonderland" had been a hit for Guy Lombardo's Band in December 1934, along with "Santa Claus Is Coming to Town" by George Hall and His Orchestra. Joel Whitburn, *Christmas in the Charts* (Menomonee Falls, WI: Record Research, 2004).
45. Bing Crosby's "White Christmas" was first recorded in May 1942.
46. *Variety*, August 20, 1947.
47. "I Call on Perry Como."
48. *Variety*, September 10, 1947.
49. Joel Whitburn, *Billboard Pop Hits 1940–1954.*
50. *Ibid.*

Chapter 6

1. *Chesterfield Supper Club*, December 24, 1948.
2. *Letter from America*, Alistair Cooke, BBC Home Service, January 19, 1951.
3. Ray Charles quoted in "Perry Como," biographical sketch by the Academy of Television Arts and Science (ATAS) Hall of Fame, 1989.
4. *TV Guide*, May 2001.
5. For a detailed description of the early years of television, see *www.tvhistory.tv*.
6. Television set sales figures from Cobbett Steinberg, *Television Facts* (New York: Facts on File, 1980).
7. Como interview by David Jacobs.
8. Como interview by Chris Stuart.
9. *TV-AM Cleveland*, 1984.
10. Charles Dexter, *Star Weekly*, Toronto, October 29, 1955.
11. *www.high-techproductions.com*.
12. *Variety*, December 29, 1948.
13. *Ibid.*
14. Ray Charles, author interview.
15. *Variety*, January 19, 1949.
16. *Ibid.*
17. *Ibid.*
18. *Ibid.*
19. *TV Guide*, May 2001.
20. Lionel Pairpoint, Malcolm Macfarlane, and Greg Van Beek, *The Chronological Bing Crosby on Television*, 2003.
21. Malcolm Macfarlane, *Bing Crosby—Day by Day* (Metuchen, NJ: Scarecrow, 2001).
22. *Variety*, June 5, 1950.
23. *New York Times*, October 10, 1951.
24. *New York Times*, April 10, 1949.
25. *TV Guide*, May 2001.
26. "Perry Como," ATAS Hall of Fame.
27. Como interview by Chris Stuart.
28. Russell Sanjek, *American Popular Music and Its Business: The First Four Hundred Years* (New York: Oxford University Press, 1988).
29. Crosby's first foray into recording his radio show was to use the old format of 16" transcription discs. He moved to tape as soon as it was commercially available.
30. *Variety*, September 14, 1949.
31. The #1 hit version of "You're Breaking My Heart" belonged to Vic Damone, who had met Como at the New York Paramount while working there as an usher and elevator operator.
32. *Billboard*, September 17, 1949.
33. *Variety*, October 19, 1949.
34. *Ibid.*
35. *Ibid.*
36. *Variety*, October 26, 1949.
37. *Ibid.*
38. John Bush, *All Music Guide*, http://www.answers.com/topic/mitchell-ayres.
39. "Nice Guys Finish First," *Collier's*, January 6, 1956.
40. George Townsend, sleeve note to RCA CD *Perry Como with the Fontane Sisters*, 2001.
41. Whitburn, *Billboard Pop Hits 1940–1954*.
42. *Ibid.*
43. Robert Jones, sleeve note to CD *Legendary Singers*, Time-Life, 1998.
44. *Time*, December 27, 1948.
45. Sanjek, *American Popular Music and Its Business*.
46. *New York Times*, June 5, 1988.
47. *Recollections—Journal of American Recorded Music*. See also *http://ronpenndorf.com/labelography 2.html*.
48. Peter Copeland, British Library Sound Archive, justified the choice of speed in scientific terms as follows: "The 45 RPM record was developed by RCA Victor company in 1948—immediately following the invention of 'vinyl' plastic and the development of the 12" LP record by CBS engineers (also in 1948). The 45 RPM speed was the only one to be decided by a precise optimization procedure. Calculus was used to show that the optimum use of a disc record of constant rotational speed occurs when the innermost recorded diameter is half the outermost recorded diameter. That's why a 7-inch single has a label 3½ inches in diameter. Given the CBS LP vinyl groove dimensions and certain assumptions about the bandwidth and tolerable distortion, a speed of 45 rpm comes out of the formula."
However, George Avakian, who worked on the development of the LP before joining RCA, offered a different rationale to Classic Records in 1998: "In 1962, when I was at RCA, someone finally told me where 45 rpm came from. They apparently took 78 and subtracted 33 which left them with 45, which they went with out of spite." As quoted on *http://www.boo-ga-loo.demon.co.uk*.
49. *Billboard*, April 2, 1949, four-page RCA advertisement.
50. Sanjek, *American Popular Music and Its Business*.
51. *Downbeat*, April 8, 1949.
52. Sanjek, *American Popular Music and Its Business*.
53. George Townsend, writing on *www.kokomo.ca*.
54. *Time*, April 4, 1949.
55. *A Perry Como Album*.
56. Whitburn, *Billboard Pop Hits 1940–1954*. Jo Stafford and Gordon MacRae's version ran neck and neck with Como's for the chart honors. The other two were recordings by Dinah Shore and Ilene Woods.
57. *Downbeat*, December 30, 1949.

Chapter 7

1. David Halberstam, *The Fifties* (New York: Fawcett Columbine, 1993).
2. *Ibid.*
3. *Ibid.*
4. Joshua Zeitz, writing on *www.americanculture.com*.
5. Sanjek, *American Popular Music and Its Business*.
6. *Ibid.*
7. *Ibid.*
8. *Ibid.*
9. *Ibid.*
10. *Ibid.*
11. *Time*, June 29, 1953.
12. *Ibid.*
13. *Ibid.*
14. Escott, *Yesterday and Today*.
15. *Newsweek*, June 29, 1953.
16. *Ibid.*
17. *The Barber Comes to Town*.
18. *Parkinson*.

19. *Perry Como and The Fontane Sisters*, booklet.
20. Whitburn, *Billboard Pop Hits 1940–1954*.
21. *www.kokomo.ca*.
22. Como interview with Chris Stuart.
23. Whitburn, *Billboard Pop Hits 1940–1954*.
24. Como had of course made a number of sides with the Fontane Sisters, but these were more solos with choral support rather than a duet, which, strictly defined, is a piece performed by two singers.
25. Whitburn, *Billboard Pop Hits 1940–1954*.
26. *The Perry Como Show*, February 21, 1951.
27. Griffis, Ken, *Hear My Song: The Story of the Celebrated Sons of the Pioneers*, rev. ed. (Northglenn CO: Norken, 1996).
28. Perry Como press release issued by Harry Sobel, date unknown.
29. Later in the fifties, however, CBS revived the simulcast by broadcasting Como's TV show on radio.
30. *Variety*, January 25, 1950.
31. *Ibid.*
32. "Cooley: Calm Approach to Como," by Richard F. Shepard, *New York Times*, January 15, 1956.
33. *Time*, June 16, 1952.
34. *Ibid.*
35. Dr Richard Doll, *British Medical Journal*, 1950.
36. *Variety*, August 29, 1951.
37. *Variety*, November 21, 1951.
38. *Variety*, March 7, 1951.
39. *New York Times*, December 9, 1951.
40. *Ibid.*
41. *Ibid.*
42. Stephen Pouliot, author interview, September 21, 2007.
43. *New York Times*, December 9, 1951.

Chapter 8

1. "Perry Como Album," *Skyline*, 1957.
2. "Nice Guys Finish First," *Collier's*, January 6, 1956.
3. David Como, author interview.
4. *A Perry Como Album* (Dell Magazines, 1950).
5. David Como, author interview.
6. "Perry Como Legend: He's 'Such a Good Boy,'" *San Antonio Light*, May 12, 1957.
7. Laura Deni, "Broadway to Vegas," August 24, 1998 (a syndicated column, published in several newspapers).
8. Ray Charles, email to author, May 20, 2008.
9. David Como, author interview.
10. *Time*, March 16, 1959.
11. *Celebrity Golf*, October 9, 1960.
12. *www.hollisny.com*.
13. *The Morning Herald*, Uniontown PA, July 29, 1960.
14. *Ibid.*
15. "About Long Island," *New York Times*, June 10, 1990.
16. *Daily Notes*, June 17, 1950.
17. Article by Mannie Sachs, RCA Records Vice President and General Manager, *Billboard*, July 4, 1953.
18. *Downbeat*, May 20, 1949.
19. "Perry Como Story," by Joseph P. Kaye, *Coronet*, May 1953.
20. *Downbeat*, July 16, 1952.
21. Dorothy Kilgallen's syndicated column as seen in *The Charleston Gazette*, May 21, 1953.

22. *AM Cleveland*, July 31, 1984.
23. *A Perry Como Album* (Dell Magazines, 1950).
24. *Billboard*, August 7, 1954.
25. *Ibid.*
26. Escott, *Yesterday and Today*.
27. Ray Charles, author interview.
28. Sleeve note to *The Incomparable Como*, Reader's Digest (U.K.), 1975.
29. Don Tyler, *Hit Songs 1900–1955: American Popular Music of the Pre-Rock Era* (Jefferson NC: McFarland, 2007).
30. Robert Jones, sleeve note to CD *Legendary Singers*, 1988.
31. Laura Deni, "Broadway to Vegas," May 13, 2001.
32. *Billboard*, November 29, 1953.
33. Whitburn, *Billboard Pop Hits 1940–1954*
34. *Newsweek*, June 29, 1953.
35. *Time*, June 29, 1953.
36. *Billboard*, April 18, 1953.
37. *Billboard*, July 4, 1953.
38. *Ibid.*
39. *The Incomparable Como*.
40. *Billboard*, June 13, 1953.
41. Although the Emmy awards were established in 1949, other TV awards developed during the 1950s, including ones sponsored by *TV Guide*, *Look*, and the Sylvania electronics company. The Michael was the brainchild of Ed Sullivan, reflecting a growing rivalry between Los Angeles, whence the Emmy originated, and New York, where Sullivan worked. Although Hollywood dominated the film industry, most television programming at this time originated in New York. Sullivan launched his own television awards, the Michaels, in 1950 and hosted an annual award event until 1953. Como won a Michael for best male vocalist in 1951 and 1952.
42. *Variety*, February 18, 1953.
43. *Variety*, August 26, 1953.
44. The Nielsen ratings had started in 1950 and soon displaced both *Variety* and the Hooper ratings as the definitive source of information on who was watching what on TV. The two most quoted Nielsen measures were the "ratings points" and "share" scores. "Ratings points" showed the percentage of households that were tuned into a program, while the "share" showed the percentage of all in-use televisions that were tuned in.
45. *Los Angeles Times*, December 15, 1953.
46. *Variety*, December 16, 1953.
47. *Los Angeles Times*, December 15, 1953.
48. *Variety*, December 16, 1953.
49. Whitburn, *Billboard Pop Hits 1940–1954*.

Chapter 9

1. Vernon Presley was born in 1916, four years after Como.
2. "A Perry Como Album," *Skyline*, 1957.
3. Joel Whitburn, *Billboard Book of Top 40 Hits* (Menomonee Falls WI: Record Research, 1989).
4. Ray Charles, author interview.
5. "A Perry Como Album," *Skyline*, 1957.
6. " Perry Como Story."
7. *Variety*, August 25, 1954.
8. Ray Charles, author interview.
9. Charles Dexter, *Toronto Star*.

10. *New York Times*, April 1, 1955.
11. *Ibid.*
12. *Billboard*, October 1, 1955.
13. *Ibid.*
14. *New York Times*, September 19, 1955.
15. Colin Escott, sleeve note to *Juke Box Baby* CD.
16. *Ibid.*
17. *Press-Telegram*, Long Beach CA, December 1, 1955.
18. Ray Charles, author interview.
19. "How to Relax the Como Way," *New York Times*, January 29, 1956.
20. "Ye Olde Free-for-All," *TV Guide*, February 1956.
21. *Ibid.*
22. *Los Angeles Times*, April 12, 1956.
23. The eighth song, the moody "Black Moonlight," was a carryover from Perry's "Zing Zing, Zoom Zoom" session of December 1950.
24. *www.kokomo.ca.*
25. Will Friedwald, *Jazz Singing: America's Great Voices from Bessie Smith to Bebop and Beyond* (New York: Scribner's, 1990).
26. Como interview with Chris Stuart.
27. Ray Charles, author interview.
28. *Ibid.*
29. Mel Tormé, quoted in notes to RCA boxed set *The First Thirty Years*, 1973.
30. Como interview with Chris Stuart.
31. *The Barber Comes to Town.*
32. *Donahue.*
33. *Perry Como's Greatest Hits* CD, sleeve note.
34. "Perry Como Story."
35. Mickey Glass, interview by Larry Trompeter and Colleen Zwack.
36. *TV-AM Cleveland.*
37. *A Perry Como Album* (Dell Magazines, 1950).
38. Nick Perito, interviewed by Alan Cass, American Music Research Center, Music Library, University of Colorado (UCL), Boulder, March 15, 2002.
39. *A Perry Como Album* (Dell Magazines, 1950).
40. Ray Charles, author interview.
41. Tyler, *Hit Songs.*
42. *Legendary Singers*, CD sleeve note.
43. Isabelle Leymarie, "Mambo Mania," *UNESCO Courier*, January 1995, Vol. 48.
44. *The Incomparable Como.*
45. Details and quotations on the making of "Papa Loves Mambo" are taken from "A Hit Is Born," *Coronet*, February 1955, under Perry Como's own byline.
46. Fred L. Worth, *Elvis: His Life from A to Z* (New York: Random House, 1992).
47. *Perry Como's Greatest Hits*, CD sleeve note.
48. Consuelo Dodge, *The Everly Brothers: Ladies Love Outlaws* (Starke FL: CIN-DAV, 1991).
49. "I Call on Perry Como."
50. *Juke Box Baby* CD sleeve note.
51. *Billboard*, July 9, 1955.
52. Ray Charles, email to author, December 31, 2007.
53. Whitburn, *Billboard Book of Top 40 Hits.*

Chapter 10

1. Dwight Hemion, interview by Michael Rosen on July 9, 2001, Archive of American Television.
2. Bob Finkel, interview by Morrie Gelman on September 10, 1997, Archive of American Television.
3. *Ibid.*
4. *TV-AM Cleveland.*
5. *Parkinson.*
6. Ray Charles, email to author March 3, 2008.
7. Robert Perrella, *They Call Me the Showbiz Priest* (New York: Trident, 1973).
8. Bob Finkel, interview by Morrie Gelman.
9. Bob Finkel, author interview, July 15, 2007
10. Bob Finkel, interview by Morrie Gelman.
11. *Ibid.*
12. *Ibid.*
13. Bob Finkel, author interview.
14. Bob Finkel, interview by Morrie Gelman.
15. Dwight Hemion, author interview, June 27, 2007.
16. Buz Kohan, author interview.
17. *Variety*, September 17, 1956.
18. *Daily Variety*, September 19, 1956.
19. *Variety*, November 21, 1956.
20. "I Call on Perry Como."
21. Escott, *Yesterday and Today.*
22. *Variety*, September 18, 1957.
23. *Daily Variety*, September 16, 1957.
24. Bob Finkel, author interview.
25. *Ibid.*
26. Ray Charles, author interview.
27. *Donahue.*
28. Perella, *They Call Me the Showbiz Priest.*
29. *Ibid.*
30. *Ibid.*
31. *Ibid.*
32. *Ibid.*
33. Ray Charles, email to author, December 13, 2007.
34. *Ibid.*
35. "I Call on Perry Como."
36. Whitburn, *Billboard Book of Top 40 Hits.*
37. Lou Stallman quoted in "Perry Como Album," *Skyline*, 1957.
38. *The Incomparable Como*, sleeve note.
39. *The Gramophone*, January 1958.
40. Escott, *Yesterday and Today.*
41. *www.kokomo.ca.*
42. *Billboard*, December 30, 1957.
43. *Billboard*, January 13, 1958.
44. Jo Rice and Time Rice, *The Guinness Book of British Hit Singles* (Enfield U.K.: Heartaches Ltd. and Guinness Superlatives, 1977).
45. *www.kokomo.ca.*

Chapter 11

1. *Time*, March 16, 1959.
2. *Ibid.*
3. Associated Press, March 5, 1959.
4. *Variety*, October 7, 1959.
5. *Ibid.*
6. Jack Gould, *New York Times*, October 1, 1959.
7. *Variety*, March 2, 1960.
8. *Variety*, March 23, 1960.
9. Ray Charles, author interview.
10. Chart information taken from Whitburn, *Billboard Book of Top 40 Hits*, and Rice and Rice, *Guinness Book of British Hit Singles.*
11. Ray Charles, email to author, April 15, 2008.

12. *Show Time*, February 7, 1960.
13. *Ibid.*
14. *Ibid.*
15. Internal memo, BBC, February 17, 1960.
16. *Ibid.*
17. *Variety*, May 4, 1960.
18. *New York Times*, April 28, 1960.
19. Clark Jones' letter to Ronnie Waldman, May 3, 1960.
20. Yvonne Littlewood, author interview, July 16, 2007.
21. Fred Danzig, UPI, June 2, 1960.
22. *All Music Guide*, quoted on *www.music.barnesandnoble.com*.
23. *Ibid.*
24. Ray Charles, email to author, March 3, 2008.
25. Felisa Vanoff, author interview, September 21, 2007.
26. *Ibid.*
27. Dwight Hemion, interview by Michael Rosen.
28. Gary Smith, interviewed by Karen Herman on July 9, 2001, Archive of American Television.
29. *Ibid.*
30. Rich Little, author interview, September 18, 2007.
31. Gary Smith, Archive of American Television.
32. *Open House*, BBC Radio 2, October 26, 1973.
33. *Variety*, October 12, 1960.
34. John P. Shanley, *New York Times*, October 16, 1960.
35. Dwight Hemion, interview by Michael Rosen.
36. *Ibid.*
37. *Variety*, December 7, 1960.
38. Andy Williams, author interview, June 23, 2007.
39. *New York Times*, October 16, 1960.

Chapter 12

1. *Variety*, October 11, 1961.
2. *New York Times*, October 19, 1961.
3. *Variety*, April 4, 1962.
4. *The Barber Comes to Town.*
5. *Variety*, October 10, 1962.
6. Ray Charles, author interview.
7. *Tucson Daily Citizen*, February 21, 1963, syndicated in other Associated Press newspapers.
8. *Ibid.* Como was echoing a quote from Bing Crosby, who when asked about the Frank Sinatra phenomenon in the mid–1940s said, "A singer like Frank Sinatra comes along once in a lifetime. Why did it have to be my lifetime?"
9. Perry Como quoted in Colin Escott's sleeve note to *Juke Box Baby* CD, 2005.
10. *Ibid.*
11. *Tucson Daily Citizen.*
12. *Joel Whitburn Presents a Century of Pop Music* (Menomonee Falls WI: Record Research, 1999).
13. *The Troy Record*, October 21, 1961.
14. *The Incomparable Como*, sleeve note.
15. Ray Charles, email to authors, May 17, 2007.
16. *The Songs I Love*, LP, 1963, sleeve note.
17. Whitburn, *The Billboard Book of Top 40 Hits.*
18. Perito, *I Just Happened to Be There.*
19. *Ibid.*
20. Ray Charles, author interview.
21. Mickey Glass, interview by Larry Trompeter and Colleen Zwack.

22. Ray Charles, email to author, December 13, 2007,
23. Yvonne Littlewood, author interview,
24. *The Barber Comes to Town.*
25. *Los Angeles Times*, February 17, 1964.
26. *Variety*, May 27, 1964.
27. *Charleston Gazette*, May 27, 1965.
28. *Ibid.*
29. *Variety*, November 23, 1966.
30. *Variety*, January 26, 1966.
31. Perito, *I Just Happened to Be There.*
32. Friedwald, *Jazz Singing.*
33. Tony Bennett, *The Good Life: The Autobiography of Tony Bennett* (New York: Simon and Schuster, 1998).
34. Friedwald, *Sinatra.*
35. Escott, *Yesterday and Today.*
36. Colin Escott, sleeve note to *The Hit Sound—The Anita Kerr Singers*, Collector's Choice Music.
37. Anita Kerr, email to author, September 28, 2007.
38. Ray Charles, email to author, May 17, 2007.
39. Anita Kerr, email to author, September 28, 2007.
40. Whitburn, *The Billboard Book of Top 40 Hits.*
41. *Stereo Review*, 1965.

Chapter 13

1. George T. Simon, sleeve notes for *A Legendary Performer*, LP, RCA 1976.
2. *Melody Maker*, March 1971.
3. *New Musical Express*, December 1970.
4. *Family Weekly*, July 2, 1972.
5. Ray Charles, author interview.
6. Perito, *I Just Happened to Be There.*
7. *Los Angeles Times*, July 24, 1970.
8. Perito, *I Just Happened to Be There.*
9. Ray Charles, author interview.
10. Mickey Glass, interview by Larry Trompeter and Colleen Zwack.
11. Perito, *I Just Happened to Be There.*
12. *Donahue.*
13. Mickey Glass, interview by Larry Trompeter and Colleen Zwack.
14. *New Musical Express*, April 14, 1971.
15. *High Fidelity*, 1971.
16. *Melody Maker*, March 1971.
17. Buz Kohan, author interview.
18. Associated Press, November 1972.
19. Ray Charles was not in the studio at the time, but what he recalls hearing about the accident is broadly similar to Kohan's story. "I heard that Perry had been told not to move on the set, but he moved and fell into the crevice," he said (email to authors, April 15, 2008).
20. Bob Finkel, author interview.
21. Associated Press.
22. David Como, author interview.
23. Associated Press.
24. Ray Charles, author interview.
25. Ray Charles, email to author, April 15, 2008.
26. *Variety*, December 13, 1972.

Chapter 14

1. Rice and Rice, *The Guinness Book of British Hit Singles.*
2. Morgan Ames, *High Fidelity*, September 1973.

3. *Ibid.*
4. Shaun Usher, *Daily Telegraph*, December 1972.
5. *The Song Stylists*, BBC Radio 2, December 17, 1973, Perry Como interviewed by Ken Barnes.
6. *Open House*, BBC Radio 2, November 1973.
7. *Variety*, December 19, 1973.
8. Robert Windeler, *Stereo Review Magazine*, 1974.
9. Peter Reilly, *Stereo Review Magazine*, 1974, quoted on *www.kokomo.ca*.
10. *Variety*, April 17, 1974.
11. *New York Times*, April 12, 1974.
12. Cecil Smith, *Los Angeles Times*, January 13, 1976.
13. *Variety*, December 24, 1975.
14. *Ibid.*
15. Stephen Pouliot, author interview, September 21, 2007.
16. *Ibid.*
17. Bob Banner, interviewed by Henry Colman on November 5, 1999, Archive of American Television.
18. *Ibid.*
19. Cecil Smith, *Los Angeles Times*, January 13, 1976.
20. *Ibid.*
21. *Ibid.*
22. Stephen Pouliot, author interview.
23. Rich Little, author interview.
24. *Ibid.*
25. *New Musical Express*, February 20, 1971.
26. *London Evening News*, May 10, 1974.
27. *Music Week*, May 18, 1974.
28. *London Evening News*.
29. *The Stage*, November 1974.
30. Ray Charles, author interview.
31. *Daily Mirror*, April 12, 1975.
32. Ray Charles, email to author, May 20, 2008.
33. *The Barber Comes to Town*.
34. *Ibid.*
35. *Daily Mirror*, April 12, 1975.
36. *The Barber Comes to Town*.
37. Ray Charles, author interview.
38. Perito, *I Just Happened to Be There*.
39. *Ibid.*
40. *Sydney Morning Herald*, May 3, 1976.
41. Earl Wilson's syndicated column *On the Town*, seen in the *Morning Herald* of Uniontown, PA, July 19, 1976.
42. *New York Times*, July 21, 1976.
43. *Ibid.*
44. *Ibid.*
45. *Variety*, December 22, 1976.
46. Ray Charles, author interview.
47. *www.kokomo.ca*.
48. The song was different from the one with the same title that Como included on his 1971 album, *I Think of You*.
49. "Mr. Relaxation Still Gets Butterflies," *Globe & Mail*, July 28, 1977.

Chapter 15

1. *TV-AM Cleveland*.
2. Interview with Bob Protzman, *Detroit Free Press*, July 6, 1984.
3. Japanese TV interview, March 1993, station unknown.
4. Nick Perito, *I Just Happened to Be There*.

5. *Ibid.*
6. *Los Angeles Times*, July 21, 1978.
7. Jay Leno quoted on ATAS Hall of Fame, 1989.
8. Ray Charles said that the main reason Perry turned down chat show invitations for so long was that once he had agreed to do one, he would have to do them all. Email to author, May 20, 2008.
9. *Parkinson*.
10. Benny Green, sleeve note to *The Best of British* LP, 1977.
11. *Ibid.*
12. *TV-AM Cleveland*.
13. *New York Times*, May 8, 1981.
14. *Washington Post*, December 17, 1983.
15. Como interview with Chris Stuart; Stephen Pouliot, author interview.
16. *Variety*, December 21, 1983.
17. Stephen Pouliot, author interview.
18. *Variety*, December 16, 1981.
19. *Variety*, December 22, 1982.
20. Kitty Kelley, *His Way: The Unauthorized Biography of Frank Sinatra* (New York: Bantam, 1986).
21. Clyde Osborne, *Asheville Citizen*, August 1979.
22. Bill Kaufman, *Los Angeles Times*, December 11, 1979.
23. *High Fidelity*, 1980.
24. *High Fidelity*, 1981.
25. *Ibid.*
26. Irving Berlin originally wrote the song in 1928 with the title "Where Is the Song of Songs for Me?" He wrote a new lyric to the same melody for the *Mr. President* score.
27. "Inside & Out," *Peoria Journal Star*, July 23, 1983.
28. Ray Charles, email to author, April 18, 2007.
29. RCA press release, June 1983.
30. *Ibid.*
31. David Como, author interview.
32. *Ibid.*
33. *Detroit Free Press*, January 18, 1984.
34. Bob Thomas, Associated Press, August 27, 1985.
35. Stephen Pouliot, author interview.
36. Stephen X. Rea, *Philadelphia Inquirer*, August 21, 1984.
37. Jack Hawn, *Los Angeles Times*, July 31, 1985.
38. *Ibid.*
39. Gerald Nachman, *San Francisco Chronicle*, July 26, 1985.
40. Ray Charles said that he thought that Roselle Como never knew that he was off the team. Email to author, May 2008.
41. Ray Charles, author interview.
42. Ed Bark, *Chicago Tribune*, November 20, 1986.
43. Greg Dawson, *Orlando Sentinel*, December 23, 1987.
44. Ed Bark, *Dallas Morning Herald*, December 6, 1986.
45. *Ibid.*
46. Dick Williams, author interview, August 1, 2007.
47. Perito, *I Just Happened to Be There*.

Chapter 16

1. Album total refers to newly recorded albums and excludes reissues and compilations.
2. In 1983, Arista Records owner Bertelsmann had

sold 50 percent of Arista to RCA. In 1985, Bertelsmann and RCA formed a joint venture called RCA/Ariola International. When General Electric acquired RCA in 1986, the company sold its 50 percent interest in RCA/Ariola International to its partner Bertelsmann and the company was renamed BMG Music for Bertelsmann Music Group. BMG brought back the lightning bolt logo to make clear that RCA Records was no longer co-owned with the other RCA entities which GE sold or closed. The only RCA unit GE kept was the National Broadcasting Company. BMG also revived the RCA Victor label for musical genres outside of country, pop and rock music.

3. Mickey Glass, interview by Larry Trompeter and Colleen Zwack.

4. Dale Kawashima, "Jeff Silbar: Writing the Classic 'Wind Beneath My Wings,'" *Songwriter Universe*, date unknown.

5. Jack Hawn, *Los Angeles Times*, July 31, 1985.

6. Roger Piantasdosi, *Washington Post*, July 17, 1987.

7. George Townsend, email to author April 16, 2007.

8. *Philadelphia Inquirer*, June 2, 1988.

9. Perito, *I Just Happened to Be There*.

10. Cassie Miller, by email, September 16, 2007.

11. Mark Taylor, *Post-Tribune*, July 23, 1989.

12. *Ibid*.

13. Writer Buz Kohan recalled that the initial falling out between Como and Davis came about because Sammy did not call him directly to explain his reasons for pulling out of the show. "That caused him to carry the Italian, 'never forget a slight' type of grudge," said Kohan. Email to authors, April 21, 2008.

14. Bob Wynn, author interview, August 1, 2007.

15. Duke Children's Classic brochure, early 1990s.

16. Duke Children's Classic brochure, 1990.

17. Diane Ketcham, *New York Times*, June 10, 1990.

18. Ray Boyce, *Syracuse Post-Standard*, December 12, 1990.

19. Ray Charles, author interview.

20. Jack Swersie, writing on *www.jackswersie.com*.

21. *Ibid*.

22. Perry Como concert, Japanese TV, March 1993.

23. *Kenny Live*, RTE, January 15, 1994.

24. David Como, author interview.

25. Bob Wynn, author interview.

26. David Como, author interview.

27. *Irish Examiner*, January 22, 1994.

28. *Irish Independent*, January 22, 1994.

29. *The Irish Times*, January 22, 1994.

30. Bob Wynn, author interview.

31. John Voorhees, *Seattle Times*, December 12, 1994.

32. Beverley Beckham, *Boston Herald*, December 3, 1994.

33. Perito, *I Just Happened to Be There*.

34. Mickey Glass, interview by Larry Trompeter and Colleen Zwack.

Chapter 17

1. Perito, *I Just Happened to Be There*.

2. *Pittsburgh-Post Gazette*, May 16, 1999.

3. *Ibid*.

4. Perito, *I Just Happened to Be There*.

5. David Como, author interview.

6. *Philadelphia Inquirer*, May 13, 2001.

7. *The Palm Beach Post*, May 19, 2001.

8. Perry Como quoted in "Perry Como, Relaxed and Elegant Troubadour of Recordings and TV, Is Dead at 88," by Richard Severo, *New York Times*, May 13, 2001.

Appendix A

1. The sessions on August 1, 6, 20 and 22 covered recordings for the Musical Smart Set *Perry Como Sings Merry Christmas Music*.

2. The sessions on March 4, 11 and 13 covered recordings for the 10" album *TV Favorites*.

3. The sessions on May 5, 18, 21 and 26 and June 22 covered recordings for the 10" album *Around the Christmas Tree*.

4. These sessions covered recordings for the 10" album *I Believe*.

5. These sessions covered recordings for the album *So Smooth*, except for "Nobody" which was released as a single. *So Smooth* was Perry's first 12" LP.

6. Ray Charles Singers not present.

7. The sessions on June 18, 1956, and February 12 and 19, 1957, covered recordings for the album *We Get Letters*.

8. These sessions covered recordings for the album *Saturday Night with Mr. C*.

9. Recorded for the album *When You Come to the End of the Day*, except for May 29 and June 5 sessions.

10. Recorded for the album *Como Swings*.

11. These sessions covered recordings for the album *Season's Greetings from Perry Como*.

12. These sessions covered recordings for the album *Songs for the Young at Heart*.

13. These sessions covered recordings for the album *Sing to Me, Mr. C*.

14. These sessions covered recordings for the album *By Request*.

15. These sessions covered recordings for the album *The Best of Irving Berlin's Songs from Mr. President*.

16. These sessions covered the recordings for the album *The Songs I Love*.

17. The Feb 9–12 sessions covered the recordings for the album *The Scene Changes*.

18. These sessions covered the recordings for the album *Lightly Latin*.

19. These sessions covered the recordings for the album *Perry Como in Italy*.

20. These sessions covered the recordings for the album *Look to Your Heart*.

21. These sessions covered recordings for *The Perry Como Christmas Album*. It is believed that the July recordings were disregarded and the entire project re-recorded during August and that it was these latter recordings that were released.

22. No documentation exists to show whether Take 1 or 2 was released as the single. From listening to the takes, Como's vocal on the song displays a greater familiarity on the originally issued single as compared to the alternate take released later. The assumption is therefore made that the original release was Take 2.

23. Recorded live at the International Hotel, Las Vegas, for the album *Perry Como in Person*.

24. These sessions covered recordings for the album *It's Impossible*.

25. These sessions covered recordings for the album *I Think of You*.

26. These sessions were for a country music oriented album which was never issued as planned. Some of the tracks were used in the *And I Love You So* album.

27. These sessions covered recordings for the album *Perry*.

28. The songs for the album *Just out of Reach* were taken from these sessions. The sessions on January 7, January 22 and May 6 were arranged and conducted by Bill Justis. The sessions on January 16, May 27 and 28, and June 6 were arranged by Mike Leach.

29. These sessions covered recordings for the album *The Best of British*.

30. These sessions covered recordings for the album *Perry Como*.

31. Recorded at the Mill Run Theatre, Niles, Illinois for the album *Perry Como Live on Tour*.

32. These sessions covered recordings for the *So It Goes* album.

33. These sessions covered recordings for the *Perry Como Today* album.

34. Recorded at The Point Theatre, Dublin, Ireland for the album *Perry Como's Christmas Concert*.

35. O Little Town of Bethlehem was replaced by "White Christmas" on post–1947 issues.

36. First dual 45/78 release.

37. Final 78 rpm release.

Bibliography

Books

Bennett, Tony. *The Good Life: The Autobiography of Tony Bennett*. New York: Simon and Schuster, 1998.

Dodge, Consuelo. *The Everly Brothers: Ladies Love Outlaws*. Starke, FL: CIN-DAV, 1991.

Edwards, Anne. *Judy Garland*. London: Constable, 1975.

Escott, Colin. *Roadkill on the Three-Chord Highway: Art and Trash in American Popular Music*. London: Routledge, 2002.

_____. *Yesterday and Today*. Booklet accompanying RCA CD boxed set, 1993.

Falcocchio, Luigi. *Abruzzo-Pensilvania Solo Andata*. L'Editrice Italica-Pescara, 2007.

Friedwald, Will. *Jazz Singing: America's Great Voices from Bessie Smith to Bebop and Beyond*. New York: Scribner's, 1990.

_____. *Sinatra: The Song Is You*. New York: Da Capo, 1997.

Giddins, Gary. *Bing Crosby: A Pocketful of Dreams*. Boston: Little, Brown, 2001.

Griffis, Ken. *Hear My Song: The Story of the Celebrated Sons of the Pioneers*. Rev. ed. Northglenn, CO: Norken, 1996.

Halberstam, David. *The Fifties*. New York: Fawcett Combine, 1993.

Hemming, Roy, and Hajdu, David. *Discovering Great Singers of Classic Pop*. New York: Newmarket, 1991.

Kelley, Kitty. *His Way: The Unauthorized Biography of Frank Sinatra*. New York: Bantam, 1986.

Laine, Frankie, and Laredo, Joseph. *That Lucky Old Son: The Autobiography of Frankie Laine*. New York: Pathfinder, 1993.

Macfarlane, Malcolm. *Bing Crosby—Day by Day*. Metuchen, NJ: Scarecrow, 2001.

Pairpoint, Lionel, Macfarlane, Malcolm, and Van Beek, Greg. *The Chronological Bing Crosby on Television*. International Crosby Circle, 2003.

Perrella, Robert. *They Call Me the Showbiz Priest*. New York: Trident, 1973.

Perito, Nick. *I Just Happened to Be There*. Philadelphia: Xlibris, 2004.

Pleasants, Henry. *The Great American Popular Singers*. London: Victor Gollancz, 1974.

Rice, Jo, and Rice, Tim. *The Guinness Book of British Hit Singles*. Enfield, U.K.: Heartaches Ltd. and Guinness Superlatives, 1977.

Sanjek, Russell. *American Popular Music and Its Business: The First Four Hundred Years*. New York: Oxford University Press, 1988.

Simon, George T. *The Big Bands*. New York: Macmillan, 1967.

Simon, George T., and Friends. *The Best of the Music Makers*. Garden City, NY: Doubleday, 1979.

Steinberg, Cobbett. *TV Facts*. New York: Facts on File, 1980.

Tosches, Nick. *Dino: Living High in the Dirty Business of Dreams*. London: Secker and Warburg, 1992.

Tyler, Don. *Hit Songs 1900–1955: American Popular Music in the Pre-Rock Era*. Jefferson, NC: McFarland, 2007.

Ward, Geoffrey C. *Jazz: A History of America's Music*. New York: Alfred A. Knopf, 2000.

Whitburn, Joel. *Billboard Book of Top 40 Hits*. Menomonee Falls, WI: Record Research, 1989.

_____. *Billboard Pop Hits 1940–1954*. Menomonee Falls, WI: Record Research, 1994.

_____. *Christmas in the Charts*. Menomonee Falls, WI: Record Research, 2004.

_____. *Joel Whitburn Presents a Century of Pop Music*. Menomonee Falls, WI: Record Research, 1999.

_____. *Pop Memories 1890–1954: The History of American Popular Music*. Menomonee Falls, WI: Record Research, 1986.

289

Willis, Chuck. *Destination America*. London: DK, 2005.

Worth, Fred L. *Elvis: His Life from A to Z*. New York: Random House, 1992.

Articles

We reviewed an extensive selection of newspaper articles and cuttings about Perry Como's life and career. Those references are cited in detail in the notes for each chapter. Articles of general interest include the following:

"Big Cheese." *Time*, March 16, 1959.

"Blue Chip." *Time*, June 29, 1953.

"Canonsburg Youth Rated as Modern Edition Bing Crosby." *Canonsburg Daily Notes*, July 16, 1934.

"Casual Como Knows What He Is Doing." *Long Beach Press-Telegram*, December 1, 1955.

"A Casual Guy and That's Fine by Him." *Montreal Star*, November 18, 1967.

"Como at 64 Is Still Packing Them In." *Long Beach Independent Press-Telegram*, July 17, 1976.

"Como Back with Better Image." *Los Angeles Times*, October 21, 1960.

"Como Enjoys Life—and Rehearsals, Too." *Long Beach Press-Telegram*, November 30, 1955.

"Como Finds Welcome Among Home Friends." *Canonsburg Daily Notes*, September 16, 1946.

"Como Has Great Expectations for His September TV Special." [Pasadena] *Star-News*, September 1, 1976.

"Como Now Rivals Crosby and Sinatra with Juke-Box Fans." *Cumberland Sunday Times*, September 1, 1946.

"Como on NBC: Singer Makes Relaxed Debut on Network in His Relaxed Manner on Hour Program." *New York Times*, September 19, 1955.

"Como Signs for $25 Million." *St. Joseph Herald Press*, March 5, 1959.

"Como Story Began Here in Canonsburg." *Canonsburg Daily Notes*, August 24, 1977.

"Como Taking Last Bow Tonight?" *Charleston Gazette*, May 27, 1965.

"Como's Golden Anniversary Tour Back on Track." AP News (syndicated), July 22, 1984.

"Cooley: Calm Approach to Como." Richard F. Shepard. *New York Times*, January 15, 1956.

"The Crooner, R.I.P." William F. Buckley. *National Review*, May 18, 2001.

"A Decade with Perry Como." *Newsweek*, June 29, 1953.

"'Dr.'" Perry Como Given His Degree for Many Reasons." *New Castle* [Pennsylvania] *News*, June 10, 1967.

"Fresh Approach Needed on TV, Perry Como Says." *Show Time*, February 7, 1960.

"He Got Rich Quick." Jack Sher. *Los Angeles Times*, March 23, 1947.

"A Hit Is Born." *Coronet*, February 1955.

"'Home Place for Me,' Says Perry Como Here on Vacation Visit." *Canonsburg Daily Notes*, August 24, 1948.

"How to Relax the Como Way." *New York Times*, January 29, 1956.

"I Call on Perry Como." Pete Martin. *Saturday Evening Post*, January 1960 (three-week series).

"'I Just Open My Mouth at Eight O'Clock and Out It Comes.'" *Stereo Review*, October 1974.

"'I Sold Them on the Idea That Screaming Was Disrespectful.'" *Washington Post*, August 24, 1977.

"'I've Been Around Too Long to Pretend.'" *Radio Times*, May 1971.

"Idea Men Behind the Como Show." *New York Times*, October 16, 1960.

"In Search of the Soul of Perry Como." *Pittsburgh Post-Gazette*, December 17, 1995.

"Inside & Out." *Peoria Journal Star*, July 23, 1983

"Like 'Working in a Shoe Factory.'" *New York Times*, December 9, 1951.

"The Lives They Lived." *New York Times*, December 30, 2001.

"Local Youth Hits Top with Weems Orchestra." *Canonsburg Daily Notes*, January 26, 1938.

"Megaphone for Mike." *Nebraska State Journal*, October 24, 1943.

"Memories Are Made of This." *New York Times*, June 10, 1990.

"Mr. Class." *TV Guide*, May 2001.

"Mr. Relaxation Still Gets Butterflies." *Globe & Mail*, July 28, 1977.

"Modest Como Marks 50 Years in Show Business." AP News (syndicated), July 10, 1983.

"NBC Lures Como from CBS with Big Contract." *Los Angeles Times*, April 1, 1955.

"New Crooner Keeps 'Em Swooning in New York." *Lowell Sun*, July 15, 1944.

"The 'New' Perry Como Is Still a Nice Guy." *Lima News*, October 16, 1955.

"New Telerecording System Brings Clearer Picture." *New Musical Express*, November 18, 1960.

"Nice and Easy Still Does It for Como." *Montreal Sun*, December 1, 1981.

"Nice Guys Finish First." *Collier's*, January 6, 1956.

"Passing the Word to Como." *New York Times*, October 26, 1958.

"Perry Como." Biographical sketch by the Academy of Television Arts and Science (ATAS) Hall of Fame, 1989.

"Perry Como a Soothing Respite for the Holiday Hubbub on TV." *New York Times*, December 13, 1976.

A Perry Como Album. Dell Magazines, 1950.

"Perry Como Album." *Skyline*, 1957.

"Perry Como Cites Need of Eight Weeks' Rest; Says Seasonal Grind Is Tiring." *Coshocton* [Ohio] *Tribune*, June 30, 1954.

"Perry Como—Ever the Dream-Maker." *Frederick News-Post*, August 16, 1977.

"Perry Como: His Song Goes On." *Good Housekeeping*, December 1990.

"Perry Como: How Much Is His $25 Million Worth?" *Look*, May 12, 1959.

"Perry Como Legend: He's 'Such a Good Boy.'" *San Antonio Light*, May 12, 1957.

"Perry Como Never Confused by Money." *Long Beach Press-Telegram*, June 24, 1955.

"Perry Como, Relaxed and Elegant Troubadour of Recordings and TV, Is Dead at 88." *New York Times*, May 13, 2001.

"Perry Como Still Seeks a Full House." *Elyria* [Ohio] *Sun*, December 1, 1985.

"Perry Como Story." Joseph P. Kaye. *Coronet*, May 1953.

"Perry Como, the Relaxed Man." *Holiday*, March 1957.

"Perry Como to Quit Weekly Show." *San Antonio Light*, February 22, 1963.

"Perry Como's Climb to Top Spot Built on One-Night Band Stands." *Charleston Gazette*, October 31, 1955.

"Regarding Mr. Como." *New York Times*, August 29, 1943.

"Remembering Mr. C—Perry Como." *Three Villages Times*, July 13, 2001.

"Suave Perry Como at 64 Is Still 'Smooth as Silk.'" *Bucks County* [Pennsylvania] *Courier Times*, July 23, 1976.

"Time Is Nice to This Guy." *Sydney Morning Herald*, April 29, 1976.

"$25 Million Contract Signed by Perry Como." *Los Angeles Times*, March 1959.

"We Thank Perry Como...." *New Musical Express*, July 10, 1959.

"Whatever Became of Perry Como, America's Favorite?" *Family Weekly*, July 2, 1972.

"A World of Nice Guys." *Time*, December 19, 1955.

"Ye Olde Free-for-All." *TV Guide*, February 1956.

We must also pay special tribute to the twin bibles of the showbiz industry, *Variety* and *Billboard* magazines. We have used these two journals for contemporary reviews of Mr. Como's TV and stage appearances. Details are included in the chapter notes.

Internet Sources

Many web sites assisted us and in particular we must mention YouTube, Redmond Nostalgia, www.newslibrary.com, www.newspaperarchive.com, www.OTRCAT.com, The Radio GOLDINdex, Wikipedia, Recording Industry Association of America, www.kokomo.ca, www.perrycomo.net, Ellis Island and Ancestry.com.

Index